CWPG - 5 PG -

CB
#1740

12/4

FIRST BLOOD

ALSO BY W. A. SWANBERG

JIM FISK: The Career of an Improbable Rascal

W. A. SWANBERG

FIRST BLOOD

THE STORY OF
Fort Sumter

LONGMANS

LONGMANS, GREEN AND CO LTD
6 & 7 CLIFFORD STREET, LONDON W I
THIBAULT HOUSE, THIBAULT SQUARE, CAPE TOWN
605 - 611 LONSDALE STREET, MELBOURNE C I
443 LOCKHART ROAD, HONG KONG
ACCRA, AUCKLAND, IBADAN
KINGSTON (JAMAICA), KUALA LUMPUR
LAHORE, NAIROBI, SALISBURY (RHODESIA)
LONGMANS, GREEN AND CO INC
119 WEST 40TH STREET, NEW YORK 18
LONGMANS, GREEN AND CO
20 CRANFIELD ROAD, TORONTO 16
ORIENT LONGMANS PRIVATE LTD
CALCUTTA, BOMBAY, MADRAS
DELHI, HYDERABAD, DACCA

This edition first published 1960

Printed in Great Britain by
Lowe and Brydone (Printers) Limited, London, N.W.10

FOR
DOROTHY

QUOTATIONS FROM COPYRIGHTED SOURCES

DIRECT QUOTATIONS from the following copyrighted books have been included in *First Blood—The Story of Fort Sumter*, on pages indicated in parentheses following each source. These quotations are used by special permission of the publishers listed below along with the titles of the works.

CAUTHEN, CHARLES EDWARD—*South Carolina Goes to War*. University of North Carolina Press, Chapel Hill, 1950. (Pp. 16, 24, 25.)

CHESNUT, MARY BOYKIN—*A Diary From Dixie*. Appleton-Century-Crofts, Inc., New York, 1905. (Pp. 14, 278, 279, 288, 294, 298.)

CRAVEN, AVERY—*Edmund Ruffin, Southerner*. Appleton-Century-Crofts, Inc., New York, 1932. (Pp. 15, 23, 294, 301, 329.)

LAWTON, EBA ANDERSON—*Major Robert Anderson and Fort Sumter*. G. P. Putnam's Sons, New York, 1911. (P. 155.)

McELROY, ROBERT—*Jefferson Davis, the Unreal and the Real*. Harper & Bros., New York, 1937. (P. 166.)

MEARNS, DAVID C.—*The Lincoln Papers*. Doubleday & Co., Inc., New York, 1948. (Pp. 159, 234.)

MEIGS, MONTGOMERY C.—*Diary, March 29—April 8, 1861*. The American Historical Review, Washington, 1920-21. (P. 256.)

MOORE, JOHN BASSETT (ed.)—*The Works of James Buchanan*. The J. B. Lippincott Co., Philadelphia, 1909. (P. 56.)

NEVINS, ALLAN, and THOMAS, MILTON HALSEY (eds.)—*The Diary of George Templeton Strong*. The Macmillan Co., New York, 1952. (Pp. 160, 167, 219, 235-6.)

RAVENEL, HENRY WILLIAM—*The Private Journal of Henry William Ravenel*, edited by Arney R. Childs. The University of South Carolina Press, Columbia, 1947. (Pp. 190, 191.)

SCHIRMER, JACOB—*The Diary of Jacob Schirmer*, 1860 (manuscript). The South Carolina Historical Society, Charleston. (Pp. 81, 138.)

TRESCOT, WILLIAM HENRY—*Trescot's Narrative*. The American Historical Review, Washington, 1908. (Pp. 53, 54.)

WELLES, GIDEON—*The Diary of Gideon Welles*. Houghton Mifflin Co., Boston, 1911. (P. 266.)

WHITE, LAURA A.—*Robert Barnwell Rhett, Father of Secession*. The American Historical Association, Washington, 1931. (P. 9.)

CONTENTS

	Map	x
I.	Damnation to the Yankees	1
II.	We Hate Each Other So	12
III.	The Unluckiest Man	26
IV.	I Picked Him Myself	34
V.	A Free-Love Arrangement	52
VI.	The Honor-Savers	64
VII.	Where's the Fire?	70
VIII.	Peaceably, if Possible	82
IX.	No Time for Tea	89
X.	My Compliments to the Governor	102
XI.	Men Do Go Mad	109
XII.	Fleas in Their Ears	122
XIII.	Blessings on You Anyhow	131
XIV.	The Disgust of Captain Doubleday	144

xv.   Sumter Is Not for Sale   *160*

xvi.   Let the Major Declare War   *172*

         Illustrations   *between pages 126-7 and 286-7*

xvii.   The South Carolina Gentlemen   *187*

xviii.   The Peacemakers   *194*

xix.   The Lion and the Lamb   *203*

xx.   "Hold, Occupy and Possess"   *219*

xxi.   A Dear, Delightful Place   *242*

xxii.   . . . To Move by Sea   *253*

xxiii.   Wait and See   *263*

xxiv.   Eleven Codfish   *272*

xxv.   Let the Strife Begin   *283*

xxvi.   The End of Long Doubt   *291*

xxvii.   Virtue *v.* Vice   *299*

xxviii. Gentlemen, Return to Your Batteries   *312*

xxix.   April 14, 1861   *326*

xxx.   April 14, 1865   *333*

         Bibliography   *340*

         Notes   *345*

         Acknowledgments   *368*

         Index   *369*

FIRST BLOOD

Is it possible there can be truth in the old notion that, in times of great national trial and excitement, so many men do go mad, so to speak, in a quiet and private way, that madness becomes a sort of epidemic?
—DIARY OF A PUBLIC MAN

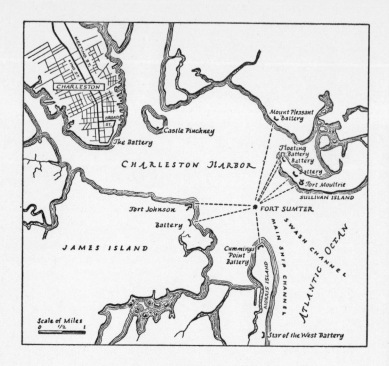

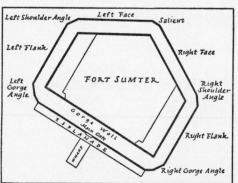

Map at top shows position of Fort Sumter in relation to Charleston and also to the Confederate batteries surrounding it. Broken lines indicate concentration of fire poured at Sumter. Simplified diagram below explains nomenclature of Sumter's various parts.

DAMNATION
TO THE YANKEES

Assistant Surgeon Samuel Wylie Crawford, U.S.A., got out of the cars and found Charleston's North Eastern Station much like a Turkish bath. A slender, erect Pennsylvanian of thirty, Dr. Crawford possessed a brain everlastingly curious about all manner of natural phenomena. Three years earlier he had climbed Popocatepetl, explored the crater, and taken periodic readings on a barometer.[1] He had no barometer with him now, but he may have reflected that the steaming heat of South Carolina's metropolis in mid-September of 1860 was entirely appropriate for the hottest political spot in the nation.

He hailed a hack and was driven through gaslit streets to the impressively balconied Charleston Hotel on the corner of Meeting and Pinckney. The night clerk eyed him doubtfully on learning that he was an officer assigned to Fort Moultrie, out in the harbor.

"Don't you think you had better go to the fort tonight?" he suggested.

He was quite courteous about it, but nevertheless his meaning was that Dr. Crawford would not be warmly welcomed as a guest. The surgeon was nettled. He had jogged over the rails all the way from Rhode Island, and he was tired.

"It is five miles or more," he said. "What means of conveyance is there? I've never been here before in my life."

"None that I know of," the clerk replied. "The steamers stop running after three o'clock, but you might get a Negro to row you over in a skiff. It is dangerous to stay here."

Crawford didn't quite believe that. The mere fact that he was a Northerner, an army officer, surely could not bring him into peril in this seat of Southern culture.

"No," he said firmly. "That is out of the question. I shall remain overnight here."

For a moment the North and the South gazed at each other across the desk. The South shrugged and handed the North a key. Crawford went to bed and was happy that no one made an effort to throttle or disembowel him as he slept. He breakfasted at the hotel in the morning without being poisoned. No one insulted or assailed him as he made his way to the wharf and boarded the steamer.[2]

It was a bracing ride, with a breeze coming in off the sea and the formidable hulk of Fort Sumter rising from the mist farther out in the harbor. Surgeon Crawford already knew that he was in for an experience unique in his nine-year army career, something that would challenge his scientific mind, and he was looking forward to it. Heretofore he had treated soldiers' bunions and bellyaches in remote frontier posts in Texas, New Mexico, and Kansas where a hoop skirt was a rarity. Now he was assigned to Fort Moultrie, a place long regarded by old army men as a veritable country club, with never an Apache or a bushwhacker to worry about and a cotillion every Saturday night.[3] There was a time when desert-weary officers pulled every string they could to get sent to Moultrie, but no one was pulling that kind of string any more. A blight had fallen on the country club. Crawford, a remarkably well-informed man, knew all about this and yet he was not intimidated. At least he could expect something different. *How* different not even smart Dr. Crawford could foresee.

He alighted at the west end of Sullivan's Island and boarded a horsecar that took him past rows of frame summer houses and dropped him off at a most tired-looking fortification. Beach sand had drifted against Fort Moultrie's sixteen-foot brick walls for years until in places it seemed all but inundated. The surgeon was admitted at the gate by a languid corporal. As he was escorted inside, he noticed no sentries parading the parapet, no sign of military activity at all. The place had such a sleepy aspect that if a soldier had clicked his heels the effect would have been startling.[4]

Crawford found the commandant, septuagenarian Lieutenant Colonel John Lane Gardner, in his quarters. Gardner greeted him and said no, sir, there was no truth at all in that rumor that there was yellow fever in Charleston. Maybe a little dengue, but that was all.[5] He introduced the surgeon to the two company commanders, Captain Abner Doubleday and Captain Truman Seymour. Between them, Doubleday's and Seymour's depleted companies, which comprised the entire garrison, totaled exactly sixty-one men—less than the strength of one regulation company. All in all, the majesty of the United States Government looked anything but fearsome as represented by its force in Charleston harbor.

This was a situation galling in the extreme to Captain Doubleday, who had carried the flag to glory at Monterey and Buena Vista and now considered it as sinking in disgrace in South Carolina. A tall, burly, forty-one-year-old West Pointer from New York State with a thick black mustache, Doubleday was a mathematical fellow with an inventive mind. Years earlier, growing tired of watching youngsters playing aimlessly with bats and balls, he had put some sense into it by devising a diamond and a scoring system that came to be known as baseball. He thought this a trivial accomplishment, but he took his politics seriously. Doubleday was second in command at Moultrie and not overly proud of the honor. To his way of thinking it was much like being first mate aboard a sinking ship. With those hotheads over in Charleston talking of capturing the fort in a swift surprise attack, he felt like a man in a trap.[6] Moultrie was built originally as a mere sea battery for the protection of the city, with the reasonable assumption that citizens would come to the aid of the fort in case of attack. No one had ever envisaged the idea that those same citizens might attack the bastion. On its landward side it was no tighter than a sieve, with a public street running directly behind it and separating it from its storehouses and shops. From the upper stories of summer homes of prosperous Carolinians nearby, and from equally convenient sand hills, sharpshooters could neatly pick off soldiers in the fort if they were so inclined.[7]

What worried Doubleday was that some of them were talking as if they *were* so inclined, or soon would be. Their leaders were itching for secession. Gusty young Lawrence Keitt, a South Carolina Representative in Congress, actually said that if the Republican Lincoln was elected in November, "loyalty to the Union will be treason to the South." [8] This sort of talk made Doubleday purple, being a strong Unionist and Lincoln man. It also made him look around with uneasiness at the sickly condition of Moultrie. The captain had never before been stationed in a fort that could be entered by a reconnoitering party of cows. That was almost literal truth, for the drifted sand made handy ramps up to the parapet in several places, and occasionally a wandering Guernsey would drop in for an unannounced visit. If cows could walk in, how about people? [9]

While Doubleday felt some sympathy for gouty old Colonel Gardner, he was also impatient with the colonel because he neither shouted loudly enough to Washington for help nor took energetic steps to batten down with what he had.[10] Gardner had won his spurs far back in antiquity as a third lieutenant in the War of 1812. He had fought gallantly in the Florida and Mexican wars, but now, after almost half a century in the army, his martial spirit was pretty well played out. His soldiers knew the old man was an easy mark and took full advantage of it. He was more interested in a dram and a game of whist at his comfortable house just west of the fort than in spit-and-polish discipline. He enjoyed the evening concerts given by the garrison band, with fashionable Carolinians promenading the parapet and his officers in dress uniforms chatting with them and admiring the view as late shafts of sunlight touched Fort Sumter a mile across the water.[11] The social amenities of military life were a comfort to the colonel, who felt he had earned them after years of hardship in frontier posts, and the thought that these nice people—so beautifully dressed, so courteous, so attractively drawly in speech—might have designs against him and his fort was repugnant.

Although he was a native of Massachusetts, Gardner was inclined to favor the South in its quarrel with the North. The South, sir, he would say, has been treated outrageously in the question of the territories. Still, he had his duty to perform.

He wished those firebrands over in town would stop talking so wildly about seizing Fort Moultrie, stop saying that the federal garrison there was an insult and a threat to the sovereign state of South Carolina.[12]

Well, sir, that was rank nonsense. It was farthest from Colonel Gardner's intention to insult or threaten anybody. A garrison had been here at Moultrie for years, aimed at the defense of the port and always mingling on the friendliest terms with the populace. Now, merely because it appeared that this uncouth back-woodsman Lincoln would be elected, some excitable Charlestonians were suddenly taking the attitude that the colonel, his eight officers, sixty-one men, and thirteen musicians were a menace. Ridiculous, to be sure, and yet these Carolinians had a hair-trigger sense of honor and there were times when cool reason seemed to have no effect on them.

Gardner had pointed out the dangers of his position in his reports to Washington, but nothing seemed to come of it. He knew that a Congressional appropriation had been made the previous June for the repair of Moultrie and the completion of vacant Sumter. They had better get a move on with it or it might be too late. The colonel and his officers were mightily relieved when Captain John Gray Foster, Corps of Engineers, arrived a few days after Surgeon Crawford and got busy.[13]

A thirty-seven-year-old West Pointer from New Hampshire, Foster was six feet of powerful Yankee topped by one of the most splendid beards in the service. Still limping slightly from a Mexican War leg wound, he went in to Charleston, opened a small office there, hired a corps of stonemasons and mechanics, and began work on Moultrie and Sumter which he had planned in a survey made the previous summer. Finding that he could not secure enough skilled workmen locally, he sent to Baltimore for a large crew who had worked for him on an earlier job at Fort Carroll, Maryland. Soon men were hauling sand away from Moultrie's seaward face to prevent the easy entrance of cows, and were also tearing apart the interior of the fort for major defensive repairs.[14]

This bustle of activity aroused irritation in Charleston and also at the state capital at Columbia. Most of the South Carolina leaders, foreseeing the election of Lincoln, had already determined that the state would secede from the Union as soon after the Republicans took over as the feat could be managed. When South Carolina proclaimed its independence, of course, it would assume its own defense. It could not tolerate the presence of "foreign" soldiers manning the harbor forts. The work now in progress at Moultrie and Sumter was extensive enough to make it appear that President Buchanan and his administration might be so ignorant of political realities as to intend maintaining possession of the forts regardless. Whoever heard of such folly? There was grumbling, and yet intelligent Carolinians understood perfectly that until secession came the forts were United States property and Old Buck with clear legality could arm them to the teeth and even turn handsprings on the ramparts if he chose. But why couldn't he read the handwriting on the wall and act accordingly? [15]

From his engineering office in Charleston, Captain Foster heard these complaints. They did not impress him in the least. It seemed to him that he had heard and read of nothing but growls from South Carolina as long as he could remember, and he took the opinion that growling must be the nature of the beast. These people had talked of separating from the Union thirty years ago, and again ten years ago. Now they were at it again. Well, let them talk. Foster didn't put any stock in it. He had a job to do on two forts in the harbor and he went ahead with it.

Possibly he would have been wiser had he given more heed to the unrest. He did not trouble to inquire into the politics of his workmen. Naturally, those from Charleston were almost solid for secession, and many from Baltimore were likewise—a fact that soon was to cause him concern.[16]

The four forts in Charleston harbor in the fall of 1860 were splendid examples of government complacency and neglect. Castle Pinckney, a small half-moon fortress on Shute's Folly Island only three-quarters of a mile east of the city's docks, contained some heavy guns but was occupied only by Ordnance Sergeant

Skillen, his wife and fifteen-year-old daughter Kate. Skillen's duty was not to repel possible boarders but to keep the equipment lacquered and oiled against rust, on the theory that should the day ever come when Pinckney would be needed, it would be ready. Farther from the city was Fort Moultrie, the only work that was garrisoned. It had been all but edged off Sullivan's Island by the encroaching resort town of Moultrieville. Across the bay from Moultrie on James Island was Fort Johnson, a small Revolutionary work which the government had abandoned entirely and was a virtual ruin. On a shoal alongside the main ship channel almost midway between Moultrie and Johnson lay Fort Sumter, a stronghold about which there was some question whether it would crumble from age before it was finished.

Work on Sumter began in 1829, after which the government spent ten years and a half million dollars building an artificial island of granite "leavings" from New England quarries. In later years another half million had been spent in constructing on this foundation the large brick pentagonal fort, designed to be one of the most powerful in the nation with a war garrison of 650 men manning 146 guns of varying calibers. Unruffled decades of peace had induced a glacial slowness in Washington. Now, after thirty-one years, Sumter was still unfinished. While its masonry shell was largely completed, there was still a great deal of work to be done before the first gun could even be mounted. Captain Foster had a job on his hands, for the interior was a shambles of building materials, equipment, and assorted artillery and carriages.[17]

If the repairs on Moultrie caused annoyance among Charleston's many disunionists, this Sumter business outraged them. Anyone with half a brain could understand that the possession of Sumter was the key to South Carolina's safety. Commanding the ship channel as it did, an unfriendly garrison in it could prevent the passage of so much as a rowboat, bottle up the state's only major port, and make a laughingstock of any claim to independence. After neglecting the bastion for years, why was the Washington government now in such a hurry to com-

B

plete it when there was no threat of foreign war whatever? Why indeed, unless it intended to occupy Sumter and hold it despite the secession that would come just as surely as fate after Lincoln was elected? [18]

The angriest man in the state was sixty-year-old Robert Barnwell Rhett, the tall, supercilious owner of the Charleston Mercury, lawyer, one-time Senator, full-time agitator, proprietor of two plantations, and master of 190 slaves. A born incendiary, Rhett had campaigned against "Northern oppression" almost without cessation for thirty years with such monomaniacal persistence that even most of his colleagues thought him a hotheaded crank. For ten years he had openly preached secession. During the greater part of his adult life he had steered a rebellious course whose ultimate goal was disunion, and like all zealots he was entirely sincere in his belief that he was right even when this premise implied that everybody else was wrong. He had long regarded himself as a martyr, a man ahead of his time. Now, at long last, his time had struck. The prophet had come into his own. The election of that political monstrosity, Abe Lincoln—rendered almost certain by the splintering of the Democratic party—was an insult no true Carolinian could stomach.[19]

How would you like, Mr. Rhett demanded, to have a mulatto for Vice President? Well, you will when Lincoln and Hamlin come in. This mischievous canard came about because Hannibal Hamlin's father in Maine, a global-minded man, had named four of his other sons America, Europe, Asia, and Africa. Some Southerners reasoned that it was impossible that anyone named Africa could be white, and rumor—plus Mr. Hamlin's swarthy complexion—had done the rest.[20] The rumor was untrue, to be sure, but it was convenient for Rhett to believe it and undoubtedly most of his readers *did* believe it, experiencing a strong Caucasian sense of revulsion. A skillful propagandist, Rhett used his red-hot Mercury as a torch, spreading the flames of sectional discord, playing on his readers' touchy sense of Southern honor as well as on their feelings of racial superiority.

He prodded a sensitive spot when he declared that the South had been threatening disunion so long that the Yankees were laughing and saying it was all bluff.

"The North claims," said Mr. Rhett, "that the South cannot be kicked into disunion." [21]

The Union, he insisted, was strictly a one-way road, with the North getting the profits and the South paying the taxes. The South was the best colony the North ever had. His pronouncements over the years had sounded the tocsin for resistance with a bullheaded disregard for national tranquillity equaled only by a few of his abolitionist opposite numbers on the far side of the Mason-Dixon line. "What, sir, has the people ever gained, but by revolution?" he demanded in 1832. He was right along with Patrick Henry in his view of treason. "The word has no terrors for me," he said in 1850. ". . . I have been born of Traitors, but thank God, they have ever been Traitors in the great cause of liberty. . . ." [22]

Now in 1860, Rhett might even have felt a sneaking fondness for Lincoln because he was doing what Rhett had been trying to do for years—pushing South Carolina right splash into the unexplored waters of secession. Long distrusted in his own state as a risky radical, the veteran revolutionist now had plenty of former conservatives shouting with him and eyeing Forts Moultrie and Sumter with mingled anxiety and exasperation. In Charleston, a group of leading secessionists founded the 1860 Association in September, with lawyer Robert Newman Gourdin as chairman, and began organizing the movement on a basis of business efficiency. The 1860 Association corresponded with disunionists in other Southern states, urging concerted action in the crisis. It issued a flood of pamphlets enumerating the wrongs of the South and picturing the booming prosperity that would result from repudiating the corrupt, money-grubbing government in Washington. It sponsored political meetings, inquired into the state's defenses, and took steps, as the *Mercury* put it, to "spot the traitors of the South, who may require some hemp ere long." [23]

There was such an uneasy feeling that Charleston was over-run with abolitionist spies and agents from the North, aiming to foment bloody insurrection among the slaves, that Vigilance Associations were formed to sniff out such plots. Unofficial military companies were blossoming all over the state, parading to martial music, and gathering on street corners to hang Lincoln in effigy. Semi-military groups called the Minute Men, organized on a statewide basis October 3rd, were campaigning for separa-tion and ready to fight if separation meant war. The October elections for the state legislature brought on a thousand picnics, barbecues, rallies, and stump speeches in which the sins of the North were listed ad infinitum.[24] "Damnation to the Yankees!" was a favorite toast. Up near Yorkville, Colonel Thomas Beards-ley and a gathering of secesh men used a cannon, probably along with a few libations, to demonstrate their feelings about Lincoln and the pro-slavery Presidential candidate, John Breck-inridge. Let's see what this cannon thinks about Lincoln, they shouted. They loaded the piece with a teaspoonful of powder, and the sickly *fffttt* it made when they discharged it had every-body in stitches. For Breckinridge they packed it with an enormous charge and touched it off. It made a mighty Breckin-ridge boom, true enough, but it exploded, wounding Beardsley and two others.[25]

Enthusiasm, it seemed, was getting a bit out of hand. Oratory and band music had their usual effect of drowning out sober reflection and inducing a reckless spirit of crusade. For two months previous to the Presidential election, the citizens of the Deep South's smallest state were exposed to an all but unanimous propaganda barrage that gained in intensity day by day and night by night until at last anyone who still had a notion that there might be some small virtue in the Union must have been an iron-willed character indeed.

Over in Fort Moultrie, Captain Doubleday viewed these portents with mounting ire. Then he went ahead and willfully committed the most awful social error possible for a man living in the vicinity of Charleston. He said—publicly—that he was opposed to slavery and intended to vote for Lincoln. Thereafter he was shunned by people on the streets and treated generally as if he were leprous, an attitude he observed with grim humor.[26]

Like Rhett, Doubleday was a man who had trouble seeing both sides of a question. A Unionist to the core, he detested the patricians of Charleston as a parcel of arrogant popinjays who had been flirting with treason for thirty years and now were ready to seize the hussy in a hot, sinful embrace. That their course was deliberately wicked was so patent to him as to admit of no argument. What if he and Mrs. Doubleday were no longer invited to dance and sip Madeira on bloom-scented verandahs with the chivalry? Those people would eventually have to be taught the facts of life. He was merely starting his own, private hostilities a little early, that was all.

WE HATE
EACH OTHER SO

Like most South Carolina political leaders, fifty-three-year-old Governor William Henry Gist was born to wealth in an atmosphere of heirlooms, servants, slaves, pride of lineage, and reverence for honor and state rights. The family sentiment on this last point was so strong that the governor's younger brother had been solemnly christened State Rights Gist. In his youthful days, William Gist had killed one Samuel Fair in a duel after "a controversy over some remarks about a lady." An ardent Methodist, he was dead set against overindulgence in alcohol and advocated restrictions on the sale of liquors.

On Monday, November 5th, 1860, however, Governor Gist seemed more in a mood for dueling than for preaching temperance, his adversary this time being nothing less than the Federal Union of thirty-three sovereign states. On that day the state legislature convened in the white-pillared statehouse at Columbia to choose Presidential electors—a quick formality, since everyone knew that all of South Carolina's votes would go to Breckinridge.[1] The feeling in the hall packed by legislators from low country and upcountry was tense. There was a grave air of history in the making. The governor had prepared the way by a private meeting eleven days earlier with the state's top politicians at which it was agreed formally to secede if Lincoln was elected.[2] Recent Republican victories in Pennsylvania and elsewhere left little doubt that the rail-splitter would win. Gist took this for granted as he got down to the business at hand.

". . . I would earnestly recommend," he said, "that in the event of Abraham Lincoln's election to the presidency, a convention of the people of this state be immediately called, to consider and determine for themselves the mode and measure of redress. . . . the only alternative left, in my judgment, is the secession of South Carolina from the Federal Union. . . .

"If . . . the government of the United States should attempt coercion, it will become our solemn duty to meet force by force. . . ." [3]

Reminding his audience that "we are contending for the safety of our homes and firesides," Gist went on to urge a thorough reorganization of the state militia, the arming of every man between eighteen and forty-five, and the immediate calling of ten thousand volunteers. The governor was not unmindful that ten thousand volunteers would be of little use unless they had ten thousand guns. Two weeks earlier he had sent an agent, Thomas F. Drayton, to Washington to negotiate quietly with Secretary of War John B. Floyd for the purchase of arms. Drayton had reported that he could buy ten thousand muskets through Floyd from the United States Government at two dollars apiece. Secretary Floyd, a Virginian, was so remarkably agreeable an official that he did not seem to mind that those guns might be used to shoot holes through the Union he served. The muskets were old smoothbores recently superseded by improved models, but still they could perforate a man at two hundred yards.[4]

So the legislature agreed to remain in session until the result of America's most momentous Presidential election—held the very next day—should become official instead of merely inevitable.

Almost without exception the state senators and representatives were in favor of secession, the main points at issue being how soon and under what circumstances. That they had ample provocation to quit the Union, few had any doubt. The victory of Lincoln on the anti-slavery Republican platform, while not sufficient cause in itself, was regarded as the last straw in a thirty-year succession of wrongs against the South.[5] John Calhoun was ten years dead, but reverence for him and his unique doctrine of state sovereignty burned like a holy flame. These men had been brought up on talk of secession, had discussed it pro and con for years, and many had opposed it previously only on grounds of expediency rather than because of any feeling that there might be something improper or illegal about breaking up the Union. South Carolina was a state unto itself, completely misunderstood in the North. Years earlier the name of Union Street in Charleston had proved annoying enough so that it was changed to State Street.[6] The feeling of loyalty toward the whole nation was much like Colonel Beardsley's cannon when it went *fffttt* for Lincoln, while the allegiance to the state was loaded with a potent and dangerous charge. Carolinians were more inclined to be "statriots" than patriots, and were perfectly convinced of the rectitude of this narrow fidelity to their state.[7]

They could give reasons galore to justify slamming the door on the Union. The slavery question, the tariff, the fight for the territories, the endless fugitive-slave quarrels—undoubtedly all of these underlay the trouble. But probably Mary Boykin Chesnut, the pretty and mettlesome wife of Senator James Chesnut, struck more to the heart of the matter.

"We are divorced," she said, "because we have hated each other so."[8]

South Carolina's aristocrats did not take kindly to being characterized by Northern abolitionists as drunken, brutal slave-beaters, or as lechers who made every slave woman a concubine. "The South," said Wendell Phillips, "is one great brothel, where half a million of women are flogged into prostitution."[9] The planter could reply that slaves in general were treated well, enjoying benefits unknown in their primitive state, and could even cite Biblical approval of slavery, but somehow this did not answer the case. Names like "sadist" and "lecher" stuck. When a South Carolina Congressman beat a Massachusetts Senator insensible in Congress in 1856, and won Southern applause for the act, it was a symptom of a national malaise. The North and South had insulted and assailed each other for several decades in Congress, in newspapers, in sermons and every other medium known to man, and perhaps hatred was a logical result. South Carolina planters resented being regarded as morally reprehensible. To make matters worse, many of them felt a mite vulnerable about slavery, for European nations frowned on it too, which put them on the defensive, a position that rankled. Now the talk was about over, to be replaced by action.

The election returns, trickling in on the telegraph, settled that. Lincoln—and his "mulatto" running mate—were minority victors over the three tickets against them. If Alabama's Senator Clay had the right information, the stage was set for the Black Republicans to free the Negroes and force the whites to intermarry with them.[10] The news made Charleston boil with excitement. Citizens paraded with shouts of "Hurrah for Lincoln!" giving the devil his due for assuring secession. A crowd of them went out to Fort Moultrie, sporting secession cockades and marching around the fort, which gave old Colonel Gardner a few uneasy moments. The booksellers of Charleston indignantly closed their accounts with the publishers of *Harper's Weekly,* returning all copies because the *Weekly* published a full-length portrait and biographical sketch of Lincoln.[11]

Up in Virginia, wealthy, sixty-six-year-old Edmund Ruffin left his plantation on the Pamunkey as soon as he had cast his vote for Breckinridge and boarded a train for South Carolina, carrying with him a pike. An eccentric genius, Ruffin had rescued Virginia's worn-out soil by his discovery of the efficacy of calcareous manures, but for years he had been more interested in secession than in fertilizers. Fanatical in his hatred of the North, he had long predicted war, preached disunion, handed out pamphlets and had encouraged "Ladies' Shooting Clubs" to prepare Southern women to defend themselves during the conflict. A year earlier he had journeyed to Charles Town to witness the hanging of John Brown, and had managed to appropriate a number of the pikes with which the old abolitionist had armed his followers. He liked to carry one of them around with him bearing the label:

SAMPLE OF THE FAVORS DESIGNED FOR
US BY OUR NORTHERN BRETHREN

Ruffin had sent a John Brown pike to the governor of each Southern state, urging that it be placed prominently in the capitol as a reminder of Northern enmity and violence. On his only trip to New York, his luggage had been stolen—a fitting example of Yankee honor. An omnivorous reader, he shunned Webster's dictionary as Yankee trash. Now he was utterly impatient with his own state of Virginia because his secesh talk got short shrift there. He was bound for South Carolina, where the people had some spirit.[12]

In Columbia he found spirit enough to warm his heart. Minute Men were marching, bands playing, and speeches were being given on every corner. The old man was transported with joy. Walking into the crowded lobby of the Congaree House, he was immediately recognized and serenaded. His eyes ablaze, his head jerking defiantly so that his long white locks danced around his shoulders, he obliged with a brief speech.

"This [secession] has been the one great idea of my life," he said in part. "The defense of the South, I verily believe, can only be secured through the lead of South Carolina. As old as I am, I have come here to join you in that lead. . . . The first drop of blood spilled on the soil of South Carolina will bring Virginia and every Southern state with you." [13]

There was something thrilling and electric in the atmosphere at Columbia that invaded men's souls and even converted skeptics—United States Senator James Chesnut for one. Until very recently the Princeton-educated Chesnut, owner of a half-dozen plantations and a thousand slaves, had been dubious about secession undertaken with no more compelling immediate reason than the election of a Republican President.[14] Now in Columbia the gale blew him down. He came out hotly for separation in a speech arraigning the "blind consciences and crazy brains" of the Republicans, who in South Carolina were always referred to as Black Republicans. "For myself," he declared, "I would unfurl the Palmetto flag, fling it to the breeze." [15] Danger of war? The Senator scoffed at such an idea.

"The man most averse to blood might safely drink every drop shed in establishing a Southern Confederacy," he said.[16]

The wind in Charleston was as strong. The United States District Court was in session there on November 7th, presided over by Harvard-educated Judge Andrew Gordon Magrath, a scholarly man whose massive head looked out of proportion to his small body. The foreman of the grand jury was Huguenot-descended Robert Gourdin, chairman of the 1860 Association. It appears that Gourdin and the judge had got their heads together before court convened and reached agreement on a startling Association project. Gourdin rose and addressed the court.

"The verdict of the Northern section of the Confederacy," he said, "solemnly announced to the country through the ballot-box on yesterday, has swept away the last hope for the permanence, for the stability of the Federal government of these sovereign states. . . . These issues involve the existence of the government of which this court is the organ and minister. In these extraordinary circumstances, the grand jury respectfully declines to proceed with the presentments."

What he was saying was that the jury was seceding from the United States court. Judge Magrath did not reprove him. He got to his feet, deliberately unfastened his silken judicial gown, tossed it away, and seceded from his federal job.

"So far as I am concerned," he said, "the Temple of Justice, raised under the Constitution of the United States, is now closed . . . I thank God that its doors have been closed before its altar has been desecrated with sacrifices to tyranny." [17]

United States District Attorney James Conner and United States Collector C. J. Colcock likewise made haste to resign. As propaganda, this dramatic retirement of well-paid United States officials could hardly have been more skillful, for it made disunionists seethe to follow the example and shake off the federal fetters with all speed, while even the laggards were impressed. A huge flag emblazoned with a palmetto-and-lone-star design was promptly stretched across the street from the upper window of Mr. Rhett's *Mercury* office. "The tea has been thrown overboard," crowed the *Mercury*. "The revolution of 1860 has been initiated." [18]

Tea was indeed pouring over the gunwales. Ex-Judge Magrath unloaded some more when he addressed a huge rally at Institute Hall, saying little but making it count.

"Fellow citizens," he said in level tones, "the time for deliberation has passed." He walked across the stage, saying nothing for a long, long moment, then turned and shouted passionately, "The time for action has come!"

The audience rose and cheered, one of them a young clergyman named A. Toomer Porter. "And I, fool as I was, yelled with the rest of them and threw up my hat," he later recalled, "and no doubt thought we could whip creation. It was very dramatic in the judge, a fine piece of acting, but alas, the prologue of what a tragedy!" [19]

Over at Fort Moultrie, things were in terrible shape. Guns had been dismounted and the workmen had torn great gaps in the wall where double capioneres were to be constructed. Colonel Gardner was nervous at the thought of trying to stave off a possible attack with his fort caught in deshabille, and yet he did nothing, saying irritably that under the circumstances he could not be held responsible for anything that might happen.[20] Out at Sumter, Captain Foster had 109 laborers working at a job that would take several months to complete even with makeshift haste, assuming that the truculent Carolinians would allow him to complete it. He had exactly one ordnance sergeant with him to make up a defense force of two. Many of the fort's lower embrasures were wide open, making excellent entrances. It appalled him to think what a ridiculous and humiliating thing it would be if a rowboat full of Charleston blades bearing fowling pieces should come in the night and snatch powerful Fort Sumter from the United States Army, as they could do at any time they were so inclined.

While many of his workmen were secessionists, Foster felt that a number of his Baltimore hands were good Union men and could be relied on. The captain wrote Washington urgently recommending that a few small arms be given the workmen to protect the government property. This suggestion was passed on to Secretary Floyd, who approved the idea provided Colonel Gardner was in favor.[21]

Colonel Gardner was not in favor. He pointed out that most of the Sumter workmen were of foreign extraction and doubtful loyalty. Putting guns in their hands might be dangerous business. Furthermore, he admitted uneasiness because right in his lap at Moultrie he had fifty laborers, known secessionists who lived in the neighborhood.

". . . I am constrained to say," he wrote, "the only proper precaution . . . is to fill these two companies [at Moultrie] with drilled recruits (say fifty men) at once, and send two companies from Old Point Comfort to occupy respectively Fort Sumter and Castle Pinckney." [22]

Gardner had asked for reinforcements before, without result. Had he known the Secretary of War better, he would have understood that asking for more soldiers was hopeless because Floyd was resolutely opposed to it. As a result, the colonel got neither the men nor the guns he needed. Moultrie was in such a defenseless condition that Captains Doubleday and Seymour were in a sweat. They repeatedly urged the commandant to take at least nominal steps for protection, and persuaded him to detail night sentries for the approaches. Knowing that the fort was short on ammunition and hand grenades, as well as maintenance supplies, they pressed him to replenish them from the United States arsenal in Charleston.[23]

This Gardner was reluctant to do, even though it was ordinary routine and plain duty. He knew the arsenal was being watched by attentive Charlestonians and feared that any withdrawal of ammunition would bring Minute Men swarming into his semi-dismantled fort. But his officers kept at him, and finally he decided to do his duty by stealth. He detailed Captain Seymour to take a squad of soldiers to the arsenal, directing that they leave after dark and that the enlisted men wear civilian clothes in the hope that the move would escape observation.[24]

Late on November 8th Seymour sailed with his men in a small schooner up the Ashley River and tied up at a private wharf near the arsenal which the garrison customarily used. No sooner had they started carrying out boxes labeled "Cartridges" than a gentleman tapped Seymour on the shoulder. Sir, he said, I am the owner of this wharf and I cannot permit you to use it for such a purpose.

As Captain Seymour parleyed with him, a crowd gathered

with a speed indicating that some vigilant observer had spread the word. There were threats and jeers. Things were looking ominous. Rather than start a battle then and there, Seymour ordered his men to desist and to carry back the ammunition already moved. The expedition returned empty-handed to the fort. Next morning, Seymour went in to town and called on Mayor Charles Macbeth at the city hall.

The mayor, a courtly individual, knew immediately that his townspeople were in the wrong. He apologized politely, said that South Carolina wished to be faithful to its obligations so long as it remained in the Union, and Seymour could take whatever he wanted from the arsenal.[25]

When Colonel Gardner learned of this, he got up on his high horse. Since when, he demanded, was the mayor of Charleston telling the commandant at the fort what he could or could not do with goverment property? He refused to avail himself of the mayor's permission, thereby depriving himself of the very ammunition he needed.[26] In truth, the old colonel was disgusted with Washington for not sending him more men, and was averse to stirring up a hornet's nest in Charleston anyway. He did not know that the arsenal fiasco had already got him in trouble with Secretary Floyd.

Some Charleston chauvinist had dispatched a telegram to Assistant Secretary of State William Henry Trescot in Washington, a native of Charleston and a statriotic Carolinian, describing the outrage. The telegram inquired whether the Secretary of War had authorized the removal of "arms" from the arsenal, warning that if he had he had better revoke it or there would be a "collision." Trescot hurried to consult his good friend, Secretary Floyd. Possibly Floyd was misled by the term "arms" into thinking his soldiers had attempted to take guns rather than ammunition. He was a man who could become confused without outside help. In any case, despite the fact that he was even then arranging to sell thousands of government muskets to the state of South Carolina through an intermediary, he was angered at the news that his own soldiers had tried to arm themselves.[27]

"Telegraph back at once," he snapped to Trescot, "say you

have seen me, that no such orders have been issued and none such will be issued under any circumstances." [28]

So Colonel Gardner soon learned that he apparently was forbidden to perform the usual routine of getting cartridges from the arsenal, which in turn led to the unpleasant thought that his men were expected to ward off possible assault with clubs or fingernails. By this time some of Gardner's officers were deeply suspicious of their own War Department, headed as it was by a man of strong Southern leanings. It looked to them as if Floyd had no intention of supporting the garrison but aimed to weaken them so they would be easy prey.

"We believed that in the event of an outbreak from Charleston few of us would survive," Doubleday later recalled.[29] So concerned was he that he bethought himself of the fact that all his mail to the North went through the Charleston post office. Who could tell when some prying clerk might take a notion to peek at what the abolitionist captain was writing? The resourceful Doubleday solved this dilemma by devising a code so that he could communicate safely with his brother Ulysses in New York City. The two brothers each owned copies of the same dictionary. In writing Ulysses anything confidential, Abner merely represented a word by two numbers, one indicating its page in the book, the other its position on the page counting from the top.[30]

More trouble piled on Colonel Gardner's gray head when an assistant inspector general, handsome young Major Fitz John Porter, arrived to take a careful look at the army's position in Charleston harbor. Porter, not knowing he was viewing a situation that would soon catapult him to two-star rank, was appalled at what he saw. From the way people were talking there was no telling when Moultrie might be attacked by excited citizens, and yet the fort was a chaos of construction work, its men in a poor state of discipline and its commanding officer too indifferent even to take proper precautions against a surprise assault.[31] The hospital and storehouses were inflammable frame buildings outside the fort, and were unguarded. "An incendiary could in a few minutes destroy all the supplies and workshops of the command," Porter wrote in his report to Washington, and went on:

> The unguarded state of the fort invites attack, if such design exists, and much discretion and prudence are required on the part of the commander to restore the proper security without exciting a community prompt to misconstrue actions of authority. I think this can be effected by a proper commander. . . . All could have been easily arranged several weeks since, when the danger was foreseen by the present commander. Now much delicacy must be practiced. The garrison is weak, and I recommend that a favorable opportunity be taken to fill up the companies with the best-drilled recruits available.[32]

Even before this stinging report reached Washington, Colonel Gardner's days at the one-time country club were numbered. He had lost the confidence of the Secretary of War. Mr. Floyd paid no more heed to Porter's recommendation for reinforcements than he had to Gardner's. He was now looking around for a new commander for the garrison, an officer who would combine all the qualities of discretion, prudence, and delicacy Porter stressed were needed for this supremely sensitive post.

Gardner's abortive arsenal expedition also put ideas into the head of Governor Gist. On November 12th, twenty South Carolina militiamen marched up to the arsenal. The lieutenant in command informed Captain F. C. Humphreys, the United States officer in charge, that the detachment was tendered by the state as a "guard" in case of an insurrection among the slaves. Humphreys, a Floridian whose Southern ties later made him join the Confederacy, was still trying to do his duty. He accepted the guard and wrote Washington for instructions that never came.[33] While this state guard over a federal arsenal would prevent Negroes from stealing any of the 22,000 muskets stored there, it also came in handy as a method of close surveillance over the arsenal. It could be interpreted as a suggestion on the part of the state that federal soldiers as well as Negroes would have trouble getting arms from the depot which was their source of supply. In surrounding the arsenal the state was making a polite but firm encroachment on federal authority at the same time as it crippled the small garrison at Moultrie. In failing to protest the "guard," Mr. Floyd was nothing if not conciliatory.

Meanwhile, Judge Magrath hurried up to Columbia to urge the legislature to get a move on with secession, sent by a group of Charlestonians who also dispatched a telegram to the capital saying in part, "Our people cannot be restrained." [34] The Union ties weighed on hotheads like a dishonor that must be cast off without palaver, and yet palaver was the order of the day. Speeches were heard from every balcony and soapbox. Edmund Ruffin was so charmed by the disunion orgy that he wrote his son, "The time since I have been here has been the happiest of my life." [35] In Columbia, Judge Magrath described the feeble federal forts in Charleston as a standing menace and insult:

"I came from a city where millions worth of property lie exposed to peril . . . where three fortresses bristle with cannon pointed against her. . . . In the name of Heaven give the word and let us raise your flag and point it to these cannons." [36]

An intelligent man, the judge must have known he was overstating the case. This kind of stentorian pugnacity, repeated in cities and hamlets all over the state, inflamed the feeling of mass injury that was growing a bit too quickly as it was. Those who feared that secession might involve some impropriety or even danger were unheard in the tumult, intimidated by the sudden groundswell against them. It took courage to stand up against the tide, particularly since it was evident that no one could stop it. One of the few who stood his ground nevertheless was witty old James Louis Petigru, the state's outstanding lawyer, who had fought disunion since the Thirties and now realized that the fight was lost. "My countrymen here in S. C.," he wrote, "are distempered to a degree that makes them to a calm and impartial observer real objects of pity." [37]

To the disunionists it was such men as Petigru who deserved pity because they could not see the plain path of honor and destiny. In Columbia, James Chesnut resigned as United States

C

Senator, and James Henry Hammond quickly followed him. The legislature whipped through a bill calling for a state convention to meet December 17th and whose sole purpose would be to walk out of the Union officially as soon as possible. Senator Hammond was one of those who was swept with the tide against his will. Although he felt there was plenty of justification for secession, he saw no reason for all the hurry and was afraid his hot-blooded colleagues might get the state in a ticklish position, leaving the Union alone with no friends at her side.

"I thought Magrath & all those fellows were great asses for resigning & I have done it myself," he wrote. "It is an epidemic and very foolish. It reminds me of the Japanese who when insulted rip up their own bowels. . . . People are wild. The scenes of the French Revolution are being enacted already. Law & Constitution are equally & utterly disregarded." [38]

Hammond knew better than to say such things publicly. Adelina Patti was singing in Charleston at the time, to disappointingly small audiences; people were more interested in secession than in sopranos. A canny Connecticut Yankee, Captain A. A. Colt, arrived in Charleston to push the sale of his arms, made in Hartford, to local officers and gentlemen. This outraged a Carolinian named A. J. Gonzales, who advertised that he sold fine rifles manufactured by "a Southern company" at thirty-three dollars each. Mr. J. P. Caulfield composed a "Grand Secession March." The proprietor of Charleston's Mammoth Boot Store suddenly discovered why customers were shunning his establishment and hastened to publish an announcement:

Information having come to us, to the effect that this firm have been connected with circulating Abolition documents, we respectfully assert that such is not the case. The rumor is entirely without foundation. Our interests, our sentiments, our lives if need be, and property, are with the South and for South Carolina.[39]

On Saturday, November 17th, Charleston staged a great public demonstration before a ninety-foot "liberty pole" erected at Meeting and Hayne Streets. Twenty thousand people heard a

100-gun salute and cheered when the band played the *Miserere* from Il Trovatore as a requiem for the departed Union, while marching groups carried banners emblazoned "Good-bye, Yankee Doodle," "Stand to Your Arms, Palmetto Boys!" and "Let Us Bury the Union's Dead Carcass." [40]

Brilliant, volatile young Lawrence Keitt pretty well struck the public temper a few days later when he was serenaded at the Charleston Hotel. Although he still represented South Carolina in Congress, Keitt was not anxious to hold his job.

"I say we have the right [to secede]," he shouted, "and by Heaven nothing but the strong hand shall put it down. . . . Let us unfurl the flag and, with the sword of State, cut the bonds of this accursed Union." [41]

But Keitt had been talking that way almost ever since he wore an Eton collar. It was different when Michael P. O'Connor of Charleston described the Union as "a dead carcass stinking in the nostrils of the Southern people." [42]

Mr. O'Connor had always been known as a Union man.

THE UNLUCKIEST MAN

Late in October 1860, Lieutenant General Winfield Scott, top dog of the United States Army for nineteen years, seized a quill pen in his New York office and began writing a document remarkable for its combination of sense and nonsense. General Scott was seventy-four, six feet four inches tall, weighed three hundred pounds net, and had a face like an eroded hillside but an eye of marvelous force. He was an American institution, a figure of legend and fable for decades. Devoid of false modesty, he took it for granted he was the nation's greatest military chieftain since Washington, which he was. He had moved the headquarters of the army from Washington to New York seven years earlier because he had lost to Franklin Pierce in the Presidential election of 1852 and could not abide being near the man who had beaten him. This did not make for efficiency or close liaison between the general-in-chief and the Secretary of War, but Scott liked it that way and he stayed.[1]

Downright inspiring as a battle leader in 1812 and 1847, long a national hero, the general was almost as famous for his tendency to pull boners when he ventured into any utterances on matters of policy. He finished this particular utterance, labeled it "Views Suggested by the Imminent Danger of a Disruption of the Union by the Secession of One or More of the Southern States," and dispatched it to his boss in Washington, Secretary Floyd.

Floyd passed it along to *his* boss, President Buchanan, who must have started at what he read.

The general wrote that should only one state secede, force might be used to bring it back into the Union. But if many states seceded and force were employed, the resulting civil war would be so bloody as to make "the intestine wars of our Mexi-

can neighbors . . . sink into mere child's play." A far lesser
evil, Scott went on, would be to go right ahead and carve up the
Union peacefully into four separate and independent confeder-
acies, each bound together by its solidarity of interest. The
Northeast Confederacy, for example, would comprise the New
England and middle states and would have its capital at
Albany.[2]

The President could be pardoned for goggling. Even if the
general-in-chief had a right to move into high political policy,
which he did not, his proposition to remedy secession amounted
to consummating it wholesale, much like killing a patient to
cure his ills. Then Scott's Views came down out of fantasy. It
was his solemn conviction, he went on, that nine United States
forts in the South, all of them vacant or weakly garrisoned, were
in danger of seizure by secessionists. Among them were Forts
Moultrie and Sumter. Garrison them strongly at once, Scott
urged, or a corporal's guard could snatch any of them.[3]

This was a military recommendation that Buchanan could
not ignore. He immediately inquired what men were available.
Scott's reply fizzled sadly. Five companies, he said—about four
hundred men.[4]

The old general could have done better than that. To think
of reinforcing nine Southern forts with 400 men when Sumter
alone called for a war garrison of 650 was laughable. It was true
that the scarcity of soldiers was not Scott's fault, for he had
asked Buchanan for more men and the President had recommended to Congress that the military establishment be enlarged,
without result. The whole United States Army, charged with
the protection of three million square miles of territory, numbered only a shade over sixteen thousand officers and men, most
of them guarding Indian country in the Far West. But it was a
question of choosing between crises, and a judicious combing
of the posts could surely have winnowed a thousand men for
reassignment. A thousand extra men could have held the more
important of those nine forts until additional recruits came
along. Now was the time of all times to reinforce them, as soon
would be demonstrated.[5]

Buchanan preferred to let sleeping dogs lie. Sending men down to those forts would inflame the Southern excitement he was trying to pacify. Like most Northerners, he underestimated the magnitude of what was brewing and hoped to baby it along until he returned to his country estate near Lancaster come March 4th.[6] So—very well, four hundred men is absurd and we will forget about it.

One of the world's unluckiest men, James Buchanan had sought the Presidency when it was a post of honor and had won it when it became a target of abuse. In four short months his term would be finished, but those four months would come near finishing him. A six-foot, privately wealthy country gentleman of sixty-nine, he had performed the miracle of immersing himself in the pitch of American politics for four decades without being personally defiled, serving his country as Congressman, minister plenipotentiary to Russia and England, Secretary of State, and chief executive. Everybody knew he was honest and conscientious, although he could be a bit foxy at times. Dignified, suave, a bachelor who delighted in female society, the President was known behind his back—never to his face—as Old Buck, The Squire, and the Old Public Functionary, or O. P. F. for short, which enemies construed as "Old Pennsylvania Fogy." He liked to conduct government on a gentlemanly basis, but during his administration things had come to a dreadful pass. Congressmen from the North and South were often the worse for liquor. They shrieked insults in the Capitol, cursed each other, swung roundhouse punches, and many had taken to carrying pistols or bowie knives for protection. Representative Daniel Sickles of New York, a close friend of the President and no bluenose, remarked, "The debate reeked with whisky. The solemn resolves of statesmanship were taken by men whose brains were feverish from whisky." [7]

All in all, Mr. Buchanan was growing tired of the vulgar tumult and was looking forward to Lincoln's inauguration as a day of deliverance. But now he had General Scott's Views to think about. Much as he wanted to, he found he could not quite forget about them. Above all, there was that tense situation in

Charleston. Old Colonel Gardner kept complaining about the threats against Fort Moultrie and asking for reinforcements. Major Porter had gone down to look things over and likewise had urged reinforcement. Rumors trickling North said the Carolinians were in an extraordinary state of excitement. That incident when the citizens came close to mobbing the soldiers at the arsenal was a nasty portent.

So the President summoned Secretary Floyd to the White House to consider what might be done.

John Buchanan Floyd, former governor of Virginia and also son of an earlier governor, was an affable, heavy-jowled man of fifty-three, probably the most chaotic executive ever to hold federal office. Careless, absent-minded, his public and private affairs were always in confusion. He had a habit of keeping records involving thousands in government funds on loose scraps of paper, some of which he lost. His neglect had the War Department in anarchy, and yet Buchanan liked him personally and could not bring himself to dismiss him. For many months, unknown to the President, he had been performing a reckless and illegal juggling act with federal money.[8] At the moment he was busy arranging to sell those ten thousand government rifles to the state of South Carolina, which was not illegal but was certainly unwise. The government had 105,000 of those outdated rifles for sale to states or private parties, South Carolina being theoretically entitled to her share. Still, a prudent Secretary of War would not have placed muskets in the hands of excited Palmetto men who were making threatening gestures toward Forts Moultrie and Sumter and the whole Union. The fact that he preferred to close the deal quietly through a New York bank as intermediary made it plain that he foresaw criticism if it were done openly. Floyd was the worst possible man to head the War Department at this critical time, and he should have been removed long before on the ground of incompetence alone. Yet there he was, at Buchanan's elbow.

Floyd assured the President that the rumors of violence at Charleston were exaggerated. He felt sure the people would not attack the forts.[9] Nevertheless, Buchanan was disturbed enough to take up the matter at a Cabinet meeting two days later on November 9th. He told his counselors that the question to be considered was the most important since he took office, namely, what course the administration should take toward the ominous activities in the South, especially South Carolina.

Ancient Secretary of State Lewis Cass spoke right up and said that while he conceded that the South had grievances, this secession doctrine was monstrous and should be put down by force if necessary. Attorney General Jeremiah Black did not go quite that far but he "advocated earnestly the propriety of sending at once a strong force into the forts in Charleston harbor." [10] This suggestion was anathema to the Dixie members of the Cabinet—Howell Cobb, Jacob Thompson, and Floyd—and Buchanan opposed it himself. The meeting came to nothing, being only the first of many in which the Northern and Southern members came to loggerheads on the question of what to do about South Carolina. This did not mean that no decision was made, for a failure to decide on sending reinforcements was as good as a decision against sending them. The President was running the show and even in his uneasiness he fell in with his Southern colleagues' dislike of any step that might smack of force, or "coercion" as everyone was calling it. So matters tended to drift in Washington while they moved at top speed in Carolina.

While the problem was receiving this passive treatment, Francis Wilkinson Pickens, Mr. Buchanan's recently resigned minister to Russia, arrived in New York with his family aboard the *Adriatic* and immediately got into a controversy with the steamship company. They lost some of his baggage, he said, plus a fine "musical box" he had bought in Europe. He valued the lost articles at $240, and when the company refused to admit blame he took steps to bring suit.[11] Then he hurried on to Washington.

Pickens had more pressing matters on his mind than lost baggage. A planter from Edgefield, South Carolina, he had been a stormy figure in local and national politics for thirty years. In some respects he was a *beau idéal* of the ruling class in the

Palmetto State. He was a kinsman of the canonized John Calhoun, owner of a vast estate near Edgefield manned by several
hundred slaves, and a firm believer in state rights. A supporter
of Buchanan, he had not been keen on going to the land of the
czars when the President tendered him the post in 1858, but his
beautiful and accomplished wife Lucy liked the idea and he had
served there for two years "without special distinction." Of late
he had found St. Petersburg an awkward place from which to
watch the surprising events in his home state. Pickens was dis-
tressed that many Europeans were laughing at the pretensions
of South Carolina, and he thought his fellow citizens were being
foolishly precipitous. He was going back to Carolina to get a
better view and also to use his considerable influence in favor
of moderation.[12]

One characteristic of Carolinians at the time was that the
closer they got to home, the less were they inclined to moderation. Pickens' conservative feelings were to undergo a rapid
change, and the change began as soon as he reached Washington. One of the first men he saw there was Charleston-born
William Henry Trescot, the Assistant Secretary of State who,
being on friendly terms with Buchanan and in close contact
with South Carolina leaders, knew exactly how the political
breezes were blowing. Only thirty-eight, Trescot was a quiet
intellectual who had no doubt that his state would secede and
was concerned only that she do it properly. Trescot had used his
good offices with Secretary Floyd to promote the sale of the
muskets to Governor Gist's agent.[13] Like Pickens, he was wealthy
and came from a patrician family, but there the resemblance
largely ended. Where Pickens was apt to be dogmatic and impulsive, Trescot was a cool, subtle individual who always looked
in every direction before he jumped.

So into the attentive ear of Francis Pickens, Trescot must
have poured information about the inner turmoil in South
Carolina which had not reached Russia. Pickens was in a difficult
position. He felt loyalty to Buchanan, his political sponsor and
always a good friend of the South. In spite of all that, if he had

to take sides in a controversy between the federal government
and the state of South Carolina, his choice was clear. The state
came first, obviously. On November 12th he dined with Trescot,
Floyd, and several other Dixie men in Washington, the talk
inevitably bearing on the question of Southern relations with
the Union. Undoubtedly Pickens urged Floyd not to send reinforcements to Charleston harbor, although the secretary needed
no coaching on that score. "The belief seemed to be that disunion was inevitable," Floyd recorded in his diary. "Pickens
. . . was excited and warm." [14]

But it appears that he cooled off somewhat when he had his
audience with the President. No doubt Buchanan made full
use of the political debt owed him by the late minister and asked
that when he return to his home state he go in friendliness and
moderation. Later events made it evident that Pickens left with
the feeling that it would be only right that secession should be
delayed until the change of administrations on March 4th so
that Buchanan should not bear the brunt of it. The Republicans brought it on—let them suffer for it when they came into
office.[15]

As for Secretary Floyd, he had been pondering a thorny question: How to safeguard the United States forts in Charleston
against the angry citizens without making them still angrier?
He saw the answer not in reinforcements, which to him smacked
of coercion and would be violently resented, but in the selection
of new commanders tactful enough so that they could soothe
the populace.[16] He viewed the matter as a diplomatic problem
rather than a military one. In his opinion, Gardner had botched
everything. His removal, and the dispatch of new and discreet
officers as good-will ambassadors, would serve as a gesture to
show South Carolina the amicable intentions of the government.

The arsenal, being right in the city, was a touchy spot, now
commanded by Captain Humphreys of Ordnance with fourteen
men under him. Floyd was about as conciliatory as a man could
be when he ordered Brevet Colonel Benjamin Huger to serve
as ambassador in charge of the arsenal, with Humphreys re-

maining under him. Huger was a native of Charleston, a member of one of its most prominent families. If he could not mollify the citizens, who could? [17]

The job of ambassador in charge of the harbor forts was even tougher. Floyd went over the list of available officers with care and finally came up with one who seemed just the right fellow. As he later said, "I selected him myself." [18] On November 15th, the headquarters of the army issued Special Orders No. 137:

"Major Robert Anderson, First Artillery, will forthwith proceed to Fort Moultrie, and immediately relieve Bvt. Col. John L. Gardner . . . who, on being relieved, will repair without delay to San Antonio, Texas. . . ." [19]

I PICKED HIM MYSELF

When Robert Anderson received his orders in New York City, where he was on furlough, he knew he was in for a difficult assignment. He hardly could have been aware that the next five months would visit him with such tension and torture as to shatter his health and speed him to the grave. He was fifty-five —four years older than Lincoln—and with a brilliant thirty-five-year army record since his graduation from West Point in 1825, he was yet a major, promotion being as slow as molasses in the tight little peacetime military establishment. Secretary Floyd had chosen well, perhaps better than he knew. No other officer in the service possessed the unique combination of qualities embodied in Anderson—characteristics that would make him fight to avert war in Charleston harbor with a dedication strange in a man of arms.

A compact, middle-sized man with iron-gray hair, a warm smile, and inbred courtesy, he had recently served with Senator Jefferson Davis of Mississippi on a commission inquiring into the condition of the Military Academy. Davis had known him since both were cadets at West Point, and later as a brother officer in the Black Hawk War, calling him "a true soldier and man of the finest sense of honor." [1] In that same war Anderson had sworn into the army a lanky young Illinois recruit named Abraham Lincoln. [2] But that was twenty-eight years ago, and right now he had the Charleston assignment to worry about. His first move was to consult with his old friend Lieutenant General Scott at his fine house on Twelfth Street.

Scott, who always called officers under him "young gentlemen" even though they might be grandfathers, was fond of Anderson, who had once been his aide-de-camp and had fought nobly under him in Mexico until three bullets felled him at

Molino del Rey. But Scott was not fond of Secretary Floyd, who ignored his Views and of late had taken to running the army without much consultation with the general-in-chief. Scott himself was partly to blame for this, since he insisted on maintaining his headquarters at such an inconvenient distance from Washington, but he had been in New York for years without being bypassed in this way. Very well. Mr. Floyd had selected the young gentleman for the post. Let Mr. Floyd tell him what to do when he got there. Scott was kindly, but he refused to give Anderson specific orders or suggestions, merely going over the situation with him in a general way.[3]

But he seems to have made one remark that must have stuck in Anderson's mind. Fort Moultrie, the general knew, was indefensible. It might be necessary for the major to transfer his command over to Sumter, which held Moultrie and the whole harbor under its guns, provided someone would get busy and mount the guns.[4]

A thorough man, Anderson wanted to learn as much as possible about what he was getting into. He had served a tour of duty at Moultrie in 1845–46, but things had changed since then. He next called on Captain George W. Cullum, West Point '33, an engineering officer then stationed at Fort Hamilton who knew Charleston like the back of his hand. Cullum had spent the better part of the five years from 1855 to 1860 working on Fort Sumter and improving the harbor, returning from Charleston only the previous summer.[5] He was blunt about conditions down Palmetto way. South Carolina would secede for a certainty, he told Anderson, and Charleston would be the center of it. Fort Sumter—well, that would be the only safe place for United States troops anywhere around.[6] That is, it *would* be if it had any guns.

So Major Anderson said goodbye to his invalid wife Eliza, his three daughters and baby son and left for Washington, where he conferred with Secretary Floyd. In selecting Anderson for the post, Floyd was influenced by the fact that the major was a Kentuckian who had married a Georgia lady—the daughter of the late General Duncan Clinch—and was known to be sympathetic with the South. Until early in 1860 he had owned a few slaves in Georgia himself.[7] For all that, he was a Union man, opposed to secession and Southern extremists, so it was felt that he could fulfill two functions that were already essentially contradictory—satisfy the Carolinians and at the same time do his duty to the United States.[8]

Yet Secretary Floyd was not quite candid with the major when the two met in the War Department building. He stressed the delicacy of the situation at Charleston, to be sure, and the great need for discretion. But he neglected to mention the one fact that the major above all should have known. Floyd did not say that he was determined to send no reinforcements to Charleston. When Anderson boarded a southbound train, he knew he was going to a fort so undermanned as to be a military jest, but he did not know it was fated to stay that way.[9]

One of the most sincerely religious of men, a seeker of divine guidance in every act, he must have done a deal of praying as the train clattered southward. Yet his new task represented an exciting challenge. He, of all officers in the army, had been chosen for this most exacting of posts. His assignment was a token of special government trust in him as well as a matter of enough political importance to make newspapers North and South comment on it as they viewed the developing drama in South Carolina. In a sense, Anderson felt a hereditary fitness to command in Charleston, almost as if it had been writ long before in the celestial scroll. His father, Virginia-born Major Richard Clough Anderson, had fought the British from old Fort Moultrie in 1779, had been captured when the city fell to the redcoats, and had spent nine months there in prison. The son was hoping for better luck at Moultrie.[10]

Born near Louisville in 1805 into a remarkable family of Scottish-Welsh ancestry, Robert Anderson was old enough to remember the nation as a loose collection of eighteen states. He could recall when Andrew Jackson and President Monroe had visited his hospitable father. He could take pride in the fact that his mother—his widowed father's second wife—was related to Justice Marshall. At West Point he had been hardly more

than an average student, standing fifteenth in a class of thirty-
seven, more known for solid plugging than brilliance—known
even better for his quiet sense of duty. On his graduation he
had taken his only long respite from army service of his adult
life, serving in Bogotá for a year and a half as secretary to his
older half-brother, Richard Anderson, United States minister
to Colombia. Since then he had been stationed at a score of
posts, had been an instructor in artillery at West Point, and had
written a textbook, *Instruction for Field Artillery*. He had survived cholera in the Black Hawk War, been brevetted for gallantry in the Florida War, brevetted again in Mexico. He
avoided voting on the principle that a soldier has no place in
politics. Said a kinsman: "The Ten Commandments, the Constitution of the United States, and the Army Regulations were his
guides in life." [11] He would need them all.

Arriving at Moultrie, Anderson relieved Gardner and greeted
his officers, some of them acquaintances from earlier assign-
ments. Aside from the new construction, the place was much as
he remembered it, a mouldering citadel with walls fifteen feet
thick that were a sandwich of brick outside and inside with
solid earth between. If it had little else, Moultrie had some history behind it. It had been erected very near the site of the old
palmetto-log Revolutionary fortress of the same name which the
Carolinians under Colonel Moultrie—and the major's father—
had defended so valiantly against the British. For years it was
the prison of Osceola, the warlike Seminole chieftain, whose
grave was just outside the walls. Edgar Allan Poe had been a
soldier here thirty years earlier, subsequently making Sullivan's
Island the scene of his "Gold Bug." More recently, such officers
as Sherman, Bragg, Reynolds, and Thomas had served tours of
duty at the fort. Now Moultrie seemed on the threshold of a
different kind of history.[12]

The abolitionist Doubleday, although he had no use for the
new commander's "pro-slavery" sentiments, reflected that he was
"a gentleman, courteous, honest, intelligent, and thoroughly
versed in his profession." [13] The major found himself in command of two undersized companies in a fort torn apart and full

of holes. The senior officers were Doubleday (Company E), Seymour (Company H), and Captain Foster, the engineer in charge of construction who was responsible to engineering head-quarters in Washington rather than directly to Anderson. The scholarly surgeon, Crawford, held a captain's rank.

There were four junior officers. First Lieutenant Theodore Talbot of Company H, an undersized Kentuckian of thirty-five, had attended military school in his home state. He was a gay, chivalrous sort despite a lung ailment that kept him in delicate health.

First Lieutenant Jefferson C. Davis, a bearded, impetuous Indianian, was the only officer who had come up from the ranks. Known as "the boy sergeant of Buena Vista," he had been com-missioned for gallantry in Mexico.[14]

First Lieutenant George W. Snyder, Corps of Engineers, was a bright New York Stater who had graduated from Union Col-lege and then gone on to win top honors in the West Point class of 1856. He was assisting Foster in the supervision of the work at Sumter. Second Lieutenant Norman Hall of Company H, a handsome young Michigander with luxuriant sideburns, was the "kid" of the outfit, a recent West Point graduate who served as post quartermaster and adjutant. Doubleday, who could be critical, regarded his fellow officers with approval and added, "The majority of the men, too, were old soldiers, who could be thoroughly relied upon. . . ."[15]

Even so, Major Anderson noticed the lax discipline resulting from the easygoing Gardner regime—something he would have to work on.[16] But what concerned him most was the defenseless condition of the fort he was ordered to hold, with its outworks agape and its parade crawling with secessionist workmen and littered with dismounted cannon and construction materials. A hundred-odd yards east were two high sand hillocks com-manding Moultrie and offering perfect cover for sharpshooters. The safety of the fort was dependent on the good will of the townspeople, who at the moment did not seem imbued with good will. The work had been defended by their ancestors of

'76, its name was sacred to them, and they were candid in saying they meant to have it.[17] People from the dwellings flanking the fort, most of them wearing secession cockades, sauntered in and out at will to watch the work in progress. Officers from Charleston military companies strode in to appraise the improvements and take notes on them.[18] Some of these visitors thought it was generous of the United States to repair Moultrie so it would be in tiptop shape when they took it over.

". . . there is a settled determination . . . ," Anderson noted, "to obtain possession of this work." [19]

He had already known something of the situation, but no one had told him that Moultrie was as public a meeting place as a grogshop. While he had anticipated wild talk on the part of younger blades, what he found was a "settled determination" that seemed unanimous among young and old, the only point in doubt being just when the fort would be seized. Judging from the citizens' temper, with Moultrie's weakness naked for all to see, it would be soon. From conversations with them he learned that Castle Pinckney, manned only by an ordnance sergeant, "they regard as already in their possession." [20] Then there was Sumter out in the harbor, unfinished and unmanned but with guns that when mounted could quickly wipe out Moultrie. Supposing they took a notion to appropriate Sumter?

A military realist, Anderson knew that the best way to prevent an attack was to make it clear to the citizens that any assault would mean at least a stout resistance in which Carolinian blood would be spilled. In Moultrie he could make no substantial resistance for weeks. He looked longingly at snug little Castle Pinckney, less than a mile from the city, with guns that could spray Charleston with metal. As commander in the harbor, he was in charge of Pinckney and Sumter as well as Moultrie, expected to defend them all. He had made a careful preliminary inspection of all three works. He was a worried man when he sat down to spend hours preparing a comprehensive report for Secretary Floyd, which he dispatched through the usual army channels to Adjutant General Samuel Cooper in Washington. In it

D

he explained clearly the complications of the defensive situation in Charleston as well as the imminent danger to the garrison— things he felt were imperfectly understood in the capital.

"The clouds are threatening," he wrote, "and the storm may break upon us at any moment." He went on to ask for reinforcements no less than six times.

Fort Sumter, he said, "is the key to the entrance of this harbor; its guns command . . . [Moultrie], and could soon drive out its occupants. It should be garrisoned at once." As for Pinckney,

> It is, in my opinion, essentially important that this castle should be immediately occupied by a garrison, say, of two officers and thirty men. . . . The Charlestonians would not venture to attack . . . [Moultrie] when they knew that their city was at the mercy of the commander of Castle Pinckney. . . . Fort Sumter and Castle Pinckney *must* be garrisoned immediately if the government determines to keep command of the harbor.
>
> I need not say how anxious I am—indeed, determined, so far as honor will permit—to avoid collision with the citizens of South Carolina. Nothing, however, will be better calculated to prevent bloodshed than our being found in such an attitude that it would be madness and folly to attack us. . . . I do, then, most earnestly entreat that a reinforcement be immediately sent to this garrison, and that at least two companies be sent at the same time to Fort Sumter and Castle Pinckney. . . . I firmly believe that as soon as the people of South Carolina learn that I have demanded reinforcements . . . they will occupy Castle Pinckney and attack this fort. It is therefore of vital importance that the troops embarked (say in war steamers) shall be designated for other duty.

By this the major meant that if the troops were dispatched openly for Charleston, secession sympathizers would send the word South. It had better be done under cover or he would be overpowered before they arrived.

"With these three works garrisoned as requested," he finished, ". . . I shall feel that, by the blessing of God, there may be a hope that no blood will be shed. . . . If we neglect, however, to strengthen ourselves, . . . South Carolina will . . . most assuredly immediately attack us. I will thank the Department to give me special instructions, as my position here is rather a politico-military than a military one." [21]

This was one of the most important reports ever penned by an American officer, the fruit of careful deliberation by an able commander at the scene, stated with the highest degree of emphasis and warning. It spelled out the military facts so that Mr. Floyd could not misunderstand them:

1. Moultrie alone was indefensible and the citizens knew it.

2. The garrisoning of Pinckney, putting Charleston in range of United States guns, would reduce the danger to Moultrie.

3. But since Sumter commanded the approaches to both Moultrie and Pinckney, Sumter also must be garrisoned.

4. All this must be done with speed and caution.

Certainly Anderson had come away from his discussion with Floyd with the feeling that the secretary wanted to know the exact state of affairs in Charleston and would support him in any reasonable request. While he waited for a reply, the major urged Captain Foster to hasten the repairs on Moultrie. Foster now gave his personal attention to Moultrie, supervising 125 workmen, while Lieutenant Snyder moved bag and baggage to Sumter to boss a crew of 115.[22]

A few days later, Foster got a surprise. The adjutant of a Charleston regiment arrived and asked him politely for his work rolls. Many of the workmen were Carolinians, he said, and he wanted to enroll them for military duty for the state. That made Foster's jaw sag a bit. No, he replied, he couldn't do that. The men were in the pay of the United States Government and could not be impressed by the state. The adjutant went his way, leaving the impression that Foster would have to give up his men whether he wanted to or not.[23]

Charleston was in a state of chronic truculence that bred false rumors. Colonel Huger, Anderson's West Point classmate now in command of the arsenal, came out to Moultrie in some trepidation to consult with the major. There was talk in the city, Huger said, that four companies of United States troops were

coming aboard the *James Adger,* and the firebrands were all for
going out and intercepting the *Adger.* Was it so? Anderson
knew nothing about it.[24] He had troubles enough of his own
without worrying about Charleston gossip. Already he was regarding Moultrie as a trap, the expensive repairs on it a waste
of money he never would have recommended had he been there
earlier. In a second report to Floyd dated November 28th he
repeated his request for reinforcements and asked what to do
about the Carolina demand for the work rolls, finishing:

> . . . if I had been here before the commencement of expendi-
> tures on this work, and supposed that this garrison would not
> be increased, I should have advised its withdrawal, with the
> exception of a small guard, and its removal to Fort Sumter,
> which so perfectly commands the harbor and this fort.[25]

It took two days, sometimes three, for mail to travel from
Moultrie to Floyd's lair in the War Department. Furthermore,
Floyd was in no great hurry to answer. Captain Seymour, on an
off-duty trip to Charleston, was astonished at the feeling there.
Several responsible citizens told him they regarded the work on
Moultrie and Sumter as "aggression" and that not a man nor
any supplies would be permitted to land.[26] Surgeon Crawford,
likewise returning from a visit to the city, said the situation was
"critical" and believed the Carolinians would first seize Sumter,
since it was ungarrisoned and controlled everything else.[27] Military companies were drilling day and night, giving vent to much
menacing talk. Colonel Huger, right in the midst of it, was
doing his best to calm his fellow townsmen, even saying that if
Moultrie were mobbed, he would go out there and fight beside
his friend Anderson.[28] The populace was now in such a wrathy
temper, whipped up by stump speakers and the daily salvoes
of Rhett's bellicose *Mercury,* that cooler heads were trying to
slow them down.

Annoyed at the army's feebleness, Doubleday resolved at any
rate to make Moultrie *look* as if it might deal out a bit of punishment. Now and then, for the benefit of the citizen audience,
he loaded an eight-inch howitzer with double canister and let

fly into the sea. "The spatterings of so many balls in the water looked very destructive," he noted, "and startled and amazed the gaping crowds around." [29] He also made a great showing of placing a few mines here and there around the walls, telling no one the mines were powderless duds.[30]

The easy Gardner days were over now with a vengeance. Discipline reappeared, with gun drill a daily chore and sentries posted night and day to guard the approaches. It got so that sleep was a luxury. With fifteen hundred feet of rampart to watch, and so few men, Anderson was forced to detail his officers to take their turn on night sentry duty. One night the Mesdames Doubleday and Seymour, wives of the company commanders, made some kind of army history when they took over as sentries to spell their weary husbands.[31] In their jumpy frame of mind, the soldiers were as vulnerable as the Charlestonians to rumor which they could not verify but were inclined to believe. It was said that the secessionists had already sent some cannon to the eastern end of Sullivan's Island which they were mounting with an eye to covering the channel and preventing reinforcements from that direction. Another report had it that two thousand of the state's best riflemen had been assigned to occupy the commanding sand hills and the roofs of adjacent houses, from which they could shoot down the garrison with ease if it tried to man the guns.[32]

As he spurred the Moultrie repairs, Anderson took what hasty steps he could to protect his other two works until reinforcements should arrive. To Pinckney he sent thirty-four workmen in charge of Lieutenant Davis to make minor repairs and to give the fort some semblance of being occupied. Davis was cautioned "to act with the greatest discretion," his workmen being picked Union men. It was Anderson's idea that these laborers could quickly be taught the rudiments of manning the guns so that any unorganized assault could be beaten off.[33] At the same time, Captain Foster visited Huger at the arsenal, asking him for a hundred muskets to divide among the loyal workmen at Sumter and Pinckney for defensive purposes. Anderson and Foster were aware that the spirit of these bricklayers and carpenters was something less than martial and that some of them had never loaded or aimed a firearm in their lives. The two officers were reduced to this pitiful makeshift for want of any other recourse, hoping that the workmen might make some show of resistance against a mob attack.

Getting arms from the arsenal was just the sort of thing that had raised a ruckus and cooked Colonel Gardner's goose back on November 8th. No, said Huger firmly, he could not issue the muskets without special permission from Washington. Foster immediately wrote Washington to ask permission. He was turned down with the notation, "Action deferred for the present." [34]

The captain was disgusted and so was Anderson. A thoroughly reasonable man who believed in the rightness of slavery and felt real sympathy for the grievances of the South, he had arrived in Charleston determined above all to establish friendly relations with the citizenry, to make every word and action soothe civic resentment and prove he was anything but aggressive. He found it impossible. His mere presence there was regarded as aggressive and insulting. The trouble arose from an irreconcilable disagreement no diplomacy could soften. The Charlestonians felt the forts should be theirs. Anderson knew the forts were federal property which he must defend. While he waited for the instructions from Floyd that took so long in coming—and waited hopefully for reinforcements—he dispatched another report to Washington on December 1st underlining the need for decisive action one way or the other:

"The question for the Government to decide—and the sooner it is done the better—is, whether, when South Carolina secedes, these forts are to be surrendered or not. If the former, I must be informed of it, and instructed what course I am to pursue. If the latter be the determination, no time is to be lost in either sending troops, as already suggested, or vessels of war to this harbor." The major showed his resentment when he said, "They [the Carolinians] are making every preparation (drilling nightly, &c) for the fight which they say must take place, and insist on our not doing anything. We are now certainly too weak to fight. Were we to guard against a surprise, our men, if surrounded by only an undisciplined mob, would soon be worn out by fatigue." [35]

In his own report to engineering headquarters, Foster was sounding the same alarm. "I regret," he wrote, ". . . that sufficient soldiers are not in this harbor to garrison these two works [Sumter and Pinckney]. The Government will soon have to decide the question whether to maintain them or to give them up to South Carolina. If it be decided to maintain them, troops must instantly be sent, and in large numbers." [36]

Major Anderson was growing increasingly impatient with the elaborate repair work that would keep Moultrie's defenses impaired for several weeks. Captain Foster's artisans had nearly completed one bastionette when they were forced to suspend operations there while waiting materials. Another bastionette was only started. This left inviting holes at corners of the fort. Other workmen were clearing a ditch and building a glacis around the outer wall. In so doing they erected planking which would serve an attacking party admirably as ladders. Anderson talked with Foster about this, urging him that time was short and he should seal the fort quickly with makeshift construction rather than building for the ages. But Foster, who worked under instructions from the Corps of Engineers, was a Yankee perfectionist who could not bear anything jerry-built and felt he must proceed according to plan.[37]

Early in December the major received two short dispatches from Washington that must have jolted him. In the first, Secretary Floyd let him know that all communications should be directed to him.[38] This meant, although the secretary did not say so, that General Scott, who normally received reports from officers in the field, was being bypassed and removed from any jurisdiction at Charleston. In the second, Floyd politely declined to send reinforcements.

"It is believed," wrote Adjutant General Cooper, "from information thought to be reliable, that an attack will not be made on your command, and the Secretary has only to refer to his conversation with you, and to caution you that, should his convictions unhappily prove untrue, your actions must be such as to be free from the charge of initiating a collision. If attacked, you are, of course, expected to defend the trust committed to you to the best of your ability.

"The increase of the force under your command, however much to be desired, would, the Secretary thinks, judging from the recent excitement produced on account of an anticipated increase, as mentioned in your letter, but add to that excitement, and might lead to serious results." [39]

Anderson must have wondered where Floyd got his reassuring information. The secretary had rejected all of his recommendations for the defense of the forts, leaving him to make do with what he had. Orders were orders. On December 5th he made the short steamer trip to Charleston to join Colonel Huger in some ambassadorial work. With Huger he visited Mayor Macbeth and several other civic leaders, suggesting that they take steps to prevent a sudden mob sortie against any of the forts. "All seemed determined," Anderson later reported, "as far as their influence or power extends, to prevent an attack by a mob on our fort; but all are equally decided in the opinion that the forts *must be theirs* after secession." [40] This left him with the disquieting feeling that their "influence or power" might not extend quite far enough. It happened that he had a previous slight acquaintance with Robert Gourdin, who had invited him to dine when he arrived. Since Gourdin was a highly influential Charlestonian as well as chairman of the 1860 Association, Anderson did not miss the opportunity to impress on him his peaceful intentions, at the same time conveying a hint that Moultrie would not be taken without a struggle. He wrote Gourdin in part:

> You need no assurance from me that, while I am exerting myself to make this little work as strong as possible and to put my handful of men in the highest state of discipline, no one will do more than I am willing to do to keep the South in the right and to avoid the shedding of blood. You may be some-

what surprised at the sentiment I express, being a soldier, that
I think an appeal to arms and brute force is unbecoming the
age in which we live.[41]

Gourdin, elected to the convention and about to leave for
Columbia to push for quick secession, was an upright lawyer
who wanted no mob action but wished to secure the forts by
negotiation when the state declared its independence. He replied with a hint of his own:

> Your sentiments in reference to war and blood-shed are such
> as I knew you to hold. . . . The Secession movement cannot be
> suppressed; it pervades the South. I trust in God that we will be
> allowed to seek our peace and happiness as a people according
> to our own consid[er]ations of right and duty, unmolested by
> the government at Washington and by the peoples of the
> North.[42]

If he was to get no more men, Anderson knew he must walk
a straight line of caution and tact. In his next report to Floyd,
he permitted himself a reminder that without reinforcements,
"in the event of our being attacked I fear that we shall not
distinguish ourselves by holding out many days." Then he added
some queries that showed how intimidated he was by his own
military insecurity as well as by the repeated admonitions from
Washington to avoid giving any excuse for offense. "I have not
yet commenced leveling off the sand hills which, within one
hundred and sixty yards to the east, command this fort," he
wrote. "Would my doing this be construed into initiating a collision? I would thank you also to inform me under what circumstances I would be justified in setting fire to or destroying
the houses [near the fort] which afford dangerous shelter to an
enemy, and whether I would be justified in firing upon an
armed body which may be seen approaching our works." [43]

The commander was now wary about drawing a deep breath.
His last query almost amounted to asking whether he was allowed to defend himself at all. Floyd's reply must have left him
still asking that question.

Under ordinary circumstances, the secretary admitted, removing the sand hills would not be considered as a hostile act. "But the delicate question of its bearing on the popular mind, in its present excited state, demands the coolest and wisest judgment. The fact of the sand hills being private property, and, as is understood, having private residences built upon them [which they did not] decides the question in the negative. The houses which might afford dangerous shelter to an enemy, being chiefly frame, could be destroyed by the heavy guns of the fort at any moment, while the fact of their being leveled in anticipation of an attack might betray distrust, and prematurely bring on a collision. Their destruction at the moment of being used as a cover for the enemy would be more fatal to the attacking force than if swept away before their approach."

Mr. Floyd had not studied at West Point. His absurd reasoning could hardly persuade a man who knew he might be shot down by marksmen in those houses before he could even reach his guns. As for an armed body approaching the fort, Floyd went on, "their purpose should be demanded at the same time that they are warned to keep off, and their failure to answer and further advance would throw the responsibility upon them."

But it was in reference to the Carolinian demand to enroll government workmen in their armed forces that he perpetrated deeper dialectical anarchy. ". . . you will," he instructed, "after fully satisfying yourself that the men are subject to enrollment, and have been properly enrolled under the laws of the United States, and of the State of South Carolina, cause them to be delivered up or suffer them to depart." [44]

Verily the secretary spake in riddles. If Anderson had been a swearing man, he could have been forgiven a few oaths. How could men be enrolled under United States laws for the purpose of defying United States laws? And who but the Secretary of War should define the legality of the question? Floyd was an expert at shrugging off responsibility and handing it right back to the commander, who was earnestly seeking clear instructions to guide him and got evasion for his pains.

In the end he did not "suffer them to depart." Although by this time he must have felt that the War Department was abandoning him, in his almost daily reports he kept hammering home to Floyd that Sumter and not Moultrie was the vital spot and that in its present condition it could be taken by the first comer.

". . . it is deemed probable that their [the Charlestonians'] first act will be to take possession of that work," he wrote, adding, "Fort Sumter is a tempting prize, the value of which is well known to the Charlestonians, and once in their possession . . . it would set our Navy at defiance and give them the perfect command of this harbor." [45]

The War Secretary had been putting some thought on Sumter himself. He reached conclusions which he decided were too delicate to entrust to the mails or even to put in writing at all. On December 7th he directed Major Don Carlos Buell of the adjutant general's staff to commit the instructions to memory and carry them in person to Anderson. Buell, another officer fated for speedy promotion to a generalship, arrived in Charleston on the ninth and immediately felt like a man in a foreign country. There was no violence in the city, but the way people talked they intended to seize Fort Sumter with or without state sanction. "There was everywhere evidence of a settled purpose," he noted.[46]

So when Buell took the boat over to Moultrie, he had a small sample of the Charlestonian temper which it might have benefited Secretary Floyd to experience. At the fort he was regarded dourly by many of the garrison who felt that a timid administration was deserting them to be massacred by a mob.

"I can hardly stand the way in which this weak little garrison is treated by the head of the Government," an officer's wife wrote bitterly. ". . . the Secretary has sent several officers, at different times, to inspect here, as if that helped. It is a mere sham, to make believe he will do something. . . . When the last man is shot down, I presume they will think of sending troops." [47]

Oblivious of this animosity, Buell made an inspection of the three forts. He also spent one night in the same room with Anderson, who could not have lost this opportunity to acquaint the visitor with the precariousness of his position. Buell gave Anderson his verbal instructions, and the two discussed the possibility of abandoning Moultrie and moving over to Sumter before the secessionists did.[48] On the morning of December 11th, just before he left, Buell said to Anderson, "You ought to have written evidence of these [Floyd's] instructions." [49] He thereupon wrote the following:

> You are aware of the great anxiety of the Secretary of War that a collision of the troops with the people of this State shall be avoided, and of his studied determination to pursue a course with reference to the military force and forts in this harbor which shall guard against such a collision. He has therefore carefully abstained from increasing the force at this point, or taking any measures which might add to the present excited state of the public mind, or which would throw any doubt on the confidence he feels that South Carolina will not attempt, by violence, to obtain possession of the public works or interfere with their occupancy. But as the counsel and acts of rash and impulsive persons may possibly disappoint these expectations of the Government, he deems it proper that you should be prepared with instructions to meet so unhappy a contingency. He has, therefore, directed me verbally to give you such instructions.
>
> You are carefully to avoid every act which would needlessly tend to provoke aggression; and for that reason you are not, without evident and imminent necessity, to take up any position which could be construed into the assumption of a hostile attitude. But you are to hold possession of the forts in this harbor, and if attacked you are to defend yourself to the last extremity. The smallness of your force will not permit you, perhaps, to occupy more than one of the three forts, but an attack on or an attempt to take possession of any one of them will be regarded as an act of hostility, and you may then put your command into either of them which you may deem most proper to increase its power of resistance. You are also authorized to take similar steps whenever you have tangible evidence of a design to proceed to a hostile act.[50]

As Buell handed this paper to Anderson, he added a meaning remark: "This is all I am authorized to say to you, but my personal advice is that you do not allow the opportunity to escape you." [51]

These instructions, despite one lamentable flaw, showed Floyd in a better light. He was not abandoning Anderson to his fate but was offering him one escape from the trap. By the time Buell left, Major Anderson had already begun to contemplate a move of modest intrinsic military significance, never dreaming it would explode a political bombshell over the land.

A FREE-LOVE
ARRANGEMENT

In 1860, honor, loyalty, and duty meant different things depending on where one stood. In the nationalized North, the federal government was paramount and the Union had come to mean something bigger and greater than any of the states, commanding allegiance and carrying final authority. In the unassimilated South, where federal power had long been viewed with suspicion, the reverse idea prevailed with a majority who swore by their state as the focus of allegiance and the ultimate authority. To be sure, the state had delegated certain powers to the federal government as a matter of convenience, but it could withdraw them as well. Let a vital issue arise between state and nation and there was no question where the average man of Dixie would stand. He was for his state, and those fellows in Washington could go hang.

In this view, the Union was not a permanent marriage, as Mr. Lincoln shocked people by saying, but a "free-love arrangement" to be persevered in only so long as "passional attraction" lasted. In all the South, this feeling of amorous independence was strongest in little South Carolina. That state's passional attraction toward Washington had cooled to such revulsion that it was ready to chuck the hussy and look for some more agreeable mistress. The question of who was right in these conflicting marital concepts was not a subject for friendly debate, because each side, North and South, believed sincerely and implacably that it was right.

Otherwise, pint-sized young Assistant Secretary of State William Henry Trescot would have been one of the greatest traitors unhanged. The urbane Charlestonian was a dexterous mental acrobat who easily executed the handspring of working for disunion while holding a key federal post, and also performed the elastic feat of keeping one ear in his home state and the other in Washington. His position in the administration would have been matched had Abraham Lincoln occupied a post high in the councils of the governor of South Carolina. He saw no disloyalty in this. On the contrary, he would have regarded himself as disloyal had he acted otherwise.

Trescot came from a wealthy, patrician family and had married into a wealthy, patrician family. He was a representative of the proud ruling class of his state, with the highborn Carolinian's acute sense of honor. A lawyer, he had served two years as secretary of legation in London, developing such an interest in international affairs that he set out to write a diplomatic history of America. Two volumes of this work had recently been published, receiving critical acclaim that established him as an authority.[1] Now the gifted Charlestonian was one of the most influential members of Buchanan's official family, working subtly and skillfully to destroy the Union, putting a face of frankness on his secession sentiments, and yet occasionally resorting to sly stratagems in Old Buck's rear. Smart as a whip, he had the President's ear, was on intimate terms with the Cabinet and enjoyed an insider's view of high government policy at the same time as he kept in constant communication with secession leaders in Carolina. Was this treason? Not at all, said Trescot.

". . . the Union was only a state of transition and . . . the United States were in no true sense ever one nation," he wrote a few months later.[2] As he saw it he was working in Washington for a decaying central headquarters which had never exercised real authority over the states. He was not only justified but forced by every worthy principle to jettison the interests of a worn-out, obsolete Union in order to protect his own state of South Carolina, to which he owed his only true loyalty. He wanted his state to secede in a correct, dignified, nonviolent way. To his mind the greatest threat to peace was the presence in Charleston harbor of Major Anderson and his garrison. During November and December Trescot was working, arranging, counseling, sending telegrams, joining in midnight conferences, marshaling every force and pulling every string he could find in a dedicated effort to get Anderson out of there or, barring that, to keep him in such a condition of military helplessness that he might as well not be there.

In this last design he was so successful that he probably altered history. In doing so he was using the President as a pawn in the South Carolina disunion program, being one of those Southern politicians who, in Trescot's own words, "were willing for reasons of their own to make the issue as peaceful as possible and lost nothing by meeting Mr. Buchanan half way." [3]

The veteran President, who had entered politics before Trescot was born, was nobody's dupe. He knew perfectly well that his Assistant Secretary of State was an active secessionist and was therefore undermining the Union and flouting the law of the land as Buchanan saw it.[4] It was a queer business, the head of the state countenancing a subordinate who—along with others—was busily wrecking it, but the Old Public Functionary entered into this fantastic arrangement with his eyes open. Trescot was personally friendly to him, was against violence or undue haste in secession, and to that extent could be used to further Buchanan's policy of delay. Furthermore, Trescot kept him posted on Carolina sentiment and served as an amicable line of communication with angry Palmetto State leaders who would otherwise be entirely estranged from the Washington government. Trescot was acting in effect as the South Carolina ambassador in Washington, and the President did not want to lose this last link with the dissident state that was moving beyond his reach too quickly as it was.

So Mr. Trescot was using Mr. Buchanan, and Mr. Buchanan was using Mr. Trescot, and the question was which of the pair would get the most usefulness out of the other.

What to do about Charleston harbor? The President had no intention of handing it over to the secessionists. He had devoted careful thought to the problem of keeping the flag flying there without causing the Carolinians to blunder into war. Any aggression would have to come from them, for Major Anderson was the soul of discretion, working under strict orders to act on the defensive. The Cabinet was sharply divided on what to do about those confounded forts. There was even some intriguing behind Buchanan's back. Trescot kept warning Secretary Floyd that the citizenry in Charleston were so inflamed that sending any reinforcements would almost certainly catapult them in an assault against the forts.[5]

Floyd himself was against reinforcement because it would look like "coercion," but on the other hand he was not going to submit to any Carolinian attempt to seize the forts. Trescot was so finicky about not sending a single man that Floyd got a little testy. He ought to be trusted, he snapped. If he sent a little ammunition or a few men South in the ordinary routine of business, that certainly was no sufficient cause to make the people go wild.

"You tell me," he said, "that if any attempt is made to do what under ordinary circumstances is done every day, you will be unable to restrain your people. Suppose you are not able to restrain them now, am I bound to leave those garrisons un-protected to the mercy of a mob—am I not bound to enable *them* to resist the unlawful violence which *you* cannot resist?" [6]

This was sound talk. It made Trescot so worried that he went to consult Howell Cobb, the influential, secessionist Secretary of the Treasury. Cobb took the problem to Jacob Thompson, the secessionist Mississippian who was Secretary of the Interior. Then both Cobb and Thompson descended that same night on Floyd and pelted him with argument. They were so successful in moulding the plastic Secretary of War that later that night Floyd called on Trescot and admitted he was wrong about what he had said a few hours earlier. If it was likely to cause violence, he said, he "would not consent that a man nor a gun should be sent to any of the Forts in the harbour of Charleston." Furthermore, he was so eager to cooperate that if his sense of duty induced any change in this policy he would inform Trescot in advance, in ample time for him and his state to counter it.[7]

The forts—the forts. It seemed to President Buchanan that all he heard about was the forts. Late in November he received

E

a letter from Robert Barnwell Rhett in Charleston, a former Senator and political associate. Rhett paid his respects to the President, then got to the point in two sentences:

"South Carolina, I have not a doubt, will go out of the Union —and it is in your power to make this event peaceful or bloody. *If you send any more troops into Charleston Bay, it will be bloody.*" [8]

This was just the sort of tough talk The Squire deprecated. Mr. Rhett was threatening him with war should he have the temerity to reinforce Major Anderson's puny garrison—something he felt he had a perfect right to do although he was uncertain as to its wisdom. To his credit, he was not entirely intimidated, for about this same time he summoned Secretary Floyd.

"Mr. Floyd," he said, "don't you intend to strengthen the forts at Charleston?"

"I do not," the secretary replied.

"Mr. Floyd, I would rather be in the bottom of the Potomac tomorrow than that these forts in Charleston should fall into the hands of those who intend to take them." The President grew warmer. "It will destroy me, sir, and if that thing occurs it will cover your name with an infamy that all time can never efface, because it is in vain that you will attempt to show that you have not some complicity in handing over those forts. . . ."

"I will risk my reputation," Floyd said, "I will trust my life that the forts are safe under the declarations of the gentlemen of Charleston."

"That is all very well," Buchanan countered, "but pardon me for asking you, does that secure the forts?" [9]

It was a good question. Floyd, affrighted, argued that reinforcements would mean certain war. Then he jumped whole-hog into appeasement and begged the President not only to send no help but to withdraw Major Anderson and the small force that was there. He seized on the word "property" which Buchanan had used in referring to the forts.

"If it is a question of property," he said, "why not put an ordnance sergeant into them—a man who wears worsted ep-

aulets on his shoulders and stripes down his pantaloons . . . ?
That will be enough to secure the forts." [10]

This was an idea so downright submissive that not even the
Carolinians themselves had as yet suggested it. Buchanan refused to consider it. Still, he was influenced enough by Floyd's
warnings so that he agreed to suspend judgment about reinforcement until General Scott could be consulted. Scott, who
had recently been so ignored that he had to get his information
about military affairs in Charleston from the newspapers, was
requested by telegraph to come to Washington.

The Virginian Floyd was talking more like a Carolina fire-
eater than a Secretary of War sworn to defend his government,
and yet at this time he seems to have been loyal to Buchanan
in his own peculiar, halfhearted way. While he thought secession unwise, he regarded it as a right a state could exercise if it
wished, and in his view war was the worst possible outcome of
the quarrel.[11] He took quick steps behind the scenes to bring
pressure on Buchanan to desist from sending reinforcements.
He dispatched messages to Senator Jefferson Davis of Mississippi
and to Senators James Mason and R. M. T. Hunter of his own
state, asking them to come to Washington at once to exert their
influence.[12] Then he consulted with Trescot and with the
Secretary of the Interior, genial Jacob Thompson.

These three Southern men anxiously pondered moves that
might dissuade the President from sending so much as a man or
a bullet to the aid of Major Anderson. They finally adopted a
stratagem proposed by Trescot, who made haste to write Governor Gist of South Carolina. Would the governor write by
return mail to Trescot—a letter that could be shown to the
President and would spell out clearly the disaster that would
be caused by any reinforcement? [13]

Governor Gist complied on November 29, penning a message
of combined assurance and threat which was addressed to Trescot
but intended for Buchanan's eyes. At the same time Gist wrote
a second and strictly private letter for Trescot alone, asking if
he would serve as the "confidential agent" of South Carolina in
Washington as soon as he resigned his federal post.[14]

Young Mr. Trescot was indeed already serving in this capacity although he was drawing his pay as Assistant Secretary of State. He promptly showed Gist's first letter to the President, who read the following:

DEAR SIR: Although South Carolina is determined to secede from the Federal Union very soon after her Convention meets, yet the desire of her constituted authorities is, not to do anything that will bring on a collision before the ordinance of secession has been passed and notice has been given to the President of the fact; and not then, unless compelled to do so by the refusal of the President to recognize our right to secede, by attempting to interfere with our exports or imports, or by the refusal to surrender the forts and arsenals in our limits. I have found great difficulty in restraining the people of Charleston from seizing the forts, and have only been able to restrain them by the assurance that no additional troops would be sent to the forts, or any munitions of war. Everything is now quiet, and will remain so until the ordinance is passed, if no more soldiers or munitions of war are sent on. . . . but the Legislature and myself will be powerless to prevent a collision if a single soldier or another gun or ammunition is sent on to be placed in the forts. If President Buchanan takes a course different from the one indicated and sends on a reinforcement, the responsibility will rest on him of lighting the torch of discord, which will only be quenched in blood. . . .[15]

Old Buck now had his second warning within a week that sending any help to Anderson meant war. His half-formed resolution to dispatch reinforcements was tottering. Unluckily, one of the few men who might have bolstered him—General Scott—failed to arrive, being laid low with dysentery in New York. No dysentery, however, stayed the steps of Senators Davis, Mason, and Hunter, who descended on the President with strong advice against reinforcement. These men were powerful Democrats who had helped elect him in 1856, political allies of many years whose opinions had great influence.

As the President wavered, he had many others things on his mind. For almost a month he had been working on his annual message to Congress, devoting his best efforts to it because in it he would be forced to recognize the Carolinian threat and announce his policy toward it.

The whole nation was waiting to hear what he had to say. When he said it on December 3rd, nobody was satisfied.

A good Democrat, Buchanan scolded the North for its "imtemperate interference" with slavery. It had no more right to meddle with Southern institutions, he said, than with matters in Russia or Brazil, and harmony could easily be restored if everyone would simply mind his own business. But he likewise reproved the South when he denied the right of a state to walk out of the Union, saying that the framers of the government "never intended to implant in its bosom the seeds of its own destruction." It was when he explained what he meant to do about the South Carolina illegality that the President wandered into a dissertation on constitutional law that confused rather than clarified. He said he did not believe he had the right to "coerce" a state—compel it by force of arms to stay in the Union. Yet he affirmed his duty to enforce the federal laws and to hold the federal property in South Carolina and elsewhere.

"It is not believed," he said hopefully, "that any attempt will be made to expel the United States from this property by force; but if in this I should prove to be mistaken, the officer in command of the forts has received orders to act strictly on the defensive. In such a contingency the responsibility for consequences would rightfully rest upon the heads of the assailants." [16]

The general howl of protest that greeted the message disclosed a national schism so wide and deep that not even the long-legged President could straddle it. Southerners, while pleased by his disavowal of any intention to coerce, were angered at the denial of the right of secession. Senator Seward neatly expressed the Republican reaction when he said, "It shows conclusively that it is the duty of the President to execute the laws—unless somebody opposes him; and that no state has a right to go out of the Union—unless it wants to." [17] With Congress in session, the Old Public Functionary was the butt of assaults aimed not only by the Republicans but also by some of his former Democratic friends of the South.

If Buchanan's message did nothing else, it served to focus national attention more strongly than ever on Charleston harbor, where it seemed the issue of war or peace would be resolved. In Charleston the nation's safety teetered on a razor's edge. What was done or not done would spell ruin or triumph depending on the geographical latitude of the onlooker. The President immediately became the center of a civil war in his own Cabinet, which was about equally divided in members coming from North and South and thus represented the quarrel in miniature. Treasury Secretary Howell Cobb of Georgia resigned with a strong defense of the right of secession, warning the people of his state to "Arouse, then, all your manhood for the great work before you. . . ." [18] Secretary of State Cass, abetted by Attorney General Black and Postmaster General Holt, were urging the President to reinforce Anderson. Floyd, Thompson, and Trescot were imploring him not to send a man unless he wanted to loose rivers of blood.

To his own assistant secretary, old Lewis Cass argued in a vein that illumined a fundamental sectional difference. "I speak to Cobb," he told Trescot, "and he tells me he is a Georgian; to Floyd, and he tells me he is a Virginian; to you and you tell me you are a Carolinian. I am not a Michigander; I am a citizen of the United States. The laws of the United States bind you, as they bind me, individually." [19]

Trescot could not agree. He was still a Carolinian. And as for the President, he was a Union man but nevertheless he was making a cautious retreat from his talk about strengthening the forts. Warnings from a dozen quarters told him that reinforcement would mean war, which he aimed to avoid even if it cost some temporary humiliation and sacrifice of strict principle. Mr. Buchanan felt hamstrung by the weakness of his own army, and he was also gripped by an error that a few days' stay in Charleston might have corrected.

Those fellows down in South Carolina, he thought, were just shouting "Wolf!" a little more loudly than before. They would secede, certainly, but skillful maneuvering should hold them alone in disunion.[20] When they found themselves a small island of secession surrounded by states that frowned on them for their hotheadedness, their wrath would cool. Buchanan believed the Republican victory only temporary, that a reaction was already beginning that would sweep the Democrats back in power in 1864 to wipe out whatever vestiges of disunion remained.[21] He could not conceive of the Carolinian movement as one designed to get out of the Union irrevocably and perpetually. Therefore the thing to do was to conciliate the grumblers, steer clear of war, and pave the way for an ultimate happy reunion. While he had no doubt of his right to put his whole army in Charleston harbor if he wished, he felt he had better abstain from exercising the right because one gunshot there might inflame the whole South. The old diplomat who had taken tea with Queen Victoria and the Czar and had successfully tilted a lance with smooth European intriguers, still felt he could handle a parcel of Carolinians who, underneath all their bluster, were fellow Democrats who had voted for him in '56.

The President had a painful time of it when Georgia-born Eliza Clinch Anderson, the ailing wife of the commander in Charleston, came from New York to call on him at the White House. Mrs. Anderson was in a high state of anxiety, fearing that her husband was in imminent danger of assault by a lawless mob, and naturally she pleaded that he be reinforced.[22] Buchanan reassured her as best he could. A few days later, on December 8th, a delegation of South Carolina Congressmen headed by William Porcher Miles and Lawrence Keitt consulted him on the same subject but with opposite advice: *no* reinforcement.

These Palmetto representatives, who were all secessionists but had not yet resigned their seats, admitted they could not speak officially but gave it as their belief that Anderson was in no danger of attack so long as no help was sent him. Let any reinforcements be sent, they warned, and violence was certain.[23]

The Congressmen had an extraordinary nerve if they expected the President to give them a binding promise to return for their

mere hopeful and unofficial opinion. Yet they came away with
the feeling that Buchanan had "solemnly pledged" the government not to alter the military status at Charleston—a misunderstanding that later was to swamp Old Buck with woe and erupt
like lava in Carolina. Such a pledge he had no power to give,
for he would be promising away the government's right to defend itself against disunion, which he had already condemned as
illegal and unconstitutional. He put nothing in writing, so there
is no proof that he even gave a flat verbal guarantee. But the
long and short of the matter was that according to his own
definition the Carolinians had no particle of authority over
the forts in the harbor, and he was moving toward a dangerous
surrender of national sovereignty in giving them any assurances
whatever.[24]

So now the President, regardless of the nature of the promise
or assurance he gave, had moved in his own mind right into
the Trescot-Floyd no-reinforcement camp. General Scott finally
put down his intestinal insurrection and hurried to Washington
on December 12th to urge Buchanan to reinforce Anderson.
No, said Old Buck, the time had not yet come for that. He saw
no danger of early secession except in South Carolina. When
that state seceded she would send commissioners to negotiate
about the forts. He would refer the commissioners to Congress
and await the result.[25]

Secretary of State Cass could stand it no longer. After pressing for reinforcements for weeks, he now made it a good deal
stronger. "These forts must be strengthened," he said. "I demand it." "I am sorry to differ with the secretary of state,"
Buchanan replied, and the popular old Cass promptly resigned.[26]

The sudden exit of Cass, known as a reinforcer, loosed a
muddy stream of invective on Buchanan's head. Mutterings of
impeachment were heard. Horace Greeley's New York *Tribune*
suggested that the President was insane. Others thought him
sane enough, but cringing, cowardly, or downright traitorous.
The Philadelphia *Press* let out a furious blast:

The administration of the Government is in the hands of the enemies of the country. The President of the United States has ceased to be the Chief Magistrate of a free people. . . . He refuses to protect the public property, and to reinforce the gallant Anderson at Fort Moultrie! . . . His confidants are disunionists. His leaders in the Senate and in the House are disunionists! and while he drives into exile the oldest Statesman in America, simply and only because he dares to raise his voice in favor of the country, he consults daily with men who publicly avow, in their seats in Congress, that the Union is dissolved. . . . Is it not time, then, for the American people to take the country into their own hands. . . ? [27]

The old gentleman in the White House was hanged in effigy in many Northern cities. Yet he stubbornly hewed to his policy as the only safe one. He went right on making "confidants" of disunionists. When Trescot did something he properly should have done weeks earlier—handed in his resignation—the President was relieved that he agreed to stay on as Acting Secretary of State until Attorney General Black could take over the job.

In those bleak days before Christmas, a change had come over the land. In the public mind Forts Moultrie and Sumter—and Major Anderson's little garrison—had assumed an enormous importance all out of proportion to their value or numbers. They had become a symbol, a principle, above all a challenge. To the North they represented the preservation of the Union, the enforcement of the laws against Southern intransigence. To the South they represented a tyrannous threat to peaceable secession. One side would have to budge or there would be war.

THE HONOR-SAVERS

As if President Buchanan were not already beset by woes aplenty, John Floyd now heaped more on him. The Secretary of War was suddenly caught not in one but in two scandalous enterprises that would have raised fumes in a government enjoying nationwide popularity. In an administration execrated both in the North and South, the exposures about Floyd caused an unhappy explosion that sent ricochets splashing around lonely Major Anderson in Charleston.

In Enterprise No. 1, the secretary played a merry game with the public funds. For two years he had joined in a quiet and illegal arrangement with Russell, Majors & Waddell, a transportation firm holding large government contracts for the horse-and-wagon delivery of supplies to army posts on the remote Western frontier. When William H. Russell, head of the company, asked Floyd in 1858 to help him out of a hole, the secretary promptly obliged. He believed Russell a man of vast resources whose financial distress was only temporary. Besides, he felt that no other firm was equipped to deliver supplies across the plains, so that unless Russell was kept solvent the army would go hungry. Floyd thereupon dedicated himself to keeping Russell solvent.[1]

He did it by accepting Russell's drafts on the War Department for government work to be performed in the future. Russell took the drafts, which were negotiable paper signed by the Secretary of War, and borrowed money on them, the theory being that he would pay off the loans with his cash earnings from the government—a theory that came to take a licking. The secretary coolly wrote various banks and capitalists, urging them to loan Russell money on the drafts, all of this being unauthorized and highly irregular. The contractor was so delighted

at this magic solution to his troubles that he began to beat a
path to Floyd's door, asking for more drafts. The Virginian, a
remarkably accommodating man, couldn't seem to turn him
down. Before long a stream of paper bearing Floyd's official
signature was circulating around the land.[2]

Although William Russell was a native of Vermont, he had
long since forgotten Yankee thrift and become a Wall Street
plunger. Far from being in a solid condition, he had taken such
losses in the panic of 1857 that he was financially shaky. The
money he borrowed on Floyd's drafts saved him for a time, but
eventually he was hard put to pay off these loans before incur-
ring new debts. The secretary, with amiable disregard for ele-
mentary fiscal prudence, made no effort to ascertain whether
Russell was retiring the old drafts before getting new ones, nor
did he trouble to keep careful records of these transactions
amounting to millions. He had no patience for bookkeeping.
He just signed the drafts and forgot about them, keeping sketchy
account of them on loose pieces of paper.[3]

Senator Benjamin of Louisiana, hearing a rumor about this
rubbery arrangement, called on Floyd and warned him it was a
risky business. Floyd thanked him and said he would stop it.
He proceeded to sign more drafts. President Buchanan ultimately got wind of it, though he had no idea of its extent,
and told him sharply it must stop. Floyd agreed—and kept on
signing more drafts.[4]

In July of 1860 Russell reached the end of his rope. Some of
his earlier drafts were due and he could not meet them. Since
they were signed by Floyd and apparently had the government
behind them, the holders would raise a howl if they were not
paid, call for an investigation, bring the whole shady business
to light, and sink the secretary in ruin. Floyd now realized that
his own honor was deeply involved. Frantically he issued Russell
more drafts to help him cover the earlier ones.[5] During the
entire last half of 1860, the Cabinet officer chiefly responsible
for handling the Charleston crisis was giving it only part-time
attention because he was in a terrible pickle of his own devising
—a state of mind that boded ill for Major Anderson.

A new character now entered the scene, an Alabamian named Godard Bailey who was a clerk in the Interior Department. Bailey, whose wife was a cousin of Floyd, had got his job through Floyd's influence. Learning that his friend was in imminent danger of exposure and disgrace, he pondered ways to save him. Although Bailey was penniless himself, he was guardian of several millions in gilt-edged bonds held in trust in the Interior Department for various Indian tribes. His anxiety to rescue Floyd preyed on him until in mid-July he took $150,000 worth of negotiable bonds from the safe in his office and delivered them to Russell at his hotel. He did this, he later explained, with no other motive than to "save Mr. Floyd's honor" by furnishing Russell with funds to pay off the drafts.[6]

Promising to return the bonds, the Vermonter hurried off to New York with them and dove into some fast financial manipulation. By September he was broke again, not only unable to make payment on more War Department drafts but now in danger of losing the bonds themselves, which he had given out as security. He returned to Washington, where the worried Bailey gave him $387,000 more in Indian bonds. But Russell was a magician who could make dollars vanish. In December he was back with the same old plea—more bonds to save Floyd's honor. This time Bailey gave him $333,000 more, doctoring his books to make it appear that the bonds were in the safe where they belonged. Protecting Floyd's honor had grown into a large-scale enterprise containing many of the aspects of embezzlement.[7]

Bailey later claimed Floyd knew nothing of the bond snatch, making himself out to be a remarkably shut-mouthed man who risked his own reputation to save his friend Floyd with nary a mention of it to Floyd. But Jacob Thompson at any rate was unaware of this iniquity in his department. The Interior Secretary, who had been born and educated in North Carolina before settling in Mississippi, had something else on his mind— a letter from Governor Pettus of Mississippi asking him to go as official commissioner of his state to North Carolina to urge the Tarheel State's cooperation with Mississippi in seceding from the Union.

Asking a Cabinet minister to undertake such an errand might seem like urging a young man to go and shoot his mother, but neither the governor nor Thompson saw anything matricidal about it. Thompson was a Mississippian first, a Cabinet member second. He knew secession was coming—permanent secession, not the temporary estrangement the hopeful President had in mind. He viewed the peaceful, orderly dissolution of the Union as an achievement that would later be hailed as a triumph of civilized American political wisdom.[8]

Besides, he was a "mild" secessionist, a good friend of Buchanan who saw no reason for disunion until The Squire's term had ended. He consulted the President, who tried to dissuade him from the mission, saying it would be "misunderstood." Thompson offered to resign, but Buchanan did not want that either, possibly fearing that such a step would speed disunion in Mississippi. So the secretary departed for Raleigh, a loyal man (Southern branch) obeying his own interpretation of loyalty. Senator Clingman of North Carolina, himself a secessionist, later admitted amazement that the President would allow such a thing.[9]

While Thompson was gone, Secretary Floyd must have realized that his exposure and dismissal from the Cabinet was inevitable. Perhaps he reasoned that if he was to be ruined in the North, he had better do something to raise his stature in the South. On December 20th he wallowed into Enterprise No. 2. He quietly ordered the Allegheny arsenal at Pittsburgh to send a bristling assortment of armament—113 heavy columbiad cannon and eleven 32-pounders—to the United States forts at Ship Island, Mississippi, and Galveston.

If there were any places where cannon would be not only useless but dangerous to the Union, it was Ship Island and Galveston. Both forts were unfinished and ungarrisoned. Ship Island would not be ready for its guns for a full year, while Galveston would still be abuilding for something like five years. Unguarded, the cannon would make a rich prize for secessionists to seize. The Secretaries of War and Interior had simultaneously gone to Dixie, but with a difference. Thompson was sincere and open in his beliefs, Floyd a foxy intriguer. In Pittsburgh, Unionists learned of the cannon order and began to seethe. Floyd was a Virginian, wasn't he—the fellow who refused to send help to Major Anderson? Was he sending those guns South as a gift to rebels who would turn them against the government? The citizens called a mass meeting in protest.[10]

Meanwhile, Clerk Bailey saw exposure ahead in the form of a routine government audit. His nerve snapped. He confessed pilfering the bonds to "help Russell," admitting that his basic motive was to shield Floyd. Thompson came back from North Carolina to find $870,000 in Indian bonds gone beyond recall. In their place in the safe was a batch of Floyd's drafts Russell had given Bailey as "security," with a face value of $870,000. As security, the drafts were roughly equivalent in value to old newspapers. The President, shocked by the scandal in his own official family, saw too late that Floyd was not merely incompetent and irresponsible but downright slippery. The newspapers splashed headlines about administration corruption, innocent redskins began to wonder whether the Great White Father could be trusted with their funds, and this time impeachment seemed a real possibility.

Buchanan's clear duty was to confront Floyd and fire him instanter, but he disliked unpleasant scenes. He asked Secretary Black to request the Virginian to resign. Not at all, Black said —that was the President's job. Still squeamish, Buchanan got Vice President John Breckinridge, a kinsman of Floyd, to handle the hot chestnuts. Breckinridge went to Floyd and told him Buchanan wished him to resign.

"But that cannot be," said the brassbound secretary, "for he has not so intimated to me."

"He has requested me to say so to you," Breckinridge insisted.[11]

After some grumbling, Floyd agreed to resign. Being a man who could say one thing and do another, he failed to get around to it. Buchanan, expecting momentarily to receive the resignation, was puzzled that it did not come.

Floyd lingered on in the Cabinet for days, discredited but not ejected, as rumblings began to come in from Pittsburgh about those 124 cannon consigned to the South—an order unknown to the administration. The President made a great error in not dismissing him, one reason being that Major Anderson badly needed a functioning Secretary of War. Another reason was that if given an inch, Floyd could easily stretch it to a mile. He would leave when he got good and ready, and when he did he would manage to sabotage the already touchy Carolina situation at the same time as he had the nerve to claim he was quitting because *his* honor was offended.

Down in a small Palmetto State the curious ones may find
A ripping, tearing gentleman, of an uncommon kind,
A staggering, swaggering sort of chap who takes his whiskey straight,
And frequently condemns his eyes to that ultimate
       vengeance which a clergyman of high standing
       has assured must be a sinner's fate;
This South Carolina gentleman, one of the present time.[1]

When Francis Wilkinson Pickens left Washington after conferring with the President, he was a moderate in the sense that
he favored delaying secession until the end of Buchanan's term,
not knowing that in the statriot view this was not moderation
but downright, contemptible reaction. When he got home he
discovered that the South Carolina ozone, different from that
breathed elsewhere, contained an airborne disunion virus that
could change one's manner of thinking in a hurry. Senators
Chesnut and Hammond, both inclined to moderation, had
drawn only a few deep inhalations in their native heath before
they became hell-for-leather secessionists. Now Pickens was exposed to the same supercharged atmosphere.

Possibly he would not have succumbed so quickly had he not
been stricken simultaneously by another contagion, a desire to
succeed Gist as governor when his term ended in December.
Pickens made a restrained speech at his home town of Edgefield,
declaring that secession should rightfully await the installation
of the Republican regime that caused it. So cool was the reaction that it was plainly not the kind of talk that led to the
governor's chair. By the time he made a full-dress oration at the
capitol in Columbia, his tune had changed. He was as eager for
speedy secession as Lawrence Keitt.

"I, for one," he said in very small part, "would be willing to appeal to the God of Battles—if need be, cover the State with ruin, conflagration and blood rather than submit. . . . Let the Convention pass the Ordinance of Secession now, and as soon as possible let them nail that flag to the mast." [2]

These sentiments showed that the man from Russia had become acclimated. The legislature shortly afterward elected him governor over Robert Barnwell Rhett, a stinging defeat for the father of secession. Pickens, who had intelligence and wide experience in public affairs but was somewhat overbearing of manner and impulsive in disposition, was to lead his state into ruin, conflagration, and blood such as he never dreamed of.

While the state moved toward secession, Major Anderson at Fort Moultrie was doing his best to make bricks without straw. He had asked for upwards of two hundred men, and on December 10th he got the utmost that Secretary Floyd would allow —one man. He was Second Lieutenant R. K. Meade, a bright young man with curving mustaches who had been second in the West Point class of 1857. A native of Petersburg, Virginia, Meade was suffering from a common complaint of the time, divided loyalties. His father, Buchanan's minister to Brazil, was getting ready to resign his post before Lincoln came in and ruined the country. The lieutenant felt a Southerner's sympathy for South Carolina, and yet he could not forget that he had sworn to defend the flag of the Union. He was immediately assigned by Captain Foster to take charge of the workmen repairing Castle Pinckney, allowing Lieutenant Davis to rejoin his company at Moultrie.[3]

Foster and Anderson were having their troubles making headway in the face of Carolinian disapproval augmented by a partial economic embargo. Some Charleston lumber merchants refused to sell to the United States Government, forcing Foster to scout around for needed materials.[4] The engineering chief was in a dilemma that gave him the fidgets. He could not do the right thing until he knew the government's plans for the ultimate disposition of the garrison at Moultrie. If the command was to be transferred, then assuredly the Carolinians would seize Moultrie and all his expensive construction there would not

F

merely be wasted but would be handed over to hostile forces. If the garrison was to remain at Moultrie, then Foster was inviting disaster should he mount the big guns at Sumter that could be taken by the Carolinians any time they chose and would make Moultrie untenable. Foster compromised by pushing the work at Moultrie, mounting only a few guns at Sumter that bore away from Moultrie, and begging Washington to clear up his doubts.

"I would respectfully, but strongly, urge," he wrote, "that more definite instructions be given me for my guidance." [5]

However, the Secretary of War was too preoccupied with eccentric pursuits of his own to furnish the guidance Foster needed. Probably no garrison in such a critical position was ever abandoned so completely by a government that should have sustained, advised, and supported it. Responsibility that should have been borne by Washington was thrust squarely on the shoulders of Major Anderson and Captain Foster, who were reduced to makeshift, day-to-day expedients in entire ignorance of any long-range plan.

Foster had a theory that a soldier ought to be armed, especially if he was expected to guard something. A fortnight earlier he had been refused when he requested a hundred muskets at the arsenal. On December 17th he visited the arsenal again with a more modest query: Could he have two muskets with which to arm the ordnance sergeants at Sumter and Pinckney?

Colonel Huger had recently left Charleston to resume his former command at the Pikesville arsenal, North Carolina, leaving Captain Humphreys once again in charge. Humphreys, a cautious fellow, said he had no authority to issue any of the arsenal's 22,000 muskets, not even two.

In his anxiety to gain some semblance of defensive strength, Foster made use of a technicality in orders. He reminded Humphreys that back on October 31st, Secretary Floyd had approved a requisition for forty muskets which had not been issued because Colonel Gardner, then commanding, had demurred. The demurral was now removed, since Major Anderson wanted the muskets and approved the order. So, Foster said triumphantly, I'll take those forty muskets.

Humphreys looked at the records and saw that this was correct. Foster could not have two muskets, but he could have forty.
The captain left with them, feeling a sense of victory.[6]

The United States arsenal at Charleston was still in the humiliating position of having a twenty-man "guard" of South
Carolina militiamen who kept a sharp watch. Foster's departure
with forty muskets was immediately reported to General Schnierle of the state militia. Schnierle came on the run to remonstrate with Humphreys. Violence was certain, he said, unless the
muskets were returned forthwith. Humphreys was intimidated.
He backtracked in a hurry and promised to see about it, writing
Foster an almost tearful letter begging him to return the
muskets or there was no telling what would happen.[7]

He might as well have asked Foster for his life's blood. The
man from New Hampshire prized those muskets above jewels
and was not going to part with them without a struggle. He
agreed to refer the matter to Washington, doubtless feeling he
would be supported.

"To give them [the muskets] up . . ." he reported, "would
place the two forts under my charge at the mercy of a mob.
Neither of the ordnance sergeants at Fort Sumter and Castle
Pinckney had muskets until I got these, and Lieutenants Snyder
and Meade were likewise totally destitute of arms. . . .

"I must say plainly that I have for some days arrived at the
conclusion that unless some arrangement is shortly made by
Congress, affairs in this State will arrive at a crisis. . . ."[8]

Foster's determination was more than matched by the Carolinians'. They had no particle of legal right to meddle in this
strictly federal matter, not even if the whole contents of the
arsenal should be transferred to the forts, but strict legality was
going by the boards. Even as they were arming themselves with
all speed, they had made an issue of their demand that there be
no strengthening of the forts which they conceived as a menace,
and they backed it up with the usual threat of unrestrainable
violence. Forty muskets Captain Foster could not have. If he
did not return them there would be violence.

Some angry Charlestonian sent a telegram to the handy Mr.

Fixit, Assistant Secretary of State Trescot, in Washington, telling of Foster's removal of the muskets. Trescot got the message late at night but considered the matter important enough to rush to Floyd's lodgings and wake him up.[9] The secretary, so generous in his sale of muskets by the thousands to South Carolina and in his willingness to ship 124 cannon South, was wroth at the idea of his own men arming themselves with forty firearms. He dispatched a peremptory telegram that reached Foster at 2:00 A.M.:

"I have just received a telegraphic dispatch informing me that you have removed forty muskets from Charleston Arsenal to Fort Moultrie. If you have removed any arms, return them instantly." [10]

Resentful beyond measure, Foster returned the arms next day. In his report to Washington, he let his anger show through just this side of insubordination:

The order of the Secretary of War of last night I must consider decisive upon the question of any efforts on my part to defend Fort Sumter and Castle Pinckney. The defense now can only extend to keeping the gates closed and shutters fastened, and must cease when these are forced. . . .

I would earnestly, but respectfully, urge that definite instructions be given me how to act in the emergency which . . . will probably arise sooner or later. . . .[11]

Instructions, instructions . . . Anderson and Foster had asked for them many times and got precious little in reply. When the story of the forty muskets got around the garrison, there was anger and gloom. The support which the men expected from their own government seemed replaced by something approaching hostility. Captain Doubleday was bitter. "So we were left to our own scanty resources," he commented, "with every probability that the affair would end in a massacre." [12] He was especially incensed at the costly construction work at the three forts without manpower to defend them. Was Secretary Floyd crazy, or had he turned traitor? Didn't he know he was building forts for South Carolina to use? In Doubleday's opinion the only reason the Carolinians had held off attacking so long was because they were foxily waiting until the forts would be entirely finished at Uncle Sam's expense.[13]

Abner Doubleday's grandfather had fought at Bunker Hill and Stony Point and had been taken prisoner by the British. His father had served two terms in Congress from New York State. He himself had fought for his flag in Florida and Mexico.[14] He was taking no back seat to the Carolinians who were so insufferably proud of their lineage and their honor and who lived in luxury gained by the sweat of their slaves. He was mad clear through at a position of humiliating helplessness to which he felt no self-respecting officer should be forced to submit, and his feelings were shared by Captains Foster and Seymour, Surgeon Crawford, and Lieutenants Snyder and Hall, all of them loyal Union men. Tension was growing among the officers, bringing with it nervousness and irritability. All of them knew there was one escape.

Sumter.

Doubleday spoke to Anderson about that, as did some of the others. Move out of this deathtrap at Moultrie, they urged, while there is still a chance. Move over to Sumter where we can command Moultrie, command the harbor, and be soldiers again.[15]

Anderson, who was laboring under a greater strain than any of them, had long been entertaining the same idea, but he wisely kept it under his hat. No, he said with a straight face, we are assigned to Moultrie and we will stay here.[16]

The major had continuously urged the government to give him some clear policy about Sumter, receiving vague generalities in return. The basic instructions he had received from Secretary Floyd by mail and via Major Buell could be summed up in two items:

1. He must act on the defensive, avoid giving offense.

2. If attacked, or if he had "tangible evidence" of a design to attack him, he could move his command to Sumter or Pinckney.

That was all he had to work on. The joker was that phrase

"tangible evidence." Where would one find it? Anderson did not anticipate that the Charlestonians would be so accommodating as to announce the precise moment when they intended to seize his fort. They would swarm at him from those nearby houses before he knew it. Any idea of moving to Sumter *during* an attack was preposterous, since the garrison's wharf and boats would be taken before the fort was assailed. The move could not be a spur-of-the-moment affair. It would take advance preparation and hours to accomplish it. If he made it at all, it would have to be well before the attack, which might come tonight, or next week, or not at all, and might come without a shred of tangible evidence. Or could he construe the widespread talk in town about taking Moultrie as tangible evidence? Or the obvious fact that the Carolinians were arming themselves with greatest haste, certainly not for mere parade? Or the report that they had provided themselves with ladders for escalading Moultrie's walls? [17]

Tangible evidence—the phrase must have haunted Anderson for many a night as he pondered the merits and perils of moving to Sumter. He was impelled by a sense of responsibility that involved not merely the safety of his garrison but also the safety of the nation itself. One misstep on his part would cause civil war, a prospect that made the civilized major shudder. Yet he had felt from the start that to remain in Moultrie was the surest road to war, because Moultrie was a pushover, so easy a conquest that the Carolinians could hardly withstand the temptation to reach out and take it—an effort he would be bound to resist as long as he could fight.[18]

"Nothing . . . will be better calculated to prevent bloodshed than our being found in such an attitude that it would be madness and folly to attack us," Anderson had written Floyd on November 23rd. The only place where he could get into such an attitude was Sumter. In powerful Sumter, with guns mounted and salt water all around him, he would be strong enough so that the Palmetto men would have to be foolish indeed to attack him. He must make a decision soon, for on December 17th the South Carolina Convention met at Columbia with the near-

unanimous purpose of drawing the papers and making secession official as quickly as men could vote.

South Carolina in 1860 was prosperous, with cotton selling at
12½ cents and negroes as high as $1500.[19] There was no eco-
nomic pain to cause discontent. While there was much grumbling that the victorious Republicans were a sectional party,
which was true, Palmetto leaders were not sincerely exercised
about democracy, for their own state government was firmly in
the hands of a most undemocratic planter aristocracy assured of
control by an undemocratically rigged system of representa-
tion.[20] Realists understood that Lincoln was elected consti-
tutionally and could do them little harm with a Congress and
Supreme Court opposed to him. There was even some disagreement in South Carolina about the relative importance of their
various long-run reasons for wishing to sink the Union. But
there was perfect agreement as to the immediate cause that fired
them. It was Lincoln.

Lincoln was uncouth, ignorant, full of hideous malice, an
ogre to frighten children with. The Black Republicans who
had elected him were motivated by "settled hostility" toward
the South. Lincoln was the catalyst that fused South Carolina's
dissident factions into unified determination to resist. His election was a direct insult, something the proud Carolinian could
not ignore. In personal matters it meant a duel. Pistols did not
answer the case here, so the next best thing was to disown
Lincoln, disown the Republicans, disown the Union. The
landed and professional gentry who ran the South Carolina
show were a tightly knit group of men lordly by habit, generally
intelligent and well-educated, accustomed to command and to
expect implicit obedience, with an exterior polish that concealed a dark strain of violence under the skin. They were perfectly convinced that most Northerners were not gentlemen—
were, in fact, inferior creatures spiritually, intellectually, and
in fighting ability.[21]

As the delegates met in convention at Columbia, they felt
they were about to take the only step left them consistent with

honor. They knew that the people of the state, conditioned by years of propaganda and a new sense of outrage, were almost solidly behind them. "Sirs, you never saw anything like it," marveled Judge A. B. Longstreet of Columbia. ". . . you might as well attempt to control a tornado as to attempt to stop them [the people] from secession." [22] Old Edmund Ruffin, the Peter the Hermit of disunion who would not have missed this event if he were at death's door, was given a seat of honor. David Flavel Jamison of Barnwell, a fifty-two-year-old scholar and planter whose two thousand acres were tilled by seventy slaves, served as presiding officer and exhorted the delegates in the words of Danton "To dare! and again to dare! and without end to dare!" [23]

Right away the members were embarrassed to discover that the state law decreed that they must swear loyalty to the United States Constitution—an oath all of them would have choked on. They agreed to dispense with this item and go ahead sans oath.[24] While they were willing to adopt Jamison's spirit of daring insofar as quitting the Union was concerned, there was another condition in Columbia that gave them pause, an incipient epidemic of smallpox. It was decided to reconvene in Charleston over the protest of Delegate William Porcher Miles, who thought this a disgraceful retreat on the part of men dedicated to daring.

"It will be asked on all sides," Miles pointed out, " 'Is this the chivalry of South Carolina? They are prepared to face the world, but they run away from smallpox.' " [25]

Charleston was aglow with enthusiasm when the convention gathered at Institute Hall on Meeting Street on the eighteenth. One could have traveled the city from end to end without finding the Stars and Stripes except at the arsenal and the post office, but many other flags and bunting designs were in evidence. One depicted Judge Magrath firing a cannon in his library. Another showed Abe Lincoln trying vainly to split a palmetto log. But the delegates were serious men, comprising some of the ablest in the state, most of them well along in years and some with records of former attachment to the Union. They knew they were taking a step of gravity and some risk—how much gravity and how much risk not one of them realized. Just as the North had misunderstood them, now these honorable men took their turn to misjudge the North. Few of them thought the issue would end in war.[26]

Among the audience was one discordant spectacle, a man wearing the uniform of a Yankee officer. He was the ever-inquiring Surgeon Crawford of the Moultrie garrison, indulging his taste for history. On the speaker's table Crawford saw a great gavel with the word "Secession" cut into it in deep letters. While he found the city loud with tumult, the deliberations of the convention were quiet and dignified. There was some discussion about the federal "property" in South Carolina, the most important property in everyone's eyes being Forts Moultrie, Sumter, and Pinckney. It was resolved to send three commissioners to Washington to inform the government there of the Palmetto State's independence and to treat for possession of the forts and other "real estate."

Delegate Miles assured the convention that President Buchanan would not try to coerce the state. He told of his meeting with Buchanan, attended by other Carolina Congressmen, at which he said there was "a tacit, if not an actual agreement" on the part of the President to make no change in the military status in the harbor.[27] This was a cheering note, since the United States military status was satisfyingly feeble and would presumably stay that way until the garrison was politely withdrawn.

At 1:15 P.M. on December 20th the ordinance of secession was passed without a dissenting vote among the 169 delegates. Fifteen minutes later Rhett's *Mercury* was on the street with an extra proclaiming: "UNION IS DISSOLVED!" The town went crazy. ". . . a mighty shout arose," one observer said. "It rose higher and higher until it was as the roar of the tempest. It spread from end to end of the city. . . ." [28] There was an impressive public ceremony that evening when the delegates

filed up to sign the ordinance. Emotion and even tears were
evident among the audience. After the last name was affixed,
Chairman Jamison announced:

"The Ordinance of Secession has been signed and ratified,
and I proclaim the State of South Carolina an independent
Commonwealth." [29]

Bells rang, cannon boomed, tar barrels were ignited, champagne corks popped, snakeline parades undulated through the
streets amid fusillades of firecrackers, and Charleston began a
fiesta of freedom that would last beyond Christmas. The young
poet Paul Hayne was so inspired that before he could sleep
that night he composed a "Song of Deliverance," one stanza
reading:

> O, glorious Mother Land!
> In thy presence stern and grand,
> Unnumbered fading hopes rebloom, and faltering hearts grow brave,
> And a consentaneous shout
> To the answering heavens rings out—
> "Off with the livery of disgrace, the baldric of the Slave!" [30]

Old Judge Petigru, a Union rock with secession waves crashing all about him, was unmoved. "South Carolina is too small
for a republic and too big for a lunatic asylum," he had said.[31]
Now, with bells tolling in every steeple, he met one of his
former law students, Joseph Pope, in the street.

"Where's the fire?" Petigru demanded.

"No fire," Pope replied. "They're ringing the bells in honor
of the ordinance of secession."

"I tell you there is a fire," Petigru corrected. "They have
this day set a blazing torch to the temple of constitutional
liberty and, please God, we shall have no more peace." [32]

But the judge was a lonely fellow, a Charleston fixture
tolerated only because of his wit and charm. "If there were any
like Mr. Petigru," one citizen commented, "they hid themselves." [33] There must have been a respectable minority of Carolinians who viewed the disunion intoxication with misgivings

but concealed their sentiments out of regard for their own health or reputation. One of them was Jacob Schirmer, a Charleston merchant of Union sympathies who vented his feelings safely in a diary: "This is the commencement of the dissolution of the Union that has been the Pride and Glory of the whole world, [and] after a few years have rolled around . . . we will find the beautiful Structure broke up into as many pieces as there are now States, and Jealousy and discord will be all over the Land." [34]

One of the unhappiest witnesses of the Charleston gayety was Caleb Cushing, a Massachusetts Democrat who had arrived only that morning as a special envoy from President Buchanan to try to stop a tornado. Though his precise instructions were secret, it was believed he was empowered to make a deal to delay secession: If Major Anderson was unmolested at Moultrie, the government would make no hostile move toward South Carolina during Buchanan's term. Cushing's railroad fare was wasted. He had seen Governor Pickens, who let him know the time of day without preamble, saying, "I must tell you candidly that there is no hope for the Union." Cushing could see that all around him. His mission was indeed a matter of amusement. He retired disconsolate to his hotel room, his ears jarred by a babel of celebration. When the Charlestonians invited him to attend the signing of the ordinance as the envoy of a foreign state, he indignantly refused and took the next train north.[35] Cushing was a symbol of Washington's ignorance of Carolinian feeling. He was a symbol of something else. When he reached Charleston, he was a Northern Democratic friend of the South. When he left, he was no longer friendly, and there were a lot of Northern Democrats like him.

But the Charlestonians, in no mood to give heed to such portents, were more inclined to feel like Lawrence Keitt when he said, "We have carried the body of this Union to its last resting-place, and now we will drop the flag over its grave." [36]

Keitt had the courage of his convictions. He was killed at Cold Harbor in 1864.

PEACEABLY, IF POSSIBLE

When the delegates signed the ordinance of secession, they performed a piece of magic on Francis Pickens. They transformed him instantly from governor of one of the thirty-three United States to head of the sovereign Republic of South Carolina, leader of 301,271 free citizens and 402,541 slaves. He was authorized to select a cabinet. He was empowered to levy war, negotiate treaties, send and receive ambassadors, and to treat with his old boss, President Buchanan, on terms of equality if he could get away with it.

Secession also wrought a change on Major Anderson and his men. They became soldiers of a foreign power menacing Charleston, a denial of Carolinian independence as long as they remained. Now, in the view of the statriots, they would *have* to get out—peaceably, if possible.

Governor Pickens—he was still called Governor—saw clearly that his first problem was to clear the harbor of the foreign garrison and take over the forts in the name of the new republic. Son of Governor Andrew Pickens, grandson of General Andrew Pickens of Revolutionary fame, the governor was proud of his lineage and confident that his own abilities lived up to the family tradition. He was famous for his reply years earlier during Nullification times when a colleague inquired whether he were not fearful of his course. "Fear!" Pickens exclaimed. "Mr. President, I was born insensible to fear!" [1] Hot for secession in 1852, he had later cooled so much as to work hand in glove with Northern Democrats—a change his enemies laid to desire for federal office. He was now known as a conservative, which in the queer Carolinian nomenclature meant simply that he was a shade less rash in his contempt for federal authority than men such as Rhett.[2]

Maybe the governor was born insensible to fear, but he had a healthy respect for the power of Fort Sumter, which the Yankee-hired workmen were increasing every hour. To be sure, there was some sort of gentlemen's agreement between the South Carolina Congressmen and Mr. Buchanan to the effect that the military status in the harbor would remain unchanged. Pickens did not quite trust this agreement. It was merely a matter of conversation, vague and informal, with no documents to prove it. In Moultrie, Major Anderson was a mouse in a trap. In Sumter he would be a formidable enemy. All he had to do was cross a mile of salt water to exchange weakness for strength, which must be tempting to a military man.

The Charleston *Mercury,* secession's sleepless watchdog, was likewise disinclined to put faith in agreements. "Major Bell [Buell] and several other officers of the Army have been sent to Fort Moultrie to look after the forts . . ." said the *Mercury.* "They were sent for no good to us. See that they make no change in the distribution of soldiers, so as to put them all in Fort Sumter. That would be dangerous to us." [3]

No sooner had Pickens taken office on December 16th than he attacked the problem with characteristic impulsiveness. The state capital was at Columbia, but the governor stayed right on in Charleston, not only because of smallpox but because Charleston was the focal point in the question of the forts. He took a luxurious suite at the Charleston Hotel and set up his offices three blocks away in the second floor of the city hall at Broad and Meeting Streets, with a fine marble bust of his kinsman Calhoun on his desk.[4] Even before the state seceded, he dispatched a message to President Buchanan with a strange request bolstered by the familiar warning that violence would be the penalty of refusal. He wrote in part:

> I am authentically informed that the forts in Charleston harbor are now being thoroughly prepared to turn, with effect, their guns upon the interior and the city. . . .
> The arsenal in the city of Charleston, with the public arms, I am informed, was turned over, very properly, to the keeping and defense of the State force at the urgent request of the

Governor of South Carolina. I would most respectfully, and from a sincere devotion to the public peace, request that you would allow me to send a small force, not exceeding twenty-five men and an officer, to take possession of Fort Sumter immediately. . . . If something of the kind be not done, I cannot answer for the consequences. . . .[5]

When Buchanan received this missive and showed it to Trescot, the Carolinian saw at once that Pickens had made his first gubernatorial blunder. For one thing, Pickens was entirely mistaken in his belief that the government had "turned over" the arsenal to the state. Captain Humphreys had perforce consented to a state "guard" at the arsenal, but the administration had not sanctioned this even as a mere guard. For another, the demand threatened to raise a new issue about Sumter which the careful Trescot did not want. He would rather trust in the pacific intentions of the President and let the matter rest until South Carolina sent commissioners to treat for Sumter and the other forts.[6] As for Buchanan, he had already made a series of concessions to South Carolina for which vituperation was heaped on him in the North. The President cannily ticked them off to Trescot:

1. He had removed Colonel Gardner from command for taking ammunition from the arsenal.

2. He had refused to send reinforcements to Charleston.

3. He had accepted the resignation of Cass, the most eminent member of his Cabinet, rather than consent to strengthen the garrison.

4. He had ordered Foster to return forty muskets taken from the arsenal.

5. He had done all this out of confidence in the assurances of the South Carolina Congressmen that there would be no attack on the forts at least until the commissioners negotiated for them.

On top of all this, Buchanan pointed out, Pickens' request was based on admitted doubt of his ability to control his own people and maintain order. Certainly this was a deplorable, Central-American sort of ground for a government to take in making any sort of demand—a kind of "Your money or your life" proposition.[7]

Trescot had to agree. Pressing Buchanan on this might make him think of withdrawing concessions already given. Trescot consulted with Senators Davis and Slidell, who likewise felt that Pickens' demand would cause only mischief. A telegram was dispatched to Pickens asking that he withdraw his letter. It was a slap for the governor, but he assented and everybody breathed more easily again.[8]

Trescot as always was working like a tartar for his state. Just to bolster his own feeling that Sumter would safely be left un-occupied by the military, he had another conference with Secretary Floyd. Floyd reassured him so firmly on that point that Trescot was able to write Pickens:

> No order has been issued that will at all disturb the present condition of the garrisons; and while I cannot even here venture into details . . . I am prepared to say, with a full sense of the responsibility, that nothing will be done which will either do you injury or properly create alarm. . . .[9]

Trescot was saying in effect, "Anderson will not move to Sumter," and yet Pickens was nervous. He was under heavy pressure from citizens who wanted him to seize the forts at once. Shortly after he took office he was visited by four members of the state legislature who did not feel he should go so far but who did urge him to take every precaution to prevent any movement of the United States force to Sumter.[10] While it was true that the new republic would send commissioners to Washington to negotiate for the forts, it was important that Anderson be kept in helplessness at Moultrie while the parley went on, not only to strengthen the commissioners' hand but to make certain that South Carolina could easily take over the forts by force should negotiation fail. Pickens, finally deciding that the "gentlemen's agreement" was too slender a reed to lean on, took a significant step.

At midnight December 18th he summoned Captain Charles H. Simonton, a Charleston lawyer and citizen-soldier who commanded the Washington Light Infantry. He told Simonton he had heard that Anderson might evacuate Moultrie and occupy Sumter, which must be prevented at all costs. Just where he "heard" this is a mystery. Perhaps he did not hear it at all but envisaged it as a logical possibility; again, the Washington administration, including the War Department, was so honeycombed with Southern sympathizers that secrecy was a myth and the gist of the Buell memorandum as well as Anderson's frequent reports about Sumter might have been duly forwarded to the governor.[11] In any case, he ordered Simonton to detail men to cruise the channel between Moultrie and Sumter, keeping a close watch. They were to avoid any conflict with the garrison if possible. But if United States troops were seen heading for Sumter, they were to be ordered back. If they refused to turn back they were to be sunk and Captain Simonton's men were to occupy Sumter themselves.[12] In giving this pugnacious order two days before the state seceded and was still legally a part of the Union even by its own definition, the governor demonstrated that if necessary he was willing to take the revolutionary road to independence before peaceable negotiation had been tried.

So Simonton's men began their surveillance of the Moultrie garrison, using two small coastal steamers, the *Nina* and the *General Clinch,* the latter ironically named after the father of Major Anderson's wife, a Georgian hero of the Seminole War. Still Governor Pickens had the fidgets about Sumter. Charleston as always was a fertile ground for rumor, one of them saying that twenty United States enlisted men had secretly been transferred from Moultrie to Sumter.

So concerned was the governor at this report that on the morning of December 20th, secession day, he went to see the nearest United States officer, Captain Humphreys, who was still commanding the arsenal behind a guard of Carolina troops. What was this, Pickens demanded, about twenty soldiers moving over to Sumter? Humphreys, surprised, said he knew nothing of such a move. To the best of his knowledge, the only soldiers at Sumter in addition to the work crew were Lieutenant

Snyder and an ordnance sergeant.[13] The governor was not satisfied. He wanted an authoritative yes-or-no answer. Humphreys hastened to oblige by writing Captain Foster:

> The governor requested as a favor that such assurance should be given him over the signature of an officer of the Army, and . . . I make known Governor Pickens' desire to you, and respectfully suggest that you send him *immediately* (as he said it was important that he had a denial of the rumor by night) such communication as you may deem best in the premises.[14]

Still seething over the affair of the forty muskets, Foster gave the governor the back of his hand in a tart reply to Humphreys:

> I regret that I cannot accede to your request to write to the governor-elect of South Carolina and assure him that twenty enlisted men had not, as he had heard, been sent from Fort Moultrie to Fort Sumter. As the governor of a state that has by an ordinance to-day decided to secede from the Union, I cannot, I conceive, properly communicate with him in matters of this kind, except through the Government at Washington.

Then Foster went on to make it plain that while he refused to hold any commerce with the governor of the self-styled republic of South Carolina, he was willing to give the information to Humphreys, a fellow officer:

> I regret exceedingly that an unfounded rumor of this kind should have obtained the serious attention of the governor of South Carolina. I, as the officer in charge of Fort Sumter, can assure you that no enlisted men have been transferred from Fort Moultrie to Fort Sumter.[15]

Foster had been putting some deep thought on the garrison's predicament. While the government had refused to give them any men, there was no scarcity of powder. Why not make use of the powder? The captain came up with an explosive idea for defense that he passed on to Washington:

> There is another thing which I propose to do, and of which I write to you in season, so that if you disapprove it you can have time to forbid it. I propose to connect a powerful Daniels

G

battery with the magazine at Fort Sumter, by means of wires stretched across under water from Fort Sumter to Fort Moultrie, and to blow up Fort Sumter if it is taken by an armed force, after Lieutenant Snyder and my men have time to escape from it.

I propose, also, to use the same battery to fire small mines around Fort Moultrie, and to explode a large mine placed in the sand hills.[16]

Captain Foster should have known that Mr. Floyd—if he ever got around to answering—would never approve *that*.

"I am sorry to have no Christmas gift to offer you," Major Anderson wrote his wife on Christmas Day. "Never mind—the day may *very* soon come when I shall do something which will gratify you enough to make amends for all the anxiety you now feel on my account."[1]

By this veiled remark he meant his surprise move to Sumter, now fully decided on. Since secession he had virtually stopped his visits to Charleston, so that there had been no opportunity for shopping, which must have pained him. A gift-giving man, he was devoted to his wife, who had been in delicate health since before the Mexican War.

The major doubtless had pondered a move to Sumter ever since his talk with Major Buell on December 11th. On returning to Washington, Buell had left a copy of his memorandum of instructions with Secretary Floyd who, in his unhurried way, got around to looking at it on December 21st. On that date Floyd endorsed it, "This is in conformity to my instructions to Major Buell," and handed it to President Buchanan.[2]

Since Floyd approved the order in writing, he evidently was satisfied with it. The President also must have read it with care, for he took exception to the line ordering Anderson to defend himself "to the last extremity." This gave him an unhappy picture of the major and his men dying at their guns when attacked by overwhelming forces, and he ordered Floyd to soften it by informing Anderson he was expected only to make the best resistance possible.

Although the order authorized Anderson to move to Sumter under certain conditions, neither the President nor Floyd seemed to think those conditions would arise. The idea that he might have to escape to Sumter apparently never entered their minds as a serious possibility—another indication that neither of them understood the Charleston situation as well as they should have.

Anderson, who had long felt this lack of comprehension on the part of the administration, likened his position at Moultrie to "a sheep tied watching the butcher sharpening a knife to cut his throat." [3] Somewhere around mid-December his doubts about the Sumter move became resolved except for one harassing item: *tangible evidence of a design to proceed to a hostile act.* Who was to decide whether there was such evidence? Who but Major Anderson himself? A man who swore by the army regulations, he found his orders too vague and contradictory for guidance. Defend the forts, they said, but in heaven's name do not offend anyone. They were the instructions of a superior who did not choose to take a clear stand but preferred to throw responsibility on his subordinate. If Anderson remained in Moultrie to be humiliatingly defeated, he could be censured for not taking the escape offered him. If he shifted his force to Sumter, he could be censured for making a hostile military move. Small wonder that he was beginning to get a case of nerves.

One thing that irked him was Captain Foster's everlasting thoroughness in the improvements on Moultrie. Foster, of course, did not know Anderson was contemplating a move to Sumter which would make the Moultrie construction useful only to South Carolina. This was a secret Anderson felt compelled to keep to himself until the last moment, so Foster, responsible directly to engineering headquarters in Washington, was proceeding according to plan. Despite the major's objections, he finished one caponiere and started another, leaving an inviting gap at one corner of the fort. In a report to Floyd, Anderson made it clear that he did not intend to reflect on Foster but he was opposed to starting that second caponiere.

"He says that he will have the 'work defensible in five more working days, and have it finished in nine more working days,'" Anderson wrote. "God knows whether the South Carolinians will defer their attempt to take this work as long as that. I must confess that I think where an officer is placed in as delicate a position as the one I occupy that he should have the entire control over all persons connected in any way with the work intrusted to him. Responsibility and power to control ought to go together." [4]

Anderson did not know that when this message reached Washington on December 26th, Secretary Floyd was in disgrace and the War Department was without an operating head at the very moment when it needed an around-the-clock genius. The major was writing reports to a Secretary of War who in effect did not exist.

Late on the night of December 20th, a watchman on the ramparts of Fort Sumter aroused Lieutenant Snyder. Following him to the parapet, Snyder was surprised to see an unlighted steamer close under the west flank, apparently taking soundings. As the two men watched, the vessel moved away about six hundred yards from the fort, where it remained. On the same night this or another steamer reconnoitered around Castle Pinckney for some time. The watchman at Pinckney hailed it and demanded its business.

"You will know in a week," a male voice shouted back.[5]

When this was reported to Captain Foster, he was furious. It seemed to him that ever since he came to Charleston he had been forced to bow to one humiliation after another. Now the Carolinians were actually spying on the forts at night, and who could tell whether they intended to walk in and occupy them? Foster dashed off a report to Washington mentioning his apprehensions and urgently asking for instructions as to the action he should take about the surveillance.[6]

Although instructions from Washington were strangely difficult to get, he was still trying. When his report reached the War Department it was read by Captain H. G. Wright at engineering headquarters. Wright was so impressed with its importance that he shot it in to Secretary Floyd's office "with the earnest request that the instructions solicited by Captain Foster may be promptly given."

There was no reply from Floyd. Wright fidgeted for two days, then again called Floyd's attention to the report "as one of great importance."

Floyd still made no answer. Determined to get action, Captain Wright visited the secretary personally later that same day and read him the report.

"Very satisfactory," Floyd said, unruffled. Possibly his mind was on the Russell-Bailey Indian bond scandal, and the fact that the President had asked him to resign. "I hope," he added, "we shall get over these troubles without bloodshed." [7]

Wright later wrote despairingly to Foster that he had done his best to get instructions from Floyd but failed.[8] The United States Army, weak at best, was further hamstrung by a complete abdication of leadership.

Anderson likewise reported to Floyd the presence of the Carolina steamers, with no more result.[9] The major now felt himself surrounded by land and sea. He could only guess whether the object was surveillance or attack. The boats could easily drop a company or two of riflemen on Sullivan's Island. The riflemen could occupy that high sandhill just east of Moultrie—the hill that still remained because Secretary Floyd had thought its removal might be regarded as a hostile move. Once there, sharpshooters could command Moultrie and make it impossible for the garrison to serve their guns. If the object of the night watch was merely to await a favorable moment to seize Sumter, that likewise would render Moultrie untenable.

Once more Anderson wrote to the nonexistent Secretary of War, spelling out the advantage of shifting his force to Sumter and seeking to get definite instructions from Floyd authorizing the move:

That the authorities of South Carolina are determined to prevent, if possible, any troops from being placed in that fort [Sumter], and that they will seize upon that most important work as soon as they think there is reasonable ground for a doubt whether it will be turned over to the State, I do not doubt. I think that I could, however, were I to receive instructions so to do, throw my garrison into that work. . . . I do not think that we can rely upon any assurances, and wish to God I only had men enough here to man fully my guns.[10]

This was another of a long line of requests that received neither consideration nor reply. Shortly after secession, plump old Judge Petigru arrived with his friend, Judge George S. Bryan, to pay a visit to the garrison. They expressed their sympathy, saying frankly they believed that if the fort was not given up it would be taken. "[Petigru] bade us farewell with much feeling," Doubleday recalled. "The tears rolled down his cheeks as he deplored the folly and the madness of the times." [11] Until then, free access to the fort had been permitted, with citizens, militia officers, newspapermen, and engineers watching the construction and making notes and sketches of it. Now Anderson ordered the gates closed to all but the garrison, a step that added to the resentment of the Charlestonians.

On December 23rd, a messenger arrived at Moultrie carrying a dispatch from Floyd which the secretary thought too important to entrust to the mails. The bearer was Captain John Withers of the adjutant general's office, a Tennesseean later to join the Confederacy. The message read:

SIR: In the verbal instructions communicated to you by Major Buell, you are directed to hold possession of the forts in the harbor of Charleston, and, if attacked, to defend yourself to the last extremity. Under these instructions, you might infer that you are required to make a vain and useless sacrifice of your own life and the lives of the men under your command, upon a mere point of honor. This is far from the President's intentions. You are to exercise a sound military discretion on this subject.

It is neither expected nor desired that you should expose your own life or that of your men in a hopeless conflict in defense of these forts. If they are invested or attacked by a force so superior that resistance would, in your judgment, be a useless waste of life, it will be your duty to yield to necessity, and make the best terms in your power.

. . . These orders are strictly confidential, and are not to be communicated even to the officers under your command, without close necessity.[12]

There is strong evidence that the even-tempered major all but blew up when he read it. He had asked Floyd again and again for guidance, and what did he get? Nothing but instructions to submit tamely without a fight. To a soldier imbued with such a high sense of duty as Anderson, looking to his government for support in his dilemma, the orders offered only a prospect of shameful surrender. They were so secret he was not even to divulge them to his officers. Of late he had come to realize that he and his men were not so much United States soldiers as they were pawns that might be sacrificed at any time in a political chess match. Now he even suspected that Floyd was treasonously handing him, his garrison and the forts over to the Carolinians, thereby allowing them to start the war that still might be avoided by decisive action. Anderson, who had never committed an insubordinate act in his thirty-nine years as a soldier, gave up on the secretary. He instantly determined to move to Sumter at the earliest opportunity.[13]

Tangible evidence? Now that the state had seceded he felt a hostile move imminent. The guard boats watching him might at any moment turn from surveillance to attack or to the occupation of Sumter. That would have to be tangible evidence enough.

On December 24th, three Carolinians boarded a Washington-bound train in Charleston for the purpose of dickering with a foreign nation, the United States. They were Robert W. Barnwell, James H. Adams, and James L. Orr, all able men with long public experience. They were empowered as commissioners "to treat with the government of the United States for delivery of the forts, magazines, lighthouses, and other real estate . . . within the limits of South Carolina." [14] The state took the stand that these properties were nothing more nor less than real estate to be bargained for like a house or factory.

Major Anderson well knew that the commissioners represented South Carolina's effort to solve by negotiation a problem which, if their overtures failed, the state would settle by force of arms. He decided to move to Sumter on the evening of Christmas Day, counting on St. Nicholas to help him. Charleston would be celebrating not only the birth of the Saviour but also Carolina's first Christmas as a "free and sovereign republic," and merriment might mean a relaxing of watchfulness.

More than a week earlier he had begun a psychological preparation for the move by misleading his own men. He let the officers know that because of his fear of early attack he was planning to send the women and children of the garrison to safety at Fort Johnson, on James Island. Later he asked Foster to refrain from mounting any Sumter guns that could be turned on Moultrie. On December 24th Foster sent to Moultrie the elevating screws and pintle bolts of the Sumter cannon to hinder Carolinian use of them. These steps convinced the garrison that Anderson had no intention of going to Sumter but meant to defend Moultrie to the last.[15] The commander's deception was not caused by any distrust of his officers, not even the Virginian Meade. But some of them such as Foster had rented quarters in Moultrieville some distance from the fort, and if they knew of the plan they might unwittingly give indications of what was afoot by packing belongings, sending the laundry, or changing their messing arrangements. The Carolinians, suspicious, would be watching.

On Christmas Day Anderson ordered his quartermaster, young Lieutenant Hall, to get transportation for the women and children of the enlisted men. Then rain came spitting in from the sea, causing him reluctantly to postpone the maneuver for a day.[16] In Charleston, money was tight but the shopping area along King Street was gaily decorated and the city fairly whooped with Christmas merriment. Some of the volunteer state soldiers let their enthusiasm get the best of them. There was so much uproarious shooting in the streets that it was a wonder no one was hurt.[17] Out on Sullivan's Island, Captain Foster and his lady had a party at their Moultrieville cottage attended by Major Anderson, his officers, and a few friendly secessionists.[18] The festivities there must have had an undertone of uneasiness, with no one knowing what tomorrow might bring, but the bachelor Lieutenant Davis thrust care aside when he chatted with the pretty younger sister of Mrs. Foster. She gave him a small pocket flask of brandy by way of a Christmas present.[19] Captain Doubleday took the opportunity to ask Anderson for authorization to buy a large quantity of wire for erecting entanglements in front of Moultrie.

"Certainly," Anderson replied, "you shall have a mile of wire, if you require it." He said it with such a quizzical look that Doubleday got the impression that perhaps something unusual was in the offing.[20]

On the morning of the twenty-sixth, the major read on parade an order assigning each officer to his duty. This was interpreted as preparation to defend Moultrie. The commander seemed to think action was imminent. Transportation for the women and children would be in the two lighters used by the engineers at Sumter and Pinckney, so the two officers in command there—Lieutenant Snyder at Sumter and Lieutenant Meade at Pinckney—were let in on the secret first.

At noon the forty-five wives and children of the soldiers boarded the two lighters at the Moultrie wharf. Four months' provisions for the entire garrison were also loaded aboard, along with some of the men's personal belongings not immediately needed. Anderson had intimated that he intended to defend Moultrie until capture was certain, whereupon he would blow up the fort. On this pretext the boats were loaded heavily.[21] The major placed Lieutenant Hall in charge of the two craft and then told *him* the secret. Hall was ordered to head toward Fort Johnson but not to land. He was to wait in midstream until he heard two signal guns from Moultrie, which would mean that the garrison had landed safely at Sumter. Hall was then to make for Sumter.[22]

The great activity at the Moultrie wharf, with soldiers carrying boxes and bags into the vessels, aroused the interest of the householders nearby. Some were curious. Why, they asked Hall, was he moving so many provisions? Hall gave them an "evasive answer." Surgeon Crawford had no suspicion that anything was in the wind. He went to Sumter on his usual medical rounds, then intended to visit Charleston. No, he couldn't visit Charleston—no boats available. Why not? He saw Lieutenant Snyder about it. Snyder eyed him meaningly.

"Crawford," he said, "go back to Fort Moultrie, and don't take your eyes off Anderson." [23]

Now aware that something was afoot, the surgeon returned to Moultrie. He found Anderson on the seaward parapet, watching a large steamer of the Savannah line that was passing toward the city.

"I hope she will not attempt to come in," he said. "It would greatly embarrass me. I intend to move to Fort Sumter tonight." [24]

The plan was still a secret, he warned. How about the hospital equipment? Crawford asked, even in his astonishment thinking first of his medical necessities. That would have to wait, Anderson replied. It was more important to get the food and supplies across first. The major had selected the hour of dusk, between 5:00 and 6:00 P.M., to begin the actual crossing of the garrison's men, so that they would be less likely to be seen by residents of Sullivan's Island. There was still another peril—the guard boats, which were in the habit of beginning their patrol an hour or two after dusk. Could the garrison cross before the watch began, or elude it if not? Anderson must have been a nervous man as he calculated the risks he had to take in the knowledge that the move he was making in the cause of peace might, on a single mishap, break out in war.

Over in the officers' quarters, Mrs. Doubleday had a table all spread for tea. Her husband left to invite Anderson to join them. He found the major on the parapet with Crawford, both men silent and preoccupied. Before Doubleday got the invitation out of his mouth, Anderson turned to him.

"I have determined to evacuate this post immediately," he said, "for the purpose of occupying Fort Sumter; I can only allow you twenty minutes to form your company and be in readiness to start." [25]

The captain was not built for speed, a man of such calm deliberation that he was afterward nicknamed "Twenty-Four Hours," but on this occasion he showed real celerity. This could mean fighting. He was concerned for the safety of his wife, but duty came first. He sprinted for the barracks, formed his company, and saw that each man was properly armed and equipped. Then he raced back and warned Mary Doubleday to leave in a hurry, to take refuge with friends outside and to get behind the sand hills if firing broke out. Mrs. Doubleday left the tea things right where they were, packed a few valuables, and fluttered out the main gate with a couple of soldiers carrying her luggage.

"We took a sad and hasty leave of each other," Doubleday recalled, "for neither knew when or where we would meet again." [26]

Major Anderson, who had a remarkable reverence for his flag, was waiting at the gate with the garrison colors rolled under his arm. Doubleday joined him there with twenty of his company. The major turned and led them out of the fort. It was still far from dark as they marched in utter silence past a group of secessionists' houses and on down the beach, but they had the good fortune to be unobserved. The citizens apparently had decided it was only natural to move the women and children away from such a risky place as Moultrie. Anderson led his party to a point on Sullivan's Island's seaward beach about a quarter mile from the fort, directly across from Sumter. There Lieutenants Snyder and Meade, with a few soldier oarsmen, were waiting huddled behind rocks of the old seawall.

"Captain, those boats are for your men," Snyder whispered to Doubleday.[27]

There were three six-oared barges waiting in a small cove formed by the rocks. The men filed into the barges, laying down their muskets for concealment. Anderson and Snyder shoved off in charge of the first boat, Meade followed in the second, with Doubleday bringing up the rear. The commander still held the precious garrison flag. Seymour and his company would be next to cross.

Anderson realized all the possibilities of the move and was prepared to back it to the hilt. Behind him he had left Lieutenant Davis with the remainder of Doubleday's company as a rear guard. Captain Foster and Surgeon Crawford had been left on the parapet at Moultrie with five enlisted men. They were stationed at two loaded cannon bearing on the channel, and they had orders to sink the guard boats if they fired on the crossing soldiers.[28]

A full moon was growing brighter as dusk thickened. The seaborne soldiers were clad in the regulation uniform of the time —greatcoats with brass buttons, big black hats with brims upturned on the right, the officers wearing similar hats decorated with plumes. They were not quite in midstream when they spied what appeared to be one of the guard boats coming down the channel from Charleston. Anderson and Meade, in their two barges, made a wide circle toward the city to avoid it. Doubleday sized up the situation and decided that with some good work at the oars he could pass safely in front of the steamer. He ordered his helmsman to steer directly for Sumter, and the oarsmen to pull with all speed.

Unluckily the men at the oars were landlubbers and a mite clumsy. They made such slow progress that Doubleday saw to his dismay that they would come within view. He doffed his officer's hat, throwing open his greatcoat to hide the shiny buttons. He ordered his men to take off their coats and lay them over their guns to prevent any telltale glint. He was hoping prayerfully that they would be taken for a party of laborers returning to Sumter.[29]

On the parapet at Moultrie, Foster and Crawford were on tenterhooks as they watched the silent drama, the latter using a telescope. The cannon were aimed. Foster was ready to order his men to fire if there was any interference.[30]

The guard boat, later identified as the *Nina*, drew closer. Doubleday now saw that it was towing a smaller vessel, giving him hope that it was not on its usual patrol duty. "The paddlewheels stopped within about a hundred yards of us," he recorded, "but, to our great relief, after a slight scrutiny, the steamer kept on its way." [31]

Because of their more direct course, Doubleday's party reached Sumter first. A crowd of workmen met them at the wharf. A few Unionists among them set up a cheer, but more of them, wearing the blue cockade of secession, were scowling. "What are these soldiers doing here?" they demanded. Doubleday took no chances. He formed his men and advanced with bayonets, driving the workers into the fort. Taking possession of the guardroom which commanded the main entrance, he posted sentinels to keep the crowd in order—not the easiest task, since there were 115 workmen there. But soon Anderson and Meade arrived with their men to get the situation in hand. The boats were sent back immediately for Seymour's company and Davis' men, who arrived later without incident.[32]

All this time Lieutenant Hall had been waiting off Fort Johnson with the two lighters containing the women, children, and provisions. With the crossing safely accomplished, Hall heard the two signal guns from Moultrie and ordered his vessels to make for Sumter. One of the captains, a Carolinian, went into such a rage when he saw that he had been deceived that he had to be forcibly overpowered.[33]

The Charlestonians were strangely lacking in alertness that night. When the two guns were fired, another of the guard boats, the *Emma*, had not yet left her wharf although it was long past the usual hour of patrol. Colonel J. Johnston Pettigrew, an aide of Governor Pickens, hurried aboard to inquire what the shooting was about. The *Emma* went out on her mission at once, but noticed nothing amiss because the crossing had already been accomplished.[34]

One of the casualties of the evening was a fine hot beef dinner prepared for the officers at Moultrie by Mrs. Rippit, wife of one of the enlisted men. It was all laid out on the table, with not a blessed officer coming to dine. Mrs. Rippit was in a pet about it, and she gave Lieutenant Davis a piece of her mind when he returned to Moultrie for some supplies. A fine thing—there was the dinner, stone cold and the gravy congealed! Where was everybody? She was incredulous when Davis told her the whole garrison had moved to Sumter. The lieutenant put her and her kettles in his boat and rowed back to Sumter.[35]

So the move that might have been a bloody little affair

turned out to be almost a lark. Major Anderson was in such high good humor that he jokingly offered to serve as Davis' counsel if they were court-martialed for what they had done. Davis produced something better than a quip in reply. He brought out the pocket flask given him by Mrs. Foster's sister— a small thing for a half-dozen officers, but it would do. Anderson proposed a toast "to the success of the garrison," and each of them in turn had a sip of brandy to celebrate their liberation from that wretched rat trap, Fort Moultrie.[36]

The camaraderie and the flask were of short duration, for the major's worries were not over. His men were in an unfinished fort, on unfamiliar ground, with embrasures wide open inviting entrance. It would be perfectly feasible for the Carolinians to land storming parties, and if they did they would be aided by many secessionist workmen inside the fort. Hurried steps were taken for defense. And yet the devout Anderson, to whom the Almighty was a constant and near presence, felt that he had been accorded divine protection in his maneuver. That same evening he reported to Colonel Samuel Cooper, Floyd's adjutant general:

COLONEL: I have the honor to report that I have just completed, by the blessing of God, the removal to this fort of all my garrison, except the surgeon, four non-commissioned officers and seven men. We have one year's supply of hospital stores and about four months' supply of provisions for my command. I left orders to have all the guns at Fort Moultrie spiked, and the carriages of the 32-pounders, which are old, destroyed. I have sent orders to Captain Foster, who remains at Fort Moultrie, to destroy all the ammunition which he cannot send over. The step which I have taken was, in my opinion, necessary to prevent the effusion of blood.

Respectfully, your obedient servant,

ROBERT ANDERSON
Major, First Artillery, Commanding.[37]

The report went off in the next mail, not to reach Washington until December 29th. Many astonishing things would happen in the meantime.

MY COMPLIMENTS
TO THE GOVERNOR

At Fort Moultrie, Captain Foster had a busy and anxious night. He and his eleven men cut down the flagstaff, began spiking the guns and preparing to burn the wooden carriages of the 32-pounders, which would let the cannon sink helplessly to the terreplein and render them useless until new carriages were provided. At the same time they had to be watchful against an assault. This apprehension diminished as they saw the guard boat *Emma* take its place in the channel between Moultrie and Sumter and remain there, its officers apparently unaware that anything unusual had happened. The Carolinians had been caught napping. The move had been made with such quiet efficiency that up to now not even the residents of Moultrieville, bordering the fort on the west, suspected anything amiss.[1]

Mrs. Doubleday had taken refuge with the family of the Reverend Matthias Harris, the elderly chaplain of the garrison, who lived in Moultrieville. Although he was an uncompromising Unionist, Rev. Harris had not been informed of the move for security reasons and was astonished to find himself temporarily a shepherd without a flock. The Harrises and Mary Doubleday walked the beach for several hours that night, watching toward Sumter for signs of trouble and feeling relief to find all tranquil. Mesdames Foster and Seymour had already fled to the city.[2]

During the night, Surgeon Crawford crossed to Sumter, while Lieutenant Davis returned to Moultrie and remained with Foster. Early on the morning of the twenty-seventh, Crawford was rowed once more over to Moultrie to direct the transfer of a few more hospital effects. To the west he could see the lovely city of Charleston, a row of stately mansions fronting on the Battery, a skyline serrated by church steeples, a home of elegance and wealth where—in the surgeon's Pennsylvania-bred opinion—the thinking was as narrow and confined as the tongue of land on which the town was built, hemmed in by the Ashley and Cooper Rivers. As he approached the fort, he saw a heavy column of smoke rising above the parapet. Foster and Davis were burning the gun carriages, evidently doing a good job of it.[3]

That morning, just about every one of Anderson's soldiers and musicians were lined on the ramparts at Sumter, grinning like Cheshire cats, feeling like men released from prison, gazing out to see what the world looked like from a fort that was surrounded by water and was defensible. When the *Nina* passed by, her crew must have goggled. She raced into town with the incredible news: Sumter was full of Yankee soldiers! [4]

This first hint of what had come to pass encountered some disbelief in the city. Confirmation came quickly, for dozens of the secessionist workmen at Sumter quit their jobs that morning either on principle or because they feared the fort might soon become a center of hostilities. They were allowed to go to Charleston, where they told crowds of excited people how the Yanks had sneaked in and surprised them.[5] Captain Foster had the temerity to go to a Charleston bank before noon to get money to pay off his Moultrie workmen, who would no longer be needed. He described his reception with New Hampshire restraint: "I saw that . . . it would not be safe for me to go to town again for some time." [6]

It was a bad morning for Governor Pickens. The very maneuver against which he had guarded with the greatest care had been consummated under his nose, making him a target of quick criticism. Some accused him of lack of vigilance, while others said that if he had not been so confoundly finicky about the political amenities he would have seized Sumter himself *before* the Yankees did. Stung, the governor dispatched his aide, thirty-one-year-old Colonel J. Johnston Pettigrew of the South Carolina militia, to make representations about it. The colonel got into a boat with young Major Ellison Capers of his regiment and they were rowed to Sumter, where Pettigrew sent in his card.

H

They were ushered into Anderson's office on the second floor of the officers' quarters. Pettigrew, a relative of Judge Petigru but no Unionist,[7] was a brilliant Charleston lawyer who should have gone on to greatness had there been time. Time was to run out on him when Federal bullets struck him down a fortnight after he covered himself with glory at Gettysburg.

But here in the Union bastion there was no clairvoyant view of things to come: only the here and now—Sumter. The Charlestonians, in full uniform, exchanged formal greetings with Anderson and declined his offer of chairs. Pettigrew eyed Doubleday, Crawford, and several other officers who were with the commander.

"Major Anderson," he said, "can I communicate with you now, sir, before these officers . . . ?"

"Certainly, sir," Anderson replied. "These are all my officers; I have no secrets from them, sir."

Pettigrew declared he was directed to say that Governor Pickens was much surprised that he had "reinforced" Sumter— a word Anderson promptly disputed. Not at all, he said. He had merely transferred his garrison from Moultrie to Sumter. Surely no one could question his right to do so, since he was in command of all the forts in the harbor.

That might be technically correct, Pettigrew admitted, but the move was a violation of an agreement. When Pickens took office he found that an understanding existed between the previous governor, Gist, and President Buchanan. According to this understanding, South Carolina would make no attempt against the public property in the state, and in return the Washington government would not alter the military status in the harbor. By moving to Sumter, Anderson had most decidedly altered the military status. Pettigrew was instructed to say that Governor Pickens had hoped for a peaceful solution, but this violation seemed to make it uncertain if not impossible.

This was news to Major Anderson. An understanding? He knew nothing whatever about it, he insisted. He had tried vainly to get information and positive orders from Washington.

Meanwhile his position was threatened every night by Carolina troops.

"How?" demanded Major Capers. Only twenty-four, he was young enough to be Anderson's son, though he equaled him in rank, and like Pettigrew he was aroused over what he conceived as a broken pledge.

"By sending out steamers armed and carrying troops," Anderson replied. "These steamers passed the fort going north. I feared a landing on the island and the occupation of the sand hills just north [actually, east] of the fort. One hundred riflemen on that hill would command the fort and make it impossible for my men to serve their guns, as any military man can see."

He went on to make it clear that he ordered the move on his own sole responsibility, that he had done it to prevent bloodshed and protect his command and had no doubt about his rights. "In this controversy between the North and South," he said, "my sympathies are entirely with the South. These gentlemen" —he indicated his own officers—"know it perfectly well." But he added that his sense of duty as commander in the harbor came first with him.

Pettigrew and Capers bowed at the major's mention of his sympathies. "Well, sir," Pettigrew replied, "however that may be, the Governor of the State directs me to say to you, courteously but peremptorily, to return to Fort Moultrie."

"Make my compliments to the Governor," Anderson said, "and say to him that I decline to accede to his request; I cannot and will not go back." [8]

The two Charlestonians bowed again and took their leave. Anderson turned his attention to a ceremony he had planned to acknowledge the divine protection to which he had not the slightest doubt he owed his safe passage to Sumter. That it was Thursday and not Sunday made no difference to him. He had managed to get Chaplain Harris rowed over from Sullivan's Island to officiate and doubtless had talked with Harris about the theme he would take in his prayer. The major wanted his men to share his deep feeling of deliverance and gratitude at the success of their enterprise—wanted them also to understand that they had not occupied Sumter as an act of defiance toward South Carolina but in the belief that the step lessened the immediate threat of war.

At 11:45 the garrison and workmen were ordered to the parade, part of which was littered with building materials, unmounted cannon, supplies, and personal effects. The band was lined on the parapet, thankful that even their instruments had not been forgotten in the move. The major marched out with military stride, carrying the folded flag he personally had borne from Moultrie, and stood by the flagstaff.

The command was brought to parade rest. Everyone uncovered as Chaplain Harris intoned a prayer of thanksgiving and hope that the flag would soon float over a united country. Anderson knelt, his head bowed, his iron-gray hair giving off glints of silver in the sunlight. The prayer ended, he rose smartly and pulled at the lanyards to make Old Glory soar upward until it cleared the high walls and was caught by the breeze.[9]

Every hardfisted trooper there was moved by an emotion of loyalty and devotion to duty that seemed personified by the commander, a quiet man, a Southerner who stood by his flag when the going was roughest, an officer who had proved his unflinching courage only the night before on the waters of Charleston harbor. The band played "Hail Columbia" as the battalion presented arms. Then the men broke spontaneously into rousing cheers "repeated again and again." Patriotism at that moment was a living thing at Sumter such as few are given to feel it. The ovation was as much for a peerless leader as for the colors he raised. Wrote Sergeant James Chester, who was there doing his share of the cheering: "If any of those who doubted the loyalty to the Union of Major Anderson could have had but one glimpse of that impressive scene, they would have doubted no longer." [10]

In Charleston, Governor Pickens, pressed hard by angry counselors, moved into his second and gravest gubernatorial error. On his order Colonel Pettigrew boarded a vessel with units of three companies and landed at Castle Pinckney. This was one of the "properties" about which the South Carolina commissioners were even then in Washington to negotiate for. It *was* federal property. The governor would have given more realistic service to the cause of peace he claimed to espouse had he kept patience and let negotiation take its course—particularly since he had Anderson's word that the movement to Sumter was his own idea and not specifically ordered from Washington. The military move on Pinckney was armed aggression at the governor's command—the first overt act of war to come—in no way justified by Anderson's transfer to Sumter.

At Pinckney, Lieutenant Meade was in command with one soldier under him—Ordnance Sergeant Skillen—and some thirty-five laborers. These workmen, who had been hand-picked by Captain Foster in the hope that they would aid in the defense of the fort, proved a sore disappointment. At word that the Carolinians were coming, they refused to resist, some of them hiding in closets and under beds.[11] The disgusted Meade closed and barred the main gate and waited the inevitable. Pettigrew's men raised scaling ladders and climbed into the fort. The colonel announced to Meade that he was taking charge of the work by order of Governor Pickens in the name of the state.

Meade, although a Virginian and Southern in his sympathies, was far from compliant. He had no means of resistance, he said, so he could only enter his protest. When Pettigrew offered him receipts for the public property, Meade sharply replied that since he did not recognize the governor's authority he would not accept the receipts. Furthermore, he refused to give his parole as he did not consider himself a prisoner of war. He asked for considerate treatment of Sergeant Skillen and his family, and was allowed to go to Sumter.[12]

As the Palmetto flag went up over the first Union fortress lost in the war, a Carolina officer found fifteen-year-old Kate Skillen, the sergeant's daughter, weeping bitterly. He patted her head and assured her she would not be harmed.

"I am not crying because I am afraid!" she sobbed.

"What is the matter then?"

"I am crying because you put that miserable rag up there," said peppery Kate, pointing at the Palmetto ensign.[13]

Shortly afterward, also under the governor's orders, Lieutenant Colonel Wilmot DeSaussure, a member of the state legislature, landed on Sullivan's Island with two hundred militiamen to take over empty Fort Moultrie. Doubleday's subtle propaganda about laying mines around the fort had made an impression. The Carolinians approached gingerly and decided to stay out for the nonce. Only Colonel DeSaussure and a few men entered that evening to hoist over Moultrie a Palmetto flag taken from the *General Clinch,* the vessel honoring Mrs. Anderson's father.[14]

Said the Charleston *Courier:*

"Maj. Robert Anderson, U.S.A., has achieved the unenviable distinction of opening civil war between American citizens by an act of gross breach of faith." [15]

In New York, the *Herald* headlined:

IMPORTANT FOREIGN INTELLIGENCE
Major Anderson Abandons Fort
Moultrie and Spikes the Guns
MAJOR ANDERSON DISOBEYS HIS ORDERS [16]

MEN DO GO MAD

"Is it possible," the Public Man wondered, "there can be truth in the old notion that, in times of great national trial and excitement, so many men do go mad, so to speak, in a quiet and private way, that madness becomes a sort of epidemic?" [1]

It was not only true but demonstrated right there before him in Washington. For weeks legislators and officials had been showing a gradually increasing condition of derangement which was now to burst out in something much like madness, and not very quiet or private either.

On Wednesday evening, December 26th, Commissioners Barnwell, Orr, and Adams arrived in the capital, having spent their Christmas uncomfortably on the train in the service of their state and the hope that they could persuade the United States Government to purchase peace by handing over the Charleston forts. They were met by William Trescot, the efficient fixer and middleman of secession. Mr. Trescot was no longer simultaneously serving under two flags. With the exit of his state from the Union he had left the government and become what in effect he always had been—South Carolina's minister without portfolio and chief shooter of disunion trouble. He figured the commissioners might be around for a long time. President Buchanan would refer them to Congress, and Congress would be as long-winded as usual getting to it. So Trescot had rented a mansion at 352 K Street, a half mile from the White House, where the envoys could do their waiting in dignity. Commissioner Orr was an old Washington hand, former Speaker of the House, and one of the most popular of men. He was greeted by many friends who "jokingly regretted to see him here as a *foreigner*." [2]

The commissioners had their argument all laid out. They

took the stand that South Carolina had ceded the sites for the forts in 1805 to be used so long as they were employed for the defense of the state. Now that this condition no longer existed, she had revoked the cession and would resume control, but was of course prepared to give the United States adequate compensation for the value of the works erected on the sites. What could be more reasonable?

Trescot no sooner got the three visitors comfortable than he went to the White House to inform the President of their arrival. Buchanan had already told him he could not recognize the commissioners in their official capacity but would be glad to receive them as "private gentlemen" and pass their proposals to Congress. This was quite acceptable to Trescot and the more conservative Carolinians who saw that delay was an advantage giving them time to arm—an interim during which other states could be expected to secede and join them. Buchanan now told Trescot he would see the envoys next day, December 27th, at one o'clock.[3]

Next morning, Trescot was discussing strategy with the commissioners at their residence when Washington's most violent and uninhibited character strode in. This was Senator Louis Trezevant Wigfall of Texas, a former South Carolinian noted for his willingness to shoot people who disagreed with him. A grim man who exuded truculence and had the eye of an old sea rover, Wigfall had wounded or killed eight dueling opponents. Twelve years a Texan, he was still a Carolinian at heart. Only two days earlier, on Christmas night, he was said to have gone to Secretary Floyd's house with a typical Wigfallian proposition: Let us kidnap President Buchanan, he said, and carry him off in close confinement. That will make Breckinridge President, and as a good Southerner he will prevent war. Floyd, though his ethics were elastic, could not make them stretch that far. He flatly refused to have any truck with kidnaping, and Wigfall's trigger temper exploded but fortunately he brought no pistols into play.[4]

Now the Senator was breathing fire. A telegram from Charleston, he told Trescot and the commissioners, said that Anderson had abandoned Moultrie, spiked his guns, and moved his command to Sumter. His listeners were incredulous.

"I will pledge my life," Trescot said, "if it has been done, it has been without orders from Washington."

At that moment Secretary Floyd was ushered in. Trescot told him the news and repeated the statement he had just made.

"You can do more that that," Floyd said with a smile. "You can pledge your life, Mr. Trescot, that it is not so. It is impossible. It would be not only without orders, but in the face of orders. To be very frank, Anderson was instructed in case he had to abandon his position to dismantle *Fort Sumter,* not Fort Moultrie." [5]

The secretary was wrong, as was common with him. Anderson had never received such orders. Another telegram now arrived for Barnwell affirming that the news was indeed true. Floyd bolted out and hurried to the War Department, where no one knew anything about the move. He dispatched a peremptory telegram to Anderson at Charleston:

"Intelligence has reached here this morning that you have abandoned Fort Moultrie, spiked your guns, burned the carriages, and gone to Fort Sumter. It is not believed, because there is no order for any such movement. Explain the meaning of this report." [6]

Trescot meanwhile drove like mad to the Capitol, where he rounded up Senators Davis and Hunter and sped with them to the White House. Buchanan must have sensed by their expressions that something momentous had happened. Davis recited the facts to him.

"And now, Mr. President," he finished, "you are surrounded with blood and dishonor on all sides."

Buchanan stood by the mantel, slowly crushing a cigar in the palm of his hand—a nervous habit of his. "My God!" he exclaimed. "Are calamities never to come singly! I call God to witness, you gentlemen, better than anybody, know that this is not only without but against my orders. It is against my policy." [7]

He then expressed disbelief. He had heard nothing about

this from the War Department, he said. He sent for Secretary
Floyd, whom he had asked to resign four days previously, and
who had agreed to resign but was still delaying his exit. Floyd
reported that his department had received no official word, and
that he had telegraphed Anderson for explanation. Davis had no
doubt the news was true and that the "implied pledge" to maintain the status had been broken. The only thing for the President to do now, he insisted, was to withdraw the garrison from
Charleston harbor altogether.[8]

To his credit, Buchanan declined this invitation to clear out
of the harbor of a state whose secession he had declared illegal
and refused to recognize. But he appears to have been embarrassed by his December 10th conversation with the South Carolina Congressmen, when he had given them some informal assurance, though no official guarantee, that the military status
would not be changed. He had never dreamed that Anderson
would move of his own accord. To the President the Sumter
maneuver was a stark nightmare. Here things were nicely in
hand, with the South Carolina commissioners coming to negotiate like gentlemen, and now Anderson had crashed everything
in ruins! In his White House ivory tower, with a nonfunction-
ing or malfunctioning Secretary of War, Buchanan had no adequate understanding of the crisis in which Anderson had acted
and felt the major had committed a terrible blunder.[9]

The men from Dixie were pressing him hard, urging him to
move fast. Unless he ordered Anderson to move right back to
Moultrie, the chances were that South Carolina would seize the
other forts, attack Sumter, and bring war over the land. The
elderly President was still reeling from the Floyd scandal when
this new blow struck him. The wonder is that he did not collapse. He did not. Although at first he was inclined to order
Anderson back to Moultrie forthwith, he decided that he could
not condemn the major unheard. He must consult the Cabinet
about it.[10]

At the War Department, the still unresigned John Floyd
received a telegram which jolted him but also presented him

with just the tailor-made opportunity for which he had been
hoping:

> The telegram is correct. I abandoned Fort Moultrie because
> I was certain that if attacked my men must have been sacri-
> ficed, and the command of the harbor lost. I spiked the guns
> and destroyed the carriages to keep the guns from being used
> against us.
>
> If attacked, the garrison would never have surrendered with-
> out a fight.
>
> ROBERT ANDERSON
Major, First Artillery.[11]

That last sentence might have seemed superfluous, but was
not. It showed exactly what Anderson thought of Floyd's order
not to make a "vain and useless sacrifice" of himself and his
garrison. The major naturally assumed that both Floyd and
Buchanan had approved Buell's instructions that he could move
to Sumter if threatened, as indeed they had. Neither of them
apparently had placed any importance in this discretion allowed
to the commander or felt there would be any need to exercise it.

Anderson did not know that his move to Sumter raised such
momentous questions that the President and his counselors
would wrestle with them for three days and four nights. Floyd,
although the other Cabinet members considered him virtually
out of office, still acted like a member of the team.

"This is a very unfortunate move of Major Anderson," he
said to Major Buell. "It has made war inevitable."

"I do not think so, sir," Buell replied. "On the contrary, I
think that it will tend to avert war, if war can be averted." [12]

With a colossal nerve, Floyd attended the first Cabinet meeting on the morning of the twenty-seventh uninvited, nor did he
come with his hat in his hand. He was in a rage. Immediately
he tilted with Secretary of State Black, who warmly approved of
Anderson's move.

"I am glad of it," Black said. "It is in precise accordance with
his orders."

"It is not," Floyd contradicted.

"But it is," Black insisted. "I recollect the orders distinctly word for word." [13]

So the orders given Anderson by Major Buell on December 11th were brought in. They had been read and approved by Floyd with his written endorsement on December 21st, and approved by the President the same day. Now they were reread, with emphasis on the last line giving Anderson authority to move from Moultrie "whenever you have tangible evidence of a design to proceed to a hostile act." There was some discussion about the tangibility of the evidence, but this was quickly settled. The orders were meaningless if they did not allow Anderson to judge the evidence for himself.[14]

That should have settled Floyd's hash, but it did not. The Virginian set up a howl about the "pledge" to South Carolina not to change the status, though how he could reconcile this with his own orders to Anderson he did not explain. It was obvious to everyone that he was putting on a well-rehearsed show designed to let him resign as the guardian of governmental honor instead of being kicked out as the official who had tossed 870,000 federal dollars to the breeze. Heatedly he insisted that the only step now that could avert war and save the administration's integrity was to remove the garrison from Charleston entirely. Black, Holt, and Attorney General Stanton, hardly concealing their contempt for the discredited secretary, were up in arms against such an idea. To take that course would be a crime equaling Arnold's, Stanton declared, and anyone participating in it should be hanged like André.[15]

"A President of the United States who would make such an order," he snapped, "would be guilty of treason."

"Oh, no! not so bad as that, my friend!" Buchanan exclaimed, raising his hands. "Not so bad as that!" [16]

But he was taking no advice from Floyd, and that veteran double-dealer made his resignation official two days later with considerable success in convincing the South and much of the North that he had quit rather than be a party to administration duplicity.

While getting rid of Floyd was a wholesome accomplishment, there still remained the question: What to do about Charleston? Buchanan was besieged by Southern legislators who warned him to get out of Charleston before shooting began. Senator Joseph Lane, the Oregon secessionist, said, "Anderson ought to be cashiered or dismissed from the service." [17] When the three South Carolina commissioners visited Buchanan, they presented him with a copy of the secession ordinance and a written ultimatum.

They had been ready to negotiate all questions, they declared, until Anderson's move made it impossible. For the past sixty days South Carolina could have occupied Sumter merely by walking in, refraining because of their trust in the President's assurances. Now Anderson had walked in, violating those assurances. Until this was righted, they must suspend all discussion. They urged the President to withdraw all the troops from Charleston harbor at once, "as they are a standing menace which render negotiations impossible and threaten a bloody issue." [18] Barnwell, the trio's chairman, tried persistently to hold Buchanan to account for that conversation he had had with the South Carolina Congressmen.

"But, Mr. President," he said at least three times, "your personal honor is involved in this arrangement."

"Mr. Barnwell," Buchanan protested, "you are pressing me too importunately; you don't give me time to consider; you don't give me time to say my prayers. I always say my prayers when required to act upon any great State affair." [19]

The commissioners retired to give him a reasonable time to pray. For long, as Trescot cannily diagnosed it, The Squire's policy had not been indecision but "really a fixed purpose to be undecided." [20] Now, because of Anderson, this strategy of drifting and delay was irrevocably ended. A decision had to be made one way or the other in the knowledge that whatever it was, one half of the nation would be outraged. After angling for weeks to set up a situation amounting in his mind to a safe truce, delaying any clear-cut issue, the President saw an army major wreck the truce and thrust the issue right into his face. From

the top down, official Washington was split on whether Major
Anderson had committed treachery or answered the deepest
promptings of patriotism. Floyd's denunciation of the move
went out over the wires to add confusion. Newspapers the
nation over headlined the governmental crisis precipitated by
the transfer of some four score of men and officers over a mile of
salt water. The devout Kentucky major was suddenly the most
famous man in the country, praised and damned with equal
heat. In the turmoil, someone must have inquired whether
General Scott could have ordered Anderson to occupy Sumter.
The reply of Scott, now in Washington for keeps, fairly crackled
that he had issued "no order, intimation, suggestion or communication" to Anderson, letting it be known that Floyd had
handled the whole Charleston matter himself and feeling privately that he had made a mess of it.[21] At the same time the old
war horse, though suffering a recurrence of his diarrhea, made
it plain that he was solidly behind his former ADC, Anderson.
Believing Floyd was still functioning as Secretary of War, he
dispatched a note to him reading in part:

> Lieutenant-General Scott, who has had a bad night, and can
> scarcely hold up his head this morning, begs to express the
> hope to the Secretary of War—
> 1. That orders may not be given for the evacuation of Fort
> Sumter.
> 2. That one hundred and fifty recruits may instantly be
> sent from Governor's Island to reinforce that garrison, with
> ample supplies of ammunition, subsistence, including fresh
> vegetables, as potatoes, onions, turnips; and
> 3. That one or two armed vessels be sent to support the said
> fort.[22]

Washington, a few days earlier convulsed by the Floyd scan-
dal, had forgotten it in the throes of a new and bitter struggle.
Reinforce Anderson . . . send him men, onions, turnips, war
vessels . . . move him back to Moultrie . . . get him out of
Charleston altogether and hand over the forts without a fight.
. . . Every man had his own solution, while Buchanan sought

the solution. Hearing the ominous thumping of war drums, he was stalling for time, sounding public opinion. He gave out that he was considering sending Anderson back to Moultrie, and cupped his ear for the reaction. One reaction came from some Union men of Lancaster, who offered to buy his estate at Wheatland if he agreed not to come back, ever.[23] His own new Attorney General, Edwin Stanton, and one of his closest friends in Congress, Daniel Sickles, were taking sly steps behind his back to stiffen his resolve. Stanton sent confidential telegrams to Unionists in Northern cities, urging them to stage celebrations and parades honoring Anderson for his move and the President for backing him. Sickles personally visited Philadelphia and New York, where he arranged for 100-gun salutes for Anderson and Buchanan.[24] In the welter of confusion and argument, few understood the simple fact that Anderson had moved to Sumter for only one purpose: to preserve peace.

The President drafted a reply to the South Carolina commissioners, tried it out on the Cabinet and found that only Secretary of the Navy Toucey approved it. Black, Stanton, and Postmaster General Holt opposed it as making too many concessions to the Palmetto State. Thompson and Secretary of the Treasury Philip Thomas opposed it for yielding too *little*.[25] One of the many Cabinet meetings on the subject was interrupted when burly Senator Robert Toombs of Georgia called on the President to ask whether he had decided what to do about Sumter. Buchanan told him the matter was still under discussion, then inquired why the question of a fort at Charleston should have any interest for Georgia.

"Sir," Toombs rumbled, "the cause of Charleston is the cause of the South."

"Good God, Mr. Toombs," the President exclaimed, "do you mean that I am in the midst of a revolution?"

"Yes, Sir—more than that," the Senator growled as he departed, "you have been there for a year and have not yet found it out." [26]

Ridicule had become a large part of the daily fare of the old gentleman from Pennsylvania, but no one could say he was not working devotedly to keep the peace and that he had not performed some kind of miracle in holding together a Cabinet whose members were diametrically at odds. Now, because of Anderson, his hold began to slip. Now emerged one of those "strong men" who seem to rise for good or ill in national crises to mould the destinies of millions. He was Jeremiah Sullivan Black, the fifty-year-old Secretary of State.

Tall, slouching, homely, untidy, with a wig that seemed always crooked and clothes that did not fit, Judge Black was a lawyer's lawyer and a classical scholar who could not open his mouth without dropping literary gems. A Pennsylvanian, he had supported Buchanan for twenty years. The pair were intimate friends, almost on a Damon-Pythias basis. A good Democrat, Black had loyally backed the President's kid-glove treatment of South Carolina until recent weeks, when he began to resent the Carolinian demands. Like Buchanan, he had opposed the "coercion" of South Carolina, but he did not regard the nonaggressive federal possession of its own forts as coercion at all. "The Union is necessarily perpetual," he had said, pressing Buchanan to reinforce Anderson at Moultrie not only as a right but as a duty. Old Buck had refused, fearing reinforcement would mean war. Black's misgivings about the hands-off policy had been growing. Now, when he heard Buchanan read his projected reply to the three commissioners, Black was ready to quit.[27]

Although Buchanan's draft has been lost, it is clear from what followed that Black considered it a disgraceful surrender to South Carolina as well as a slap at Major Anderson. Early on Sunday, December 30th, the President heard of Black's intention to resign and sent for him in great trepidation. He knew that if Black left, Stanton and Holt would undoubtedly follow, leaving his administration in ruins.

"Is it true that you are going to desert me?" he asked.

It was a painful moment for Black. "I promised as long as there was a button to the coat I would cling to it," he said. "But your action has taken every button off, and driven me away from you. . . . I would not leave you for any earthly consideration so long as I could stay by you with self-respect, but I cannot do it, if the paper you have prepared is sent to the gentlemen from South Carolina." [28]

Buchanan pointed out the need for avoiding war, with the North divided, the army pitifully small, and a hostile Congress refusing to do anything about it. He also apparently admitted that to some extent he had made an agreement and his honor was involved. Black was adamant. There was a long discussion before the President capitulated. He gave Black the letter and told him to suggest changes, even though the Secretary said his changes would mean virtual recasting. But Black must hurry because the reply would have to be ready by nightfall.[29]

The Secretary of State hastened to Attorney General Stanton's office. There he wrote as fast as he could, with Stanton copying as the sheets were tossed at him. When Black finished, he had read the President a lesson in governmental law as well as presenting a vividly clear picture of one man's analysis of the crisis that was giving the nation the shakes. He wrote in part:

> The President erred in seeming to acknowledge that South Carolina had a right to be represented in negotiations with the United States government. There could legally be no negotiation with them.
>
> The forts in the harbor of Charleston belong to this Government, are its own, and cannot be given up. It is true they might be surrendered to a superior force. . . . But Fort Sumter is impregnable, and cannot be taken if defended as it should be. It is a thing of the last importance that it should be maintained, if all the power of this nation can do it. . . .
>
> The implied assent of the President to the accusation which the commissioners make of a compact with South Carolina by which he was bound not to take whatever measures he saw fit for the defense of the forts, ought to be stricken out. . . . The paper signed by the late members of Congress from South Carolina does not bear any such construction. . . . The fact that he pledged himself in any such way can not be true.
>
> The remotest expression of a doubt about Major Anderson's perfect propriety of behavior should be carefully avoided. He is not only a gallant and meritorious officer, who is entitled

I

to a fair hearing before he is condemned; he has saved the country, I solemnly believe, when its day was darkest and its peril most extreme.

He has done everything that mortal man could do to repair the fatal error which the administration have committed in not sending down troops enough to hold *all* the forts. He has kept the strongest one. He still commands the harbor.

It is a strange assumption of right on the part of that state [South Carolina] to say that the United States troops must remain in the weakest position they can find in the harbor. It is not a menace of South Carolina or of Charleston, or any menace at all: it is simply self-defense. If South Carolina does not attack Major Anderson, no human being will be injured, for there certainly can be no reason to believe that he will commence hostilities.

. . . I entreat the President to order the *Brooklyn* and the *Macedonian* to Charleston without the least delay, and in the mean time send a trusty messenger to Major Anderson to let him know that his Government will not desert him. The reinforcement of troops from New York or Old Point Comfort should follow immediately. If this be done at once all may yet be not well, but comparatively safe. If not, I can see nothing before us but disaster and ruin to the country.[30]

Until he read that paper, Buchanan had been a gentleman trying to be nice to everybody, and especially careful not to offend his Democratic friends in the South. Now, moved by Black's eloquence and his own sense of peril, he could no longer be nice to everybody. He had to choose. He told a friend, "If I withdraw Anderson from Sumter, I can travel home to Wheatland by the light of my own burning effigies." [31] He also feared another very possible result—impeachment. But for all his wavering, he must have seen that Mr. Toombs was right—this was no mere incident in Charleston harbor that confronted him. It was massive revolution. Major Anderson in Fort Sumter was the only visible token that the administration meant to oppose the revolution with anything more than polite protest. Anderson would have to stay.[32]

On that same historic Sunday, the President received another of General Scott's remarkable third-person notes:

> Lieutenant-General Scott begs the President of the United States to pardon the irregularity of this communication.
>
> It is Sunday; the weather is bad, and General Scott is not well enough to go to church. But matters of the highest national importance seem to forbid a moment's delay, and if misled by zeal, he hopes for the President's forgiveness.
>
> Will the President permit General Scott, without reference to the War Department and otherwise, as secretly as possible, to send two hundred and fifty recruits from New York Harbor to reinforce Fort Sumter, together with some extra muskets or rifles, ammunition, and subsistence stores . . . ? [33]

The President would. A man at the crossroads, he took the fork turning North. Anderson would not only have to stay. He would have to be reinforced. The peace-loving Buchanan knew exactly what that meant.

FLEAS
IN THEIR EARS

When John Floyd read his curtain speech and left the Cabinet, he automatically sent up a danger flare for the benefit of South Carolina. Floyd had generously let it be known that he was opposed to coercion and would resign instantly if the administration undertook to use force. In the whole South his resignation was taken as a signal that the kid-glove treatment was over,[1] and no one was more aware of it than Louis Wigfall.

"Holt succeeds Floyd," he telegraphed General M. L. Bonham of the South Carolina military in Charleston. "It means war. Cut off supplies from Anderson and take Sumter soon as possible." [2]

This was a fairly unusual message for a United States Senator to be sending, but Wigfall was following his own concept of loyalty. He would sneer at the Union for eleven more weeks in the Senate while he kept his eyes and ears alert and dispatched a succession of confidential messages to Charleston on his favorite subjects: the defying of coercion and the efficient dismemberment of the nation.

This word "coercion" had been bandied about by so many individuals of diverse prejudices that it came to have almost as many meanings as the word "loyalty." To Judge Black, coercion meant sending an army into South Carolina to crush secession by force of arms—something he did not believe the government had a right to do. On the contrary, merely keeping possession of the federal forts was decidedly not coercion. It was the administration's plain duty. The Carolinians, along with many other Southern fire-eaters like Wigfall, said this was poppycock. From where they stood, the presence of Anderson's garrison even in forlorn Moultrie was a species of coercion. His move to Sumter was indubitably coercion. To send him reinforcements now —well, that would be coercion in large capitals.

Now that Buchanan had decided on reinforcement ("coercion" south of the Potomac), he set out with what appeared to be real earnestness, moving Postmaster General Joseph Holt into the Secretary of War's spot. One of Holt's first moves was to countermand that inexplicable order of Floyd's to send 124 cannon south.[3] The cannon stayed. Winfield Scott, so long an unhappy outsider, was pulled out of the dust heap as Holt went into conference with him. Things began to move. Scott sent an order to Fortress Monroe to ready four companies to embark for Sumter on the *Brooklyn,* a formidable twenty-five-gun sloop of war, adding a sharp warning: *"Look to this."* [4] The President wrote his new reply to the Carolina commissioners, stiffened à la Black. In it he admitted that his "first promptings" had been to order Anderson back to Moultrie, until he learned that South Carolina had immediately taken armed possession of Castle Pinckney, Fort Moultrie, the United States arsenal, custom house, and post office. These seizures made even the pacific Buchanan boil, and he let the commissioners know it:

"It is under all these circumstances that I am urged immediately to withdraw the troops from the harbor of Charleston, and am informed that without this, negotiation is impossible. This I cannot do; this I will not do." He would defend Fort Sumter, he said, but "I do not perceive how such a defense can be construed into a menace of the city of Charleston." [5]

Governor Pickens had indeed blundered. Had he refrained from these seizures and contented himself with asking his commissioners to complain about Anderson's move, the chances are strong that Buchanan would have moved the major right back to Moultrie.

Yet for all his stout talk the President still shrank from action. His fixed determination to be undecided had suffered only a temporary eclipse. At this critical moment his new-found determination wilted on a queer ground: politeness. He felt it would not be courteous to send the *Brooklyn* to reinforce Anderson until the commissioners had had time to read his letter and reply to it. General Scott, a gentleman of the Virginia school, agreed. Neither seemed to comprehend that if Anderson was to be reinforced, every hour and every minute counted. Both knew that South Carolina, with unchivalrous neglect of niceties, was arming to the teeth, commissioners or no commissioners. It was courtly of the President and Scott to delay on this score, but their politeness was to pay them back in bitter failure.[6]

Meanwhile, there was still great commotion about the "pledge" Buchanan was said to have given, although its sanctity seemed to be held very lightly by Governor Pickens when he sent out the guard boats. Trescot and Attorney General Stanton had a set-to about the pledge, with Stanton laying down some good hard sense. He told Trescot he knew nothing of any pledge, but for the sake of argument would admit that one had been given.

"Anderson's conduct has broken that pledge," he went on. "You had two courses to choose: you had a right to either. You could have appealed to the President to redeem his pledge, or you could have . . . acted as you saw fit, but you have no right to adopt both. . . . Now you have chosen; you have, by seizing the remaining forts and arsenals, undertaken to redress yourselves. The President's pledge may be broken or not, that *now* concerns him individually—as to the Government, you have passed by the pledge and assumed, in vindication, a position of hostility; with that alone I have to deal." [7]

Trescot, well knowing his state was not yet prepared, was still working to prevent open conflict. Buchanan's chief embarrassment and indignation, he felt, was caused by the Carolina seizure of the other forts. If Anderson were to be ordered out of Sumter now, he had nowhere to go but away—out of the harbor entirely —and this was a move Northern public sentiment would not stand for. Trescot galloped in a hansom to the home of Senator Hunter of Virginia. Would Hunter submit a proposition to the President that the state would withdraw from the forts they had seized if Anderson would return to Moultrie? Hunter agreed, and called on Buchanan. He came out looking agitated.

"Tell the Commissioners it is hopeless," he said. "The President has taken his ground. I *can't* repeat what passed, but if you can get a telegram to Charleston, telegraph at once to your people to sink vessels in the channel of the harbor." [8]

By this method of respecting a confidence, Hunter might as well have said that the whole United States Navy was bound for Charleston. The commissioners promptly wired home: ". . . We believe reinforcements are on their way. Prevent their entrance into the harbor at every hazard." Turmoil there was, and yet social custom had to be served. The next day being January 1st, 1861, official business was suspended as the President held his traditional New Year's reception at the White House—anything but a frolicsome affair. A number of the guests flaunted secession cockades while others "purposely insulted the President by refusing to take his hand." [9] Washington had the eerie aspect of a city whose most important public figures were walking through a dream. Not included among the dreamers were the South Carolina commissioners, who were polishing off their reply to Buchanan.

On January 2nd, the Cabinet resumed its consideration of the Sumter problem. Floyd was gone, but Secretary Thompson was still there, a secessionist determined that no reinforcements would be sent to Charleston while he was in office. Thompson, hewing to the warm-climate definition of coercion, let it be known that when coercion was adopted he would resign. There was noisy wrangling until a resolution was proposed, concurred in by Buchanan, to send an officer posthaste to Anderson to inquire whether he wanted or needed reinforcement. This aroused Secretary Black's apprehension. Three days earlier the President had been firmly decided on reinforcement. Now he was acting as if it were a subject for discussion.[10]

"Does the sending of a messenger imply," Black asked, "that no additional troops are to be sent until his return?"

"Judge Black," Buchanan replied, impatiently raising his hands, "it implies nothing." [11]

Black knew better. The Old Public Functionary was weakening, and how far he might have receded no one can tell had not at that moment the reply of the commissioners arrived to fortify his hardihood. They rejected all of his arguments and were quitting Washington, their hope for a peaceful adjustment glimmering. Their letter was a bitter arraignment of the President for defaulting on his alleged pledge. Secretary Floyd, it said, had resigned his seat because he wanted no part of such dishonor. The commissioners should have found a less shopworn upholder of honor than Mr. Floyd, but they were determined that Buchanan had broken his word. "You did not deny it," they wrote; "you do not deny it now; but you seek to escape from its obligations. . . ."

There was no threat against Anderson, they insisted, and yet he had moved "under cover of the night, to a safer position. This was war." South Carolina, relying on the President's word, had been deceived and cheated. Now he had resolved to hold by force what he had gained through their "misplaced confidence." His course probably made civil war inevitable, the commissioners wrote, and if he chose to force the issue on them, the state of South Carolina would accept it.[12]

"After this letter," Black said triumphantly, "the Cabinet will be unanimous." [13]

The President was a shade paler than usual. The commissioners had called him double-faced, lying, deceitful. The Union had suffered divers discourtesies of recent weeks without Buchanan's taking noticeable offense, but this time his own person had been insulted.

"It is now all over," he said heavily, "and reinforcements must be sent." [14]

Secretary Thompson, the man who aimed to resign as soon as coercion began, was present but did not hear the remark. Strangely, he left the meeting still under the impression that no decision had been made to reinforce Anderson.[15] For days Thompson's notion of loyalty had been carrying him in a new direction—a correspondence with Judge A. B. Longstreet of South Carolina. This came about when Longstreet, president of South Carolina College, went to Charleston to see what he could do to aid the secession cause. There he found that Governor Pickens was the prey of dozens of wild and often contradictory rumors telegraphed daily from Washington by friends who wished to help or enemies who wished to confuse. The governor was in a swivet, not knowing what to believe. Longstreet volun-

Major Anderson with his wife Eliza and their son Robert

Sumter, the fort where the nation's fate hung by a thread for twenty weeks

Note barrack roofs that later made such vulnerable targets

Interior view of Sumter shows a 10-in. columbiad
that was later hoisted to the top tier

Fort Sumter National Monument, from Harper's Weekly

Major Anderson's men enter Fort Sumter—a move
that shook the nation, North and South

teered to get him information right from the horse's mouth, and thereupon opened his communion with the Secretary of the Interior. Was Thompson acting as a spy in relaying confidential information from the government in whose Cabinet he was serving? Not at all, in his opinion. He was promoting the cause of peace—urging South Carolina not to attack Anderson, and on the other end using his influence against sending reinforcements. Thompson was to discover, just as Buchanan had, that in this quarrel one who tried to serve both parties was flirting with disaster.[16]

So now the President's three days of courtesy were over and the cannon-bristling *Brooklyn* could steam on its way to Charleston. It could have, but it did not. For here gigantic old General Scott suddenly shrank to a pygmy. The general had been thinking about the *Brooklyn*, and the more he pondered the more he doubted. The *Brooklyn* was a deep-draft vessel that might have trouble getting over the bar at Charleston harbor except at high tide. Furthermore, Scott was averse to stripping Fortress Monroe of even two hundred men. He told Buchanan it would be better to send two hundred well-drilled recruits from New York instead—not on the *Brooklyn* but on an unarmed merchant steamer. This, he said, would best insure secrecy and success as well as avoiding the appearance of coercion.

The President "yielded reluctantly"—an assent he never should have given. The decision changed the open, forthright reinforcement of one of the nation's forts into a clandestine enterprise as sneaky as a smuggler's voyage. It also delayed matters for at least another two precious days.[17]

The orders to Fortress Monroe were canceled. New orders went to New York, where the government succeeded in chartering a private merchantman, the side-wheeler *Star of the West,* for $1,250 a day. Hours slipped by while arrangements were made, supplies procured, and the vessel was loaded. Since New York was teeming with Southern sympathizers, extraordinary precautions were taken for secrecy. It would take three days for the *Star* to make Charleston, but a telegram would get there in a matter of minutes. The ship was cleared for New Orleans, ostensibly on a routine cargo voyage. After loading, she embarked late on January 5th, then anchored in the darkness off Staten Island while two hundred "well-drilled recruits" came aboard from a steam tug. The vessel was captained by John McGowan, a merchant skipper, the troops being under the command of First Lieutenant Charles R. Woods. A New York pilot was aboard to navigate the tricky Charleston harbor. The *Star,* a perfect example of too little and too late, steamed southward with orders for its soldiers to hide below decks on reaching Charleston—a maritime equivalent of Colonel Gardner's trick of sending soldiers in civilian clothes for ammunition. The United States Government, it seemed, did not have the courage to do its duty honestly and openly.[18]

A message—also too late if not too little—was dispatched to Major Anderson instructing him to fire if the relief boat was attacked and that he would receive more troops if necessary. It went on to say that his "conduct meets with the emphatic approbation of the highest in authority"—General Scott's words, and not quite correct, since President Buchanan had still not recovered from the shock. Unhappily, this vital letter, which could easily have been dispatched days earlier, was not posted until about the time the boat cleared. It was not sent by special messenger but via the regular mails.[19]

The effort at secrecy fizzled. Several newspapers, sniffing a scoop, published stories suggesting that the *Star* was heading for Charleston with reinforcements. The New York *Tribune* of January 7th said:

> Rumors were rife that she was to convey troops to Charleston, but the story was ridiculed at the office of the owners. . . . Several belonging to the vessel said that she was going to Charleston, and would take on troops in the stream during the night. The freight taken was nearly all pork, beef and pilot bread.

Interior Secretary Thompson knew nothing about all this. In Charleston, Governor Pickens had received all sorts of vague warnings that United States soldiers might come, but nothing he could depend on. So Judge Longstreet dispatched a query to Thompson: Were reinforcements coming? The cooperative Thompson replied on January 5th, the very day the *Star* sailed:

"I can not speak with authority, but I do not believe that any additional troops will be sent to Charleston while the present status lasts. If Fort Sumter is attacked, they will be sent, I believe." [20]

It was not until January 8th that Thompson picked up a copy of the Washington *Constitution* and was dumfounded to read that the *Star of the West* had sailed on the fifth with reinforcements and should now be nearing Charleston. A few inquiries disclosed that this was indubitably true. Thompson was in a rage. He felt that the President had deceived him, kept secrets from him—as indeed the President should have done if he wanted any secrets kept. The secretary thought bitterly of the telegram he had sent Longstreet, reassuring him with the opinion that no reinforcement would come unless Sumter was attacked—an assurance that might give the Charlestonians a false sense of security, put them off their guard, and result in disaster to them. On top of this, he now received another telegram from Longstreet. It was a direct query. They had received word in Charleston that the *Star* was coming with troops. Was it true? [21]

Perhaps Thompson pondered the Biblical warning that no man can serve two masters. He was in a dilemma from which he could not escape without disrepute on one side or another. Should he keep quiet and let the Charlestonians suffer a possible reverse because of his misleading advice? Or should he betray his good friend Buchanan and the United States of America and send an alarm?

Thompson had to choose. A good statriot, he did not have too much trouble deciding. The Secretary of the Interior dispatched not one but two telegrams to Longstreet warning him that the *Star* would soon be in Charleston with reinforcements, in the full knowledge that he might be sending those troops to the bottom. Then Thompson did something he should have done long, long before. He resigned from the Cabinet.[22]

Not that this made any great difference outside of establishing the true status of Jacob Thompson. For Louis Wigfall was on the *qui vive,* and although still a United States Senator had long since chosen his side. That same morning Wigfall telegraphed Governor Pickens:

"The *Star of the West* sailed from New York on Sunday with Government troops and provisions. It is said her destination is Charleston. If so, she may be hourly expected off the harbor of Charleston." [23]

In the North, where the more spirited citizens had come to regard Buchanan as a chronic disease that had to be borne stoically until March 4th, the late news was stirring. "We have a Government at last," cheered the New York *Times,*[24] and the New York *World* commented: "The South Carolina commissioners have gone home with fleas in their ears. Five days ago we did not suppose Mr. Buchanan would ever give any honest man an opportunity to praise him." [25]

BLESSINGS ON YOU
ANYHOW

In occupying Sumter, Anderson had no idea that he had prostrated the President, convulsed the Cabinet, forced out the Secretaries of War and Interior, brought apoplexy to the South Carolina commissioners, created hysteria in the nation's newsrooms, sent a thrill of exultation into the hearts of millions of Northerners, and even caused a few poets to woo the muse in his praise. He was merely an army major doing his duty, placing his force in a position so secure that the Carolinians would hardly venture to assail him and thereby giving strength to the drooping dove of peace. Now the gentlemen on the opposing sides of the question would have time to consult and possibly come to nonviolent agreement.

A good Southerner, the major would have been embarrassed had he known that he was being toasted in Northern champagne and beer, that Republican legislators were urging his promotion in rank, and that urchins in Northern streets were cheering him with a bouncy rhyme:

> Bob Anderson, my beau, Bob, when we were first aquent,
> You were in Mex-i-co, Bob, because by order sent;
> But now you are in Sumter, Bob, because you chose to go,
> And blessings on you anyhow, Bob Anderson, my beau.[1]

With no such intent, he had inspired the North with a jubilation that swept like a hurricane from Maine to the far frontiers. For weeks Northern patriots had smouldered at Carolinian cheek and chafed as they felt the Union to be crumbling through default of resistance by the Buchanan administration. For weeks they had yearned for stout action, hungered for a hero. Now they had both the action and the hero. Who had cocked a snook in the face of the arrogant Palmetto leaders? Who had made an honest man of Old Buck, driven the traitors from his Cabinet, and let the world know that the Union had a little life in it yet? Why, no one but Bob Anderson, bless him!

In his isolation at Sumter, the major as yet was unaware of this adulation. He was careful to make it plain in letters to Robert Gourdin that he knew of no agreement forbidding his transfer to Sumter and that he had moved on his own responsibility in a sincere desire for peace.[2] Gourdin replied kindly but pronounced the step "most unfortunate."[3] Anderson watched from Sumter's parapet in indignation as the South Carolina troops seized Pinckney and Moultrie, promptly sending Lieutenant Hall to Moultrie to ask by what authority that work was occupied. The new commandant, the courtly Colonel De-Saussure, replied that it was occupied by order of the governor of the sovereign state of South Carolina. Militarily speaking, DeSaussure said, Anderson's move to Sumter was one of "consummate wisdom" but would greatly complicate matters.[4]

The Sumter garrison also watched Palmetto troops occupy dilapidated Fort Johnson on James Island, but one seizure they could not see—the December 30th occupation of the United States arsenal in Charleston by two hundred troops. Captain Humphreys surrendered with his fourteen men under protest, nervous because "so many inexperienced persons are at every turn with loaded arms."[5] In the arsenal, the captors found a rich prize—22,000 muskets, a few cannon, and large quantities of ammunition and military stores, the whole valued at a half million dollars. Captain Foster's engineering office in Charleston, containing maps and diagrams of the forts, was also taken over. The city was still in a rage at Anderson. The captains of the lighters that transported the women and children to Sumter were threatened.[6] Some citizens took out their spleen on luckless Louisa Seymour, the landbound wife of the Sumter captain.

"Two different boarding houses refused to take Mrs. Seymour," Surgeon Crawford noted in his diary, "and the third one replied that if the editor of the *Mercury* gave his consent, she might come."[7]

There were other annoyances. Governor Pickens forbade all

communication of the Sumter garrison with Charleston except for mail. When Lieutenant Snyder was rowed to the city by a couple of men, their boat was seized by the police, who later relented and allowed them to return but refused to let them take fresh provisions they had bought. On a trip to Fort Moultrie, Captains Foster and Seymour were temporarily arrested by order of Brigadier General R. G. M. Dunovant, now commanding Sullivan's Island. Anderson was incensed at being treated like an enemy, and by being called "a traitor to the South" in the South Carolina Convention.[8]

"The Governor does not know how entirely the commerce and intercourse of Charleston by sea are in my power," he wrote Gourdin. "I could, if so disposed, annoy and embarrass the Charlestonians much more than they can me. With my guns I can close the harbor completely to the access of all large vessels, and I might even cut off the lights, so as to seal the approach entirely by night. I do hope that nothing will occur to add to the . . . bad feeling which exists in the city. No one has a right to be angry with me for my action. . . ."[9]

The major was talking stronger than he felt. He was in a bleak-looking fortification that rose out of the sea in a tent-shaped pentagon, its apex pointing northeast toward the ship channel and Fort Moultrie. The long gorge wall measured 380 feet. The brick walls were fifty feet high. They tapered from a twelve-foot thickness at the base to eight and a half feet at the parapet. Sumter was four times the size of Moultrie, potentially the strongest citadel on the South Atlantic, but right now it was a sorry shambles and Anderson knew it. Building materials littered the wharf, esplanade, and the big parade, the latter also being choked with sixty-six guns, 5,600 shot and shell, piles of sand, masonry, and temporary wooden shacks for equipment. Defensively the place was an artilleryman's horror. It was built for three tiers to take a full complement of 146 guns served by a garrison of 650 men. So far only three guns had been mounted on the upper or barbette tier, and eleven on the lower. The second tier was so incomplete that only one gun had been mounted. Forty-one embrasures there were unfinished, leaving yawning holes eight feet square. There were no flanking defenses. The enlisted men's barracks were still under construction, and where tenable were occupied by the workmen. The officers' quarters, fully completed, were occupied by the garrison.[10]

As it stood, Sumter could easily have been taken by a few hundred men with scaling ladders.[11] A whale of a lot of work was necessary before it would be reasonably defensible. Anderson was well aware of his weakness, but he did not have too much respect for the untrained South Carolina militia, and there were two other factors working in his favor. For one, the Carolinians thought Sumter impregnable. *"Twenty-five well-drilled men could hold it against all Charleston,"* said the *Courier* in mistaken alarm. "Its batteries could level Fort Moultrie with the ground in a few hours, and shell the city effectively if turned against it." [12]

For another, Governor Pickens entertained a strong hope that his commissioners would persuade Buchanan to send the garrison back to Moultrie. When Lieutenant Snyder came ashore with a message from Anderson to the governor, Pickens asked Snyder if he thought the major would return to Moultrie if ordered by the President. Snyder replied that Anderson would promptly obey any Presidential order.[13] The idea that the garrison would be ordered back also seemed to be held by ex-Senator Chesnut. The Rev. A. Toomer Porter met Chesnut walking on the Battery and said sadly, "We are at the beginning of a terrible war."

"Not at all," Chesnut corrected. "There will be no war, it will be all arranged. I will drink all the blood shed in the war." [14]

An uneasy lull prevailed as the Sumter men worked like stevedores to plug holes and mount guns. Many of the hired workmen, sure that fighting was about to begin, drew their pay and went ashore, where some spread false rumors—one of them to the effect that Anderson tried to press them into military service. Captain Foster, with his two engineering aides, Lieutenants Snyder and Meade, supervised the remaining laborers in cleaning up debris and sealing open embrasures. The soldiers fell in with a will to work for which they had never enlisted, manning shovels, carrying ammunition, hoisting ponderous guns with makeshift equipment. Finding a coil of heavy rope severed by a knife-cut, they knew they had to watch for sabotage on the part of secessionist workmen.[15]

If the workmen could not be entirely trusted, Anderson knew he had his garrison behind him to a man. The move to Sumter had braced them like a tonic. They had stolen a march on the Carolinians they viewed with unanimous dislike, and the impressive flag-raising ceremony—an event they would remember to their dying day—had imbued them with a sense of dedication and duty. Even Captains Doubleday and Foster, who did not see entirely eye to eye with the major, cheered the Sumter move as a masterpiece of planning and execution.[16]

And now, as the mail brought in newspapers and letters, the garrison discovered with some surprise that they had made 72-point headlines in every journal that came to hand, and that their commander was hailed as a hero. Anderson was astonished at the excitement he had caused. Insulated from the public, he had been unaware of the slow groundswell of Northern resentment against South Carolina. True, the Floyd propaganda had sunk in and some papers erroneously said Anderson had "disobeyed orders." The Northern press lauded him all the more in the belief that he had. Said the New York *World* of the Sumter maneuver: "It was unauthorized, it is true, but it is indispensable." [17] The New York *Tribune* said Anderson had to make the move "almost in defiance of orders," praising him as possessing "the highest order of military genius." Salutes in his honor were fired at New York, Boston, Schenectady, Chicago, and dozens of other cities. At a huge public banquet in Philadelphia honoring Anderson, a reporter noted, "Every mention of his name drew out a hurricane of applause. . . . This community fairly worships him." [18]

A trickle of personal letters began reaching Anderson, increasing to a stream and then a flood. They came from cities, hamlets, and farms all over the North, most of them from utter

K

strangers, most of them placing the modest major in a niche with Washington.

"I will take the liberty of informing you . . . that you are today the most popular man in the nation," wrote an enthusiastic Chicagoan. "This day thirty-three guns have been discharged in this city, and all the bells in the meantime were ringing. . . ." [19]

". . . loyal Kentucky thanks you for your soldierlike conduct," wrote an old soldier of 1812. "God save the Union and damn all traitors." [20]

Leverett Saltonstall wrote from Boston: "It is indeed refreshing in these sad days of demogagues, traitors, fanatics, idiots and rascals in high places, to see *one true man,* who, occupying a most important and serious position, knows his duty and most determinately fills it. Your name is a watchword for Patriots, and while you hold Fort Sumpter, I shall not despair of our noble, our glorious Union." [21]

"The Lord bless your noble soul!" wrote Edmund Morris from Burlington, New Jersey. ". . . such excitement, such unanimous & whole souled approval of and rejoicing over your masterly stroke, you cannot imagine. Your name was in every man's mouth. God bless you and preserve you . . . God bless you again. . . . Oh, my dear sir, the whole country will triumphantly sustain you. . . ." [22]

The major, who had made his move not for headlines but for security and peace, was disturbed. He had done what he least intended—fired the North by an act he saw was misinterpreted as a challenge hurled in the Carolinians' teeth. In his answers he conscientiously explained his pacific intent, but explanations were futile. He was still "Bob Anderson, my beau," the man who had thumbed his nose at haughty Charleston and confounded the minions of disunion.

Governor Pickens, smarting under criticism for having allowed the foreign soldiers to escape from Moultrie, was hoping to have them returned via the easy road of negotiation but ready with prompt steps should negotiation fail. The regard for the amenities that hamstrung the President and General Scott did not stay the hand of the governor. On December 29th he ordered Major P. F. Stevens, commander of the Citadel Academy in Charleston, to take forty cadets to Morris Island and erect a battery of 24-pounders there. A ninety-man company of infantry was detailed to help them. The fortifying of Morris Island, a barren waste of sand almost directly south of Sumter, was a move of greatest military significance. It commanded the main ship channel into the harbor—the channel which would have to be used by any large vessel bringing aid to Sumter.[23]

Keeping a sharp watch on harbor activity, Anderson correctly deduced that a battery was going up on Morris Island and reported it to Washington. He was still in the dark as to whether his move might be disavowed and the administration would slap him down and send him back to Moultrie.

"The more I reflect upon the matter the stronger are my convictions that I was right in coming here," he wrote anxiously. "Whilst we were at Fort Moultrie our safety depended on their forbearance. A false telegram might, any night, have been seized upon as an excuse for taking this place [Sumter], and then we would have been in their power." [24]

In Charleston, Governor Pickens was astounded at word from Washington that Buchanan was showing signs of backbone. Not only did he refuse to send Anderson back, but an apparently well-founded report said that the armed United States revenue cutter *Harriet Lane* was steaming south with 250 regulars to reinforce Sumter. The governor got a telegram from the commissioners imploring him to prepare for war. Charleston officialdom went into a turmoil. Brigadier General James Simons of the state militia was ordered to make an immediate survey of the harbor defenses. All communication with Sumter was suspended and the mails cut off. The harbor lights were extinguished, leaving Sumter's beacon the only one remaining. "O God, wilt thou bring confusion upon our enemies," prayed the Reverend Dupree before the state convention. Pickens in person rushed to Fort Moultrie to spur defense preparations. Workshops in the city were busy making new gun carriages for those the garrison had burned. The Carolina artillerists could be thankful Anderson had not blown up Moultrie, and in fact had been so considerate in his spiking of the guns that they were quickly repaired. But what good did that do if he could level Moultrie with a curtain of fire from Sumter? [25]

Something near panic swept the city. The banks suspended specie payment. Surgeon General R. W. Gibbes, anticipating bloodshed, asked the ladies to make bandages. "We think our Leaders have acted rather too hastily," Jacob Schirmer told his diary.[26] Governor Pickens was discovering that it took time and training to mould willing recruits into efficient soldiers. As for General Simons, he made a tour of the defenses and threw up his hands in despair.

". . . your lines of communication . . . are directly within the range and effective power of Fort Sumter—the citadel of the harbor—controlling every point," he wrote Pickens. ". . . . A single gun from Fort Sumter would sink your transport, and destroy your troops and supplies." Of Fort Moultrie he said, "This post is wholly untenable," adding that in its garrison "there is probably not a single man . . . who ever loaded a siege gun." Moultrie, he felt sure, must "fall to the enemy, after a very short and bloody contest." Simons, who had no compunctions about referring to the United States troops as "the enemy," pointed out that they were experienced soldiers while the Carolinians were "raw militia, who never saw a battle." Fort Johnson, he said, was garrisoned by light infantry "who never handled a heavy gun" and would be driven out by the first shells from Sumter. Conditions on Morris Island were worse, if possible. The battery of three 24-pounders there was not completed and the force was made up of cadets and recruits "not one man of whom, probably, ever saw a twenty-four pounder manipulated or fired." General Simons did not think they had a chance to hit the *Harriet Lane,* which would steam by at fourteen knots per hour and land its reinforcements at Sumter unopposed. "Why, then," he demanded, "all this preparation and expense, if the work cannot but terminate in disastrous failure?"

The general's report was indeed a parade of anguish. In occupying Sumter, "the enemy" had Charleston by the throat.

"He can demolish our other posts when he pleases, from one of the most impregnable fortresses in the world, and so our posts live at his will, and remain in our possession at his sufferance." Simons ended by begging Pickens not to start hostilities now because "nothing but bloody discomfiture must attend the opening campaign." [27]

It would have been instructive had President Buchanan been able to scan this report. As for Governor Pickens, his choler rose as he read it. What was Simons telling him to do—quit? If inexperienced troops were worthless against regulars, should he evacuate all South Carolina because he had no regulars? Perhaps the state was weak, he admitted, but so was the United States. If he were to follow Simons' advice he would call in all his troops, allow Sumter to be reinforced, and yield every point he had fought for without a struggle. "I shall do no such thing," he snapped. [28]

Even so, Pickens was sensible to nervousness if not fear. He must have been as relieved as General Simons was when the rumor that the *Harriet Lane* was coming was learned to be false. This was one of the mistaken scares that resulted in the installation of Judge Longstreet as official-in-charge-of-seeking-truth. Defense work went on at top speed nevertheless. Recruiting was intensive, aimed at creating a ten-regiment South Carolina army more than half the size of the whole United States force. Enlistment increased as the spirited young women of Charleston vowed they would secede from any man who shirked his duty. White-haired Edmund Ruffin, who had been in Florida preaching secession, hurried back to "commit a little treason" by shoveling dirt for strengthening Moultrie. From Sumter the men could see a bustle of activity as Carolinian ships carried soldiers, workmen, and armament to the harbor posts. [29]

Was this war, peace, or something vaguely in between? To the Sumterites there was an air of unreality about it all. All around them ships were plying with men and materials of war aimed at surrounding Sumter, isolating it from help, reducing the fort, destroying its garrison. Even with their few guns they could have sunk some of those vessels and closed the harbor. They did not raise a hand. They had orders to act "on the defensive."

On January 4th Governor Pickens announced the selection of his cabinet, including among them Judge Magrath as Secretary of State and David Jamison as Secretary of War. Still ashore and unhappy were the Mesdames Foster, Doubleday, and Seymour, wives of Sumter officers. Mrs. Foster succeeded in getting Pickens' permission to join her husband, but Mrs. Doubleday, a staunch Republican, was asking no favors from a slaveholding secessionist. She coolly climbed into a boat carrying laborers who stared at her in surprise but allowed her to ride with them to Sumter. Louisa Seymour made the mistake of asking permission of General Dunovant, whose answer was a blunt "No." So Mrs. Seymour had to wait until nightfall, when she was rowed over to the fort by two sons of Dan Sinclair, sutler of the post.[30]

Captain Doubleday was overjoyed to see his wife, although Sumter was anything but a cozy place for women. In the hurried move from Moultrie only a small supply of coal had been brought. Fuel was strictly rationed for cooking and hospital use, the chill invading the barracks so that one could see one's breath. Doubleday had to break up a good mahogany table for fuel to keep his wife warm during her brief stay.[31]

The presence of the women "threw a momentary brightness over the scene," as Doubleday noted.[32] Even though the accommodations were Spartan, they wanted to stay with their husbands. But with no one knowing when hostilities might begin, the fort was no fit place for domesticity. Anderson was already troubled about the forty-five wives and children of soldiers he was forced to shelter until he could make arrangements for their removal. There was no use adding to the hazard. Next day the Mesdames Foster, Doubleday, and Seymour bade their husbands goodbye and left the fort. Mary Doubleday and Louisa Seymour went surreptitiously at midnight in a boat rowed by the helpful Sinclair boys, taking refuge at Moultrieville with the family of Chaplain Harris.[33]

Meanwhile, forty-eight-year-old John Hugh Means, a former governor of South Carolina, had heard about General Dunovant's refusal to allow Mrs. Seymour to visit her husband. Means, a huge man whose amiability matched his size, thought this excessively harsh of the general. He went over to the Harris home and chivalrously assured the chaplain that he would see to it that Mrs. Seymour received a pass. Rev. Harris was in a dilemma. He did not want to admit that Mrs. Seymour had already visited the fort without authorization, for this might get the Sinclair boys into trouble. The chaplain allowed himself an unchaplainlike fib. Mrs. Seymour, he said, had such a headache that she was confined to her room and could not make the trip. The kindly Means went his way, with death awaiting him a year and a half later at Second Manassas.[34]

Another wife, far away in New York, was enduring a different kind of travail. Eliza Anderson, spending the winter at the Brevoort Hotel with her children, was downright furious at the Carolinians who in her opinion wore a graceful and charming outward manner to conceal inner brutality. The "Christmas present" her husband gave her—the move to Sumter—was inspiring, true enough, but she was skeptical of all the talk about Sumter's impregnability, and newspaper reports that Anderson had resolved to "die at his post" if necessary were scarcely reassuring. On New Year's Day hundreds of enthusiastic New Yorkers who poured into the Brevoort to heap praise on her husband found her too unwell to receive them. They noted that her young son, twenty-one months old, wore a uniform that was "an exact facsimile" of that worn by her husband at Sumter.[35]

Because of the interruption of communications with Sumter, she had received no letters from the major for days. Pondering some way to help him, she decided on a mission that would have done credit to a Scott novel.

She recalled that during the Mexican War Anderson had an orderly, Sergeant Peter Hart, who was devoted to him. It struck her that if Hart were only at his side now, he would be a great comfort. The first problem was to find the sergeant, who had been out of the Army for years and was believed to be somewhere in New York. Although it must have seemed almost hopeless, she began a canvass that encountered implausible luck when Hart was located, now a burly member of the police force. Mrs. Anderson interviewed him and asked a momentous question: Would he rejoin his old commander at Sumter? Asking a man to go to that isolated and menaced fortress was much like asking him to go to Tasmania. She was overjoyed when Hart, although he was a married man, agreed to quit the force and join the colors under Anderson. A Union man to the core, he had been thrilled by the major's move to Sumter and the idea of helping defend that bastion was like powder in the old artilleryman's nostrils.

Despite her fragile health, Mrs. Anderson left New York by train with Hart on January 3rd. As the cars rattled through Virginia they heard secessionist passengers damning Anderson as a man who had violated a sacred pledge. Arriving in Charleston, they put up at the Mills House, where Mrs. Anderson met her brother, Bayard Clinch, a prominent Georgia disunionist. Also there to meet her was her husband's brother, Larz Anderson of Cincinnati, who had come down to see what he could do for the garrison. Clinch and Larz Anderson succeeded in getting Governor Pickens' permission for Mrs. Anderson to visit Sumter. Pickens, who had known old General Clinch, was anxious to accommodate the daughter, but he drew the line at allowing Hart to go out there. That would add one more fighting man to Sumter's strength. The answer was no.

It began to appear that Hart had resigned his job and made the long journey southward in vain. Then the governor relented. Hart could go to Sumter and remain, but not as a soldier. It would have to be strictly as a civilian workman.[36]

On Sunday, January 6th, Major Anderson was pleasantly astonished when a small boat docked at Sumter and his wife stepped out. "My glorious wife!" he was reported to have said as he embraced her. With her were Clinch, Larz Anderson, Robert Gourdin, and the *pièce de résistance*, Peter Hart. The party brought both bad news and good. Several other Southern states were expected soon to join South Carolina in secession. But the House of Representatives, by an overwhelming majority, had approved Anderson's "bold and patriotic act" in occupying Sumter. The major knew he no longer faced the humiliation of being returned like a naughty boy to Moultrie.[37]

Mrs. Anderson remained just two hours, dining with her husband, telling him the children were well and undoubtedly imploring him to be careful. Then she returned with her companions to Charleston, where some kindly citizens urged her to stay. But she boarded a northbound train with Larz Anderson that same night, finding the trip so difficult in her frail condition that she was almost unconscious when she reached Washington and had to rest at Willard's for two days before she could go on to New York.[38]

The Mesdames Foster, Doubleday, and Seymour, Northerners all, received no invitations to stay, sensing rather an unspoken frigidity. After applying for boarding accommodations and getting polite refusals, the trio gave it up and decamped for the North. At the fort, Captain Doubleday once more succumbed to gloom.

"If we ascended to the parapet," he wrote, "we saw nothing but uncouth State flags, representing palmettos, pelicans, and other strange devices. . . . Our glasses in vain swept the horizon; the one flag we longed to see was not there. . . ." [39]

It was not there, quite, but the *Star of the West* was on the way.

THE DISGUST
OF CAPTAIN DOUBLEDAY

While South Carolina claimed to have thrown off the Union yoke and established herself as an independent nation, in one respect she remained as Yankee as the state of Maine. The United States mails functioned as before, with Carolina nationals using foreign United States stamps and Carolina postmasters rendering their accounts to a foreign postmaster general in the foreign capital of Washington, whose officials obstinately refused to recognize the state's independence.[1] Normally it took two days for a letter to travel from Charleston to Washington. After Anderson's move to Sumter, however, there was a temporary closing of communications and also a bit of meddling with the Sumter mail on the part of the Charlestonians.[2] For these reasons it took six days for Anderson's official report of December 31st to reach Secretary of War Holt in Washington.

Holt read it on January 5th with the sinking feeling of a shipwrecked sailor who watches a vessel pass by unheeding. In the report Anderson made two statements that smote him with the realization that all the preparations for reinforcing the major were a ghastly error likely to bring on immediate war. For one thing, the major said that for the present he felt safe at Sumter, adding, "Thank God, we are now where the Government may send us additional troops at its leisure."

This was a sad mistake on the part of the usually perceptive Anderson. As events were to prove, if he was to be reinforced at all there could be no leisure about it and no half measures. Only determined naval power, ready to hurt and be hurt, would do it for a certainty. Furthermore, his air of security seemed contradicted by his second statement: that the Carolinians were building a battery, possibly more than one, on Morris Island which commanded the ship channel leading to Sumter.[3]

To Holt, all this was a double blow. Anderson, whom the administration thought would be howling for help, was not precisely asking for it but rather leaving it up to the government. Earlier, when he begged repeatedly for more men, they were refused him. Now the men had been sent and he appeared almost indifferent. Worst of all, they had been sent in an unarmed merchantman which would have to run a gauntlet of island batteries previously unknown to Holt. There would be firing, very possibly the *Star* would be sunk, and how better could you lose a ship with all its occupants and start a war?

A despairing telegram was sent to New York to stop the *Star*. Too late. She had already sailed. In hasty conference, Holt, General Scott, and Buchanan agreed they must do what they could to protect the defenseless ship. Yet it was January 7th before the Secretary of the Navy sent orders to Fortress Monroe instructing the *Brooklyn*, under Captain David Farragut, to steam south, find the *Star*, and give it whatever aid it could without crossing the Charleston bar. How it could render any aid at all without crossing the bar was a mystery no one explained.[4]

On January 8th, some of Captain Foster's workmen rowed to Sumter from the city, bringing a Charleston *Mercury* that bore strange tidings. The *Star of the West*, it said, was en route to Charleston carrying reinforcements for the garrison. The papers —above all the *Mercury*—were such incorrigible spreaders of false rumors that no one in the fort put much stock in this one. "We do not credit it entirely," Surgeon Crawford jotted in his diary. ". . . Major A. thinks Genl. Scott would not send troops except by a War vessel." [5]

Major A. had good reason to think that. Who would dream that the forthright old general would resort to subterfuge, or would send aid without notifying Anderson? A few sentries were walking the Sumter parapet near midnight that night, unaware that the *Star* had arrived off the bar with darkened lights. Only one beacon, Sumter's, shone in the harbor and the ship's pilot did not know which one it was. With all the buoys removed, he found it impossible to enter in darkness. The vessel waited until dawn. As soon as the harbor landmarks were visible Captain McGowan headed her into the main channel, her troops concealed below decks.

Her officers had no idea that their supposedly secret mission was as well advertised in Charleston as the minstrel show at Secession Hall. Governor Pickens had received telegrams from Interior Secretary Thompson, Senator Wigfall, and others. The citizens had read newspaper stories about it. The Palmetto defenders were on the watch. As the *Star* bore in with daylight brightening, she saw a small steamer ahead that evidently spied her, for she burned red and blue signal lights before turning toward Charleston. The *Star* kept going, paralleling Morris Island. As she drew within two miles of Sumter, McGowan and Lieutenant Woods heard a muffled report from the island and saw a cannonball arc above them. An American ensign fluttered from her flagstaff, and they now hoisted another large flag at the fore, but in Woods's words "the one was no more respected than the other." [6] Another shot whistled above them. The balls came from a battery on Morris Island that was only about a thousand yards distant but was concealed by sand dunes, though its red palmetto flag was visible.

The first shot of the War Between the States had been fired by a young Citadel cadet named George E. Haynsworth of Sumter, South Carolina. His historic feat later won him plaudits despite his indifferent aim. No more than Rhett, nor Ruffin, nor Governor Pickens, did Cadet Haynsworth realize the national convulsion his shot signalized. [7]

Although it was not yet seven, Captain Doubleday happened to be on the Sumter parapet with his spyglass. He saw the vessel flying the Stars and Stripes being fired at by the Carolinian battery. That newspaper story must be true after all! He dashed downstairs to the officers' quarters where he found Anderson not yet dressed, and gave him the news. Anderson ordered him to have the long roll beaten and to post the men at their guns, then scrambled into his uniform with less than his usual military meticulousness. By the time he reached the ramparts, every man of the command—and some of the soldiers' wives—were there, all gazing at the tableau to the south. Some wondered whether it might be a United States vessel come to evacuate them—an idea that offended them, for they now felt themselves a match for the Carolinians. Soldiers were manning the three barbette 24-pounders facing Morris Island, one gunner named Oakes holding a lanyard and all ready to jerk it.[8]

Every officer and artillerist there must have felt the uneasy thrill of men who know they are about to open a conflict whose end no one could foresee. Yet most of them were itching to fire. They had a long grudge to settle. Doubleday and Surgeon Crawford, in particular, expected an order to fire. It did not come. The *Star* was still plowing full speed toward them, the battery still firing at her with uncertain aim. Crawford, with his glass on the steamer, reported that the *Star* was apparently trying to signal with its flag. Anderson ordered that signals be returned, but the halyards were so fouled that the Sumter flag could not be budged.

"There seemed to be much perplexity among our officers," remarked Sergeant James Chester of the garrison.[9] Major Anderson appeared "excited and uncertain what to do." [10] The arrival of the ship was a complete surprise. He had his orders to act "strictly on the defensive." Normally any firing on the United States flag would admit only of instant retaliation, but his situation was anything but a normal one and to make a snap judgment inaugurating war was difficult. Moreover, as he knew, the Carolinians had cunningly built the Morris Island battery beyond his range. Any fire in that direction would be a mere demonstration.

Now the *Star of the West*, after suffering two insignificant hits, was virtually out of range of Morris Island but would soon come within range of Fort Moultrie. At Moultrie, Lieutenant Colonel Roswell Ripley, West Point '45, an Ohioan turned Carolinian, was now in command. Ripley ordered his cannoneers to get ready, fully expecting a withering return fire from Sumter. "Now, boys, we'll give 'em a shot or two," he shouted, "and then we'll catch the devil from Sumter!" [11]

Moultrie fired, its shot falling a half mile short. It did not catch the devil at all. At Sumter, the men anxiously awaited the order to let fly at Morris Island when Lieutenant Davis turned to Anderson. "Don't fire that, Major, it is of no use," he said. He pointed at Moultrie. "That's the place." [12]

Anderson seemed to acquiesce. He directed Davis to go below, take command of a battery of two 42-pounders in the casemate tier bearing on Moultrie and await orders. Young Lieutenant Meade, the serious Virginian with many secessionist friends, was having his own inner struggle in determining where duty lay. He urged the major earnestly not to fire at all.

"It will bring civil war on us," he said. Furthermore, he was of the opinion that the firing on the vessel was unauthorized, the work of some hothead Carolinians, and that Governor Pickens would repudiate it. [13]

Moultrie fired again, without effect. At Sumter the men still awaited a signal, a word that would let them blaze away. Anderson seemed frozen in uncertainty. The Virginia-born wife of Private John H. Davis could stand it no longer. She seized a friction tube, sprang to a gun, and vowed she would fire it herself. Doubleday gently dissuaded her. [14] Captain Foster was in a rage. He smashed his hat down, muttering something about the flag in which the words "trample on it" were audible to the men nearby. [15]

Aboard the *Star of the West*, McGowan and Woods saw they were in a ticklish position. To reach Sumter they would have to draw even closer to the Moultrie guns, and Sumter was giving them no protection. When a South Carolina steamer approached them with what seemed an armed schooner in tow, they decided the risk was too great. In a circumstance where they might have won eternal fame—or Davy Jones's locker—had they accepted the risk and held their course, they turned and headed out the channel toward sea, forced once more to take the fire from Morris Island as they fled. Anderson reached a decision as he saw her head away.

"Hold on; do not fire," he said. "I will wait. Let the men go to their quarters, leaving two at each gun—I wish to see the officers at my quarters." [16]

General Simons' January 1st opinion of the abilities of the Morris Island artillerists was borne out as the *Star* side-wheeled past the battery unscathed. Anderson's officers meanwhile gathered for a council. They had come within a hair's breadth of war and the moment had passed. The flag had been fired on. Sumter had remained silent. Crawford, Foster, Seymour, and undoubtedly others were deeply resentful. As for Doubleday, he thought it was nothing less than shameful that this affront to the flag had not been answered by the full spite of Sumter's guns whether or not they could reach the Morris Island battery.[17]

Robert Anderson, a man who valued honor and duty above all else, must have known that in the eyes of some of his officers and men he had lost stature. The major was as enraged as any of them. For him it had taken a far greater degree of soul-searching and self-control to hold his fire than to say the word that indignation made him yearn to say, but would have started war. He had deliberately sacrificed his own pride, quelled his own impulse to strike back in the faint but still visible hope of peace—a forbearance not at all in the swashbuckling American tradition of Ethan Allen or Mad Anthony Wayne.

But now the major was so consumed with a build-up of wrath that he seemed ready to inaugurate the war that a few minutes ago he had declined to accept. He told his men that he proposed immediately to close the harbor with his guns and fire at any South Carolina vessel that came within range. What did they think of that?

Surgeon Crawford was on hand to record some of the replies. Lieutenants Hall and Snyder, along with Captain Doubleday, were agreed that this was the proper course. Doubleday urged immediate action. Every day's delay, he said, would add to the enemy's strength, and he called them "the enemy" advisedly.

Next to Hall, Meade was the youngest officer there, but he felt strongly enough to oppose this idea. It would mean war, he said, and since the garrison was ordered to act only on the defensive it would be a breach of orders. Bushy-bearded Lieutenant Davis thought it would be best first to ask Governor

Pickens whether he sanctioned the attack. Surgeon Crawford spoke good sense: They had allowed the opportunity for immediate action to pass, he pointed out. Now it would be best to let the governor know their determination. Anderson saw the logic of this.[18] He prepared the following dispatch, addressed to "His Excellency, the Governor of South Carolina":

> SIR: Two of your batteries fired this morning upon an unarmed vessel bearing the flag of my Government. As I have not been notified that war has been declared by South Carolina against the Government of the United States, I cannot but think that this hostile act was committed without your sanction or authority. Under that hope, and that alone, did I refrain from opening fire upon your batteries. I have therefore respectfully to ask whether the above-mentioned act, one I believe without a parallel in the history of our country or of any other civilized government, was committed in obedience to your instructions, and to notify you, if it be not disclaimed, that I must regard it as an act of war, and that I shall not, after a reasonable time for the return of my messenger, permit any vessel to pass within range of the guns in my fort. In order to save, as far as lies within my power, the shedding of blood, I beg that you will have due notice of this, my decision, given to all concerned. Hoping, however, that your answer may be such as will justify a further continuance of forbearance on my part. . . .[19]

Lieutenant Hall was given the message and rowed to Charleston in a boat carrying a white flag—an ominous sign of the turn of events. At the wharf, Hall had to make his way through a crowd of excited people who quickly spread the rumor that he had come to announce that Charleston would be bombarded. Some nervous souls began thinking of shelter. The lieutenant entered the city hall, where Governor Pickens promptly broke up a cabinet meeting to give him audience. The governor read Anderson's note, then asked Hall to wait while he conferred with his cabinet once more. After some delay, Pickens personally handed Hall his reply and the lieutenant returned to Sumter with it.[20] Reading it, Anderson saw that the governor was doing anything but disavowing the attack.

The major did not seem to comprehend the situation, Pickens wrote. South Carolina had seceded. Anderson's occupation of Sumter was the first hostile act against the state. President Buchanan knew full well that to send reinforcements to Sumter would be treated as a further act of hostility against South Carolina, and to repel such an attempt was "only too plainly its duty." The *Star of the West* had insisted on entering despite warning given by a South Carolina vessel stationed at the bar, and further warning shots across her bows by the Morris Island battery. "The act is perfectly justified by me," wrote the governor, adding that if Anderson carried out his threat to close the harbor it would amount to "imposing upon the State the condition of a conquered province." [21]

Pickens' reply was forthright, devoid of bluster, and even containing a touch of humility in the "conquered province" line. Humility was not his habit. Possibly it was inspired by his awareness that he was not ready for war, that Sumter's guns *could* close the state's only sizable harbor and ruin Charleston's thriving commerce. By now Anderson's indignation had cooled, as had that of some of his officers. On reflection, bearing in mind the warnings to the *Star* of which he had not been aware, he decided not to carry out his threat of closing the harbor until he had received specific instructions from Washington—a decision that made Doubleday groan. He chose Lieutenant Talbot, the consumptive but dashing Kentuckian, as his courier. Talbot went to Charleston accompanied by Crawford and saw Governor Pickens, who said he was "very glad indeed" that Anderson had suspended his rash threat about closing the harbor. The governor would be happy to give Talbot a safe conduct to leave for Washington for instructions. To Talbot and Crawford it seemed obvious that Pickens and his aides were uncommonly relieved to know that they would not be bottled up after all.[22]

The governor, knowing his vulnerability, was thankful for all favors. On the same day he dispatched a curt order to three

L

South Carolina artillery experts, Colonels Walter Gwynn, Edward White, and J. H. Trapier:

> You are ordered to come together, immediately, and consider and report the most favorable plan for operating upon Fort Sumter, so as to reduce that fortress, by batteries or other means in our possession; and, for this consultation you are authorized to have with you Colonel Manigault, the State Ordnance Officer.[23]

The four colonels made haste to "come together." On the very next day they submitted a long report advising additional "batteries of heavy ordnance" on Sullivan's, James, and Morris Islands, as well as more mortar batteries. The batteries would be placed not only to surround Sumter with cannon but also to prevent reinforcements from reaching the fort. After "an incessant bombardment and cannonade of many hours' duration," the colonels felt that the Sumter garrison's morale would be impaired enough so that an assault would take the fort. Possibly assault would not even be necessary, for "the slow (but sure) process of starvation would yet put Fort Sumter in our possession." [24]

Unlike President Buchanan and Major Anderson, the four colonels were speaking the language of war. So was the Charleston *Mercury*, belching some of the smoke exhaled by the fire-eatingest fire-eater of them all, Robert Barnwell Rhett:

> . . . Yesterday the 9th of January will be memorable in history. Powder has been burnt over the decree of our State, timber has been crashed, perhaps blood spilled. . . . The expulsion of the steamer *Star of the West* from the Charleston Harbor yesterday morning was the opening ball of the Revolution. We are proud that our harbor has been so honored. . . . Entrenched upon her soil she has spoken from the mouth of her cannon, and not from the mouths of scurrilous demagogues, fanatics and scribblers. . . . she has not hesitated to strike *the first blow*, full in the face of her insulter. . . . We would not exchange or recall that blow for millions! It has wiped out a half century of scorn and outrage. . . .[25]

The *Star of the West* was limping back to New York. The *Brooklyn*, which had not left Fortress Monroe until after the *Star* was attacked, made a futile search for her and then returned to its base. The whole expedition was so bungled in conception and execution as to make the American eagle appear a sorry bird indeed.

The reinforcement of Fort Sumter was a story of what might have been had ordinary initiative and enterprise been shown. *If* the powerful *Brooklyn* had been sent in the first place, with its twenty-two nine-inch guns, it would have steamed grandly into the harbor, outshooting the South Carolina batteries. *If* the President and General Scott had not been so extraordinarily polite, delaying the expedition out of courtesy to the commissioners, it would have arrived days earlier to find the feeble Morris Island battery even less ready. *If* the *Star of the West* had had a Navy captain with the traditional Navy reaction to the smell of powder, or *if* Captain McGowan had been carried away by that fine recklessness that inspires heroic deeds, the *Star* had an excellent chance of making Sumter as it was.[26] *If* the government had got word to Anderson in time—a failure for which there seems no conceivable excuse—the major would have had his orders and would have supported the *Star* with every piece he could load.

As for Governor Pickens, he had to face the possibility that the next step of the newly militant Buchanan might be to send a whole fleet of men-of-war blasting into Charleston. There was truth in the *Mercury* taunt that the President had only a thousand soldiers at his command from Boston to New Orleans, far less than South Carolina had under arms.[27] But men under arms did not necessarily signify a trained army. Worse yet, the state had not a single fighting ship worthy of the name, while the United States Navy was a power formidable enough by comparison to give the governor the horrors. The four colonels were busy men now. Anderson's men saw even greater activity in the harbor as defenses were added at Moultrie and boats plied in the shadow of Sumter's battlements to carry workmen, soldiers, and materials for batteries on James and Morris Islands.

To Doubleday, watching all this preparation aimed at Sumter's isolation and destruction without raising a hand against it was military suicide. He urged Anderson to forbid it, or at least to remonstrate. To Doubleday's disgust, the major refused.[28]

The attitude, motives and hopes of Robert Anderson are mirrored with almost perfect clarity in his acts, his official reports, and in the many private letters he wrote to friends. That he was in the most difficult position in which an American officer had ever been placed was apparent to him. In his view, a civil war was the most awful prospect the mind could conceive. He was willing to make any honorable concession that might avert it. So powerful was his repugnance to war, so personal his awareness of an almighty Being, that it seems strange he did not enter the ministry rather than West Point. "I think that killing people is a very poor way of settling National grievances," he wrote his wife from Mexico in 1847.[29] If he felt that way about killing Mexicans, his abhorrence was multiplied a hundredfold at the thought of brother killing brother—no mere figure of speech to him. In a civil war, Bayard Clinch and many other of his wife's relatives, possibly some of his own, would be on the other side. In a civil war he would be fighting officers such as his good friend Benjamin Huger—Southern men who had shared with him the hardships of Mexico or had become comrades of garrison days since. In a civil war his home state of Kentucky would become a darker and bloodier battleground than it ever had been in Indian days, with neighbors at each others' throats. The sensitive Anderson regarded such an issue with a revulsion the blunt Doubleday could not comprehend, for Doubleday was a pragmatist who had already decided war was inevitable, a Southern-hating abolitionist with Northern antecedents and relatives who had no such stake involved. Though he avoided politics, Anderson viewed slavery as an institution not only right but expressly sanctioned by the Bible, and he was by nature and upbringing far closer akin to the South than to the North. Yet he loved the Union and was thoroughly out of patience with South Carolina, looking on her as "a spoiled child that needed correction." [30] A man as devoid of guile and deviousness as mortal could be, in his inner travail he prayed constantly for light to see his duty, always regarding his oath of allegiance as sacred. He did not agree with a Southern officer who told him he loved his flag but loved his state better.

"The selection of the place in which we were born," Anderson replied, "was not an act of our own volition; but when we took the oath of allegiance to our Government, it was an act of our manhood, and that oath we cannot break." [31]

For weeks at Fort Moultrie he had vainly begged for reinforcements. In his move to Sumter, taken in the cause of peace, he had been astonished at the national sensation he had created as well as saddened to find that the move had speeded other states into secession. He well knew he had come perilously close to being ordered back to Moultrie. It is not surprising that the unexpected storm he raised heightened his caution, made him resolve to take no other decisive step without clear authorization from his government. The voice of the North was confusing and divided, with leaders like Greeley and Beecher saying "Let the South go." The administration itself, as the whole nation could see, was vacillating and uncertain, groping for some policy to meet the crisis. If the administration was uncertain, perhaps an army major in Charleston harbor could be forgiven a trace of hesitation.[32]

Adding to Anderson's uneasiness was the fact that the situation was daily growing more menacing. When he arrived in Charleston, only South Carolina seemed irreconcilable and there was hope that disunion might be isolated there. But now Mississippi and Florida had joined her in secession, with Alabama, Georgia, and others heading in the same direction. The little disagreement had swollen to formidable proportions. The "spoiled child" treatment no longer applied. In common with many other Union men, Anderson found it difficult to believe that the administration would take up arms against such a powerful segment of the South and was still hopeful that the dispute could be settled by some miracle at the conference table. Robert Anderson, a man with a simple desire for peace, was baffled emotionally and intellectually by a political problem so complex and frightening that James Buchanan, a politician for decades, all but despaired of solving it. In Sumter, Anderson was at the focus of the quarrel, the spot where a mistake would fire the fuse touching off national slaughter. He would never, never forgive himself such a mistake. Doubleday could grumble all he wanted, but caution thereafter made the commander weigh every move and every word in the light of one criterion: Would it keep the peace?

All these considerations and many more preoccupied the major on January 11th, two days after the *Star of the West* fiasco, when Governor Pickens made his next gambit on the Charleston chessboard. Although the governor was straining every resource to gain strength enough to surround Sumter and take it by force, he was not forgetting that this might be a bloody business and that it would be much nicer for all concerned if he could get the fort simply by asking for it. That morning, the Sumterites watched steamers tow four stone-loaded hulks, donated by the sympathetic citizens of Savannah, past the fort and sink them across the entrance of the channel to keep out deep-draft vessels such as United States men-of-war.[33] Possibly this was timed as a bit of stagecraft to impress Anderson with his isolation, for soon thereafter a small steamer bearing a white flag tied up at the Sumter wharf. Little Judge Magrath, secretary of state of the self-proclaimed South Carolina republic, stepped out, followed by the secretary of war, David Jamison. Anderson met them, escorting them to the guardroom inside the sally port, where they handed him a letter from the governor:

> Sir: I have thought proper, under all the circumstances of the peculiar state of public affairs in the country at present, to appoint the Honorable A. G. Magrath and General D. F. Jamison, both members of the Executive Council and of the highest position in the State, to present to you considerations of the gravest public character, and of the deepest interest to all who deprecate the improper waste of life, to induce the delivery of Fort Sumter to the constituted authorities of the State of South

Carolina, with a pledge on its part to account for such public property as is under your charge.

Your obedient servant
F. W. PICKENS [34]

Boiled down, this was a polite request to surrender the fort, or as Doubleday put it, "a grand effort to negotiate us out of Fort Sumter." [35] Anderson knew what his reply had to be, but it would seem curt to answer "No" then and there. For propriety's sake he called a council of his officers in another room. They were unanimous for rejection. Even the Virginian Meade, anxious as he was to avert war, pointed out that Lieutenant Talbot was now en route to Washington and it would be best to await the instructions he would bring. Anderson gave his reply to the Carolina gentlemen with his regrets.[36]

Andrew Gordon Magrath, unlike Jamison and most other Palmetto leaders, was not of the planter aristocracy but had won eminence through intellect and ability. He came by his revolutionary instincts naturally, for his father had been forced to flee Ireland in "the troubles" of 1798. One of the state's most stirring orators, he gave a speech to the assembled Sumter officers in the chill guardroom.[37]

The United States soldiers were representing a government that was tottering and all but dissolved, he said. More states were leaving the Union almost every day. President Buchanan, a man in his dotage, had even denied that reinforcements were sent to Sumter with his authority. All was such confusion and dismay in Washington that it was high time for the garrison to look to its own safety, since South Carolina was determined to possess the fort at any cost. He entreated Anderson to listen to "the refined dictates of humanity," for if he did not, "thousands will howl around these walls and pull out the bricks with their fingers." [38]

The judge said these things with eloquent feeling, undoubtedly believing them to be true. This direct proposal to the Sumter commander was an insult to the United States government, which properly was the authority that should have been consulted, but Magrath put a fatherly note into his appeal. His speech was a skillful effort to convince the garrison's officers of the futility of defending a government that was itself crumbling, and when he finished with "May God Almighty enable you to come to a just decision!" he had made a considerable impression on his listeners.

". . . but I cannot do what belongs to the Government to do," Anderson pointed out. "The demand must be made upon them, and I appeal to you as a Christian, as a man, and as a fellow-countryman, to do all that you can to prevent an appeal to arms. I do not say as a soldier, for my duty is clear in that respect. . . . Why not exhaust diplomacy, as in other matters?" [39]

If Governor Pickens would send a commissioner to Washington to present the demand, he went on, he would send one of his officers to report on the condition of the fort. Magrath and Jamison returned to Charleston carrying Anderson's letter to Pickens urging that the matter be referred to Washington and ending, "Hoping to God that . . . we shall so act as to meet His approval, and deeply regretting that you have made a demand with which I cannot comply. . . ." [40]

The governor must have cheered when he read it. He had bluffed and won while holding deuces. It was going to take more than howls and clutching fingers to capture Sumter—namely, additional heavy batteries that could not be constructed for weeks. Had Anderson called Pickens' bluff and simply returned a peremptory refusal to hand over the fort—an answer fully authorized by his orders—the governor would have been discomfited, caught in a palpable artifice, unable to carry out his threat. Instead, he had gained a bloodless victory. Anderson's proposition amounted to the offer of a truce that might last many days. Time was just what Pickens needed to get those batteries in place. It would be time of double value to him because as long as the truce continued the major could get no help from outside. Pickens accepted the offer with almost indecent haste. [41]

Anderson had clearly fallen into an error, but not out of fear that he could not hold his position. He now had enough guns

mounted so that he felt able to beat off any attack.[42] There
seems little doubt that what he feared was that the governor—
a man not always moved by wisdom or moderation—might
carry out his threat and launch an assult which, even if re-
pulsed, would surely start war. The major had hopes that the
Star of the West defeat, providentially accompanied by no casualties, might be overlooked. Insensibly he had moved beyond his
purely military obligation to defend his fort and taken on a
higher duty of preserving the peace. He knew that time worked
in favor of South Carolina, but a breathing spell might also give
time for peaceful negotiation.

The next day, Attorney General Isaac W. Hayne of South
Carolina left for Washington as Pickens' commissioner to demand Sumter, with Robert Gourdin as his assistant. Accompanying them as Anderson's representative went Norman Hall,
a twenty-three-year-old second lieutenant from Michigan who
had never dreamed of becoming involved in such a momentous
mission.

In Abner Doubleday's opinion, things were going from bad
to worse. He wrote to his wife, now in New York, complaining
that Anderson was allowing the Carolinians to surround the
fort with batteries without lifting a finger against them. The
spirited Mary Doubleday was incensed. She showed the letter
to Doubleday's brother, Ulysses Doubleday. Ulysses, as uncompromising a Republican Unionist as Abner, was seized by
dark suspicion. That Anderson fellow—a Kentuckian who believed in slavery—must be a traitor at heart or at the very least
must be flagging in his loyalty.

Ulysses enclosed his brother's note in a letter to President-
elect Lincoln at Springfield, pointing out that the Carolinians
were arming right under Sumter's guns even though Captain
Doubleday "constantly urged" Anderson to forbid it. "Depend
upon it," Ulysses wrote Lincoln, "Maj. A.s heart is not with his
duty." [43]

It was a warning Lincoln would have reason to remember
when inauguration time rolled around.

SUMTER IS NOT FOR SALE

As Colonel Hayne rolled northward with his companions, he could savor the knowledge that he represented a government that knew exactly what it wanted in a parley with another government that seemed divided, stunned, unhinged. Secession, sweeping the South like a religion, unifying it in new solidarity, had exactly the opposite effect in the North, where the sounds of confusion rose in earsplitting discord. Never had the young nation faced a crisis like this one. Secession raised questions never before answered. There were no precedents to follow, no ready-made solutions, no convenient rules of statecraft to apply, not even a coherent public opinion to give guidance. The no longer United States, which had prided itself as a shining model of liberty and freedom before the world, staggered like a drunken giant near a chasm, and where was the strong hand that would save him? [1]

One measure of the apathy was in the reaction to the inglorious *Star of the West* affair. While a few hotheads raged that this was war, the public which had so wildly cheered Anderson for his Sumter coup was inclined to accept the humiliation without reprisal. No one got shot, did they? "The nation pockets this insult to the national flag," snarled George T. Strong, "a calm, dishonorable, vile submission." [2]

If the nation pocketed it, so would President Buchanan, hamstrung by military weakness and a return to caution. The 1860 appropriation for the army was the smallest in five years. [3] If General Scott had barely enough men to keep the Cherokees and Sioux in check, what could be done with a throng of artillerized Carolinians? In the House a Committee of Thirty-three was scratching for some agreement that might bring the broken pieces of the Union together again. In the Senate a

Committee of Thirteen pondered the same problem. The venerable Senator John Crittenden of Kentucky was capping a long career with a heroic effort at compromise, only to see legislators indulge in windy debates on constitutional law while the government's authority crumbled. Stephen Douglas warned his colleagues it was time to stop theorizing and face facts. "South Carolina had no right to secede," he said, *but she has done it. . . .* Are we prepared in our *hearts* for war with our own brethren and kindred?" Senator Benjamin of Louisiana sneered to a friend that in permitting South Carolina to force the *Star of the West* to flee cannonballs, the government had practically relinquished whatever sovereignty it claimed.[4] The faith of bankers in the future of the United States was so low that Treasury Secretary Thomas was begging for loans.[5] Another reason was that the bankers' faith in Thomas, a Marylander with Southern leanings, was equally low and it was feared he would head South with the federal funds.[6] The War Department was so full of big-eared Dixie clerks that Secretary Holt had to use General Scott's office to maintain any secrecy at all.

In the North there was talk, in the South action. In Washington, Jefferson Davis met with the Senators from Alabama, Georgia, Florida, Louisiana, and Texas in a caucus that urged the speedy secession of all Southern states and the calling of a convention at Montgomery, Alabama, no later than February 15th to found a Southern Confederacy, but thought it might be a good idea for the Senators to stay at their posts as long as possible in order to "keep the hands of Mr. Buchanan tied, and disable the Republicans from effecting any legislation that will strengthen the hands of the incoming Administration." [7] Georgia seized Fort Pulaski. Mississippi seized the unfinished fort at Ship Island, missing the rich store of ordnance John Floyd intended for them. A wave of seizures began in the South —arsenals, forts, revenue cutters, custom houses—with the federal government powerless.

The gathering storm whisked up odd little eddies. Some Northerners were indignant because Colonel Sam Colt, the enterprising Yankee firearms manufacturer who was shipping boatloads of guns South, was building himself a princely mansion in Hartford on the profits.[8] Arming the enemy? Not at all, he said. The seceded states were still part of the Union in the administration's view, weren't they? A munitions manufacturer at Hazard's Mill, Connecticut, took the same attitude when he sold three hundred thousand pounds of powder to Governor Pickens of South Carolina.[9] Congressmen in the Southern states were making use of their franking privileges to stir up secession, happily employing Union funds and facilities to destroy the Union. Representative J. D. Ashmore of South Carolina must have had a twinge of conscience about this, recollecting that his state was now a republic, for he wrote Postmaster General Horatio King to ask if it was all right if he continued franking. King replied snappishly that while the United States still considered South Carolina a part of the Union, "it will be for you to determine how far you can conscientiously avail yourself of a privilege the exercise of which assumes that your own conviction is erroneous, and plainly declares that South Carolina is still in the Union. . . ." [10] Some found wry humor in the fact that Major Pierre Beauregard of Louisiana was about to take over as commandant at West Point, and wondered if the Military Academy was to be seized like the Southern forts.

The Southern contention that the North was interested only in vulgar trade and had no stomach for war could find a thousand proofs. The once powerful nation was the butt of derision and insult. "Can there not be found men bold and brave enough in Maryland," demanded the Richmond *Enquirer*, "to unite with Virginians in seizing the Capitol at Washington?" [11] Georgia's Senator Alfred Iverson aroused laughter in the Senate when he said, "I see no reason why Washington City should not be continued the capital of the Southern confederacy." [12] A Bladensburg physician exclaimed, "Noble South Carolina has done her duty bravely. Now Virginia and Maryland must immediately raise an armed force sufficient to control the district, and never allow Abe Lincoln to set foot on its soil." [13] This sort of talk swelled until it seemed ominous rather than

funny. General Scott hurriedly took steps to defend the seces-
sionist-infested capital, scraping up a few regulars and appoint-
ing Colonel Charles P. Stone to work against time in drumming
up some volunteer companies that could be relied on.

"We are now in such a state," said the general, "that a dog-
fight might cause the gutters of the capital to run with blood." [14]

Hoary Lewis Cass, older than the nation, saw nothing but
disaster ahead for the Union he had helped build. "The people
in the South are mad; the people in the North are asleep," he
groaned. "The President is pale with fear. . . . God only knows
what is to be the fate of my country!" [15]

When Colonel Hayne arrived on January 13th, he entered a
capital torn by dissension and pervaded by distrust and downright fright. Yet through all the gloom there penetrated a few
faint rays of hope for the nation. Old Buck, for all his irresolu-
tion, had not been intimidated into any open admission that
his jurisdiction had collapsed in large segments of the South.
"I have no more power . . . in South Carolina than I have in
China," he privately conceded.[16] But if his authority was only
a shadow, he upheld the shadow. His Cabinet had been cleansed
of Floyd, Trescot, and Thompson. With the removal of Treasury Secretary Thomas and his replacement by the doughty
General John Dix of New York, the Cabinet presented a front
rightly to be expected from such a body—a new unanimity for
the Union, with none of its members sending guns or telegrams
South or tampering with federal funds. In homely Jeremiah
Black the President had a Secretary of State who had gained a
new view of coercion.

"Coercion," he said, "—well, I would not care about coercing
South Carolina if she would agree not to coerce us. But she
kicks, cuffs, abuses, spits upon us, commits all kinds of outrages
against our rights, and then cries out that she is coerced if we
propose to hide our diminished heads under a shelter which
may protect us a little better for the future." [17]

When Isaac Hayne called at the White House on January
14th, the President heeded Black's warning that there could be
no official intercourse with representatives of the so-called Pal-

metto republic and declined to hold any conversation with him. Everything must be in writing, he said. Hayne came on the same errand as the commissioners three weeks earlier, to demand Fort Sumter and the rest of the federal "property" in South Carolina at a sale price to be negotiated. He was also to serve warning that any further attempt on the part of the President to send troops to South Carolina "will be regarded as his declaration of war against the State of South Carolina." [18]

Before he had time to put this admonition on paper he was cornered by Senator Clement C. Clay of Alabama, representing the same ten cotton-state Senators who had hatched the secession manifesto recommending the formation of a Dixie confederacy. Clay had an admonition for *him*. These Senators did not want war. They had laid out a blueprint for the partition of the Union and the creation of their own government in the South, a move most of them felt could be achieved peacefully if ordinary prudence were used. But the Palmetto men seemed strangers to prudence. Their diplomacy consisted largely of cannonballs and threats. Unless something was done to stop them, they were just the fellows who would ruin the blueprint by starting a shooting war in Charleston harbor over some trivial incident and dragging the whole South into it.

Slow down, the Senators advised. They told Hayne they had a "common destiny" with South Carolina, asked him to defer delivering his demands to the President, and urged a cautious course that would avoid hostilities at least until the Southern government was an actuality. The state was in no danger, they said, for "we have the public declaration of the President, that he has not the Constitutional power to make war on South Carolina, and that the public peace shall not be disturbed by any act of hostility toward your State." [19] They even asked that Major Anderson be furnished with food and supplies.

The colonel agreed to hold up and ask his government for further instructions on one condition: that he be assured there would be no reinforcement of Sumter in the interval. This proposition was submitted to Buchanan, beginning a strange exhibition of forensic shadow-boxing in which neither side was quite candid. The President well knew that Hayne had come to demand Sumter. He knew he must refuse. Hayne likewise knew he would be refused. His business in a sense was over before it started. Yet it dragged on for almost a month for a potent reason: As long as Hayne remained in Washington, the truce arranged between Anderson and Governor Pickens continued in effect and there would be no war.

What Buchanan did not know was that Hayne, who professed to be impatient to get on with his mission, was actually quite willing to cool his heels and give his state time to build more batteries.[20] The "truce" was precisely equivalent to one man standing with hands tied while another gathered brickbats to assault him. Every day of it saw more cannon readied in a ring around Sumter while the fort remained in status quo.

What Hayne did not know was that Buchanan, though he made out to be annoyed at Anderson for suggesting the truce in the first place, was equally happy to delay the issue. He had some forty-seven days remaining of his Presidency and was counting them on his fingers, regarding each day gained without facing the dread finality of war as a victory. Had he sincerely wished to end the truce he could have done so instantly, with a word. So the President, the colonel, and the Senators were all playing for time, each with his own motive.[21]

Secretary of War Holt was in no hurry about drafting the President's reply to Hayne's proposition. A quiet, seam-faced Kentuckian, fifty-three years old, Joseph Holt was not by nature a temporizer. As a young man he had served a brilliant term as prosecutor in Louisville before going to Mississippi, where he amassed a fortune in five years by his eloquence as a pleader and gained a sympathy for the Southern point of view. Under his mild exterior he was a hardheaded executive, and this sympathy had taken punishment of late. Like Black, Holt had seen his attitude change to one of resentment toward South Carolina, but he had to accept the fact that Floyd had left him a depleted military establishment and he was in no position to bluster. Holt replied on January 22nd that while it was the "fixed purpose" of the President to preserve peace, as had been amply proved by the forbearance to use force when the *Star* was fired on, it was impossible to give assurance that no reinforcement would be sent to Sumter. The President was bound to protect the public interest. It was not thought necessary to reinforce Anderson because he was considered secure. "Should his safety, however, require reinforcements, every effort will be made to supply them." [22]

This rejected Hayne's prime condition, but the Southern Senators were still working on him, still angling to keep South Carolina from wrecking their blueprint for a new confederacy. They argued that Buchanan plainly did not want to stir up another hornet's nest by sending reinforcements, even if he was too cagey to say so. So the colonel, probably thinking of those batteries accumulating in Charleston, agreed to send home for further instructions anyway. Every day he remained in Washington, South Carolina grew stronger and Anderson relatively weaker, so the Hayne mission was already a resounding success even though it got nothing it demanded.

Jefferson Davis, who was one of the Senators seeking to slow down the Palmetto men, put the case plainly in two letters to Governor Pickens. Davis was following the Trescot-Thompson concept of loyalty when, from his seat in the Senate, he counseled Pickens, "I take it for granted that the time allowed to the garrison at Fort Sumter has been diligently employed by yourselves, so that before you could be driven out of your earthworks you will be able to capture the fort which commands them." He added later, "The little garrison [at Sumter] in its present condition presses on nothing but a point of pride," going on, "you can well afford to stand still, so far as the presence of a garrison is concerned, and if things continue as they are for a month, we shall then be in a condition to speak with a voice that all must hear and heed. . . ." [23]

While Hayne waited for instructions, Secretary Holt turned to another matter, the assumption by Major Beauregard of command at West Point. Beauregard was a brother-in-law of Senator Slidell of Louisiana, long a political crony of Buchanan, and Slidell had aided in getting the appointment months earlier.

Learning that Beauregard was frank in saying he would join the South if Louisiana seceded, Holt decided it was high time to insist on unwavering allegiance at the Military Academy. With Buchanan's approval he removed Beauregard from the post after he had occupied it exactly five days—an act that brought an icy note from Slidell to the President ending, "May I take the liberty of asking you if this has been done with your approbation?" [24]

"Mr. President," Holt exploded when he saw the note, "we have heard the crack of the overseer's whip over our heads long enough." [25]

Buchanan agreed. He sent a cool reply to Slidell backing up Holt, and thereafter Slidell was another old friend turned enemy. To Old Buck, a man morbidly sensitive to criticism, anxious to please everybody, these last few weeks of a blighted administration were a nightmare. Men who had been his allies for decades were cutting him, denouncing him, or plotting to kidnap him. Newspapers insulted him. Plain citizens he never saw damned him. Wrote George Templeton Strong: "Old James Buchanan, the 'O.P.F.,' stands lowest, I think, in the dirty catalog of treasonous mischief-makers." [26] When Senator Benjamin Fitzpatrick of Alabama paid a farewell call on the President before leaving for his seceded state, Buchanan said to him, "Governor, the current of events warns me that we shall never meet again on this side of the grave. I have tried to do my duty to both sections, and have displeased both. I feel isolated in the world." [27]

In the midst of this hurtful enmity, one crisis followed another to force a succession of risky decisions out of the tired old man. As if Sumter were not trouble enough, violence suddenly exploded in Florida.

That thinly populated state, not long since rescued from warlike Indians, likewise decided to become a republic. On January 12th, two days after the state seceded, a regiment of secesh volunteers advanced on the United States Navy Yard at Pensacola, whereupon the aged and timorous commander, Commodore James Armstrong, promptly surrendered. But the army

M

commander at Fort Barrancas nearby, bespectacled Lieutenant Adam Slemmer, got wind of the attack and took a page out of Major Anderson's book. With his forty-six-man company and thirty seamen from the yard, Slemmer spiked his guns and escaped across the bay to powerful Fort Pickens on Santa Rosa Island, until then unoccupied. Slemmer would have been able to hold off all Florida in this bastion, named after the South Carolina governor's grandfather, except that it called for a war garrison of 1,260 men and his small command was almost lost in it. A company of artillery was sent from Fortress Monroe aboard the *Brooklyn* to reinforce him, the question being whether it would arrive on time. Fort Pickens was one of those strongholds General Scott had urged the President to garrison, so the general could now take an I-told-you-so attitude.[28]

From Virginia came a hollow echo from John Floyd, who had been forced to borrow money to get his family back home. Under indictment for malversation in the bond-and-draft scandal, he was to escape prosecution on a lucky technicality. If he was poor in pocket, he was still rich in histrionics. Tendered a banquet in Richmond by admiring friends, he made a speech, described Major Anderson as "a man of honor, truth and courage," then went on to punish truth by saying that Anderson had "no authority" to occupy Sumter and to paint himself as a virtuous public official who had resigned in protest at the administration's shameful treatment of South Carolina. "Let you men of Virginia and the South prepare," Floyd warned, and was applauded by listeners apparently credulous enough to believe him.[29]

Buchanan meanwhile was besieged by peace-at-any-price men who implored him to evacuate Sumter, and Unionists advising him to reinforce the fort. A remarkable citizen of Massachusetts named Gustavus Vasa Fox wrote in to insist that it was perfectly feasible to reinforce Sumter, telling in detail how it could be done and asking the privilege of risking his life in leading the expedition. A naval officer for nineteen years, Captain Fox had retired to private life as a textile agent but was anxious to get back with the colors to meet a challenge that aroused him. An-

other man anxious to meet the challenge was Secretary of State
Black, who was urging the President to make up his mind, fix
on some policy other than delay. In a letter rising to high eloquence in its urgency and sense of peril, Black asked that Anderson be reinforced, going on:

> . . . There certainly would be no hurry about it, if it were
> not for the fact that the South Carolinians are increasing their
> means of resistance every day, and this increase may be such
> as to make delay fatal for his safety. . . .
>
> In the forty days and forty nights yet remaining to this ad-
> ministration, responsibilities may be crowded greater than
> those which are usually incident to four years in more quiet
> times. I solemnly believe that you can hold this revolution in
> check, and so completely put the calculations of its leaders out
> of joint that it will subside after a time into peace and harmony.
> On the other hand, by leaving the Government an easy prey,
> the spoilers will be tempted beyond their powers of resistance,
> and they will get such an advantage as will bring upon the
> country a whole iliad of woes. The short official race which yet
> remains to us, must be run before a cloud of witnesses, and to
> win we must cast aside every weight . . . and look simply upon
> our duty and the performance of it as the only prize of our
> high calling. . . .[30]

The weight was too heavy for the President to cast aside. With
Hayne still in Washington there was a state of truce and he would
observe it. Besides, Anderson had not asked for reinforcements,
and Lieutenant Hall, now in the capital, said the major felt
secure at Sumter. Another development Buchanan seized on
with hope was the leadership of the Virginia legislature in
organizing a Peace Convention to meet in Washington February
4th and to be attended by delegates from every state interested
in finding a peaceful solution where the government had failed.

At long last Colonel Hayne got instructions that ended his
Washington sojourn. With all due respect to the cotton-state
Senators, Judge Magrath informed him, the continued occupa-
tion of Sumter by a foreign garrison could not be tolerated.
Hayne then went ahead and presented his original demand to

the President, stressing South Carolina's right of "eminent domain" over Sumter and pledging the state to make compensation "to the last dollar" if the fort was surrendered. "No people not completely abject and pusillanimous," he wrote, "could submit, indefinitely" to the armed occupation of a fort commanding their principal harbor where even the ferryboats had to sail "at the sufferance of aliens." [31]

Secretary Holt, who answered for the President, took his time about it. In his reply a week later on February 6th he demonstrated a rare gift of expression in expounding a concept of the Union and its responsibilities that secessionists could neither understand nor accept. Hayne's proposition, he wrote, boiled down to an offer to buy Sumter under a threat to seize it by force if the purchase were not permitted—a most unusual request. Fort Sumter, said Mr. Holt, was not for sale. The President could not sell it even if he were willing, for it represented something far more important than property.

"The title of the United States to Fort Sumter," he went on, "is complete and incontestible. . . . [The nation] has . . . political relations to it, of a much higher and more imposing character than those of mere proprietorship. It has absolute jurisdiction over the fort and the soil on which it stands. . . . This authority was not derived from any questionable revolutionary source, but from the peaceful cession of South Carolina herself, acting through her legislature, under a provision of the Constitution of the United States. . . . South Carolina can no more assert the right of eminent domain over Fort Sumter than Maryland can assert it over the District of Columbia. The political and proprietary rights of the United States in either case rest upon precisely the same grounds.

". . . The property of the United States has been acquired by force of public law, and can only be disposed of under the same solemn sanctions. The President . . . can no more sell and transfer Fort Sumter to South Carolina than he can sell and convey the Capitol of the United States to Maryland, or to any other State or individual seeking to possess it."

The right of the United States to reinforce Sumter, he added, was likewise incontestible, finishing, "If, with all the multiplied proofs of the President's anxiety for peace and of the earnestness with which he has pursued it, the authorities of that State shall assault Fort Sumter and peril the lives of the handful of brave and loyal men shut up within its walls, and thus plunge our common country into the horrors of civil war, then upon them, and those they represent, must rest the responsibility." [32]

Thus did Joseph Holt inform South Carolina that Sumter was not a thing with a price tag on it. It was a trust, an inescapable federal obligation, a part of the Union itself that could be surrendered only in battle, not in bargaining.

Colonel Hayne, who so sincerely disagreed with every word Holt said that he considered the Secretary insulting, dashed off an angry reply that was indeed insulting and took the next train South. With him, it seemed, departed the last chance to avert war.

LET THE MAJOR DECLARE WAR

Sing a song of Sumter,
A fort in Charleston bay;
Eight and sixty brave men
Watch there night and day.

Those brave men to succor,
Still no aid is sent;
Isn't James Buchanan
A pretty President!

In Sumter, the garrison was entering upon a trial whose reality was not at all impaired by the fact that no one could quite understand it, estimate its duration, or appraise its significance. The men became aware that they were in a prison, shut off from the joys of the world just as surely as if they were condemned felons. Discomfort became routine. January was cold, with frequent fogs and chill rain, so that sometimes the fort was a point in space surrounded by gray mist. In the hurried move from Moultrie the band instruments had not been forgotten but other important items had. Surgeon Crawford, taking over as quartermaster in Lieutenant Hall's absence, made an inventory and found alarming shortages. Little coal was left. There was scant coffee, sugar, and salt. Candles and soap were almost gone. Crawford's list of the provisions on hand showed the following:

> 38 bbls pork
> 37 bbls flour
> 13 bbls hard bread
> 2 bbls beans
> 1 bbl coffee
> ½ bbl sugar
> 3 bbls vinegar

10 lbs candles
40 lbs soap
¾ bbl salt [1]

At Moultrie the garrison had regularly supplemented its staples with purchases of fresh meat and vegetables from Charleston, but now the authorities there seemed unwilling to allow
such luxuries to foreigners. Anderson wrote to Daniel Mc-
Sweeney, the Charleston butcher who had formerly supplied
him, but got no reply, leading him to assume that McSweeney
refused to do business with him or was afraid to. While there
was plenty of water in the cisterns and plenty of barreled pork,
a constant diet of salt pork could be tiresome. Dissipation was
a thing unknown, for there was no whiskey and—worse yet—
only a few lucky men still had tobacco.

The soldiers were sleeping on prickly mattresses made of
shavings. They saw their breaths and shivered as they ate unin-
spiring fare. They made do with half rations of coffee. They
had not been paid for weeks, although what good mere money
would do them was a metaphysical question. They had lost
prized personal possessions in the move from Moultrie. They
were confined to deadliest routine in a fort with walls so high
that the sun, on those occasions when it shone, peered in for
only a few hours a day. If ever men had reason to bellyache,
these men had it. Strangely, they did nothing of the kind.[2]

"Morale is very high," Captain Foster noted,[3] while Anderson
described his command as "in excellent health and in fine
spirits." [4] Sergeant Chester, himself one of the less privileged
enlisted men, said, "There never was a happier or more contented set of men in any garrison than the Sumter soldiers." [5]
Chester remarked on the alacrity with which they pitched into
the armament, laboring with makeshift block and tackle to
hoist a ten-inch columbiad—a cannon weighing 15,400 pounds
—to the barbette tier high above the parade. This gun threw
a 128-pound shot, so it was normally derrick work to hoist the
shot as well. Knowing that the lone derrick was badly needed for
heavier work, one beefy sergeant, after retreat roll call, carried

one of the ponderous balls up the stairway and demanded
whether anyone else was man enough to do the same. This challenge had dozens of men following suit until all the balls were
delivered to the ramparts.[6]

There were reasons for this spirit. While no one could be
expected to understand the machinations of politicians in Washington, the men were keenly aware that they alone represented
the Union in this hostile harbor and were proud of the distinction. Not a day went by that they were not mentioned in the
papers. Speeches were made in Congress about them, sermons in
churches, lectures in auditoriums, arguments on street corners.
They were easily the most famous band of soldiers since Leo-
nidas and his Spartans. In Moultrie they had gone to bed with
the uneasy feeling that they might be massacred before they
awoke. In Sumter they could deal out punishment as well as take
it. And—an important point in morale—they had a commander
they admired, a disciplinarian but no martinet, a man who was
kindly even though firm.

In Charleston, Governor Pickens was once again a man in the
middle. There was indignation in Congress about Anderson's
inability to get provisions, and the governor was urged to relent
even by other Southern leaders. Although Rhett and like firebrands complained that Anderson was already treated too gently
when he ought to be blasted out of the harbor with gunpowder,
Pickens gave in. The Sumtermen were overjoyed on January
20th when a boat arrived from Charleston carrying provisions
supplied by the South Carolina quartermaster—two hundred
pounds of red beef, bags of turnips, potatoes, and other delicacies the men had known only in dreams since they left Moultrie
almost a month earlier. Their mouths watering, a detail of
soldiers began carrying the provender into the kitchen. Then
Anderson found out about it.

He was sorry, he said, but the provisions would have to be
sent back. He was not accepting charity from the governor,
although he put it in more diplomatic language: "As commandant of a military post, I can only have my troops furnished
with fresh beef in the manner prescribed by law, and I am com-

pelled, therefore, with due thanks to his excellency, to decline his offer." [7] Either he would get his supplies direct from a Charleston merchant or not at all.

Captain Doubleday, a big man who could have done something with a joint of beef, had to cheer the commander for this. "Anderson showed a good deal of proper spirit," he admitted.[8] The soldiers, Crawford noted, returned the viands to the boat with regret but "without complaint." [9]

The rosy path of secession, Pickens was finding, had thorns along the way. Trade in Charleston's once thriving harbor was stagnating. Some Northern shippers, intimidated by the firing on the *Star of the West*, decided to use the port of Savannah instead. The news about the four hulks—donated by the sympathetic citizens of Savannah—being sunk at the channel entrance caused other ships to play safe and use the Georgia port even though Charleston's harbor could still be entered with care. Savannah was reaping a commercial harvest at the expense of Charleston, and some wondered whether the Georgians had been generous or shrewd. With merchants complaining at the slump in trade, Pickens hurried a telegram to the Dixie-born G. B. Lamar, president of the Bank of the Republic in New York:

"Please have it authoritatively published that no flag and no vessel will be disturbed or prevented from entering our harbor unless bearing hostile troops or munitions of war for Fort Sumter.

"All trade is desired, and all vessels in commerce only will be gladly received." [10]

Although his defensive position in Sumter was a vast improvement over Moultrie, Major Anderson was anything but freed from care. This state of hostile truce could not last indefinitely, with many Charlestonians bitterly resenting his presence. "They are determined," he observed, "to bring on a collision with the General Government. Everything around us shows this to be their determination and their aim." [11] A decision would soon have to be made in Washington. Either he would have to be withdrawn or there would be eventual war, while any effort to reinforce him would mean immediate war. Anderson was overly optimistic about his strength early in January, before new batteries began to menace him.

"My position will . . . enable me to hold this fort against any force which can be brought against me," he reported to Holt, "and it would enable me, in the event of a war, to annoy the South Carolinians by preventing them from throwing supplies into their new posts except by the out-of-the-way passage through Stono River. . . . I shall not ask for any increase of my command, because I do not know what the ulterior views of the Government are." [12]

While this gave Holt a comforting idea of Anderson's security at the moment, it also should have warned him that the major, isolated from the world as he was, ignorant of the plans in Washington but aware that the political considerations of his position were far more important than the military ones, was leaving the question of reinforcements entirely up to the administration. Holt's basic instructions in reply echoed those of the late Secretary Floyd in one respect. He praised Anderson for his "brilliantly executed" transfer to Sumter and went on: "You will continue, as heretofore, to act strictly on the defensive; to avoid, by all means compatible with the safety of your command, a collision with the hostile forces by which you are surrounded." [13]

By January 16th Holt had the benefit of conversations with both Lieutenants Talbot and Hall, who described the Charleston situation to him in detail. When Talbot returned to Sumter on the nineteenth, he brought with him two messages. One was for Doubleday, to the effect that the Charleston hotheads were "howling for his Black Republican head." [14] The other was a dispatch from Holt to Anderson:

> You rightly designate the firing into the *Star of the West* as an "act of war." . . . Had their act been perpetrated by a foreign nation, it would have been your imperative duty to have resented it with the whole force of your batteries. As, however, it was the work of the government of South Carolina, which is a member of this confederacy, and was prompted by

the passions of a highly-inflamed population of citizens of the United States, your forbearance to return the fire is fully approved by the President. Unfortunately, the Government had not been able to make known to you that the *Star of the West* had sailed from New York for your relief, and hence, when she made her appearance in the harbor of Charleston, you did not feel the force of the obligation to protect her approach as you would naturally have done had this information reached you.

Your late dispatches, as well as the very intelligent statement of Lieutenant Talbot, have relieved the government of the apprehensions previously entertained for your safety. In consequence, it is not its purpose at present to reinforce you. The attempt to do so would, no doubt, be attended by a collision of arms and the effusion of blood—a national calamity which the President is most anxious, if possible, to avoid. . . . Whenever, in your judgment, additional supplies or reinforcements are necessary for your safety, or for a successful defense of the fort, you will at once communicate the fact to this Department, and a prompt and vigorous effort will be made to forward them.[15]

That last sentence, so determined on its surface, was actually a subtle evasion of duty. Holt, speaking for the President, was passing the biggest buck ever passed. He was handing the obligation of deciding on reinforcements right back to Anderson. Since both Holt and Anderson knew perfectly well that reinforcement meant war, the secretary was saying in effect, "We leave it to you to decide when or whether war shall begin"— certainly the first time a United States administration had shrugged off such a responsibility and put it on the shoulders of an army major. Holt had no real justification for his complacent view about the garrison's safety. As evidence that "safety" was not a proper description, he had Anderson's earlier statement, "We are now, or soon will be, cut off from all communication, unless by means of a powerful fleet, which shall have the ability to carry the batteries at the mouth of this harbor." [16] He had the unpleasant knowledge that the *Star* had been driven off by those batteries and that more Carolinian guns were being added. He knew that Sumter was designed for a war garrison of 650 men, and that Anderson with his force of some seventy could hardly be expected to hold off any formidable attack.

The discerning Holt knew these things, knew that from a military point of view not a moment was to be lost if the fort was to be reinforced. Above all he knew that the fateful decision of reinforcing Sumter was now almost entirely a *political* one, the duty of no one less than the President to decide. But he was suffering from previous errors not his own, and he was only the agent of a President who was postponing the fatal issue with every stopgap device he could maneuver in the hope that some witchcraft would avert it entirely. Anderson was known to be calm, judicious, strongly opposed to war. Let him decide.

In addition to the dispatch from Holt, Talbot brought back a story about the President that put Old Buck in a pitiful light. Talbot said that when he reached Washington and went to the White House, Buchanan greeted him in great trepidation, laid a hand on Talbot's shoulder and quavered, "Lieutenant, what shall we do?"

For the nation's executive to put such a question to a mere subaltern staggered Talbot. "I never felt so in my life," he admitted to Lieutenant Snyder. "The President seemed like an old man in his dotage." [17]

Talbot, with his weak lungs, resumed his duties in a fort pervaded by such a cavernlike chill that Surgeon Crawford was worried about a possible epidemic of illness. One way to keep warm was to work. Captain Foster had only forty-three civilian workmen left, the rest having found the boom of cannon so unpleasant that they quit and skipped out immediately after the *Star of the West* incident—good riddance, in the captain's opinion. Those remaining were loyal and might be of some help in an attack. Foster was working under handicaps other than inclement weather. His cement and bricks had given out, a boatload of these materials having been seized by the Carolinians. The lack of fuel prevented burning for lime, so all masonry had to be laid with dry stone. [18]

While Foster kept one eye on his own work he turned the other on the projects of the Carolinians, who were working

vigorously on a plan that was all too obvious. Several hundred
Negroes were building solid merlons between the guns at Moultrie for protection from Sumter's fire—a defense considered so
urgent that the slaves worked by torchlight at night as well as by
day. Moultrie's burned gun carriages had been replaced, the fort
now having thirteen guns bearing on Sumter. Rumor said there
was a new five-gun battery about three hundred yards west of
Moultrie and another at the eastern end of Sullivan's Island,
both of these hidden behind houses. Two new batteries neared
completion at Fort Johnson, 2,400 yards west of Sumter, one of
three guns, the other of three guns or mortars. The Morris
Island battery, now called the *"Star of the West* battery" because of its recent triumph, was believed to have been enlarged
from two to at least four guns. Even more ominous to the Union
garrison was a gang of Negroes building a huge new battery on
Cummings Point, the northern tip of Morris Island, big enough
for six or eight guns. Cummings Point was only thirteen hundred yards almost due south of Sumter. This nearest installation
promised to be a powerful one that would bear on Sumter's
weakest point, its gorge wall. The chivalry had not as yet decided on a state flag, for the one on Morris Island had a white
palmetto on a red field, the one at Moultrie a green palmetto
on a white field with a red star in the corner. Captain Foster
relayed news of all this hostile activity to Washington in careful,
detailed reports complete with sketches by Captain Seymour,
who had once taught drawing at West Point.[19]

Being "strictly on the defensive," the Sumtermen could do
nothing about the work aimed at their destruction except to
tighten their own defenses. By January 21st they had fifty-one
guns in position, twenty-four of the heaviest on the barbette
tier, twenty-four more on the lower tier. The second tier was
not used at all. Two ten-inch columbiads—the most powerful
guns in the fort—were too heavy to lift when the derrick grew
rickety. They were mounted as mortars, along with four eight-
inch columbiads, in timbered trenches in the parade to bear on
Morris Island, Moultrie, and the city of Charleston. Sumter had
no army-issue cartridge bags to hold artillery charges, so a few

men were detailed to sew bags from shirts taken from the quartermaster's stores. The stone flagging was removed from the parade so that if shells fell there they would bury themselves and do less damage.[20]

Sumter, being designed to repel naval assault, was vulnerable to attack by storm. Only eight men could be assigned to defend each of its five walls. The rear or gorge side was unarmed, the large main gate in its center leading to the broad granite-paved esplanade and thence to the wharf—a fine landing spot for an attacking party. Foster's men laid mines around the wharf. They reinforced the main gate with a solid wall of masonry three feet thick, leaving only a narrow passage wide enough for one man. An eight-inch howitzer was mounted at the entrance to sweep the wharf with direct fire. Two guns were mounted outside on either side of the sallyport. Fougasses were installed along the wall—innocent-looking piles of stones, each containing a magazine of gunpowder that could be detonated from inside to explode as a deadly mine. Captain Seymour, the ingenious Vermonter, devised a "flying fougasse"—a barrel of stones placed atop the walls and containing a canister of powder. When pushed over the wall, it could be exploded at ground level by means of a long lanyard, hurling stones in all directions. Captain Doubleday, a man who believed in psychology, tried out one of these fougasses one day as a Carolinian schooner passed nearby. It made a handsome explosion, churning up water some distance from the fort and causing thoughtful comment in Charleston about the "infernal machines" devised by the foreigners.[21]

At Doubleday's suggestion, mâchicoulis galleries were built on each flank and face of the work—large, boxlike structures, armored with iron plates and extending four feet over the edge of the parapet. These galleries were loopholed so that marksmen could fire at stormers no matter how close to the wall, or drop grenades on them.[22] A German carpenter named Wittyman, who spoke little English, was ordered to build a cheval-de-frise at the outside angle of the gorge nearest Cummings Point to hinder enemy movement should they succeed in making a landing. Wittyman listened gravely to his instructions, said *Ja*, and set to work. No one had time to watch him, and when he was finished it was seen that his comprehension had been imperfect. Wittyman's cheval-de-frise was a fantastic structure, a well-built mystery of dizzily projecting scantlings and no military value whatever. The whole garrison had a good laugh about it, repeated every time they looked again. Carolinian observers were baffled by the nameless contrivance. Every time a boat went by, glasses were trained on it, some Charlestonians deciding it must be a device for the exploding of mines.[23]

Major Anderson, the man who was to decide when war would begin, had other problems on his mind of less consequence but still costing him worry and thought. As commanding officer he was responsible for the well-being of sixty-eight enlisted men, eight musicians, nine officers, forty-three workmen, and forty-five wives and children of soldiers—a total of 173 people. The constant fare of salt pork was a threat to health and morale. He had asked his friend Robert Gourdin, as a member of the state convention, to see if arrangements could be made for the garrison to buy provisions in the customary way. Gourdin, who had returned from Washington ahead of Hayne, was no member of the Rhett "starve-them-out" school. He would do what he could. The candles and soap were gone, leaving the long winter nights unlighted and cleanliness an approximation. The major, out of writing paper, had to borrow scraps from others and request Washington for a supply. In the midst of many petty annoyances he was disturbed by word from New York that his wife was ill. One forgetful gun crew made the mistake of practice-firing the new howitzer at the main gate without opening the windows, with the result that most of the glass on the gorge wall was shattered, letting wind and rain blow into the barracks. Some of the workmen and the soldiers' families, who had moved into the barracks, had to find room once more in the officers' quarters for some semblance of warmth.[24]

With war possible at any time, the presence of the forty-five women and children was an embarrassment as well as a drain on the larder. Anderson wrote the governor for permission to send the women and children to New York, pointing out that this was an indulgence granted "even during a siege, in time of actual war." He was relieved at Pickens' prompt agreement. Many of the women were reluctant to leave, but on February 3rd they departed with their youngsters aboard the steamer *Marion* for Fort Hamilton, New York, with Anderson honoring them with a one-gun salute. He had honored them in a quieter way, arranging that the wives be paid the soldiers' salaries at Fort Hamilton.[25]

"As they passed the fort outward-bound," Doubleday wrote, "the men gave them repeated cheers as a farewell, and displayed much feeling; for they thought it very probable they might not meet them again for a long period, if ever." [26]

Another worry besetting the major was the mail. After the Sumter move, his communications had been stopped by the angry governor and there had also been some "surveillance" of his private dispatches at the Charleston post office. In mid-January Pickens permitted the restoration of mail service, ruling that the garrison must not pick up the pouch at Charleston as before because of the risk of "collision" with excited citizens. Thereafter the Sumter mail was sent to Fort Johnson and picked up there by a boat sent across the shallow stream from the federal fortress. Anderson was in the uneasy position of having his communications at the mercy of hostile authorities who might at any time spy on his reports and instructions or stop them entirely. He took the precaution of sealing all his dispatches with wax so that any tampering could be detected, writing Holt:

> [The mail] is entirely under the control of the governor of this State, who may, whenever he deems fit, entirely prohibit my forwarding any letters, or prevent my sending any messenger, to my Government. I shall, however, as long as I can do so, send daily a brief note to the Department, the reception of which will show that the channel is still open, and the failure will indicate that our communication has been cut off.[27]

Anderson meanwhile saw a tarnish dull his status as the shining hero of the North. While he still received admiring letters, there was also criticism. The New York Assembly, which had

proposed presenting him with a sword, now tabled the resolution.[28] "If Major Anderson was aware that the *Star of the West*
brought reinforcements for Fort Sumter," said the New York
Times, "we confess we do not see the necessity of his forbearance," adding later, "It is useless to deny that the conduct of
Major Anderson stands in need of some explaining." [29] Some
Southerners misinterpreted his failure to open fire as proof that
he was a true Dixie man getting ready to abandon the Union.
"Major Anderson is a Southern man," one of them declared,
"born and raised in the noble old 'Dark and Bloody Ground.'
He will be found on the side of the South when this Govern-
ment is dismembered. . . ." [30]

During that bleak month of January the major wrestled with
the puzzle of what was to become of the Union he loved, the
Union his soldier father had helped to bring to life, the Union
that was disintegrating with each week that passed in a movement now rolling in a mighty swell over the South and causing
only bickering and dissension in the North. A change had come
over his thinking. Earlier he had believed that unruly South
Carolina could be contained and won back, and if military force
could achieve this end, however much he deplored force it
would be justified. Now, with a whole block of Southern states
seceded, he had come to the belief that war would be not only
monstrous and inhuman but hopeless—that instead of reuniting
the states it would bathe the nation in blood and divide it in
eternal hatred. War now would be national suicide, the ultimate
calamity. Better to let the seceding states go in peace, in the
hope that wise counsels later would bring them back.[31]

"The time is at hand," he wrote in reply to a congratulatory
letter from Albany, "when all who love the glorious Union
. . . shall show themselves good and true men. Our fellow-
countrymen in this region have decided to raise another flag.
I trust in God that wisdom and forbearance may be given by
Him to our rulers, and that this severance may not be 'cemented
in blood.' " [32]

"Be assured," he wrote another correspondent in Connecticut,
"that not a life shall be taken, not a dwelling demolished, unless

N

there be an absolute necessity for it. . . . I trust in God that time may now be gained, and that instead of resorting to the arbitrament of the sword, reason and good sense will regulate the actions of those in authority." [33]

President Buchanan, who did not want war, had handed over the responsibility of starting hostilities to Robert Anderson, who did not want it either. He would avoid it as long as honor permitted. He would avoid it even at the expense of having Northern patriots topple him off the pedestal they had raised for him and call him coward or traitor. This firm resolution, amounting almost to a holy vow, is the key to Anderson's conduct thereafter. He would keep his government informed about his condition and about Carolinian movements, but he would not make a direct appeal for reinforcements unless the necessity was extreme.

"I do hope," he wrote Adjutant General Cooper, January 20th, "that no attempt will be made by our friends to throw supplies in; their doing so would do more harm than good." A fortnight later he reported, "Their [the Carolinians'] engineering appears to be well devised and well executed, and their works, even in their present condition, will make it impossible for any hostile force, other than a large and well-appointed one, to enter this harbor, and the chances are that it will then be at a great sacrifice of life." But a significant postscript showed that he did not believe reinforcement impossible: "P.S.—Of course, in speaking of forcing an entrance, I do not refer to the little stratagem of a small party slipping in." [34]

Two days later he again mentioned the subject of reinforcements—as well as a growing doubt about his own security—in a report to Cooper: "I observe in the last English papers that a shipment of three rifled cannon has been made from England to Charleston. Such an addition to their battery would make our position much less secure than I have considered it; and if we are to have a collision, which God forbid, would render it necessary to send on reinforcements in a few days after the commencement of hostilities." [35]

Captain Foster, who shared not a particle of Anderson's

Southern sympathies, was in perfect agreement with him in his feeling that it would be the part of wisdom for the administration to accept the inevitable and evacuate Sumter. In a report to engineering headquarters, Foster wrote:

> I do not . . . consider it good policy to send reinforcements here at this time. We can hold our own as long as it is necessary to do so. If any force is sent here it must have the strength and facilities for landing and carrying the batteries on Morris or Sullivan's Island. . . . But if the whole South is to secede from the Union, a conflict here and a civil war can only be avoided by giving up this fort sooner or later. We are, however, all prepared to go all lengths in its defense if the Government requires it.[36]

Anderson echoed that sentiment to the letter. As long as he was ordered to hold Sumter, he would defend it to the last. Just to make sure the Carolinians did not mistake his determination on that score, he wrote Gourdin January 28th to say that if he were attacked and overwhelmed, *he would blow up the fort and everyone in it.*

> . . . if an attack is made [he warned], and I am convinced that the work will be carried, God willing, the Fort will fall into the possession of the state in such a condition that no flag can be raised on its walls. I am opposed to this shedding of blood, but if the strife be forced upon me, and we are overcome by numbers, not a soul will, probably, be found alive in the ruins of the work.[37]

Gourdin, a humane man personally fond of the major, knowing him not one to make empty threats, was appalled. He wrote an eight-page reply, well-reasoned and plausible despite its urgency. The irritation of the Carolinians was not directed against Anderson, he insisted, but against the government that so wrongly kept him there.

> . . . can you believe [he asked], that the honour and safety of the Government you represent are so involved in the defense of Fort Sumter that, if it is to fall, it must be reduced to ruin, even though every human being within its walls shall perish?

Review this determination, my friend, it is not the legitimate sequence of your convictions of the right and wrong of this quarrel; it does not bear the test of sober reason, it is not justified by any principle of duty; I am quite sure that humanity and religion condemn it. . . .

. . . I believe, as I live in the presence of Almighty God, that the authorities and the people of South Carolina would assail you and your small force *only* under the solemn conviction that the time had come when it is absolutely necessary to have fort Sumter. You have friends here who pray night and morning that this strife may be averted. . . . No, my friend, in no aspect of this issue can I discover any justification for [your] resolution. . . .

. . . If it should be your fate to be overcome, would you terminate the unhappy struggle by the horrible tragedy indicated in your letter? God of mercy and Justice forbid it, and save you from an error so fatal. It seems to me that having faithfully, bravely, and gallantly defended your post, if defend it you must, duty to yourself, and to those committed to your charge would require you to submit to that which you may not have the power to avert. . . .

God bless and direct you. . . .[38]

The letter did honor to its writer. But Anderson had taken an oath "in his manhood" and could not disown it for all his understanding of Southern grievances. Both Gourdin and the major were swept up in a surge of events too powerful for either of them to stop.

CHAPTER XVII

THE SOUTH CAROLINA GENTLEMEN

Of course he's all the time in debt to those who credit give,
Yet manages upon the best the market yields to live,
But if a Northern creditor asks him his bill to heed,
This honorable gentleman instantly draws his bowie-
knives and a pistol, dons a blue cockade, and
declares that in consequence of the repeated
aggressions of the North, and its gross violations
of the Constitution, he feels that it would
utterly degrade him to pay any debt whatever,
and that in fact he has at last determined to SECEDE,
This South Carolina gentleman, one of the present time.[1]

As of family-conscious Boston, it could whimsically be said that Charleston was a place where the Hugers spoke only to Pinckneys and the Pinckneys spoke only to God. This little city, which liked to be known as the Athens of the South, had a population of less than fifty thousand but swung its weight as if it were ten times that large because it reflected the prestige and influence of a class of landed barons who, in ex-Senator Hammond's words, were "the nearest to *noblemen* of any possible class in America"[2] and aimed to stay that way. Since Charleston was the social center of the state, it was also the political hub because aristocracy also implied political power. A planter might till a domain 150 miles upcountry, but it was to Charleston that he repaired for the theater, the horse races and cockfights, the St. Cecelia Ball, the winter shopping and social season. It was said that in one parish five planters owned all the land and all the slaves on it, so for many years it was the custom of these five to have in turn a dinner party on each election day "and to elect one of their number to the senate, by a *viva voce* vote at the table, over their wine."[3]

Charleston in the winter of 1861 was full of such statriot grandees, Francis Pickens being one of them, who owned balconied town houses or lived at the best hotels. These men regarded authority as their birthright, took pride in their public service and their guardianship of the social order, and accepted their superiority to citizens of other states not boastfully "but in a quiet and axiomatic way." Their background deprived them of several essentials of the democratic spirit, among them an ability to see beyond their own narrow horizon, to grant the validity of other points of view, to bend, compromise, admit of any need for change. They were unanimously secessionists *per se,* long past looking for concessions from the federal government that would lure them back into the Union. For many years they had lived on a basis of separate maintenance from Washington. Now they wanted outright divorce, final and perpetual. Socially they were a closed corporation, self-sufficient, suspicious of strangers but hospitable to those visitors from without who bore proof of distinction.[4]

That winter, Major Anderson was a visitor to whom they no longer extended hospitality even though he was admittedly a distinguished man with a fine war record and family background. Anderson had to get out. "You can form no idea of the feeling that exists here," wrote one Charlestonian. "Major Anderson will be driven out of Fort Sumter if it costs 10,000 lives. . . . He has now more than half his force in irons for refusing to obey him." [5] The city was a rumor factory where every wild report spread like a blaze. Among the gentry in residence were many who were willing to advise Governor Pickens on what he should do, and some who suggested that everything he had done to date was wrong. The radicals were howling for action on Sumter, some saying that a little bloodletting was just what was needed to unify the South, and what was the governor waiting for? He was called a peace-at-any-price man who kept sending commissioners to Washington to be insulted. The jingoistic *Mercury* as usual took the lead, saying "let us be ready for war" and demanding that "every foreign soldier" be driven out. Was proud South Carolina afraid of Anderson's corporal's guard? [6]

"Border southern States will never join us," the *Mercury* argued, "until we have indicated our power to free ourselves— until we have proven that a garrison of seventy men cannot hold the portal of our commerce. The fate of the Southern Confederacy hangs by the ensign halliards of Fort Sumter." [7]

The governor was criticized for allowing Anderson to receive mail and for considering the idea of sending him fresh provisions instead of a salvo of hot shot. There was a story that Rhett was so outraged at this that he rushed to Pickens' office on Meeting Street to demand that Sumter be reduced and captured with no more shilly-shallying.

"Certainly, Mr. Rhett," Pickens purred, a little weary of being whipsawed. "I have no objection! I will furnish you with some men and you can storm the work yourself."

Rhett drew back. "But, sir, I am not a military man!"

"Nor I, either," said the governor, "and therefore I take the advice of those who are." [8]

Jerked in one direction by the firebrands, Pickens was pulled in the other by local conservatives and by foreign Southern statesmen like Jefferson Davis who feared that touchy South Carolina might unilaterally start a war that would at once become the burden of the unready South. It was the belief of these outside conservatives that when the Confederate government was formed it could arrange a peaceable separation from the Union if only Pickens did not upset the applecart in the meantime by attacking Sumter.

So the governor was under endless pressure. Not by nature an equable man, he was growing testy under the strain. The process of seceding from the Union, which had seemed such a joyous step a few months earlier, was beset by difficulties no one had dreamed of. Who could have imagined, for example, that Old Buck would find resolution enough to insist on holding Sumter? Despite his bold front, Pickens was willing to delay the issue, knowing the state's weakness, knowing that his army, for all its formidable numbers, was composed largely of militia groups that had degenerated into social clubs whose members were more suited to picnicking than to military discipline. But while the delay continued, Charleston's harbor commerce was languishing so badly that business was in the doldrums. The sheer cost of preparing for war was a crushing burden said to total twenty thousand dollars every day. That added up to more than seven million a year, causing one observer to remark, "Our State will soon be bankrupt at that rate." [9]

Governor Pickens was working many hours daily at his city hall office, and his work went right on evenings at his suite at the Charleston Hotel. Friends, politicians, and know-it-alls bearded him at either place to point out his errors and explain what *should* be done. While the war fuse sputtered, he had to take time from pressing duties for such chores as officially accepting with thanks the offer of the Catawba Indians of South Carolina to enter into the state service. He was receiving a mountain of mail, much of it telling him what he should do. One of his letters, from a gunsmith in Beloit, Wisconsin, named W. H. Calvert, was a queer one. "I write a few lines to you stating that I have two or three dozen Rifles that I will send to you if you want such an artcel," Calvert proposed, "and will make two or three hundred if you want them. I will sell you those that I have on hand at low figgers." Pickens endorsed the letter, "Needs no answer." [10]

His suit was pending in New York for the recovery of $240, the value of his lost luggage and musical box, leading the *Herald* of that city to comment, "The question will here arise as to whether the plaintiff (Governor Pickens) can maintain action in this State, he being, as he claims, a citizen of an independent sovereignty." [11]

The governor, who had a three-thousand-dollar balance due him on his salary as United States minister to Russia, wrote to Washington for it—a fairly cheeky move considering that on his order the United States subtreasury in Charleston was forbidden to cash any more drafts from Washington. Mr. Secretary Dix settled that neatly. He sent Pickens a draft on the subtreasury whose payments he had stopped.[12] But the governor had more important things on his mind than $240, or even $3,000. One of his anxieties was that Britain might now attempt to reassert her old sovereignty over South Carolina on the theory that she had recognized the government of the original thirteen states, and that government's authority had passed away in Palmetto-land. Pickens wrote the Russian minister in Washington gravely urging Russia's influence against such a monstrous assumption.[13] Overriding all these cares was the question of Sumter. He was losing face with a large part of his constituents with every day of inactivity on that sore point and he knew it.

The trouble was, Carolina's more aggressive citizens could see only the pretty surface of things about which the governor knew the disturbing inner core. Charleston's aristocrats had absorbed the idea of war in stride and put it on a social footing like everything else. The men were raising money for the volunteer companies. The women were scraping lint for bandages and sewing soldiers' uniforms. There was no doubt as to what the result would be. After the *Star of the West*, did anyone need to be told the Yankees were afraid to fight? They knew that Anderson had only seventy men while the state forces now numbered in the thousands. Wealthy planters were not only giving their sons to the army but also sending slaves by the hundreds to work on the Charleston batteries. Anderson was surrounded by guns. Why did the governor hesitate? Pickens had once said he was insensible to fear, but he was not insensible to irritation. His nerves were getting frazzled.

"There is great dissatisfaction prevailing in the city at the course of Gov. Pickens in making the appointments to the army & in all his official acts," wrote Henry W. Ravenel, a scholarly planter and botanist. "He is overbearing, haughty & rude, & has given offence in numerous cases. He has caused many resignations & has made himself so unpopular since his election, that were it not for the critical state of affairs now existing, he would be called to account & perhaps impeached. . . . Pickens ought never to have been elected Governor." [14]

The South Carolina gentlemen were dead serious about this secession business, which they felt concerned their honor as well as their interest. Few could find any humor in it. They left that to old Judge Petigru who, for all his sadness at the breakup of the Union, could still muster a quip at the imponderable paradoxes of disunion. When a young friend told him that Louisiana had seceded, Petigru replied, "Good Lord, William, I thought we *bought* Louisiana." [15]

So uneasy was Pickens at the situation in Charleston that he wrote other Southern leaders for advice. One of them, Governor Joseph E. Brown of Georgia, replied with canny counsel. He appreciated Carolina's irritation at the foreign menace in her harbor, Brown wrote, and yet political considerations dictated forbearance. If war was begun now during the Buchanan administration, the Northern Democrats would sustain Buchanan and Lincoln could take up the war as "unfinished business actually commenced." But if a rupture with Buchanan could be avoided, then Lincoln would be saddled with the onus of starting the war, the Northern Democrats would oppose him and the North would be divided.[16]

That seemed to make sense, and while Colonel Hayne was negotiating in Washington, Governor Pickens had a plausible excuse for inactivity. But when Hayne was rebuffed by Holt's refusal to sell Sumter and departed for Charleston claiming he had been insulted, the firebrands were after Pickens again. Here was the second mission South Carolina had sent to Washington for peaceable parley only to meet affront! The governor was now in such a hot spot in his own little republic that he may have wished he had stayed in chill St. Petersburg. Possibly it was in an effort to ease the pressure in Charleston that he embraced an idea that would transfer pressure elsewhere: Let Virginia and Maryland seize the capital at Washington and take over the reins of government. Revolutionist Pickens urged this course in a letter of February 7th to J. Thomson Mason, a secessionist friend who was United States Collector at the port of Baltimore:

> . . . It is a great mistake to suppose that for Virginia and Maryland to remain neutral, leads to peace, it is the reverse, it leads to confusion and aggression, which must end in conflict. . . .
>
> I see Scott is strengthening Washington by pouring in federal troops under circumstances of the deepest degradation to Mary-

land and Virginia. If you can bear this, then you can bear anything. I am sure the only way to secure fort McHenry and Fort Monroe is for Maryland and Virginia, or citizens of these states, to seize immediately Washington, and by throwing the head into convulsion, and through that, to get possession of Fort Monroe and Fort McHenry in the convulsion. This would force Lincoln to seek another point for the inauguration, and thus throw the Northern States into apparent revolution. . . . It would be all over in three weeks, and as far as the South is concerned there would be peace and the North would be in confusion and divided. It looks violent at first, but I sincerely believe it would be the most certain mode of saving the country from a permanent, bloody and civil war. . . .[17]

While Pickens' shaky syntax hinted at some convulsion of his own, he was plainly ready for desperate measures—anywhere but in Charleston.

THE PEACEMAKERS

In Washington that winter a pale, slight, beak-nosed Senator spoke soothingly through a cigar that dripped ashes on his vest, telling legislators North and South that the nation's troubles would be solved as soon as he was running the government, so would everybody please sit tight and hold their tempers until March 4th? He was William Henry Seward of New York, a man who was to accomplish short-term benefits by spreading sincere but erroneous beliefs. Long a foe of slavery, he was famous or infamous for his prediction of the "irrepressible conflict" between North and South. Now that his prediction seemed well on the way to reality, he was working like a tartar to make himself out a liar. He was accurately described as a lawmaker "whom the convulsions of the country have terrified into moderation. He has been overcome by the complete fulfillment of his own prophecy." [1]

Seward had missed the Presidency by an eyelash when the dark horse Lincoln surprisingly stole the nomination from him at Chicago—a stunning blow he cushioned with the thought that he was top dog in the Republican Party and would be President in fact even though Lincoln bore the title. Once called by Henry Clay "a man of no convictions," the New Yorker was one who could trim his sails to catch any political breeze, fruitful in expedients, persuasive, and a wee bit devious. Consistency worried him not a whit. In December he pronounced secession a "humbug" that was already on the wane. A week later he found it no humbug at all but a gigantic peril. His letters during the next month reveal a mistaken man discovering his mistakes and finding also a new sense of personal responsibility toward the whole nation:

December 28th: "I will try to save freedom and my country."

December 29th: "Treason is all around and amongst us; and plots to seize the capital, and usurp the Government."

January 3rd: "I have assumed a sort of dictatorship for defense; and am laboring night and day, with the cities and States."

January 23rd: "Mad men North, and mad men South, are working together to produce a dissolution of the Union, by civil war. The present Administration and the incoming one unite in devolving on me the responsibility of averting these disasters." [2]

Untroubled by false modesty, Seward's frank opinion was that the only man who could save the nation was Seward, an estimate that contained some truth. By this time it was known he would be Lincoln's Secretary of State. He was regarded by legislators of all sections as the real leader of the Republicans who would control the new administration when it came in, a seasoned politician whose long experience in national affairs would make Lincoln—by comparison an amateur—lean on him for policy. The Senator, it was thought, *was* the Lincoln administration, residing right there in Washington during the last weeks of the Buchanan regime. If he took the hard line, all hope for the Union was lost. If he was conciliatory, there might yet be a faint chance for agreement.

Seward, the old rabble-rouser whose extreme views had won him odium in the South, made a fast change of coat, threw his party's platform out the window, decked himself with olive branches, and became the most peaceable man in the capital. All this fuss was ridiculous, he protested. When he took charge a compromise would be effected that would suit everybody and save the Union too. "Nay," he said, "if this whole matter is not satisfactorily settled within sixty days after I am seated in the saddle, and hold the reins firmly in my hand, I will give you my head for a foot-ball." [3]

He was indeed "laboring night and day" in a laudable effort to avoid disunion and disaster, sincerely trying to bridge the gap between Buchanan and Lincoln. He had put serious thought on the problem and come up with some theories, not all of them leakproof. He thought Major Anderson had been foolish in the first place to occupy Sumter, accomplishing nothing but to arouse Southern anger. The slavery quarrel, he felt, had been overdone, talked to death—better to drop it now in favor of the one vital issue, saving the Union. He held an immovable conviction that in the dissident Southern states—even South Carolina—there was a powerful Union sentiment derailed temporarily by excitement. Give this sentiment time and it could not fail to reassert itself. Recognizing the cold fact that a parcel of states had seceded and could not be brought back in a day, he was in favor of giving them a cooling-off period, perhaps as much as two or three years, after which the true Southern nationalism would be in the ascendant and there would be a happy reunion.[4]

Seward's theories, strangely, were much like those of President Buchanan, a man he professed to believe wrong in everything, but he advanced them as his own creation with convincing optimism. Talkative, amiable, charming, he made it his business that winter to assure Southerners they had nothing to fear from the Lincoln, or *Seward*, administration. He was an indefatigable ambassador of good will, conveying the impression that he had all the answers in his vest pocket. He conferred with Secretary of State Black and General Scott. He held secret meetings with Attorney General Stanton, who visited him after dark under the alias of "Mr. Watson" to keep him informed of Buchanan's moves. He let it be known he favored the withdrawal of Anderson from Sumter. If anything, Seward was more conciliatory than Buchanan himself, influencing the President to even greater caution. Certainly, he felt, it was more than ever his duty to keep the peace if the next administration intended likewise.[5]

So the Senator from New York succeeded in reducing the Washington hysteria a fraction, never dreaming he was wrong in his two basic assumptions—that he was going to run Abraham Lincoln and that there was any great devotion for the Union left in such states as South Carolina. As a peacemaker he was aided by the arrival of seventy-year-old ex-President John Tyler from Virginia to head the Peace Convention sponsored by that state, a last-ditch effort at mediation, carrying considerable moral force despite its unofficial character. Old Tyler reached Washington at a time when General Scott had managed to scrape together a few men and guns to defend the capital against a possible surprise attack, presenting a martial appearance that offended the peace man.

"What are you doing here with all these preparations?" he demanded of Black and Stanton, who met him. "Are you going to make war? Nothing could be more exciting to the Southern people than these preparations. I have come here for peace." [6]

Tyler was also disturbed by a rumor—correct—that the *Brooklyn* had sailed southward from Fortress Monroe with a contingent of soldiers. If those soldiers were intended to reinforce Sumter, then Tyler and all his delegates might as well pack up, for there would be war. The Virginian dispatched a note to Buchanan asking a fairly nosey question: Where was the *Brooklyn* going? The President tried to conceal the vessel's confidential mission by replying that she was "on an errand of mercy and relief . . . in no way connected with South Carolina," an answer that made it plain she was en route to reinforce Fort Pickens in Florida.[7] Another worry haunting Tyler was the abrupt departure of Colonel Hayne, claiming he had been insulted by the government—a development that might easily cause Governor Pickens to let cannon replace negotiation. Tyler called on the President to press his droll theory of mediation— that the United States should do all the conciliating and disarming. He urged Buchanan to snuff out the threat by removing "that noble boy," as he referred to the fifty-five-year-old Anderson, and his garrison from Sumter.

He found Buchanan remarkably stubborn on this point. He refused to withdraw the garrison, refused to make any pledge that Anderson would not be reinforced, though at present he was considered safe.[8] Old Buck wished the Peace Convention nothing but well, and in fact looked to it hopefully as an influence that might stave off war by creating another unofficial "truce" between the administration and South Carolina.

He had receded on other issues but on Sumter he was immovable. It was his visible protest against the illegality of secession and the continuing seizures of federal property in the South, a symbol that the administration still considered the Union intact, and Anderson would stay.

South Carolina had been invited to send delegates to the Peace Convention, but declined with thanks. It would not be fitting, it was felt, to take part in parleys aimed at saving the Union when the state was already out of the Union and had no further interest in it. The Palmetto men instead were sending delegates to another conclave meeting the same day as the peace men—the convention in Montgomery, Alabama, opening February 4th to form a new government for the seceded states. Tyler telegraphed an appeal to Governor Pickens:

"Can my voice reach you? If so, do not attack Fort Sumter. You know my sincerity. The Virginia delegates here earnestly unite." [9]

Pickens replied that while he could make no pledge, his course might be controlled by the provisional Confederate government then forming in Montgomery. "Everything which can be done consistently with the honor and safety of this State," he telegraphed, "to avoid collision and bloodshed, has been and will be the purpose of the authorities here." [10]

This was hardly candid, coming from the man who at the same time was egging on secessionists in Maryland to join with Virginians in making collision and bloodshed certain by seizing Washington by armed force. The Southern honor of Governor Pickens was fraying. But Tyler hastened to give the purport of this message to Buchanan as proof that Sumter should not worry him. The President was not entirely reassured, and meanwhile problems were popping up in other quarters, one of them Pensacola.

Lieutenant Slemmer was still holding Fort Pickens there with a pocketful of soldiers, but the complexion of things had changed. The United States men-of-war *Sabine, St. Louis,* and *Macedonian* had arrived off the harbor, and the *Brooklyn* was on the way with a company of regulars under Captain Israel

Vogdes. A powerful naval force was anchored there, just waiting. Senator Stephen Mallory of Florida looked over the situation and possibly decided that these vessels were perfectly
capable of steaming in and retaking the navy yard and forts the
state had recently appropriated. Mallory dispatched an urgent
appeal to three friendly Senators in Washington proposing a
truce at Pensacola: He would pledge there would be no attack
on Fort Pickens if the administration in turn would pledge not
to reinforce the garrison. This proposal was passed on to the
President, who agreed to it despite his resolve to eschew all such
pledges. His ships could easily repossess the navy yard, but that
would be war. The *Brooklyn* was ordered to land supplies for
Slemmer but no reinforcements, and to wait there with the
other vessels, ready to repel any attack. This was the peculiar
"Fort Pickens truce," a truce favorable to the secessionists since
by its terms the administration voluntarily agreed not to exercise its ability to retake bastions stolen from it. Lieutenant
Slemmer was left with a token force in a position similar to that
of Major Anderson, with one notable exception: There was
nothing to prevent Slemmer from being reinforced should the
truce be broken.[11]

One of the most persistent rumors in Washington had it that
secessionists were plotting to seize the capital on February 13th,
the day when the electoral votes would be officially counted at
a joint session of Congress and Lincoln would formally be declared the winner. General Scott had taken what steps he could
to prevent this, embroidering his action with vivid utterance.

"I have said," he growled, "that any man who attempted by
force . . . to obstruct or interfere with the lawful count of the
electoral vote . . . should be lashed to the muzzle of a twelve-
pounder gun and fired out of a window of the Capitol. I would
manure the hills of Arlington with fragments of his body, were
he a senator or chief magistrate of my native state! It is my duty
to suppress insurrection—*my duty!*" [12]

The electoral count was made without incident except for
the grumbling of Southern legislators who chose to regard a
sensible defense of the capital as an insult, calling Scott an

o

"ungrateful son of the South" and a "Free-state pimp." [13] The general was busy with another chore—planning an expedition to reinforce Major Anderson. Gustavus Fox, the navy officer turned businessman, hurried to Washington to explain his plan to force an entrance with tugboats supported by warships. He conferred with Lieutenant Hall, the Sumter officer still lingering in Washington, who was convinced that the fort could be reinforced via the Swash Channel, a shallow passage entering the harbor east of the main channel. Captain Fox was eager to get his expedition under way, pointing out that Hall could return to Sumter and inform Anderson of the details. Scott thought Fox's plan feasible but seemed to favor another designed by Commander Ward of the navy, who proposed making an entrance with four or five small coast-survey steamers.[14] Both plans were submitted to Secretary Holt and the President, who ordered the Ward expedition to be fitted out at once in New York. Rumors leaked out as usual, and Senator Wigfall was listening. The Senator promptly telegraphed a warning to Governor Pickens:

"Attempt to reinforce Anderson by stealth at night in small boats determined on." [15]

But for all his pondering about reinforcing Anderson, the President's heart was not in it. It was contrary to his basic policy, to keep the peace. The Ward expedition was readied in New York with great speed only to stay there, marking time, awaiting the signal that never came. Buchanan decided at length to respect the appeal of the Peace Convention, provided Governor Pickens would do the same. Besides, it appeared now that the new, so-called Confederate government at Montgomery would take the Sumter problem out of the nervous hands of Pickens and possibly open diplomatic overtures. Buchanan, critics snarled, was willing to "give up part or even the whole of the Constitution to save the remainder." [16] Time was being gained. The forty days and forty nights remaining to the suffering President had dwindled to less than twenty, and he could see something like daylight ahead. The time for reinforcing Anderson without inviting a blood bath was likewise dwindling with every day that passed.

In the House, Representative Daniel Sickles of New York had put through a resolution calling for a special observance of Washington's birthday. Secretary Holt, thinking this a logical time for a patriotic parade of the military, gave orders for it which appeared in the Washington papers February 21st. Old John Tyler, who had been looking down his nose at the army detachments in the capital—some six hundred men—was incensed at this idea of military display. In three weeks' time Tyler would make a fiery speech in Virginia calling for secession and the seizure of the Norfolk navy yard, but now he felt this parade to be a hostile demonstration, a reflection on peaceable Virginia and Maryland. He asked the President to stop it. Buchanan gave in, calling off the parade despite Holt's protests.

Sickles heard about this on the morning of February 22nd. He was the only member of Congress who was also a killer, having slain his wife's lover near the White House and won an acquittal, and he was a man not at all diffident about pressing his opinions. He rushed into the War Department, where Buchanan was closeted with Holt, and demanded to see the President. Holt came out to warn him that Buchanan could not be disturbed. Sickles characteristically went right in and disturbed him.

"Mr. President," he snapped, "there are ten thousand people out on the streets of Washington today to see the parade which was announced. I have just heard that it has been countermanded. . . ."

Just how, he inquired, could anyone take offense at a procession in honor of the national hero? He pelted the President with such logical arguments that Old Buck threw up his hands. "Go ahead with the parade," he said to Holt.[17] So the parade went on as the President wrote John Tyler the perfect excuse for the display that needed no excuse:

"The troops everywhere else join such processions in honor of the birthday of the Father of our Country, and it would be hard to assign a good reason why they should be excluded from the Capital founded by himself. . . ." [18]

Washington was indeed a place of serio-comic paradoxes, and what happened next day proved it. Abraham Lincoln arrived quietly, hours ahead of schedule, having taken an earlier train to thwart a rumored plot to assassinate him in Baltimore. The report that he had disguised himself in Scotch cap and long cloak was untrue, but there was no denying that he had sneaked into his own capital fearful for his life, to be met by Senator Seward, the man who intended to tell him how to run the government. If secessionists needed any further scorn to heap on the rail-splitter, they had it now. With many predicting that rebels would seize Washington, with husbands sending their wives and children away to escape violence, with the President-elect arriving secretly to escape murder, the city seemed more like a Central American capital than the seat hallowed by Jefferson and Jackson.

Lincoln entered a dreary, frightened city under the most humiliating circumstances. Washington, like the nation, seemed to be falling apart. The signs of disintegration were everywhere. The Peace Commissioners were still at work, but the general opinion was that they were wasting their breath. The Senate gravely appointed a committee of conference on the tea and coffee amendments to the tariff bill. Southern Congressmen were making their farewells and leaving by every train. Southern officers of the army and navy were handing in their resignations and heading South. Lieutenant-Colonel George W. Lay, the Virginia-born military secretary of General Scott who was privy to much of the general's confidential affairs, was quietly planning to quit.[19]

But Senator Wigfall was not quitting. He was staying on in Washington as long as he could do some good. Then he was planning to open a recruiting office in Baltimore. For *Confederate* soldiers, sir!

THE LION
AND THE LAMB

Governor Francis Pickens in February was talking tough and acting with caution, keeping an attentive ear toward Montgomery. He doubtless would have loved the honor of taking Sumter himself, thereby silencing the Charleston critics and recovering some measure of popularity, but he knew he would be condemned by other Southern leaders if he started war before the Confederacy was organized.[1]

On February 4th, delegates from the seceded states met at Montgomery to form a government in a hurry, electing Howell Cobb as president of the convention. One of the reasons for their hurry was their fear that the Carolinians, so long known for impulsive action, would begin a war when none was necessary. Most of these men were opposed to war and confident it could be avoided. One of the hackneyed pleasantries used by Southern politicians when they were urging their constituents to embrace secession was that they would drink all the blood spilled in any war that would ensue. Leroy Pope Walker, the handsome, bearded Alabamian who was to become Confederate secretary of war, created a variation on that: He would wipe up all the blood with his handkerchief.[1] While events had taken a more difficult course than expected, the feeling was still almost universal that the Confederacy would quit the Union in peace if Governor Pickens would hold his temper. Quick attention was paid to Pickens' temper. Robert Toombs, soon to be Confederate secretary of state, wrote the governor February 9th urging that no attack on Sumter be made "without the sanction and jurisdiction of our joint Government."[2] The congress speedily elected Jefferson Davis president and on February 12th voted to assume all questions about forts and other United States property in the Confederacy—a decision that was promptly telegraphed to Pickens.

The governor—he was now only a governor again after seven
weeks as head of a republic—seemed to be saying yes and no at
the same time. To Toombs he stressed the need for an early
attack on Sumter, writing, "I hope to be ready by Friday night
[February 15th], and think I am prepared to take the fort or
silence it," adding that if his attack was resisted, "the slaughter
of the garrison is inevitable." [3] This talk of attack and slaughter
came only three days after Pickens had assured John Tyler of
his pious aim to avoid "collision and bloodshed." The governor
was a lamb or a lion, depending on whom he was addressing.
To Cobb he wrote acknowledging the superior authority of the
Confederate government but urging that South Carolina's interests demanded the reduction of Sumter before Lincoln took
office.

"Mr. Buchanan cannot resist," he reasoned, "because he has
not the power; Mr. Lincoln may not attack because the cause of
the quarrel may be considered by him as past." He went on to
become entangled in ambiguities which Cobb must have had
some trouble piercing:

> If an attack is delayed till after the inauguration of the in-
> coming President of the United States, the troops now gathered
> in the Capitol [sic] may then be employed that which previous
> to that time, they could not be spared to do. They dare not
> leave Washington *now* to do that which *then* will be a measure
> too inviting to be resisted. . . . [4]

What Pickens was saying was that the time to attack Sumter
was now while all the available federal soldiers had to stay in
Washington to guard the inauguration. Instead of avoiding collision and bloodshed, he was using all his influence to bring it
on. He did not share the view of the gentlemen in Montgomery
that the new Confederacy could be born without pain. And yet
the governor, for all his violent talk, consented to let Mr. Davis
handle the Sumter problem if he would get a move on with it—
a transfer of authority that angered some statriot Carolinians
who thought it a reflection on the state and feared it would delay
the attack on Sumter. Bishop Thomas F. Davis of the Episcopal

diocese of South Carolina took official cognizance of the new situation in a circular to the clergy:

> Beloved Brethren: South Carolina having now become one of the "Confederate States of America," a Provisional Government having been established, and the President inaugurated, permit me to request that hereafter, in the prayer for *"all in civil authority"* now used, you substitute for the words *"Governor of South Carolina,"* the words *"President of the Confederate States of America,"* and that in the *"prayer for Congress,"* instead of the words *"United States,"* the words *"Confederate States"* be used. . . .[5]

Many clergymen were far ahead of the bishop in this respect. It was said that one Presbyterian parishioner complained to his pastor, threatening to quit the church unless he prayed for the Union. "Why," the pastor replied, "our church does not believe in praying for the dead." [6]

Courtenay's bookstore on Broad Street reported a good sale on Barnard's *Notes on Seacoast Defence* and *Instruction for Heavy Artillery*.[7] The city had long been indignant about articles appearing in the abolitionist New York *Tribune* abusing secessionists and signed "by our Charleston correspondent." The correspondent was not known, and many believed his diatribes were dreamed up in Washington. One day in February a man mounted a barrel in front of the post office and gathered an appreciative crowd with a speech about the virtues of disunion. Growing warmer, he stamped to emphasize his words, broke the barrelhead, fell through, and fractured his leg. Taken to a hospital, he was discovered to be the Charleston correspondent of the *Tribune*. There was angry talk against him, but he was allowed to depart for New York with his leg in braces.[8]

At a Charleston drydock, construction was well under way on a weird engine of war, a "floating battery" built under the direction of Lieutenant John Hamilton, late of the United States Navy and son of a former governor of South Carolina. It took shape as an enormous houseboat about a hundred feet long and twenty-five feet wide, made of stout pine timbers buttressed by palmetto logs and armored with a double layer of railroad iron. On one side were four siege cannon, so heavy that the other side had to be counterweighted with sandbags. The monster even carried its own hospital in a small shed attached. Lieutenant Hamilton had great hopes for his contraption, which could be towed out into a position to blaze away at Sumter's weak gorge wall.[9]

II

At Sumter, the beleaguered garrison was building its grudge against the Charlestonites into full-blown hatred. Who was to blame for all their troubles? Why, those ———— in Charleston! The men had run out of tobacco and were reduced to chewing spun cotton, which produced "some of the loudest grumbling ever listened to." [10] On one trip to Fort Johnson to pick up the mail, a couple of Sumtermen managed to buy some tobacco from an amiable Carolinian, then were enraged to have it taken away from them by other militiamen.[11] There were numerous petty indignities. Many of them had left private belongings of some value behind them in the move to Sumter and had never seen them since although their return had been promised. Captain Foster had lost considerable property in the move. Packages mailed to soldiers were sometimes withheld in Charleston. The women were gone, the children were gone, the men were pent up in their chill fortress without even a dram to warm their innards, with no recreation or enjoyment, and today was just like yesterday only a shade worse. There was a strong suspicion that their mail was being scrutinized in Charleston.

"The traitors and rascals open our letters in town," exploded Sergeant Eugene Scheiber of Company E, "and I must write German, though there are enough of them [Germans in Charleston] to translate it for them." [12]

Valentine's Day came as usual on February 14th, but there was no one handy to kiss. The men made sardonic jokes on reading in Northern papers that their confinement in Sumter was the subject of stage dramas in New York and Boston, one of them a pantomime titled *Fort Sumter by Moonlight*. "It was quite amusing," Doubleday noted, "to see our names in the play-bills, and to find that persons were acting our parts and spouting mock heroics on the stage." [13]

Major Anderson had become silent and thoughtful, saying he was "in the hands of God." [14] "I have lost all sympathy with the people who govern this State," he wrote a friend. "They are resolved to commence their secession with blood." [15] In his view the sensible thing for the administration to do now was to withdraw from the harbor, but in his reports he confined himself to his own sphere, the military. The garrison now had no chaplain, a deficiency noted by one Rev. Mr. Menes of Bath, Maine, who wrote to apply for the post. For all his churchly inclinations, the major felt that "in the present condition of affairs" it would be best for the Reverend Menes to stay in Maine.[16]

Anderson was wrestling with an inner problem: What course should he take if his own state of Kentucky seceded? It tormented him because he could not satisfy his sense of honor with either alternative. His wife, for whom his pet name was Eba, seemed to have no doubts on that score. Aroused by the garrison's privations, she had such a contempt for South Carolina that she was ready to disown her natal Southland. Henry Ravenel, the kindly Carolinian planter, who was a friend of Robert Gourdin, had called on her during a recent visit in New York only to get a polite piece of her mind.

"We talked over *secession* and Fort Sumter, of course," she wrote her husband. ". . . I told him most decidedly, that I *did* know what *you* intended to do if there should be a Northern & Southern confederacy, and as for *myself*, he might rest assured I might never be found in the same Confederacy with *South Carolina*, that he must pardon me, but that, really, for the first time in my life, I was ashamed of being a *Southerner,* since the whole North was crying out at the little pitiful, contemptible course *his* State was pursuing towards the fort in her harbor. Indeed, I said a great many very unpleasant truths, in the most pleasant manner possible. . . .

". . . I do hope they come to some amicable arrangement, but still, I must say, that I, for one, will *not* be satisfied if you are made to leave . . . Fort Sumter to the Carolinians. Do ask those in authority at Washington. *I* would make it a special request—to let you blow it up, sky high, on leaving it." [17]

Ravenel proved his Carolinian courtesy and capacity for punishment by calling on Mrs. Anderson again. That spirited lady apparently assumed that her husband would remain with the Union, but if so she did not consider the hard question of Kentucky. Despite his reverence for the Union, Anderson could scarcely bring himself to fight against friends and relatives in his own state. For most Southern officers it was a matter they solved easily by going with their respective states, but for the upright major it was a soul-wrenching problem in which he could not satisfy his exacting sense of duty by taking either side should Kentucky decide against the Union. He was considering a third course, itself an unhappy one but less repugnant than either of the other two: If Kentucky seceded he would resign his commission and go with his family to Europe.[18]

For Robert Anderson, this was a winter of spiritual misery that far transcended mere bodily discomfort. All that he held dear was going to smash with such appalling certainty that again and again, in his letters and even in his official reports, he indicated that he had lost hope in everything but God. Although he had been upheld by the administration in failing to support the *Star of the West*, he was nevertheless haunted by the thought that his flag had been fired on and he had not replied. Some Northern newspapers were still questioning his loyalty. A few of his own officers—notably Doubleday and Crawford—much as they admired him personally, felt that his Southern sympathies were leading him away from plain duty. He received a significant letter from the Reverend S. W. Crawford of Philadelphia, father of the surgeon, reading in part:

I have one son with you & I would cheerfully send another. I think he loves his country; & I am persuaded will defend the Stars & Stripes to the last; or make them his winding sheet. If he would not he is no son of mine.

I have no words to express my abhorrence of the Imbecile at the head of the gov't—his gross neglect of his duty, particularly of you & your Command. I need not say to *you* stand up fearlessly for your country.[19]

Anderson could easily translate the meaning of that last line to read: "My son has expressed some misgivings about you."

The major was also troubled by a lack of explicit instructions from Washington. The dispatch from Holt brought by Talbot contained only the oft-repeated "strictly-on-the-defensive" order. Lieutenant Hall returned February 11th with nothing more enlightening. The administration seemed content to let Anderson handle all details above that one basic instruction himself—a heavy responsibility in dangerous Charleston harbor. He kept sending in almost daily reports and getting precious little in reply. Possibly a reason for Holt's silence was his suspicion that the mails were being opened and read in Charleston; yet an occasional dispatch concerning mere routine would have aided the isolated commander's morale. Anderson asked specific questions about a few delicate points:

"I would thank the honorable Secretary to give me instructions in reference to vessels bearing the flags of foreign governments in the event of the commencement of hostilities. I presume that no vessel should pass the fort." Again: "I should like to be instructed on a question which may present itself in reference to the floating battery, viz: What course would it be proper for me to take if, without a declaration of war, . . . I should see them approaching my fort with that battery? They may attempt placing it within good distance before a declaration of hostile intentions." [20]

This last question posed such problems that it was taken up in a Cabinet meeting. The President's first reaction was that he would "crack away at them," but he quickly stressed his aversion to firing the first gun and his hope that the Peace Convention might bear fruit.[21] In his reply to Anderson, Holt admitted the question was not an easy one to answer at a distance and showed clearly that if the major was willing to make concessions in the cause of peace, the administration was even more so. Repeating the hackneyed warning that Anderson must continue to act "*strictly* on the defensive," Holt went on:

> If . . . you are convinced by sufficient evidence that the raft of which you speak is advancing for the purpose of making an assault upon the fort, then you would be justified on the principle of self-defense in not waiting its actual arrival there, but in repelling force by force on its approach. If, on the other hand, you have reason to believe that it is approaching merely to take up a position at a good distance should the pending question be not amicably settled, then, unless your safety is so clearly endangered as to render resistance an act of necessary self-defense and protection, you will act with that forbearance that has distinguished you heretofore.

Holt was all but telling Anderson to do nothing until the enemy was swarming at his gates, but he made it even stronger. Noting that the Confederate government "claimed" to assume the question of the forts, he wrote: "[This] has impressed the President with a belief that there will be no immediate attack on Fort Sumter, and the hope is indulged that wise and patriotic counsels may prevail and prevent it altogether." He finished by remarking that the labors of the Peace Convention added another powerful motive to avoid collision.[22]

If ever a man was cautioned, warned, adjured to keep the peace at almost any cost, it was Robert Anderson. Reading the newspapers avidly as he did, he must have scanned the speeches made by Abraham Lincoln as he proceeded to Washington. In Pittsburgh he smiled and said, "There is no crisis but an artificial one." Did Mr. Lincoln really mean that? In Trenton he said, ". . . it may be necessary to put the foot down firmly." What did Mr. Lincoln mean by that—war? The major had little respect for President Buchanan, but he was downright suspicious of the Republican Lincoln.

Relations were still far from cordial between Anderson and Captain Foster, who had had sharp disagreements at Moultrie. The two were of conflicting temperaments and beliefs, the New Hampshireman resenting the Kentuckian's Southern sympathies, the major in turn annoyed by the technicality in command making Foster responsible to engineering headquarters in Washington rather than to him. They differed about such things as the construction of the fougasses at Sumter. While there is no record of open quarrels between them, the clash of wills smouldered quietly as the undermanned staff of officers was stretched thin and deprived of sleep in filling night guard and day duty. Surgeon Crawford, who could have stood on his rights and confined himself to medical routine, gladly pitched in as officer of the day, and Lieutenants Snyder and Meade were willing to double as line officers, but Foster demurred at this as contrary to precedent. With Lieutenant Talbot's health forbidding him from doing any extra duty at all, the major doubtless was irked at Foster's adherence to army ritual under circumstances where ritual was going by the boards. Nervous tension, overwork, poor food, and everlasting sameness made Sumter a place where small annoyances were magnified, and the wonder is that the men were not frequently at each others' throats.[23]

Foster later relented on this, permitting Snyder and Meade to take their turns as officers of the day. The engineering captain was a busy man, rushing his own defenses and simultaneously watching and reporting on enemy works. With Anderson restricting his armament to the first and top tiers, open embrasures in the unused second tier were closed with masonry or lumber. The coping of the gorge parapet was cut away in front of one gun to allow it to be depressed so as to sweep the wharf with canister. The coal was long since gone, one of the construction sheds had been burned for fuel and the second was torn down and split—a process that also had the effect of clearing the parade.[24]

Using a spyglass, Foster noted with some concern the ever-increasing number of guns aimed at him. It was said that five big columbiads had arrived in Charleston from the Tredegar Iron Works in Richmond. Gangs of slaves were working far into the night to finish the battery at Cummings Point only thirteen hundred yards away, giving it a slanted armor of railroad iron. Now the Carolinians began a new three-gun battery just east of this one. Foster retaliated by mounting heavy barbette guns to bear on Cummings Point, feeling confident that Sumter's guns could knock out the bombproof batteries by concentrating on the embrasures. Yet he was well aware that Sumter's position was growing relatively weaker.[25]

"The troops on Fort Moultrie," he reported, "practiced with ball to obtain the ranges of the channel and especially of that point in the main channel where it turns toward the city. . . . The practice was excellent, all the shots striking the water nearly in the same spot; so it will be seen that the ranges are well understood now, and any vessel coming in must not expect to fare as well as the *Star of the West*." In another report he wrote with monumental formality: "I have the honor to acknowledge the receipt of a roll of letter paper from the Engineering Office." Foster noted that South Carolina had finally decided on its official state flag and raised it at Moultrie—a white palmetto and crescent on a dark blue field. In his partisan view it resembled the Jolly Roger more than anything else: "It is not a handsome or pleasant flag to look at. . . . At a distance it is not unlike a black flag, with the piratical emblem (head and cross-bones) upon it."[26]

At dawn on February 22nd, Castle Pinckney's guns boomed a thirteen-gun salute in honor of George Washington. At noon Sumter's guns responded with their own salute. Both sides honored the great patriot, certain that if he were living he would be on *their* side. Anderson was relieved that there was no sickness in his command despite the cold, and that morale was high. There could have been no higher proof of this than when two enlisted men whose terms were up decided to stay and share the fate of the garrison. The men roundly cheered a Charleston Irishman named McInerney who risked his life to row out to Sumter, ruining his white shirt by using it as a flag of truce and delivering a small supply of tobacco for the soldiers.

"I did not cross the broad Atlantic to become the citizen of only one Shtate," said McInerney.[27]

With ordinary conveniences denied them, the men became fertile in expedients. The lack of candles and lamps was an affliction on long winter nights, so the "Sumter lamp" was invented. Oil borrowed from the small supply left in the light-house was put in a coffee cup, and a wick arranged in a tin holder floated with a disc of cork.[28] There was great speculation among the soldiers as to whether their biggest guns, the ten-inch columbiads, could reach Charleston, 5,500 yards away. No one wished any harm to McInerney, but there were other Charles-tonians they would cheerfully give a little powder. The big columbiad's effective range was listed as 4,828 yards. "By making this shell eccentric," one Sumterman wrote North, "at least 500 more can be gained; and all intelligent artillerists know of certain other expedients by which the difference between this total (5328 yards) and 5500—the distance to Broad Street—can be overcome." [29]

A squad of gunners got permission to try with caution one big columbiad mounted as a mortar in the parade and aimed at Charleston. The full charge was eighteen pounds of powder, so they put in only two pounds and touched it off when the harbor was clear, certain it would carry only a short distance. The ball soared in a high arc with such carrying power that the men soon saw that two pounds was not a small charge when the gun was used as a mortar. Up and up the projectile went, the watchers suddenly growing fearful that it might reach the city's wharves. But it fell considerably short, splashing not far from one of the South Carolina guard boats, which forthwith headed for Sumter to demand an explanation. After that the gunners were satis-fied they could reach Charleston and there were no more experi-ments.[30]

The forty-five wives and children had arrived safely but in straitened circumstances at Fort Hamilton in New York, where they were given a warm welcome along with financial help by Henry Ward Beecher and his parishioners at Plymouth Church. The abolitionist Beecher had long characterized Major Ander-son as a saint, and the general Southern opinion of Beecher was aptly summarized in a Charleston news item mentioning the death of a Brooklyn man known in South Carolina: "He was a member of Beecher's church, otherwise a good man." [31]

Captain Doubleday was not surprised to receive an insulting

letter from Charleston, "informing me that, if I were ever caught in the city, an arrangement had been made to tar and feather me as an Abolitionist." [32] A different sort of letter came from Captain Edward McCready, commander of the Meagher Guards in Charleston, who had been friendly with the officers back in the pre-secession days at Moultrie. McCready urged Anderson and his men to throw off their allegiance to the United States and enter into the Confederate service—an appeal no one bothered to answer. George Cook, a Charleston photographer, came out to the fort and persuaded the officers to sit for a group portrait, even Doubleday consenting despite his conviction that the man was a spy. There was great curiosity in the city about the strange breed of officers at Sumter, and the pictures later enjoyed a brisk sale. [33]

Anderson had faithfully reported the expanding Carolina armament to Washington, but on February 28th he decided this was not enough. He called his officers together, asking each to submit in writing his estimate of the force that would be needed to relieve the fort. They were not to consult each other, and he wanted an immediate reply.

The officers furrowed their brows and went to work. When they had finished, all agreed that naval help was essential but differed as to the number of men. Anderson himself believed it would take 20,000 regulars to storm and carry the Carolina batteries and reach the fort. Foster's estimate, reflecting his mistrust of untrained men, was 10,000 regulars or 30,000 volunteers. Doubleday felt that 10,000 men with naval support could do it, while the most optimistic, Lieutenant Davis, suggested 3,000 men and six war vessels. In Captain Seymour's opinion, the enemy defenses were now so powerful that while it might be possible to sneak in a few men with a small supply of provisions, any large-scale relief or reinforcement was "virtually impossible." [34]

Anderson sealed all these opinions along with his own in a dispatch and sent it to Washington. Undoubtedly he intended it as guidance for the new President Lincoln, who would be inaugurated about the same time the dispatch reached the capital.

III

In Charleston there was disgruntlement because South Carolina, which had blazed the risky trail of secession alone, had been handed only one seat in the Confederate Cabinet and not the most important at that—the treasury, given to Charleston's own Christopher Memminger. Rhett, the archangel of secession, got nothing at all. Some hotheads even talked of seceding from the Confederacy. Memminger, a conservative, joined the chorus of Montgomery officials who were writing and telegraphing Governor Pickens to urge him to hold his horses, refrain from attack, relinquish all decision and authority to the Confederate government. Pickens, who seemed to have some difficulty in accepting his demotion in rank, was in an excited condition. He had received Wigfall's telegram and other tips from Washington warning him that reinforcements might be on the way. He wired Memminger testily:

> . . . if you do not act immediately and appoint a commander-in-chief to take charge, it will be too late. Act quickly, now, or I shall be compelled to act. Send your Commissioners to Washington now, right off, and telegraph me, or it will be beyond your control. Things look bad in Washington.[35]

Another problem was South Carolina's volunteer army, which had swollen to prodigious size, filling Charleston and the islands in the harbor with young bloods irked at inactivity and spoiling for a fight. Many of them said Pickens was a fool and maybe a mite cowardly for hesitating to snatch Sumter. Wasn't it the state's own property? Soldiering had become a Palmettoland craze, with the patricians leading the way and "best names" like Rutledge, Lowndes, and Ravenel taking their places in the ranks as well as accepting commissions. "There is a single regiment now stationed at one of the forts," an observer remarked, "whose destruction would put every distinguished family in the

P

State in mourning." [36] One company of soldiers had an aggregate wealth of more than a million dollars. Another company was commanded by an Episcopal clergyman and had ten divinity students in its ranks. Enlistment had taken all but about 150 of the students at South Carolina College. While the officers were generally clad in blue frocks with red sashes, there was great disparity among the enlisted men, who wore tunics of blue and white, green and yellow, brown and olive, and other combinations.[37]

The privations of these young aristocrats were not bitter, for they were ordering from Charleston's best provisioner, Klinck & Wickenberg, such delicacies as champagne, madeira, *pâté de foie gras,* French green peas, and Spanish cigars—Lucullan fare that would have made a Sumter man swoon. Growing bored with fine food, the men were getting restive and out of hand. In tomfoolery at Fort Moultrie, young Private Thaddeus Strawinski was killed by an accidental revolver wound. In similar horseplay among soldiers stationed at Moultrie House, Private James Allen ran into his companion's bayonet, which pierced his eye and killed him.[38]

Richard Lathers, a former Carolinian now heading a New York insurance company, picked this unpropitious time to arrive in Charleston with talk of mediation and re-cementing the Union. He was the official emissary of a group of well-intentioned Democrats in New York who held the delusion that South Carolina officials might have anything but loathing for the Union, and thought it likely that a friendly parley might bring them around. Lathers' illusions were shattered with the sudden shock of a plunge into ice water. "Secession was held to be so far above dispute," he noted, "that Unionist ideas were rather to be pitied than resented." Yet Governor Pickens received him kindly, honored him at a dinner, and said he was sorry that "this effort at the North to placate the South had come too late." [39] General Jamison took him out with a party to Fort Moultrie to witness the proficiency of the recruits there. A salute was fired for them, and Jamison was mortified to see one of the cannon, not being properly secured, tumble off the parapet when it was fired.[40]

Pickens had been howling to Montgomery for an engineering officer and a "commander-in-chief," and late in February he got the engineer in the person of Captain William Whiting, an able West Pointer from Mississippi. Whiting, the first representative in Charleston of the fledgling Confederate army, was perhaps not as diplomatic as he should have been. He made an inspection of the harbor armament and criticized much that was done. In his judgment there were too many guns aimed at the reduction of Sumter and too few placed to prevent naval entrance into the harbor—an attitude that so wounded the sensitive Charlestonians that some demanded his removal.[41]

On March 1st, Pickens got his commander-in-chief. He was Pierre Beauregard, the Louisiana Creole who had skyrocketed from major in the federal army to brigadier general in the Confederate army since his removal from command at the Military Academy. Beauregard, West Point '38, was a hero of the Mexican War, in which he had been twice wounded. A skillful man with artillery, he agreed entirely with Whiting's criticism of the gun concentration. Much as he respected Major Anderson, he saw instantly that there would be no problem in overpowering Sumter's meager garrison, or starving it into submission. The only problem was to make certain that no reinforcements or supplies could reach the fort, an end to which he bent immediate efforts. But he was tactful, careful not to offend these touchy people. Beauregard soon became a social lion in Charleston, an ambassador of good will who persuaded the chivalry that the Confederacy was worthy of their support.[42]

From Sumter, Anderson watched these developments thoughtfully. He knew Major—or rather *General* Beauregard very well. Back in 1837 when Anderson was instructor in artillery at West Point, one of his students had been Cadet Beauregard, such a keen young fellow that Anderson had marked him as a comer. When Beauregard graduated in 1838, he had been given at Anderson's request the post of assistant instructor of artillery and the two had worked together in imparting the lore of cannon to undergraduates. Yes, he knew Beauregard—vain as a peacock but generous, brilliant, magnetic—knew he would be a formidable adversary. Anderson reported to Washington:

> The presence here, as commander, of General Beauregard, recently of the U. S. Engineers, insures, I think, in a great measure the exercise of skill and sound judgment in all operations of the South Carolinians in this harbor. God grant that our country may be saved from the horrors of a fratricidal war![43]

"HOLD, OCCUPY
AND POSSESS"

> *James is in his Cabinet*
>   *Doubting and debating;*
> *Anderson's in Sumter,*
>   *Very tired of waiting.*
>
> *Pickens is in Charleston,*
>   *Blustering of blows;*
> *Thank goodness March the Fourth is near,*
>   *To nip Secession's nose.*[1]

"Thank God," wrote the diarist Strong, "the disgraceful reign of James Buchanan draws near its close. . . ."[2] Millions in the North agreed. Buchanan himself, who said wearily, "The office of President of the United States is not fit for a gentleman to hold," was overjoyed that the end was in sight. Most Southerners were not so sure. Even if Old Buck was, as Senator Benjamin said, "a senile Executive under the sinister influence of insane counsels,"[3] would not Lincoln be worse? Senator Wigfall, who had shrewd insight as well as colossal effrontery, got up in the Senate March 2nd and told the North off:

> This Federal Government is dead. The only question is, whether we will give it a decent, peaceable, Protestant burial, or whether we shall have an Irish wake at the grave. . . . I think myself it would be for the benefit of both sections that we do not have an Irish wake at our funeral; but that is for the North to decide, and not for us. . . . not if you were to hand us blank paper, and ask us to write a constitution, would we ever again be confederated with you. . . . I suppose commissioners, in a few days, will be here from the Confederate states. . . . Turn your backs upon these commissioners, attempt to reinforce the forts and retake those which we now have . . . and you will have war, and it will be war in all its stern realities.[4]

The commissioners Wigfall mentioned were Martin J. Crawford of Georgia, John Forsyth of Alabama, and A. B. Roman of Louisiana, all political veterans but handed a job that required sheer magic. They had been appointed by the Confederate government to do what two Carolina missions had failed to do, secure Sumter by negotiation. On top of that they were to negotiate for Fort Pickens, ask the government's blessing for all the federal property seized in the South, secure a recognition of Confederate independence, and conclude treaties of amity and good will between the two nations.[5]

Commissioner Crawford arrived in Washington first on March 3rd with some idea of parleying with Buchanan, but quickly gave this up. "His fears for his personal safety," Crawford wrote Confederate Secretary of State Toombs, ". . . together with the cares of state and his advanced age, render him wholly disqualified for his present position. He is as incapable now of purpose as a child." [6] Crawford stayed to see what could be done with Lincoln—that is, if Lincoln was allowed to be inaugurated.

For weeks there had been talk that Washington's many secessionists would join with rebels from outside the city, await a master signal, and take advantage of the public inaugural parade to assassinate the President-elect, seize the public buildings and the government, and proclaim Jefferson Davis ruler of the land. "O'er all there hung a shadow and a fear," remarked Virginia's handsome, secessionist Congressman Roger Pryor. Violence seemed so likely that women and children left town in droves. General Scott was as ready as he could be, but there were difficulties in maintaining secrecy. His military secretary, Lieutenant Colonel Lay, who wrote out the confidential orders for the defense of the capital, resigned a few hours later and went South. All night on March 3rd, "orderlies were dashing to and fro at breakneck speed; and guard details were marching to all points of possible danger." When March 4th dawned, the capital looked like a city bracing for a siege.[7]

Heeding rumors of a plot to blow up the Capitol, Captain C. W. Dunnington, chief of the Capitol police, examined "all sewers and secret places" in the building, finding nothing. Dunnington may not have been too conscientious, for he likewise soon went South. Thirty thousand spectators lined the streets when Mr. Buchanan called at Willard's for Mr. Lincoln and the two were driven up an avenue bristling with cavalry and squads of sharpshooters on rooftops ready to shoot anyone who made a false move. The report of a plan to dynamite the platform on which Lincoln would take the oath of office caused a detail of soldiers to be stationed around and under it. Flying artillery was posted at strategic intersections. Had some wag exploded a firecracker, blood might have flowed.[8]

There was no violence. The retiring and incoming Presidents rode up the street behind a huge float in which the states—all of them, seceded or not—were represented by little girls dressed in white and waving small American flags. One Unionist took courage at the sight. "The venerable form, pallid face, and perfectly white hair of Mr. Buchanan," he reflected, "contrasted powerfully with the tall figure, coal-black hair, and rugged features of Mr. Lincoln, and suggested that the exhausted energies of the old were to be followed by the vigorous strength of the new administration." [9]

On the platform near the domeless Capitol, Lincoln put steel-bowed spectacles on his nose, unaware of the soldiers under him, and read the words the whole nation was waiting for, the words that would tell whether this awkward-looking man had some solution for the challenge his predecessor had avoided and could be avoided no longer. What would he do about Sumter, about Fort Pickens, about the whole Confederacy? Unlike most orators of the South, Lincoln spoke in pacific tones, without bluster or threat. Two of his statements gave clues that men would ponder everywhere:

". . . no state, upon its own mere motion, can lawfully get out of the Union. . . ."

"The power confided in me will be used to hold, occupy and possess the property and places belonging to the government. . . ."

After his memorable closing appeal that "We must not be enemies," and the swearing-in by ancient Chief Justice Taney, the listeners dispersed. Senator Wigfall rushed to the nearest telegraph office and dispatched a message to Governor Pickens saying in part: "Inaugural means war. There is strong ground for belief that reinforcements will be speedily sent. Be vigilant." [10] James Buchanan, private citizen, went to the home of his good friend Robert Ould, United States Attorney for the District of Columbia—another official soon to head South—and received farewell calls from his Cabinet. There his counselors exclaimed about a report received that morning from Major Anderson that had Joseph Holt dumfounded. Buchanan was like a small boy at school's end heading for the swimming hole. He washed his hands of the report, saying it was a matter for the new administration. But Holt could not shrug it off because it seemed to reflect on his stewardship and also because he was going to carry over as Secretary of War until Lincoln's man, Mr. Cameron, arrived in Washington.

In the report, Anderson wrote, "I confess that I would not be willing to risk my reputation on an attempt to throw reinforcements into this harbor within the time for our relief rendered necessary by the limited supply of our provisions, and with a view of holding possession of the same, with a force of less than twenty thousand good and disciplined men." He enclosed the estimates of his nine officers, all agreeing that it would take a large force plus strong naval support. He added a list of his provisions—a good supply of salt pork, but bread for only twenty-eight days, and coffee, beans, rice, and sugar for periods of only eight to forty days.[11]

It is safe to say that Anderson, in an effort to steer the new President away from reinforcing Sumter and starting war, was giving an outside estimate of the forces needed. Yet his estimate was not appreciably higher than Foster's. Even the radical Doubleday, who was itching to stop stalling and let the slaveocrats have war, gave a figure of ten thousand men, and the Vermonter Captain Seymour doubted the success of any expedition at all.

Until then, Holt had believed he was handing over to Lincoln a fort that, if he wished it, stood a reasonable chance of being

reinforced. It would hardly do credit to the Buchanan regime
to present the new President with a bastion that was lost and
beyond help. Yet if Anderson and his officers were right, this
was precisely the case, because there was no force available such
as they named.

Appalled, Holt called on Lincoln next day and showed him
the report. The President read it carefully, undoubtedly turning over in his mind the letters he had received from Ulysses
Doubleday. Was Anderson exaggerating the strength of the
rebels so that Sumter would be handed over to them? He asked
Holt a confidential question: Did he have any doubts of Anderson's loyalty? Holt said he did not, although he admitted later
that his faith in the major was shaken.[12]

He told Lincoln the report took him wholly by surprise. He
reviewed Anderson's dispatches saying he was now where "the
Government can reinforce me at its leisure," that he could
command the harbor "as long as the Government wishes to
keep it." He explained how Anderson had been informed that
an effort would be made to reinforce him whenever he felt it
necessary. Anderson had not asked for it except on February
5th, when he suggested "a small party successfully slipping in"
—an idea the administration had rejected as impracticable.
Captain Foster, too, had written, "I do not consider it good
policy to send reinforcements here at this time. We can hold
our own as long as it is necessary to do so." In the light of all
this, Holt said, he was simply staggered at the estimate that it
would take thousands of men and a fleet of warships to reach
the fort and hold it.[13]

The secretary made out a superficially convincing case that
in reality was full of holes. He did not mention that Anderson
had reported on January 6th: "We are now, or soon will be,
cut off from all communication, unless by means of a powerful
fleet, which shall have the ability to carry the batteries at the
mouth of this harbor." Nor did he cite the major's February
5th report that the Carolina armament was so formidable that
it "will make it impossible for any hostile force, other than a
large and well-appointed one, to enter this harbor, and the

chances are that it will then be at a great sacrifice of life." That report alone, a full month earlier, should have been warning enough for Holt.

Added to that, both Anderson and Foster, ignorant of administration policy, had thought it possible that they would be peacefully withdrawn from Sumter, as indicated by Foster's statement, "a conflict here and a civil war can only be avoided by giving up this fort sooner or later." Holt, walking on eggs, had not disabused them of this notion, had not informed them that Sumter was to be held permanently, regardless of consequences. On the contrary, he had repeatedly warned Anderson to keep the peace, stay "strictly on the defensive," let the floating battery come up and get ready so long as it did not actually start shooting. Too much responsibility had been laid on the major's shoulders, and Holt was unworthy in blaming him for Sumter's present situation when the fault was the administration's own. Neither Holt nor Buchanan were justified in abdicating responsibility for the top-level decision of reinforcement and war, and handing it over to an artillery officer who was ordered to preserve the peace. While Anderson was temporarily overoptimistic in the flush of his successful move to Sumter, he and Foster thereafter had reported faithfully the ominous buildup of South Carolina batteries as well as Sumter's own supply situation. A subaltern with a pencil in the War Department could have added up these reports to arrive at an inescapable conclusion: that reinforcement was daily becoming more difficult and dangerous, and that Anderson's supplies were getting low. The administration had been too concerned about Sumter as a political problem to think of it in terms of logistics. Now Anderson had tossed the logistics at them and it floored them.[14]

Lincoln, unaware of all this, logically had misgivings about Anderson's loyalty. He had never contemplated giving up the few Southern forts still held by the government, nor had he intended to allow the Confederacy to keep unprotested those illegally seized. Ten weeks earlier he had let General Scott know through an intermediary, "I shall be obliged to him to be as well prepared as he can to either *hold* or *retake* the forts, as the case may require, at and after the inauguration." [15] In his original draft of his inaugural speech he had written, "All the power at my disposal will be used to reclaim the public property and places which have fallen; to hold, occupy and possess these. . . ." Seward, who had gone over the inaugural with him, all but choked on this. At his earnest entreaty, Lincoln excised the "reclaim" part and let it go with the much milder promise to "hold, occupy and possess" the forts.[16] Now even that limited stipulation seemed impossible to make good. Sumter, the most important fort of all—the one in secession's birthplace, the one the nation had come to regard as the ultimate test case in the government's ability to maintain itself—seemed beyond hope. It must have been a shaken President who asked General Scott's advice in the matter. Scott replied that he agreed entirely with Anderson's estimate, finishing:

"Evacuation seems almost inevitable, and in this view our distinguished Chief Engineer (Brigadier General Totten) concurs—if indeed the worn-out garrison be not assaulted and carried in the present week." [17]

The new administration was faced by disaster from the very moment of its inauguration. In Lincoln's own words, his duty seemed reduced "to the mere matter of getting the garrison safely out of the fort." [18] This was precisely what Seward wanted to do, but the idea was so repugnant to the President that he could not bring himself to give the order. Anderson's provisions could be stretched for more than a month. Lincoln would see if some alternative could be found. Meanwhile there was Fort Pickens at Pensacola to think about, still being held by Lieutenant Slemmer and his small force. By the terms of the truce between Buchanan and the Floridians, Captain Vogdes and his command of eighty-six artillerymen and 115 marines had not landed but still waited in the *Brooklyn,* which remained offshore with three other men-of-war. Lincoln regarded the truce as ended with Buchanan's retirement. An order was sent via the warship *Mohawk* for Vogdes to land his men and reinforce Slemmer— a step which it was felt would secure Pickens and remove any worries on that score. The big question, as it had been for three months, was Sumter.[19]

On this question—as on almost the whole problem of policy toward secession—Lincoln and Secretary of State Seward were diametrically opposed. During the previous winter Seward had managed to give such a strong impression that he would run the new administration that newspapers had freely predicted he would be the "master spirit." Lincoln had been annoyed enough to tell a reporter that "Seward was not nominated at Chicago" and to suggest that he would lead his own administration, but the Secretary of State was a hard man to slap down. He assumed the attitude of kingpin of the Cabinet with such breezy assurance that some of its members were annoyed. He sincerely believed that appeasement was now the only possible policy, regarding himself as the new Henry Clay who would tide the nation over its crisis and bring it together again in eventual reunion.

To be sure, Lincoln was against this at the moment. But Lincoln was a backwoods lawyer, a newcomer in Washington with almost no experience in national affairs, and Seward seemed to have no doubt that the logic of events plus the influence of Seward would win him around. The Secretary of State dove headlong into incredible error because of one bad mistake: He thought he could run Lincoln.[20]

II

Commissioner Crawford, the envoy from secessia, now let it be known that he was in Washington in the expectation of negotiating with the government, and if the administration should refuse to recognize him there would be no preventing an attack on the forts. Seward knew better than to fall into Buchanan's error of granting audiences to emissaries of seceded states—a step which would automatically give them official standing and imply recognition that they represented a foreign state. He was just as determined to save the peace by parleying with them indirectly, through intermediaries.

Through ex-Senator William Gwin, a California secessionist,

Seward assured Crawford on March 6th of the government's determination to settle the quarrel peacefully. Lincoln, he said in effect, did not fully understand the condition of the country but could be expected to learn fast under Seward's tutelage. The South need not worry at all about Lincoln's promise to "hold, occupy and possess" the forts because he had qualified it with the words "so far as practicable" and in other ways. Two days later, Seward repeated through Gwin that "war must be averted" and gave in a kernel his policy for rescuing the nation: "Saving the border states to the Union by moderation and justice, the people of the cotton states, unwillingly led into secession, will rebel against their leaders, and reconstruction will follow." [21]

John Forsyth, the second Confederate commissioner, had now arrived. He and Crawford had to chuckle about Seward's delusion that the Southern people would soon be clamoring to get back into the Union. Let the secretary dream his dreams. He was as wrong as a man could be, but as long as it inspired his peace policy it was just what the commissioners wanted because it would allow the Confederacy to organize itself in tranquillity and instead of causing any Southern states to seek return to the Union, as Seward so naively believed, would cement the new nation to the South in prosperity and self-sufficiency. The commissioners—just as Hayne had been seven weeks earlier—were anxious to gain time, which was on their side. Yet they had instructions not to *show* they were playing for time. They let Seward know, again through Gwin, that he had better get on with his negotiations because the Confederacy could not countenance delay while the foreign United States flag flew over Forts Sumter and Pickens.[22]

Seward, in his reply through the same roundabout channel, said he could not be expected to act quickly. The administration was snarled in the confusion of its first days in office, the President was besieged by office seekers and pressed by radical Republicans who wanted war. If he was compelled to take a stand now, Seward warned, he could not answer for the result.[23]

The commissioners got better news by reading the papers.

Their first and most essential condition was that Sumter be evacuated, and the newspapers were printing reports that it *would* be evacuated. One of Seward's closest friends among the newspapermen was James E. Harvey, a former Charlestonian who for some years had been Washington correspondent for the New York *Tribune*. Indeed, Seward was so fond of Harvey that he would soon persuade Lincoln to nominate him as minister to Portugal. Harvey had gone to school with Judge Magrath in South Carolina, and on March 11th Harvey telegraphed his old friend Magrath that Anderson would be withdrawn. If Harvey, who was so close to Seward and ordinarily so well informed, said this, there must be something in it.[24]

The commissioners set a clever trap for Seward. Gwin had now left town, so they found another intermediary in Robert M. T. Hunter, the secessionist Senator from Virginia. Through Hunter they informed the Secretary of State that they would give him a twenty-day breathing spell on the condition that he would in turn give them an honor-bound written pledge that there would be no change in the military status at Sumter and Pickens. As they reported to Toombs, if Seward signed such an agreement, it "would be a virtual recognition of us as the representatives of a power entitled to be treated with by this government." [25] So far the secretary had been busily communicating indirectly with them, but avoiding them personally as if they had smallpox. They now added a demand that he give them at least an informal interview.

When Hunter handed this message to Seward on March 11th, the secretary was visibly uneasy, saying he would have to consult the President. Next day he handed Hunter a note showing that Lincoln refused to snap at such bait:

"It will not be in my power to receive the gentlemen of whom we spoke yesterday. You will please explain to them that this decision proceeds solely on public grounds, and not from any want of personal respect." [26]

It must have made Crawford and Forsyth feel like lepers indeed that the secretary not only refused to see them but even avoided mention of their names or official capacities. They decided they could no longer permit being unrecognized and forced to deal with the United States clandestinely, like small boys passing notes at school. On March 13th their secretary visited the State Department to present their first formal announcement of their presence in Washington and their request for an official audience.

This put Seward in a fearful dilemma. He had tried to keep the commissioners satisfied with indirect dealings and had failed. Their formal note meant that either he must recognize them, meet them officially, or they would quit Washington in anger. As Wigfall had said, "Turn your backs upon these commissioners, and it will be war with all its stern realities." Seward's whole peace policy, his assurance that he would dominate the administration and bring about agreement, teetered on the edge of ruin. The secretary, a man of expedients, cast about for a new expedient that would save him. He delayed his reply to the note a day. He delayed it another day. But he could not delay it forever.

Although Seward did not know it, the commissioners were not quite in such a hurry as they made out. True, Toombs in Montgomery informed them, "you [are] not supplicants for its [the United States'] grace and favor, and willing to loiter in the antechambers of officials to patiently await their answer to your petition. . . ." But Forsyth replied March 14th to Montgomery: "We are playing a game in which time is our best advocate. . . . There is a terrific fight in the Cabinet. Our policy is to encourage the peace element in the fight, and at least blow up the Cabinet on the question." [27]

Seward must have been near the end of his rope on March 15th when he addressed a memorandum to the commissioners denying that they represented a foreign power or that he had any authority to recognize them. But he did not send this note to them. He merely filed it in the State Department. The note meant war, and he was still hoping for something to turn up to save him. That very same day something did turn up in the person of Associate Justice John Archibald Campbell of the Supreme Court.

An able, taciturn Alabamian, Campbell was a believer in state rights who yet wanted to save the Union—a ticklish position for him since his own state had seceded two months earlier. On March 15th Seward had a conversation with Campbell's colleague, Justice Samuel Nelson, telling Nelson something of his dilemma. He wanted peace, he said, and was working tooth and nail for it, but now he was embarrassed by the presence of the Confederate commissioners, demanding a reception which the administration would not allow him to give them.

Nelson, a New Yorker and a good friend of Seward, spoke to Campbell about this. Campbell returned with Nelson to talk with Seward, both justices urging him to receive the Confederate emissaries. The secretary admitted he could not do so even if he wanted to because Lincoln and the rest of the Cabinet were unanimously against it.

"Talk with Montgomery Blair and Mr. Bates," he said, "with Mr. Lincoln himself, they are Southern men, and see what they say. No, if Jefferson Davis had known of the state of things here, he never would have sent those Commissioners. It is enough to deal with one thing at a time. The evacuation of Sumter is as much as the administration can bear." [28]

If Justice Campbell had been a swooning sort, he might have collapsed into a chair. He was aware that the abandonment of Sumter was an essential condition with the Confederacy. There had been rumors of it in the papers, but here was the Secretary of State himself admitting it had been decided. Campbell well knew that the commissioners would be overjoyed to learn that this cardinal point had been granted. He must have had trouble concealing his elation as he agreed that quitting Sumter was a long step in the direction of peace. He instantly offered to serve as intermediary to inform the commissioners of this, adding that if Seward consented he would write Jefferson Davis about it— a consent the secretary gladly gave.

"What shall I say on the subject of Fort Sumter?" Campbell asked.

"You may say to him [Davis]," Seward replied, "that before that letter reaches him—how far is it to Montgomery?"

"Three days," Campbell replied.

"You may say to him that before that letter reaches him the telegraph will have informed him that Sumter will have been evacuated."

The justice could have been forgiven a desire to pinch himself. And what, he went on, should he inform Davis about the forts in the Gulf? By this he referred chiefly to Fort Pickens, still held by Lieutenant Slemmer.

"We contemplate no action as to them," the secretary said. "We are satisfied with the position of things there." [29]

It seems hardly possible that Seward did not know that three days earlier General Scott had ordered the reinforcement of Pickens with Captain Vogdes' force—an order still en route South by warship. If Seward knew this, he was punishing truth when he said no action was contemplated there. The secretary was playing a perilous game. When Justice Campbell left, he was jubilant in the belief that he had the administration's pledge that Sumter was about to be evacuated and Pickens would not be reinforced. He had nothing of the sort. He had Seward's word, which in the case of Pickens was either false or misinformed, and as to Sumter was misleading and premature. The administration had *not* decided to quit Sumter and Seward knew it. He was gambling everything on the belief that he could speedily influence Lincoln to give up the fort, sure that the President had no other course.

Campbell immediately visited the commissioners to tell them he had "perfect confidence" that Sumter would be handed over to the Confederacy within five days, thereby giving Seward two extra days of grace. He likewise expressed his perfect confidence that no change in the military status was planned at any of the forts. The Washington administration, he said, was convinced "the secession movements were short-lived and would wither under sunshine." He therefore urged the commissioners not to press their demand for a reception, asking for a ten-day delay to give time for the effect of the evacuation of Sumter to be measured.

The commissioners were only too happy now to let that slide.

Q

The winning of Sumter was their first diplomatic victory and a big one, even if they personally had little to do with it. Crawford said he was willing to risk a little sunshine. But from whom, he asked Campbell, did he get his assurance? Was it from Seward? Campbell replied firmly that he could not name his informant. They would have to trust him, Campbell. But the commissioners knew it had to be Seward, and they happily dispatched a message to Montgomery with the good news.[30]

III

While Abraham Lincoln was embarrassed by a shortage of men bearing arms for the Union, he had a large surplus of men anxious to draw pay—an army of office seekers who hounded him night and day, all but invading his bedroom. The New York *Herald* suggested a solution: "Major Anderson says twenty thousand men can relieve him and reinforce Fort Sumter. There are over fifty thousand patriots now at the command of Mr. Lincoln, waiting for office. Send them along." [31]

The President had to cope with jobhunters while he wrestled with the Sumter problem. At his first full-dress Cabinet council on March 9th, his advisers—Seward excepted—were stunned at the news that General Scott had given up on Sumter. All of them—Seward excepted—had taken it for granted that the fort must be held. They realized that Sumter had become a principle, representing in miniature the quarrel between the United States and the so-called Confederacy which none of them recognized as a legitimate government.[32] A backdown on Sumter would be not only a humiliating defeat for the new administration but also a cruel blow to the prestige of the Union in the eyes of the nation and of the world. It was the Cabinet's youngest and lowest-ranking member, Postmaster General Montgomery Blair, who held this view so strongly that it fairly oozed from his pores.

Blair, the tall, spare, forty-seven-year-old son of "Old Man" Frank Blair, who had counseled Jackson, had been watching developments all winter from his Maryland home with increasing suspicions of William Seward. He felt that the New Yorker had been hobnobbing with traitors, laying plans to junk the Republican platform and steamroller Lincoln into granting more concessions to the South. In his opinion the Buchanan administration had already made far too many concessions, and if Lincoln made any more the Union would be, as Dixie statesmen were so fond of putting it, dead. It happened that Blair and Gustavus Fox were brothers-in-law. For many weeks Blair had encouraged Fox in his plan to reinforce Sumter, had used whatever influence he had with General Scott to promote it, and now that he was in the Lincoln Cabinet was pushing it with all his might. From the start, Blair recognized Seward as the opponent he must somehow beat if the administration was to be kept from a course he considered fatal.[33]

Blair and his Cabinet colleagues now watched Lincoln parade a group of military and naval experts before them to give their views on the practicability of reinforcing Major Anderson. It did not simplify matters to find that the navy advisers differed sharply from the army chiefs. Commodore Stringham and Captain Ward felt that the danger of running the enemy's batteries was slight, since light and speedy vessels would be crossing the line of fire in darkness, offering the poorest of targets. They agreed that the greatest danger would be in landing at Sumter, on which there was a heavy concentration of Carolina batteries. General Scott and General Totten, the seventy-two-year-old chief engineer of the army, thought there would be disastrous losses in forcing an entrance without even mentioning the dangers of landing at Sumter in a hail of shot and shell.[34]

". . . the time for succoring Sumter has passed away nearly a month ago," Scott said. He insisted that, brushing all question of danger aside, reinforcement was logistically impossible. In his view it would require five thousand regulars and twenty thousand volunteers, plus a fleet of war vessels. The navy was so scattered that it would take four months to assemble the necessary ships, while to get the men needed would require a special act of Congress and six or eight months to raise and organize. Since Anderson's food could last only about a month, the futility of such a plan was plain to be seen.[35] Feeling it perfectly

demonstrated that the garrison had to get out, the general felt
that the sooner it quit Sumter the better, and he had already
drafted an order to Anderson to that effect which he wished to
send:

> SIR: The time having been allowed to pass by when it was
> practicable to fit out an expedition adequate to the succor of
> your garrison, before the exhaustion of its means of subsistence
> —you will, after communicating your purpose to His Excellency,
> the Governor of So. Carolina,—engage suitable water transpor-
> tation, & peacefully evacuate Fort Sumter—so long gallantly
> held—& with your entire command embark for New York. . . .[36]

The prestige of General Scott was enormous, his military
ability unquestioned. When even the navy officers began to lose
their optimism about reinforcing Sumter, most of the Cabinet
came around to the reluctant opinion that evacuation was a hard
necessity. Even Lincoln began to share this view. But not Montgomery Blair. Blair, who had been tapped for West Point by
Andrew Jackson and had served in the Florida War before resigning his commission to enter law, was the only Cabinet member with military experience. He remembered Old Hickory,
remembered his prompt and effective dealing with the nullification crisis in South Carolina three decades earlier and his ringing declaration, "The Union must and shall be preserved." Blair
felt that way now. He suspected—and rightly—that General
Scott had come under the influence of Seward and was following
Seward's lead in advocating evacuation. Therefore Scott's opinion might be founded less on strictly military considerations
than on Seward's pet theory that secession was just a temporary
political difficulty and if you let it take its course it would soon
"wither in the sunshine."

Blair held this theory to be dangerous nonsense. A combative
man, when he took hold of an idea he seized it like a bulldog.
The idea he was gripping now was that the very life of the
Union was at stake at Sumter, that its evacuation would be a
deathblow. On March 12th he telegraphed his brother-in-law
Fox in New York, asking him to come to Washington.[37]

Captain Fox arrived on the next train. On the morning of the thirteenth Blair hurried him to the White House, where Fox outlined his plan to Lincoln. The expedition he proposed would consist of a transport, two warships, and three powerful light-draft tugs to be hired in New York. The boilers and engines of the tugs would be protected on each side by layers of cotton bales. At Charleston the soldiers would be transferred from the transport to the tugs. The men-of-war—and Major Anderson's guns—would keep any enemy naval opposition at a distance. At night, two hours before high water, the tugs would steam for Sumter via the Swash Channel, within relieving distance of each other, with only the Moultrie and Cummings Point batteries to contend with. Since both of these batteries would be about thirteen hundred yards distant and would be firing in the darkness at rapidly moving targets, Fox thought the danger only nominal and the chances of success excellent—so good that he was not only willing but anxious to risk his life in the effort.[38]

Lincoln must have been impressed by the enthusiasm of this thirty-nine-year-old ex-navy man who had no official responsibility and yet was eager to assume it. Blair argued that the plan was perfectly feasible, and the President was at least partially convinced. The nation's interest in Sumter was attested by the hundreds of letters coming in from ordinary citizens, some suggesting schemes for relieving the fort. One man wrote that a "submarine vessel" could carry reinforcements unnoticed to Sumter. Another advised the use of balloons to drop supplies within the walls. The rumors that the fort would be evacuated had aroused strong protest. The Philadelphia *Bulletin* remarked, "The Inaugural declared that he [Lincoln] would 'hold, occupy and possess' the forts, and in a week's time after that we have the announcement that Fort Sumter is to be given up."[39] George T. Strong's reaction to the evacuation rumor came out in a wail of disgust: "The bird of our country is a debilitated chicken disguised in eagle feathers. We have never been a nation; we are only an aggregate of communities, ready to fall apart at the first serious shock. . . . We are a weak, divided, disgraced people, unable to maintain our national existence.

. . . I shall never go abroad. That question is settled. I should be ashamed to show my nose in the meanest corner of Europe." [40]

All reports to the contrary, Lincoln was not yet ready to give up on Sumter. He did not let Scott send the withdrawal order. He had a month before Anderson would be starved into submission, unless South Carolina meanwhile should take the initiative by attacking the fort. Entirely apart from the military problem, he was concerned about the political effect that would be produced by reinforcing the fort or by evacuating it. There was an intermediate step possible—that of making an effort merely to send provisions rather than sending troops. On March 15th he asked his Cabinet to give him written answers to this question:

"Assuming it to be possible to now provision Fort Sumter, under all the circumstances is it wise to attempt it?" [41]

This was the same day on which Seward had given Justice Campbell his assurance that Sumter would be evacuated within three days. The question was still far from settled, but the Secretary of State was cocksure it would be settled his way. In his reply to Lincoln's query, Seward opposed any attempt to supply the fort, because it would start war just as surely as an effort to send in reinforcements and was just as certain to fail. He returned to his familiar theme that conciliation—that is, the voluntary abandonment of Sumter—would cement the border states on the Union side and ultimately win the seceded states back to the Union:

. . . I have believed firmly that everywhere, even in South Carolina, devotion to the Union is a profound and permanent national sentiment, which, although it may be suppressed and silenced by terror for a time, could if encouraged, be ultimately relied upon to rally the people of the seceding states to reverse . . . all the popular acts of Legislatures and conventions by which they were hastily and violently committed to disunion. . . . [42]

Secretaries Welles of Navy, Cameron of War, Smith of Interior, and Attorney General Bates agreed in substance with

Seward that the risk was greater than the gain and that since Sumter's loss seemed only a question of time it was the part of wisdom to withdraw. Secretary Chase of Treasury returned a qualified opinion containing a good many hedgings before expressing his judgment that an attempt should be made to reach the fort.[43] Only Postmaster General Blair came out with a flat-footed appeal to provision *and* reinforce Sumter that sounded like a clarion call:

> . . . [Secession] has grown . . . into the form of an organized government in seven States, and up to this moment nothing has been done to check its progress or prevent its being regarded either at home or abroad as a successful revolution.
>
> Every hour of acquiescence in this condition of things, and especially every new conquest made by the rebels, strengthens their hands at home and their claim to recognition as an independent people abroad.
>
> It has from the beginning, and still is treated practically as a lawful proceeding, and the honest and Union-loving people in those States must by a continuance of this policy become reconciled to the new Government, and, though founded in wrong, come to regard it as rightful government. . . .
>
> I believe that Fort Sumter may be provisioned and relieved by Captain Fox with little risk. . . . This would completely demoralize the rebellion. . . . No expense or care should therefore be spared to achieve this success. . . . Nor will the result be materially different to the nation if the attempt fails and its gallant leader and followers are lost. It will in any event vindicate the hardy courage of the North, and the determination of the people and their President to maintain the authority of the Government, and this is all that is wanting, in my judgment, to restore it.
>
> You should give no thought for the commander and his comrades in this enterprise. They willingly take the hazard for the sake of the country, and the honor which, successful or not, they will receive from you and the lovers of free Government in all lands.[44]

Blair was emphatic and eloquent, but he was a voice alone. None of these gentlemen knew that the question they were debating so gravely had already been decided by Seward, and that he had gone ahead on his own to assure the South that Sumter *would* be evacuated, and very soon too, as if the President and the rest of the Cabinet had no concern in the matter. The Secretary of State must have been relieved nevertheless to find four Cabinet members on his side, one on the fence and only one opposed. General Scott was with him too, as was General Totten. True, the decision was still the President's to make, but surely he would never go against such a weight of military and political counsel.[45]

So Seward went full speed ahead while Lincoln continued to withhold judgment. The President considered the idea of quitting Sumter if in return he could win a compensating victory such as an assurance that pivotal Virginia would remain on the Union side. Barring such a gain, he could not forsake his feeling that Sumter was an obligation he had assumed when he became President, that his promise to "hold, occupy and possess" the forts certainly meant Sumter above all. He was skeptical of Seward's rosy picture of the South—even South Carolina—as being vibrant with a powerful Union sentiment temporarily muzzled by fear, a sentiment that needed only a little coddling to bring it out of hiding.

Lincoln needed more light. Mrs. Doubleday, now in Washington, was surprised when the President called on her to ask if he might see her husband's letters to help him form a better picture of the situation in Sumter.[46] That was not enough. He sent Captain Fox off to Charleston to confer with Major Anderson and learn the actual condition of the fort and its garrison. A few days later he dispatched his good friends Ward Lamon and Stephen Hurlbut to Charleston to measure the temper of the people and find if Mr. Seward was right in his belief that hordes of Unionists there were merely letting their national loyalty lie dormant for the nonce.

IV

A devotee of chess, General Winfield Scott played to win and hated to lose. In the midst of one game he left the table to spit into the fireplace, returned, and was soon checkmated. He brooded over the loss for a time, then said bitterly, "Do you know why I lost that game? It was because I got up to spit." [47]

Throughout his career he had covered himself with laurels as long as he concentrated on the military chessboard, and taken croppers when he strayed away to spit into the political grate. Now he was leaving the table again.

After his lifetime of loyal service, it is not surprising that the general felt he had risen above the limited status of military adviser and had some claim to influence policy. His chief error lay in his belief that Seward was running the new administration—a belief Seward had fostered since he held it himself. When Scott ran for President in 1852, Seward had been his most intimate counselor and the two had been warm friends ever since. Now Scott quickly accepted the New Yorker as top man and, with his strong aversion to civil war, fell in easily with Seward's theory that if secession were given its head, it would "wither in the sunshine." The general was Seward's man, entirely unaware that his king was in danger. He had long advocated Anderson's reinforcement, but now he thought the garrison should be withdrawn not only because of the risk of a reinforcing attempt but because withdrawal would, as Mr. Seward predicted, have such a happy effect in the South that Unionism would stage a triumphant comeback there.[48]

If Scott was straying, Seward was far afield. On March 15th he had assured Campbell that Sumter would be evacuated within three days. On the twentieth, Commissioner Crawford telegraphed Beauregard in Charleston asking if Anderson was preparing to quit the fort. Not at all, Beauregard replied. In fact, his men could be seen working on the defenses. Next day, Campbell once more called on Seward, again taking with him Justice Nelson. His reason for this was that neither he nor the commissioners held complete faith in Seward, whose reputation for veracity was not without flaw, and Nelson's presence would hold the secretary to account for what he said.[49]

Seward reassured the two justices, speaking cheerfully about the prospects for peace. They must not worry, he said, about a little delay. The President was merely taking a bit more time than expected about ordering the evacuation of Sumter, but they could depend on its being done. He also repeated his assurance about Fort Pickens, saying that status there would not be altered.

"You shall know," he said, "whenever any contrary purpose is determined on." [50]

Campbell returned to the commissioners and reported to them in writing his "unabated confidence" that Sumter would be given up and there would be no change at Pickens. The commissioners did not mind the delay so long as they could depend on the promise, since their secret instructions were to "play with Seward" and gain time for the South to prepare. But Campbell's confidence was not quite as unabated as he made out. The commissioners—in fact the Confederate government itself—were depending on *him* to make good the promises, and if he defaulted he would be in a pretty pickle. Uneasy, Campbell saw Justice Nelson that night before he left for New York and asked him if Seward could be trusted.

"He will not deceive you," Nelson said firmly—an opinion that quieted the Alabamian's doubts, for Nelson had known Seward for years.[51]

The secretary was deceiving no one any more than himself. In his sublime self-confidence he had made commitments he felt sure he could fulfill. He still thought he could fulfill them, but Lincoln was moving so slowly that Seward could not make good within the time limit he had set, and he was feeling a trace of uneasiness himself. The third Confederate commissioner, André Roman, had been delayed by illness but had recently arrived in Washington. Through another intermediary, Seward set about to reassure Roman and explain the delay. On March 23rd he had a heart-to-heart talk with his good friend Baron Stoeckl, the veteran Russian minister in Washington. He was certain his peace policy would prevail, he said, but he had to fight the "ultra-Republicans" to bring it to reality and the difficulties he was working under should be considered. He suggested that Baron Stoeckl invite him to the Russian legation for tea on the twenty-fifth, and that he also invite Commissioner Roman. Thus the two men could meet "accidentally" and have a chat over a cup of tea. The baron, anxious to aid the cause of peace, was delighted. He reported the entire conversation to Roman, as Seward intended. Mr. Roman said he would be pleased to have tea with the secretary even on an accidental basis. So far none of the commissioners had had so much as a glass of water with him.

Next day Seward ruined the tea party. He sent his regrets to Baron Stoeckl. If the newspapers should learn he was munching a scone with the Confederate commissioner even by pure coincidence, there would be the devil to pay.[52]

A DEAR,

DELIGHTFUL PLACE

Marooned at Sumter, Major Anderson had to depend for news on the papers, which everybody knew were full of nonsense, and on personal letters, which were as untrustworthy. Mr. Cameron, the new Secretary of War, seemed even less inclined than Holt to communicate with the fort. He sent not a word. A curtain of silence shut the garrison off from Washington at a time when a letter of mere greeting or acknowledgment would have given a cheering lift. The men wondered if they were disowned by the new administration.

Anderson did not know that his report on the number of men needed to reinforce him had agitated the President and caused several tension-filled Cabinet meetings. He did not know that Mr. Lincoln entertained some doubt as to his loyalty. He was likewise unaware that Mr. Seward would make and break a date for tea, all because of Sumter. What he did know was that under General Beauregard the Carolinians were showing even more energy than before and that during the first week in March nine more 24-pound guns along with cargoes of ammunition were landed on Cummings Point. It was evident they were strengthening their batteries on Morris Island and adding more.

"It appears to me," he reported to Washington, "that vessels will even now, from the time they cross the bar, be under fire from the batteries on Morris Island until they get under the walls of this work. I do not speak of the batteries which have been constructed on Sullivan's Island, as I am not certain of their positions. Fort Moultrie will, of course, be a very formidable enemy." [1]

Unlike General Scott, the major knew he would be overstepping his duty if he offered advice on policy, and yet his fervent hope that the new and untried Lincoln administration would not make the mistake of "putting the foot down" at Sumter was implicit in his measured words. As always, he sent this report to Colonel Samuel Cooper, adjutant general of the army for twelve years. He was unaware that Cooper, a native of New York who had married a relative of Virginia's Senator Mason, had resigned two days earlier and gone South to take an identical post with the Confederate army.

On March 8th one of the Cummings Point guns loosed a ball that soared across the intervening water and lit with a splash very close to the mine-surrounded Sumter wharf. The garrison was immediately alive with excitement. The guns facing the point were readied, the men itching to blaze away at the enemy responsible for their troubles. "One and all desired to fight it out as soon as possible," Doubleday noted.[2] To their disgust, black-bearded Major P. F. Stevens—still toasted in Charleston for sending the *Star of the West* packing—was rowed over from the island to offer his apologies for the accidental shot.

By this time Sumter had become a dank prison of such boredom and discomfort that the men would have welcomed war if for no other reason than the change it would bring. The supply of fresh meat and vegetables that had come irregularly from Charleston for a time was now cut off and once again they were condemned to a dreary fare consisting largely of salt pork. The third construction shack on the parade had been demolished for fuel; the blacksmith shop would have to be next, and its equipment was already being moved into a second tier casemate.[3]

Sumter's only connection with the outer world was the daily boat plying by Governor Pickens' permission to Fort Johnson to pick up the mail. It must have been through talk heard on one of these trips that Captain Foster learned that hot-shot furnaces had been furnished to some of the Carolina batteries. The increasingly heavy Confederate armament on Cummings Point worried the captain because it bore obliquely on the weak gorge wall, the fort's backside, which was lined with windows and ventilators. Foster's crew essayed to protect the windows by applying heavy iron shields. Two 32-pounders were added to the gorge's armament, and one of the monster ten-inch columbiads mounted near the right gorge angle would roar a destructive answer to Cummings Point.[4]

The question uppermost in the minds of both Anderson and Foster was: What would the new administration do? No word came from Secretary Cameron. No word came from General Scott. To the beleaguered officers, awaiting the instructions that would decide their fate, the continued silence from Washington seemed almost a studied affront. In Charleston, the *Courier* echoed the problem of the hour: "Well, what is it, peace or war?" [5]

Anderson must have been overwhelmed with conflicting doubt and hope when the newspapers reported March 11th "on high authority" that Sumter would be evacuated as a military necessity. Was this another blown-up rumor? Apparently not, for the reports became firmer the next day, and the next. "THE EVACUATION OF FORT SUMTER DETERMINED ON," headlined the *Courier*. "ANDERSON TO GO TO FORT MONROE." [6] The garrison got word from shore that a telegram had been received verifying the report. Evidently the Carolinians believed it, for they burst into a fusillade of artillery celebration, firing about a hundred guns at Moultrie and fifty from the other batteries. On top of that, they quit work on the harbor fortifications.

"The news . . . that orders were issued to evacuate this fort," Captain Foster reported to General Totten, "seem to have caused an almost entire cessation of work on the batteries around us. I am not ceasing work on the preparations, although I am taking an inventory of the materials on hand, and otherwise getting ready for such orders should they actually arrive. . . .

"Unless otherwise directed I shall discharge my force when the orders for evacuation arrive, and leave with the command, with my assistants, and report to you at Washington." [7]

The news seemed to be true. It cannot be doubted that the devout Anderson sent up a heartfelt prayer of thanksgiving to the God who had not forsaken him. He had suffered humiliation at the hands of the Carolinians, he had felt shame at his own failure to support the *Star*, he had been feebly backed and at times almost abandoned by his own government, and he had lived through sixteen weeks of mounting anxiety such as only a sensitive man faced with a terrible responsibility could realize. Now all his forbearance was vindicated, his trials repaid. The Lincoln administration, from which he had expected so little wisdom, had recognized the inevitable and there would be peace.

"There is now a prospect," he wrote, ". . . that the separation which has been inevitable for months, will be consummated without the shedding of one drop of blood. . . . God has, I feel, been pleased to use me as an instrument in effecting a purpose which will, I trust, end in making us all a better and wiser people. . . . A hope may be indulged in that our errant sisters, thus leaving us, as friends, may at some future time be won back by conciliation and justice." [8]

In Charleston, the report that Sumter would be given up was first received with suspicion, then with joy by the populace and annoyance on the part of the firebrands who felt cheated of their chance to assault the fort. After the inauguration, Rhett's *Mercury* had fulminated about Lincoln's "brutality" and said the South must adopt a "war strategy," [9] but the situation was confusing because of the reports of Mr. Seward's conciliatory attitude. The city as usual was swept by rumor. It was said that the Sumter soldiers were in open mutiny, that Major Anderson was resigning his commission, that the Black Republican Captain Doubleday had gone insane and was in irons.[10] A false report that the United States brig *Crusader* was en route with reinforcements for Anderson threw Colonel Ripley, commanding Fort Moultrie, into dismay. He asked what he could be expected to do with a command consisting of "290 indifferent artillerymen" and "318 helpless infantry recruits." [11]

Ripley as well as Governor Pickens must have been relieved at the news, quickly gaining the sound of reality, that Sumter would be handed over to them. Louis Wigfall, the Confederacy's Washington eyes and ears, telegraphed from the capital his belief that "Anderson will be ordered to evacuate Sumter in five days." [12] Pickens had been buying more cannon and had seen his Palmetto army swell to ten regiments totaling 8,835 men, but discipline could be better and there were jealousies to contend with. The commander of the Carolina forces was Major General Milledge L. Bonham, a Mexican War veteran who did not relish the idea of taking orders from Brigadier General Beauregard, one grade lower in rank. The floating battery, of which much had been expected, turned out to be so unwieldy that some men refused to serve in it, calling it the "Slaughter Pen." [13]

The Confederate secretary of war, L. P. Walker, was at first skeptical of the evacuation reports, telegraphing Charleston, "Give but little credit to the rumors of an amicable adjustment. Do not slacken for a moment your energies. . . ." [14] Five days later his doubts faded and he was worried that when Sumter was handed over it might be a smoking ruin instead of a fort in good commission. Spies in the Washington War Department must have relayed the news that Anderson had mined the wharf, and the major's remarks that he would blow up the fort rather than see it fall to the enemy had been misconstrued. Walker warned Beauregard that he must get positive assurances from Anderson that there were no "mines laid with trains within the fort." It might be a good idea, Walker suggested, to keep Captain Foster in the fort for a time on the theory that the garrison would not blow up Foster. [15]

From New York, Governor Pickens received annoying news. A court there had decided that he *could* sue the steamship line, since South Carolina was still a part of the Union and he was a citizen of the United States despite his claim that he was not. A jury heard the case and returned a verdict against him, denying him any redress for his lost baggage. [16] What else could one expect from Yankees? The governor shrugged it off and went to the theater with General Beauregard to see Bulwer's *Lady of Lyons,* where the handsome general was "the cynosure of all eyes." A springlike softness in the air combined with the news of Lincoln's backdown to produce a holiday atmosphere. There

was a sportive St. Patrick's Day parade featuring the Irish Volunteers and capped with a dinner at the Hibernian Society. A
boatload of crinolined ladies were escorted by General Jamison
on a visit to the harbor fortifications, drawing a grand salute
from the Morris Island batteries. Society began to promenade
on the Battery again, with gentlemen renewing the pretty custom of flattering ladies by sending them bouquets. Mrs. Chesnut, still sparkling at thirty-seven, was delighted to get two of
them at once, one from Robert Gourdin and another from Captain H. J. Hartstene. It was all so pleasant, along with her conviction that there would be no war after all, that she exclaimed,
"What a dear, delightful place is Charleston!" [17]

The good news even induced a relaxation in sternness toward
the garrison in the harbor. Lieutenant Colonel A. R. Chisolm,
a prosperous planter who had brought his Negroes to Charleston
to work on the batteries and had himself joined the cause as an
aide to Governor Pickens, went out to Sumter one day on an
official errand and lingered to chat with the officers. A couple of
them admitted jokingly that it had been a long time since they
enjoyed a good cigar. Well, said Chisolm, he would see what he
could do about that. With General Beauregard's permission, on
his next trip out he brought not only cigars but also—wonder
of wonders!—several cases of claret for the officers.[18]

On March 20th Colonel George W. Lay arrived, put up at
the Charleston Hotel, and had a long conference with Governor
Pickens and General Beauregard.[19] Out of his years of experience as General Scott's right bower and his intimate knowledge
of confidential orders and Washington talk, Lay must have had
much of interest to tell them. The next day produced a visitor
not quite so welcome—Captain Gustavus V. Fox, formerly of
the United States Navy, whose efforts to get sanction for an expedition to reinforce Sumter had been published everywhere.
Fox indeed demonstrated real nerve to show his face in Charleston. He talked with a former navy colleague, Captain Hartstene,
a native of South Carolina who had gone with his state. Hartstene took him to Governor Pickens, who asked him suspiciously
if his mission was peaceful. Fox said it was, that he had come

R

to learn the actual condition of Anderson's garrison and the extent of his provisions. Getting Pickens' somewhat reluctant approval, Fox made the trip out to Sumter that evening with Hartstene as companion to keep him honest.[20]

Major Anderson must have been surprised at the identity of his visitor. Fox, the apostle of reinforcement and therefore a war man, hardly seemed a proper emissary if the government intended to evacuate the fort. But the captain made almost no mention of the reinforcement plan that was so much in his mind, merely pointing out one likely landing place at the fort. He got Anderson's estimate that his provisions could not hold out beyond April 15th even if he put his command on short rations. The major gave his opinion that it was too late to relieve the fort by any other means than by landing an army on Morris Island. ". . . but," Fox later recalled, "as we looked out upon the water from the parapet, [an entrance from the sea] seemed very feasible, more especially as we heard the oars of a boat near the fort, which the sentry hailed, but we could not see her through the darkness until she almost touched the landing." [21] Fox, yearning as he was to lead an expedition into the harbor, kept these thoughts to himself as he appraised the fort and its approaches in the hope that he would yet get permission to make the attempt.

Fox also brought Anderson news that General Scott had not forgotten him even though he had been remiss about letter writing. The general had recommended to the late Secretary of War Holt that Anderson be brevetted lieutenant colonel for moving his command from Moultrie, and brevetted colonel for maintaining his position at Sumter—recommendations which President Buchanan, no admirer of Anderson, had ignored. After a visit of less than two hours, Fox and Hartstene returned to Charleston, where the latter reported to General Beauregard.

"Were you with Captain Fox all the time of his visit?" Beauregard asked.

"All but a short period, when he was with Major Anderson," Hartstene replied.

Beauregard nodded reflectively. "I fear that we shall have occasion to regret that short period," he said.[22]

Although Fox had mentioned the possible landing place only casually, Anderson thought it advisable to warn Washington next day, "A vessel lying there will be under the fire of thirteen guns from Fort Moultrie. . . . The Department can decide what the chances will be of a safe debarkation and unloading at that point under these circumstances." [23] But he could not seriously believe that the government was still toying with the idea of reinforcing him. A few days later came a dispatch from General Totten to Captain Foster giving him instructions what to do "should the fort be evacuated"—something he would hardly do unless evacuation was intended.[24] If the major had any further doubts, they were dissipated when another Yankee visitor appeared on the scene—Ward H. Lamon, one of Lincoln's closest friends.

Lamon registered at the Charleston Hotel March 24th and got a rough welcome when he was recognized and threatened by some truculent Carolinians who had a rope they wanted to try on his neck—a crisis averted by Lawrence Keitt, who greeted him in friendly fashion and invited him to have a drink.[25] Lamon had a drink, and he soon had an interview with Governor Pickens, telling him he was the "confidential agent" of the President and had come to make preparations for the removal of the Sumter garrison—a mission that made him welcome indeed. He also went out to the fort and talked with Anderson, to whom he gave the impression that the command would soon be withdrawn. Returning to the city, Lamon conferred once more with Pickens, discussing details of the removal of the force. By the time Lamon left Charleston, there was no doubt in anyone's mind that Anderson and his men would clear out, although Mr. Lincoln was taking an unholy time getting about it.[26]

A third Yankee visitor called on neither Pickens nor Anderson. Stephen Hurlbut of Illinois was born in Charleston, had studied law under Judge Petigru, and still had a sister living in the city. Hurlbut arrived with Lamon, but ostensibly as a private citizen with no more serious purpose than a stay with his sister. He talked with friends and relatives and had an illuminating discussion with Petigru. It did not take him long to learn that Mr. Seward's idea that "devotion to the Union" was strong in South Carolina was nonsense. Hurlbut wrote a short, pungent essay on the real situation that should have been an eye-opener to the cheery Secretary of State:

[Petigru] is now the only man in the city of Charleston who avowedly adheres to the Union. . . . From these sources I have no hesitation in reporting as unquestionable—that separate nationality is a fixed fact, that there is an unanimity of sentiment which is to my mind astonishing, that there is no attachment to the Union. . . . There is positively nothing to appeal to. The sentiment of national patriotism, always feeble in Carolina, has been extinguished and overridden by the acknowledged doctrine of the paramount allegiance to the State. False political economy diligently taught for years has now become an axiom, and merchants and business men believe, and act upon the belief, that great growth of trade and expansion of material prosperity will and must follow the establishment of a Southern republic. They expect a golden era, when Charleston shall be a great commercial emporium and control for the South, as New York does for the North.[27]

General Beauregard, happy that he would not be required to hurl metal at his old friend Anderson after all, wrote him that no "formal surrender or capitulation" would be necessary when he left. But he had strict orders from Walker to make certain that the major did not leave demolition charges that would blow up the fort after he left it. Beauregard put this point as politely as possible:

All that will be required of you on account of the public rumors that have reached us will be your word of honor as an officer and a gentleman, that the fort, all public property therein, its armaments, &c., shall remain in their present condition, without any arrangements or preparation for their destruction or injury after you shall have left the fort.[28]

Offended at the suggestion that he had a plot in mind, Anderson replied immediately:

> . . . you must pardon me for saying that I feel deeply hurt at the intimation in your letter about the conditions which will be exacted of me, and I must state most distinctly that if I can only be permitted to leave on the pledge you mention I shall never, so help me God, leave this fort alive.[29]

Beauregard saw his error. Anderson could be trusted. Orders or no orders, he wrote back dropping the demand for a pledge, disclaiming any intention of wounding "so gallant an officer," and admitting regret that he had even mentioned the subject. After that there was a friendly exchange of notes in which the former instructor and pupil addressed each other as "dear general" and "dear major" and expressed hope that they would soon meet personally.[30]

Chivalry prevailed between the two commanders, but what was taking the Lincoln government so long? Certain he would be withdrawn in a day or two, Anderson had not added to the discomfort of his men by putting them on short rations, their fare being humdrum enough at best. The last barrel of flour was issued March 29th. Still there was no word from Washington.

Long denied the solace of smoking, the men were overjoyed to receive a large shipment of tobacco from John Anderson, the New York tobacconist, which the Charleston post office let pass on the theory that the soldiers could be permitted luxuries as long as they were clearing out. But the expected withdrawal order did not come. The situation was growing embarrassing for Anderson, and the city was developing a wrath at the delay.

"If Lamon was authorized to arrange matters," Governor Pickens wrote Beauregard, "Anderson ought now to say so, in reply to yours; and if he does not, I shall begin to doubt everything." [31]

The Charleston *Courier* exploded: "We have endured long enough the dilatory and delusive rumors from the feeble fanatics who preside at Washington. . . . It is time this game of procrastination and vacillation, and double-dealing jugglery, were stopped." [32]

But Mrs. Caroline Howard Gilman of Charleston had no doubt that the garrison was getting out. She took the trouble to get a pass so that she could visit her summer home on Sullivan's Island, now under military law, and although astonished at the machinery of war she saw there, her confidence was unimpaired. "Such is my faith in peace," she wrote, "that I carried down a gardener to arrange my flower beds." [33]

Anderson had often gnawed his nails while awaiting instructions from Secretaries Floyd and Holt. The new Secretary Cameron was even slower. The major had reported several times about his dwindling supplies, getting no reply. On April 3rd he repeated the warning to Washington, adding a stronger appeal:

"I must, therefore, most respectfully and urgently ask for instructions what I am to do as soon as my provisions are exhausted. Our bread will last four or five days." [34]

In Washington, the three Confederate commissioners were still cooling their heels, unwelcomed, unrecognized, but feeling chipper enough for all that. Although their reception had been unflattering, they felt their mission to be moving toward triumphant completion. True, Mr. Seward had been overoptimistic, but the Messrs. Crawford, Forsyth, and Roman were sure he would make good his promises. The Lincolnites were backed into a nasty political corner, that was all. The public announcement of Seward's peace policy, the commissioners believed, had to be held in abeyance temporarily because the administration was afraid it would lose them the pending elections in Connecticut and Rhode Island. To the commissioners' way of thinking, time was in their favor because while the Lincoln government vacillated, neither declaring war nor coming out for peace, the Confederacy had the advantages of both.[1]

On his part, Secretary Seward was irked that his solution of the whole North-South quarrel was blocked simply because Lincoln could not seem to understand its perfect workability. "Understand" was not the right word. The President was deeply skeptical of Seward's policy. Hurlbut's report from Charleston made it seem that if the nation were to wait with Seward for the seceded states to clamor for a return to the Union, it would be like waiting for the second coming.

The government still held only four bastions in secessia— Fort Taylor at Key West, Fort Jefferson in the Dry Tortugas, Fort Pickens at Pensacola, and Sumter. Taylor and Jefferson were secure, only Pickens and Sumter challenged by secessionist arms. Lincoln took it for granted that by this time reinforcements had been landed at Fort Pickens to render it safe for the Union. That boiled the question down to one fort, Sumter alone. Secretary Seward said that giving up the fort would be farsighted statesmanship. Mr. Blair said it would wreck the nation. They agreed only on one point—that what was done or not done there was terribly important. Militarily, Sumter's value was lost to the Union. Politically and emotionally its significance was incalculable. It was the first fort to defy the first state in secession, and still defied the Carolinians whom many Northerners had come to regard as the mischief-makers who started it all. For the Lincoln administration to hand it over tamely after the wobbly Buchanan regime had at least held it, might mean the collapse of any unified feeling of nationality in the North. It was easy for the man in the street to forget that unlike Buchanan, Lincoln did not have only one dissident state to contend with but a powerful Confederacy of seven states with a voice so strong, as Jefferson Davis put it, that all creation had to "hear and heed."

When Lincoln held his first state dinner March 28th he was in high good humor, spinning some of his Illinois yarns with such zest that he seemed unburdened by care. General Scott had arrived at the White House only to be seized again with dysentery and forced to return home. Although the general was not there, he was much on the President's mind. At the dinner's end he invited the Cabinet into an adjoining room and dropped his mask of pleasantry. He showed real emotion as he announced that General Scott that day had advised the evacuation of *both* Sumter and Pickens in the following words:

> It is doubtful . . . whether the voluntary evacuation of Fort Sumter alone would have a decisive effect upon the States now wavering between adherence to the Union and secession. It is known, indeed, that it would be charged to necessity, and the holding of Fort Pickens would be adduced in support of that view. Our Southern friends, however, are clear that the evacuation of both the forts would instantly soothe and give confidence to the eight remaining slave-holding States, and render their cordial adherence to the Union perpetual. . . .[2]

The Cabinet—Seward excepted—was staggered. Giving up both forts would mean a complete surrender, a triumph for the new Confederacy. All of them thought Fort Pickens to be held safely. Montgomery Blair, who was ready to resign if Sumter was abandoned, saw red. The words, he was certain, were the words of Seward, spoken by the voice of General Scott. Seward was using Scott as his catspaw. Blair pointed out that no one pretended there was any military necessity to quit Pickens. This indicated to him that *all* of Scott's advice had better be re-examined, as politically inspired.

"Mr. President," Blair said, fixing a gimlet gaze on Seward so that no one could mistake his meaning, "you can now see that General Scott, in advising the surrender of Fort Sumter, is playing the part of a politician, not of a general." [3]

The Secretary of State—if Blair's supposition was correct—had overreached himself. Next day, Lincoln sent notes to the Secretaries of War and Navy: "I desire that an expedition, to move by sea, be got ready to sail as early as the 6th of April next. . . ." [4] He had not fully decided to try relieving Sumter, but he wanted to be ready. Captain Fox, the light of glory in his eyes, hurried to New York to get things rolling.

William Seward was in the worst predicament of his long career. Unless he could perform some quick magic, his whole policy was wrecked, all his easy talk of "running" the administration exposed as a delusion, and himself unmasked and discredited. On top of that, the Confederate commissioners with some truth would brand him a liar even though he had intended to keep his promises. A proud man, he could not allow this to happen. For the next few days he skated fast on thin ice in an effort to save the peace and save Seward, succeeding only in entangling the administration in utter confusion.

Still hoping to make good on Sumter, he wrote Lincoln an earnest opinion urging its immediate evacuation as "untenable," but advising the speedy reinforcement of Fort Pickens. The latter fort had been thought secure, but now its status was in doubt. With the telegraph at Pensacola in rebel hands, the only communication with the fort was by boat around the Florida peninsula or by messenger through the rebel lines. Word had trickled North that the *Brooklyn,* the ship with reinforcements for Pickens, was not at Pensacola at all but was at Key West, 450 miles southeast. This had given Lincoln a cold chill, for it appeared that the orders for the reinforcement had somehow misfired. Actually, the *Brooklyn* had merely sailed down to Key West for supplies, leaving the troops in the man-of-war *Sabine* off Pensacola, but the government had no way of knowing this. Lincoln had never for a moment intended to give up Fort Pickens, whose holding might better enable the North to swallow the loss of Sumter. The prospect that Pickens itself might be imperiled not only induced some panic but caused the President to feel further doubts about General Scott, who had written the orders for its reinforcement. While no one questioned the general's loyalty, it appeared that he was so bogged down with political considerations that his value as a military adviser was a puzzle.[5]

Seward seized on this situation with a quick change of course, becoming the chief apostle for rescuing Fort Pickens. Knowing Scott to be out of favor, he dropped the general like a hot potato and scooped up a new military adviser. This was his friend Captain Montgomery C. Meigs, a forty-four-year-old engineering officer then in charge of completing the Capitol dome and extensions. With never a blush, the secretary told Meigs they needed a man who could counsel on military matters without allowing politics to enter in—a young and vigorous man who, unlike Scott, could mount a horse if need be. He took Meigs to see Lincoln, urging that the captain was just the man to lead an expedition to Fort Pickens. "He complimented me much," Meigs later recalled, also remembering that Seward pressed the idea on Lincoln with the greatest urgency.[6] Meigs had recently returned from duty at Key West and Tortugas and also had a knowledge of the Pensacola fortifications—a fact that Seward stressed as fitting him for the command.

Lincoln agreed, and the secretary promptly kidnaped Meigs from his own boss, Secretary Cameron. Properly such an expedition would be the responsibility of the Secretaries of War and Navy, but not this one. This would be Seward's own enterprise, and he was not even going to let the other two secretaries in on the secret. Next morning he visited General Scott and broke the news.

"Lieutenant General Scott," he said, "you have advised the President that in your opinion it is impossible to reinforce Fort Sumter or Fort Pickens. I now come to you from the President, to say that he orders that Fort Pickens shall be reinforced, and that you give the necessary instructions."

The general rose and drew himself up to his full six feet four, looking down on the small Seward. "Well, Mr. Secretary of State," he rumbled, "the great Frederick used to say that when the King commands, nothing is impossible. The President's orders shall be obeyed, sir." [7]

Scott took the rebuff with vast dignity, but it hurt him nevertheless. His new military secretary, Lieutenant Colonel Erasmus D. Keyes, noticed that the old giant was troubled as he had his Negro servant hoist his feet up on a stool and muttered, "A dull man would be the death of me now." As for Seward, he was juggling several fragile balls in the air, facing ruin if he lost control. That same day, March 30th, he got another call from a man he must have hated to see, Justice Campbell.

The five days allowed for the evacuation of Sumter had now stretched to fifteen, and Campbell was wondering. He showed Seward a telegram the commissioners had received from Governor Pickens complaining that Lamon had promised evacuation but nothing had happened. The secretary imperturbably took the telegram, saying he would show it to Lincoln and give Campbell an answer on Monday, April 1st. His control of events was growing shakier by the minute. Had Campbell known that Seward was even then planning a secret expedition to reinforce Fort Pickens, the justice would rightly have considered himself deceived.[8]

On Easter Sunday morning, Colonel Keyes was talking with General Scott, telling him how hard it would be to land heavy ordnance for Fort Pickens on the beach at Santa Rosa Island. Scott listened attentively, then pulled out a map of Pensacola harbor he had been studying. "Take this map to Mr. Seward," he directed, "and repeat to him exactly what you have just said to me about the difficulty of reinforcing Fort Pickens." [9]

Keyes left a bit early so he would have time for a brief talk with the secretary, then go on to church. Finding Seward at his home on F Street, he explained that he had come on Scott's order to outline the difficulties of reinforcing Fort Pickens.

"I don't care about the difficulties," Seward said brusquely. "Where's Captain Meigs?"

"I suppose he's at his house, sir."

"Please find him and bring him here."

"I'll call and bring him on my return from church," Keyes suggested.

"Never mind church today," the secretary snapped. "I wish to see him and you here together without delay." [10]

Thus was Keyes kidnaped in turn. Somewhat miffed at this peremptory treatment, he hurried off and returned with Meigs. Seward told the pair to draw up a plan to reinforce Fort Pickens and bring it to the White House at three that afternoon. This was a large order, somewhat like asking a lawyer to prepare a difficult brief during his noon hour. The two officers hastened to the engineer's office, got out maps on Pensacola harbor and its fortifications, and went to work with silent speed, making lists of the fort's needs, calculating weight and bulk, the tonnage required, the number of troops, subsistence, equipment, ammunition, and scores of other details. They finished a general plan and got to the executive mansion a few minutes before deadline. Seward was there with Lincoln, who had one foot on his desk, the other on a chair. "I never saw a man who could scatter his limbs more than he," Keyes reflected.

The President may have appeared relaxed, but he was so beset by problems demanding urgent action that he was falling into error. Meigs, an able engineer who was also the inventor of a successful fire hydrant, was not bashful about laying down his requirements. Absolute secrecy was essential, he insisted. If news of the expedition leaked out the rebels would swoop down, gobble up Slemmer's force, and take Fort Pickens. Lincoln, knowing the War and Navy Departments were still staffed by many Southern sympathizers, agreed to an amazing proposition: that Seward should remain the executive in charge and that the expedition should be kept secret even from the Secretaries of War and Navy—the two officials directly concerned, whose men and facilities would be drawn on. The use of regular army or navy funds would instantly disclose the secret, so Seward was authorized to provide Meigs with ten thousand dollars from the State Department "secret service" fund to defray expenses. Lincoln delegated the whole project to Meigs and Keyes, acting under Seward's orders and with the approval of General Scott.[11]

"I depend upon you gentlemen to push this thing through," he said.[12]

Part of Meigs' plan was to send a warship to run the Confederate batteries and enter Pensacola harbor to prevent the rebels from crossing over to Santa Rosa Island and attacking Pickens from the rear—a hazardous maneuver almost certain to start hostilities. Who would handle this assignment? "Providence supplies the man and the means," Meigs remarked.[13] He suggested his good friend, Navy Lieutenant David Dixon Porter for the command and said the side-wheel man-of-war *Powhatan,* which the newspapers said had just returned to New York, would be a fine ship for the job. The President, a man in a hurry, approved both suggestions and in fact all but gave the planners carte blanche. Seward, the author and kingpin of the expedition, was handed an unlimited opportunity to cause mischief. Porter was then under navy orders to go to the Pacific, but the secretary brushed this aside and kidnaped Porter from the Navy Department. He even sought an immediate promotion for his man Meigs, a captain who could not command majors and colonels involved in the expedition. General Scott showed him this was impossible under army regulations, remarking that it was a shame to take Meigs away from his "great works" on the Capitol.

"There is no use in a Capitol unless we have a country," Seward replied.[14]

The Secretary of State seemed gripped by the "quiet and

private madness" so prevalent at the time, an official playing several games in opposition to each other, a gambler betting both ways, a peacemaker planning war but still hoping to avert it. His project for Fort Pickens, which would almost surely start cannon booming, ran directly contrary to his policy of concilia- tion. Possibly he felt that if his peace policy was to go smash he had best recoup what standing he could by winning credit for saving Fort Pickens.[15] Running Mr. Lincoln had proved more of a chore than he had anticipated, and yet he had not quite given up his hope of putting his feet into the President's shoes. All Fool's Day dawned, bringing a new crop of freakish events. Meigs, Keyes, and Porter were working like madmen, writing orders, getting Lincoln to sign them, and whipping Seward's expedition into shape. The secretary, staking his reputation in a last throw of the dice, sent a memorandum to Lincoln un- equaled for effrontery.

In it he said that after a month in office the administration was still fumbling and blundering without a policy "either domestic or foreign." He urged once again the evacuation of Sumter. He advocated a demand for explanations from France and Spain for meddling in Mexico and Santo Domingo, and a declaration of war against both countries if their replies were not satisfactory. He suggested clearly that since Lincoln had failed as President, Seward was willing and able to assume com- mand and set things right: "I neither seek to evade nor assume responsibility." [16]

While it was true that the President had procrastinated about forming a policy so that the entire nation was growing restive, Seward's medicine was exceedingly strong. More desperate words were never penned, but the secretary was a desperate man. Evidently he hoped Lincoln would step out and let him take charge so that he could make good his policy and his prom- ises to the Confederates by stopping both the Sumter and Pickens expeditions, and unify the nation by inviting foreign war—as if the nation did not already have trouble enough on its hands. He was a harried man, for Justice Campbell was call- ing again. Seward saw him and explained that the President was upset by Governor Pickens' telegram saying that Ward Lamon had "promised" the evacuation of Sumter. Mr. Lincoln wanted the governor to understand that Lamon had not been authorized to make promises of any kind. In fact, Lamon was waiting in the next room to answer any questions on that score the justice might want to ask.[17]

No, said Campbell, that was beside the point. What he wanted to know was, what should he report to the commissioners about Sumter?

Seward began to hedge. He did not know yet whether the President would be willing to abdicate in his favor. Instead of replying, he sat down and scribbled a note reading in part, "the President may desire to supply Fort Sumter, but will not undertake to do so without first giving notice to Governor Pickens."

"What does this mean?" Campbell exclaimed, appalled. "Does the President design to attempt to supply Sumter?"

"No, I think not," Seward replied. "It is a very irksome thing to him to evacuate it. His ears are open to every one, and they fill his head with schemes for its supply. I do not think that he will adopt any of them. There is no design to reinforce it."

Campbell, who had staked his own good name as well as his hopes for peace on Seward's word, was deeply disturbed—so much so that he asked no questions about Fort Pickens. He argued that he had regarded Sumter's evacuation as already settled, and now the secretary was talking about sending supplies there. Seward hesitated, then left to consult the President. He was gone for a few minutes while Campbell waited, then came out and wrote a slightly revised note: "I am satisfied the Government will not undertake to supply Fort Sumter without giving notice to Governor Pickens." [18]

This was no help at all to the man who had been promised evacuation. Campbell talked earnestly and long with Seward, who was a persuasive speaker and must have managed with comforting words to undo the clear impression he had put in writing. When Campbell left he was entirely reassured that Seward's earlier promise of evacuation still held good except for the delay. He reported this to Commissioner Crawford, who in turn passed the word on to Toombs in Montgomery, urging that Lincoln's "vacillating course" be indulged because he was still waiting for those elections in Connecticut and Rhode Island. The delay was actually an advantage, Crawford pointed out, since the Confederacy could go right on arming while the administration was committed to make no hostile move. Crawford and his colleagues had another idea which they telegraphed to Toombs. Lincoln, they said, simply did not have the courage to execute the order for evacuation which would be so unpopular in the North. He was going to "shift responsibility upon Major Anderson by suffering him to be starved out." [19]

That same April 1st Lincoln replied to Seward's suggestion that he move out and let a professional take charge. The answer was a polite, firm No.

The secretary had gambled and lost. That night he dashed off a note to his wife saying, "Dangers and breakers are before us"—a sentence in which "me" could have been substituted for "us." [20]

WAIT AND SEE

As if the United States did not have trouble enough fighting disunion, it was using up precious energy fighting itself. Thanks to Mr. Seward, with some blame also touching the President, the administration was lurching into a morass of confusion unexplored even in the days of Secretary Floyd. In New York, two expeditions were fitting out with furious speed at the same time, unknown to each other, one of them for Fort Sumter, the other for Fort Pickens.

The one for Sumter was under Captain Fox, a good man fallen on evil days, and while it was strictly secret it was operating through the regular channels of the War and Navy Departments. At the time there were only three war vessels in Atlantic waters, the *Powhatan, Pocahontas,* and *Pawnee.* The Sumter expedition was regarded as so important that Navy Secretary Welles assigned all three to Fox, adding also the five-gun cutter *Harriet Lane.* The eleven-gun *Powhatan,* biggest of the lot, was in ghastly shape. On her recent return from the West Indies she had been decommissioned for repairs, and her hull was found to be rotten, her boilers worn out. On top of that, her engines had been dismantled. But Fox needed her, so Welles sent urgent orders to Captain Andrew H. Foote, commandant at the Brooklyn navy yard, to get her back together again. Foote, who was not informed about the expedition or Fox's part in it, had mechanics working day and night to ready the *Powhatan* for sailing, rotten hull and all. All he knew was that she was wanted for some important but unnamed mission.[1]

The Fort Pickens expedition was under Captain Meigs, Colonel Keyes, and Lieutenant Porter, three men who bore confidential orders signed by Lincoln and, under the heady influence of personal talks with the President, were determined to do their duty even if it meant tossing ordinary rules out the window.

S

Their project was even more secret than Fox's because it was outrageously irregular, carried on in defiance of army and navy channels and known only to the three young officers plus Lincoln, Seward, and General Scott. It was a government secret so tightly kept that not even the top government officials who in all propriety should have known of it, did know. Seward, who was pushing it with all his energies, wanted it that way, but why Lincoln should allow the Secretary of State to take this devious course is a mystery. If clerks in the War and Navy Departments were unreliable, could not Secretaries Cameron and Welles at any rate have been taken aside and told what was afoot? The President was not at his best during these feverish hours, as he was later to admit. When Meigs, Keyes, and Porter arrived in New York, the latter carried an astonishing order for Captain Foote at the navy yard:

> SIR: You will fit out the *Powhatan* without delay. Lieutenant Porter will relieve Captain Mercer in command of her. She is bound on secret service, and you will under no circumstances communicate to the Navy Department the fact that she is fitting out.
>
> ABRAHAM LINCOLN [2]

The *Powhatan,* of course, was the vessel Fox was depending on to serve as flagship of *his* expedition to Sumter.

When Captain Foote read the order, he was in a swivet. It did not make sense. All he knew was that Welles had ordered the *Powhatan* to be made seaworthy with all speed, not knowing the purpose. Now the President gave the same orders as if he did not know Welles had already given them. Furthermore, Foote scented something fishy in the displacement of Captain Samuel Mercer, the ship's regular skipper, by Lieutenant Porter, his junior in rank. True, the President was an important man, but Foote always got his orders through the Secretary of the Navy. What was going on? Porter was a gay blade who had been so chummy with the fashionable Southern crowd in Washington that the Navy Department was not quite certain of his loyalty, and Foote had a few doubts himself.[3]

"Porter, these are ticklish times," he exploded. "How do I know that you are not going to run off with the ship? I must telegraph immediately to the Secretary." [4]

By no means, Porter insisted. He waved the President's signature under Foote's nose, allowing that it ought to be authority enough for anyone. Foote finally gave in, with great misgivings. Meigs and Keyes meanwhile were hard at work getting supplies and equipment and renting the passenger steamers *Atlantic* and *Illinois* to transport five companies of men to Fort Pickens under Colonel Harvey Brown. They were unaware that Fox was preparing an expedition for Sumter at another wharf in the same city. Fox on his own part knew nothing of the Pickens expedition, nor that the flagship whose boats he needed was being snatched from him. Fox had trouble enough chartering in strict secrecy the three tugboats for his operation, finally securing the *Freeborn, Yankee,* and *Uncle Ben* by paying through the nose for them.[5] All this martial activity had newspaper reporters aflutter with curiosity, but their inquiries got them nowhere.

"Whatever else the opponents of Mr. Lincoln's Administration may say or think," one of them commented, "they are compelled at least to acknowledge that it possesses . . . one great merit over its predecessors. It knows how to keep a secret. Extensive as have been the naval preparations at this port during the past week, all the prying and persistent ingenuity of the New York press has failed to discover to what specific end these preparations are made." [6]

The newsmen at first were certain an expedition was being prepared for either Sumter or Pickens, but when three hundred horses were driven aboard the *Atlantic* they threw up their hands. What good would horses do at Sumter or Pickens? The vessels must be bound for Texas.[7]

The Lincoln administration was indeed keeping secrets, even from itself. The *Powhatan* was ready to sail April 5th when Captain Foote got another puzzling message from Secretary Welles ordering him to hold the vessel for further instructions. Then came the crusher, the final proof that Washington's top brass had gone crazy. Welles sent orders to Captain Mercer instructing him to take command of the *Powhatan* as part of an expedition to relieve Fort Sumter.[8]

Foote's equilibrium was tottering. President Lincoln said give the *Powhatan* to Porter. Secretary Welles said give her to Mercer. What to do? Foote pondered and decided he must obey the Secretary of the Navy, since his order was the latest. Lieutenant Porter let out a roar of protest. "Would he [Welles], think you, dare to countermand an order . . . of the President?" he demanded.[9] Meigs rushed over to the navy yard to join the melee. He did not care if Welles' order was later, he cried, the President's order took precedence nevertheless. There were excited words between Meigs, Foote, and Mercer. In disgust, Meigs finally dispatched a telegram to Secretary Seward in Washington asking him *please* to straighten out the mess.[10]

When Seward read the message at about eleven that night, he must have realized that his highhanded methods had got him into trouble. But he was determined that his own pet expedition must not be hampered. He hurried over to Willard's, where Welles was staying, and found the Navy Secretary about to retire. Welles could not understand the telegram, or the conflict over the *Powhatan*. He pointed out that Lieutenant Porter had no command and that the *Powhatan* was the flagship of the Sumter expedition. Seward had the grace to be somewhat embarrassed. He muttered that there was "some mistake," and from his circuitous remarks Welles finally gathered that the Secretary of State had been doing some undercover meddling in navy affairs. Welles, who bore little love for the self-styled prime minister anyway, clapped on his hat and said they would see Lincoln about it.

"On our way thither," Welles later recalled, "Mr. Seward remarked that, old as he was, he had learned a lesson from this affair, and that was, he had better attend to his own business and confine his labors to his own Department. To this I cordially assented." [11]

It was about midnight when they reached the White House, but Lincoln had not yet retired. He read Meigs' telegram in surprise, then looked at Welles. Wasn't the secretary in error? Wasn't some other ship designated as flagship for the Sumter expedition? Not at all, Welles said firmly. In fact, earlier that day he had read to the President the orders to Captain Mercer to take the *Powhatan*. Yes, Lincoln said, he remembered the orders but thought it was some other ship. Just to clear all doubt, Welles hurried to the Navy Department, dug out the orders and brought them back. The President immediately turned to Seward and told him the *Powhatan* must be restored to Mercer, that the Sumter expedition must not be crippled.

Seward hesitated, stalled, remonstrated. Wasn't the Pickens expedition as important as the Sumter one? If the *Powhatan* was taken away from him, his mission might fail. Lincoln replied that the Pickens relief could wait better than Sumter could. Seward kept demurring, even saying it would be hard to get a telegram through to the Brooklyn navy yard at this hour. At last Lincoln told him imperatively that he must send the message without delay. The Secretary of State, disconsolate, departed—to do some more stalling.[12]

Welles had good reason to resent the President's implied mistrust of him, and Lincoln was apologetic. He explained that Seward had set his heart on the Pickens project, and Lincoln had signed a good many orders for those young fellows—Meigs, Keyes, and Porter—without really looking at them. The President took the whole blame for the mixup, admitting he had confused the two names, *Powhatan* and *Pocahontas*.[13]

Secretary Seward could not have been in any great hurry to get that telegram off to New York. Morning came, and Meigs had received no reply. Once more he pelted Foote and Mercer with urgent arguments that they must let Porter take the *Powhatan*. At last he succeeded in convincing them. Porter, so intent on secrecy that he had spent most of his time in his room at the Astor House, came out in mufti and sneaked aboard the ship. The *Powhatan* sailed at 1:00 P.M. April 6th with Captain Mercer on the bridge and Porter lurking in a stateroom. Not until the ship got opposite Staten Island did Porter come out of hiding, whereupon Mercer introduced him to the executive officer as the commander of the ship, then went ashore.

This was when Mr. Seward's telegram to Porter finally reached the navy yard. A fast launch was sent out, overtaking the *Powhatan* at the Narrows, where the telegram was handed to Porter. It must have staggered the lieutenant:

"Give the *Powhatan* up to Captain Mercer.—SEWARD." [14]

Porter had plenty of nerve, as he was to demonstrate in later engagements. He thought it over, saw no reason why he should obey, and dashed off a snappy reply:

"I received my orders from the President and shall proceed and execute them." [15]

Porter steamed south. If Seward had signed the telegram in the President's name as he should have done, the lieutenant would have had to turn back. There is still speculation as to whether the Secretary of State made the mistake intentionally, hoping to hamstring the Sumter expedition, which he opposed, and to aid his own secret Pickens expedition.[16] His undercover meddling had indeed choked the navy's gears with sand and caused many earnest men to labor for nothing—especially when, as it later developed, the *Powhatan* was not needed at Pensacola and went unused there.[17]

Seward's private madness continued. Although his Fort Pickens expedition was so secret that he kept the Secretaries of War and Navy out of it, he was not so careful about the Sumter mission. He let his tongue wag in the presence—of all persons—of a newspaperman. Worse yet, it was a newsman from South Carolina, his friend James Harvey whom he was pushing for United States minister to Portugal. Harvey sprinted to a telegraph office and dispatched the following message to his old Charleston crony, Judge Magrath:

"Positively determined not to withdraw Anderson. Supplies go immediately, supported by naval force . . . if their landing be resisted." [18]

So Captain Gustavus Fox, working hard in New York to get his ships afloat and save Sumter for the Union, was combating obstacles of many kinds, not the least of them being the Secre-

tary of State. Fox was properly annoyed that his plan, which he
had been urging since January, was not accepted until the
eleventh hour, and then on such short notice that he had to rush
everything and hope for the best. By dint of valiant effort he
managed to embark in the chartered steamer *Baltic* on April
10th with two hundred recruits and plenty of supplies to keep
Sumter going a year. By this time Washington was so lost in
confusion that even normal navy channels were in a condition
later to become known as snafu. Although the *Powhatan* had
been taken from him four days earlier, no one informed Fox
about it. He sailed in the belief that the flagship he was depending on was part of his force, to rendezvous 632 miles south
outside Charleston harbor.[19]

II

Possibly one of the reasons for Lincoln's hesitation on Sumter
was his uncertainty about the commander's loyalty. The suspicions of Ulysses Doubleday and other bellicose Republicans, in
addition to Anderson's 20,000-man estimate and the fact that
he had been selected by the ambiguous Mr. Floyd put the
major's allegiance in a dubious light in the view of the President, who was not privy to the long history of difficulties Anderson had coped with at Charleston. In fact, Lincoln had said
privately a few days earlier, "Anderson has played us false." [20]
Unhappy experience had proved there was no telling when a
Southern-born officer might cross over to the other side. If there
was any question at all about the practicability of relieving Sumter, the doubts would be multiplied if the commander's heart
had left the Union and gone to Dixie. It was just another chance
Lincoln decided he had to take.

In his inaugural he had told the South, "You can have no
conflict, without yourselves being the aggressors," a promise he
meant to keep. While even Buchanan had upheld the government's right to reinforce a federal fort at any time, and Lincoln
exercised this right at Fort Pickens, he was more cautious about
Sumter. Captain Fox was instructed first to make an effort to
send a boatload of provisions only to Major Anderson so that,

in the President's words, if the Confederates resisted this "they will be firing on a boat filled with bread." If they did not resist, Fox was to do no more. If they did, he had orders to attempt an entrance into the harbor not only to supply the fort but to reinforce it as well.[21]

In addition, Lincoln determined to give Governor Pickens formal notice of the attempt, a step removing any suggestion of stealth from the movement and placing the onus of whatever hostilities might follow on the Southerners. This was to be no *Star of the West* stratagem. The United States Government, ignoring the Confederacy it did not recognize, was informing the governor of South Carolina it was sending provisions to Sumter, leaving to the governor the hard choice of allowing food to enter peacefully or starting war. The man selected to deliver this notice was Robert L. Chew, a State Department clerk who lives in history only because of this brief moment of drama. Chew's military companion on the trip to Charleston was Captain Theodore Talbot, the consumptive lieutenant of the Sumter garrison who had just arrived in Washington to be promoted in rank and given a post in the adjutant general's office. Talbot and Chew left the capital for Charleston by train on the evening of April 6th, four days before Captain Fox sailed from New York.[22]

Meanwhile the three unrecognized Confederate commissioners felt doubt creep into their conviction that Mr. Seward's policy of conceding everything would soon prevail. They heard reports of the formidable military preparations in New York. At first they believed it had to do with the Santo Domingo trouble, none of their worry. This assurance faded and, since they had no source of reliable information, they gave heed to rumor. Daily they telegraphed to Toombs such a series of wild stabs that the Confederate secretary of state must have grown dizzy.

On April 4th they telegraphed: "Strengthen the defenses at the mouth of the Mississippi."

April 5th: "The statement that the armament is intended for St. Domingo may be a mere ruse."

April 6th: "The rumors that they are destined to use against Pickens, and perhaps Sumter, are getting every day stronger."

April 7th: "It may be Sumter and the Mississippi; it is almost certain that it is Pickens and the Texas frontier." [23]

Of their statements, the truest of all was, "We know nothing positive on the subject." But of one thing they were certain— things were looking ominous, not at all as Mr. Seward had led them to believe. Commissioner Crawford had a grim conference with Justice Campbell. How about that promise to evacuate Sumter? he demanded.

Campbell himself was full of forebodings. Despite moments of uneasiness, he had believed in Seward. On April 7th he sent the secretary a note expressing his and the commissioners' alarm at the warlike preparations and asking whether the rumors were "well or ill founded." [24]

That Seward had deceived Campbell about Sumter may be in some degree excused by the fact that he had deceived himself. But he had knowingly misled Campbell for more than a week about Fort Pickens, and all in all his dealings, carried on without Lincoln's knowledge, had been so reckless and unscrupulous that they put the whole administration in a deceitful light. Next day Seward sent Campbell an enigmatic reply, unsigned and undated:

"Faith as to Sumter fully kept; wait and see. . . ." [25]

From this the commissioners made a pretty good guess that an expedition was being sent to Fort Pickens, and that Sumter would not be reinforced but might be provisioned. They were understandably in a rage about the whole affair, feeling that they had been systematically betrayed, and they took some of their rage out on Campbell. The well-intentioned jurist, who had pledged his reputation on saving the peace, lost the peace and his reputation as well. When he later returned to Alabama he discovered that he was regarded as a traitor to the South.

At Sumter the men had long since finished packing their belongings in preparation for departure and were wondering why the government took so long to say the word. Washington was always slow, but now it seemed frozen. "We shall certainly leave here on Saturday," one soldier wrote a friend in Baltimore.[1] The Charleston papers had reported that Major Anderson was to be transferred to Fortress Monroe, to Kentucky on recruiting duty, to Fort Washington on the Potomac, to Fort Hamilton in New York. They explained that the delay in the evacuation came about because Lamon brought only verbal orders to Anderson, and the major demanded written orders for so momentous a move.[2] "I have been informed for the hundredth time," the *Courier's* Washington correspondent wrote in towering annoyance, "that Fort Sumter will be evacuated within three days."[3]

Major Anderson was in a condition of nervousness and resentment for which he had ample reason. He had received no instructions from his government since Secretary Holt's dispatch of February 23rd, five weeks earlier. The Lincoln administration had been in office almost a month, and he had yet to receive a word from Secretary Cameron although he had reported almost daily to Washington, warned of his diminishing supplies, and asked pointedly for orders.

All he knew was what he read in the papers. To get reports of evacuation from all sources but the official one was maddening. The government was according miserable treatment to this officer who was shut off from the world in a position of crucial importance and had been under a virtual state of siege for more than three months. Whether the cause was the confusion attendant on a new administration or the considerable doubt of Anderson's loyalty, the result was to impose needless hardships on a commander who had already had more than enough.

The food problem was becoming more critical daily. Foster's forty-three laborers were hungry men, and the captain was forced to report to Washington that his provisions for them had dwindled to a half barrel of corn meal, one-seventh barrel of grits, and eleven codfish. Whatever else they ate would have to come from the soldiers' rations. Anderson sought to ease this drain on the larder by discharging all but a few of the workmen, but was foiled by his friend Beauregard. Beauregard had strict orders from the Confederate government, now growing decidedly impatient and knowing that Sumter's food was low, that no one could leave the fort unless *everybody* left. The general made an exception in the case of Lieutenant Talbot, however, who was ordered to a new post in Washington as captain. Talbot was allowed to leave on the theory that his departure would weaken the command and also that he would report in Washington the true condition of the fort, which the Carolinians believed to be deplorable.[4]

At 2:00 P.M. on April 3rd, the garrison heard one of the Morris Island batteries let loose. Watchers on the ramparts were amazed when they saw a disreputable-looking little schooner flying the American flag appear out of the outer fog and sail in the main ship channel. One of the island guns had fired a warning shot across her bows, and now fired another. At Sumter the long roll was beaten, the men in sudden excitement took their posts and the battery on the northeast angle was readied for firing. Anderson, greatly concerned, was eyeing the vessel from the parapet. Surely the government would not send such an insignificant ship to aid him—or would it?

The major was faced again with the last thing he wanted, a crisis involving the flag. Lieutenant Davis reported the battery ready. Anderson told him to wait. Hurriedly he summoned his officers into council and asked their opinions on what should be done. They knew their batteries could not reach the Morris Island guns, but five of the officers—Doubleday, Foster, Crawford, Davis, and Hall—were in favor of retaliating immediately against Moultrie and the other batteries they could reach. Seymour, Snyder, and Meade opposed this and advised sending an officer to Morris Island to inquire into the circumstances.

Anderson, in visible distress, sided with the minority. Much as it had hurt him, his failure to fire during the *Star of the West* incident had proved a blessing. Another personal humiliation, however painful, was a small thing when measured against the immeasurable need for peace. By this time the Palmetto gunners were done with warning and were doing their best to sink the ship, but with ineffective aim. Having plenty of evidence that she was unwelcome, the schooner turned about, taking one ball through her mainsail before gaining the safety of the bar. On Anderson's order, Captain Seymour and Lieutenant Snyder were rowed to Morris Island under a white flag while Doubleday fumed over the unpunished affront.[5]

"In amplifying his instructions not to provoke a collision into instructions not to fight at all," he later commented, "I have no doubt he [Anderson] thought he was rendering a real service to the country. He knew the first shot fired by us would light the flames of a civil war that would convulse the world, and tried to put off the evil day as long as possible. Yet a better analysis of the situation might have taught him that the contest had already commenced, and could no longer be avoided." [6]

On Morris Island, Colonel DeSaussure told the two Sumter officers that he had merely obeyed orders, which were to fire at any vessel bearing the United States flag that tried to enter the harbor. Rowing on out to the schooner, Seymour and Snyder interviewed the master, Joseph Marts, who seemed in complete bewilderment. His ship, the *Rhoda Shannon,* had become so hopelessly lost in storm and fog while en route from Boston to Savannah with a cargo of ice that he had turned into Charleston harbor in the belief that he had reached Savannah. The captain himself was in a fog. Why, he wanted to know, were people shooting at him? He understood when he was informed that he was at Charleston, for he had read of some little difficulties there. Marts, described as "an ignorant man" with an imperfect knowledge of navigation, flatly refused when he was told he could take refuge at Charleston. He headed for Savannah, where honest men did not get shot at.

Major Anderson sent Lieutenant Snyder to Charleston with a protest to Governor Pickens, declaring that a boat should have been stationed at the bar to warn off such mistaken mariners. Pickens, who had considerable respect for the major, expressed regret over the incident, explaining that the guard boat *Petrel* had been stationed there for that very purpose but had left its post because of rough seas. Its captain, he promised, would be dismissed.[7]

So the amenities were observed, an apology received, and anyone could see the folly of starting civil war over the likes of slow-witted Captain Marts and his tub of ice. In the light of common sense, Anderson had been wise to hold his fire. But at Sumter, common sense was no longer a dependable measure. The plain fact was that for the second time the major had failed to resent an affront to the flag, a failure some of the officers privately condemned. Feeling shame himself, Anderson sensed this silent disapproval all the more. It was noticed that he seemed almost in despair. "I was convinced," Doubleday recorded, "that it acted a great deal upon his mind. . . . he was very sensitive to every thing that affected his honor." [8]

The lonely, unhappy Anderson felt such a need for understanding of his forbearance that he did something unprecedented. He told his officers for the first time of the instructions he had received on January 10th and February 23rd to act strictly on the defensive and avoid any collision if consistent with his safety.[9] His soreness of spirit brimmed over in a report on the incident he sent to Washington:

> The truth is that the sooner we are out of this harbor the better. Our flag runs an hourly risk of being insulted, and my hands are tied by my orders, and if that was not the case, I have not the power to protect it. God grant that neither I nor any other officer in our Army may be again placed in a position of such mortification and humiliation.[10]

Another simultaneous development struck him with a cold chill. When Snyder was in Charleston conferring with Pickens, the governor showed him a dispatch from Commissioner Crawford in Washington reading:

> I am authorized to say that this Government will not under
> take to supply Fort Sumter without notice to you [Pickens].
> My opinion is that the President has not the courage to execute
> the *order agreed on in Cabinet* for the evacuation of the fort,
> but that he intends to shift the responsibility upon Major
> Anderson by suffering him to be starved out.[11]

The governor was willing to show this to Snyder, feeling it
might cause Anderson to suspect his own government. He was
right. The major, normally skeptical of rumor, could not shake
this one off when Snyder told him about it. It was corroborated
by an identical news story in the Charleston *Courier* April 3rd.
Anderson had long felt that he and his men were being sacrificed to a political necessity. Now Crawford's appraisal seemed
substantiated by apparent inconsistencies that had troubled him
—the long-continued rumors of evacuation that were never realized, the continued failure of Washington to send him so much
as a word of instructions. Was the administration turning him
adrift without orders, condemning him to the final humiliation
of being forced to surrender when his food ran out, making
him the scapegoat because it did not know what else to do?
Fearing it was true, Anderson sent the adjutant general a virtual
prayer for orders:

> I cannot but think that Mr. Crawford has misunderstood
> what he has heard in Washington, as I cannot think that the
> Government would abandon, without instructions and without
> advice, a command which has tried to do all its duty toward
> our country.
> I cannot but think that if the Government decides to do
> nothing which can be construed into a recognition of the fact
> of the dissolution of the Union, that it will, at all events, say to
> me that I must do the best I can, and not compel me to do an
> act which will leave my motives and actions liable to misconcep
> tion.
> . . . After thirty odd years of service I do not wish it to be
> said that I have treasonably abandoned a post and turned over

to unauthorized persons public property intrusted to my charge.
I am entitled to this act of justice at the hands of my Government, and I feel confident that I shall not be disappointed.
What to do with the public property, and where to take my
command, are questions to which answers will, I hope, be at
once returned. Unless we receive supplies I shall be compelled
to stay here without food, or to abandon this post very early
next week.[12]

Former Senator Wigfall, himself a one-man example of secession, ready to secede from anything and everything, had quit
the Senate and spent a busy fortnight establishing a secret Confederate recruiting station in Baltimore. He had sent sixty-four
recruits to Charleston when the trend of events warned him
there might be war over Sumter after all.[13] A native Carolinian
and a combative man drawn irresistibly to any scene of strife,
Wigfall dropped his Baltimore enterprise, went to Charleston
and registered April 3rd at the Mills House, where he strode out
on the balcony and gave a fighting speech to a crowd of sere-
naders.

"Whether Major Anderson shall be shelled out or starved
out," he said, "is a question merely of expediency. The honor
of South Carolina was vindicated when the flag of the United
States was fired at, and it has remained vindicated, because they
have never resented that shot. . . . that flag was never fired at
with impunity until it covered a crew of Black Republicans."

Then Wigfall spoke sense: "We have a new flag; that flag
has not yet been baptized in blood. I hear someone say, God
forbid.

"I tell you, fellow citizens . . . South Carolina became a
nation, South Carolina became a people and declared their independence before the 4th of July, 1776. But it was not acknowledged until after seven years of suffering and shedding of blood,
and if you suppose this is going to be gained without blood, I
think you are mistaken." [14]

A change had come since those blithe early days of secession.
Unlike so many others, Wigfall did not offer to drink all the
blood spilled over disunion. He could see that plenty of it was

going to be spilled. He was immediately accepted by General Beauregard as an aide with the honorary rank of colonel, although Beauregard and Pickens already had plenty of aides and were more in need of good, solid information. They were getting a flood of reports from Washington so conflicting that one canceled the other. Anderson would be evacuated in a few days. . . . Anderson would be abandoned by the government and left to be starved out. . . . A large expedition was organizing in New York. . . . Anderson would be supplied but not reinforced. . . . Anderson *would* be reinforced. . . .

What to believe? The Confederate commissioners in Washington were spreading as much confusion as anyone. Pickens did not even credit the telegram arriving from James Harvey, Mr. Seward's friend, saying: "Positively determined not to withdraw Anderson."

The uncertainty was getting on everybody's nerves. Mrs. Chesnut had *pâté de foie gras* salad, *biscuit glacé,* and champagne frappé with the Isaac Hayneses but was too upset to enjoy it. "How can one settle down to anything?" she asked. "One's heart is in one's mouth all the time." [15] William Trescot, secession's great fixer, was in Charleston now and so unhappy about the way things were going that he "grumbles all the time." [16] Old Judge Petigru, his summer house on Sullivan's Island removed to make room for cannon, thought the world was going crazy. White-haired Edmund Ruffin was still in town, refusing to leave lest he miss the start of the bloodshed he believed necessary to unify the South. He had sat for photographer Quinby and his pictures were on sale as an inspiration to Dixie statriots. Fire-eater Rhett, an unwitting architect of slaughter, stalked the streets with triumph in his eye. A couple of sharp-looking Northerners breezed into Charleston and took hotel rooms. They were pioneers of a hardy breed—George Salter of the New York *Times* and F. G. Fontaine of the *Herald,* first of the war correspondents.[17]

General Beauregard, who had found time in a busy schedule to pose for a full-length portrait, had little leisure after receiving an ominous dispatch from Confederate Secretary of War Walker at Montgomery. "The Government has at no time placed any reliance on assurances by the Government at Washington in respect to the evacuation of Fort Sumter," Walker wrote not quite truthfully, warning Beauregard to be on the alert and act "precisely as if you were in the presence of an enemy contemplating to surprise you." [18] Work on the harbor fortifications, which had lagged during the peace talk, began full blast again.

"The plot thickens," Mrs. Chesnut remarked, "the air is red hot with rumors; the mystery is to find out where these utterly groundless tales originate." [19] Governor Pickens could have amended that. The real mystery was to find out which of the rumors, if any, were correct. In his ignorance he turned to the Confederate commissioners in Washington whose reports had already run the gamut of confusion, telegraphing them April 7th:

> We have so many extraordinary telegrams, I would be glad to know from you if it is true that they have determined to reinforce Sumter, and if a naval force is sent to our harbor. Be so good as to answer as soon as convenient, for something [is] desired to govern our conduct.[20]

The commissioners' reply, received next day, proved to be just another extraordinary telegram which could hardly govern anyone's conduct:

> We are assured that you will not be disturbed without notice, and we think Sumter is to be evacuated and Pickens provisioned.[21]

That same evening of April 8th, a few hours after this ludicrous intelligence was received, Captain Talbot and Robert Chew arrived at the North Eastern station, hurried to the Charleston Hotel, and soon had an audience with Governor Pickens and General Beauregard. A tremor in Chew's voice would have been excusable as he held a square of paper near the candlelight and read the message that put an end to rumor and gave Pickens something that would indeed govern his conduct:

T

I am directed by the President of the United States to notify you to expect an attempt will be made to supply Fort Sumter with provisions only, and that if such attempt be not resisted, no effort to throw in men, arms or ammunition, will be made, without further notice, or in case of an attack upon the Fort.[22]

Chew then handed Pickens a copy of the message. It was unaddressed and unsigned, not at all according to formal protocol between the President and the governor of a state. It was Lincoln's subtle way of taking Pickens down a peg—no salutation, no courtesies, just the bare message and nothing more, delivered by the humblest of clerks. The governor was so astonished at this gross disregard for his importance that for a moment he even suspected a hoax. But Talbot, a Sumter man himself, was there to affirm its authenticity. When Pickens spoke of an answer, Chew said no, he was not authorized to accept one—another blow at the governor's pride. Lincoln was informing him, that was all, and had not the slightest interest in anything he might have to say.[23]

Captain Talbot, who had been reluctant to leave his comrades at Sumter, asked Beauregard if he might now proceed to the fort and report to Anderson for duty. Certainly not, the general snapped. He and the governor were a trifle stunned. They were also more than a little angry, feeling with some justification that the United States Government had been devious in its dealings with the Confederacy. Talbot and Chew were advised that "their immediate departure northward would be prudent." People had gathered outside the hotel, and it was evident that Chew was nervous.

"The crowd you see around this building," Beauregard assured him, "shows the eagerness of the people to be informed of the news you bear us, and nothing more." [24] But just to be on the safe side, the Northerners were escorted to the railroad station by two Carolina aides.

Major Anderson, also in need of intelligence to govern his conduct, got his notification through the regular mail. It was his first instructions from the Lincoln government, his first com-

munication of any kind from them, and was therefore Secretary
Cameron's way of saying how-do-you-do to the commander at
Sumter:

> SIR: Your letter of the 1st instant occasions some anxiety to the
> President.
>
> On the information of Captain Fox he had supposed you
> could hold out till the 15th instant without any great incon-
> venience; and had prepared an expedition to relieve you be-
> fore that period.
>
> Hoping still that you will be able to sustain yourself till
> the 11th or 12th instant, the expedition will go forward; and,
> finding your flag flying, will attempt to provision you, and, in
> case the effort is resisted, will endeavor also to reinforce you.
>
> You will therefore hold out, if possible, till the arrival of the
> expedition.
>
> It is not, however, the intention of the President to subject
> your command to any danger or hardship beyond what, in your
> judgment, would be usual in military life; and he has entire
> confidence that you will act as becomes a patriot and soldier,
> under all circumstances.
>
> Whenever, if at all, in your judgment, to save yourself and
> command, a capitulation becomes a necessity, you are author-
> ized to make it.
>
> Respectfully,
>
> SIMON CAMERON,
Secretary of War [25]

Surgeon Crawford, an expert at understatement, said that
Anderson was "deeply affected" by this letter.[26] He must have
been crushed. Cameron's instructions represented the defeat of
his hopes, sounded the crack of doom. He had endured long
hardship and great strain, but above all he had accepted humiliation to himself and his flag on two separate occasions, so that in
some degree he had sacrificed the respect of his own men. Nothing could have hurt him more. The only thought that had sustained him was that if his personal mortification could buy
peace, the price was cheap enough. Now he had the mortification
and he had war too. He had been neglected by the Lincoln
administration, left in ignorance, allowed to fall into error

through that ignorance. He had every reason to believe that the administration had not only vacillated and bungled but also had indulged in trickery, for—thanks to Mr. Seward—it had. Under the circumstances, his reply to Secretary Cameron through Adjutant General Thomas was extraordinarily restrained:

I had the honor to receive by yesterday's mail the letter of the honorable Secretary of War, dated April 4, and confess that what he there states surprises me very greatly, following as it does, and contradicting so positively the assurance Mr. Crawford telegraphed he was authorized to make [that Sumter would be evacuated]. I trust that this matter will be at once put in a correct light, as a movement made now, when the South has been erroneously informed that none such will be attempted, would produce most disastrous results throughout our country.

It is, of course, now too late for me to give any advice in reference to the proposed scheme of Captain Fox. I fear that its result cannot fail to be disastrous to all concerned. Even with his boat at our walls the loss of life (as I think I mentioned to Mr. Fox) in unloading her will more than pay for the good to be accomplished by the expedition, which keeps us, if I can maintain possession of this work, out of position, surrounded by strong works, which must be carried to make this fort of the least value to the United States Government.

We have not oil enough to keep a light in the lantern for one night. The boats will have, therefore, to rely at night entirely upon other marks. I ought to have been informed that this expedition was to come. Colonel Lamon's remark convinced me that the idea, merely hinted at to me by Captain Fox, would not be carried out. We shall strive to do our duty, though I frankly say that my heart is not in the war which I see is to be thus commenced. That God will still avert it, and cause us to resort to pacific measures to maintain our rights, is my ardent prayer. . . .[27]

Secretary Cameron doubtless would have been a little taken aback by this report, but it never reached him. It fell into the hands of General Beauregard instead.

LET THE STRIFE
BEGIN

For three weeks Sumter's sixty-eight enlisted men had confidently expected to quit their prison, go back North, breathe free air again, flirt with pretty girls, enjoy warm baths, plenty of tobacco, pork chops and apple pie, and possibly a nip or two. Now they discovered that all these pleasures were denied them. They were going to stay right there at Sumter and fight, and with a glorious kind of combative cussedness they cheered when they learned of it.

They exhibited the "greatest enthusiasm," Surgeon Crawford noted approvingly.[1] "The news acted like magic upon them," Doubleday observed. "They had previously been drooping and dejected; but they now sprung to their work with the greatest alacrity, laughing, singing, whistling. . . . They had felt themselves humiliated by the open supervision which South Carolina exercised over us, and our tame submission to it. . . ."[2]

Major Anderson's heart was not in the war, but he moved energetically to put the fort on a war footing. Men were detailed to carry ammunition to the guns. The flagstones from the parade were piled in tiers under the open casemate arches to offer more protection to the gunners. The ship bringing them supplies and men, if it got by the enemy batteries, would anchor at the fort's left flank. Foster's workmen opened one of the sealed embrasures on that flank to permit the entry of men and supplies. It would be hot work under heavy shelling, so a ladder and runway was prepared to speed it up. Anderson had no illusions that the enemy would allow provisions to enter unopposed. That meant that the expedition would attempt to send him provisions *and* reinforcements.

The men and officers were each given one biscuit morning and evening, none at noon, and required to save any unfinished crusts of bread. Secretary Cameron had said the expedition should arrive by "the 11th or 12th instant," and by these economies Anderson could hold out. A fact he had to consider was that his men had been weakened by long confinement and poor diet so that they would have to economize on energy as well. One vital item in low supply was cartridge bags, which would be filled with a measured charge of powder, rammed into the guns and demolished with each discharge. Lieutenant Meade set to work with a detail of men in cutting up surplus blankets and woolen shirts, sewing them into crude cartridge bags.[3]

On Sunday morning, April 8th, the Sumtermen got a shock. The Confederates blew up a house on Sullivan's Island just west of Fort Moultrie, unmasking a previously hidden battery of four heavy guns, well constructed with sod revetments. Anderson, Doubleday, Foster, Seymour, and Davis, all of them Mexican War veterans who knew what artillery could do, were sobered by this development that threw off all their calculations. The new battery would not only pour a hail of enfilading fire on the flank where the relief ship would anchor. It would also take in reverse Sumter's barbette-tier guns bearing on the Cummings Point batteries and make it impossible to man them without protection. Captain Foster got busy to furnish what protection he could. There were no sandbags, so Foster had his workmen construct a traverse of heavy timbers obtained by dismantling unused gun carriages, filling it with earth hoisted from the parade. Another traverse of masonry was begun to protect the main gates from the oblique fire of the formidable Cummings Point batteries.[4]

That same day Anderson received a note from General Beauregard, who had now dispensed with the "dear major" salutation, informing him that no further mail would be allowed to or from Sumter. In a later communication Beauregard admitted that Anderson's official dispatches already at the Charleston post office had been seized "in return for the treachery of Mr. Fox, who has been reported to have violated his word given to Governor Pickens before visiting Fort Sumter."[5]

This was putting the cart before the horse, for Fox's alleged "treachery" was not discovered until Anderson's dispatches had been read. A better explanation for opening the mail was given by Pickens when he wrote, "I did this because I consider a state of war is now inaugurated by the authorities at Washington, and all information of a public nature was necessary to us." [6] The mail was brought to the governor's office, where he, Judge Magrath, and General Beauregard gazed at the wax-sealed envelopes. Pickens handed them to the judge to open.

"No," Magrath demurred, "I have too recently been a United States judge, and have been in the habit of sentencing people to the penitentiary for this sort of thing. . . . Let General Beauregard open them."

"Certainly not," Beauregard protested. "Governor, you are the proper person to open these letters."

Pickens hesitated, then growled, "Well, if you are all so fastidious about it, give them to me." [7]

So they swallowed their fastidiousness and read two highly confidential reports, one written by Anderson, the other by Foster. Foster's report told of enemy activity, carefully listing his steps to defend against it. Anderson's was his letter to Cameron saying "my heart is not in the war," disclosing important facts about Sumter's condition and mentioning that Captain Fox had "merely hinted at" his relief plan. It was this hint that the trio seized on, claiming that Fox, who had said he was visiting Sumter on a peaceful mission, had broken his word. The letters were sent on to the Confederate government at Montgomery, where President Davis and his cabinet were already gathered in a historic conference.

They had received Beauregard's notification of Mr. Lincoln's expedition to supply the fort with "provisions only" unless resisted. Should they resist, knowing that resisting meant war? Davis, never one of those who believed separation could be won peacefully, thought they should. Much as he hated to be maneuvered into the position of firing the first shot, he took the stand that the Washington government had been so repeatedly an aggressor that the matter of who started the shooting was a mere technicality. Moving to Sumter in the first place had been aggression, holding it was aggression, the *Star of the West* was aggression, and now this new expedition was aggression piled on top of all the rest.

Meekly allowing Sumter to be provisioned might lose the new Confederate government popular support. One Alabamian had warned Davis, "Unless you sprinkle blood in the face of the Southern people they will be back in the old Union in less than ten days." [8] A sprinkle of blood, too, should bring the fence-sitters—Virginia and the other border states—into the Confederate fold. There was vast indignation against the Lincoln administration that was believed to have promised to evacuate Sumter and now had broken the promise. If the Confederacy did not take Sumter, it was entirely probable that the impatient Carolinians would thumb their noses at Montgomery and reduce the fort on their own, which would be a terrible blow at the authority of the Davis government. [9]

The state rights idea, Davis must have seen, had its draw-backs. Despite all these considerations, the burly Toombs was against resistance.

"Mr. President, at this time it is suicide, murder, and will lose us every friend at the North," he said. "The firing upon that fort will inaugurate a civil war greater than any the world has yet seen. . . ." [10]

Prophetic words, but Toombs was overruled. War Secretary Walker telegraphed Beauregard, ". . . you will at once demand its [Sumter's] evacuation, and if this is refused proceed, in such manner as you may determine, to reduce it." [11]

Although Beauregard got this order April 10th, he was in no hurry to execute it, being beset by last-minute troubles. He had called out five thousand more soldiers, who were now arriving in Charleston in streams, and something had to be done with them. The general did not trust the Washington government any farther than he could throw a columbiad after the way the commissioners had been cozened. The "provisions only" story he believed another deception, feeling sure the federals were coming with the intention of attacking and aimed to land a large force on Morris Island to take the batteries there from

*Fort Sumter
National Monument,
from Frank Leslie's*

e impressive flag-raising ceremony at Sumter,
Major Anderson hoisting the colors as
aplain Harris ends prayer

New York Public Library

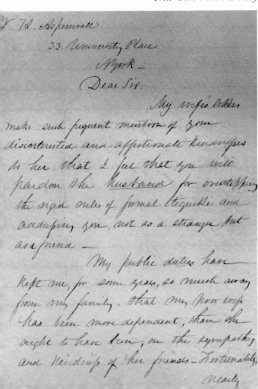

Cornelius Greenway Collection

After Sumter, Anderson showed
the marks of ordeal. (*Left*) A
portion of a letter he wrote from
the fort to W. H. Aspinwall
thanking him for kindnesses
shown to his wife.

New York Library, from Harper's Weekly

Citizen collapses after perusing papers with conflicting news: Sumter will be reinforced, it will be evacuated, has been evacuated, etc.

The sorry ruin of Sumter at the war's end. Compare this photograph with the engraving of the fort at the beginning of the war.

The floating battery looked l

val nightmare, but Beauregard made use of it

Sumter's officers. (*Front row l. to r.*): Doubleday, Anderson, Crawford, Foster. (*Back row*): Seymour, Snyder, Davis, Meade, Talbot. Lieut. Hall was in Washington at this time.

Harper's artist sketches spectators on Charleston rooftops as Sumter burns like a smudge fire

the rear. The only convenient way he could get men to Morris Island was under the guns of Sumter, making it necessary to keep those guns quiet until he got the men there. Charleston's shipping was taxed, getting hundreds of men and tons of equipment out to the island. One of the men was the fierce Wigfall, eager to officiate at the Union's funeral. Another was Edmund Ruffin, the "Nestor of the South," carrying a carpetbag and a musket he had obtained at the Citadel, a hoary zealot going to glory, cheered by companions young enough to be his grandsons. Morris Island soon became a chaos, glutted with equipment and recruits not knowing what to do next. Beauregard hastily sent Major Whiting, recently promoted, out to the island to restore order.[12]

The general also was in a sweat to mount two new guns just arrived. One of them, a heavy Dahlgren, he wanted at the western end of Sullivan's Island, writing General Dunovant: "This is one of those moments when the word impossible must be ignored, for the fate of Anderson and Sumter depends upon the results of this night's firing." [13] For all Beauregard knew, the fleet might be outside even now, the attack be made that very night of April 10th.

The other gun was a thing of beauty, the latest word in ordnance—a rifled Blakely gun just in from Liverpool, the gift of a Charlestonian in business in England, Charles K. Prioleau. On it was engraved, "Presented to the State of South Carolina by a citizen resident abroad, in commemoration of the 20th December, 1860." The Blakely, which would throw a shell or 12-pound shot with the accuracy of a dueling pistol, using only a half pound of powder, was promptly shipped to Cummings Point in the hope that it would pound holes in Sumter's gorge wall.[14]

Out on Morris Island, Major Whiting was going frantic with more than two thousand men falling over each other, losing their muskets, getting separated from their commands, and creating unholy anarchy. "For God's sake have this post inspected by yourself, or someone else competent, before you open fire," he appealed to Beauregard. "I am expected to be

engineer and everything else." [15] Beauregard sent him a couple
of officers and told him to cool off: "Things always appear worst
at first sight when not perfect." [16] The general was not as calm
as he sounded. Organization was tottering just at the most
critical moment. South Carolina's General Bonham, disgruntled
at being left out of the picture, demanded command of all the
Carolina troops under Beauregard—a ticklish point because
General Dunovant would resent Bonham ranking *him*. Bonham
was told he would have to wait.[17] Beauregard, the brain of a
large and complicated military movement, was sending out
orders as fast as he could write them. The floating battery, too
clumsy for its original purpose, would come in handy at the
west end of Sullivan's Island, and he sent it there. He ordered
Captain Hartstene, in charge of naval operations, to prepare
barges containing great piles of wood, ready to be set ablaze
at the entrance to the harbor so the enemy could not enter
unseen.[18]

Although the Confederacy now had some six thousand men
surrounding Major Anderson and his minuscule command,
Governor Pickens was not without fears. "I trust we are ready,"
he wrote President Davis with surprising uncertainty for a man
who had talked of being "ready" weeks earlier, "and if they
come we will give them a cordial reception, such as will ring
through this country, I think. I hope we are not mistaken,"
adding later, "I think you will hear of as bloody a fight as ever
occurred." [19]

Charleston's streets were clogged with marching soldiers,
rumbling wagons of powder, excited citizens. "Why did that
green goose Anderson go into Fort Sumter?" Mrs. Chesnut
wailed in her diary. "Then everything began to go wrong." [20]
Despite all the turmoil, the races were run as usual in the
nearby Metairie course, Equinox beating Bettie Ward and Twi-
light. The Charleston *Courier* let out a blast at Lincoln's "ignorance and vulgarity," trumpeting: "We are prepared to apply
the last argument. . . . We are sick of the subject of evacuation. . . . Let the strife begin—we have no fear of the issue." [21]

That April 10th another distinguished visitor arrived at the

Charleston Hotel—tall, black-haired young Roger Pryor, the
Virginia ex-Congressman and secessionist who, like Ruffin, was
out of patience with his own state for failing to join the disunion parade. Pryor had come to urge an attack on Sumter as
the sure way to get cautious Virginia to move. A fiery orator
who knew how to sway a crowd, he quickly obliged with a
balcony speech when he was serenaded that night.

"I thank you," he said in part, "that you have at last an-
nihilated this accursed Union. . . ." He poked fun at his own
state for its slowness. "Give the old lady time. . . . She is a
little rheumatic. . . . But I assure you that just as certain as
tomorrow's sun will rise upon us, just so certain will Virginia
be a member of the Southern Confederacy; and I will tell your
Governor what will put her in the Southern Confederacy in less
than an hour by Shrewsbury clock. *Strike a blow!*" [22]

When April 11th dawned bright and clear, Anderson and his
men received another unpleasant surprise. The floating battery
had been towed from the city and firmly stranded at the west
end of Sullivan's Island behind a stone breakwater that would
protect it from richochet shots. Now it added its two 42-
pounders and two 32-pounders to the heavy guns already enfilading Sumter's left flank where the relief boat would anchor.
If it was lucky enough to reach the fort, the boat and its occupants would be in for a screaming welcome. General Beauregard was indeed a canny artillerist. There was no help for it
now. The garrison was cut off from the world, and no warning
could be given to the fleet. [23]

Captain Foster was still struggling with makeshift traverses
against the unsuspected weight of metal. The remaining bread
was eaten that day, leaving nothing but salt pork and a few
broken crackers in the larder. Someone remembered that on
the floor in one of the barracks rooms was a quantity of rice
which had been dampened in shipment six weeks earlier and
was spread out to dry. When the salute to Washington was fired
February 22nd, the windows had broken, mixing fragments of
shattered glass with the rice. The glass was now sifted out of the

rice which, although a trifle mouldy, was a welcome addition to the provender.[24] "D. [Doubleday?] found a potatoe today, and put it away," Crawford noted in his diary. "He said somebody had tramped on it, but had not hurt it much." [25]

The harbor was alive with craft, most of them carrying men and munitions past Sumter to Morris Island. The rebels were rushing to completion still *another* battery at the end of Sullivan's Island near the floating battery, this one of one gun, a big nine-inch Dahlgren. Although he was ill and taking vile medication, Surgeon Crawford was busy arranging hospital facilities in one of the unused bombproof casemates. By Anderson's order, everybody moved their bedding from the vulnerable barracks and officers' quarters to the protection of the casemates, where they would live as well as fight. The major could see no logic in defending this fort which he considered lost anyway, but he would defend it nevertheless, resigned to what he considered sheer madness in Washington. The observant Crawford noticed an unforgettable contrast: the men working with "greatest alacrity" on their defenses, Major Anderson pacing alone in a casemate, head bowed, face grim, a man who saw nothing but tragedy ahead for the nation.[26] Yet his report for April 11th, which might never be read, mirrored no despair but rather the determination of a soldier to do his duty.

"Although not permitted to send off my daily report," he wrote, "I shall continue, as long as I can, to prepare them, so that if an opportunity is afforded me I shall have them ready." He outlined enemy activity and his own, finishing, "The officers and men, thank God, are in pretty good health; and, although feeling aware of the danger of their position, have greater anxiety about the fate of those whom they expect to come to their succor than they entertain for themselves." [27]

THE END
OF LONG DOUBT

Surgeon Samuel Crawford, a man with a sense of history, somehow continued to find time to dash off an occasional line in his diary. It made his Union blood race to know that an expedition was en route to fight its way into the harbor, help the garrison so long neglected, fill Sumter with fresh new men and plenty of provisions, and give the fort the strength it needed to deal out righteous punishment to the wicked inventors of secession.

"We are looking for the relief promised to us," he wrote April 11th, "and men can be seen at all hours on the parapet." [1] They saw no warships, but at 3:30 that afternoon they spied a small boat bearing a white flag approaching from the city. Lieutenant Jefferson Davis, who had endured much joshing at the fort because his name had such a rebel sound, was officer of the day at the time. He met the boat at the wharf as Colonel Chesnut got out, followed by Captain Stephen D. Lee and Colonel Chisolm, and escorted them to the guardroom where Anderson met them. Lee, like Chesnut one of Beauregard's many aides, was a young Carolinian West Pointer who had gone with his state. Chisolm was well remembered, having once brought wine and cigars. They greeted the major and handed him a dispatch from Beauregard. In it the general said the Confederacy could wait no longer to assume "actual possession of a fortification commanding the entrance of one of their harbors," going on:

> I am ordered by the Government of the Confederate States to demand the evacuation of Fort Sumter. . . . All proper facilities will be afforded for the removal of yourself and command, together with company arms and property, to any post in the United States which you may select. The flag which you have upheld so long and with so much fortitude, under the most trying circumstances, may be saluted by you on taking it down. [2]

The three Southerners waited while Anderson summoned his officers into council in another room. He told them he had a decision to make which involved not only their position but possibly their lives. Then he read them Beauregard's message.

The phrasing was courteous, the terms generous. As Crawford put it, "was ever such terms granted to a band of starving men?" In the next breath he wrote, "we to a man unanimously refused to give up our trust." [3] Doubleday, Foster, Seymour, Snyder, Davis, Hall, Crawford—even the young Virginian Meade, who would later join the Confederacy—all voted No. Anderson wrote his reply:

> GENERAL: I have the honor to acknowledge the receipt of your communication demanding the evacuation of this fort, and to say, in reply thereto, that it is a demand with which I regret that my sense of honor, and of my obligations to my Government, prevent my compliance. Thanking you for the fair, manly and courteous terms proposed, and for the high compliment paid me,
>
> I am, general, very respectfully, your obedient servant,
>
> ROBERT ANDERSON
> Major, First Artillery Commanding [4]

The major informed the three aides of the decision as he accompanied them out to the wharf. "Will General Beauregard open his batteries without further notice to me?" he asked.

Colonel Chesnut pondered. "I think not," he said. "No, I can say to you that he will not, without further notice."

"I shall await the first shot," Anderson said, "and if you do not batter us to pieces, we shall be starved out in a few days."

It was a remark which in strict military propriety he should not have made—would never have made had he considered these men enemies who must be destroyed rather than gentlemen who had a legitimate grievance. Chesnut, surprised, asked if he might report this to Beauregard. Anderson declined to give it the character of a report but said it was true. The boat pushed off. [5]

General Beauregard did not want to shell his friend Anderson. More important, it would take some time to reduce the

fort, during which time the relief fleet would surely arrive and
he would have a naval enemy to combat as well. How much
better if he could have the fort handed over to him intact and
undamaged before the fleet arrived. He telegraphed Secretary
Walker, quoting Anderson's remark and asking for instructions.
At Sumter, the men kept glancing out to sea. No warships were
visible. Late that afternoon three hulks were towed out from
Charleston, anchored and ready to be set ablaze at the spot
where the Main and Swash channels met and where the relief
boats would have to turn.[6]

Dinner that night consisted of salt pork and rice—eaten with
care lest some bits of glass might remain—but it was served to
the officers with customary éclat by a mulatto servant from
Charleston who, along with the workmen, had been forced to
remain. Over the *pièce de résistance* Anderson announced a
decision that jolted his officers. He was restricting the garrison
to the use of the sheltered guns in the lower casemate tier only.
In view of the greatly increased enemy batteries on Sullivan's
Island and the hail of metal that would whistle around the
poorly protected guns on the parapet, he forbade the men to
use those guns at all. He took sole responsibility for this important step. Had he had anything near the fort's proper war
garrison of 650 men, doubtless he would have acted otherwise.
With just about a tenth that number, his men were not ex-
pendable.[7]

This was a blow, for the heaviest artillery was on the barbette
tier, which afforded a better view of enemy emplacements and
a more advantageous angle of fire. Among the twenty-seven guns
there were five 42-pounders, six eight-inch columbiads, and two
mighty ten-inch columbiads. Of the twenty-one guns in the
casemate tier, the heaviest were three 42-pounders at the right
shoulder angle, the rest being 32-pounders. The decision rendered useless the long toil expended in raising and mounting
guns on the parapet as well as Captain Foster's valiant work in
building a traverse to protect the barbette guns on the right
flank, which must have disgruntled the captain.

That night, sentinels kept a close watch but saw no sign of

the fleet. It is doubtful that Major Anderson got any sleep at all. Thirteen hundred yards south on Cummings Point, Edmund Ruffin had been made an honorary member of the Palmetto Guards under Captain G. B. Cuthbert. Cuthbert shouted to the old man, who was somewhat deaf, that the company had chosen him to fire the first shot of the fight. "I was highly gratified by the compliment, and delighted to perform the service," he wrote, and went to bed without undressing to make sure he would be ready.[8] In Charleston, Mrs. Chesnut had attended "the merriest, maddest dinner we have had yet. Men were audaciously wise and witty. We had an unspoken foreboding that it was to be our last pleasant meeting," This brilliant woman had more forebodings than most. She knew her husband was on a climactic errand that night. "I do not pretend to go to sleep," she wrote. "How can I? If Anderson does not accept terms at four, the orders are, he shall be fired upon." [9]

If he had any nerves, Captain Foster did not sleep well either. He had long been sizing up the enemy batteries bearing on Sumter, and as he figured it they were distributed as follows:

SULLIVAN'S ISLAND

The iron-clad floating battery at the west end of the island had two 42-pounders and two 32-pounders.

Next to it, the lone but potent nine-inch Dahlgren.

Next to that, a battery of two 32-pounders and two 24-pounders.

Just west of Fort Moultrie, a battery of three ten-inch mortars.

Behind Moultrie, a battery of two ten-inch mortars.

In Moultrie itself, three eight-inch columbiads, two eight-inch seacoast howitzers, five 32-pounders, and four 24-pounders.

MOUNT PLEASANT

(On the mainland beyond Sullivan's Island.)

Two ten-inch mortars.

JAMES ISLAND

The Fort Johnson battery, one 24-pounder.

South of this, a battery of four ten-inch mortars.

Four batteries on Cummings Point: (1) a battery of two 42-pounders and one rifled Blakely gun; (2) a battery of four ten-inch mortars; (3) the Iron-Clad Battery of three eight-inch columbiads; (4) a battery of three ten-inch mortars.

That added up to thirty guns and eighteen mortars firing on Sumter from four different points of the compass. In return, Sumter had twenty-one guns in its casemate tier, not a single mortar, most of its guns being only 32-pounders. It was not enough, and Foster knew it.[10]

At 12:45 A.M. April 12th, the Sumter sentinels hailed a boat approaching under a white flag. It was the three Confederate aides again, this time accompanied by a fourth, Roger Pryor, now an aide of General Beauregard and a quick colonel. Pryor had a sudden qualm. Recalling that his state had not yet seceded, he did not go in with the others but remained in the boat. Chesnut, Lee, and Chisolm handed Anderson another dispatch from Beauregard. In it the general said he had communicated Anderson's remark about being "starved out" to the Confederate government, and he was ordered to ask the major to state precisely when he would be forced to evacuate the fort.[11]

Anderson aroused his officers and put the question to them. They were all tired from many a night watch and too much work for too few men. The major asked Dr. Crawford for his professional opinion: How long could the men last and do any fighting?

Crawford said the lack of food was already being felt, but estimated that the garrison could last for five days, "when they would then be three days entirely without food."[12] There was considerable reference to Secretary Cameron's letter of instructions, so remarkably mild in tone. The secretary wrote, "Hoping still that you will be able to sustain yourself until the 11th or 12th instant, the expedition will go forward. . . . You will therefore hold out, if possible, till the arrival of the expedition." This, along with the authorization to Anderson to capitulate when necessary, was anything but a peremptory order to hold

U

out at all costs. The orders could be interpreted to mean that the government wished to make only a token defense before surrendering the fort to superior forces. It was now early in the "12th instant" and the expedition had not arrived. The officers debated so long that Chesnut and his companions, waiting in another room, grew impatient.

"Major Anderson made every possible effort to retain the aides till daylight," Captain Lee later wrote, "making one excuse and then another for not replying." [13]

Possibly the major was playing for time, but it was also a hard decision to make. On one occasion when the aides pressed him for an answer, his resentment boiled over for a moment.

"You have twice fired on my flag," he said, "and if you do it again I will open fire." [14]

At last the Sumter officers agreed that waiting until noon on April 15th, the last date mentioned by Cameron, would give the expedition sufficient time to arrive if it was coming at all. Anderson wrote a reply to Beauregard agreeing to evacuate the fort at that time unless the Confederates meanwhile made a hostile move, "should I not receive prior to that time controlling instructions from my Government or additional supplies." [15]

Chesnut, who was instructed to act for Beauregard, read it and shook his head. There were too many conditions in it. He wrote a reply and handed it to the major:

SIR: By authority of Brigadier-General Beauregard, commanding the provisional forces of the Confederate States, we have the honor to notify you that he will open the fire of his batteries on Fort Sumter in one hour from this time.[16]

Although he could have expected nothing else, Anderson was deeply moved. "He seemed to realize the full import of the consequences," Captain Lee wrote, "and the great responsibility of his position. Escorting us to the boat at the wharf, he cordially pressed our hands in farewell, remarking, 'If we never meet in this world again, God grant that we may meet in the next.'" [17]

It was nearing 3:30 when the aides were rowed off into the darkness. Anderson and his officers went through the casemates where the soldiers were sleeping, arousing them one by one, giving each the same message: We will soon be attacked. Stay where you are until further orders. We will not fire until morning.[18]

Chesnut and his mates were cutting water in the direction of Fort Johnson, where they found Captain George S. James, commander of the mortar battery. They ordered James to open fire at 4:30 with a gun that would give the signal that the crews of the forty-seven other guns surrounding Sumter had been awaiting so long—start the war.

Captain James had a full appreciation of this historic moment and his own never-to-be-forgotten part in it—something he could tell to his children and his children's children with pardonable pride. But James was a great admirer of Roger Pryor, standing there so tall and slim and eager. The captain thought a moment, then achieved a decision of real self-denial. Would Colonel Pryor be so kind as to fire it?

"You are the only man to whom I would give up the honor of firing the first gun of the war," he said.

Some thirty hours earlier the Virginian had spoken to a cheering crowd from the Charleston Hotel balcony, saying, "Strike a blow!" Yet now he was strangely agitated by the opportunity to strike it himself. "His manner was almost similar to that of Major Anderson as we left him a few moments before," observed Captain Lee, who was taking in the colloquy. After a long moment, Pryor shook his head.

"I could not fire the first gun of the war," he said in a husky voice.[19]

So Chesnut, Lee, Chisolm, and Pryor got back into their boat and headed for Fort Moultrie while Captain James aroused his command. The four aides glided across a calm sea under a canopy of stars and scudding clouds, undoubtedly gripped by mixed emotions—relief at the end of long doubt and indecision, the thrill of impending combat, the elation of men about to settle a sore grievance combined with a solemnity in the knowledge that the settling might be painful.

They were not far north of Sumter when they saw a flash of

flame from one of James's ten-inch mortars, moments later hearing its throaty roar—a sound that "woke the echoes from every nook and corner of the harbor." [20] The shell soared in a high arc, its burning fuse spitting like a small rocket. It curved downward and burst almost directly over Fort Sumter. A few statriot watchers on Charleston's Battery later swore that when it exploded it formed a pattern in flame of an almost perfect palmetto.[21]

Over on Cummings Point the Palmetto Guards had been aroused at four, their pieces loaded and ready. Edmund Ruffin, erect and proud, was standing by one of the columbiads of the Iron Battery when the signal gun was fired from Fort Johnson. Ruffin, with none of Pryor's qualms, jerked the lanyard and sent a shell crashing into Sumter's parapet.[22] Then the darkness was split by thunder as a dozen batteries broke loose from various points in the harbor.

In her suite at the Mills House, Mrs. Chesnut had not slept a wink. "At half-past four the heavy booming of a cannon," she wrote. "I sprang out of bed, and on my knees prostrate I prayed as I never prayed before." [23]

VIRTUE v. VICE

Flashing, flashing, along the wires,
The glorious news each heart inspires,
The war in Charleston was begun,
Its smoke obscured the morning sun,
As with cannon, mortar and petard
We saluted the North with our Beauregard.

Being weary, Captain Doubleday had gone to bed in an empty magazine on the right flank even though he knew that a lot of gratuitous metal would come his way at 4:30. He was awake when the signal shot boomed. Then came another that jarred him a bit, one he described in the manner of a man who would never spoil a good story by a too rigid adherence to fact: ". . . by the sound, [it] seemed to bury itself in the masonry about a foot from my head, in very unpleasant proximity to my right ear. This is the one that probably came with Mr. Ruffin's compliments." [1]

As the firing became a continuous roar, Doubleday showed his contempt for the slave oligarchy by staying right in bed. Sumter's failure to return the fire caused surprise and disappointment among the Confederates. Some wondered if Anderson could be quitting without a fight. Even before dawn, Charleston's noncombatant citizens found vantage points on wharves, on the Battery, and on rooftops to see the show. Mrs. Chesnut climbed with many others to the roof of the Mills House and in her excitement sat down on a chimney, suddenly becoming aware that her dress was on fire and friends were beating it out. [2]

Reveille was at six at Sumter that morning, as if anyone needed any awakening. Some took quick, vain glances out to sea for the fleet. The men were formed in the bombproofs instead of the open parade, where shells were falling at a lively clip, throwing dirt and masonry in splendid confusion. "The roll was called as if nothing unusual was going on," noted Sergeant Chester of the garrison.[3] Breakfast was a quick, two-course affair—fat pork and water—although the officers' mess had a slight advantage in this respect. Surgeon Crawford triumphantly brought in a bit of farina he had found in a corner of the hospital.[4] The mulatto waiter, usually so efficient, was wincing at each explosion and wishing he were back in Charleston. "He leaned back against the wall," Doubleday wrote, "almost white with fear, his eyes closed, and his whole expression one of perfect despair." [5] The men fell in again when assembly was beaten, and Major Anderson gave them special instructions. He was a humane man, and on top of that he had a garrison of nine officers, sixty-eight soldiers, eight musicians, and forty-three noncombatant workmen—128 men all told, including himself. He would need them all. He gave them strict orders to stay in the casemates as much as possible.

"Be careful of your lives," he said. "Make no imprudent exposure of your persons to the enemy's fire; do your duty coolly, determinedly and *cautiously*. Indiscretion is not valor. . . ." [6]

The major appointed three details to serve the guns under Doubleday, Davis, and Crawford. Most army sawbones did not know a cannon's muzzle from its breech, but Crawford, the inquiring scientist, was as interested in artillery as he was in Popocatepetl. As commander, Anderson could have exercised the privilege of firing the first gun—an honor he willingly forbore. Doubleday, as second in command, accepted it with relish. He led his men to a battery of two 32-pounders in the right gorge angle, bearing on the spiteful mass of armament gathered on Cummings Point. The burly, black-mustachioed, abolitionist captain, himself an embodiment of one of the reasons why war had come, was girded by a feeling of unassailable rectitude.

"In aiming the first gun fired against the rebellion," he reflected, "I had no feeling of self-reproach, for I fully believed that the contest was inevitable, and was not of our seeking. The

United States was called upon not only to defend its sovereignty, but its right to exist as a nation. . . . To me it was simply a contest, politically speaking, as to whether virtue or vice should rule." [7]

It was just short of seven o'clock when he gave the order and the 32-pounder belched its projectile at Vice across the way. It should have been a historic shot, but its emotional impact was impaired by the fact that the Confederates had already been blazing away for two and half hours, and besides, it had no punishing effect at all. The ball struck the slanted T-rail roof of the Iron Battery and bounced off harmlessly as if it were one of the captain's baseballs.[8] Yet the shot produced an instantaneous sensation among the hostile thousands at Cummings Point, Fort Johnson, Sullivan's Island, Mount Pleasant, and Charleston. Anderson was going to make a fight of it after all! Until then they had felt the frustration and slight sense of shame of a man belaboring another who refuses to fight back; they had been robbed of the decent, respectable resistance they felt they deserved.[9] War was new to most of them, and there was a tendency to view it as a spectacle, a grand jousting of armored knights on the field of honor, not as the thing of casualty lists and black ruin it was to become. Over at Cummings Point, Edmund Ruffin was gratified when he saw the first ball from Sumter come whistling across the water and bounce off the T-rails. Until then he had been disgruntled, certain that nonresistance would "cheapen the conquest of the fort." [10]

Doubleday began a steady, deliberate fire on the Iron Battery, while Davis and his men assailed the James Island mortars and Crawford's detail took the floating battery as target. They were working at a disadvantage, for Sumter's guns were not equipped with breech sights. The inventive Doubleday had sought to repair this deficiency by devising makeshift vertical marking rods to denote the elevation of barrel, a useful but imperfect substitute.[11] Although the smoke was thickening, a breeze carried enough of it away so that the gunners could often watch the trajectory of the ball they fired, note where it struck, and make a correction of aim or elevation. Firing soon became a me-

chanical operation, each of the four men at each gun performing
his part of it: sponge barrel, load cartridge, ram it, load ball
and wad, ram it, *fire*. Peter Hart, the New York police officer
who had been allowed to go to Sumter on his promise to serve
as a workman, regarded this obligation as dissolved now that
war was a roaring reality. He helped serve one of the guns with
a skill not forgotten from the old Mexican days.

The forty-two other workmen were in an anomalous position,
honest artisans caught in a conflict they had never contemplated
experiencing as participants. While they were loyal Unionists,
they were not soldiers, and some had turned a little green when
they learned that the Confederates refused to let them leave the
target of all those encircling guns. Now they were stuck and
they made the best of it. Some carried ammunition and powder
to the guns while others worked with six needles—the fort had
six and no more—sewing shirts and sheets into cartridge bags
to replace those being blasted to smithereens with each shot.[12]

The enemy, at first inclined to fire too high, soon improved
his range. Sumter became a place of walled-in thunder, flying
metal whining as it ricocheted, chunks of broken masonry sailing in crazy abandon. The Confederate mortar men were lobbing shells that soared aloft before they plopped down to explode on the parapet or inside the fort. The brick-and-frame
barracks and officers' quarters, built three stories high along
the gorge wall, began to take a dreadful beating. Yet the men
in the stone-arched casemates, protected from missiles from
within by the piled-up flagstones, were comparatively safe from
anything but an unlikely shot directly through an embrasure.
The pesky Blakely gun on Cummings Point was sending projectiles at terrific velocity, one shot dislodging a piece of embrasure stone that knocked Sergeant Thomas Kernan flat on his
face. His companions anxiously asked if he was wounded. "No,"
growled Kernan as he picked himself up, "I was only knocked
down *temporarily*." [13]

Warfare was not allowed to rule out levity. When Captain
Seymour arrived with a detail to relieve Doubleday and his

exhausted gunners, Seymour shouted over the din, "Doubleday, what in the world is the matter here, and what is all this uproar about?"

"There is a trifling difference of opinion between us and our neighbors opposite," Doubleday yelled back without cracking a smile, "and we are trying to settle it." [14]

But the sad fact was that while Sumter's interior took a pounding, it could not seem to dent the well-protected Confederate batteries. For a couple of hours Crawford threw 32-pound balls at the floating battery, shielded by the stone sea wall and armored with railroad iron. He scored a number of good hits but saw to his disgust that the balls bounced off harmlessly. A 32-pound ball with range at a mile simply did not have enough weight or power. Now, those eight-inch and ten-inch columbiads upstairs, hurling projectiles weighing 65 and 128 pounds respectively, could have dealt out real punishment, but the major's strict orders were to stay down in the casemates, and he had justification because the ramparts were a screaming chaos unsafe for man or beast. Crawford went hunting for Anderson to ask permission to switch his fire to Moultrie. He finally found him looking over the main magazine, whose exposed position was causing him considerable worry. If its 300-odd barrels of powder exploded, it would blow the fort and everyone in it to eternity.[15]

With Anderson's approval, Crawford shifted his men to three casemate guns bearing on Moultrie and began blazing away at his former home. Moultrie's guns were so heavily protected with sandbags and cotton bales that they seemed impervious. The Sumter gunners felt like men assailing a stone wall with peashooters, an unsatisfying sensation that caused Private John Carmody of Company H to disobey orders. Knowing that the guns on the ramparts were already loaded and trailed, he stole up the circular stairway and fired, one by one, every barbette gun on the Moultrie side of the work.

"The contest was merely Carmody against the Confederate States," his friend Sergeant Chester later observed, "and Carmody had to back down, not because he was beaten, but because he was unable, single-handed, to reload his guns." [16]

This valorous insubordination was contagious. On the other side of the fort, two veteran sergeants who were sick and tired of pea-shooting thought longingly of the mighty ten-inch columbiad mounted *en barbette* on the right face. They sneaked up there and fired it. The aim was perfect, the range a trifle high, the huge ball sailing just over the Iron Battery. Although enemy metal was screeching around them, they could not resist trying another shot, giving the elevating screw half a turn down. They managed to reload the gun but could not throw the carriage in gear, a job taking the combined effort of six men. Recklessly they let her go as she was. Having been fired "from battery," the eight-ton monster recoiled and plunged off its carriage, dismounting an eight-inch seacost howitzer next to it, and came near rolling down the stairs. Luckily unhurt, the sergeants noted with regret that this shot was a mite low, spraying the Iron Battery with a deluge of sand. [17]

Many of the men were eager to take their chances on the parapet, and there was some disgruntlement at the order to stay in the casemates. Yet, hungry and tired as they were, they worked with an enthusiasm that gratified Surgeon Crawford, who watched them with a questioning professional eye for signs of exhaustion. Anderson was badly crippled by his lack of mortars as well as by his inability to fire shell, which might have been more destructive than plain ball. The garrison had plenty of shells but not a single fuse to fire them—a deficiency the men tried vainly to overcome by improvising crude fuses of bored-out pine filled with caked gunpowder. They did not work. In the parade were mounted two ten-inch and four eight-inch columbiads as mortars bearing on Charleston, Moultrie, and Cummings Point. Some of the soldiers were itching to try them —particularly the one aimed at Charleston—but they were so exposed to enemy fire that they went unused. [18]

If the Sumter men were making little impression on the enemy, they had the satisfaction of knowing that their own walls, about twelve feet thick at the first tier level, were turning away shot with fine disdain. It was on the exposed parapet that the damage was beginning to show, and the two upper stories of the barracks were steadily being reduced to wreckage. Shells just clearing the parapet crashed squarely into the barracks. The enemy mortars were doing good work too, some of their shells dropping through the barracks roof to explode inside the building. Other shells buried themselves in the dirt parade so that "their explosion shook the fort like an earthquake." [19] Crawford penned hasty impressions in his diary: ". . . splintering of brick and cement flying every where— Four men are wounded slightly. . . . Our quarters being riddled with shot and shell— chimney knocked away. . . ." [20]

The barracks were supposed to be fireproof, but somone had made an error there. In midmorning, when the upper story caught fire, Peter Hart took charge of a group of workmen and put it out with water from the cisterns. As a New York policeman, Hart had often watched the fire laddies at work, and he was soon called on to extinguish another blaze in the barracks. It became apparent that the Moultrie gunners were making use of their hot-shot furnaces and firing red-hot balls.

Sumter could use some beefsteak and some more men. Where was the relief expedition Mr. Cameron said would arrive on the "11th or 12th instant"? A watch was kept at an unused embrasure in the right flank, but nothing more cheering could be seen than a steady flow of projectiles coming from smoke-clad Cummings Point. Although Second Lieutenant R. K. Meade hailed from Petersburg, Virginia, had many secessionist friends, and was himself painfully torn on the question of right and wrong in this national struggle, he could see nothing friendly about the secessionists throwing shells at him. Meade relieved Crawford in charge of the guns bearing on Moultrie and hurled shot with such spirit that he won the approval of Doubleday, a man suspicious of anyone who came from south of the Potomac. "Hall, Snyder and Meade had never been under fire before," Doubleday commented, "but they proved themselves to be true sons of their Alma Mater at West Point." [21]

Sumter started the day with only seven hundred cartridge

bags, a large part of them handmade from clothing and bedding. By noon they were so depleted that Anderson ordered the firing confined to six guns, two bearing on Cummings Point, two on Moultrie, and two on the batteries at the west end of Sullivan's Island. The six needles were busy making more, but the bags could be blown apart much faster than they could be manufactured. A throng of some five thousand people, almost entirely women, could be seen watching the battle from Charleston's Battery, another group of spectators crowding the shore of Sullivan's Island out of the line of fire. Some reckless citizens put out in small boats to get a better view. When Doubleday came on duty again, taking over the battery firing on Moultrie, he gazed with distaste on these civilians who seemed to regard an assault on the nation as a sort of public jubilee. To the east of Fort Moultrie hulked the large frame summer hotel, the Moultrie House, where the teetotaling, nonsmoking captain had often enjoyed a cup of tea back in the friendly days. The hotel had recently been used as a barracks for Carolina troops, but its palmetto flag had been removed just before the bombardment started.[22]

"I saw no reason why the mere lowering of the flag should prevent us from firing at them," Doubleday observed.[23] Changing his aim, he let loose with a 42-pound ball. The shoreline spectators saw it coming toward them and scattered pell-mell. The ball crashed squarely into the hotel's second story with a rending of clapboard, timber, and plaster. ". . . a party of gentlemen were setting [sic] in the parlor, watching the fight," a newsman reported. "The gentlemen scattered miscellaneously." [24] To Doubleday, the sight of people plunging out of the hotel in undignified haste was a small but satisfying repayment for the many discourtesies he and his colleagues had suffered.

Early in the afternoon the watchers set up a shout. United States men-of-war out beyond the bar! The word passed from mouth to mouth. The fleet! There they were, two ships steaming closer, still distant but gloriously visible through wisps of smoke, flying the Stars and Stripes which had not been seen anywhere for many a moon except on Sumter's own flagstaff.

To the men so long penned in lonely isolation, circled by hostility, the sight was one to warm the heart and bring a catch to the throat. These were fighting ships, the kind of ships that should have come instead of the *Star of the West*, the kind they had been hoping to see day after day during the long three months since the *Star* had been chased away in such humiliation. The two vessels were soon joined by a third. They were about as late as they could be without being *too* late, but now they were here in wonderful reality, the might of the United States Navy bringing men, ammunition, beef, potatoes, and maybe a spot of rum. They would have hot work delivering those essentials even under cover of night, but who could doubt that they would succeed? To the men in Sumter it meant everything they needed with a most aching need. Let them get reinforcements and provisions during the night and on the morrow they would be manning all of Sumter's forty-eight guns, upper and lower, giving the Palmetto boys a real taste of Yankee metal.[25]

Major Anderson ordered the colors dipped as a signal to the vessels—an effort that failed when a bursting shell cut the halyards and the flag stuck at half-mast. The men fought on with new spirit, but soon Hart and his firemen were fighting another blaze in the barracks. Recalling that he had left a chest full of belongings in the officers' quarters, Doubleday asked the mulatto servant to help him carry it out to safety. Hugging the protection of the outer wall, the man politely declined, explaining, "De major, he say, I muss not expose myself." [26]

If there was one man Doubleday felt doomed to eternal hellfire, it was Lieutenant-Colonel Roswell S. Ripley, commanding the Moultrie artillery and doing an excellent job of it. Ripley had fought under the old flag in Mexico and now was shooting at it, but his cardinal sin in the captain's estimation was that he was a native of Ohio and therefore a renegade. After resigning from the army, Ripley had gone into business in Charleston as agent for a rifle company and when hostilities loomed had accepted a commission in the Carolina army. "Like all Northern converts, he thought it necessary to be overzealous in his new position," Doubleday wrote, "to do away with the suspicions excited by his birth and education. I was told . . . that for this purpose he took pains to denounce me as an Abolitionist, and to recommend that I be hanged by the populace as soon as caught." [27]

Although every man at Sumter by now had conceived an earnest loathing for salt pork, salt pork was what they had for dinner that night, the gun crews downing it as they worked. The heady wine of battle had converted many of Foster's workers from men who sought safe corners into enthusiastic fighters. Along with the musicians they did good work filling cartridge bags with powder and carrying ammunition. One group of a half-dozen workmen even took instruction from the soldiers and manned a gun themselves for a time. [28]

The barracks were still burning despite all efforts to extinguish the flames, when help came from an unexpected quarter. An enemy shot punctured three of the iron cisterns just under the roof, sending water cascading down over the blazing timbers. A heavy rainstorm came around seven o'clock to finish the firemen's job. As it grew dark, Anderson ordered the firing stopped for the night because of the critical shortage of cartridges. Lieutenant Meade kept busy with a detail of men cutting up shirts, sheets, and even coarse paper and sewing the pieces into bags. [29]

The major and Captain Foster had an anxious duty: to ready the fort and give what help was possible if boats should run the enemy batteries and make it to the work during the night. The enemy had now restricted his activity to the mortars, lobbing shells at fifteen-minute intervals. Foster went outside in the storm, making sure with his own eyes that the preparations for receiving men and supplies at the left flank were still intact. Although the men were bone-weary, Anderson had to station watchers at strategic embrasures to sound the alarm if help arrived. [30]

Here was a situation ticklish enough to make a man queasy. It was entirely possible that the enemy would attempt a storming assault during the night. How to tell friend from foe? "Both would come in boats," Sergeant Chester observed, "both would answer in English. It would be horrible to fire upon friends; it would be fatal not to fire upon enemies." [31]

They would have to do the best they could. The Confederates had problems too. In the teeth of a wild wind and occasional rain, a string of rowboats went out from Charleston, each carrying a huge torch, to watch near the bar and guard against surprise from the sea. Around midnight, Surgeon Crawford, though still not quite recovered from his illness, went out with Lieutenant Snyder and made an inspection. All five sides of the fort, but most of all the gorge wall and the faces opposite Moultrie, were pocked by solid shot. The eight-inch columbiad balls had penetrated the brick about twelve inches, making wide craters. The Blakely gun had gone a trifle deeper, penetration in places being twenty inches, and one shot had blasted through the main gate. Although the parapet was badly battered, the fort's power of resistance was little affected, its lower casemates and guns undamaged, and no one in the garrison suffering any injury of consequence.[32]

By midnight no relief boats had come. Major Anderson ordered Lieutenant Meade to cease his destruction of government-issue shirts and sheets and to get some rest. Surgeon Crawford took a dose of evil-tasting medicine, went to bed, and "slept all night well but hungry." [33] The major, serving out the final hours of his unhappiest duty, probably got no sleep at all.

II

Never was a man so balked by circumstances beyond his control as Captain Gustavus Vasa Fox, who had neglected his textile business at some sacrifice to volunteer out of sheer patriotism for a duty involving peril as well as skill and found himself frustrated by the elements, by departmental confusion, and above all by Secretary Seward. *Everything* went wrong. The voyage south was made in a howling gale that cost more precious time and had many sailors seasick. Fox arrived in the *Baltic* at the rendezvous ten miles out of Charleston harbor at 3:00

A.M. on the twelfth, at the very time when the Confederate aides were waiting so impatiently at Sumter for Anderson to give his reply. The five-gun paddle-wheeler *Harriet Lane*, Captain John Faunce, was the only ship already there. Still to come were the men-of-war *Powhatan, Pocahontas,* and *Pawnee,* and the three tugs *Yankee, Uncle Ben,* and *Freeborn.*

Fox still did not know that the big frigate *Powhatan,* on whose boats and guns he was counting, had been taken from him by Seward. Nor did he know that the tug *Uncle Ben* had been driven by the storm into Wilmington, North Carolina, and the *Yankee* buffeted clear past Charleston to Savannah. The *Freeborn,* the third of the tugs, never left New York because her owners got squeamish at the last moment about the hazards of the mission. The captain could do nothing but wait in heavy seas for the six additional ships of his expedition, four of which—the vital four—would never come.[34]

At 6:00 A.M. the *Pawnee,* skippered by Commander Stephen C. Rowan, put in her appearance. Fox boarded the *Pawnee* and asked Rowan to "stand in for the bar" with him. Not on your life, snapped Rowan. His written orders told him to stay ten miles out and await the arrival of the *Powhatan* for further instructions—another pretty little item of confusion.

"I am not going in there to begin civil war," Rowan said.[35]

Fox left him there and headed in with the *Baltic,* accompanied by the *Harriet Lane.* As they neared the bar they heard the batteries booming, saw smoke trailing across the harbor. The war had already begun, thereby invalidating Fox's first orders to supply Sumter peaceably with provisions and making effective his alternative orders—to run the batteries and attempt to reinforce the fort as well as supply it. Now that the war was on, Rowan changed his tune. He was in favor of going in immediately and sharing the fate of the garrison. Fox vetoed such a risky effort, knowing that the men-of-war would offer prime targets and would almost certainly be sunk. He would wait for the *Powhatan,* with its three hundred sailors, and the three tugs, in which the sailors could fight their way into the channel.

Surely, he thought, they would arrive during the day so that the attempt could be made the following night.

Fox was in an agony of suspense as they waited there all day of the twelfth without another vessel of the fleet showing up. When darkness came, he began signaling with lights for the *Powhatan,* keeping it up all night without success. By that time he realized that something was terribly, terribly wrong.[36]

GENTLEMEN, RETURN
TO YOUR BATTERIES

Now glory be to Uncle Abe, and Scott, his bully pet,
And Seward, cook and bottle-washer of the Cabinet;
And glory to the mighty fleet that stood off Charleston Bar,
And left the dauntless Anderson to bear the brunt of war![1]

All that stormy night the Sumter sentinels kept watch as the enemy sent mortar-shell greetings at fifteen-minute intervals. Nobody came, friendly or otherwise. At dawn the garrison awoke to the realization that the fleet had not even made an attempt to send in relief boats—discouraging intelligence to the many who had confidently expected to be bolstered with fighting men and something new in the way of victuals. At daybreak that Saturday, April 13th, the ships were still off the bar. Had they come down just to watch the fireworks? The Sumter men uttered some earnest curses. The Confederate gunners, sensing a strange sympathy for the garrison they were trying to exterminate, felt the same way, expressing contempt for the "timorous inactivity" of the fleet that came to help and did nothing but rubberneck.[2]

After reveille, the Sumter men sat down to fat pork, someone dourly remarking that at any rate the enemy artillerists were giving them "hot rolls for breakfast."[3] They went to the casemates and began a brisk fire concentrated mainly on Moultrie because the other targets seemed impervious. Although they could not disable Moultrie's well-protected guns for any length of time, they scored numerous hits on the fort's barracks with satisfyingly destructive results. They were making history in more ways than one, for this was said to be the first battle on record between two forts firing at each other. Perhaps Major Anderson did not know that at least one of his brothers-in-law was among the enemies shooting at him—a small token of the split in families that was to come.[4]

The night's storm culminated in a heavy rainfall between seven and eight o'clock, but even the downpour failed to drive spectators from Charleston's Battery and other vantage points. The city was gripped by such a fever of excitement that all business was suspended, upsetting the plans of Wilbur & Son, furniture dealers at 176 Meeting Street. Wilbur & Son announced:

> The furniture sale, which was to have taken place yesterday . . . was postponed in consequence of the bombardment of the harbor by the renegade who commands Fort Sumter, and who has been allowed all the luxuries our city could give him, for the last three months. The sale will positively take place as soon as Fort Sumter is taken.[5]

Around eight o'clock the rain ended, the skies cleared, sunshine turned the harbor waters a vivid blue, and it grew warm. The Iron Battery at Cummings Point was beating a devastating tattoo on Sumter's gorge wall with particular attention to the stone traverse Foster had erected to protect the main gates. As the traverse crumbled, the heavy wooden gates began to take direct punishment. Only a few of Moultrie's guns were firing now, the rest being held in readiness to blast at any boats that might enter. Then it happened again. The Sumter barracks caught fire.

The soldiers were muttering incivilities against the engineers who had designed the "fireproof" barracks. The buildings were faced with brick, but their slate roofs were fastened on wooden sheathing and their floors, doors, and window frames were wooden. To add another element of shortsighted design, the powder magazine was located in the ground floor of one of them. Hart and a detail of men picked their way through the shattered barracks in imminent danger of extinction by enemy missiles and succeeded in extinguishing the blaze. But by this time a dense column of smoke arose to apprise the attentive Colonel Ripley that the fire-resisting qualities of the barracks were purely theoretical. The men at Moultrie began plying their hot-shot furnaces with vigor. All of the Moultrie batteries went to work on Sumter, sending in a hail of projectiles including many red-hot balls. In no time at all the barracks were burning again in several places. After some futile effort to control the blaze, Anderson ordered the men to desist and let the wreckage burn.[6]

The danger now was the magazine. Flames were licking toward it, only one set of quarters away. Powder had been carried out of it all the previous day in considerable haste so that some had been spilled in a trail on the ground, making a first-rate fuse that could carry a train of fire into the room where well over 275 barrels of powder still remained. Sergeant Chester recorded a memorable scene:

"Major Anderson, his head erect as if on parade, called the men around him; directed that a shot be fired every five minutes; and mentioned that there was some danger of the magazine exploding." [7]

At his order, the gun crews remained at their batteries while the rest of the soldiers, officers, workmen, and musicians streamed out of the casemates and into the shot-torn parade to see what they could do to keep from being blown up en masse. Some took axes to the flaming woodwork, but this was useless. Anderson ordered the magazine door opened and a line formed. The tired men rolled barrel after barrel out of the room, across the parade and into the casemates. Still the fire was gaining. Something over fifty barrels had been removed when showers of sparks and burning debris began to fall, rendering any further transfer of powder suicidal. The major ordered the copper magazine door closed. A trench was hopefully dug in front of it and the door banked with earth.[8]

To the enemy, Sumter looked like an inferno, with flames leaping high in the air. Feminine watchers on the Battery began to entertain sympathy for the garrison. Surely they would have to surrender now, before they were all burned to a crisp! Yet Sumter kept firing. Gunners at Cummings Point and Fort Moultrie were so amazed at this exhibition of gallantry—men fight-

ing from a fort that was ablaze—that they ripped out a volley
of cheers for Major Anderson and his men. Then they got down
to the business at hand and fired more hot shot, expecting to
see a white flag at any moment.[9]

Cartridges now were so short that Sumter restricted its firing
to one gun every ten minutes. The hope that the fire might
burn itself out proved a vain one. It got worse. For fireproof
buildings, the barracks produced a conflagration of heroic proportions. Stockpiles of shells and grenades had been left at
strategic points along the gorge wall to repel assault. As the
heat reached them they exploded, sending down showers of
brick and burning timber. Sumter was being assailed by its own
ammunition. For the Confederates to fire hot shot now was
redundant, yet they kept coming, one red-hot ball bouncing on
the parade, rolling into a casemate, and setting a soldier's bed
ablaze. The heat from the fire became so oppressive that soldiers
began to remove outer clothing. The air filled with flying, fiery
particles that drifted everywhere, even into the casemates, causing Anderson to feel apprehension about the powder that had
been moved there.

The anxious commander sent Surgeon Crawford up to the
parapet to see if the fleet had moved. Before he got there a pile
of shells and grenades exploded on the left gorge angle, destroying the staircase so that the surgeon had to pick his way up like
a mountain climber. He gazed out through smoke to see that
the vessels were still out beyond the bar, unmoving. The major
must have received this news with mixed emotions. An attempt
to run the batteries by daylight might result in slaughter, and
yet what were the ships there for if not to help? Ignorance of
the government's intentions had been his fate during most of
his stay in the harbor. Now, with his fort in extremity and the
fleet doing nothing, the purposes of the Lincoln administration
must have seemed an inscrutable riddle.[10]

As the barracks burned more fiercely, sending great flurries
of crackling debris into the casemates, the powder barrels
moved there for "safety" became a menace instead. Anderson
ordered all but five of them jettisoned. Sweating men rolled

them to the embrasures and dumped them out, protecting the remaining five with wet blankets. A solid shot bounced and hit the magazine door, jamming it permanently so that when the five barrels were gone there would be no more powder. The breeze moved around to the west, bringing a new enemy— smoke. The barracks, wet by rain and the still leaking cisterns, burned like a smudge fire, hissing as it sent clouds of thick, piny smoke into the casemates. Choking, red-eyed, almost smothered by heat and fumes, the men were forced to leave the guns and seek air.[11]

"It seemed impossible to escape suffocation," Doubleday wrote. "Some lay down close to the ground, with handkerchiefs over their mouths, and others posted themselves near the embrasures, where the smoke was somewhat lessened by the draught of air." [12] The men were in such agony that many took refuge in the Almighty. "We now prayed for the relief," Crawford recorded.[13] The relief did not come. "The roaring and crackling of the flames, the dense masses of whirling smoke, the bursting of the enemy's shells, and our own which were exploding in the burning rooms, the crashing of the shot, and the sound of masonry falling in every direction, made the fort a pandemonium." [14]

A few men crawled out the embrasures to sit on the outer edges—a risky business, for some of Ripley's guns were spattering the fort with case shot. The main gates now were aflame. Discipline suffered as both officers and men abandoned everything else in a search for air, but it did not collapse into anarchy. When the breeze shifted some time later, affording partial relief, the half-blinded gunners returned to their batteries and went to work again, not knowing that the Confederates were cheering them for every shot they fired. Swirling smoke was still thick enough at times so that they could not see beyond the muzzles of their own guns. With their cartridges almost gone, the gunners resorted to an ingenious substitute for cartridge bags— socks. "We fired away several dozen pairs of woollen socks belonging to Major Anderson," Sergeant Chester noted.[15]

A red-hot ball touched off a couple of jettisoned powder barrels at the water's edge in an explosion that knocked an un-manned casemate gun clear out of the battery. The fort was an island of smoke, heat, din, of the kind of eerie unreality one might experience in a nightmare. It was no wonder if some of the exhausted men reacted to the unreality, to the incessant pounding on their senses, with a touch of madness. Undoubtedly some felt it was about time to quit—a thought that must have occurred to the major himself. Secretary Cameron's orders gave him carte blanche on that point, saying it was not the intention of the President "to subject your command to any danger or hardship beyond what, in your judgment, would be usual in military life," and adding, "Whenever . . . a capitulation be-comes a necessity, you are authorized to make it." The orders made it apparent that the administration had no great hope of holding the fort but had decided that voluntary evacuation would be hurtful politically. As the fire raged around those 275 barrels of powder in the magazine, Anderson must have wondered if the political necessity had not been properly served, and whether the hardships suffered by his men were not suf-ficiently beyond the usual in military life, and whether the few guns still being manned were doing the United States or the Confederate States any possible good or harm politically, mili-tarily or in any other way.

If so, he did not quit, nor did his men. When noon came Sumter was still a flame-swept bastion hurling an occasional 42-pound missile at Moultrie. Shortly before one o'clock, an enemy ball decapitated the high flagstaff. The flag, already hanging precariously on broken halyards, fell to the parade. See-ing it go, young Lieutenant Hall reacted with a West Point re-flex. He dashed out on the parade into searing heat that singed his hair and made his gilt epaulets so hot that he had to rip them off. He emerged dirty-faced, his eyebrows gone, beating out the smouldering edges of the flag. Peter Hart, who but for patriotic impulse could have been safely pounding a New York police beat, found a long spar. Accompanied by Hall, Captain Seymour, and Lieutenant Snyder, he made his way to the rubble-strewn parapet, where the four were cheered by the garrison as they fastened the spar to a gun carriage and raised the flag again "without undue haste" despite the enemy guns firing at them—a scene similar to one later to be enacted at Iwo Jima.[16]

Over on Cummings Point, Louis Wigfall, the Confederacy's most ferocious colonel, had been witnessing the Irish wake over the Union's grave which he had deplored in the Senate. He saw the Sumter flag go down. It was obvious that Anderson was in distress. A tough customer, Wigfall was also an admirer of gallantry, and he thought the major had shown enough of it. Brushing aside the objections of his superior, General Simons, he got into a boat with Private Gourdin Young and two Negro oarsmen and headed for Sumter to suggest a surrender—a mad, Wigfallian errand, well intentioned but unauthorized.

The Cummings Point batteries stopped firing, but all the others were still throwing iron. The oarsmen rowed for dear life on a risky mission they did not relish. Reaching the fort, Wigfall got out with a white flag draped on his sword, saw that the main gates were burning, and walked around to an open embrasure. Sumter was now in such a condition that the approaching boat had not even been seen. With balls and masonry falling uncomfortably close, the two slave oarsmen decided this was no place to stay. They pushed off and were about to make for Cummings Point when Young, a relative of Robert Gourdin, aimed his revolver at them, forced them back, and vowed he would shoot the first one who moved.[17]

At the embrasure, a Sumter private named Thompson was surprised to see the wild-eyed man with a white flag on his sword. Wigfall climbed into the stifling fort, saw Lieutenant Snyder nearby, identified himself, and asked for Major Anderson. As Snyder departed to summon the major, Wigfall encountered Lieutenant Davis.

"Your flag is down," the Texan shouted excitedly, "you are on fire, and you are not firing your guns. General Beauregard desires to stop this."

"No, sir," Davis corrected. "Our flag is not down; if you will step this way you will see it floating on the ramparts."

"Let us stop this firing," Wigfall insisted. "Will you hoist this?" He indicated the white flag on his sword.

"No," said Davis, "it is for you stop it."

Impatiently Wigfall went to an embrasure facing Fort Moultrie, which was still firing. Squirming past the gun, he poked the flag out and waved it. Davis relented. As long as Wigfall had put the flag out himself, he said, he would let one of the soldiers hold it for him. He directed Corporal Bringhurst of Company E to wave the white flag out the embrasure. It was something Davis had no right to do, capitulation being strictly a decision for Anderson to make. The actions of both Davis and Wigfall were a little daft, a reflection of pressures and surroundings scarcely less than infernal. Bringhurst had waved the flag for only a moment when a solid shot from Moultrie crashed into the wall above the embrasure.

"God damn it!" he shouted, springing back inside. "They don't respect this flag—they are firing on it!"

"I have been fired upon with that flag two or three times," Wigfall remarked. "I should think you might stand it once."

He turned as Anderson came up. "Major Anderson, I am Colonel Wigfall. You have defended your flag nobly, sir. It's madness to persevere in useless resistance. General Beauregard wishes to stop this, and to ask upon what terms you will evacuate this work."

Anderson exhibited such coolness that Wigfall remarked on it later in his report. The major knew his visitor was right—further resistance was indeed useless. "I have already stated the terms to General Beauregard," he replied. "Instead of noon on the 15th, I will go now."

"Then, Major Anderson, I understand that you will evacuate the fort upon the same terms proposed to you by General Beauregard?"

"Yes, sir," Anderson nodded, "and upon those terms alone."

A shell exploded across the parade. The two retired to a bombproof and discussed the conditions. Anderson was to quit the fort with his command, taking all arms and company property and saluting his flag. Wigfall complimented the major again and took his leave, an emissary of confusion who had not come from Beauregard and had no authority to offer terms. The major gave the order to his officers. At 1:30 P.M. on Saturday, April 13th, 1861, after thirty-three hours of bombardment, the flag Hart had raised from a gun carriage was taken down and a hospital sheet placed there instead.[18]

Meanwhile the considerate Beauregard, concerned by the flames at Sumter and noticing the disappearance of the flag, had sent three aides to offer assistance to Anderson. The three, Captain Lee, Pryor, and William Porcher Miles, had rowed halfway across the stream from Moultrie when they saw the colors replaced on a spar by Hart. They turned back toward Moultrie. Before reaching Sullivan's Island, they looked back to see a white flag fluttering from the ramparts. Once more they pulled for Sumter, reaching there about 2:00 P.M. They found the usually impeccable major's face smudged by soot, his uniform stained, but his observance of the formalities in no wise impaired.

"Present my compliments to General Beauregard," he said, "and say to him I thank him for his kindness but need no assistance." His expression mirrored puzzlement. "Gentlemen, do I understand you have come direct from General Beauregard?" They said they had. "Why," the major went on, "Colonel Wigfall has just been here as an aide to and by authority of General Beauregard, and proposed the same terms of evacuation offered on the 11th instant." [19]

The three aides stared. Wigfall, Captain Lee informed the major, had been on Morris Island for the last two days and had not seen Beauregard during that time. He could not have brought any terms from the general.

Anderson was vexed at being placed in an awkward position. He had been granted terms, and now learned that Colonel Wigfall represented only Colonel Wigfall. The terms were void.

"Very well, gentlemen," he said, sweeping his hand toward Fort Moultrie, "you can return to your batteries." [20]

He was perfectly serious about it. He would raise his flag

again, he said, and the battle could continue. The major, too, had been affected by his ordeal so that he was not quite a normal man. Lee, Pryor, and Miles, sweating in the heat of the still burning fort, urged that this was useless. They retired to parley in the only habitable casemate handy, the one occupied by Surgeon Crawford as his quarters. Roger Pryor flung himself down on a chair and noticed an interesting-looking black bottle on the table next to the surgeon's cot. Feeling the need of a bracer, he forgot his usual Virginia courtesty. Without a by-your-leave he poured himself three fingers and tossed it off at a gulp.

His face puckered instantly. What he had drunk was not whiskey but Crawford's potent medicine containing iodide of potassium, a mixture dangerous in anything but small doses.

Pryor let out a strangled cry of alarm. Crawford came on the run. "If you have taken the amount of that solution that you think you have," he said to Pryor, probably without real sympathy, "you have likely poisoned yourself."

"Do something for me, doctor!" Pryor pleaded, gagging.

Crawford took him out on the parade, applied a stomach pump, and soon brought him around. If nothing else, Colonel Pryor had furnished the first belly-laugh of the war.[21]

"Some of us questioned the doctor's right to interpose in a case of this kind," Doubleday observed. "It was argued that if any rebel leader chose to come over to Fort Sumter and poison himself, the Medical Department had no business to interfere with such a laudable intention. The doctor, however, claimed, with some show of reason, that he himself was held responsible to the United States for the medicine in the hospital, and therefore he could not permit Pryor to carry any of it away." [22]

Lee and Miles continued the parley with Anderson while the Virginian was being purged. The major was persuaded not to resume battle, and ultimately Beauregard extended the same terms he had offered before, including the salute to the flag, "as an honorable testimony to the gallantry and fortitude with which Major Anderson and his command had defended their post." [23] The garrison would leave on the morrow. As the three aides left—Pryor still somewhat pale—Miles remarked that no one had been wounded by the Sumter fire.

"Thank God for that!" Anderson exclaimed.

That made Doubleday writhe. "As the object of our fighting was to do as much damage as possible," he commented, "I could see no propriety in thanking Heaven for the small amount of injury we had inflicted." [24]

Miles was not quite correct. Four men had been slightly injured at Fort Moultrie, and Pryor might be considered a near casualty. Strangely, four men also had been injured at Sumter by flying brick or pieces of shell, none of them seriously. The only fatality of the battle was a horse killed on Morris Island by a Sumter ball. As Horace Greeley later said, it was a comparatively bloodless beginning for the bloodiest war America ever knew.[25]

For the men of Sumter, it was all over. They had arrived here on December 26th in exultation. They had seen exultation fade into doubt and puzzlement and finally into grinding boredom that engendered hate for the fort and for the secessionists who kept them in it. Now, through the cockeyed logic of war, the prison that had walled them in for fifteen weeks while they were circumspect and peaceable, had opened its doors and rewarded them with freedom because for thirty-three hours they had been violent and homicidal. Now they would go north, be granted furlough and in perfect liberty enjoy all those things they had dreamed about—pork chops, foaming steins, wives and children, waltzing to sweet music, all of these pleasures and more without let or hindrance or any high-and-mighty Carolinian to say them nay. Yet they were not jubilant. Some began gathering their things in silence, like automatons. Others just lay down and slept.

"The enthusiasm that had so long inspired them seemed to have gone," noted Crawford with superlative understatement.[26] Another observer put it more strongly: "The appearance of both Major Anderson, his officers and the men, indicated the terrible nature of the ordeal from which they had just emerged. . . .

they looked worn, haggard, and ready to drop with sheer exhaustion." [27]

The fort looked haggard too. Its previously smooth brick outer walls bore the raw craters of some six hundred direct hits by enemy solid shot. Its gates were gone, its parapet a ruin, the parade a shambles, the officers' quarters and barracks burned-out skeletons with fire still blazing somewhere down in their depths, the whole giving an effect as if "the hand of the destroying angel had swept ruthlessly by." [28] Yet Sumter's basic defenses were scarcely impaired. Had it been furnished with its full war garrison, well supplied, and manning a full complement of guns, the battle undoubtedly would have been a titanic one with heavy casualties on both sides. As it was, the enemy had not gone unscathed, several guns having been knocked out temporarily and the Moultrie barracks being demolished. [29]

As yet no one on either side knew that the bombardment of Sumter was entirely useless, unnecessary, and in fact a loss to the victors. Had the Confederates known the true helplessness of the federal naval force, all they would have had to do was guard against the entry of men and supplies—an easy task, since Fox had no facilities for making any effective attempt at forcing an entrance. They would have had the fort handed over to them undamaged, in perfect shape, in a few days at most, when the garrison would be facing starvation. It is even possible that not a shot would have been fired, the command would have evacuated the fort peacefully, and the Sumter crisis would have ended without war, postponing the conflict to another day. [30]

But no one knew that General Beauregard's batteries had fired a total of 3,341 destructive shot and shell to no more purpose than a man setting fire to his own house. [31] Charleston was in a paroxysm of victorious delight. People were still streaming in from fifty miles around to see the excitement, most of them camping out overnight. Business was at a standstill, the whole town taking holiday. Wilbur & Son's furniture sale would still have to wait a few days. Governor Pickens, who had watched the bombardment through a telescope, could feel that he had more than evened the score for his lost baggage and music box. Inevitably, he gave a speech that night from the balcony of the Charleston Hotel. Perhaps he had celebrated with a toast or two, for his tone was lacking in the humility becoming a victor:

> They have vauntingly arrayed their twenty millions of men against us; they have exultingly, also, arrayed their navy, and they have called us but a handful of men. . . . But we have rallied; we have met them . . . and we have conquered. We have defeated their twenty millions, and we have made the proud flag of the stars and stripes, that never was lowered before to any nation on this earth—we have lowered it . . . before the Palmetto and Confederate flags, and we have compelled them to raise by their side the white flag. . . .

The governor made more wind than sense. He had not defeated 20,000,000 men at all. Some 7,000 of his men had defeated 128 hungry soldiers, musicians, and workmen who might more properly be called "a handful of men." But he admitted, "The man who defended that fort has many of the attributes of a brave soldier," then went on to say something most of his listeners must have thought fantastic:

"Remember that the danger is not yet over. We, perhaps, may have just commenced the opening of events that may not end in our day and generation." [32]

One of the few who believed that was Judge Petrigru. "It is an odd feeling to be in the midst of joy and gratulations that one does not feel," he wrote. ". . . The universal applause that waits on secessionists and secession has not the slightest tendency to shake my conviction that we are on the road to ruin. . . ." [33]

Out beyond the bar, Captain Fox was sick with chagrin. The *Powhatan* and the three tugs had never come. The *Pocahontas* finally arrived at two that afternoon, just at the time Sumter was surrendering. Not until then was Fox informed that the *Powhatan* had gone on another mission. The nonappearance of the tugs was still a mystery. In desperation, Commander Rowan seized an ice schooner from Boston that was standing by, and preparations were made for a do-or-die attempt to run the batteries that night with the sluggish schooner carrying a few soldiers and provisions. Before nightfall, Fox saw that Sumter's flag was down and the battle was over.[34]

". . . with the *Powhatan* a reinforcement would have been easy," he wrote in his report. "In justice to itself as well as an acknowledgment of my earnest efforts, I trust the Government has sufficient reasons for putting me in the position they have placed me." [35]

He sent the report to War Secretary Cameron. The man who should have got it was Mr. Seward.

APRIL 14, 1861

Sunday morning, April 14th, 1861. . . . It was a bright morning, sunlight sparkling on the waves, the towers of St. Michael's and St. Philip's perfectly visible, poking up like spikes among the high-piazzaed houses of Charleston. The harbor was swarming with rowboats, skiffs, dories, sailing vessels, launches—anything that would float and hold people. It was victory Sunday, a gala day combining history and destiny and just plain statriotic joy. It was the day when Anderson was getting out at last, when Sumter was to be given over to its rightful owners and the Palmetto and Confederate flags would go up side by side over the battered fort that had come to have such a deep and terrible meaning to millions who never set eyes on it.

Ferryboat men were doing a thriving business transporting gaily dressed passengers at fifty cents a head to stare at the fort, still occupied by the foreign garrison who, it had to be admitted, had fought with spirit. Women, children, aged crones, bearded patriarchs, shiny-faced Negroes, all had deserted Charleston to witness a scene fit to be engraved ineffaceably on the memory. Troops and spectators lined the shores of Sullivan's, James, and Morris Islands, gazing at the fallen bastion from which wisps of smoke still issued. While most of the watching thousands had an imperfect knowledge of the motives, intrigues, beliefs, prejudices, and errors that for thirty years had built up steam until it finally exploded at Sumter, they were pretty well agreed on one point. The old order—the United States of America—was truly dead, as Mr. Wigfall had put it. Ahead of them—perhaps after a punitive expedition taught the Yankees the facts of life—they saw a new era whose outlines were still as nebulous as a faint rainbow but which would surely be one of limitless freedom, glory, and prosperity in the South.

In Fort Sumter, Major Anderson had a pleasant chore. He was handing out to his men the mail which had been withheld for many days and now was released. "He appeared to be in perfect health," a newsman reported. "He was all smiles, and chatted in an easy vein." [1] Appearances were deceptive, for the major was sick with a deep-down sickness, so broken by strain that he would never fully recover. The Confederate authorities had been most considerate, extending all facilities to aid his departure. President Jefferson Davis had not forgotten his old army comrade, converted by ruthless events to an enemy. Davis telegraphed Beauregard from Montgomery: "If occasion offers, tender my friendly remembrance to Major Anderson." [2] This the general did not do in person. Moved by a chivalrous sentiment, Beauregard abstained from visiting Anderson lest his presence "add to the distress and natural mortification of a gallant officer." [3]

Probably never was a defeated enemy treated with greater courtesy. Brandy was brought from shore to the fort and accepted with thanks. Medical help was tendered and declined. The major had been permitted to communicate with the fleet still waiting beyond the bar, and to arrange for the transportation of his command to New York. Thus he had learned the reason for the navy's failure to aid him—a reason not fully appreciated by some of his men, who still expressed the "utmost contempt" for the sailors they accused of cowardice.[4] Fire continued to smoulder in the bowels of the ruined barracks and officers' quarters. Only three cartridges had been left when the fort capitulated, and the men were hard put to find enough shirts and blankets to sew into cartridge bags for the salute to the flag.

This farewell salute, generously permitted by Beauregard, was held in peculiar importance by Anderson, whose sensitive spirit had suffered wounds incalculable because of that same flag. When the Charleston steamer *Isabel,* which had been placed at his disposal, arrived at Sumter, he stepped aboard to greet its captain. An unidentified gentleman on the vessel inquired anxiously whether the salute would be of thirty-four guns—a

Y

number that would be a studied discourtesy, since there were thirty-four states and such a number would imply South Carolina's continuing membership in the Union.

"No," the major replied, "it is one hundred, and those are scarcely enough." Then he was shaken by sobs that gripped him for several moments before he regained his poise.[5]

At two o'clock that afternoon, Governor Pickens and his lovely wife, General Jamison, General Beauregard, Judge Magrath, and Roger Pryor were among the thousands of high and low degree watching Sumter from assorted craft as the salute began booming from the barbette guns whose use had been denied Anderson's men during the battle. The gunners under Lieutenant Hall were firing from a parapet littered with broken masonry, charred wood, and Confederate shot. Down on the torn parade the entire command not at the guns—soldiers, workmen, musicians, officers—stood at attention, some of them feeling a lump in the throat, as the Stars and Stripes, raised on the ramparts for the occasion, was slowly lowered. Then occurred an accident that cast a pall over an already solemn event.

Private Daniel Hough inserted a cartridge for another fire. Apparently the barrel had not been fully sponged from the previous shot, for some flame remained in it, exploding the cartridge prematurely. Hough's right arm was blown off and he was killed almost instantly. Fire dripping from the muzzle was caught by the breeze and carried to a pile of cartridges beside the gun, exploding them all and sending fragments of stone flying in all directions. Five other men were wounded, and the scene on the parapet took on an aspect of ghastly carnage unknown in the battle itself.[6]

In Private Hough the Union had its first dead—the first of many to come—and Surgeon Crawford had grim work on his hands. The tragedy cut short the salute at fifty guns, after which Hough was buried with honors in the Sumter parade. Privates Edward Galloway and George Fielding were taken to a Charleston hospital, where Galloway died five days later and Fielding subsequently recovered. The other three victims, less seriously wounded, were cared for by Crawford.

It was four o'clock before the command was ready to leave. Major Anderson, his head bowed, had something infinitely precious under his arm—the Sumter flag, a little torn, a little burned, bearing the wounds of glorious battle. At his order Captain Doubleday formed the men on the parade. The drums began their stirring *rat-a-tat-tat* and the band struck up "Yankee Doodle"—a tune fit to rouse the blood even in the midst of sadness—as the double file marched out of the fort's ruined gate and boarded the waiting *Isabel*. A Carolinian officer took Doubleday aside for a moment. He had a bone to pick. Why, he wanted to know, had that ball been sent crashing into Moultrie House?

"Not caring to enter into a discussion at that time," Doubleday recorded, "I evaded it by telling him the true reason was, that the landlord had given me a wretched room there one night, and this being the only opportunity that had occurred to get even with him, I was unable to resist it. He laughed heartily, and said, 'I understand it all now. You were perfectly right, sir, and I justify the act.' " [7]

Captain Cuthbert's Palmetto Guard immediately took possession of the fort, one of his men being Edmund Ruffin, who had served with the company throughout the bombardment and now had the honor of being one of the first to set foot in the conquered fort. It was a moment of rare triumph for the old warrior. Shucking his canteen and blanket roll, he set about gathering fragments of shells as souvenirs to send his friends in slowpoke Virginia. Could he have looked into the future he would have seen his home vandalized and wrecked by Union soldiers who scribbled on the walls, "This house belonged to a Ruffinly son-of-a-bitch." In four years, his cause lost, Ruffin would send a bullet into his own brain after penning a last page of vitriol:

"And now with my latest writing and utterance . . . I here repeat . . . my unmitigated hatred to Yankee rule . . . and the perfidious, malignant and vile Yankee race." [8]

Because of the delay, the *Isabel* missed the tide and the command was forced to wait on board until the morrow—a circumstance that made them unwilling witnesses of a mighty celebration inspired by their defeat. Men cheered, women wept, cannon boomed, whistles tooted, and bells rang in a victorious din that encompassed the whole harbor as the Confederate Stars and Bars went up on Sumter's ramparts alongside the Palmetto ensign of South Carolina. Who could dream that the equality of those two flags, representing as it did a state allegiance that had wrecked the Union, represented also a dividing and disrupting force that would come to play its part in wrecking the Confederacy? In the midst of the festivities the smouldering barracks began burning hotter than ever, with thirty thousand pounds of powder still sealed in the magazine. Two fire companies were rushed over from Charleston to pump water for more than twenty-four hours before they got the blaze under control.[9]

On Monday morning the major and his men sailed out past Morris Island, astonished to receive a remarkable demonstration of respect from the enemy who had shot them out of Sumter. The gunners and infantry on Cummings Point "lined the beach, silent, and with heads uncovered, while Anderson and his command passed before them," some shaking their fists at the fleet out yonder.[10]

The men of Sumter boarded the *Baltic* and soon were on their way north, catching up on sleep and piling into luxurious fare such as they had not seen for weeks. Their desperate battle for a doomed fortress had performed a mass miracle, unified overnight a formerly divided North, made Sumter a new Lexington, transformed Anderson's name into a rallying cry of fierce Union inspiration that blew down the doubters and peacemakers in a surge of unanimity from "Penobscot's waters to San Francisco's bay" that meant one thing: War. They were heroes, every one of them, their commander the greatest hero of all. The New York *Leader* sounded a trumpet call typical of a thousand others:

"When has the world witnessed a spectacle of nobler heroism? . . . It is to Major Anderson, a slaveholder of the border slave states . . . that we stand indebted for this evidence of national spirit, and that we have still a flag for which heroes are proud to die." [11]

II

Major Robert Anderson, the Galahad of the North, was exhausted physically and mentally. The death of Hough and the wounding of the others was a cruel blow, but worst of all was his overpowering sense of failure. The man the Union hailed as its savior saw only disaster in what he had been forced to do. In his keeping he had held a fort that had come to symbolize the last outpost of honor and right that neither side could surrender. He had held it like precious glass, an awareness of enormous responsibility shaping every move. He had made mistakes—even come close to compromising his duty as a soldier—always on the side of peace. After long travail, it seemed that he had won. Then had come the dispatch from Cameron, the utterly useless fleet, the ruin of everything. To him, every gun fired from Sumter, every return salvo from the enemy, sounded the defeat of reason and humanity.

Somehow the nation had lurched and careened into awesome error, conceived and multiplied by men on both sides, most of them men of honor and good intentions but many of them so bemused by misunderstanding that it was hard to tell where the blame lay. Blame now was academic, a thing of yesterday, a metaphysical point of no consequence. The issue of today was war and speedy victory. In Montgomery, Secretary of War Walker—the man who had vowed his handkerchief would absorb all the blood spilled in the war—ventured a new prediction. "No man can tell where the war this day commenced will end," he said, "but I will prophesy that the flag which now flaunts the breeze here will float over the dome of the old Capitol at Washington before the first of May." [12] The New York *Tribune* had other information: "Jeff Davis & Co. will be swinging from the battlements at Washington at least by the 4th of July." [13] The same men who had mistaken the possibility of war were now mistaking its meaning.

On April 18th the *Baltic* entered New York harbor, the tattered Sumter flag flying proudly at her fore, saluted by the welcoming din of whistles and bells from every steamer and tug in sight. It was precisely the same clamor the soldiers had heard in Charleston, but inspired by sentiments violently opposed. It was New York's answer to Charleston, the North's answer to the South, the end of an era, the beginning of an ordeal unimagined. In the metropolis, Anderson and his men would be seized by the populace as living creators of a new and slightly hysterical national spirit, would touch off an impassioned public demonstration, would be cheered, petted, paraded, feted, lionized, given medals.

As the *Baltic* stood off Sandy Hook, with all this acclaim yet to come, Major Anderson was still too weary to write any sort of official report of the battle. He got Captain Fox to write a brief report as he dictated.[14] Fox jotted down a single long sentence addressed to Secretary Cameron that somehow captured the major's mingled emotions of pride and failure:

> Having defended Fort Sumter for thirty-four hours, until the quarters were entirely burned, the main gates destroyed by fire, the gorge walls seriously impaired, the magazine surrounded by flames, and its door closed from the effects of the heat, four barrels and three cartridges of powder only being available, and no provisions remaining but pork, I accepted terms of evacuation offered by General Beauregard, being the same offered by him on the 11th instant, prior to the commencement of hostilities, and marched out of the fort on Sunday afternoon, the 14th instant, with colors flying and drums beating, bringing away company and private property, and saluting my flag with fifty guns.
>
> ROBERT ANDERSON, Major, First Artillery [15]

APRIL 14, 1865

On Good Friday, April 14th, 1865, exactly four years after Anderson had surrendered, Sumter was the scene of another flag-raising. President Lincoln had directed that the date be marked by an observance commemorating the federal repossession of the fort that had started all the trouble. Secretary of War Stanton had fallen in enthusiastically with the idea, ordering Assistant Adjutant General E. D. Townsend to organize "suitable ceremonies" to be attended by military and naval units as well as civilians, and climaxed by an address by Henry Ward Beecher. Mr. Stanton was not without a sense of the dramatic, for his directive read in part:

> *Ordered: First.* That at the hour of noon, on the 14th day of April, 1865, brevet Major-General Anderson will raise and plant upon the ruins of Fort Sumter, in Charleston Harbor, the same United States flag which floated over the battlements of the fort during the rebel assault, and which was lowered and saluted by him and the small force of his command when the works were evacuated on the 14th day of April, 1861.[1]

The Confederacy was beaten, although the beating had taken years longer than anyone had expected. The destroyer Sherman had wheeled through South Carolina, not forgetting to burn the home and prized library of David F. Jamison, president of the convention that had voted the state out of the Union.[2] The Carolinians, who had stubbornly held Sumter against repeated Union attacks during the war, were never driven out by direct military action but had been forced to withdraw because of Sherman's threat to their rear. Now Lee had surrendered in Virginia, Edmund Ruffin had blown his brains out, and it was all over but for a few formalities, one of them being the ceremony at Sumter.

From small beginnings, this blossomed into a large affair. The Reverend Mr. Beecher, who never did things in a small way, was one of those beating the drum for it. The return of the symbolic fortress to its proper owner, settling once and for all Colonel Hayne's arguments about real estate, struck Northern imaginations as a peculiarly fitting end to the long struggle. Hundreds decided it was something they could not miss. There even seemed to be cosmic assistance in the project, making Good Friday fall on April 14th. Large delegations had come from New York and Washington aboard the steamers *Arago* and *Oceanus,* so that Charleston—badly damaged by General Quincy Gillmore's Swamp Angel and other federal cannon— was a Southern city under temporary Northern occupation.

Many of the visitors wanted to make speeches, read poems, or present tableaux at the flag-raising. They pestered General Townsend so that he was obliged to put his foot down to keep the affair from ballooning into a week-long orgy. "I conceived it necessary to form a program which should strictly limit the performances," as he put it.[3]

April 14th turned out to be warm and sunny, much like its counterpart four years earlier. Once again, too, the harbor was filled with vessels, but this time many of them were part of Admiral Dahlgren's fleet, brilliantly decked out with victory flags. Small steamers brought visitors all morning from the city to the fort, where Townsend had made extensive preparations. A wooden stairway had been built to allow guests to climb over the wall and down again to the central parade. A double line of Union soldiers and sailors formed a welcoming guard, some of them Negroes from a Massachusetts regiment—an omen that could not have been lost on the Charlestonians, who had no part in the program nor any authority to regulate it.

There was applause when General Anderson arrived shortly before noon with his family, escorted by General Gillmore. Anderson was fifty-nine, but he looked older. His hair was a more silvery gray, he was thinner, and there was a noticeable pallor on his formerly bronzed face. Yet he bore himself with the military erectness that had become the habit of a lifetime. His army career had reached its apogee during his fifteen weeks in Sumter, and when the fifteen weeks were finished, so was Anderson.

True, President Lincoln, his doubts about the major settled by the valiant defense of Sumter, had recognized the debt the nation owed this unassuming officer by making him a brigadier general and sending him off to Kentucky to use his prestige and ability in holding his home state in the Union. But Anderson's health soon broke down and he was obliged to retire from active service. His physician forbade him even to write letters, so he never got around to writing a detailed official report of the battle of Fort Sumter.[4] The officer whose name had been on the lips of millions at the start of the conflict had receded into the background, other heroes taking his place in the headlines. A combat casualty just as surely as if he had been hit by bullets, he had spent the war years in New York, a gray, quiet man occasionally seen walking with his young son. He did not think he had long to live.[5]

Now, as Anderson climbed the temporary stairway to the parapet and got a full view of the fort that had made his fame and also ended it, he must have been shocked at the change. Sumter was a place of incredible ruin and desolation, so battered by Union artillery that its original lineaments were only dimly discernible, its ramparts chopped and truncated, its interior a waste of rubble. The fort had remained a symbol to both sides, the Yankees wasting tons of metal on it throughout the war, the Carolinians defending and holding it even when it was reduced to a great pentagonal windrow of loose brick and debris.

"General Anderson . . . could see nothing by which to recognize the Fort Sumter he had left four years ago," a newsman reported.[6]

In the parade, wreckage had been cleared away for the construction of a large diamond-shaped wooden platform, covered by an arched canopy and surrounded by stands for four thousand spectators. The seats were already filled and many people were standing, among them some five hundred "old citizens" of Charleston, drawn to this demonstration of their own defeat by some horrid fascination. Cheers mingled with a ripple of handclapping as Anderson ascended to the platform, taking his six-year-old son Robert Jr. by the hand. With him was Peter Hart—the same, solid Hart who had fought with him in the Mexican War and had battled flame, fired cannon, and planted the flag on the ramparts of Sumter. The affection between these two men, so different in background and rearing, was that of soldiers with implicit trust in each other proven in many fields over the years.

Anderson's duty this day, cherished in one respect, in another was almost as painful as it had been four years earlier. To replace the Sumter flag with his own hands was a tribute whose honor he could not deny. Yet he had been opposed to turning the event into a celebration of the crushing of the Confederacy, feeling that a short religious service stressing thankfulness that the war was ended would be more fitting. He had urged that the program be brief and quiet. Instead it was going to be long and noisy, with a 100-gun salute. But he was there by order of the Secretary of War, just as he had been four years before, and he obeyed.[7]

As he gazed out over the throng, he could take pride in the knowledge that his garrison, which had fought so well here, had gone on to win laurels in battlefields from Pennsylvania to Florida, from Virginia to Arkansas. No less than five of his officers—Doubleday, Foster, Crawford, Seymour, and Davis— had become Union generals. Seymour, in fact, had been severely wounded in leading an assault against a Confederate stronghold on Morris Island in 1863. Young Lieutenant Hall had risen to colonel, leading a brigade at Gettysburg. These men had figured in action at places whose names had won ominous fame—Bull Run, Antietam, Fredericksburg, Chancellorsville, Cold Harbor, many others.

Captain Talbot and Lieutenant Snyder had died of illness early in the conflict, as had Lieutenant Meade, the only one of the officers who had joined the Confederacy. Meade had gone along when Virginia seceded—with considerable anguish, it was said—and thus became one of the few who fought on both sides.[8]

As Anderson had foreseen, the war had split the nation in monstrous hatred, leaving wounds of the spirit that would be a long time healing. The chivalry so evident when the Carolinians cheered the major and his men at Sumter had soon settled down to a grim struggle for survival in which glory took a back seat to killing and winning. Now the killing was over, but not the vindictiveness. Jefferson Davis would soon be in prison, as would Judge Magrath, who had been Carolina's last war governor. Here in the throng filling the stands were some moved chiefly by humble gratitude that peace had come at last, and others not averse to rubbing Carolinian noses in the dirt. Among those present were men who had figured in the Sumter crisis of '61—Chaplain Matthias Harris, former War Secretary Holt, General Doubleday, General Dix, Commodore Rowan, and Captain Fox, now Assistant Secretary of the Navy.[9]

Some had urged Lincoln to attend, but the President was a tired man. He stayed in Washington. Mrs. Lincoln was coaxing him to take her to the theater that night, and although he was not keen on the idea, his lady usually had her way.

The chattering crowd on the parade grew silent as white-haired old Chaplain Harris, who had led the service at Sumter the day after Anderson occupied the fort, spoke a prayer. General Townsend then rose and read in a clear voice Anderson's memorable dispatch to Cameron from the *Baltic* ending, "saluting my flag with fifty guns." The major had kept that tattered flag as a treasure ever since. As he stepped forward, with Peter Hart beside him carrying the flag, the spectators leaped to their feet and cheered him. "The burst of joy was uncontrollable," noted the New York *Herald's* correspondent.[10] Hart, with memories of his own, made the flag fast to the halyards.

"Commingled joy and sadness struggled upon [Anderson's] manly face," wrote another observer. ". . . He seemed wrestling with intense emotion, as if living over again, in that moment, the terrible scenes of four years before, and as if conscious that through the ten thousand eyes of that vast assemblage, the whole nation was looking at him." [11]

Anderson gazed out over the crowd, seated near where the barracks had burned so fiercely in '61. He must have put considerable thought on what he would say, wanting to strike the right note, feeling strongly that the time for martial music was over and this was a time for a hymn.

"I am here, my friends, my fellow-citizens, and fellow soldiers, to perform an act of duty to my country dear to my heart," he said. "Had I observed the wishes of my heart, it should have been done in silence; but in accordance with the request of the Honorable Secretary of War, I make a few remarks, as by his order, after four long, long years of bloody war, I restore to its proper place this dear flag which floated here during peace, before the first act of this cruel Rebellion. I thank God that I have lived to see this day"—here he had to wait for applause to subside—"and to be here to perform this, perhaps the last act of my life, of duty to my country."

He took hold of the halyards. "I thank God who has so signally blessed us," he went on. "May all the nation bless and praise the name of the Lord, and proclaim, 'Glory to God in the highest, and on earth peace, good will towards men.' " [12]

Many people were weeping, some shouting amens, the *Herald* and *Tribune* writers noted, as Anderson pulled firmly at the halyards and the flag went up, carrying with it a garland of roses. When it neared the top and was caught by the breeze, "there was one tumultous shout." [13]

After that came the 100-gun salute—repeated in scores of Northern cities simultaneously celebrating the Sumter flag-raising—and then a long, long oration by Mr. Beecher. There was no denying that Beecher, who used a good portion of his time in denouncing the rebellion, had a sweeping command of the language. Yet some felt that General Anderson's few words, so sincerely from the heart and so clearly urging an end to hatred, were a better expression of the need of the hour.

One of the many changes wrought by the struggle was that Robert Anderson and Abraham Lincoln, who had viewed each other with mistrust in 1861, were in perfect accord in 1865. No soldier, North or South, had felt more keenly than Anderson the tragedy of the war. His petition for "peace, good will to-wards men," was an echo of the President's resolution to have done with conflict and "bind up the nation's wounds."

That night, General Gillmore gave a full-dress dinner at the Charleston Hotel, where Governor Pickens four years earlier had spoken with premature pride of defeating the North's twenty millions. Pickens had long since retired to his estate near Edgefield, his slaves gone, debt staring him in the face, himself a victim of ruin he had not foreseen. That night also the Battery was crowded again, just as it had been four years earlier, this time with spectators watching fireworks displayed from Admiral Dahlgren's ships in the harbor. Reverberations from the fire-works could be heard in the ghost-haunted hotel dining room as speeches were given by victorious Unionists including that inflexible old abolitionist, William Lloyd Garrison.[14]

The dinner began well before the President, in Washington, left the White House for Ford's Theater, but it went on and on. General Anderson, although an honored guest, was not one for public speaking. He listened to others not so averse to it. Later, when he rose to propose a toast, it was in words of moderation, using the symbol of a nation reunited to honor the President whose aim was moderation and reunion:

"I beg you, now, that you will join me in drinking the health of . . . the man who, when elected President of the United States, was compelled to reach the seat of government without an escort, but a man who now could travel all over our country with millions of hands and hearts to sustain him. I give you the good, the great, the honest man, Abraham Lincoln." [15]

The toast was drunk with a will, a tribute to the President who at that same moment was chuckling at a rather feeble farce in the Washington theater. No hand sustained him that night. Less than an hour after Anderson spoke the words, Lincoln lay dying with a bullet in his brain.[16]

BIBLIOGRAPHY

The writer has aimed to place heaviest reliance on those sources nearest the time and place—the *Official Records*, the accounts of actual participants, and articles in contemporaneous newspapers and periodicals. Wholesale instruction has been taken from *The Genesis of the Civil War* by the amazing Samuel Wylie Crawford, the army surgeon who observed the entire Sumter crisis on the spot and went on to become general, geographer, and historian. Because of the large cast of characters in the Sumter drama, the *Dictionary of American Biography* was a constant source. The following is a list of those works actually cited or quoted:

BOOKS

Abstracted Indian Trust Bonds, House of Representatives, Report No. 78, 36th Congress, 2nd Session.

Alexander, E. P., *Military Memoirs of a Confederate*, New York, 1907.

American Historical Review, Vol. XIII, 1908, for Narrative of William H. Trescot; Vol. XXVI, 1920-21, for Diary of Montgomery C. Meigs.

Anderson, E. L., *Soldier and Pioneer: A Biographical Sketch of Lieutenant Colonel Richard C. Anderson*, New York, 1879.

Anderson, Robert, *An Artillery Officer in the Mexican War: Letters of Anderson from Mexico*, New York, 1911.

Anderson, Thomas M., *The Political Conspiracies Preceding the Rebellion*, New York, 1882.

Auchampaugh, Philip G., *James Buchanan and His Cabinet on the Eve of Secession*, Lancaster, Pa., 1926.

Bancroft, Frederic, *Calhoun and the South Carolina Nullification Movement*, Baltimore, 1928.

——, *The Life of William H. Seward*, 2 vols., New York, 1900.

Basso, Hamilton, *Beauregard, the Great Creole*, New York, 1933.

Battle of Fort Sumter and the First Victory of the Southern Troops (pamphlet), Charleston, 1861.

Beale, Howard K., ed., *The Diary of Edward Bates, 1859-1866*, Washington, 1933.

Black, Chauncey F., ed., *Essays and Speeches of Jeremiah S. Black*, New York, 1886.

Blaine, James G., *Twenty Years in Congress*, 2 vols., Norwich, Conn., 1884.

Boucher, C. S., *The Nullification Controversy in South Carolina*, Chicago, 1916.

Bowes, Frederick P., *The Culture of Early Charleston*, Chapel Hill, N. C., 1942.

Brooks, U. R., *South Carolina Bench and Bar*, Columbia, S. C., 1908.

Buchanan, James, *The Administration on the Eve of the Rebellion*, London, 1865.

——, *The Works of James Buchanan*, ed. by John Bassett Moore, 12 vols., Philadelphia, 1910.

Buel, Clarence C., and Johnson, Robert U., eds., *Battles and Leaders of the Civil War*, 4 vols., New York, 1884-87.

Carson, James Petigru, ed., *Life, Letters and Speeches of James Louis Petigru*, Washington, 1920.

Cauthen, Charles Edward, *South Carolina Goes to War*, Chapel Hill, N. C., 1950.
Chadwick, French Ensor, *Causes of the Civil War*, New York, 1906.
Chapman, John A., *A History of Edgefield County*, Newberry, S. C., 1897.
Charleston, South Carolina: The Centennial of Incorporation, 1883, Charleston, 1884.
Chesnut, Mary Boykin, *A Diary From Dixie*, edited by Isabella D. Martin and Myrta Lockett Avary, New York, 1905.
Chittenden, L. E., *Recollections of President Lincoln and His Administration*, New York, 1891.
Coleman, Mrs. Chapman, *The Life of John J. Crittenden*, 2 vols., Philadelphia, 1871.
Columbia Historical Society, Records of, Vol. XXXX–XXXXI. Article about Montgomery C. Meigs.
Connor, Henry G., *John Archibald Campbell*, Boston and New York, 1920.
Craven, Avery, *The Coming of the Civil War*, New York, 1942.
———, *Edmund Ruffin, Southerner*, New York, 1932.
Crawford, Samuel Wylie, *The Genesis of the Civil War: The Story of Fort Sumter, 1860–1861*, New York, 1887.
Cullum, George W., *Biographical Register of the Officers and Graduates of the United States Military Academy*, third ed., Boston and New York, 1891.
Curtis, George Ticknor, *The Life of James Buchanan*, 2 vols., New York, 1883.
Davis, Jefferson, *Rise and Fall of the Confederate Government*, New York, 1881.
DeLeon, T. C., *Four Years in Rebel Capitals*, Mobile, Ala., 1890.
Diary of a Public Man (anonymous), Chicago, 1945.
Dix, Morgan, ed., *Memoirs of John Adams Dix*, 2 vols., New York, 1883.
(Doubleday, Abner, as subject) *Major-General Abner Doubleday and Brevet Major-General John G. Robinson in the Civil War*, Albany, N. Y., 1918.
Doubleday, Abner, *Reminiscences of Forts Sumter and Moultrie in 1860–'61*, New York, 1876.
Dumond, Dwight L., *The Secession Movement, 1860–1861*, New York, 1931.
Elliott, Charles Winslow, *Winfield Scott, the Soldier and the Man*, New York, 1937.
Fahrney, Ralph Ray, *Horace Greeley and the Tribune in the Civil War*, Cedar Rapids, Iowa, 1936.
Foote, Henry S., *Casket of Reminiscences*, Washington, 1874.
Foster, Major General John G., Report of, in *Supplemental Report of the Joint Committee on the Conduct of the War*, Vol. II, Washington, 1866.
Fuess, Claude M., *Caleb Cushing*, 2 vols., New York, 1923.
Gobright, L. A., *Recollections of Men and Things at Washington*, Philadelphia, 1869.
Gorham, George C., *Life and Public Services of Edwin M. Stanton*, 2 vols., Boston and New York, 1899.
Grayson, William J., *James Louis Petigru*, New York, 1866.
Greeley, Horace, *The American Conflict*, 2 vols., Hartford, 1864.
Hagood, Johnson, *Memoirs of the War of Secession*, Columbia, S. C., 1910.
Hale, William Harlan, *Horace Greeley, Voice of the People*, New York, 1950.
Harper's Pictorial History of the Civil War, Chicago, 1866.
Harris, W. A., *The Record of Fort Sumter* (pamphlet), Columbia, S. C., 1862.
Hart, Albert Bushnell, ed., *American History as Told by Contemporaries*, 4 vols., New York, 1901.
Hendrick, Burton J., *Lincoln's War Cabinet*, Boston, 1946.
———, *Statesmen of the Lost Cause*, New York, 1939.
Heyward, DuBose, and Sass, Herbert R., *Fort Sumter, 1861–65*, New York, 1932.
Irving, John Beaufain, *The South Carolina Jockey Club*, Charleston, 1857.
Jones, Katherine M., *Heroines of Dixie*, Indianapolis and New York, 1955.
Keyes, Erasmus Darwin, *Fifty Years' Observation of Men and Events*, New York, 1884.

Kibler, Lillian Adele, *Benjamin F. Perry, South Carolina Unionist*, Durham, N. C., 1946.

King, Horatio, *Turning On the Light*, Philadelphia, 1895.

Lamon, Ward Hill, *Recollections of Abraham Lincoln, 1847–65*, Chicago, 1895.

Lathers, Richard, *Reminiscences of Richard Lathers*, ed. by Alvan F. Sanborn, New York, 1907.

Lawton, Eba Anderson, *Major Robert Anderson and Fort Sumter*, New York, 1911.

Leech, Margaret, *Reveille in Washington*, New York, 1941.

Leiding, Harriette Kershaw, *Charleston, Historic and Romantic*, Philadelphia, 1931.

Lincoln, Abraham, *Complete Works of Abraham Lincoln*, ed. by John G. Nicolay and John Hay, 12 vols., New York, 1894.

Lossing, Benson J., *Pictorial History of the Civil War*, 3 vols., Philadelphia, 1866.

McClure, Alexander K., *Abraham Lincoln and Men of War-Times*, Philadelphia, 1892.

McElroy, Robert, *Jefferson Davis, the Unreal and the Real*, 2 vols., New York, 1937.

McLaughlin, Andrew C., *Lewis Cass*, Boston and New York, 1899.

Mason, Edward G., "A Visit to South Carolina in 1860," *Atlantic Monthly*, Vol. LIII, 1884.

Mazyck, Arthur, *Guide to Charleston*, Charleston, n.d.

Mearns, David C., ed., *The Lincoln Papers*, 2 vols., Garden City, 1948.

Meigs, Montgomery C., Diary, March 29–April 8, 1861, in *American Historical Review*, Vol. XXVI, 1920–21.

Meneely, A. Howard, *The War Department, 1861*, New York, 1928.

Milton, George Fort, *The Eve of Conflict*, Boston and New York, 1934.

Molloy, Robert, *Charleston, a Gracious Heritage*, New York, 1947.

Moore, Frank, ed., *Anecdotes, Poetry and Incidents of the War, North and South*, New York, 1866.

———, ed., *Fort Sumter Memorial*, New York, 1915.

———, ed., *The Rebellion Record*, 12 vols., New York, 1861–65.

Nicolay, John G., and Hay, John, *Abraham Lincoln, a History*, 10 vols., New York, 1890.

Official Records of the Union and Confederate Navies in the War of the Rebellion, 27 vols., Washington, 1894–1917. Only Series I, Vol. IV, is cited here.

Paine, Albert Bigelow, *A Sailor of Fortune*, New York, 1906.

Phillips, Ulrich Bonnell, *Life of Robert Toombs*, New York, 1913.

Pollard, Edward A., *Lee and His Lieutenants*, New York, 1867.

Poore, Ben Perley, *Reminiscences of Sixty Years in the National Metropolis*, 2 vols., Philadelphia, 1886.

Porter, A. Toomer, *Led On! Step By Step*, New York, 1898.

Porter, David Dixon, *Incidents and Anecdotes of the Civil War*, New York, 1885.

Pryor, Mrs. Roger A., *Reminiscences of Peace and War*, New York, 1904.

Randall, J. G., *Lincoln the President: Springfield to Gettysburg*, 2 vols., New York, 1945.

Ravenel, Henry William, *The Private Journal of Henry William Ravenel*, edited by Arney R. Childs, Columbia, S. C., 1947.

Ravenel, Mrs. St. Julien, *Charleston, the Place and the People*, New York, 1927.

Rhodes, James Ford, *History of the United States, 1850–1877*, 7 vols., New York, 1910.

Roman, Alfred, *The Military Operations of General Beauregard*, 2 vols., New York, 1884.

Ropes, John Codman, *The Story of the Civil War*, Part I, New York, 1933.

Russell, Sir William H., *The Civil War in America*, Boston, n.d.

Sandburg, Carl, *Abraham Lincoln: The War Years*, 4 vols., New York, 1939.

Schultz, Harold S., *Nationalism and Sectionalism in South Carolina, 1852–1860*, Durham, N. C., 1950.

Scott, Winfield, *Memoirs of Lieutenant General Scott, LL.D., Written by Himself*, 2 vols., New York, 1864.

Seward, Frederick W., *Seward at Washington*, New York, 1891.

Simkins, Francis B., and Patton, James W., *The Women of the Confederacy*, Richmond, 1936.

Smith, William Ernest, *The Francis Preston Blair Family in Politics*, 2 vols., New York, 1933.

Snowden, Yates, ed., *A History of South Carolina*, 5 vols., Chicago and New York, 1920.

Stampp, Kenneth M., *And the War Came*, Baton Rouge, La., 1950.

Starr, Louis M., *Bohemian Brigade*, New York, 1954.

Stephenson, N. W., *The Day of the Confederacy*, New Haven, 1919.

Stevens, William Oliver, *Charleston, Historic City of Gardens*, New York, 1939.

Stovall, Pleasant A., *Robert Toombs*, New York, 1892.

Strode, Hudson, *Jefferson Davis, American Patriot, 1808–1861*, New York, 1955.

Strong, George Templeton, *The Diary of George Templeton Strong*, edited by Allan Nevins and Milton Halsey Thomas, 4 vols., New York, 1952.

Taylor, Rosser H., *Ante-Bellum South Carolina*, Chapel Hill, N. C., 1942.

Thomas, John Peyre, *A History of the South Carolina Military Academy*, Charleston, 1893.

Tilley, John Shipley, *Lincoln Takes Command*, Chapel Hill, N. C., 1941.

Townsend, E. D., *Anecdotes of the Civil War*, New York, 1884.

Trescot, William Henry, Narrative of, in the *American Historical Review*, Vol. XIII, April 1908.

The Trip of the Steamer Oceanus, by a committee of passengers, Brooklyn, 1865.

Tyler, Lyon G., *The Letters and Times of the Tylers*, 2 vols., Richmond, 1885.

Van Deusen, John G., *Economic Bases of Disunion in South Carolina*, New York, 1928.

Wallace, David D., *The History of South Carolina*, 3 vols., New York, 1934.

War of the Rebellion: A Compilation of the Official Records of the Union and Confederate Armies, 128 vols., Washington, 1880–1901. Only Series I, Vol. I, is cited here.

Welles, Gideon, *Diary of Gideon Welles*, with introduction by John T. Morse, Jr., 3 vols., Boston and New York, 1911.

————, *Lincoln and Seward*, New York, 1874.

West, Richard S., Jr., *Gideon Welles, Lincoln's Navy Department*, Indianapolis and New York, 1943.

White, Laura A., *Robert Barnwell Rhett, Father of Secession*, New York, 1931.

Williams, Kenneth P., *Lincoln Finds a General*, Vol. I, New York, 1949.

Williams, T. Harry, *P. G. T. Beauregard, Napoleon in Gray*, Baton Rouge, La., 1954.

Wilson, William Bender, *A Few Acts and Actors in the Tragedy of the Civil War*, Philadelphia, 1892.

Within Fort Sumter, by One of the Company (anonymous), New York, 1861.

Wright, Mrs. D. Giraud, *A Southern Girl in '61*, New York, 1905.

Year Book, 1895, City of Charleston, S. C., Charleston, n.d. Biographical sketch of James Gordon Magrath by L. F. Youmans, pp. 365–75.

Young, John Russell, *Men and Memories*, New York, 1901.

NEWSPAPERS AND PERIODICALS

Charleston, S. C.
  The *Courier*
  The *Mercury*
New York, N. Y.
  The *Herald*

Z

The *Leader*
The *Times*
The *Tribune*
The *World*
American Historical Review
Atlantic Monthly
Harper's Weekly
Frank Leslie's Illustrated Newspaper
Dawson's Historical Magazine, issues of January and March, 1872, containing article, "The Story of Fort Sumter."

MANUSCRIPTS

The Robert Anderson Papers; the S. W. Crawford Papers; the S. W. Crawford Diary; the Papers of Francis W. Pickens and Milledge L. Bonham—all in the Library of Congress.
The Francis W. Pickens Papers, New York Public Library.
The Diary of Jacob Schirmer, South Carolina Historical Society.

NOTES

CHAPTER I. DAMNATION TO THE YANKEES

1. *Harper's Weekly*, March 23, 1861.
2. *The Genesis of the Civil War*, by Samuel Wylie Crawford; preface, pp. vi, vii. This work, repeatedly cited hereafter, will be referred to as "Crawford."
3. *Battles and Leaders of the Civil War* (hereafter called "*B. & L.*"), ed. by Clarence C. Buel and Robert V. Johnson, Vol. I, p. 50. Article by James Chester, a member of the Moultrie garrison.
4. Note the report of Major Fitz John Porter, Chap. II.
5. Crawford, preface, p. vii.
6. *Reminiscences of Forts Sumter and Moultrie in 1860–'61*, by Abner Doubleday, pp. 14–15.
7. Crawford, p. 6.
8. Charleston *Mercury*, July 20, 1860.
9. *B. & L.*, Vol. I, p. 40.
10. Doubleday, p. 18.
11. Crawford, p. 7.
12. Doubleday, p. 19.
13. The same, p. 20.
14. Crawford, p. 7; Doubleday, p. 31.
15. *Causes of the Civil War*, by French Ensor Chadwick, p. 136; *The American Conflict*, by Horace Greeley, Vol. I, p. 330; Crawford, p. 7.
16. *B. & L.*, Vol. I, p. 40; Doubleday, p. 33.
17. *A Pictorial History of the Civil War*, by Benson J. Lossing, Vol. I, p. 118; Crawford, p. 4.
18. Crawford, p. 66; also, "A Visit to South Carolina in 1860," article by Edward G. Mason in *Atlantic Monthly*, Vol. LIII, 1884.
19. *Robert Barnwell Rhett, Father of Secession*, by Laura A. White, pp. 101, 133, and 135.
20. *Abraham Lincoln: The War Years*, by Carl Sandburg, Vol. I, p. 155; Doubleday, 16.
21. White, p. 177.
22. The same, pp. 24, 108–09, and 127.
23. Charleston *Mercury*, Oct. 6, 1860; also, *South Carolina Goes to War*, by Charles Edward Cauthen, pp. 34–36.
24. Cauthen, pp. 45–47; also, *Nationalism and Sectionalism in South Carolina, 1852–1860*, by Harold S. Schultz, pp. 226–27.
25. *Frank Leslie's Illustrated Newspaper*, Dec. 1, 1860, quoting the Yorkville *Enquirer*.
26. Doubleday, pp. 25 and 32.

CHAPTER II. WE HATE EACH OTHER SO

1. South Carolina was the only state where there was no popular vote for President, electors being chosen by the legislature.
2. Greeley, Vol. I, p. 330; Chadwick, p. 136.

3. Greeley, Vol. I, p. 331.
4. *Life and Public Services of Edwin M. Stanton,* by George C. Gorham, Vol. I, p. 85.
5. *The Secession Movement, 1860–1861,* by Dwight L. Dumond, p. 118; Greeley, Vol. I, p. 345; Cauthen, p. 38.
6. *Charleston, Historic City of Gardens,* by William Oliver Stevens, p. 250.
7. *Ante-Bellum South Carolina,* by Rosser H. Taylor, p. 49; *Benjamin F. Perry, South Carolina Unionist,* by Lillian A. Kibler, p. 153. The term "statriots" was used by Frederic Bancroft, *Calhoun and the South Carolina Nullification Movement,* p. 173.
8. *A Diary From Dixie,* by Mary Boykin Chesnut, p. 20.
9. *The Eve of Conflict,* by George Fort Milton, p. 161.
10. *The Coming of the Civil War,* by Avery Craven, p. 424.
11. Doubleday, pp. 32–33. *History of the United States, 1850–1877,* by James Ford Rhodes, Vol. III, p. 124.
12. The items about Ruffin are all from Avery Craven's *Edmund Ruffin, Southerner,* pp. 12, 54–60, 105, 176–79, 182, and 188.
13. Spoken Nov. 7; Greeley, Vol. I, pp. 335–36.
14. White, p. 175; Cauthen, p. 50.
15. Greeley, Vol. I, p. 332.
16. Cauthen, p. 53.
17. *Year Book, 1895, City of Charleston, S. C.,* pp. 368–69; *A History of South Carolina,* ed. by Yates Snowden, Vol. II, pp. 658–59.
18. Charleston *Mercury,* Nov. 8, 1860.
19. *Led On! Step By Step,* by A. Toomer Porter, p. 119.
20. Doubleday, p. 25.
21. *War of the Rebellion: A Compilation of the Official Records of the Union Confederate Armies,* Series I, Vol. I, pp. 67–68, Craig to Floyd. This work hereafter will be cited as *"O. R.,"* and all citations are from Series I, Vol. I.
22. *O. R.,* pp. 68–69, Gardner to Craig, Nov. 5, 1860.
23. Doubleday, p. 29.
24. Crawford, p. 57.
25. *O. R.,* p. 71; Doubleday, pp. 30–31.
26. Crawford, p. 58.
27. *Lee and His Lieutenants,* by Edward A. Pollard, p. 791; also Gorham, Vol. I, p. 90.
28. Narrative of William Henry Trescot, in *American Historical Review,* Vol. XIII, p. 533. This work will hereafter be cited as "Trescot."
29. *B. & L.,* Vol. I, p. 43.
30. Doubleday, p. 24.
31. Crawford, p. 60.
32. *O. R.,* pp. 70–72, Porter to Cooper, Nov. 11.
33. *O. R.,* p. 72, Humphreys to Craig, Nov. 12; Crawford, p. 19.
34. Charleston *Courier,* Nov. 10, 1860.
35. Craven's *Ruffin,* p. 196.
36. Charleston *Courier,* Nov. 12, 1860.
37. Kibler, p. 332.
38. Cauthen, p. 61.
39. Charleston *Courier,* items taken from issues of Nov. 15, 16, 17, and 19.
40. Rhodes, Vol. III, p. 120; Lossing, Vol. I, p. 98.
41. Charleston *Courier,* Nov. 21.
42. Cauthen, p. 51.

Chapter III. THE UNLUCKIEST MAN

1. *Winfield Scott, the Soldier and the Man,* by Charles Winslow Elliott, p. 649; *Fifty Years' Observation of Men and Events,* by Erasmus Darwin Keyes, p. 45.

2. *The Administration on the Eve of the Rebellion,* by James Buchanan, p. 101; *The Life of James Buchanan,* by George Ticknor Curtis, Vol. II, pp. 297–98.
3. *Memoirs of Lieutenant General Scott, LL.D., Written by Himself,* Vol. II, pp. 609–10.
4. Buchanan, *The Administration on the Eve of the Rebellion,* p. 103.
5. Chadwick, pp. 185–86; Rhodes, Vol. III, p. 129.
6. Trescot, p. 547.
7. *Men and Memories,* by John Russell Young, pp. 56–57.
8. *The War Department, 1861,* by A. Howard Meneely, pp. 30 and 38; Rhodes, Vol. III, p. 237. Also, *James Buchanan and His Cabinet,* by Philip G. Auchampaugh, pp. 92–95.
9. Pollard, pp. 790–91.
10. The same, p. 792.
11. Charleston *Courier,* Feb. 13, 1861, quoting New York *Herald.*
12. *The Diary of George Templeton Strong,* Vol. III, p. 76. According to a fellow passenger on the *Adriatic,* Pickens said his fellow citizens in South Carolina were making themselves the "laughing-stock of Europe."
13. Pollard, p. 791; Gorham, Vol. I, p. 86.
14. Pollard, p. 794.
15. Rhodes, Vol. III, p. 195; Snowden, Vol. II, p. 660.
16. Trescot, p. 533.
17. *O. R.,* pp. 6 and 74.
18. Floyd speech, New York *Herald,* Jan. 17, 1861. Also, Trescot, p. 533.
19. *O. R.,* p. 73. *Dawson's Historical Magazine,* January 1872, p. 37, says Anderson was recommended for the post by his "intimate friend," Fitz John Porter, as does *A Few Acts and Actors in the Tragedy of the Civil War,* by William Bender Wilson, pp. 41–42.

CHAPTER IV. I PICKED HIM MYSELF

1. *Rise and Fall of the Confederate Government,* by Jefferson Davis, p. 216.
2. *Jefferson Davis, American Patriot, 1808–1861,* by Hudson Strode, pp. 39, 66, and 69.
3. *Abraham Lincoln, a History,* by John G. Nicolay and John Hay (hereafter cited as "Nicolay and Hay"), Vol. II, p. 349.
4. Elliott, p. 678.
5. *Biographical Register . . . of the United States Military Academy,* by George W. Cullum, Vol. I, pp. 535–37.
6. Cullum, Vol. I, pp. 347–52.
7. *Charleston, Historic and Romantic,* by Harriette Kershaw Leiding, p. 209.
8. Doubleday, p. 42; Crawford, p. 61.
9. Had Anderson known this, he would not have besieged Floyd with requests for reinforcements.
10. *Soldier and Pioneer: A Biographical Sketch of Lieutenant Colonel Richard C. Anderson,* by E. L. Anderson, pp. 26–27.
11. *The Political Conspiracies Preceding the Rebellion,* by Thomas M. Anderson, p. 7. Also, *Fort Sumter Memorial,* by Frank Moore, pp. 61 and 65.
12. *Guide to Charleston,* by Arthur Mazyck, pp. 37 and 108–09.
13. Doubleday, pp. 41–42.
14. The same, pp. 22–23.
15. The same, p. 23.
16. *O. R.,* p. 78.
17. Crawford, p. 4.
18. The same, p. 95.
19. *O. R.,* p. 75, Anderson to Cooper, Nov. 23.
20. The same.

21. The same—full report is on pp. 74–76.
22. *O. R.*, p. 86.
23. The same, p. 79, Anderson to Cooper, Nov. 28.
24. The same.
25. The same.
26. *O. R.*, pp. 81–82, Anderson to Cooper, Dec. 1.
27. The same.
28. Doubleday, p. 42.
29. The same, p. 40.
30. The same.
31. The same, p. 50.
32. The same, p. 43.
33. *O. R.*, p. 75.
34. The same, pp. 83–84.
35. The same, pp. 81–82, to Cooper, Dec. 1.
36. The same, p. 85, Foster to DeRussy, Dec. 4.
37. Crawford, pp. 92–93; *O. R.*, pp. 87–88.
38. *O. R.*, p. 77, Cooper to Anderson, Nov. 28.
39. The same, pp. 82–83, Cooper to Anderson, Dec. 1.
40. The same, p. 87, Anderson to Cooper, Dec. 6.
41. Crawford, p. 69.
42. Anderson Papers, Library of Congress, Dec. 16.
43. *O. R.*, p. 88, Anderson to Cooper, Dec. 6.
44. The same, pp. 92–93, Cooper to Anderson, Dec. 14.
45. The same, p. 89.
46. Crawford, p. 74.
47. Lossing, Vol. I, p. 126.
48. Crawford, pp. 72 and 74.
49. The same, p. 73.
50. *O. R.*, pp. 89–90.
51. Crawford, p. 74.

Chapter V. A FREE-LOVE ARRANGEMENT

1. Trescot, pp. 528–29.
2. The same, pp. 551–52.
3. The same, p. 548.
4. Trescot (p. 537) made no secret of this in discussions with Buchanan.
5. Trescot, p. 534.
6. The same, pp. 533–34.
7. The same, pp. 534–35.
8. *The Works of James Buchanan*, edited by John Bassett Moore, Vol. XI, p. 5, dated Nov. 24.
9. Floyd's later speech, quoted in New York *Herald*, Jan. 17, 1861. *Turning On the Light*, by Horatio King, p. 120, records the same conversation.
10. New York *Herald*, Jan. 17, 1861.
11. Pollard, p. 794; Trescot, p. 532.
12. New York *Herald*, Jan. 17, 1861.
13. Trescot, pp. 535–36.
14. Crawford, p. 32.
15. The same, pp. 31–32.
16. The entire message is given in Buchanan's *The Administration on the Eve of the Rebellion*, pp. 114–33.
17. *Seward at Washington*, by Frederick W. Seward, p. 480.
18. Nicolay and Hay, Vol. II, p. 392.

19. Crawford, p. 23.
20. Buchanan, *The Administration on the Eve of the Rebellion*, p. 164.
21. Trescot, p. 532.
22. *O. R.*, p. 125.
23. The same, pp. 125–28, statement of Miles and Keitt.
24. *The Story of the Civil War*, by John Codman Ropes, pp. 32–35 and 56–60. Also, *And the War Came*, by Kenneth Stampp, pp. 59–60. There has been endless discussion as to just what was said at this conversation, for Buchanan later denied giving any pledge at all. Yet the Carolinians left with the distinct impression that he *had* given them assurances, and the President later acted like a man who had committed himself to some extent.
25. Winfield Scott's *Memoirs*, Vol. II, pp. 614–15.
26. *Lewis Cass*, by Andrew C. McLaughlin, p. 344.
27. Philadelphia *Press*, Dec. 21, 1860, cited in Lossing, Vol. I, p. 143.

CHAPTER VI. THE HONOR-SAVERS

1. *Abstracted Indian Bonds*—House of Representatives, Report No. 78, 36th Congress, 2nd Session, pp. 101 and 351–52.
2. The same, pp. 302–05.
3. The same, p. 83, Floyd's testimony.
4. The same, pp. 296–97. Also, Auchampaugh, p. 94.
5. *Abstracted Indian Bonds*, p. 88.
6. The same, pp. 270–71.
7. The same, p. 9.
8. Auchampaugh, pp. 174–76.
9. The same, pp. 118–19. Also, *The Eve of Conflict*, by George Fort Milton, p. 510.
10. New York *Herald*, Dec. 28, 1860.
11. Crawford, p. 215; *Essays and Speeches of Jeremiah S. Black*, by Chauncey F. Black, p. 13. The Floyd scandal is discussed in Rhodes, Vol. III, pp. 239–40; in Greeley, Vol. I, 408; and in Meneely, pp. 38–48. The entire testimony of Floyd, Russell, and many others before a House investigating committee is in *Abstracted Indian Bonds*.

CHAPTER VII. WHERE'S THE FIRE?

1. *Anecdotes, Poetry and Incidents of the War, North and South*, collected by Frank Moore, p. 15.
2. Charleston *Courier*, Dec. 3, 1860.
3. Doubleday, p. 112; *O. R.*, pp. 90–91.
4. Crawford, p. 96.
5. *O. R.*, pp. 90–92, Foster to DeRussy, Dec. 13.
6. *O. R.*, pp. 100–01.
7. The same.
8. The same, pp. 95–96, Foster to DeRussy, Dec. 18.
9. Trescot, p. 539.
10. *O. R.*, p. 100, Dec. 20.
11. The same, p. 101, to DeRussy, Dec. 20.
12. Doubleday, p. 44.
13. The same, pp. 44 and 49.
14. *Major-General Abner Doubleday and Brevet Major-General John G. Robinson in the Civil War*, pp. 61–62.
15. *B. & L.*, Vol. I, p. 42; Doubleday, p. 59.

16. The same, both sources.
17. Doubleday, p. 47.
18. Crawford, p. 111.
19. *The Coming of the Civil War*, by Avery Craven, p. 405; also, *The History of South Carolina*, by David D. Wallace, Vol. III, p. 167.
20. Kibler, p. 226.
21. *Ante-Bellum South Carolina*, by Rosser H. Taylor, pp. 41-49.
22. Charleston *Courier*, Dec. 13, 1860.
23. Nicolay and Hay, Vol. III, p. 115.
24. Lossing, Vol. I, p. 100.
25. The same, p. 101.
26. Snowden, Vol. II, p. 662.
27. Lossing, Vol. I, p. 102; *Harper's Pictorial History of the Civil War*, p. 33.
28. A. Toomer Porter, p. 118.
29. Snowden, Vol. II, pp. 663-64.
30. Lossing, Vol. I, p. 104.
31. Doubleday, p. 56.
32. Snowden, Vol. II, p. 664.
33. A. Toomer Porter, p. 118.
34. The Diary of Jacob Schirmer, South Carolina Historical Society, entry for Dec. 20.
35. *Caleb Cushing*, by Claude M. Fuess, Vol. II, pp. 273-74.
36. Greeley, Vol. I, p. 345.

CHAPTER VIII. PEACEABLY, IF POSSIBLE

1. *Harper's Weekly*, Jan. 19, 1861.
2. *A History of Edgefield County*, by John A. Chapman, pp. 143-44.
3. Charleston *Mercury*, Dec. 13, 1860.
4. New York *Herald*, Jan. 12, 1861.
5. *The Record of Fort Sumter*, by W. A. Harris, pp. 7-8, letter dated Dec. 17.
6. Trescot, p. 541.
7. Harris, pp. 9-11.
8. Trescot, p. 541.
9. Harris, pp. 9-11, letter dated Dec. 21.
10. Crawford, p. 90.
11. The same, p. 91; New York *Tribune*, Jan. 9, 1861.
12. Crawford, p. 88.
13. *O. R.*, p. 101.
14. The same, letter dated Dec. 20.
15. The same, p. 102, Dec. 20.
16. The same, pp. 97-98, Foster to DeRussy, Dec. 19.

CHAPTER IX. NO TIME FOR TEA

1. Nicolay and Hay, Vol. III, p. 46.
2. *O. R.*, p. 117.
3. *Major Robert Anderson and Fort Sumter*, by Eba Anderson Lawton, p. 9.
4. *O. R.*, p. 105, Anderson to Cooper, Dec. 22.
5. *O. R.*, p. 106.
6. The same, Foster to DeRussy, Dec. 22.
7. *O. R.*, p. 107; Crawford, p. 99.
8. *O. R.*, p. 107, letter dated Dec. 27, 1860.
9. The same, p. 105, Anderson to Cooper, Dec. 22.

10. The same.
11. Doubleday, p. 56; Crawford, p. 95.
12. *O. R.*, p. 103, letter dated Dec. 21.
13. *Major Anderson and Fort Sumter*, by Eba Anderson Lawton, pp. 3-4; and *The Political Conspiracies Preceding the Rebellion*, by Thomas M. Anderson, pp. 29-30. Both writers were close kin of Major Anderson, and declare that the major regarded this Floyd order as treason. Actually it was not treason at all. Floyd on Dec. 21 showed his original orders to Anderson via Buell instructing him to defend the fort to the "last extremity" to the President. Buchanan himself ordered Floyd to soften the order and instruct Anderson merely to make the best defense possible.
14. Rhodes, Vol. III, p. 215.
15. Nicolay and Hay, Vol. III, pp. 47-48.
16. Crawford, p. 102.
17. Charleston *Courier*, Dec. 27.
18. Nicolay and Hay, Vol. III, p. 46.
19. *Dawson's Historical Magazine*, January 1872, p. 48.
20. Doubleday, p. 60.
21. Nicolay and Hay, Vol. III, p. 48.
22. Crawford, pp. 102-03.
23. The same, p. 103.
24. The same, p. 104.
25. Doubleday, p. 62.
26. The same, p. 63.
27. *B. & L.*, Vol. I, p. 45.
28. Crawford, p. 106.
29. Doubleday, p. 65.
30. Crawford, p. 106.
31. Doubleday, pp. 65-66.
32. The same, p. 66.
33. Crawford, p. 106.
34. The same, p. 105.
35. Nicolay and Hay, Vol. III, p. 54.
36. *Dawson's Historical Magazine*, January 1872, p. 52.
37. *O. R.*, p. 2.

CHAPTER X. MY COMPLIMENTS TO THE GOVERNOR

1. Crawford, p. 107; Nicolay and Hay, Vol. III, p. 54.
2. Doubleday, p. 67.
3. Crawford, p. 107.
4. Doubleday, p. 68.
5. Crawford, p. 108.
6. *O. R.*, p. 109.
7. Judge Petigru, formerly Pettigrew, had changed his name years earlier to conform with the original Huguenot spelling.
8. This entire scene is related in Crawford, pp. 109-12, and partially in Doubleday, pp. 79-80.
9. Crawford, p. 112; Doubleday, p. 71.
10. *B. & L.*, Vol. I, p. 65.
11. Doubleday, p. 73.
12. Crawford, p. 114.
13. Doubleday, p. 73.
14. Charleston *Courier*, Dec. 31; Crawford, p. 116.
15. *Courier*, Dec. 28, 1860.
16. New York *Herald*, Dec. 28, 1860.

CHAPTER XI. MEN DO GO MAD

1. *Diary of a Public Man*, p. 90.
2. Charleston *Courier*, Jan. 3, 1861; Lossing, Vol. I, p. 147.
3. Trescot, pp. 537 and 542.
4. *Recollections of Abraham Lincoln, 1847–65*, by Ward Hill Lamon, pp. 264–65. Also, *Public Man*, p. 34.
5. Trescot, p. 543.
6. *O. R.*, p. 3, Dec. 27.
7. Trescot, p. 544.
8. *Rise and Fall of the Confederate Government*, by Jefferson Davis, pp. 213 and 215.
9. Auchampaugh, p. 167; Rhodes, Vol. III, p. 228; Stampp, pp. 59–60.
10. Trescot, p. 544.
11. *O. R.*, p. 3, dated Dec. 27.
12. Crawford, p. 146.
13. Auchampaugh, p. 158. Also, Gorham, Vol. I, p. 135.
14. Black, p. 12.
15. Black, p. 13; Curtis, Vol. II, p. 409.
16. Gorham, Vol. I, pp. 158–59.
17. New York *Herald*, Dec. 28, 1860.
18. *O. R.*, pp. 109–11, dated Dec. 28.
19. Crawford, pp. 148–49.
20. Trescot, p. 551.
21. *O. R.*, p. 111, Scott to Buchanan, Dec. 28.
22. The same, p. 112, Scott to Floyd, Dec. 28.
23. *Frank Leslie's Illustrated Newspaper*, Dec. 29, 1860.
24. *Military Memoirs of a Confederate*, by E. P. Alexander, p. 11; also, Young, pp. 25–26.
25. Black, p. 14.
26. Trescot, p. 546.
27. *Twenty Years in Congress*, by James G. Blaine, Vol. I, pp. 230 and 233. Also, Gorham, Vol. I, pp. 121–22; Rhodes, Vol. III, p. 188.
28. Auchampaugh, pp. 161–62.
29. *Abraham Lincoln and Men of War-Times*, by Alexander K. McClure, p. 278. Also, Black, p. 14.
30. Black, pp. 14–17.
31. Trescot, p. 552.
32. Blaine, Vol. I, p. 233.
33. *O. R.*, p. 114, dated Dec. 30.

CHAPTER XII. FLEAS IN THEIR EARS

1. *The Day of the Confederacy*, by N. W. Stephenson, p. 5.
2. *O. R.*, p. 252, Jan. 2, 1861.
3. Auchampaugh, p. 91.
4. *O. R.*, p. 119, Dec. 31, 1860.
5. The same, pp. 115–18, Dec. 30, 1860.
6. Black, p. 19; Rhodes, Vol. III, p. 234.
7. Trescot, pp. 552–53.
8. The same, pp. 545–46.
9. New York *Tribune*, Jan. 5, 1861.
10. Nicolay and Hay, Vol. III, p. 93.
11. Black, p. 20.

12. *O. R.*, pp. 120–25, Jan. 1, 1861. Also, Ropes, pp. 40–41.
13. Nicolay and Hay, Vol. III, p. 93.
14. The same. Also, Black, p. 20.
15. Black, p. 20.
16. Charleston *Courier*, Jan. 18, 1861. Also, Black, p. 20.
17. *The Administration on the Eve of the Rebellion*, by James Buchanan, pp. 189–90; Rhodes, Vol. III, p. 245.
18. *O. R.*, pp. 128–29, Scott to Thomas, Jan. 2; Elliott, p. 685.
19. The same Scott-to-Thomas letter cited above. Also, *Lincoln Finds a General*, by Kenneth P. Williams, Vol. I, pp. 26–27. Gen. Scott sent Col. Lorenzo Thomas to New York to arrange for the *Star of the West*. Thomas was also to notify Major Anderson. This could have been done in general terms the moment the expedition was decided on, but for some reason Thomas waited until arrangements were completed and the *Star* was ready to embark.
20. Black, p. 20.
21. Milton, p. 514. Thompson had made plain his intention to resign if reinforcements were sent. It seems likely that Buchanan and Holt did deceive him, knowing this was the only way to maintain secrecy.
22. Black, pp. 20–21; King, pp. 97–98; Buchanan's *Works*, Vol. XI, pp. 100–01.
23. *O. R.*, p. 253, Jan. 8, 1861.
24. New York *Times*, Jan. 3.
25. New York *World*, Jan. 4.

Chapter XIII. BLESSINGS ON YOU ANYHOW

1. *Harper's Weekly*, Jan. 26, 1861.
2. Two letters, Anderson to Gourdin, in Crawford, pp. 128–30.
3. The Robert Anderson Papers, L. C., Dec. 27, 1860.
4. *O. R*, pp. 112–13.
5. The same, pp. 8–9.
6. Crawford, pp. 129 and 136.
7. Crawford Diary, L C., dated Jan. 4, 1861.
8. Crawford, pp. 118–19; *O. R.*, p. 120; Lossing, Vol. I, p. 131.
9. Crawford, p. 129, dated Dec. 29.
10. Crawford, p. 131; Doubleday, pp. 77–78; *B. & L.*, Vol. I, pp. 52–53.
11. Doubleday, p. 78.
12. Charleston *Courier*, Dec. 31, 1860.
13. Crawford, p. 118.
14. A. Toomer Porter, p. 122.
15. *B. & L.*, Vol. I, p. 55.
16. Doubleday, p. 64.
17. New York *World*, Jan. 4, 1861.
18. New York *Tribune*, Jan. 10, 1861.
19. Anderson Papers, C. Ballance to Anderson, Jan. 8, 1861.
20. The same, Leslie Combs to Anderson, Jan. 1, 1861.
21. Anderson Papers, Jan. 3.
22. The same, Dec. 28, 1860.
23. *A History of the South Carolina Military Academy*, by John Peyre Thomas, p. 107; Crawford, pp. 124–25.
24. *O. R.*, p. 120, to Cooper, Dec. 31.
25. Charleston *Courier*, Dec. 31, 1860; Crawford, p. 134; *O. R.*, pp. 136–37.
26. Schirmer Diary, last entry of 1860.
27. Harris, pp. 14–17.
28. The same, pp. 19–21.
29. *The Women of the Confederacy*, by Francis B. Simkins and James W. Patton,

p. 15. Also, Cauthen, p. 62; *Edmund Ruffin,* by Craven, p. 202; Crawford, p. 137.

30. Crawford Diary, entry Jan. 4. Also, Doubleday, pp. 95–96; Crawford, pp. 117–18; *B. & L.,* Vol. I, p. 46.
31. Doubleday, p. 96; Crawford, p. 134.
32. Doubleday, p. 100.
33. Doubleday, p. 96; *B. & L.,* Vol. I, p. 46.
34. Doubleday, p. 97; Thomas, pp. 121–25.
35. New York *Tribune,* Jan. 4, 1861.
36. Doubleday, p. 99.
37. *Fort Sumter Memorial,* by Frank Moore, p. 21.
38. The entire account of Mrs. Anderson's hunt for Hart and journey to Charleston is in Lossing, Vol. I, pp. 132–35.
39. Doubleday, p. 100.

CHAPTER XIV. THE DISGUST OF CAPTAIN DOUBLEDAY

1. King, p. 102.
2. Letter of Postmaster Huger of Charleston to Secretary Holt, published in Charleston *Courier,* Jan. 17, 1861. Huger admitted there had been some "surveillance" of the mail.
3. *O. R.,* p. 120, Anderson to Cooper, Dec. 31.
4. Rhodes, Vol. III, pp. 248–49; *O. R.,* p. 134; Crawford, p. 176.
5. Crawford Diary, dated Jan. 8.
6. *O. R.,* p. 10, Lt. Woods's report dated Jan. 13.
7. Charleston *Courier,* Jan. 23.
8. *B. & L.,* Vol. I, p. 61; Crawford, p. 186.
9. *B. & L.,* Vol. I, p. 61.
10. Crawford, p. 186.
11. *Frank Leslie's Illustrated Newspaper,* Jan. 26, 1861.
12. Crawford Diary, Jan. 9.
13. The same; also Crawford, p. 186.
14. *Within Fort Sumter,* by One of the Company, p. 15.
15. *B. & L.,* Vol. I, p. 61.
16. Crawford, p. 186. The *Star of the West* incident is taken from Crawford Diary, April 9; Crawford, pp. 183–86; Woods's report, Jan. 13, *O. R.,* pp. 9–10; McGowan's report, New York *Times,* Jan. 14; *B. & L.,* Vol. I, pp. 61–62; Charleston *Courier,* Jan. 10; Doubleday, pp. 101–04; *Within Fort Sumter,* p. 15; and Foster's later report, in *Supplemental Report of the Joint Committee on the Conduct of the War,* Vol. II, p. 7.
17. Doubleday, pp. 103–04; Crawford, p. 187. At this time Anderson had received no word from the government since his move to Sumter except the outraged telegram of Floyd. He knew the move had caused a national convulsion, and while Congress had approved it, the administration had maintained what must have seemed to him a stony silence. He undoubtedly felt uncertain of his ground and unsupported by the government.
18. Crawford, pp. 187–88.
19. *O. R.,* p. 134, Jan. 9, 1861.
20. Crawford, p. 189.
21. *O. R.,* pp. 135–36, Jan. 9.
22. Crawford, p. 191.
23. Harris, p. 21.
24. The same, pp. 21–23, Jan. 10.
25. Charleston *Mercury,* Jan. 10.
26. Chadwick, p. 231.

27. Quoted in New York *Tribune*, Jan. 7.
28. Doubleday, p. 111. Anderson's orders, to remain on the defensive and avoid provoking Carolinian ire, forbade resistance to anything but outright assault and possibly even forbade protest.
29. Anderson, Robert, *An Artillery Officer in Mexico: Letters of Robert Anderson*, p. 93.
30. Doubleday's words: Doubleday, p. 74.
31. Lawton, p. 17.
32. *The Lincoln Papers*, edited by David C. Mearns, Vol. II, p. 405; *Horace Greeley and the Tribune in the Civil War*, by Ralph Ray Fahrney, pp. 44–45; *Horace Greeley, Voice of the People*, by William Harlan Hale, pp. 228–29.
33. *O. R.*, pp. 143–44, Anderson to Holt, Jan. 21.
34. Crawford, p. 192.
35. Doubleday, p. 108.
36. Crawford, pp. 192–93.
37. Sketch of Magrath in *South Carolina Bench and Bar*, by U. R. Brooks, Vol. I, pp. 328–37.
38. Crawford, p. 193; Doubleday, p. 108.
39. Crawford, p. 193.
40. The same, p. 194; Nicolay and Hay, Vol. III, pp. 110–12.
41. Cauthen, p. 103; Chadwick, p. 240; *The Administration on the Eve of the Rebellion*, by James Buchanan, p. 193.
42. *O. R.*, p. 133, Anderson to Cooper, Jan. 6.
43. Mearns, *The Lincoln Papers*, Vol. II, pp. 403–04.

Chapter XV. SUMTER IS NOT FOR SALE

1. *Lincoln the President*, by J. G. Randall, Vol. I, p. 211.
2. *Diary of George Templeton Strong*, Vol. III, p. 89.
3. Meneely, p. 22.
4. *Diary of a Public Man*, p. 37.
5. *Memoirs of John Adams Dix*, edited by Morgan Dix, Vol. I, p. 362.
6. Auchampaugh, p. 68.
7. *O. R.*, p. 443, Jan. 7, 1861.
8. Charleston *Courier*, Jan. 18, 1861.
9. Cauthen, p. 116.
10. King, pp. 48–49.
11. Quoted in Rhodes, Vol. III, p. 300.
12. Nicolay and Hay, Vol. III, p. 137.
13. Lossing, Vol. I, p. 142.
14. *B. & L.*, Vol. I, p. 13.
15. Lossing, Vol. I, p. 141.
16. Washington dispatch of Charleston *Courier*, Mar. 7, 1861.
17. Black, pp. 21–22, letter to A. V. Parsons, Jan. 17, 1861.
18. Harris, pp. 30–32.
19. The same, pp. 32–34.
20. Cauthen, p. 105.
21. Nicolay and Hay, Vol. III, p. 157.
22. *O. R.*, pp. 149–50. Also, *Casket of Reminiscences*, by Henry S. Foote, pp. 96–97; and Auchampaugh, pp. 80–81.
23. Two letters, Davis to Pickens, in *Jefferson Davis, the Unreal and the Real*, by Robert McElroy, Vol. I, pp. 252–53 and 255.
24. King, p. 57; also, *P. G. T. Beauregard, Napoleon in Gray*, by T. Harry Williams, pp. 45–46.

25. Crawford, p. 277.
26. *Diary of George Templeton Strong*, Vol. III, p. 103.
27. *Harper's Weekly*, Feb. 2, 1861.
28. *B. & L.*, Vol. I, pp. 26-31; *O. R.*, pp. 112.
29. New York *Herald*, Jan. 17, 1861. Although both Floyd and Russell were
    indicted, neither came to trial because it was discovered belatedly that
    an earlier law forbade criminal prosecution of persons who had testified
    before a House committee in the same case. Thus was lost an opportunity
    to clear or convict the two and throw more light on the bond-and-draft
    scandal.
30. Crawford, pp. 242-43, letter dated Jan. 22, 1861.
31. The same, pp. 226-28, letter dated Jan. 31.
32. *O. R.*, pp. 166-68, Feb. 6, 1861.

Chapter XVI. LET THE MAJOR DECLARE WAR

1. *O. R.*, pp. 153-54; Crawford, p. 203.
2. *Within Fort Sumter*, p. 10; Crawford, p. 203.
3. *O. R.*, p. 157.
4. The same, p. 133.
5. Chester's narrative, *B. & L.*, Vol. I, p. 56.
6. The same, pp. 55-56.
7. *O. R.*, pp. 144-45, Anderson to Jamison, Jan. 19.
8. Doubleday, p. 113.
9. Crawford, p. 202.
10. *Harper's Weekly*, Jan. 26, 1861.
11. *O. R.*, p. 158, Anderson to Cooper, Jan. 29.
12. *O. R.*, p. 133, Jan. 6.
13. The same, pp. 136-37, Jan. 10.
14. Doubleday, p. 113.
15. *O. R.*, p. 140, dated Jan. 16.
16. *O. R.*, p. 133.
17. Lossing, Vol. I, p. 313.
18. *O. R.*, pp. 156-57; New York *Tribune*, Jan. 4.
19. Crawford, p. 210; *O. R.*, pp. 143 and 146-48.
20. Crawford, p. 199; *O. R.*, p. 163.
21. Doubleday, p. 122; Crawford, p. 200; *B. & L.*, Vol. I, pp. 57-58 and 60.
22. *B. & L.*, Vol. I, p. 59; Crawford, p. 200.
23. *B. & L.*, Vol. I, p. 60.
24. Anderson Papers, Gourdin to Anderson, Jan. 31, 1861; *O. R.*, pp. 139, 150,
    and 160; *Within Fort Sumter*, pp. 22-23.
25. Crawford, p. 207; *Within Fort Sumter*, p. 24; *O. R.*, p. 158.
26. Doubleday, p. 117.
27. *O. R.*, pp. 123-24, Jan. 21.
28. Stampp, p. 99.
29. *Times*, issues of Jan. 11 and 16, 1861.
30. Anonymous letter in Charleston *Courier*, Jan. 17, 1861.
31. Anderson's views are quoted in a letter from Robert Gourdin, Anderson
    Papers, Feb. 2, 1861.
32. Jan. 15 letter quoted in *Harper's Weekly*, Feb. 2, 1861.
33. Jan. 27 letter to J. C. Peak quoted in Charleston *Courier*, Feb. 12, 1861.
34. *O. R.*, p. 163, dated Feb. 5.
35. The same, p. 169, dated Feb. 7.
36. The same, pp. 138-39, dated Jan. 14.
37. This is quoted verbatim in Gourdin's reply, dated Feb. 2, Anderson Papers.
38. The same Gourdin letter.

Chapter XVII. THE SOUTH CAROLINA GENTLEMEN

1. *Anecdotes, Poetry and Incidents of the War, North and South*, edited by Frank Moore, p. 15.
2. *Life, Letters and Speeches of James Louis Petigru*, edited by James Petigru Carson, Introduction, p. v.
3. "A Visit to South Carolina in 1860," by Edward G. Mason, in *Atlantic Monthly*, Vol. LIII, 1884, p. 247. Also, *The South Carolina Jockey Club*, by John B. Irving, pp. 11–12; *Ante-Bellum South Carolina*, by Rosser Taylor, p. 33; *Charleston, a Gracious Heritage*, by Robert Molloy, pp. 86–87.
4. Taylor, p. 37; *The Culture of Early Charleston*, by Frederick P. Bowes, Chap. VII, pp. 115 ff.
5. Anonymous letter in *Harper's Weekly*, Jan. 26, 1861.
6. Cauthen, p. 106; White, p. 193.
7. Quoted in *The Rebellion Record*, edited by Frank Moore, Vol. I, Diary section, pp. 15–16.
8. Doubleday, p. 114.
9. *The Private Journal of Henry William Ravenel*, edited by Arney R. Childs, p. 51.
10. Pickens-Bonham Papers, L. C., dated Jan. 24.
11. Quoted in Charleston *Courier*, Feb. 13, 1861.
12. *Harper's Pictorial History of the Civil War*, p. 40.
13. Cauthen, pp. 83–84.
14. *The Private Journal of Henry Willam Ravenel*, entry Jan. 31, pp. 51–52.
15. *The History of South Carolina*, by David D. Wallace, Vol. III, pp. 157–58.
16. Crawford, p. 266, letter dated Feb. 2.
17. Francis Pickens Papers, New York Public Library, letter dated Feb. 7.

Chapter XVIII. THE PEACEMAKERS

1. Charleston *Courier*, April 4, 1861, quoting London *Times*, Mar. 14.
2. Excerpts from four letters in *Seward at Washington*, pp. 487, 488, 491, and 497.
3. *The Life of John J. Crittenden*, by Mrs. Chapman Coleman, Vol. II, pp. 337–38.
4. *Diary of a Public Man*, p. 29; *The Life of William H. Seward*, by Frederic Bancroft (hereafter cited as "Bancroft"), Vol. II, pp. 15, 18, and 37; *Reveille in Washington*, by Margaret Leech, pp. 25–26.
5. *Seward at Washington*, p. 492; Bancroft, p. 7; *Lincoln's War Cabinet*, by Burton J. Hendrick, p. 159; *Lincoln and Seward*, by Gideon Welles, p. 50.
6. Crawford, p. 243.
7. Nicolay and Hay, Vol. III, pp. 166–67; Curtis, Vol. II, p. 466.
8. *The Letters and Times of the Tylers*, by Lyon G. Tyler, Vol. II, pp. 610–11. Buchanan's *Works*, edited by John Bassett Moore, Vol. XI, pp. 141–42.
9. *O. R.*, p. 254.
10. Tyler, Vol. II, p. 612, dated Feb. 9.
11. Nicolay and Hay, Vol. III, pp. 167–68; Chadwick, pp. 250–51.
12. *Recollections of President Lincoln and His Administration*, by L. E. Chittenden, p. 38.
13. The same, p. 45.
14. *O. R.*, pp. 177 and 201–03; Crawford, pp. 249–50.
15. *O. R.*, p. 257, dated Feb. 20.
16. Chittenden, p. 34.
17. Nicolay and Hay, Vol. III, pp. 149–51. See also King, p. 53; Tyler, Vol. II, p. 615; and Crawford, pp. 273–74.
18. Crawford, p. 274.

19. *Four Years in Rebel Capitals*, by T. C. DeLeon, p. 17; *Harper's Weekly*, Mar. 9, 1861.

CHAPTER XIX. THE LION AND THE LAMB

1. Strode, pp. 421–22.
2. Crawford, p. 266.
3. Crawford, pp. 267 and 270, letter dated Feb. 12.
4. Francis Pickens Papers, New York Public Library, dated Feb. 13.
5. *Harper's Weekly*, Mar. 16, 1861.
6. Charleston *Courier*, Mar. 12.
7. *Courier*, March 12 and April 1.
8. *Reminiscences of Richard Lathers*, edited by Alvan F. Sanborn, p. 125.
9. Lossing, Vol. I, p. 312.
10. *B. & L.*, Vol. I, p. 56.
11. Crawford, p. 204.
12. Letter printed in Charleston *Courier*, Mar. 13.
13. Doubleday, p. 123.
14. Crawford, p. 295.
15. Auchampaugh, p. 156, dated Jan. 11.
16. *O. R.*, p. 176.
17. Anderson Papers, dated Feb. 5.
18. Doubleday, p. 126.
19. Anderson Papers, dated Feb. 4.
20. Both reports to Cooper, Feb. 13 and 16, *O. R.*, pp. 170 and 175.
21. King, p. 45.
22. *O. R.*, pp. 182–83, Holt to Anderson, Feb. 23. Also, Ropes, pp. 50–51.
23. Crawford, pp. 298, 372, and 471–72; Doubleday, pp. 86–87. While Anderson remained on cordial terms with his other officers after the Sumter siege, apparently the resentment between him and Foster lingered. Anderson was later offended when Foster received promotion in rank before the other officers, feeling he had done less to deserve it. Foster implied criticism of Anderson in an 1865 report to the Committee on the Conduct of the War, saying that Sumter could have been reinforced at any time.
24. *O. R.*, pp. 172–73.
25. *O. R.*, pp. 170, 172–73, and 175–76; *Charleston, S. C.: The Centennial of Incorporation, 1883*, p. 230.
26. Excerpts from three Foster reports, *O. R.*, pp. 172–73, 175–76 and 186–87.
27. *B. & L.*, Vol. I, pp. 63–64.
28. The same, p. 63.
29. Anonymous letter in *Harper's Weekly*, Feb. 16, 1861.
30. *B. & L.*, Vol. I, p. 56.
31. Charleston *Courier*, Mar. 27, 1861.
32. Doubleday, p. 119.
33. Doubleday, pp. 119–20 and 122; Charleston *Courier*, Feb. 14.
34. *O. R.*, pp. 197 and 202; Crawford, pp. 283–84.
35. Crawford, p. 248.
36. *Reminiscences of Richard Lathers*, p. 128.
37. *The Civil War in America*, by Sir William H. Russell, p. 34.
38. A. Toomer Porter, p. 123; *O. R.*, p. 158; Charleston *Courier*, Feb. 14.
39. *Reminiscences of Richard Lathers*, pp. 121 and 124.
40. The same, p. 122.
41. Crawford, pp. 271–72; *O. R.*, p. 259.
42. *The Military Operations of General Beauregard*, by Alfred Roman, Vol. I,

p. 29; *Beauregard,* by T. Harry Williams, p. 53. *Beauregard, the Great Creole,* by Hamilton Basso, p. 24.
43. *O. R.,* p. 191, to Col. Cooper, Mar. 6.

Chapter XX. "HOLD, OCCUPY AND POSSESS"

1. *The Rebellion Record,* Vol. I, Poetry, p. 23.
2. *Diary of George Templeton Strong,* Vol. III, p. 104.
3. Blaine, Vol. I, p. 233.
4. *American History as Told by Contemporaries,* edited by Albert Bushnell Hart, Vol. IV, pp. 172–75.
5. *Lincoln's War Cabinet,* by Burton J. Hendrick, pp. 154–55.
6. Nicolay and Hay, Vol. III, p. 398.
7. *Reminiscences of Peace and War,* by Mrs. Roger A. Pryor, pp. 118–19; *B. & L.,* Vol. I, pp. 24–25; DeLeon, p. 19.
8. *Recollections of Men and Things at Washington,* by L. A. Gobright, pp. 289–90; Leech, pp. 41–45; *Diary of a Public Man,* pp. 72–73.
9. Chittenden, pp. 85–86.
10. *O. R.,* p. 261.
11. Nicolay and Hay, Vol. III, pp. 377.
12. Crawford, p. 285; Buchanan's *Works,* Vol. XI, pp. 195–97.
13. Crawford, pp. 284–89.
14. Ropes, pp. 54–55 and 77–78.
15. Letter to Washburne, Nicolay and Hay, Vol. III, p. 250.
16. Sandburg, Vol. I, p. 125.
17. Nicolay and Hay, Vol. III, p. 378.
18. *Complete Works of Abraham Lincoln,* ed. by Nicolay and Hay, Vol. VI, p. 301.
19. Randall, Vol. I, pp. 315, 331–32.
20. Welles, *Lincoln and Seward,* pp. 49 and 53; *Diary of Gideon Welles,* Vol. I, p. 7.
21. Crawford, p. 322; Bancroft, Vol. II, pp. 108–09.
22. Bancroft, Vol. II, p. 110.
23. The same.
24. *Bohemian Brigade,* by Louis M. Starr, p. 27; Randall, Vol. I, pp. 342–43.
25. Bancroft, Vol. II, p. 111.
26. Crawford, p. 324.
27. Nicolay and Hay, Vol. III, pp. 403–04.
28. Crawford, p. 328.
29. *John Archibald Campbell,* by Henry G. Connor, pp. 123–24.
30. Connor, pp. 125–26; Crawford, pp. 328–30; Bancroft, Vol. II, p. 114.
31. Quoted in Charleston *Courier,* Mar. 18, 1861.
32. Welles, Diary, Vol. I, p. 13.
33. *The Francis Preston Blair Family in Politics,* by William E. Smith, Vol. II, p. 7; Crawford, p. 347; Welles, *Lincoln and Seward,* pp. 64–68.
34. *O. R.,* pp. 197–200.
35. The same, p. 197. Also, *Diary of Gideon Welles,* Vol. I, pp. 5–6.
36. *The Lincoln Papers,* edited by David Mearns, Vol. II, p. 476.
37. Crawford, p. 347.
38. *O. R.,* pp. 203–04; Crawford, p. 347.
39. Quoted in Charleston *Courier,* Mar. 18, 1861.
40. *Diary of George Templeton Strong,* Vol. III, p. 109.
41. *O. R.,* p. 196.
42. Crawford, pp. 349–52.
43. *Diary of Edward Bates,* edited by Howard K. Beale, pp. 178–80. Also, Crawford, pp. 357 and 361; Nicolay and Hay, Vol. III, pp. 387–88.

Aa

44. Crawford, pp. 358–60.
45. Welles, *Lincoln and Seward*, pp. 56–57; Bancroft, Vol. II, p. 106.
46. Doubleday, p. 130.
47. Keyes, p. 56.
48. Elliott, p. 697.
49. Bancroft, Vol. II, p. 116; Connor, pp. 125–26.
50. Connor, pp. 126–27.
51. Crawford, p. 333.
52. The same, p. 334.

Chapter XXI. A DEAR, DELIGHTFUL PLACE

1. *O. R.*, p. 192, to Cooper, Mar. 9.
2. Doubleday, p. 130.
3. *O. R.*, pp. 195–96 and 218–19.
4. The same, p. 191; Crawford, pp. 295 and 297.
5. *Courier*, Mar. 11.
6. *Courier*, Mar. 13.
7. *O. R.*, p. 196, dated Mar. 14.
8. Crawford, p. 290.
9. Charleston *Mercury*, Mar. 5, 1861.
10. *Within Fort Sumter*, pp. 19 and 31; New York *Herald,* April 14.
11. Crawford, p. 305.
12. *O. R.*, p. 273.
13. Doubleday, p. 127.
14. *O. R.*, p. 276, to Beauregard, Mar. 15.
15. *O. R.*, pp. 276 and 279, Mar. 15 and 21.
16. Charleston *Courier*, Mar. 23.
17. Chesnut, p. 25.
18. *B. & L.*, Vol. I, p. 82.
19. Charleston *Courier*, Mar. 21.
20. Crawford, pp. 369–70.
21. Nicolay and Hay, Vol. III, p. 389.
22. Crawford, p. 372.
23. *O. R.*, p. 211, Mar. 22, to Col. Thomas, the new adjutant general who had succeeded Cooper.
24. *O. R.*, p. 217, Mar. 26.
25. Lamon, pp. 76–77.
26. *The Record of Fort Sumter*, pp. 35–36; *O. R.*, pp. 281–82.
27. Nicolay and Hay, Vol. III, pp. 391–92.
28. *O. R.*, p. 222, dated Mar. 26.
29. The same, pp. 222–23, same date.
30. The same, pp. 223 and 226.
31. *O. R.*, pp. 281–82, dated Mar. 26.
32. *Courier*, Mar. 22.
33. *Heroines of Dixie*, by Katherine M. Jones, pp. 16–17.
34. *O. R.*, p. 232.

Chapter XXII. . . . TO MOVE BY SEA

1. Crawford, p. 336.
2. *O. R.*, pp. 200–01.
3. Crawford, p. 366. Also, Welles, *Lincoln and Seward*, pp. 57–58; Bancroft, Vol. II, pp. 123–24.
4. *O. R.*, pp. 226–27; Nicolay and Hay, Vol. III, pp. 433–44.

5. Nicolay and Hay, Vol. III, p. 434; Seward, p. 536.
6. *American Historical Review*, Vol. XXVI, p. 299.
7. Seward, p. 534.
8. Connor, p. 127; Bancroft, Vol. II, p. 128.
9. Keyes, p. 380.
10. The same, pp. 380–81.
11. The same, p. 382. *The Conspiracies Preceding the Rebellion*, by T. M. Anderson, pp. 45 and 49; Crawford, pp. 410–11.
12. *American Historical Review*, Vol. XXVI, p. 300.
13. *Conspiracies Preceding the Rebellion*, by T. M. Anderson, p. 44.
14. *American Historical Review*, Vol. XXVI, p. 301.
15. Bancroft, Vol. II, p. 132.
16. Seward, p. 535.
17. The activities of Lamon in Charleston are unexplained. Although at the time he left Washington there was strong belief that Sumter would be evacuated, if he did assure Governor Pickens that he had come to arrange for the evacuation he was apparently exceeding his authority.
18. The Seward-Campbell conversation is from Connor, pp. 127–28.
19. *O. R.*, pp. 283–84.
20. Bancroft, Vol. II, p. 131.

Chapter XXIII. WAIT AND SEE

1. Crawford, p. 412.
2. *Official Records of the Union and Confederate Navies in the War of the Rebellion* (hereafter called "*O. R. N.*"; all citations are from Series I, Vol. IV), p. 109.
3. *Diary of Gideon Welles*, Vol. I, p. 19.
4. Crawford, p. 412.
5. *Incidents and Anecdotes of the Civil War*, by David Dixon Porter, pp. 20–21; *O. R. N.*, pp. 248–49.
6. New York dispatch to Charleston *Courier*, April 11.
7. The same. The horses actually went with flying artillery to Fort Pickens.
8. *O. R. N.*, p. 235, dated April 5.
9. The same, pp. 111–12.
10. *American Historical Review*, Vol. XXVI, pp. 301–02; *The Conspiracies Preceding the Rebellion*, by T. M. Anderson, p. 48; Crawford, pp. 413–14.
11. *Diary of Gideon Welles*, Vol. I, p. 24.
12. The same, pp. 24–25. *Gideon Welles, Lincoln's Navy Department*, by Richard S. West, Jr., pp. 104–06.
13. Nicolay and Hay, Vol. IV, pp. 4–6.
14. *O. R. N.*, p. 112; Crawford, pp. 414–15.
15. *O. R. N.*, p. 112; also Porter, *Incidents and Anecdotes*, pp. 21–22.
16. Bancroft, Vol. II, p. 144.
17. *Diary of Gideon Welles*, Vol. I, p. 26.
18. *O. R.*, p. 287. Recommended by Seward, Harvey soon thereafter went to Portugal as American minister. While there, his telegrams to Magrath were discovered, raising a furore, but Seward refused to recall him. Harvey, who had been working for peace, had sent previous telegrams to Magrath assuring him Sumter would be evacuated. When he learned of the expedition, he felt honor bound, just as Secretary Thompson had previously, to correct the error.
19. *O. R.*, p. 11, Fox report dated April 19.
20. Keyes, p. 378.
21. *O. R. N.*, p. 232, Cameron to Fox, dated April 4.
22. *O. R.*, pp. 251–52. Doubtless partly because of confusion between the two

expeditions, there was a feeling in the South that Lincoln treacherously intended the Fox expedition to get to Sumter before the warning did, and launch a surprise attack. Jefferson Davis, in *The Rise and Fall of the Confederate Government*, p. 274, made this charge, saying the only reason Fox failed to arrive before the messengers did was because he was delayed by storms. Fox would have had to make startling time indeed to get there first, fair weather or foul, since Talbot and Chew delivered the notification to Pickens in Charleston on April 8, a day and a half before Fox even left New York. Fox's orders were clear that he must first notify the Confederates that he would attempt to send provisions only to Sumter, and make no attempt to reinforce the fort unless this was resisted. Yet the suspicion of treachery may still linger. In *Fort Sumter—1861–65*, by DuBose Heyward and Herbert R. Sass, published in 1932, the same implication appears on p. 12.

As pointed out by Randall (*Lincoln the President*, Vol. I, pp. 333–36), Lincoln's reluctance to send the Sumter expedition is shown by the fact he waited not only until the last day but the last hour to order it to sail. Although Fox was directed to ready the expedition days earlier, it was on a tentative basis until April 6, when he was ordered to sail as soon as possible. Also on April 6 was sent the letter from Cameron notifying Anderson the attempt would be made, though this was dated April 4. April 6 likewise was the date Lincoln learned that the orders to reinforce Fort Pickens had not been carried out. There is some evidence that it was this failure at Pickens that made Lincoln resolve to send the Sumter expedition. He could not afford to let both forts fall in default of any effort to save them.

23. *O. R. N.*, pp. 257–59.
24. Connor, p. 129.
25. Crawford, p. 340.

Chapter XXIV. ELEVEN CODFISH

1. Charleston *Courier*, Mar. 27, 1861.
2. The same, Mar. 29.
3. The same, April 1.
4. *O. R.*, pp. 241–43 and 290; Crawford, pp. 375 and 377.
5. Crawford, pp. 375–77.
6. Doubleday, pp. 136–77.
7. *O. R.*, pp. 236–40; Crawford, pp. 375–80; Doubleday, pp. 135–36.
8. Doubleday, p. 136.
9. Crawford, p. 376.
10. *O. R.*, p. 245, dated April 6.
11. *O. R.*, pp. 242–43.
12. The same, p. 241, dated April 5.
13. *O. R.*, pp. 276 and 278.
14. Charleston *Courier*, April 4.
15. Chesnut, p. 31.
16. The same, p. 29.
17. Charleston *Courier*, April 8.
18. *O. R.*, p. 285, dated April 2.
19. Chesnut, p. 31.
20. *O. R. N.*, p. 258.
21. The same, p. 259.
22. *O. R.*, p. 291.
23. *Lincoln Finds a General*, by Kenneth P. Williams, Vol. I, p. 44.
24. Roman, *Military Operations of Beauregard*, Vol. I, p. 33.

25. *O. R.*, p. 235, dated April 4. The fact that neither the Secretary of War nor General Scott had written Anderson for a full month after Lincoln took office perhaps reflects the indecision of the new administration. There was no urgent need to write Anderson until he could be told what to do, and not for a month was this decided. Scott had a letter ready to send Anderson, instructing him to withdraw, but of course this was never sent.

26. Crawford, p. 382.

27. *O. R.*, p. 294, Anderson to Colonel Thomas. As if in afterthought, deciding this report too critical of the government, Anderson added a postscript asking Thomas to destroy it.

Chapter XXV. LET THE STRIFE BEGIN

1. Crawford, p. 398.
2. Doubleday, p. 139. Although the men were not yet officially told, they sensed immediately what was brewing.
3. *O. R.*, pp. 17 and 249; Crawford, pp. 383 and 398; *B. & L.*, Vol. I, p. 53.
4. *O. R.*, pp. 16–17 and 249; Crawford, p. 383; Doubleday, p. 140.
5. *O. R.*, pp. 248–9, dated April 9.
6. *O. R.*, pp. 292–93, Pickens to Walker, April 9.
7. Crawford, p. 384.
8. Blaine, Vol. I, p. 295.
9. Milton, p. 550; Stephenson, p. 14.
10. *Robert Toombs*, by Pleasant A. Stovall, p. 226; Crawford, p. 421.
11. *O. R.*, p. 297, dated April 10.
12. *O. R.*, pp. 292–93 and 299; *Day of the Confederacy*, p. 15. Although the usually careful Crawford (p. 422) says the reason Beauregard delayed giving the ultimatum to Anderson was because he was short of cannon powder, this seems in error. According to an official report of Secretary of War Jamison published in the Charleston *Courier* April 8, there was 240,450 pounds of cannon powder on hand March 25. The reasons given here seem ample. Johnson Hagood, in his *Memoirs of the War of Secession* (pp. 30–31) tells of the difficulties encountered by troops arriving after the bombardment started who were forced to reach Morris Island by a circuitous route, crossing the Ashley River to James Island, then crossing swamp and creek to Morris Island.
13. *O. R.*, p. 300, to Gen. Dunovant.
14. Charleston *Courier*, April 10; *O. R.*, pp. 292–93; Crawford, p. 397.
15. *O. R.*, p. 302.
16. The same.
17. *O. R.*, pp. 302–03.
18. The same, p. 300.
19. The same, pp. 292–93.
20. Chesnut, p. 34.
21. Charleston *Courier*, April 10.
22. *Courier*, April 11; Crawford, p. 305.
23. *O. R.*, pp. 250–51.
24. *O. R.*, p. 17; Crawford, p. 399.
25. Crawford Diary, entry April 11.
26. Crawford, pp. 398–99; also, *O. R.*, pp. 249–51.
27. *O. R.*, pp. 250–51.

Chapter XXVI. THE END OF LONG DOUBT

1. Crawford Diary.
2. *O. R.*, p. 13, April 11.

3. Crawford Diary, April 11.

4. O. R., p. 13.

5. The same, p. 59; Crawford, pp. 422–24; Lee's account, B. & L., Vol. I, p. 75; Chisolm's account, the same, p. 82.

6. Crawford Diary.

7. The same, April 11. There is some doubt on this point, some newspaper accounts having it that Anderson did make brief use of the barbette guns April 12. But the writer can find nothing in the accounts of those actually in Sumter indicating any use of the barbette guns except by a few soldiers who did so against orders. Crawford's manuscript Diary in portions during the battle is understandably incoherent but indicates that Anderson announced his decision to use only the casemate guns on the evening of April 11. Crawford's book, p. 445, says flatly, "The guns of the lower tier were the only ones used," with the exceptions mentioned.

8. Edmund Ruffin, by Avery Craven, pp. 216–17.

9. Chesnut, p. 35.

10. The list of enemy guns is from Foster's engineering journal, O. R., pp. 18–19, with a few corrections based on later Confederate reports. In some instances Foster had to guess about the size and number of guns.

11. O. R., pp. 13–14; Crawford, p. 424; B. & L., Vol. I, pp. 75 and 82.

12. Crawford, p. 425. Doubleday, p. 141, contradicts this, saying there was enough pork on hand to last two weeks. In general Crawford's account is far more detailed, comprehensive, and statistically accurate than Doubleday's.

13. Lee's account, B. & L., Vol. I, p. 75.

14. Chisolm's account, the same, p. 82.

15. O. R., p. 14.

16. The same, dated April 12, 1861, 3:20 A.M.

17. B. & L., Vol. I, p. 76.

18. Crawford, p. 426.

19. This entire scene is narrated by Lee, B. & L., Vol. I, p. 76.

20. The same.

21. Charleston Courier, April 15.

22. Edmund Ruffin, by Avery Craven, p. 217.

23. Chesnut, p. 35.

Chapter XXVII. VIRTUE VS. VICE

1. Doubleday, pp. 143–44.

2. Chesnut, p. 36.

3. B. & L., Vol. I, p. 66.

4. Doubleday, p. 145. Foster's engineering journal, O. R., p. 21, says there was still a little rice left.

5. Doubleday, pp. 144–45. The abolitionist captain was careful to point out that Negro troops proved their valor later in the war.

6. Within Fort Sumter, p. 44.

7. Doubleday, pp. 145–46.

8. The same, p. 146.

9. Roman, Vol. I, p. 43.

10. Edmund Ruffin, by Avery Craven, p. 217.

11. B. & L., Vol. I, pp. 62–63.

12. O. R., p. 18; Crawford, p. 431; B. & L., Vol. I, p. 52; Within Fort Sumter, p. 44.

13. Greeley, Vol. I, p. 446.

14. Doubleday, p. 148.

15. Crawford, p. 430.

16. Chester's account, B. & L., Vol. I, p. 69.

17. The same, p. 70; O. R., p. 20.

18. Crawford, pp. 431 and 445; *B. & L.*, Vol. I, p. 69.
19. Doubleday, p. 147.
20. Crawford Diary, April 12.
21. Doubleday, p. 165. Also, Crawford, p. 432; *O. R.*, p. 20.
22. *O. R.*, p. 19; Jones, p. 18; Stephenson, p. 20.
23. Doubleday, p. 161.
24. New York *Herald*, April 13. Also, *B. & L.*, Vol. I, p. 68.
25. *O. R.*, p. 19; Crawford, p. 432.
26. Doubleday, p. 153.
27. The same, pp. 153–54.
28. The same, p. 152; Crawford, p. 431.
29. *O. R.*, p. 21; *Within Fort Sumter*, pp. 48 and 50; Crawford, p. 432.
30. *O. R.*, p. 21; Crawford, p. 434.
31. *B. & L.*, Vol. I, p. 70
32. Crawford, p. 432. Luckily for Sumter, the Blakely gun was used only sparingly, having limited ammunition.
33. Crawford Diary, April 12.
34. Crawford, pp. 418–19.
35. Fox report, *O. R. N.*, Series I, Vol. IV, p. 249.
36. The same.

Chapter XXVIII. GENTLEMEN, RETURN TO YOUR BATTERIES

1. *The Rebellion Record*, ed. by Frank Moore, Vol. I, Poetry and Incidents, p. 92, quoted from Charleston *Mercury*.
2. Roman, Vol. I, p. 46. Several merchant vessels waited with the navy ships, causing the Confederates to believe the fleet a formidable one.
3. Charleston *Courier*, April 16.
4. Doubleday, p. 99; *Charleston, the Place and the People*, by Mrs. St. Julien Ravenel, p. 492.
5. Charleston *Courier*, April 13.
6. Crawford, p. 435; *O. R.*, p. 41; *The Conspiracies Preceding the Rebellion*, by T. M. Anderson, p. 66.
7. *B. & L.*, Vol. I, p. 72.
8. Crawford, p. 435; Doubleday, pp. 156–57; *O. R.*, p. 122.
9. Roman, Vol. I, p. 46.
10. *O. R.*, p. 23; Crawford, p. 437.
11. *Within Fort Sumter*, p. 54; *B. & L.*, Vol. I, p. 71.
12. Doubleday, p. 157.
13. Crawford Diary, April 13.
14. Doubleday, p. 158.
15. *B. & L.*, Vol. I, p. 54. Also, *O. R.*, p. 32.
16. *B. & L.*, Vol. I, p. 72; *Within Fort Sumter*, p. 55; Doubleday, p. 159; Crawford, pp. 437–38; *O. R.*, p. 23.
17. Charleston *Courier*, April 15.
18. The entire Wigfall sequence is taken from Crawford, pp. 439–41; Crawford Diary, April 13; *O. R.*, pp. 23 and 37–39; *A Southern Girl in '61*, by Mrs. D. Giraud Wright, pp. 41–44 and 46; *Within Fort Sumter*, pp. 57–59; and Doubleday, pp. 162–63.
19. *O. R.*, pp. 63–64, report of the Confederate aides; *B. & L.*, Vol. I, pp. 78–79.
20. *B. & L.*, Vol. I, p. 73.
21. Crawford, p. 442.
22. Doubleday, p. 170.
23. *O. R.*, pp. 30–35, Beauregard to Cooper.
24. Doubleday, p. 167.

25. *O. R.*, p. 66; Crawford, p. 470; Charleston *Courier*, April 15.
26. Crawford, p. 446.
27. *Battle of Fort Sumter and the First Victory of the Southern Troops*, p. 22.
28. The same, p. 21.
29. *O. R.*, p. 311; Russell, p. 41.
30. Crawford, p. 445.
31. *The Rebellion Record*, ed. by Frank Moore, Vol. I, Rumors and Incidents, p. 77.
32. Harris, pp. 45–46.
33. *Life, Letters and Speeches of Petigru*, ed. by J. P. Carson, p. 378.
34. *O. R. N.*, Series I, Vol. IV, p. 250, Fox's report.
35. *O. R.*, p. 11. It was later found that the *Powhatan's* gunboats, which Fox would have used, were in a bad state of disrepair. However, it seems he would have had a good chance of success had he had the tugs. Captain Hartstene of the Confederate naval arm feared that the mission would get through to Sumter. Major Whiting, on the morning of April 13, thought some relief boats *had* got through the previous night. Later in the war, Confederate boats often sneaked in and out despite the Union blockade. But Sumter, to remain in Union hands, would have required a continuous stream of supplies.

CHAPTER XXIX. APRIL 14, 1861

1. Charleston *Courier*, April 15.
2. Roman, Vol. I, p. 52.
3. The same, p. 48.
4. Charleston *Courier*, April 15.
5. *The Battle of Fort Sumter*, p. 23.
6. Crawford, pp. 446 and 470; Doubleday, pp. 171–72.
7. Doubleday, p. 162.
8. *Edmund Ruffin*, by Avery Craven, pp. 218, 240, and 259; *The Battle of Fort Sumter*, p. 12.
9. *Battle of Fort Sumter*, p. 23; *O. R.*, pp. 28 and 56.
10. *O. R.*, p. 28, report of Beauregard.
11. New York *Leader*, April 13.
12. *Rebellion Record*, ed. by Frank Moore, Vol. I, Documents, p. 188.
13. Quoted in *Horace Greeley, Voice of the People*, by William Harlan Hale, p. 243.
14. Crawford, p. 449.
15. *O. R.*, p. 12, dated April 18, 1861. Bradley S. Osbon, a New York *World* reporter who accompanied Fox's expedition, later claimed that he took Anderson's rough-draft report and whipped it into shape for him (*A Sailor of Fortune*, by A. B. Paine, p. 126), but Osbon was a swashbuckling fellow not known for false modesty. Crawford, who was there, says Anderson "dictated" it to Fox. The report has the ring of Anderson's prose and his tendency to run sentences together.

CHAPTER XXX. APRIL 14, 1865

1. *Anecdotes of the Civil War*, by E. D. Townsend, p. 211.
2. Snowden, Vol. II, p. 667.
3. Townsend, p. 213.
4. Crawford, pp. 471–72.
5. In addition to losing his health, Anderson suffered financial loss in the war. In March 1860, he had sold his twenty-nine slaves to one John G. Cocks

of Georgia, taking Cocks's note for $13,500 in payment. Cocks still owed him this sum after Sumter and repudiated the debt, writing, "I ask no more than to cancel the sale, restore to you your property, and let each assume his original position; then your present efforts may be considered less selfish, because at your expense, and not mine." (*Rebellion Record*, ed. by Frank Moore, Vol. I, Rumors and Incidents, p. 129.)

6. New York *Herald*, April 18, 1865.
7. Townsend, p. 212.
8. Crawford, pp. 450–57; Doubleday, p. 112.
9. New York *Tribune*, April 18, 1865.
10. *Herald*, April 18.
11. *The Trip of the Steamer Oceanus*, pp. 50–51.
12. New York *Times*, April 18, 1865.
13. New York *Herald*, April 18.
14. Townsend, p 219.
15. The same, p. 220.
16. Kentuckians naturally took a special pride in Anderson. In his farewell speech to the Senate, Senator Crittenden of Kentucky said, "Long after Fort Sumter shall have crumbled away, brightly will stand forth the example of Anderson as that of a soldier true to his standard, and of an American true to his country." In 1864 the Kentucky General Assembly approved resolutions asking Congress to retire Anderson with full pay and resolving, "That the people of this State cherish with pride the recollection of the gallant services rendered the nation by her distinguished son, Major General Robert Anderson [brevet rank], in defending Fort Sumpter and replying with his batteries on the ranks of the conspirators against the Union who made their first war demonstration in the very nursery of treason."

His health still failing, Anderson went abroad with his family early in 1871. He died at Nice on October 26, 1871, and was buried at West Point. His last surviving child, Sophie, died in 1934. It appears that there are no living descendants of the hero of Sumter.

ACKNOWLEDGMENTS

The writer is warmly grateful to Colonel Vincent J. Esposito, professor and head of the Department of Military Art and Engineering, United States Military Academy, for insight into the military aspects of the Sumter crisis; to Professor R. S. West, Jr., Department of English, History, and Government, United States Naval Academy, for counsel on the naval aspects; to Mr. William W. Luckett, Superintendent, and Mr. Horace J. Sheely Jr., Historian, Fort Sumter National Monument, for technical advice about the fort; to Miss Mabel C. Weaks, Archivist, the Filson Club, Louisville, Kentucky, for information about the Anderson family; to Mr. Samuel G. Stoney of Charleston, for counsel on that city's past; and to Mr. John Walsh of New York, a student of Sumter who gave aid and comfort out of his own extensive knowledge.

Special thanks go to Miss Maud Kay Sites of Washington for discriminating researches at the Library of Congress; and to Dr. C. Percy Powell of the Manuscript Division, Library of Congress.

A debt of gratitude for help given in a variety of ways is owed to Mrs. Granville T. Prior of the South Carolina Historical Society, Charleston; Mrs. Slann L. C. Simmons of Charleston; Rev. Cornelius Greenway of Brooklyn; Mr. Herbert K. Clinch of New York; Miss Frances Coleman, Librarian, Kentucky Historical Society, Frankfort, Kentucky; Mr. Emmet Crozier of Bethel, Connecticut; Mr. C. Gordon Fredine of Bethesda, Maryland; Mrs. E. A. Lindberg of Minneapolis, Minnesota; and Mr. Herbert E. Kahler, Chief Historian, National Park Service, Washington.

INDEX

Adams, James H., 94, 109
Allen, James, 216
Anderson, John, 251
Anderson, Eliza Clinch, 35, 61, 141-43, 181, 207-8
Anderson, Larz, 142-43
Anderson, Richard, 37
Anderson, Richard Clough, 36
Anderson, Maj. Robert, assigned to Charleston, 33-39; asks reinforcements, 40-46; 47, 48, 49, 50, 53, 54, 56, 71-72, 75-77, 82-83, 89, 90-91; plans and executes move to Sumter, 94-101; 104-106, 113; public reaction to Sumter move, 131-43; in Star of the West episode, 146-51; 154-56, 157-59, 174, 175, 176, 181, 182, 183, 184, 185, 186, 200, 207-11, 214-15, 218-22; Lincoln doubts his loyalty, 223-24; 233, 234, 242-45, 248-49, 252, 269, 272-78; orders from Sec. Cameron make war inevitable, 280-85, 290; refuses to surrender and returns Confederate fire, 291-308; bombardment and capitulation, 313-23; evacuation and return to New York, 326-32; re-raises flag at Sumter, 1865, 333-39
Anderson, Robert Jr., 141, 336
Armstrong, James, 167
Arsenal, U.S., in Charleston, 19, 32, 72-73, 83
Ashmore, J. D., 162

Bailey, Godard, 66-68
Barnwell, Robert W., 94, 109, 111, 115
Barrancas, Fort, 167
Bates, Edward, 230, 236
Beardsley, Col. Thomas, 10, 14
Beauregard, Pierre, 161, 166-67, 217-18, 239, 242, 246, 247, 248-49, 250-51, 273,

278, 284-85, 286-88, 291-93, 296, 318, 320, 321-22, 327, 328
Beecher, Henry Ward, 155, 213, 333, 334, 338
Benjamin, Judah, 65, 161, 219
Black, Jeremiah S., 30, 60, 63, 68, 113-14, 117, 118-20, 125, 163, 169, 196, 197
Blair, Montgomery, 230, 232-35, 237, 254, 255
Blakely gun, 287, 295, 302, 309
Bonham, M. L., 122, 246, 288
Breckinridge, John, 10, 15, 68, 110
Brooklyn, warship, 120, 123, 127, 145, 153, 168, 197, 198, 199, 225, 255, 256
Brown, Col. Harvey, 265
Brown, John, 15
Bryan, Judge George S., 93
Buchanan, James (U.S. Pres., 1857-61), 6, 26, 27, 28-30, 31, 32, 54, 55, 56, 58, 59-60; "pledge" to South Carolina, 61-62; 65, 66, 79, 83-85, 110, 111-16, 117-20; sends Star of the West, 123-30; 137, 139, 145, 157, 160; deals with Hayne, 163-71; 178, 184, 192, 196, 197, 200, 201-202, 209, 218, 220, 221, 222, 224, 248, 254, 269
Buell, Maj. Don Carlos, 49, 50, 51, 75, 83, 89, 93, 113, 114
Bulletin, Philadelphia, quoted, 235

Calhoun, John, 13, 31, 83
Cameron, Simon, 222, 236, 242, 244, 252, 255, 256, 259, 264, 272, 282, 284, 295, 305, 317, 325, 331, 332
Campbell, Justice John A., 229-32, 236, 239, 240, 257, 260-61, 271
Capers, Maj. Ellison, 103-105
Carmody, John, 303-304
Cass, Lewis, 30, 60, 62-63, 84, 163
Charleston Hotel, 1, 25, 83, 190, 247, 249, 289, 339

Chase, Salmon P., 237
Chesnut, James, 14, 16, 23, 134, 291,
    292, 295, 296, 297
Chesnut, Mary Boykin, 14, 247, 278,
    279, 288, 294, 298, 299
Chester, Sgt. James, 106, 147, 173, 300,
    303, 309, 314, 316
Chew, Robert L., 270, 279-80
Chisolm, A. R., 247, 291, 295, 297
Clay, Sen. C. C., 15, 164
Clinch, Bayard, 142
Clinch, Gen. Duncan, 35, 142
Clingman, Senator, 67
Cobb, Howell, 30, 55, 60, 203, 204
Colcock, C. J., 17
Colt, Capt. A. A., 24
Colt, Col. Sam, 161
Commissioners, Confederate, 231, 240,
    253, 270-71, 278, 279
Conner, James, 17
Cook, George, 214
Cooper, Adj. Gen. Samuel, 39, 45, 101,
    184, 243
Courier, Charleston, 108, 244, 251, 272,
    276, 288
Crawford, Martin J., 220, 226, 227, 228,
    232, 239, 253, 261-62, 271, 276, 282
Crawford, Rev. S. W., 208-209
Crawford, Surgeon S. W., 1-3, 38, 42,
    75, 79, 96-97, 99, 102-103, 145, 147,
    149, 150, 172, 175, 178, 211, 273, 281,
    283, 290, 291, 292, 295, 300, 303, 304,
    309, 315, 316, 321, 322, 328, 336
Cullum, Capt. George W., 35
Cushing, Caleb, 81
Cuthbert, Capt. G. B., 294, 329

Dahlgren, Adm. John, 334
Dahlgren gun, 287 290, 294, 339
Davis, Jefferson, C.S.A., 34, 57, 58,
    111-12, 161, 166, 189, 203, 204, 220,
    230-31, 254, 285-86, 288, 327, 331, 336,
    337
Davis, Lt. Jefferson C., U.S.A., 38, 43,
    71, 95-96, 98, 100, 101, 102, 148, 149,
    214, 273, 284, 291, 292, 300, 318-19
DeSaussure, Col. Wilmot, 108, 132, 274
Dix, Gen. John, 163, 190, 337
Doubleday, Capt. Abner, 3-4, 10-11, 19,
    21, 37, 42, 74, 75, 93, 97-100, 135, 140,
    143, 146-49, 154, 157, 159, 175, 176,
    180, 182, 207, 213-14, 222, 243, 245,
    273, 274, 283, 284, 292, 299, 300-301,
    302-303, 305, 306, 307-308, 316, 321,
    322, 329, 336, 337
Doubleday, Mary, 11, 97, 98, 102, 140,
    143, 159, 238
Doubleday, Ulysses, 21, 159, 223, 269
Douglas, Stephen, 161
Drayton, Thomas F., 13
Dunnington, C. W., 220-221
Dunovant, Gen. R. G. M., 133, 140, 287,
    288

Emma, guard boat, 100, 102

Fielding, George, 328
Fitzpatrick, Sen. Benjamin, 167
Floating battery, 205, 209, 224, 246, 288,
    294
Floyd, John B., 13, 18, 20-21, 22, 23,
    26, 29, 30, 31, 32, 35, 39, 41, 42,
    45-49, 51, 55-57, 60; involved in
    scandal, 64-68; 74, 85, 89-92, 110-11,
    112-14, 116, 122, 126, 161, 168, 176,
    252, 262, 269
Forsyth, John, 220, 227, 228, 229, 253
Foster, Capt. John G., 5-7, 18, 38, 41,
    43, 44, 45, 71-74, 91; Christmas party,
    95-96; 99, 101-103, 133-35, 148, 149,
    173, 178, 179, 184-85, 206; differs with
    Anderson, 210-11; 212, 222, 223-24,
    243-44, 249, 273, 283, 284, 285, 289,
    292, 293; appraises Confederate ar-
    tillery, 294-95; 308, 313, 336
Foster, Mrs. John G., 102, 140, 143
Fox, Gustavus, 168, 200, 233, 234-35,
    237, 238, 247-49, 255, 263, 264, 265,
    268-69, 270, 280, 282, 284-85, 309-311,
    324-25, 332, 337
Freeborn, tug, 265, 310

Galloway, Edward, 328
Galveston, Fort, 67-68
Gardner, Col. John L., 2, 4-5, 15, 18,
    20, 21, 22, 29, 32, 37, 44, 84, 128
General Clinch, guard boat, 86, 108
Gibbes, R. W., 138
Gillmore, Gen. Quincy, 334, 339
Gist, Gov. William, 12-13, 22, 57-58, 70
Gourdin, Robert Newman, 9, 17, 46,
    47, 132, 142, 159, 181, 185-86, 207,
    247, 318

Greeley, Horace, 62, 155, 322
Gwin, Sen. William, 226-27, 228
Gwynn, Col. Walter, 152

Hall, Lt. Norman C., 38, 75, 95, 96,
    100, 132, 149, 150, 159, 169, 176, 200,
    209, 273, 292, 305, 317-18, 328, 336
Hamilton, Lt. John, 205-206
Hamlin, Hannibal, 8
Hammond, James Henry, 24, 187
Harper's Weekly, 15
Harriet Lane, warship, 137, 138, 139,
    263, 310
Harris, Rev. Matthias, 102, 105, 140,
    141, 337
Hartstene, Capt. H. J., 247, 248-49, 288
Harvey, James E., 228, 268, 278
Hayne, Isaac W., 159, 160, 163-66, 192,
    197, 227, 278, 334
Hayne, Paul, 80
Haynsworth, George E., 146
Herald, New York, 108, 190, 232, 278,
    337, 338
Holt, Joseph, 60, 114, 117, 118, 123,
    144-45, 161; deals with Hayne, 165-
    71; 176-78, 182, 192, 200, 201, 209-10,
    222-24, 242, 248, 252, 272, 337
Hough, Daniel, 328, 331
Huger, Col. Benjamin, 32-33, 41-42, 43,
    44, 46, 72, 154
Humphreys, Capt. F. C., 22, 32, 72-73,
    84, 86-87, 132
Hunter, Sen. R. M. T., 57, 58, 111,
    123-24, 228
Hurlbut, Stephen, 238, 249-50, 253

Illinois, steamer, 265
Institute Hall, Charleston, 17, 78
Iverson, Sen. Alfred, 162

Jackson, Andrew, 36, 232, 234
James, Capt. George S., 297, 298
Jamison, David F., 78, 80, 140, 156-58,
    216, 247, 328, 333
Jefferson, Fort, 253

Keitt, Lawrence, 4, 25, 61, 70, 81, 249
Kernan, Sgt. Thomas, 302
Keyes, Col. Erasmus D., 257, 258, 260,
    263, 264, 265, 267
King, Horatio, 162

Lamar, G. B., 175
Lamon, Ward H., 238, 249, 251, 257,
    261, 272, 282
Lane, Sen. Joseph, 115
Lathers, Richard, 216
Lay, Col. George W., 202, 220, 247
Leader, New York, 330-31
Lee, Capt. Stephen D., 291, 295, 296,
    297, 320, 321
Lincoln, Abraham (U.S. Pres., 1861-65),
    4, 8-10, 12, 14, 15, 34, 52, 77, 78, 159,
    192, 194, 196, 202, 204, 210, 214, 219;
    inaugurated, 220-22; 223-26, 227, 228,
    230, 232-38, 240, 245, 246, 251; pre-
    pares expedition for Sumter, 253-62;
    263-67, 269-70, 280, 333, 335, 337, 338,
    339
Longstreet, Judge A. B., 78, 126-27, 129,
    139

McCready, Edward, 214
McGowan, John, 128, 146-48, 153
McInerney, 212, 213
McSweeney, Daniel, 173

Macbeth, Mayor Charles, 20, 46
Macedonian, warship, 120, 198
Magrath, Judge A. G., 16-18, 23, 24,
    78, 140, 156-58, 169, 228, 268, 285,
    328, 337
Mallory, Sen. Stephen, 199
Manigault, Col., 152
Marts, Joseph, 274
Mason, J. Thomson, 192-93
Mason, Sen. James, 57, 58, 243
Meade, Lt. R. K., 71, 95, 96, 98, 99,
    100, 107, 134, 148, 149, 157, 211, 274,
    284, 292, 305, 308, 309, 336-37
Means, John Hugh, 140-41
Meigs, Capt. Montgomery, 256, 258, 259,
    260, 263, 264, 265, 266, 267
Memminger, Christopher, 215
Mercer, Capt. Samuel, 264, 266, 267,
    268
Mercury, Charleston, 8, 17, 42, 79, 83,
    145, 152, 153, 188-89, 245
Miles, William Porcher, 61, 78, 79, 320,
    321, 322
Mills House, Charleston, 142, 277, 298,
    299
Minute Men, 10, 16, 19

Monroe, Fortress, 123, 127, 145, 197, 244, 272
Morris, Edmund, 136
Moultrie House, 306, 329
Moultrieville, 7

Nelson, Justice Samuel, 230, 239, 240
Nina, guard boat, 86, 99, 103

Oceola, Seminole chief, 37
O'Connor, Michael P., 25
Orr James L., 94, 109
Ould, Robert, 222

Patti, Adelina, 24
Pawnee, warship, 263, 310
Peace Convention, 169, 197, 200, 202, 209, 210
Pensacola, 167, 198, 199, 225, 253, 255-56, 257-58, 259, 268
Petigru, James Louis, 23, 80, 93, 191-92, 249-50, 278, 324
Petrel, guard boat, 275
Pettigrew, J. Johnston, 100, 103-105, 106-107
Pettus, Gov., 66
Phillips, Wendell, 14
Pickens, Fort, 168, 198, 199, 220, 221, 225, 227, 228, 231, 240, 253, 254-60, 263, 267, 269, 271
Pickens, Gov. Francis W., 30-32, 70-71, 81, 82, 83-84, 85-87, 103, 106, 123, 124, 126, 128, 130, 132, 134, 136-37, 138-39, 140, 142, 146, 150-52, 153, 156, 158, 162, 174, 175, 182, 188; his unpopularity, 190-93; 198, 200, 203-204, 215, 216, 222, 243, 245, 246, 247, 249, 251, 257, 261, 270, 275, 278, 279-80, 285, 288, 323-24, 328, 339
Pierce, Franklin (U.S. Pres., 1853-57), 26
Pocahontas, warship, 263, 267, 310, 324
Poe, Edgar Allan, 37
Pope, Joseph, 80
Porter, Rev. A. Toomer, 18, 134
Porter, Lt. David Dixon, 259, 260, 263, 264, 265, 266, 267, 268
Porter, Major Fitz John, 21-22, 29
Powhatan, warship, 259, 263, 264, 266, 267, 268, 269, 310, 324, 325
Press, Philadelphia, quoted, 62-63
Prioleau, Charles K., 287

Pryor, Roger, 220, 289, 295, 297, 320, 321-22, 328
Pulaski, Fort, 161

Ravenel, Henry W., 191, 207, 208, 215
Rhett, Robert Barnwell, 8-9, 10, 17, 42, 56, 71, 146, 152, 174, 189, 215, 245, 278
Rhoda Shannon, vessel, 273-75
Ripley, Col. Roswell, 147, 245, 307-308, 313-14, 316
Rippit, Mrs., 100
Roman, Andre B., 220, 240, 241, 253
Rowan, Cmdr. Stephen C., 310, 324, 337
Ruffin, Edmund, 15, 23, 78, 139, 146, 278, 287, 294, 298, 299, 301, 329, 333
Russell, William H., 64-68

Salter, George, 278
Saltonstall, Leverett, 136
Scheiber, Sgt. Eugene, 206
Schirmer, Jacob, 81, 138
Schnierle, Gen., 73
Scott, Gen. Winfield, 26-27, 28, 34-35, 45, 57, 58, 62, 116, 121, 123-24, 127-28, 145, 161, 163, 168, 196, 197, 199, 220, 224-25, 231; gives up on Sumter, 232-34; 238-39, 242, 244, 248, 254-55, 256, 257, 259, 264
Seward, William Henry, 59, 194-96, 202, 225, 226-32, 233, 236, 238, 239-41, 242, 245, 250, 253, 255; plans Ft. Pickens expedition, 256-62; 263, 264, 266, 267, 268, 270, 282, 309, 325
Seymour, Louisa, 102, 132, 140, 141, 143
Seymour, Capt. Truman, 3, 19-20, 38, 42, 75, 98, 100, 133, 149, 179, 180, 214, 222, 274, 284, 292, 302-303, 317, 336
Ship Island, Fort, 67-68, 161
Sickles, Daniel, 28, 117, 201
Simons, Gen. James, 137-39, 149, 318
Simonton, Capt. Charles H., 84-85
Sinclair, Dan, 140
Skillen, Kate, 107-108
Skillen, Ordnance Sergeant, 6-7, 107
Slemmer, Lt. Adam, 168, 198-99, 225, 231, 258
Slidell, Sen. John, 166-67
Smith, Caleb, 236

Snyder, Lt. George W., 38, 41, 75, 87, 88, 91, 96, 97, 98, 133, 134, 149, 178, 211, 274, 275, 292, 305, 309, 317, 318, 336

Stanton, Edwin M., 114, 117, 118-19, 124, 196, 197, 333

Star of the West, vessel, 127-30, 143, 145, 146-49, 151, 153, 159, 160, 161, 166, 175, 176, 178, 183, 191, 208, 212, 245, 270, 274, 286, 307

Stevens, Maj. P. F., 137, 243

Stoeckl, Baron, 240-41

Stone, Col. Charles P., 163

Strawinski, Thaddeus, 216

Stringham, Commodore, 233

Strong, George Templeton, 160, 167, 218, 235-36

"Sumter lamp," 212-13

Swash Channel, 200, 293

Talbot, Lt. Theodore, 38, 151, 157, 176, 177, 178, 209, 211, 270, 273, 279-80, 336

Taney, Justice Roger, 221

Thomas, Col. Lorenzo, 282

Thomas, Philip, 117, 161, 163

Thompson, Jacob, 30, 55, 58, 60, 66-68, 117, 125, 126-30, 146

Times, New York, 130, 183, 278

Toombs, Robert, 117, 120, 203, 204, 220, 228, 229, 262, 270, 286

Totten, Gen. Joseph, 225, 233, 238, 244, 249

Toucey, Isaac, 117

Townsend, Gen. E. D., 333, 334, 337

Trapier, Col. J. H., 152

Tredegar Iron Works, 211

Trescot, William Henry, 20, 31, 52-58, 60, 63, 74, 84-85, 109-111, 115, 124, 278

Tribune, New York, 128, 135, 205, 228, 331, 338

Tyler, John, 196-98, 201, 204

Uncle Ben, tugboat, 265, 310

Vogdes, Capt. Israel, 198-99, 225, 231

Walker, Leroy Pope, 203, 246, 250, 278-79, 286, 293, 331

Ward, Cmdr., 200, 233

Welles, Gideon, 236, 255, 259, 263, 264, 265-68

White, Col. Edward, 152

Whiting, Capt. William, 217, 286-87

Wigfall, Sen. Louis T., 110-11, 122, 130, 146-48, 200, 202, 215, 219-20, 222, 229, 245-46, 277-78, 287, 318-20, 326

Withers, Capt. John, 93

Wittyman, carpenter, 180-81

Woods, Lt. Charles R., 128, 146

World, New York, 130, 135

Wright, Capt. H. G., 91

Yankee, tugboat, 265, 310

Young, Gourdin, 318

FOOD LOVERS' SERIES

Food Lovers' Guide to Montreal

First Edition

Best Local Specialties,
Markets, Recipes, Restaurants
& Events

Patricia Harris & David Lyon

gpp

Guilford, Connecticut

Editor: Amy Lyons
Project Editor: Lynn Zelem
Layout Artist: Mary Ballachino
Text Design: Sheryl Kober
Illustrations: © Jill Butler with additional art by Carleen Moira Powell
Maps: Sue Murray © Morris Book Publishing, LLC

ISBN 978-0-7627-7121-9

Printed in the United States of America
10 9 8 7 6 5 4 3 2 1

All the information in this guidebook is subject to change. We recommend that you call ahead
to obtain current information before traveling.

Contents

Introduction: Montreal—French Roots, North American Panache, ix

How to Use This Book, xiii
Getting Around, xv
Food Events, xvii
The Best of Montreal, xix

Old Montreal & the Old Port, 1

Foodie Faves, 4
Landmarks, 20
Specialty Stores, Markets & Producers, 21
Cooking Schools & Classes, 24
Food Events, 28

Westmount, Little Burgundy & NDG, 29

Foodie Faves, 32
Landmarks, 40
Specialty Stores, Markets & Producers, 43

Downtown & Chinatown, 49

   Foodie Faves, 51
   Landmarks, 67
   Specialty Stores, Markets & Producers, 69
   Food Events, 74

Latin Quarter & the Village, 77

   Foodie Faves, 79
   Landmarks, 88
   Specialty Stores, Markets & Producers, 89

Plateau Mont-Royal, 90

   Foodie Faves, 94
   Landmarks, 125
   Specialty Stores, Markets & Producers, 127
   Food Events, 141

Mile End & Outremont, 143

   Foodie Faves, 144
   Landmarks, 154
   Specialty Stores, Markets & Producers, 157

Little Italy & Parc Extension, 173

      Foodie Faves, 174
      Landmarks, 181
      Specialty Stores, Markets & Producers, 182

Eastern Townships, 188

      Foodie Faves, 192
      Specialty Stores, Markets & Producers, 199
      Food Events, 227

Appendix A: Glossary of French Terms, 230

Appendix B: Eateries by Cuisine, 234

Appendix C: Dishes, Specialties & Specialty Food, 239

Recipe Index, 244

Index, 245

About the Authors

Patricia Harris and David Lyon met over ratatouille made from fresh garden vegetables and courted over *potage d'oignon gratinée* on rue McGill and *steak-frites* on rue Peel. Decades later, they remain convinced that Montreal is one of the best places in the world for both romance and food. They are co-authors of The Globe Pequot Press's *Food Lovers' Guide to Massachusetts* and *The Meaning of Food*. They have written about Spanish cheese, Belgian beer, Tahitian poisson cru, Neapolitan pizza, white truffles of Alba, and a slew of other foodstuffs for such publications as the *Boston Globe, The Robb Report, Cooking Light, Food Arts,* and the *Washington Post.* They live in Cambridge, Massachusetts, and are the authors of the food and travel blog HungryTravelers.com.

Dedication

To every diner who has ever said, "I'll start my diet tomorrow."

Acknowledgments

People who raise, harvest, catch, and prepare food are some of the nicest and, we think, noblest people in the world. We would like to thank the Montreal and Eastern Townships chefs, bakers, chocolatiers, pastry chefs, farmers, winemakers, brewmasters, baristas, and restaurateurs who gave us good reason to write this book. Their extraordinary talents and their generosity in sharing information, ideas, recipes, and good food made this book a labor of love.

We would also like to thank Bard Nordby of Tourisme Quebec, Danie Béliveau of Tourisme Cantons-de-l'Est, and Tanya Churchmuch of Tourisme Montreal for their good counsel and great mealtime companionship. We are additionally grateful to our friend Gilles Bengle, who introduced us to Montreal's most decadent breakfast—a croissant smeared with *pâté de foie gras*—and to our ever-flexible Montreal landlords, Jean and Monique Dontigny.

Finally, we send our heartfelt appreciation to Globe Pequot Press editor Amy Lyons for letting us sneak over the border to write this book, to project editor Lynn Zelem for swiftly ushering it into production, and to the late Laura Strom, who conceived the Food Lovers' series.

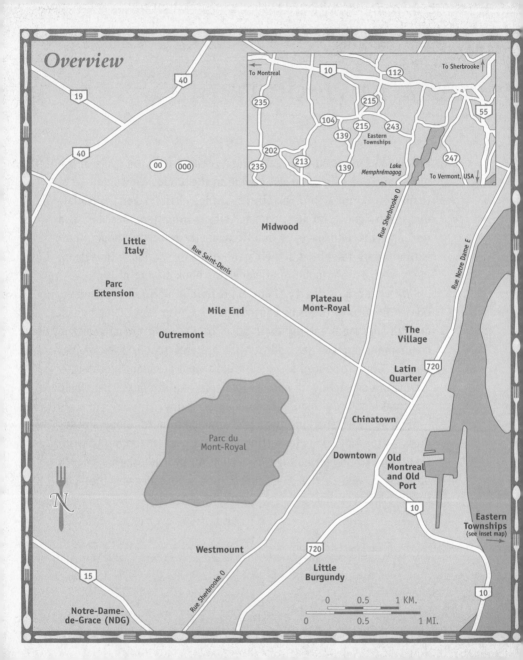

Overview

19

40

40

00 **000**

Inset map (Eastern Townships)

To Montreal ←

10

112

To Sherbrooke ↑

235

215

55

104

215

243

139

Eastern
Townships

202

235

213

139

Lake
Memphrémagog

247

To Vermont, USA ↓

Main map

Midwood

Little
Italy

Rue Saint-Denis

Rue Sherbrooke O

Rue Notre Dame E

Parc
Extension

Mile End

Plateau
Mont-Royal

The
Village

Outremont

Latin
Quarter

720

Parc du
Mont-Royal

Chinatown

Downtown

Old
Montreal
and Old
Port

N

Eastern
Townships
(see inset map)
→

Westmount

720

10

15

Little
Burgundy

Notre-Dame-
de-Grace (NDG)

Rue Sherbrooke O

10

0   0.5   1 KM.

0   0.5   1 MI.

Introduction: Montreal—French Roots, North American Panache

Chocolate ice cream tastes even better when it's made with a little *fleur de sel*. French fries cooked in duck fat are addictive. And seared *foie gras* is fantastic with apricots. Those are just three of the things we discovered in rounding out our research for this book.

Simply put, Montreal is a great city for people who love to eat. Its roughly 5,000 bistros, bars, luncheonettes, cafes, brasseries, pubs, delis, restaurants (and at least one *buvette*) make up the warp and weft of the the city. Stop a Montrealer somewhere in the 4900 block of boulevard Saint-Laurent and ask for directions to The Sparrow (where the sign is hard to see at night), and you'll get instructions something like this: Walk up past Cuisine et Dépendance and you'll see La Montée de Lait across the street. Keep going past Soy Cuisine Asiatique and L'Atelier. Sparrow will be there on the left. When you smell the cabbage in the bubble-and-squeak, you'll know you're in the right place. If only slightly prompted, he will also recite every dish he has ever eaten at each establishment.

Montrealers measure their days by the city's wonderful food—from the wake-up croissant and *bol* of *café au lait* on the way to work to the redemptive plate of *poutine* consumed on the way home after a night on the town.

We still laugh every time we recall the title of Adam Gollner's 2009 *Gourmet* essay, "Montreal: We're French and You're Not." It is true that Montreal is the second-largest French-speaking city in the world, but the French attitude is tempered by Canadian *bonhomie*. Compared to Paris, Montrealers are much quicker with a *s'il vous plaît*, a *merci*, and that ubiquitous bilingual greeting, *Bonjour-hi!* What they share with their distant French cousins is a devotion to good food and the habit of dressing up a little for dinner, even at a casual neighborhood bistro.

As North America's predominant French-speaking city, Montreal has been a magnet for francophone immigrants to Canada who brought their home cuisines in their suitcases. It is a cinch to eat your way around the old French empire at restaurants featuring the cuisines of French-speaking Africa, the Caribbean, Lebanon, and Southeast Asia. But the cosmopolitan nature of Montreal does not smother its French-Canadian roots. Mom-and-pop eateries still serve *tourtières* (meat pastries), *poutine* (french fries with brown gravy and fresh cheese curds), *fèves au lard* (baked beans), and anything drowned in maple syrup.

Over the last two decades, a younger generation of chefs—many of them trained in Quebec—have forged an authentic new Montreal cuisine. Its vocabulary is drawn from classical French gastronomy, but it is provincial in the very best sense of the word. The new Montreal cooking is heartily locavore. The chefs rely on the bounty of the Gulf of St. Lawrence and the nearby Atlantic for scallops, lobster, char, and salmon. They frequent the farms of the Eastern Townships for Lac Brome duck, *foie gras,* sweet corn, and winter squash. The old monastery villages provide them with cheeses and hard cider, the northern woods with wild game. You'll find we use the word *terroir* frequently in this book. Traditionally a term used to describe wines that reflect the taste of a specific place, we think it also applies to a highly localized foods that reflect the land, climate, and culture from which they spring.

With some notable exceptions, Montreal eating establishments are bistros, with or without the final French "t." They tend to be small, somewhat casual neighborhood places with hearty food and—except the BYOB places—plentiful drink. Montreal chefs have put their own stamp on this classic French style.

At the slightly more formal pole is what we call *bistro-plus,* where the chef is always determined to give his or her patrons a little something extra—whether it's an unexpected *amuse-bouche,* some *mignardises* with the bill, or a surprise shaving of truffles or dollop of *foie gras.* Service at a *bistro-plus* tends to be polished and attentive, if still friendly and casual.

On the other hand, what we have dubbed *bistro-grunge* is Montreal's answer to London's gastropubs and contemporary Spanish tapas bars. Both the kitchen and waitstaff are often young, tattooed, and pierced. You might

Keeping Up with the Foodie News

EatWellMontreal, www.eatwellmontreal.com
Chef Deck offers his honest opinions on Montreal restaurants for, as he puts it, "readers with short attention spans." We don't always agree, and think he's biased in favor of overly hearty portions, but the site makes good reading.

***The Gazette*, www.montrealgazette.com**
Montreal's leading English-language newspaper carries regular restaurant news and reviews, mostly by Lesley Chesterman, the paper's reviewer since 1999.

Lesley Chesterman, www.lesleychesterman.com
Blog and review database of long-time *Gazette* restaurant reviewer. She trained as a pastry chef, and while thoroughly Anglophone, is married to a French speaker.

RestoMontreal, www.restomontreal.ca
Commercial site with pretty thorough listings in both French and English. Good listing of jobs in the restaurant trade.

Montreal for Insiders, www.montrealforinsiders.com
Brazilian-born journalist Alexandra Forbes comments on the hotels and restaurants she visits for other publications and websites. As the ex-spouse of a top hotelier, she knows whereof she speaks.

La Route des Vins, www.laroutedesvins.ca
Guide to the wineries in the Eastern Townships has news about special events and sales.

Explorateurs Culinaires, www.explorateursculinaires.tv
Wacky French-language video website features a different Québecois chef each week.

Les Chefs!
This Télévision de Radio-Canada show features aspiring celebrity chefs in cooking contests judged by such real celebrity chefs as Daniel Vézina, Normand Laprise, and Martin Picard. Irregular schedule.

expect some of the diners to roll up on skateboards, or at least motorcycles. The food at a *bistro-grunge,* however, is usually just as good, just as inventive, and just as locavore as at a bistro-plus. But it has more swagger, and the chefs often vie to be a little outrageous. A *bistro-grunge* usually has a good beer list and nowhere near enough seats.

With choices like these, it's no wonder that Montrealers love to eat. But as much as they enjoy dining out, they love to talk about food and endlessly debate which *poutine* is superior, whether *foie gras* really is the new dark meat, whether one chef's halibut is better than another chef's skate, and so on. We hope this book will join that conversation.

How to Use This Book

This guide is separated into chapters by Montreal neighborhood and one additional chapter covering the Eastern Townships. The Townships, which lie southeast of the city next to the New York and Vermont borders, are historically English-speaking farm communities that serve as the origin of much of the city's good food and as a destination for weekend gourmet getaways. The neighborhood divisions include Old Montreal and the Old Port; Westmount, Little Burgundy and NDG (all west of Downtown); Downtown and Chinatown; the Latin Quarter and the Village (east of Downtown); Plateau Mont-Royal (east of the mountain and north of rue Sherbrooke); Mile End and Outremont (the traditional Jewish immigrant neighborhoods); and Little Italy and Parc Extension (the immigrant neighborhoods north of the Plateau). Within the chapters you'll find these categories:

Neighborhood Map

We've marked all the shops and eating establishments here for easy navigation.

Foodie Faves

This section is broad enough to include any restaurant we think you should check out. It could be an old standby, or a newcomer with buzz.

Landmarks

Many one-time gastronomic icons of Montreal have dropped by the wayside. The establishments celebrated here are proud reminders that good dining in Montreal is not a new development. These are establishments that have demonstrated great staying power.

Specialty Stores, Markets, & Producers

We enjoy shopping for food as much as we enjoy eating out. We bet you do, too, or you wouldn't be reading this book. This category frames our favorite farmers, cheesemakers, wineries, butcher shops, bakers, coffee roasters, tea importers, pastry shops, chocolatiers, cheesemongers, delis, and charcuteries.

Cooking Schools & Classes
The explosion of locavore cuisine in Montreal has led to a surge of interest in learning how to cook, so we have added this category where necessary.

Food Events
We think every meal should be cause for celebration, but this category gives you the skinny on most annual events that celebrate specific foods or cultures—or just celebrate. But with food, of course.

Recipes
These recipes come from people who make great food. We have chosen them because they represent the breadth of Montreal cuisine. We have translated from French where necessary, have adapted them for home cooks, and have largely converted metric to Imperial measures. Any errors or omissions are our fault alone and should not reflect on the people who supplied the originals.

Getting Around

Montrealers can skip this section. You already know how easy it is to get around the core city on the Metro, or to hop between Metro lines using the buses that run east-west on rue Sherbrooke, avenues Mont-Royal, Saint-Joseph, and Laurier, or north-south on boulevard Saint-Laurent and rue Saint-Denis. This book is divided into neighborhoods, and once you reach an area on public transit, it is easy to walk to almost every spot in the chapter. We have included the nearest Metro stop (or stops) for every shop and eatery.

For more information on public transit in general, see the Société de Transport de Montreal website, www.stm.info. The site gives you access to Tous Azimuts and Google Maps for planning a trip. We also favor the Montreal City Transit Planner (a commercial site) for quick answers on which mode of transit to use. The website is www.busMontreal.com.

Monolingual readers will notice that we occasionally slip into French in this book. In fact, we have used French for all street names and directions because the street signs are all in French. If we told you an address was on "Mountain Street" you'd have a tough time finding it because it's really on "rue de la Montagne." We have also used the French proper names for restaurants rather than translate into English. Quebec law requires French to be bigger than English on signs, and directories list places by their French names.

It's also true that almost everything tastes better in French. But while food is clearly enhanced by speaking *la langue de cuisine,* it is rarely a handicap to be limited to speaking English in Montreal. Staff at most establishments are bilingual, and menus are often translated. As an aid, we have included a short glossary of some of the more unfamiliar French terms you might encounter. When you find yourself asking for a *croissant au beurre* instead of a butter croissant, you're on your way to bilingualism.

Food Events

Predictably, food is a big part of all of Montreal's summer festivals—especially street food. The events listed below focus on celebrating food and drink.

January

Happening Gourmand, Old Montreal, www.happeninggourmand .com. Old Montreal restaurant dining promotions offer choice of three different price levels.

February

Montreal Highlights, Downtown and City-Wide; (514) 844-3500; www.montrealenlumiere.com. Festival laughs in the face of winter with concerts, parties, dances, and a whole slew of food events. Most dining celebrations take place at restaurants, but the big SAQ showcase of Quebec cheeses, with a cookoff among top chefs (and public tasting of their work), happens at L'Astral (305 rue Sainte-Catherine Ouest).

March

Salon des Vins et Spiritueux de Montreal, Palais de Congrès de Montreal, 1001 place Jean-Paul-Riopelle; www.salondesvins .com. Winemakers, sommeliers, and other authorities offer a wide range of lectures. More than 100 producers offer tastings.

May

A Taste of the Caribbean, Place Bonaventure; (514) 620-6612; www.atasteofthecaribbean.ca. Joyful whirlwind of music, dance, traditional arts and crafts—and food—celebrates flavors of more than twenty different Caribbean islands.

June

La Clé des Champs de Dunham, www.cledeschampsdunham.ca. Two-day epicurean tasting of wines, beers, ciders, pastry, chocolate, and charcuterie made in Quebec—mostly in the Eastern Townships.

Mondial de la Bière, Place Bonaventure; (514) 722-9640; www .festivalmondialbiere.qc.ca. Roughly 500 brands exhibited (and can be tasted) during the five-day extravaganza.

July

Dunham Folk and Wine Festival, www.festivalfolkvinsdunham .com. Folk-singing and wine-tasting make for a two-day party.

September

Brome Fair, www.bromefair.com. Old-fashioned country agricultural fair spotlights farms and farm life of Eastern Townships.

Fête des Vendanges Magog-Orford, www.fetedesvendanges .com. Harvest festival features 140-plus food product exhibitors ranging from fine honey to fine wine.

Lac Brome Duck Festival, www.canardenfete.com. Lots of family fun augments the duck-centric restaurant menus, cooking demonstrations, and sales of duck products over two weekends.

Les Comptonales de Automne, www.comptonales.com. Farm tour and tasting event spotlights agriculture and local artists in the Coaticook Valley.

Montreal Ukrainian Festival, Parc d'Ukraine; (514) 885-6419; www.ukefestmontreal.org. Eastern European singing, dancing, folk art exhibitions, and food—especially food.

October

Salon des Vins et Fromages du Quebec à Montreal, Complexe Desjardins, 150 rue Sainte-Catherine ouest; (888) 847-2050; www.salonvinsfromages.ca. Three-day event focuses on Quebec provincial cheese and wine.

The Best of Montreal

Best *Poutine*, Traditional: La Banquise (Plateau Mont-Royal), p. 105

Best *Poutine*, Gourmet: Au Pied de Cochon (Plateau Mont-Royal), p. 94

Best Bagel: St-Viateur Bagel (Mile End), p. 156

Best Pizza: Pizzeria Napoletana (Little Italy), p. 177

Best Smoked Meat: Schwartz's Smoked Meat (Plateau Mont-Royal), p. 126

Best Ice Cream: Bilboquet (Outremont, Westmount), p. 157 & p. 45

Best Burger: La Paryse (Latin Quarter), p. 82

Best Butter Croissant: Fous Desserts (Plateau Mont-Royal), p. 130

Best Almond Croissant: Maestro Traiteur (Mile End), p. 166

Best *Tarte Au Sirop:* Les Sucreries de l'Érable (Frelighsburg, Eastern Townships), p. 198

Best *Steak-frites:* Lémeac (Outremont), p. 150

Best Macaron: Point G (Plateau Mont-Royal), p. 137

Best Ice Cider: Clos Saragnat (Frelighsburg, Eastern Townships), p. 206

Best White Wine: Chardonnay from Vignoble Les Pervenches (Farnham, Eastern Townships), p. 227

Best Brownie: Cocoa Locale (Plateau Mont-Royal), p. 129

Best Rotisserie Chicken: Rôtisserie Romados (Plateau Mont-Royal), p. 122

Best Coffee: Faema (Little Italy), p. 183

Best Shortbread: Le Gryphon D'Or (NDG), p. 34

Best Grilled Cheese Sandwich: La Maison du Cheddar (Outremont), p. 163

Best Comfort Food: *pâté chinois* at La Binerie (Plateau Mont-Royal), p. 125

Best Breakfast Dish: breakfast skillets at Quoi de N'Oeuf (Little Burgundy), p. 39

Old Montreal & the Old Port

Old Montreal may have the city's largest concentration of atmospheric dining rooms with centuries-old stone walls and heavy timbers. There's nothing faux about this architecture—it survives from the era when Montreal was the easternmost navigable port from the Canadian interior, and the westernmost navigable port coming from Europe. That put Montreal smack in the middle of the fur and grain trade, and made it the richest city in Canada. Those atmospheric dining rooms were once stone warehouses.

Montreal began at the Old Port—literally on the site now occupied by the archaeological museum Pointe-à-Callière. The streets still follow a plan laid out in 1672, and the outlines of Old Montreal are nearly identical to the walled fortifications that the British removed when they seized Quebec from the French in the 18th century.

Old Montreal & the Old Port

N

| 0 | 100 | 200 M. |

| 0 | 500 | 1000 FT. |

Boulangerie Olive + Gourmando 28
Boutique des métiers d'art 3
Brit & Chips 33
Chez L'Épicier 5
Chez Queux 8
Claude Postel, Pâtissier, Chocolatier, Traiteur 16
Cluny ArtBar 35
DNA 30
Espace Boutique Europea 15
Gibby's 27
La Gargote 29
L'Autre Version 6
Le Club Chasse et Pêche 4
Le Jardin Nelson 7
Les Delices de l'Érable 10
Les Trois Brasseurs 9
Marché de La Villette 26
Marché du Vieux 12
Pointe-à-Callière 21
Restaurant BBQ 31
Restaurant Fourquet Fourchette 23
Restaurant Le Local 34
Restaurant Les Filles du Roy 2
Ristorante Quattro 14
Stash Cafe 22
Steak-Frites Vieux Montreal 13
Toqué! 24
XO Le Restaurant 25

Académie Culinaire 1
Accords Bar à Vin 18
Aix Cuisine de Terroir 17
Ateliers & Saveurs 19
Auberge Saint-Gabriel 11
Bar & Boeuf 32
Bonaparte Restaurant 20

After decades of decay and depopulation, Old Montreal was revived as a tourist attraction in the years following World War II—a trend that reached a fever pitch in the citywide makeover for the 1967 Montreal Exposition. Many streets were repaved with stone and antique-style street lamps were installed to augment the anachronistic ambience. Now the clip-clop of the hooves of carriage horses punctuates the pauses between bells at the Notre-Dame basilica. A revival of quite another kind came about at the turn of the millennium when the upper levels of beautiful old buildings were transformed into condos and serious restaurants began to sprout in locations once ceded entirely to the tourist trade. Resident Montrealers began to return to Old Montreal to drink and dine and play.

The small footprint of Old Montreal has even led more adventurous entrepreneurs to locate west of the Old Port and rue McGill. The grid of streets was briefly called Multimedia City, but of late the 19th-century moniker of Griffintown has returned to vogue for this once-residential neighborhood that endured a half century of being zoned light industrial. Now that most of the industry has gone, the warehouse- and factory-filled streets are being repopulated by hipsters, coders, artists, and musicians—and by visionary restaurants that understand that even creative types like to go out to eat. This chapter includes that westward expansion, so when you cross rue McGill and the street pattern changes, the eating opportunities only multiply.

Accords Bar à Vin, 212 rue Notre-Dame ouest; (514) 282-2020; www.accords.ca. Metro: Place d'Armes. Virtually in the shadow of the Notre-Dame basilica, Accords really shines on a summer afternoon when you can sit on the terrace inside the wrought-iron gate and sample from a large variety of wines available in full-size and 2-ounce pours. Tasty nibbles include the likes of smoked mackerel with pickled fennel or duck sausage with gnocchi. Full-scale meals are so hearty that even white-wine drinkers will shift to red for rack of piglet or braised veal cheek and marrow. One of the popular plates to share is a trio of spicy duck—confit in a curry sauce, smoked breast with smoked-tea jelly, and seared breast with date chutney. The sommelier offers an "accords/discord" wine choice. The "accords" pairing is the intuitive choice—say, a Côtes-du-Rhône with a steak—while the "discord" is counterintuitive, like a sparkling rosé with the same dish. It's fun to try the options and often a good lesson in suiting your own tastes instead of some abstract oenological dictate.

Aix Cuisine de Terroir, 711 Côte de la Place d'Armes; (514) 904-1201; www.aixcuisine.com. Metro: Place d'Armes. This elegant little room tucked into the lower level of the tony Place d'Armes Hôtel & Suites champions Quebec haute cuisine, and there are few places in the city with such dedication to the taste of place. Start with the choice of oysters—or, if oysters are out of season, with the charcuterie plate of sausages, *rillettes,* and a homemade terrine. The meat course emphasizes farmed Quebec game, often paired with strong flavors. For example, bison steak is scented with licorice, and the elk tenderloin is stuffed with chestnuts. Lamb raised along the Gulf of St. Lawrence in chilly Kamouraska is braised for seven hours, resulting in a dish that hardly calls for a knife. The beef fillet (from heritage cattle raised in Charlevoix) is graced with seared *foie gras.* If there's any shortcoming to Aix, it's the stream of bar patrons from upstairs who pass through the sedate restaurant to reach the bathrooms.

Auberge Saint-Gabriel, 426 rue Saint-Gabriel; (514) 878-3561; www.lesaint-gabriel.com. Metro: Champs de Mars. The arrival of young Provençal chef Éric Gonzalez (and his Michelin star) transformed this ancient dining room into one of the hottest restaurants in Old Montreal. The original 17th-century architecture of the inn has been preserved, with massive stone walls and ancient timbers giving the interior a medieval demeanor. It is quickly undercut by playful touches like the lamps installed in two stuffed moose. For years the Saint-Gabriel was, frankly, a tourist trap, and the place still has a highly theatrical feel. But now it has superb food to go with the ambience. For example, Gonzalez serves a 1-kilogram (yes, 2.2-pound) prime rib for two that is roasted on the auberge's giant rotisserie that looks borrowed from a Loire Valley castle. But he's also true to his Provençal roots with dishes like lamb shoulder with smoked eggplant, and roasted sea bream with lemon, fennel, and caramelized peppers. *Table d'hôte* lunches are lighter, brighter, and bargain priced.

Bar & Boeuf, 500 rue McGill; (514) 866-3555; www.baretboeuf .com. Metro: Square Victoria. Anglophones might easily mistake this hot little restaurant for a steak and martini joint, but the "bar" of its name is French for sea bass. Chef Alexandre Gosselin often cooks the signature fish in a temperature-controlled water bath to get the flaky texture just right, then kicks the flavor up a notch by accompanying the bass with smoked pig cheeks and braised Brussels sprouts topped with Rice Krispies. Robust, in case you hadn't guessed, could be Gosselin's middle name. He has a strong commitment to local products (he's a big fan of Stanstead rabbit), the audacity to pair strong flavors (said rabbit stuffed with *foie gras* and apricots), and the skills to make it all seem natural and easy. The wine list is one of the best and most eclectic in Old Montreal, featuring a lot of southern French wines and a healthy helping of bold Spanish reds and crisp Spanish whites. You'll even find a few Canadian Rieslings from the Okanagan Valley.

Bonaparte Restaurant, 443 rue Saint-François-Xavier; (514) 844-4368; www.restaurantbonaparte.com. Metro: Place d'Armes. Steps from the Centaur Theatre, Bonaparte's pretheater menu (5:30

to 6:30 p.m.) is a favorite for playgoers. But it's a shame to eat and run, since two of the three dining rooms have intimate little tables for savoring the refined modern French cooking. One room even has a gas fireplace. Bonaparte is a restaurant, not a bistro. The menu features *steak au poivre* flamed with brandy instead of *steak-frites,* for example, but prices are low for a restaurant and the atmosphere is relaxed if not entirely informal. We like the kitchen's inventive take on the *de rigueur* appetizer of *foie gras.* Here it's served as a crème brûlée with apple jelly and toast points. The lobster stew is worthy of a Channel Islands version, scented with vanilla and sweet Muscat wine. The upper floors of the building house a lovely little inn of similar style.

Brit & Chips, 433 rue McGill; (514) 840-1001; www.britandchips .com. Metro: Square Victoria. Brought to you by the same folks behind the fabulously successful British-style **Pub Burgundy Lion** (see p. 38) in Little Burgundy, this fish-and-chips shop departs slightly from the formula of the motherland to offer different fish in different batters. The cod in Burgundy Lion (i.e., beer) batter is the most traditional. Haddock is treated to a maple-syrup batter, salmon to a Guinness batter, and hake to a sweet batter based on an orange soft drink. What sets the shop off from other chippies, though, are the pasties (turnovers) and pot pies of either steak and ale or lamb and mint.

Chez L'Épicier, 311 rue St-Paul est; (514) 878-2232; www.chez lepicier.com. Metro: Champ de Mars. Montreal foodies are rarely lukewarm about chef-restaurateur Laurent Godbout, whom some champion as the master of complexity and others consider operatically overwrought. Although this Montreal spot started long ago as a simple market restaurant (founded by a former grocery-chain heir), it gave up its simplistic fare when Godbout took over. We like to think of his food as the Adobe Flash version of contemporary Québecois cooking. When it works, it's utterly magical. Godbout is at his best when he goes a little mad for one ingredient, as he does with fall squashes. One recent creation was a vegetarian dish of squash au gratin with a black garlic puree, spaghetti squash with porcini mushrooms, and a risottolike creamed Arborio rice and turban squash topped with a smoked quail egg. As you might expect in a restaurant whose name can be translated as the house of the spice merchant, the extensive wine list verges on the baroque with some obscure bottles chosen to match the food. During much of the day, Chez L'Épicier functions as a bustling wine bar with at least a dozen choices by the glass.

Claude Postel, Pâtissier, Chocolatier, Traiteur, 75 rue Notre-Dame ouest; (514) 844-8750; www.claudepostel.com. Metro: Place d'Armes. Back in the 1980s, M. Postel operated one of the most daring and game-centric haute restaurants in Montreal, but a couple of economic downturns later, he is comfortably ensconced in this shop-cum-bistro where he serves delicious bargain bistro fare for lunch or very early dinner and sells his exquisite pastries and

Olden Days & Nowadays

Both a museum and an archaeological site, the striking modern building of Pointe-à-Callière squats above the archaeological dig of the 1642 settlement of Ville-Marie, the beginning of Montreal. Its permanent exhibit traces six centuries of history from Amerindian encampments to the present day—with a strong emphasis on Montreal's French roots. Throughout the year, special events flesh out the story and often highlight the strong link between food and history.

In late August, the museum sponsors a weekend-long **18th-Century Public Market.** It's held at Place Royale, the site of the settlement's first public market and in many ways the center of life in the early colony. Interpreters dress in period costume and visitors can sample a variety of typical products from wild-fruit jams and jellies to preserved fiddlehead ferns, from mead and cider to spruce beer. An Amerindian encampment features medicinal herbs and edible plants.

Pointe-à-Callière does not dwell exclusively in the past. Its very popular **Cultural Feast,** a two-day event held in May also at Place Royale, brings Montreal foodways into the 21st century with a celebration of traditional cuisine from the city's many ethnic groups and lectures by some of the city's most cutting-edge chefs.

Pointe-à-Callière, 350 Place Royale; (514) 872-9150; www .pacmusee.qc.ca. Metro: Place d'Armes.

chocolates. We love the fact that you can pop in for a quiche and salad for under $10 or delicious vegetable, roast pork, or chicken panini at the same price point. The Art Deco–inspired decor of the high-ceilinged room makes you feel like you're dining instead of grabbing lunch, and you can always finish with an almond tart and a perfect espresso.

Cluny ArtBar, 257 rue Prince; (514) 866-1213; www.cluny.info. Metro: Square-Victoria. Set into the Darling Foundry building that was renovated in 2002 as a contemporary art space, Cluny ArtBar is a popular lunch spot for office workers in the Griffintown neighborhood west of Old Montreal proper. Artists who work in the building hang out in the space in the afternoon, and on Thursday night it even stays open for dinner. The food is starving-artist chic, which is to say a lot of sandwiches on whole-grain breads, récherché brownies and cookies, bread pudding, and mango smoothies. But the kitchen also makes a daily hot meal (braised lamb shank, for example) and the bar has a good list of wines by the glass.

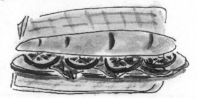

DNA, 355 rue d'Youville; (514) 287-3362; www.dnarestaurant.com. Metro: Square Victoria. Not the easiest restaurant to find, DNA faces the west end of the Old Port waterfront with a nondescript entrance. But as soon as you walk in the door you know you're not in Kansas anymore—or even in what you'd expect in Old Montreal.

The interior design is nightclub chic, with black-leather banquettes, swiveling leather-upholstered armchairs, bead curtains, and probably too much neon. Chef Derek Damman did a two-year London stint as Jamie Oliver's chef de cuisine, so his food has an Oliver-like theatrical flair and penchant for bold flavors with Italian accents. His grilled Quebec lamb leg, for example, is served on a mound of *caponata,* resulting in a dish that might be described as an operatic tenor duet. Yet just when you think all his chops are bold strokes and bluster, he can send out a lobster salad with blood oranges and watercress that is downright ethereal. The long wine list comes on a clipboard, which makes it hard to peruse. Fortunately, maître d' and sommelier Alex Cruz can cut through the confusion to give you choices of pairings for every dish.

Espace Boutique Europea, 33 rue Notre-Dame ouest; (514) 844-1572; www.europea.ca. Metro: Place d'Armes. Chef Jérôme Ferrer's flagship **Restaurant Europea** (see p. 63) is one of the city's top gourmet destinations. The "Gourmand Lunch" at this weekday-only spot offers a taste of Ferrer's style at a fraction of the cost, though it involves a difficult choice. Once you've selected your sandwich (prosciutto and blue cheese with grapes and figs, perhaps, or sliced lamb with onion confit and grilled vegetables), you can select a soup or a salad (such as marinated vegetables with smoked duck and Parmigiano Reggiano cheese or greens with gravlax, fresh dates, and mango) or a dessert (lemon and chocolate cream tart, for example, or a miniature chocolate mousse cake). Healthy or decadent? The choice is up to you. And after you've eaten at one of the tables in this elegant minimalist space, browse the small but select display of merchandise—from beautiful coffee sets to dessert-inspired body products. If you opted for the salad, treat yourself to some crème-brûlée hand lotion or dark-chocolate bath oil.

La Gargote, 351 place d'Youville; (514) 844-1428; www.restaurant lagargote.com. Metro: Square Victoria. The name is French slang for a diner, but this little mom-and-pop bistro looks, feels, and tastes like a small-town bistro lifted straight from an early 1950s French  film. La Gargote would be French provincial—if Quebec were still an overseas province of France. The oxblood-red interior (except for one stone wall) and beamed ceiling make the place look older than it is, and the cute blue-and-white awning wouldn't be out of place in Brittany. The menu wouldn't either, with dishes like calf's liver with parsley, Atlantic salmon roasted with tarragon, or a *pot-au-feu* called "seven-hour beef stew." Outdoor tables flow into Place d'Youville in the summer, but we like the homey interior, especially on a cold winter's night when a plain water glass of the house red wine seems especially warming.

L'Autre Version, 295 rue Saint-Paul est; (514) 871-9135; www .restoversion.com. Metro: Champ de Mars. It's a difficult trick to follow a famous chef-owner in a good restaurant spot, but new owners Stéphanie Gemme and Benoît Marcotte managed to right the ship at L'Autre Version when Laurent Godbout sold the place to concentrate on **Chez L'Épicier** (see above). The first amuse-bouche they offered was a simple slice of hot baguette with balsamic vinegar, olive oil, and a dried-tomato pesto—and the kitchen has followed through with Quebec-sourced food presented with deft Mediterranean flair ever since. Current chef David Chaussé likes to pair seared halibut with beets, a black-currant sauce, and Israeli couscous, for example. At lunch he offers a game burger with Hércule cheese from Charlevoix, his homemade ketchup, and *frites* cooked in duck fat. Don't let the burger mislead you—L'Autre Version is far from a bistro. It's a rather formal fine-dining restaurant with superb service.

Le Club Chasse et Pêche, 423 rue Saint-Claude; (514) 861-1112; www.leclubchasseetpeche.com. Metro: Champ de Mars. The hunting/fishing decor of this amazing restaurant is a tongue-in-cheek homage to the previous occupant (a private club) of this out-of-the-way spot near the Château Ramezay. But the outdoorsy theme does carry through to the menu, where bison, venison, and partridge make regular appearances and wild-caught fish is always a staple. Chef Claude Pelletier doesn't range very far in sourcing his ingredients. If it's fall, then the roasted cod comes with ruta-baga, and the braised piglet risotto is topped with *foie gras* shavings instead of foreign truffles. The cooking style is minimalist—only what's necessary and not a whit more. Yet the flavors are unabashedly Québecois. Even dessert—like a pumpkin and maple tart with crème fraîche—speaks Canadian French.

Le Jardin Nelson, 407 place Jacques Cartier; (514) 861-5731; www.jardinnelson.com. Metro: Champ de Mars. Its location on busy place Jacques Cartier guarantees that Le Jardin Nelson attracts its fair share of tourists. But locals favor it also for its delightful hidden garden and menu of unusual crepes, including Lac Brome duck, saddle of rabbit, mushrooms, and *blanquette de veau* (cubes of veal in a rich cream sauce) and satisfying salads with tuna, fresh salmon or roasted beets. Open early May through mid-October.

Les Trois Brasseurs, 105 rue Saint-Paul est; (514) 788-6100; www.les3brasseurs.ca. Metro: Champ de Mars. This Old Montreal outpost of the chain of brewpubs born in northern France always has white, blonde, amber, and brown ales on tap as well as a seasonal brew. The Alsatian menu is predictable but hearty (sauerkraut and sausages, steamed mussels, and North American bar food like nachos and chicken wings), and the beer rarely disappoints. Chain dining isn't so bad when it includes fresh beer.

Restaurant BBQ, 372 rue Saint-Paul ouest; (514) 284-0444; www.bbqMontreal.com. Metro: Square Victoria. From the same folks behind **Bar & Boeuf** (see p. 6), this comfort food restaurant bears only the slightest resemblance to the pit barbecue of the American South. Here the ribs, chicken, and pork all speak French. For example, laden with fresh cheese curds and slathered with a very Canadian barbecue sauce, "pig chuck" is only a distant Québecois cousin of Carolina pulled pork. One of the best starters on the menu is chef Alexandre Gosselin's charcuterie plate, and you have to love a roast-meat joint that understands that French onion soup with melted Gruyère also constitutes comfort food. The picnic table seating and low ceilings make this a pretty raucous place on a Saturday night. We've always been tempted to end the evening by ordering a Hangover Tart to go so we could warm it up for breakfast: smoked meat, *mozzarella di bufala*, *foie gras*, and tomato confit.

Restaurant Fourquet Fourchette, 265 rue Saint-Antoine ouest; (514) 789-6370; www.fourquet-fourchette.com. Metro: Square Victoria. About as locavore as it gets in Montreal, this large restaurant in the Palais des Congrès (in the corner of Old Montreal called the "International Quarter") sources 95 percent of its products from the Montérégie region southwest of the city. The menu complements the popular Quebec-made beers of Unibroue, maker of the Chambly beers brewed in a Trappist style, as well as Trois Pistoles, Raftman, La Maudite, La Fin du Monde, and other beers with fanciful labels that reference the days of the fur-trappers and early colonists. In keeping with the theme, a "New France" menu designed to evoke Quebec before the British (i.e., pre-1763) is available every meal except Saturday night. Dishes include First Peoples and fur-trapper novelty foods like pemmican and caribou pot pie. At all meals, à la carte selections include both grilled and smoked meats, stewed rabbit, and duck, duck, duck. As the license plates say, *Je me souviens* (I remember).

Restaurant Le Local, 740 rue William; (514) 397-7737; www
.resto-lelocal.com. Metro: Square Victoria. Set in an ivy-covered
building (behind an ivy-covered and therefore illegible sign), Le
Local lives up to its name. It even feels like a "local," as Brits and
Irish like to call their home neighborhood pubs—except that here
the Griffintown neighborhood is post-industrial, and thus so is the
interior design with its concrete floor, unadorned support columns,
and bare-bulb light fixtures. All this serves as a counterpoint
to the rustic food that has learned urban manners.
Chef Charles-Emmanuel Pariseau makes his sea-scallop
chowder with smoked pig's feet instead of salt pork
and even bakes the crackers to crumble on top. The
dishes hop back and forth between northern France and
Quebec, so you can get the Arctic char with a cauliflower
mousseline, or opt for a grilled burger of Quebec
veal dressed with mushroom jam and Quebec Brie
and served on a house-baked bun. Le Local quickly
won a following for its excellent list of wines by
the glass at reasonable (for Montreal) prices. If you
like quieter dining, ask for the *côté-maison,* or "house section" on
the left as you enter.

Ristorante Quattro, 17 rue Notre-Dame ouest; (514) 903-2909;
www.ristorantequattro.com. Metro: Place d'Armes. The foursome of
the name refers to the owners who hail from different parts of Italy.
So does the menu, but it's truly Italian, not Italian-Canadian, and
ranges from north (grilled meats, scallopini, delectably grilled fish

with a splash of lemon and herbs) to the south (ribbon pappardelle as they make in Puglia, savory gnocchi and sweet cannoli in the Sicilian style). The establishment also calls itself a wine bar, which is what it becomes after dinner with a broad selection of Italian and Chilean pours.

Stash Cafe, 200 rue Saint-Paul ouest; (514) 845-6611; www.stash cafe.com. Metro: Square Victoria/Place d'Armes. After more than 30 years, this restaurant featuring old fashioned Polish comfort food is something of an Old Montreal institution. It's also a good bet for a quick lunch of the stew of the day or a filling plate of potato pancakes with sour cream or pierogis stuffed with meat, cheese or cabbage. The evening "primer" menu offers a crash course in Polish cuisine from *borscht* to cabbage stew with mushroom and sausages to meat-filled pancake rolls. Other special menus concentrate on roast duck or roast of wild boar (in season) prepared from a recipe passed down from the owner's grandmother.

Steak-Frites Vieux Montreal, 200 boulevard Saint-Laurent; (514) 842-0972; www.steakfrites.ca. Metro: Place d'Armes. It's hard to go wrong with this restaurant's formula: a menu based on the classic French bistro dish of steak and french fries, combined with a BYOB policy to make it even more affordable. That might explain why there are five branches of the local chain in the central city alone offering good meat, terrific fries, and fair prices. True, the menu is limited, but it's a great chance to sit down to a good meal in a pleasant setting for a low price. BYOB.

Toqué!, 900 place Jean-Paul-Riopelle; (514) 499-2084; www .restaurant-toque.com. Metro: Square Victoria. We have to confess a certain bias. When we started writing about fine cuisine in Montreal more than two decades ago, Normand Laprise—a young chef fresh out of Quebec hotel school—bowled us over with his sheer inventiveness, uncanny ability to combine and contrast flavors, and his showmanship on the plate. Over the decades he has revolutionized Montreal gastronomy. His restaurant Toqué! in the International Quarter is a big room of serious gastronomic aspirations tempered by some of the same wit and whimsy Laprise brings to his food. If you order à la carte here, you must be the same kind of person who visits the Louvre and only glances at the Mona Lisa from across the hall. Budget be damned, take the tasting menu—which is likely to be different on Friday from what it was on Tuesday, so attuned is Laprise to harvest of the moment. In fact, he was among the first chefs in Quebec (along with Roland Ménard of the **Manoir Hovey** in the Eastern Townships, see p. 198) to forge alliances with producers—promising farmers that he would take a certain percentage of their crops if they grew what he wanted, or contracting all his lamb from one farm, all his duck products from another, and so on. What sets Laprise apart from other Montreal *terroir* toques is the refinement of his food—the color-field composition on the plate, the contrast of textures and flavors, the element of surprise. The restaurant's name is French slang for "crazy," and every dish has an element of unpredictability. Who else in Montreal would oven-dry strawberries and oyster mushrooms to complement lobster tail in a salad? Well, maybe Laprise's first-ever chef de cuisine, Charles-Antoine Crête, whose previous credits include a stint with Ferran Adrià at elBulli in Spain.

XO Le Restaurant, 355 rue Saint-Jacques; (514) 841-5000; www .xolerestaurant.com. Metro: Square Victoria/Place d'Armes. This super-swank dining room is located in the so-called Banker's Hall of the Hôtel Le Saint-James. The ceilings soar, the chandeliers glitter, the silverware clanks, and the crystal tinkles. All gold and cream, it may be the most formal and most classically glam dining room in the city—all of which means nothing if the food doesn't rise to the same bar. Under chef Michele Mercuri it does. As is the mode in Montreal these days, the product is strongly Québecois (they even name the farm that supplies the pork), but Mercuri is also a young master of artful presentation. He does a free-form lasagna of duck confit and lobster meat flavored with a lobster emulsion and a little well-aged cheese that not only manages to hold together, but each layer heightens the flavor of the others. The wine list completely bypasses the SAQ in favor of private imports, and may be the best classical list in the city. The quintessential special-occasion restaurant, XO is also a perfect venue for marking the conclusion of a multimillion-dollar merger—or watching other celebrants with a little envy.

Chez Queux, 158 rue Saint-Paul est; (514) 866-5194; www.chez queux.com. Metro: Champ de Mars. Be still our hearts—this spot may be one of the last old-fashioned French restaurants left in the world, including France, and it must be appreciated on its own terms. First the setting: the tables in the wood-paneled dining room are laid with white linens, set with a full complement of six utensils, and lit by very 19th-century-looking silver candlesticks. In short, dress for dinner. Then there is the menu—chateaubriand for two, honest-to-god-flown-in-from-Europe Dover sole *meunière*, sweet-breads sautéed with morel mushrooms. There is a cheese plate. For dessert, choose between a lemon tart and (honest!) cherries jubilee flamed at the table. *Wine Spectator* says Chez Queux has one of the greatest wine lists in the world. We won't attest to that, but it's certainly one of the most French this side of France, and laden with massive (and pricy) Bordeaux and Burgundies. Restaurants like Chez Queux don't exist anymore except in old movies and romance novels. You'll pay dearly for the nostalgia, but it's worth it.

Gibby's, 298 place d'Youville; (514) 282-1837; www.gibbys.com. Metro: Square Victoria. The stone walls, the beamed ceilings, the rustic fireplaces—the setting for Gibby's (the former stables of a hospital and convent) couldn't be more *ancien régime*. Ditto for the menu. If **Moishes** (see p. 125) was the steakhouse of the Jewish middle class, Gibby's became the steakhouse of the Anglophone bourgeoisie. The meat is great, the sides competent, and the desserts as rich as the local clientele. Gibby's is the perfect spot for a celebratory meal for well-heeled folks with meat and potatoes taste. There's nothing wrong with that, but know in advance that the bill will be about the same as you'd pay at Toqué!, Milos, or XO.

Restaurant Les Filles du Roy, Maison de Pierre du Calvet, 405 rue Bonsecours; (514) 282-1725; www.pierreducalvet.ca. Metro: Champ de Mars. There's hardly a more atmospheric place in Montreal than this historic 1725 home with stone walls and beamed ceilings. The restaurant of this small auberge is named for the intrepid young women sent by the king to marry and help populate the new colony and is furnished with dark woods, rich fabrics, and trophy heads on the wall. Menu offerings such as braised pork belly with maple syrup or duck breast with honey and rosemary pay homage to French culinary traditions as adapted to Quebec provender. For a romantic repast, ask for the table for two on the tiny balcony above the main dining room.

Specialty Stores, Markets & Producers

Boulangerie Olive + Gourmando, 351 rue Saint-Paul ouest; (514) 350-1083; www.oliveetgourmando.com. Metro: Square Victoria/Place d'Armes. We have been known to skip hotel breakfast to come here for croissants and a bowl of *café au lait*. That's how good O+G is. Partners Dyan Solomon and Éric Girard worked the bake ovens at **Toqué!** (see p. 18) before opening this bakery cafe, where they make soups and sandwiches available at lunch and sell breads, croissants, and pastries all day. Olive + Gourmando really calls into question the old saw that man does not live by bread alone.

Boutique des métiers d'art, 350 rue Saint-Paul est; (514) 878-2787; www.metiers-d-art.qc.ca. Metro: Champ de Mars. The works of more than 150 Quebec artists and craftspeople are featured in this gallery in a historic 1847 market building. Among them is Sylvain Tremblay, a woodworker who has crafted an imaginative line of pepper mills in natural woods and rich colors. His works range from elegant curvy forms to mini lighthouses, weathervanes, pigs, fish—and even the Eiffel Tower. Tremblay guarantees the stainless-steel mechanism for life and can fit any design with a corrosion-resistant plastic mechanism for grinding salt.

Les Délices de l'Érable, 84 rue Saint-Paul est; (514) 765-3456; www.mapledelights.com. Metro: Place d'Armes. A modest museum in the basement recounts that native peoples first discovered maple sap, which has little color or sweetness when it is tapped from trees in late winter. The sap must be boiled to bring out the rich, sugary flavor. If you think the resulting syrup is just for pancakes, you're in for a surprise in the upstairs retail shop where maple flavors everything from coffee and pepper to vinegar and mustard. Check out some of the taste combinations in the small cafe, perhaps a maple cappuccino with a maple almond croissant.

Maple Syrup Pie

While you could get the idea from Les Délices d'Erable that maple folks add the flavoring to almost anything, this recipe from the Maple Syrup Producers' Cooperative (www.mapledelights.com) represents one of the classics of Québecois cuisine. It's gilding the lily, but slices of the pie are delicious with a small scoop of vanilla ice cream or a dollop of whipped cream.

Makes two 8-inch pies

- ¾ cup plus 3 tablespoons maple syrup
- ½ cup plus 1 tablespoon maple sugar
- ½ cup plus 1 tablespoon brown sugar
- 2 tablespoons evaporated milk
- 3 tablespoons all-purpose flour

- 1 large egg
- 2 cups heavy cream
- 2 Golden Delicious apples, peeled, cored, and cut in ½-inch thick slices
- 2 tablespoons butter, melted
- 2 unbaked 8-inch pie shells

Preheat oven to 350°F.

Blend the maple syrup (reserving 2 tablespoons), sugars, evaporated milk, flour, and egg with a whisk.

Bring the cream to a boil. Add maple mixture to the cream and cook for four minutes, stirring constantly.

Allow mixture to cool. Divide evenly between uncooked pie shells.

Toss apple slices with 2 tablespoons melted butter, then with 2 tablespoons maple syrup. Decorate tops of pies with apple slices.

Bake for approximately 45 minutes until set and beginning to brown on top. Cool on racks before serving.

Marché de La Villette, 324 rue Saint-Paul ouest; (514) 807-8084. Metro: Square Victoria/Place d'Armes. This mom-and-pop deli can get a little noisy and the tables are a bit cramped, but it's still a great option for a good-value lunch in the Old Montreal tourist district. To channel Paris, opt for the onion soup, quiche, and salad combo or a ham and Brie crepe. Sandwich options include spicy merguez sausage, smoked salmon, turkey, tuna, or *foie gras* mousse. Waffles with hot chocolate sauce are the favored dessert.

Marché du Vieux, 8 rue Saint-Paul est; (514) 393-2772; www.marcheduvieux.com. Metro: Champ de Mars. There's certainly maple syrup on the shelves, but this *boutique du terroir* casts a much wider net and stocks a broad array of Quebec products from tins of smoked duck to apple cider vinegar and Dijon-style mustards. Of course there is an array of jams, jellies and pickled vegetables, but the most unusual product might be the olive oil infused with the sweet, salty flavor of lobster from the Magdalen Islands. A small cafe offers soups, salads, sandwiches and homemade gelato (including maple).

Cooking Schools & Classes

Académie Culinaire, 360 rue Champ-de-Mars; (514) 393-8111; www.academieculinaire.com. Metro: Champ de Mars. The academy opened in 1985 and the classes that fill the calendar in this modern facility on the edge of Old Montreal are a good reflection of changing tastes. Offerings in chocolate and pastry fill up fast and those featuring duck are always popular. But while there's a constant demand for courses in traditional French and Italian cuisine, newer courses in Thai, Szechuan, and Indian cooking are gaining ground and during May and June the academy focuses almost exclusively on barbecue. Three-hour demonstration classes are held in a well-designed room that puts all students up close to the chef, while a large professional kitchen is the site of practical classes that usually last six or seven hours. All classes, of course, include tastings or a full meal and some combine wine tasting with cooking. Classes are mostly in French, but English speakers are accommodated and you'd be surprised how much you can learn by simply watching and tasting. (See recipe on p. 26.)

Ateliers & Saveurs, 444 rue Saint-Francois-Xavier; (514) 849-2866; www.atelierssetsaveurs.com. Metro: Place d'Armes. Ateliers & Saveurs takes an all-inclusive approach to the pleasures of the table with classes in tasting wine and mixing cocktails, as well as cooking classes. Rodolfo Martins, one of the two instructors, previously worked in the kitchen of the Michelin three-star restaurant Le Meurice in Paris, but is committed to empowering the home chef. "I want to show people that good food is not about being complicated," he says, "and that they can do it at home." Of course, good food requires good ingredients and some classes begin with shopping at the nearby **Marché Atwater** (see p. 40). All classes are hands-on. In popular 1-hour lunchtime classes students master

Pâté Chinois (Québecois Shepherd's Pie)

In 2007, Montreal's French-language newspaper Le Devoir surveyed 500 people to determine the "national plate of Quebec." Despite its odd name, pâté chinois took the title, beating out pouding chomeur (white cake baked with a syrup of maple and cream) and even the more celebrated poutine. The Académie Culinaire created a jazzed-up version of this humble dish of ground meat, corn, and mashed potatoes. We call for cooking this version of pâté chinois in a 9x13 pan, but individual portions can be cooked in six small casseroles.

Serves 6

- 3 large potatoes, peeled and cut in cubes
- ½ cup heavy cream
- 1 tablespoon white truffle oil
- salt and pepper to taste
- 12 oz. creamed corn
- 1 cup fresh or frozen corn kernels
- 2 tablespoons olive oil

- 1½ pounds ground veal
- ¼ pound pancetta
- 3 tablespoons sun-dried tomatoes packed in oil, diced
- ½ cup brown stock
- salt and pepper to taste
- 2 tablespoons butter

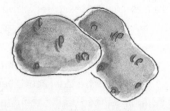

Place the potatoes in a sauce pan and cover them with cold water. Season the water with a generous pinch of salt, and cook the potatoes until they are fork tender (7–10 minutes).

Place the cooked potatoes in a food mill and process them to prepare the mashed potatoes. Add cream and truffle oil and mix well to obtain a smooth texture. Season the potatoes to taste with salt and pepper. Reserve.

Mix the two types of corn together and reserve.

In a sauté pan, heat olive oil and sauté veal and pancetta. After a few minutes, add the sun-dried tomatoes and the brown stock and continue cooking until the meat has completely lost its pink color and the sauce has become thick. Season to taste with salt and pepper.

Preheat oven to 400°F. In 9x13 pan, create three even layers for the shepherd's pie starting with the meat, followed by the corn and finishing with the mashed potatoes (using a piping bag fitted with a star tip will add flair to the finish).

Cut remaining 2 tablespoons of butter into small cubes and distribute over top of potatoes. Place in oven until the potatoes start to brown, 25–30 minutes.

Recipe courtesy of Académie Culinaire (p. 24).

a simple plate, such as a roasted pork chop with apple chutney accompanied by a roasted beet salad. During 2½-hour evening classes, students prepare a 3-course meal, such as chickpea soup, flank steak with pumpkin sauce, and apple and maple upside-down cake. Classes are taught in French and English and fill very quickly.

Food Events

Happening Gourmand, www.happeninggourmand.com. To entice diners out on a cold winter night, Old Montreal serves up its own version of "restaurant week" dining promotions but stretches it over three weeks in January. Alas, only a few of the restaurants in the neighborhood participate, but the range is wide enough to offer diners a choice of three different price levels that all represent a significant savings over ordering à la carte. In every case, diners select from a special three-course menu with two choices each of appetizer and dessert and three choices of entrée.

Salon des Vins et Spiritueux de Montreal, Palais des Congrès de Montreal, 1001 place Jean-Paul-Riopelle; http://salondesvins .com. Metro: Square-Victoria. Montrealers have a definite loyalty toward wines from France, but this extravaganza gives them a chance to broaden their horizons. Winemakers, sommeliers, and other authorities offer a wide range of lectures. But the proof is in the bottle—and more than 100 producers from around the world are on hand to offer tastings.

Westmount, Little Burgundy & NDG

This chapter focuses on three primarily residential neighborhoods west of downtown Montreal: Westmount, Notre-Dame-de-Grâce, and Little Burgundy. Each has a distinctive character (as the wide range of asking prices in the newspaper real estate section reveals), but they share in common a casual approach to dining. Each district has its own enclave of cafes and restaurants that mainly cater to residents who live within a few blocks. Their neighborhood feel speaks volumes about how Montrealers live and how they love good food. It doesn't take a special occasion to socialize over a meal—dinner is occasion enough.

Of the three neighborhoods, Little Burgundy (and the western edge of neighboring Griffintown) has recently emerged as a bona-fide dining destination, with a core of homey breakfast and lunch spots and a handful of new casual bistros at the cutting edge of the Montreal restaurant scene. Verging south toward the Lachine

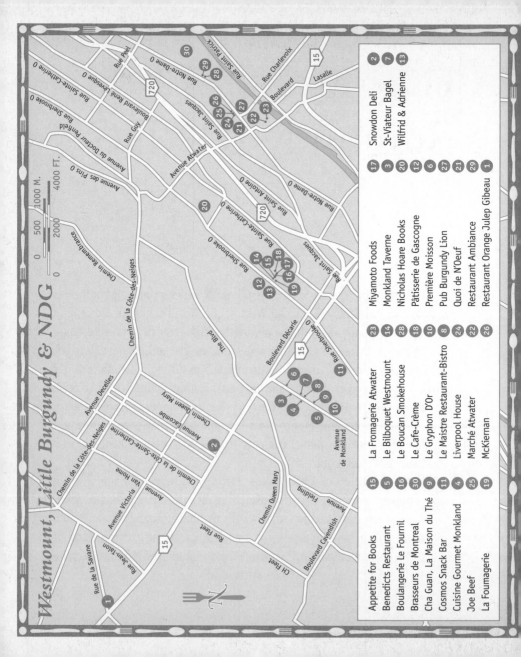

Westmount, Little Burgundy & NDG

Appetite for Books	15
Benedicts Restaurant	5
Boulangerie Le Fournil	16
Brasseurs de Montreal	30
Cha Guan, La Maison du Thé	9
Cosmos Snack Bar	11
Cuisine Gourmet Monkland	4
Joe Beef	25
La Foumagerie	19

La Fromagerie Atwater	23
Le Bilboquet Westmount	14
Le Boucan Smokehouse	28
Le Cafe-Crème	18
Le Gryphon D'Or	10
Le Maistre Restaurant-Bistro	8
Liverpool House	24
Marché Atwater	22
McKiernan	26

Miyamoto Foods	17
Monkland Taverne	3
Nicholas Hoare Books	20
Pâtisserie de Gascogne	12
Première Moisson	6
Pub Burgundy Lion	27
Quoi de N'Oeuf	21
Restaurant Ambiance	29
Restaurant Orange Julep Gibeau	1

Snowdon Deli	2
St-Viateur Bagel	7
Wilfrid & Adrienne	13

Canal, Little Burgundy was a center of smokestack industries in the late 19th century. An influx of African-Americans who came to work for the Canadian Pacific Railway established the area as Montreal's English-speaking black neighborhood. From the '30s into the '60s, Little Burgundy was a center of jazz culture in Canada. Swiftly gentrified at the end of the 20th century, Little Burgundy now boasts new townhouse condominiums (built over the former rail yards) as well as a cluster of architectural and design offices—all contributing to a critical mass of residents and workers to nurture the dining scene.

The neighborhood of Notre-Dame-de-Grâce lies north of Little Burgundy. Its Monkland Village section also underwent rapid gentrification at the end of the 20th century, becoming a preferred neighborhood for young professionals. On weekends, the sidewalks are full of dog-walkers and stroller-pushers and the smart cafes do a bustling business from breakfast and brunch through lunch. English has an edge over French as the preferred language, which might explain why Montrealers tend to refer to the area by the initials NDG rather than its decidedly French proper name.

Historically Montreal's English-speaking neighbor, Westmount remains the most British sector of the city despite an influx of French speakers of varied ethnic backgrounds. It's also one of the richest municipalities in Canada and its main shopping drag, rue Sherbrooke, has the shops to prove it. Although only a fifth of Westmount residents do not speak French, it is possible to wander the streets for a whole day hearing only English. That said, Westmounters usually go outside their own turf to dine in French.

Foodie Faves

Benedicts Restaurant, 5950 avenue Monkland; (514) 481-6075. Metro: Villa-Maria. There's an outdoor terrace for warm weather, a sleek bar with big-screen TV, and a dinner menu of pastas, burgers, and grilled chicken and fish. But for its NDG neighbors, Benedicts is the go-to place for convivial weekend breakfasts and brunches of crepes, omelets, French toast, steak and eggs, and six versions of eggs Benedict (including asparagus, salmon, and mushroom with Brie).

Brasseurs de Montreal, 1485 rue Ottawa; (514) 788-4505; www .brasseursdeMontreal.ca. Metro: Lucien-L'Allier/Georges-Vanier. It's not as if Montrealers are going to stop drinking Molson and Labatt, but microbreweries thrive in this city of ale lovers. Brasseurs brews a style for every taste, from the bright American-style ale of Le Griffintown to the malty brown Scotch ale of La Black Watch. Easily recognized by the photographs of different eyes on the labels, bottled BdM beers are available at most *dépanneurs*. At the resto-bar headquarters in Griffintown, they're on tap to accompany burgers, sandwiches, or comfort-food hot dishes like mac and cheese, *pâté chinois,* or—for a twosome—the full-on treatment of *choucroute.*

Cosmos Snack Bar, 5843 Sherbrooke ouest; (514) 486-3814. Metro: Vendôme. This sliver of a luncheonette is something of an NDG legend, not least for its founder, Tony Koulakis, who was the subject of a touching and funny documentary called *Man of Grease*. Cosmos is the ultimate greasy spoon, serving breakfast, burgers, and hash browns from around dawn to 5 p.m. Tony's son Nick now runs the joint, but he hasn't touched the menu, which still includes neighborhood favorites like the "Creation Sandwich" (fried egg, bacon, salami, cheese, mayo, and to slightly offset the concentration of animal fat, lettuce and tomato). Equally popular is the humongous "Mish Mash Omelette" of eggs, tomato, onion, cheese, bacon, ham, salami, and sausage, served with toast with the usual hash browns. There are just 11 stools, so while it takes a while to get a seat, you're bound to make new friends at either elbow.

Joe Beef, 2491 rue Notre-Dame ouest; (514) 935-6504; www .joebeef.ca. Metro: Lionel Groulx. Casual almost to a fault, this gutsy and macho bistro spearheaded the transformation of Little Burgundy's formerly fussy Antiques Row into an urban-hip dining destination. The Victorian armoires and lace doilies are long gone, and the tables are bare with just a painted outline showing where the plates go. The soundtrack is Led Zeppelin and heavy metal. Fortunately, the food is far less affected, offering big and bold contemporary interpretations of classic bistro fare—like *skate-frites,* roast chicken with morel mushrooms, and even a twist on the shore dinner using poached trout.

Le Boucan Smokehouse, 1886 rue Notre-Dame ouest; (514) 439-4555. Metro: Georges-Vanier. In a city where "barbecue" traditionally means grilled meat, and "smoked meat" is a distinctive local take on corned brisket, this establishment looks much farther south for its inspiration—all the way to the Mississippi Delta country. Smoke infuses everything from soup to dessert, the latter being a big crumbly brownie containing a slice of bacon and covered in chocolate sauce. (Oddly enough, it works.) The burgers are smoked, the ribs are smoked, and the chicken is smoked. The standard barbecue sauce here is based on cider vinegar, and the staff is generous with it. The "five-napkin chicken sandwich," for example, definitely lives up to its name. For a perfect blend of Montreal and Mississippi, try the pulled-pork *poutine*.

Le Gryphon D'Or, 5968 avenue Monkland; (514) 485-7377; www .gryphondor.com. Metro: Villa-Maria. "I grew up with my Scottish grandmother and I try to make shortbread just like hers," says Peggy Regan, who welcomes visitors to her tearoom as if they were long-lost friends. Although Regan laments that her grandmother never wrote her recipes down, the proprietor of Gryphon D'Or has managed to create near-perfect shortbread—and scones. Both figure in her proper afternoon tea, along with Welsh pancakes with cream cheese and smoked salmon, chopped egg and fresh cucumber sandwiches (with the crusts removed from the bread, of course), and cakes and tea breads. Regan also serves comfort food lunches of soups, chili, Guinness stew, quiches, meat tourtières, and very popular salmon pattie cakes. For Christmas she makes her own mincemeat and plum puddings and decorates the shop with a gingerbread village. (See recipe on p. 36.)

Le Maistre Restaurant-Bistro, 5700 avenue Monkland; (514) 481-2109. Metro: Villa-Maria. The cozy dining room in an old house-turned-restaurant is the perfect setting to enjoy traditional bistro fare, and it's a favorite of NDG locals on a budget. The menu keeps it simple with a choice of three starters (soup, salad, or whim of the chef) and three desserts, such as crème brûlée, chocolate mousse, or *nougat glacé* (a frozen meringue studded with fruit and nuts). In between, main courses might include osso buco and risotto, pork medallions with honey and mustard, grilled salmon, or a classic *steak-frites*.

Liverpool House, 2501 rue Notre-Dame ouest; (514) 313-6049; www.joebeef.ca. Metro: Lionel Groulx. Like the neighboring Joe Beef, this oyster bar-cum-casual market restaurant is the brainchild of partners David McMillan and Frédéric Morin. The menu on the chalkboard (it changes daily) includes many French market classics—no surprise given that Marché Atwater is only a block away—and some inventions of the staff, like lobster spaghetti. Pâtissière Jacinthe Turcotte wins big plaudits for her French pastry desserts, but the biggest attraction is the bustling bar scene. Gin and tonic, anyone?

Scottish Shortbread

Peggy Regan of Le Gryphon D'Or has exactly the perfect touch for shortbread, a treat she learned from her Scottish grandmother. The recipe is deceptively simple, as the tenderness of the final result depends on rolling out the dough until it just barely coheres. Regan says, "Traditionalists, my grandmother being one of them, insisted on waiting at least a month for the shortbread to 'ripen' before tasting it. If the shortbread has been well-baked, it has a good long shelf life and a month's wait is worth it." (Further proof of the stereotype of Scots as self-denying Calvinists.) Regan uses Imperial measurements (as opposed to metric) because "after all, this is a very English treat!"

Makes 3 dozen, 1" x 2" x ½" shortbreads

½ pound butter, room temperature but not warm

¼ pound sugar (fruit sugar is wonderful but regular, refined white sugar will do)

½ pound all-purpose white flour (up to 2 tablespoons flour can be replaced with rice flour for more delicate shortbread)

¼ pound additional white flour

Using a large stand mixer, use the paddle attachment to blend sugar and butter, but switch to the dough hook once that first combination is well mixed. (Or, with a hand mixer, blend sugar and butter before switching to a heavy wooden spoon.)

Add first ½ lb. of flour gradually with mixer running. Add remaining ¼ lb. of flour by hand kneading. It will warm the butter slightly and help to incorporate the flour into the butter. Dough should be satisfyingly plump and break a bit when rolled over on itself in the kneading action. Unlike classic pie pastry, shortbread is very forgiving and cannot be over-kneaded.

Preheat oven to 325°F.

Roll dough out to your favored thickness and cut into favorite shapes. Fingers are best at about ½-inch thickness, petticoat tail rounds are good at about ¼-inch, and small medallions or Christmas shapes can be a bit thinner. (A petticoat tail is made by pressing into a round pan and scoring pie-like slices.)

Place on baking sheet and bake until just beginning to brown at the edges (20–30 minutes). Check frequently after 15 minutes.

Regan does many variations on her basic dough, including some savory short-breads. Here are two of the sweet variants:

Almond shortbread: Add a few drops of almond extract to sugar and butter. Press a whole blanched almond into the top of each shortbread before baking.

Maple shortbread: In Quebec, Scottish settlers would extend their limited supplies of beet sugar with local maple sugar—a mix that didn't work with everything but was fine with shortbread. Regan mixes equal parts maple sugar and white sugar and puts a teaspoon of maple flavoring into the sugar mix before combining with the butter.

Recipe courtesy of Le Gryphon D'Or (p. 34).

McKiernan, 2485 rue Notre-Dame ouest; (514) 759-6677; www .joebeef.ca. Metro: Lionel Groulx. This 12-seat luncheonette annex of Joe Beef serves weekday lunch and weekend brunches, with lines literally out the door for the breakfast seafood platter, pancakes with sausages and eggs, lobster scones, and shrimp tacos. On weekend evenings, it functions as the bar for Joe Beef. One secret weapon for the kitchen is the tiny organic garden out back.

Monkland Taverne, 5555 avenue Monkland; (514) 486-5768; www.monklandtaverne.com. Metro: Villa-Maria. Whether you like Monkland Taverne or not depends a lot on how much you enjoy a good martini, how much you enjoy being seen in the company of the young and well-heeled, and how much tolerance you have for a no-reservations policy that means you'll be two martinis in before you get to sit down. That said, the cachet has yet to fade after more than a decade as NDG's top people-watching place, and the pasta-centric, largely Italian menu emphasizes good, fresh ingredients. The kitchen will whip up real vegetarian meals (beet risotto, for example) on request, but the best dishes are for carnivores: braised lamb shank, hanger steak, or ziti with meatballs.

Pub Burgundy Lion, 2496 rue Notre-Dame ouest; (514) 934-0888; www.burgundylion.com. Metro: Lionel Groulx. The proprietors of this Little Burgundy establishment aim to meld the laid-back feel of a traditional British pub with a chic sense of Montreal style. The menu does feature such great British pub standards as bangers and mash, shepherd's pie, and fish-and-chips, but the kitchen aims higher than a corner local in London with chicken tikka masala, a fish-lover's take on shepherd's pie, and even crustless cucumber and tuna sandwiches at tea time. In addition to more than fifty brands of whisky by the glass, bartenders can pull a dozen ales or hard ciders on tap, including a few that the pub brews itself. The place is a madhouse when British football is on the telly, and it doesn't fare so badly either when the Habs of the Canadian Football League are playing.

Quoi de N'Oeuf, 2745 rue Notre-Dame ouest; (514) 931-3999. Metro: Lionel Groulx. The most original dishes at this popular Little Burgundy breakfast spot near **Marché Atwater** (p. 40) are the "breakfast skillets," which come to the table piping hot. Combinations such as bacon and ham; smoked salmon, capers, and spinach; or Italian sausage, home fries, asparagus and peppers are sauteed in the pan and topped with scambled eggs. The dishes are so filling, you'll probably want to skip lunch. Other options include waffles, French toast, several variations of eggs Benedict, and excellent crepes. Wait staff keep the coffee refills coming and encourage customers to linger.

Restaurant Ambiance, 1874 rue Notre-Dame ouest; (514) 939-2609; www.restaurantambiance.ca. Metro: Georges Vanier. Ensconced in a neighborhood full of antiques shops, Ambiance went with the flow, coining itself a "bistrot antique," and filling the dining room with old wooden tables and chairs and vintage culinary gadgets and mirrors. There's nothing antique about the food, though, as the market-driven menu focuses on simple preparations of fresh vegetables, a fish and meat of the day, and homemade ice cream and sorbet for dessert. The French market bistro style always includes a number of organ meats, including sweetbreads, kidneys, and (often) brains.

St-Viateur Bagel, 5629 avenue Monkland; (514) 487-8051; www .stviateurbagel.com. Metro: Villa-Maria. Bagels are still the heart of this operation born at **Mile End** (see p. 156), but this NDG branch does a booming business in bagel sandwiches, salads, burgers, and beer—especially on the outdoor terrace on summer afternoons.

Landmarks

Marché Atwater, 138 avenue Atwater; (514) 937-7754; www .marchespublics-mtl.com. Metro: Lionel Groulx. When this public market opened in 1933, it sat in the center of a close-knit working class neighborhood. As the area has grown increasingly gentrified, the market has morphed into a gourmet destination with its own sushi shop and pizzeria, along with outlets of **Fromagerie Hamel** (see p. 131), **Première Moisson** (see p. 47), and **Chocolats Geneviève Grandbois** (see p. 160). One of our best friends (who introduced us to many of the delights of Montreal dining) lives nearby and we never miss a chance to accompany him on a shopping and eating excursion.

Covered stalls outside the market building feature fruits and vegetables, but unlike traditional farmers' markets, some of the vendors purchase the produce from distributors rather than growing it themselves. Among the actual growers, **Gilbert Jodoin and Louise Marc-Aurèle** sell the fruits and vegetables harvested from their Rougemont farm, along with cranberries and a few other products from other Quebec farms. They also make their own maple

MUSIC OF THE SPHERE

A busy roadway and shopping strip cannot eclipse the classic roadside architecture of **Restaurant Orange Julep Gibeau,** 7700 boulevard Decarie; (514) 738-7486; Metro: Namur. The original two-story-high orange sphere was built in 1945 to dispense the Gibeau family's secret-recipe orange drink. The building was enlarged to three stories in the 1960s and the recipe remains as secret as ever. The frothy drink (similar to Orange Julius) is made daily with fresh oranges and has a slight acidity to cut the sweetness. It's perhaps best with a scoop of vanilla ice cream, but is also a fine accompaniment to such fast-food classics as hot dogs, hamburgers, and grilled-cheese sandwiches. There's only one picnic table for sitting inside and a few more outside in the big parking lot, where classic rock blasts from speakers. Best time to visit is on a Wednesday night between May and October when classic cars converge on the "Big Orange." Limited winter hours.

syrup. Another farm, **Aux Vergers Serge Bourcier,** transforms much of its produce into jams, jellies, and pickled vegetables, including a delicious confit of onions in maple syrup. Inside the market, **Fruiterie Atwater** always has an amazing display of fresh mushrooms, while **Au Paradis du Fromage** (one of the market's three cheese shops) also stocks St-Viateur bagels (see p. 40).

The market's nine butcher shops include an outlet of sausage impresario **William J. Walter** (see p. 140) and **Adelard Belanger,** favored by some of Montreal's top chefs. The shop is particularly known for its *foie gras*. For home chefs, **Les Deux Frères** has a great selection of *tourtières,* including red deer, lamb, duck, or turkey and mushrooms. It's impossible not to work up an appetite in this temple of food—and the best simple snack to still that hunger is a grilled peanut butter sandwich and a bowl of *café au lait* from the coffee roaster **Aux Quatre Vents.**

Snowdon Deli, 5265 boulevard Décarie; (514) 488-9129; www .delisnowdon.ca. Metro: Snowdon. Such a place! Located at the edge of Côte-des-Neiges and NDG in what was largely an Anglophone neighborhood until the Décarie Expressway was built in the 1960s, Snowdon Deli is the home of Jewish soul food in the outer arrondissements. Not that it's kosher, mind you, since the grill does make a pretty credible cheeseburger. But this is the place to come for chicken soup with a matzoh ball, borscht with a ladle of sour cream on top, or a not-too-spicy tongue sandwich (choice of tip or center). Dessert should be potato knishes with sour cream and apple slices. To drink? Bubbie, you have to ask? Diet black cherry soda, of course.

Specialty Stores, Markets & Producers

Appetite for Books, 388 avenue Victoria; (514) 369-2002; www .appetitebooks.ca. Metro: Vendôme. Stop in at Christmastime and staff will be handing out cookies baked in the demonstration kitchen at the back of the store. Actually, the kitchen is busy all year with classes as well as demonstrations by visiting chefs and authors. The extensive cookbook selection features titles in both French and English and the knowledgeable and very friendly clerks are equally adept at recommending a book or a good restaurant for lunch.

Boulangerie Le Fournil, 364 avenue Victoria; (514) 485-6647. Metro: Vendôme. The three sisters who operate this tiny bakery were inspired by the recipes of their Jewish grandmother and their shop has become known for its challah. From the kitchen in the back, they turn out a wide variety of breads, cakes, cookies (almond is the best-seller), pies (including a very popular lemon version), quiches, and *tourtières* using all-organic flour. At Easter, their hot-cross buns sell like, well, hotcakes. A few choices of soups and sandwiches make a nourishing take-away lunch.

Cha Guan, La Maison du Thé, 5756 avenue Monkland; (514) 303-8238; www.chaguan.ca. Metro: Villa-Maria. Even in an espresso-loving city like Montreal, tea is making inroads and this lovely little shop offers something different. "It's important to us to share the Chinese tea culture," says Daniel Ng, whose family started the business in 2007. "It's the tea we know." Family members visit China several times a year to taste and select teas and tea sets, including delicate glass teapots that make it easier to tell when the tea is properly brewed. The shop carries more than 90 black, green, white, and red teas. Pride of place goes to puerh, an artisanal black tea that is sold by brick. "It was the first tea that existed and it's the most widely drunk in China," says Ng. "It ages like wine and is good for digestion and for circulation." To sample teas in the shop, customers can sit at tables and chairs or on pillows around a low table in the front window. "We want everyone to be comfortable," says Ng.

Cuisine Gourmet Monkland, 5683 avenue Monkland; (514) 564-3424. Metro: Villa-Maria. Most Montreal kitchenware shops seem to favor French-made Opinel knives, but this shop opts for the Laguiole brand for its upscale picnic and steak knives. In fact, there's a good knife selection overall along with sharpeners and bamboo cutting boards to go with them. Amid all the serious cookware and tableware, Cuisine Gourmet carries a whimsical line of breakfast gadgets with egg-themed handles—toast tongs, egg and pancake pans, spatulas, whisks, boiling spoons—that make clever gifts.

La Foumagerie, 4906 rue Sherbrooke ouest; (514) 482-4100; www.lafoumagerie.qc.ca. Metro: Vendôme. The slightly crazed cheese shop (the name combines French words for "fool" and "cheesemonger") also sells sandwiches organized by cheese theme. Thus the "Stilton" group includes a roast beef-Stilton-celery remoulade sandwich as well as a turkey-Stilton-cucumber-pickle sandwich. The shop also sells several exotic olive oils, three kinds of caviar, and a bunch of artisanal vinegars.

La Fromagerie Atwater, 134 rue Atwater; (514) 932-4653; www.fromagerieatwater.ca. Metro: Lionel Groulx. Many Quebec cheese aficionados are convinced that their local cheeses can hold their own against the best in the world—and this Marché Atwater shop is just the place to put that contention to the test. Among the 850 cheeses stocked by owner Gilles Jourdenias are about 175 from Quebec makers. Of the 400 or so Quebec cheeses, Jourdenias estimates that about half are very good. "We don't decide what to carry," he says, "the customers decide." But Jourdenias and his clerks are quick to make suggestions, and they seem to know every cheesemaker in the province personally. Perhaps because good Quebec cheddars are readily available even in supermarkets, Fromagerie Atwater tends to give extra shelf space to the soft cheeses of the region. Ask for advice on how best to store—and when to consume—these little miracles of milk.

Le Bilboquet Westmount, 4864 rue Sherbrooke ouest; (514) 369-1118. Metro: Vendôme. Just so the Westmount folk don't have

to make the trek to the Outremont base (see p. 157) of this artisanal ice-cream maker, this outlet has all the wonderful inventive
flavors.

Le Cafe-Crème, 357 avenue Victoria; (514) 484-3105. Metro:
Vendôme. Bialetti, Bugatti, Carimali, Gaggia, Pavoni, Mokita,
Moretti—the names alone are music to the ears of espresso lovers.
This is the place to come to marvel over the dials and styles of
Italian coffee makers—and to pick up the store's signature brand
of coffee beans. The machines tend to be expensive, but at $2 to
$3 per sip for coffee-shop espresso, they would pay for themselves
in no time. (At least that's our justification . . .)

Miyamoto Foods, 382 avenue Victoria; (514) 481-1952. Metro:
Vendôme. In some ways the center of the small Japanese-Canadian
community in Montreal, Miyamoto has been a Westmount fixture
since moving from the Plateau in 1981. It is the most dependable
spot in the city to find specialty Japanese foods, kitchen equipment, and cookbooks (in English, French, and Japanese). The store
sells its own sushi and also offers weekend classes in making sushi
and infrequent multi-session classes in Japanese cuisine.

Nicholas Hoare Books, 1366 avenue Greene; (514) 933-4201;
www.nicholashoare.com. Metro: Atwater. Elegant wooden shelves
and furniture give this multilevel shop a clubby feel that seems
only fitting for the primarily British inventory. Books about food
and spirits fill an entire wall and cover the cuisines of the world.

Titles of local interest include guides to Quebec cheese, a history of beer in Canada, and even a history of **Schwartz's** (see p. 126). If you're worried about the number of *frites* or *macarons* you have been consuming, check out the titles about why French women stay slim and hope that the principles apply to dining in the world's second largest French-speaking city as well.

Pâtisserie de Gascogne, 4825 rue Sherbrooke ouest; (514) 932-3511; www.degascogne.com. Metro: Vendôme. French-style pastry and good ready-to-heat meals are the attraction of this Westmount branch of the Mile End institution (see p. 168).

Première Moisson, 5500 avenue Monkland; (514) 484-5500; www.premieremoisson.com. Metro: Villa-Maria. The NDG outlet of the city's leading bakery chain (see p. 71) has more seating than most, so it emphasizes individual sandwiches and pastries over take-away breads and whole cakes.

Wilfrid & Adrienne, 4919b rue Sherbrooke ouest; (514) 481-5850. Metro: Vendôme. Fancy window displays are a hallmark of this shop that stocks a wide selection of elegant cookware, porcelain, and delicate glass decanters. To liven things up, they also carry flamboyant hand-painted Italian pottery featuring fish, chicken, sheep, pigs, and other barnyard creatures. Quirky utensils include goggles to wear while chopping onions. There's also a select line of products from Fauchon gourmet store in Paris.

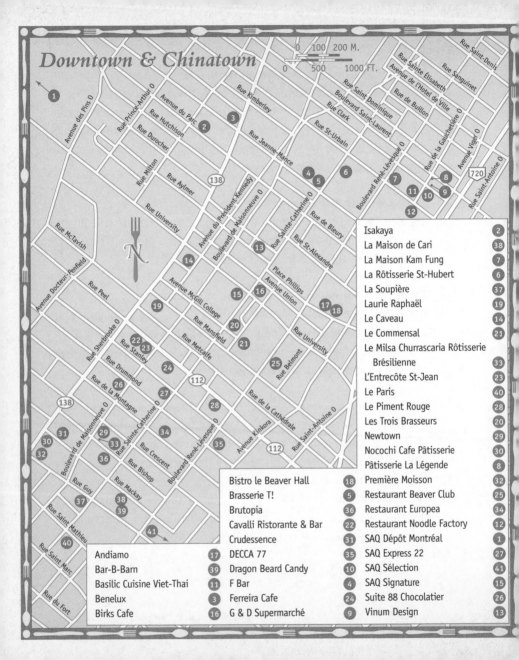

Downtown & Chinatown

0	100	200 M.
0	500	1000 FT.

Isakaya — 2
La Maison de Cari — 38
La Maison Kam Fung — 7
La Rôtisserie St-Hubert — 6
La Soupière — 37
Laurie Raphaël — 19
Le Caveau — 14
Le Commensal — 21
Le Milsa Churrascaria Rôtisserie Brésilienne — 33
L'Entrecôte St-Jean — 23
Le Paris — 40
Le Piment Rouge — 28
Les Trois Brasseurs — 20
Newtown — 29
Nocochi Cafe Pâtisserie — 30
Pâtisserie La Légende — 8
Première Moisson — 32
Restaurant Beaver Club — 25
Restaurant Europea — 34
Restaurant Noodle Factory — 12
SAQ Dépôt Montréal — 1
SAQ Express 22 — 35
SAQ Sélection — 10
SAQ Signature — 4
Suite 88 Chocolatier — 26
Vinum Design — 9

Bistro le Beaver Hall — 18
Brasserie T! — 5
Brutopia — 36
Cavalli Ristorante & Bar — 22
Crudessence — 31
DECCA 77 — 39
Dragon Beard Candy — 11
F Bar — 3
Ferreira Cafe — 3
G & D Supermarché — 16

Andiamo — 17
Bar-B-Barn — 39
Basilic Cuisine Viet-Thai — 11
Benelux — 3
Birks Cafe — 16

Downtown & Chinatown

Montreal's downtown is the city's main business district—full of banks and office buildings along with the large department stores, the hockey arena, and vast subterranean parking garages. Speaking of "subterranean," it is also the home of the Underground. Starting in the 1960s, a vast network of corridors and retail spaces has developed under the streets, allowing shoppers and commuters to escape the Montreal weather and walk between Metro stations. The anthill even extends down to the so-called International District at the edge of Old Montreal. The Underground does not let shoppers starve. Food courts are strategically placed, with the best ones located beneath Simons department store and Les Promenades de la Cathédrale, both with above-ground entries on rue Sainte-Catherine. They offer a surprising range of mostly ethnic fast foods at reasonable prices.

A few of Montreal's finest restaurants are found downtown, and many of them offer extraordinarily good deals on sit-down lunches for business clientele. There are also a lot of cafes and take-out shops serving the less well-heeled workers. Unlike many North American cities, Montreal's downtown does not empty out at the end of the workday. The presence of Concordia and McGill universities ensures a substantial population of students, and the downtown hotels provide an unending stream of visitors. Brewpubs and other casual, convivial eateries thrive in the *arrondissement,* serving students and visitors alike.

Much of the downtown belongs to the historically English-speaking part of the city, a distinction that becomes more meaningless every year. But it is reflected in street names like Peel, Bishop, Mackay, Stanley, and Guy—a ladder of streets linking Francophone rue Sainte-Catherine to Anglophone rue Sherbrooke, where the English-speaking elite once shopped for furs, fine art, and Cuban cigars. Many of these streets with English names contain vestiges of their British heritage in the pubs that evoke the old sod.

Located between the east end of downtown and Old Montreal, the small Chinatown is a remnant of the days when Chinese laborers built the Canadian railroads (then headquartered in Montreal). Chinatown now reflects the immigration from Southeast Asia. Certain Chinese institutions survive, but even the grocery stores show a distinctively more Cambodian, Thai, and Vietnamese cast in their goods. The central drag of Chinatown, rue de la Gauchetière, is pedestrian-only, making it easy to study the faux food displays in restaurant windows and the piles of exotic produce in front of the grocers.

Andiamo, 1083 Côte du Beaver Hall; (514) 861-2634; www .andiamo.ca. Metro: McGill. Part of the Jérôme Ferrer empire (see **Restaurant Europea** on p. 63), this dining room with blue-and-white checked tablecloths spotlights Ferrer's Mediterranean bent with plates that recall the sunny Greek isles, the lush seaside promontories of Italy, and the Catalan coast. It's lusty cooking—dishes like grilled veal flank steak accompanied by shallots stewed with spicy chorizo, or deep-fried calamari with a crust of Parmesan and poppy seeds. The wine list is a similar tour of the Mediterranean basin, though stronger in Spain and Italy than France. You want French? Go next door to Ferrer's **Bistro Le Beaver Hall** (see p. 53). Weekday lunch is the busy time at Andiamo.

Bar-B-Barn, 1201 rue Guy; (514) 931-3811; www.barbbarn.ca. Metro: Guy-Concordia. The menu here is so simple that it all fits on the yellow paper place mats set before each diner. "We do ribs and chicken," the waitress tells newcomers after they have studied the photos of hockey stars at the door and entered the faux-rustic dining room with dark wood walls. In fact, Bar-B-Barn has been serving ribs and chicken slathered with a sweet, tangy sauce for more than 40 years and sees no reason to

alter a winning format. Add fries, onion rings, or coleslaw but be sure to save room for a slice of homemade apple pie.

Basilic Cuisine Viet-Thai, 83 rue de la Gauchetière ouest; (514) 875-1388; www.basilic.ca. Metro: Place d'Armes. Ostensibly a pan-Asian restaurant in Chinatown, Basilic's strengths are Southeast Asian. It's one of the better spots to get a bowl of Tonkinese pho soup full of crunchy bean sprouts and heaven-scented with Thai basil. The pad Thai is also good, and available in beef, chicken, and vegetarian versions. House specialty beverages include a durian smoothie (definitely an acquired taste) and taro, mango, or coconut bubble teas.

Benelux, 245 rue Sherbrooke ouest; (514) 543-9750; www.brasserie benelux.com. Metro: Place des Arts. While most Montreal brewpubs are essentially English-style locals with a copper brew kettle set off to the side, Benelux is the microbrewery analog of a nightclub. Set inside the ground-level corner of a Neo-Brutalist apartment building (probably not Montreal's finest era of architecture), the owners go with the flow of the structure to create a post-modern beer hall. Ceilings stretch three stories high, duct work is exposed, and the decor (such as it is) is hard-core industrial chic, including some decorative abstract neon. Food choices are minimal—panini, *frites*, and other bar fare—but the ales brewed on premises have real character. As the name suggests, Belgian-style beers are among the specialties (fruit beers fare well with the students from nearby UQÀM), but Benelux also brews an excellent blonde (Lux), a crisply sharp American ale (Yakima), and a Vancouver-style IPA (Cuda) that some drinkers rank among Canada's best of the breed.

Birks Cafe, 1240 place Phillips; (514) 397-2468; www.birkscafe .ca. Metro: McGill. This jewel box of a cafe sits attentively on the mezzanine of Montreal's most exclusive jewelry store. Yet another corner of the **Europea** empire (see p. 63), the cafe gleans some straightforward dishes from Europea's menu (ricotta-stuffed pasta with wild mushroom sauce, for example) for its daily *table d'hôte* luncheon. Sweets served at Europea as a prelude to the dessert course are the perfect bite here after lunch. Weekend brunch is a social affair—reserve far ahead, or plan instead on a proper after- noon tea. Food and service alike are simply perfect, and the bill is fair, given the quality. Whenever we eat here we hope to catch a marriage pro- posal at a neighboring table. The happy couple could then go downstairs to select a ring.

Bistro le Beaver Hall, 1073 Côte du Beaver Hall; (514) 866-1331; www.beaverhall.ca. Metro: McGill. Jérôme Ferrer (see **Restaurant Europea,** p. 63) does French bistro fare as well as he does haute cuisine. This spot is simply jammed every day at lunch with busi- nesspeople who know one of the best bargains in town, with simple dishes like calf's liver with pepper sauce, wild mushroom canelloni with ricotta, or cassoulet with a confit duck leg. In the evening, more glasses and tableware appear on the white linens, the menu expands slightly, and the dessert list (flaming *crèpes Suzette* included) gets much longer. If you're smart, you'll order the sublime and ethereal macarons, a specialty made at Europea.

Brasserie T!, 1425 rue Jeanne-Mance; (514) 282-0808. Metro: Place des Arts. Superchef Normand Laprise of **Toqué!** (see p. 18) is known for his extravagant presentations and always surprising food, constantly pulling rabbits (or *foie gras*) out of his toque. For everyone who ever wondered what his food would be like if he kept it simple, Brasserie T! is the answer, with dishes like steak and salmon tartares, a *hamburger-frites* to die for, butternut-squash bisque, or seared scallops. Prices, too, are much lower than at Toqué!, as befits a casual but chic eatery on the plaza of Place des Arts. Wine choices are excellent and don't break the bank.

Brutopia, 1219 rue Crescent; (514) 393-9277; www.brutopia.net. Metro: Peel/Lucien L'Allier. Opened in 1997, Brutopia was exactly the right idea at the right place at the right time. A pioneer among brewpubs in Montreal, its three-story interior and three outdoor terraces entice the thirsty travelers holed up in the hotels so close that you could scale a beer coaster out the window and hit a doorman. Happy hour is all day and night on Monday, and from opening until 8 p.m. the rest of the week. With eight house brews on tap (five classics and three seasonal), there is never a shortage of choices; the Nut Brown ale with its complex hops is the best. Food choices are broad and tend more toward sandwiches and quesadillas than finger-food munchies.

Cavalli Ristorante & Bar, 2040 rue Peel; (514) 843-5100; www.ristorantecavalli.com. Metro: Peel. This elegant restaurant owes its *Milano puro* look to the Paris-Brussels design whiz Miguel Cáncio Martins, and we'd say they got their money's worth. This designer Italian restaurant is a haunt of the rich and the beautiful. The official dress code is "casual" but anyone who believes that will feel woefully out of place being served by the silk-sheathed waitresses and bowtie-wearing barmen. The glam factor makes Cavalli's bar a hot nightlife spot, but it's also worth visiting to dine. The menu is a creative modern take on northern Italian tradition—mushroom-spelt risotto and grilled artichokes with pine-nut-crusted filet mignon; grilled halibut with Israeli couscous; or linguine tossed with seared tuna, fire-roasted eggplant, and San Marzano tomatoes. The wine list is full of show-off bottles—a double magnum of 1992 Cristal is $5,000—but some good Barbarescos and super-Tuscans are much more affordable. The main grappas at the bar are Jacapo Poli's excellent firewaters from the heart of the Veneto.

Crudessence, 2157 rue Mackay; (514) 664-5188; www.crudessence.com. Metro: Guy-Concordia. We realize that it's hard to imagine what could be on the menu at a restaurant that is not just organic, but also vegan, gluten-free, and refuses to cook its food. But you'd be surprised what you can do making "spaghetti" noodles from threads of zucchini or crepes from pressed Brazil nuts, chia, and flaxseed. Diners with even more restricted diets can ask to be steered to the nut-free offerings.

DECCA 77, 1077 rue Drummond; (514) 934-1077; www.decca77.com. Metro: Bonaventure. Smart and sleek, this contemporary market restaurant across a plaza from the Bell Centre hockey arena is both a perfect place to get a prix-fixe meal before the puck drops or to drop by for a more serious dinner. Take time to savor the hamachi tuna poached in olive oil with corn, pepper, and braised bacon, or a roasted guinea hen with a root vegetable stew. Executive chef Daren Bergeron mixes it up at the slightest provocation—for example, featuring Ontario foodstuffs when the Maple Leafs come to town to play the Canadiens.

F Bar, 1485 rue Jeanne-Mance; (514) 289-4558; www.fbar.ca. Metro: Place des Arts. In case you hadn't guessed, the blue-and-white *azulejo* tiles should signal that this incredibly popular, almost diner-narrow resto-bar on Place des Arts is the little sister of **Ferreira Cafe** (see p. 57). It may be even better attuned to Montreal dining tastes, emphasizing comfort food like a salmon burger, grilled sardines, braised pork served with anise-scented clams, or, in summer, a chilled green pea and mint soup. Literally dozens of wines are available by the glass, making F Bar a great stop at lunch or a perfect place to get a bite before a concert on the plaza.

Ferreira Cafe, 1446 rue Peel; (514) 848-0988; www.ferreiracafe .com. Metro: Peel. Thanks to generations of immigrants, Portuguese cuisine has a higher profile (and more respect) in Montreal than almost anywhere in North America. This busy, busy restaurant is the city's top Portuguese venue—maybe one of Canada's best. Diners compare the porcini-crusted roasted black cod (actually, sablefish) with a port reduction and mashed potatoes to Japanese chef Nobu Matsuhisa's signature version with miso. Executive chef Marino Tavares cooks with bold strokes, kicking *cataplana* up a notch to make it a veritable *bouillabaisse,* and taking the mixed grill to new heights by marinating and skewering filet mignon, quail, and *chouriço* and serving them on the same plate. The Ferreira family does its own private importing of Portuguese wines and the cellar represents a nearly comprehensive collection of the best from the Douro, Dão, Alentejo, and Beiras regions.

Isakaya, 3469 avenue du Parc; (514) 845-8226; www.bistroisakaya .com. Metro: Place des Arts. Being located in the ghetto of cheap hotels that time forgot doesn't exactly add to the ambience of Isakaya, but once you're seated in the cheery dining room, you'll focus on the clean, straightforward flavors of the mostly seafood menu and forget the ugliness outside. It's one of the most reliable places in Montreal for excellent sushi and sashimi (artfully cut, we might add), and the bistro approach to traditional Japanese food works surprisingly well. Tokyo's answer to sole in lemon butter, for example, is grilled sea bass with lemon miso. The luncheon specials, including some featuring maki rolls, are an especially good value.

La Maison de Cari, 1236 rue Mackay; (514) 845-0326. Metro: Guy-Concordia/Lucien L'Allier. This Indian restaurant has been in business in Montreal through half a dozen locations over the last quarter century, but regulars follow it loyally for probably the best curries in the city. The current second-floor townhouse incarnation on Mackay can be tricky to find, but it's worth hiking up the stairs for the mild lamb curry or the buttered chicken with candied papaya—a surprising but excellent dish.

La Maison Kam Fung, 1111 rue Saint-Urbain; (514) 878-2888; www.maisonkamfung.com. Metro: Place d'Armes. Located on the second level of a small commercial center, La Maison Kam Fung can be difficult to locate: Just look for the big red neon sign in the window. It's a local favorite for dim sum, which is served from 7 a.m. to 3 p.m. Regulars suggest taking a table near the kitchen to have first choice as the carts roll out carrying shrimp and snow-pea dumplings, steamed barbecue pork buns, steamed spare ribs, vegetarian spring rolls, and other tiny treats. For dessert, don't miss the sesame balls with red bean paste.

La Rôtisserie St-Hubert, 100 rue Sainte-Catherine ouest; (514) 284-3440; www.st-hubert.com. Metro: Place des Arts. It's probably just our American myopia, but we've always thought of the St-Hubert mascot as looking an awful lot like the roadrunner that Wile E. Coyote could never quite catch. Founded in 1951, the St-Hubert group now numbers more than 100 chicken-centric restaurants in eastern Canada and serves 13.4 million pounds of *frites* a year, not to mention 23 million pounds of *poulet*. This location at Place des Arts is not the original, but it's one of the most stylish, as it has a full bar, nice dining rooms, and a pretty comprehensive menu. But when you get right down to it, the St-Hubert experience is about roast chicken, fries, and gravy. It's not so much fast food as medium-fast food, and they do it well.

Laurie Raphaël, 2050 rue Mansfield; (514) 849-1437; www.laurieraphael.com. Metro: Peel. Chef Daniel Vézina was the main reason many Montreal foodies used to visit Quebec City, but with the opening of a branch of Laurie Raphaël in the boutique design hotel Le Germain, they have to go no further than rue Mansfield. Back in the '90s, Vézina was Quebec's *enfant terrible* of experimental cuisine, but he has since trimmed his sails to celebrate the gastronomic riches of the province and subordinate his technical mastery of foams, sous-vide cookery, and other kitchen chemistry to the greater good of fabulous flavors. Cynthia Moreau serves as chef de cuisine, faithfully replicating Vézina's concepts. But the food still makes you stop and think as you eat. His grilled fillet of beef, for example, comes with a deconstructed béarnaise (*beurre blanc* with a soft-poached egg), and he makes a cucumber-agar colloid (i.e., jelly) to accompany salmon tartare. It's a joy to dine on food with wit and finesse.

Le Commensal, 1204 rue McGill College; (514) 871-1480; www .commensal.com. Metro: McGill. Are vegetarians more polite? The buffet lines for salads, hot dishes, and desserts are always smooth and orderly at this stalwart of vegetarian cuisine. With seasonings from China, the Mediterranean, and even the US southwest, the dishes are full of flavor—and are priced by weight, so make sure that your eyes aren't bigger than your stomach. Desserts, by the way, carry a slightly heftier price per gram.

Le Milsa Churrascaria Rôtisserie Brésilienne, 1445 rue Bishop; (514) 844-4550. Metro: Guy-Concordia. This giant (230-seat) emporium offers both the grill from Brazil and, on many nights, the scantily clad girls from Ipanema gyrating like it was Carnival all year around. Le Milsa is an all-you-can-eat churrascaria, which means that the servers circulate through the room with sword-like skewers of sausage, chicken, lamb kebabs, roast pork, filet mignon, rib-eye, and even pieces of turkey wrapped in bacon. These meat-laden rapiers come hot off the charcoal grills, so the meat is literally sizzling as it's sliced onto your plate. The food may not always represent the tenderest cuts, but the price is right and if you don't fill up on salads or the fresh pineapple for dessert, you can certainly get your money's worth. Le Milsa welcomes groups— you shouldn't have much trouble spotting the bachelor parties or the tables of hungry field reps visiting the home office. A lot of the regulars are men who shop for clothes in the "husky" section.

L'Entrecôte St-Jean, 2022 rue Peel; (514) 281-6492; www .lentrecotestjean.com. Metro: Peel. Diners only have to make one choice at L'Entrecôte St-Jean: whether to have a salad or soup as a first course before tucking into a strip loin steak served with a secret-recipe cream sauce and french fries. For dessert? Profiteroles with hot chocolate sauce. It may be somewhat of a tourist trap, but L'Entrecôte offers a good value meal in a classic bistro setting with mirrors on the walls to reflect the light and comfy deep red banquettes where diners can settle in for a relaxing meal.

Le Paris, 1812 rue Sainte-Catherine ouest; (514) 937-4898. Metro: Guy-Concordia. Every time we go into Le Paris, we can imagine Maurice Chevalier singing his 1939 hit, "Paris sera toujours Paris." This bistro has been a fixture on the west end of downtown since 1956, and it's fair to say that the menu is the very model of casual bourgeois cuisine, with dishes like *boeuf bourgignon,* pork steak in tarragon sauce, a confit duck leg with all the traditional garniture. Maybe the only change is that the kitchen has started using walleye (northern pike) instead of flounder for its version of sole *meunière.* The dishes are all à la carte, but you can add soup and dessert for just a few dollars more. That was a deal even in 1956.

Le Piment Rouge, 1170 rue Peel; (514) 866-7816; www.piment rouge.ca. Metro: Peel/Bonaventure. Located in the surviving wing of the architecturally distinct former Windsor Hotel, Le Piment Rouge is the epitome of an elegant, formal Chinese restaurant. The storied history of the restaurant includes hosting film stars, heads of state, athletes, and other celebrities, but this soaring two-level establishment does not need to rest on past laurels. While the menu nods to the regional cuisines of many areas of China, it is basically a two-cuisine combination of spicy, strong-flavored Szechuan and more subtle Cantonese. Some of the 100-plus dishes on the menu are perennial favorites, like the shredded beef tenderloin with fresh mango or the Hunan dumplings with peanut-sesame sauce. The presentation is as elaborate as the room—gleaming white plates on white tablecloths. The restaurant has an unusually good wine cellar, and counts itself a pioneer in pairing wines with Chinese food.

Les Trois Brasseurs, 732 rue Sainte-Catherine ouest; (514) 788-6333 (Metro: McGill) and 1356 Sainte-Catherine ouest; (514) 788-9788 (Metro: Guy-Concordia/Lucien L'Allier); www.les3brasseurs .ca. Born in France, this mini-chain of brewpubs has flourished in Montreal. The two rue Sainte-Catherine locations are the largest, but they stay true to their roots by brewing white, blonde, amber, and brown ales on premises. (There's usually a seasonal brew as well.) The food is beer-friendly and more North American than French—lots of burgers and brochettes, and thin-crust pizza masquerading as Alsatian *flammekueche*.

But food and drink are both well-made, and Les Trois Brasseurs make a good beer-lover's alternative to Rôtisserie St-Hubert.

Newtown, 1476 rue Crescent; (514) 282-6555; www.lenewtown .com. Metro: Guy-Concordia/Lucien L'Allier. Best known as a night-club and glam socializing spot, Newtown's kitchen got a new lease on life when Daniel Bergeron (also of **DECCA 77,** see p. 56) became executive chef. Both restaurants share a lot of dishes, but Newtown does them with a straighter face, making it a great place for couples to go out for a nice meal that satisfies both the foodie and the meat-and-potatoes diner. Plates like bison short rib with horseradish potatoes or grilled veal chop with polenta are great for hearty appetites. Since Bergeron and his fellow chefs are strict about following seafood sustainability guidelines, the fish side of the menu tends to be brief.

Restaurant Europea, 1227 de la Montagne; (514) 398-9229; www.europea.ca. Metro: Peel/Lucien L'Allier. Chef and co-owner Jérôme Ferrer is one of the great success stories of Montreal. The young French chef arrived in 2002 to open a restaurant and found himself penniless when his financial manager in France absconded with the funds. So he started small in a 35-seat space that had held a previous restaurant of questionable taste (if the faux snakeskin banquettes were any indication) and built an empire on sheer talent and determination. Eventually Europea expanded to take over the whole building, and the decor now exudes a contemporary sophisti-cation that matches Ferrer's food. The affordable way to experience

Macarons á l'Atelier Europea

Makes 5 dozen cookies (30 sandwiches)

Montrealers are as crazy for macarons as the Parisians, and the macarons from Restaurant Europea are considered among the city's best. The Atelier Europea offers classes in making them, and they fill almost immediately. This is the Atelier's recipe. We have kept the original metric weights for ingredients because, as with all meringue-based recipes, weighing ingredients gives more consistent results than measuring by volume.

300 grams almond flour	**90 grams water**
300 grams powdered sugar	**300 grams granulated sugar**
6 egg whites	

In a large bowl, combine almond flour and powdered sugar. Mix well. Add 3 egg whites and blend until thoroughly mixed to a smooth paste.

Add water to a non-reactive pot and stir in granulated sugar. Heat on low, stirring until sugar is well dissolved. Raise heat to high and monitor temperature with candy thermometer while preparing egg whites for meringue. Do not allow syrup to exceed 121°C (250°F).

Place 3 egg whites in a metal mixing bowl (ideally in a stand mixer) and whip to medium peaks—not soft, but not stiff.

When sugar syrup reaches a temperature of 121°C (250°F), remove pot from heat. With mixer running, slowly pour syrup down side of bowl into egg whites. Increase speed of mixer and whip until whites form very glossy high peaks. Set meringue aside to cool.

Once meringue is cooled to warm room temperature, stir about a third of the meringue into the almond-sugar paste to incorporate well. Gently fold in the rest of the meringue.

Using a pastry bag with a ⅜-inch round tip, deposit about a teaspoon of batter per cookie onto parchment-covered baking sheet. Space about 1 inch apart. When baking sheet is covered, tap on counter to make batter settle. (Cover remaining batter with plastic wrap before assembling the next tray.)

Let sit uncovered for 15–30 minutes to allow a light crust to form. This helps ensure the desired texture of creamy interior and crunchy outer shell.

Preheat oven to 180°C (350°F).

Bake for 6 to 7 minutes, rotating pan halfway through.

Let fully cool on parchment paper. Then remove and make sandwiches. Europea macarons are often filled with rich and complex sweets like caramel fleur de sel buttercream, raspberry buttercream, chocolate ganache, or lemon curd. But we have found that purchased lemon curd or raspberry jam—or fresh berries—is sure to impress our friends.

Recipe courtesy of Restaurant Europea (p. 63).

Europea is the nightly *table d'hôte* "Discovery Menu" of Ferrer's classics in four courses. But for complete immersion, choose the 10-course tasting menu for 50 percent more. It's likely to highlight a couple of fish dishes, a few meat dishes, his signature lobster cappuccino with shaved truffles, some treatment of *foie gras*, a pasta that inevitably has truffles in there somewhere, and a couple of desserts. It is truly a tasting of Ferrer's approach to cuisine. Europea is naturally a top choice for special occasions, and the wait for a reservation can be even longer than at any flavor-of-the-month new bistro. But it's worth planning ahead for an evening that is truly an event—from the impeccable service to the little extras, such as an *amuse-bouche* to get you in the right frame of mind, a little unannounced palate cleanser between courses, a "pre-dessert" before the real one arrives, and the *mignardises* (little sweets) that soften you up for the check. Ferrer is on record as saying restaurants should serve dishes that people can't make at home, but he does offer some limited cooking classes in the basement at Atelier Europea. (See recipe on p. 64.)

Restaurant Noodle Factory, 1018 rue Saint-Urbain; (514) 868-9738. Metro: Place d'Armes. If you are lucky, a chef will be standing behind the glass window making long, thin noodles by hand in this small, no-nonsense Chinatown eatery. They certainly go through a lot of them each day, either as the basis for a variety of filling soups (pork and vegetable, for example, or smoked fish) or stir-fried dishes with chicken, beef, pork or vegetables. Each dish is cooked to order in a big wok in the open kitchen and the combination of big portions, fast service, and low prices makes this a popular—and crowded—lunch spot.

Landmarks

Le Caveau, 2063 rue Victoria; (514) 844-1624; www.lecaveau.ca. Metro: McGill. This utterly splendid French restaurant believes that if a dish was good enough for Auguste Escoffier, the great chef who codified classic French cuisine, then it should be good enough for their diners. And it is. The 1901 Victorian house that became this three-level restaurant in 1949 is almost a fairy-tale venue in a forest of glass and concrete skyscrapers. Almost everyone who dines here, especially at lunchtime, is a regular and they all order off the bargain-priced menu (as opposed to à la carte). The choices barely change at dinner, except that the portions are larger and the prices slightly higher. That said, you can eat pork tenderloin with plum sauce, calf's liver with raspberries, veal kidneys in mustard sauce, pepper steak, or herb-encrusted rack of lamb at a beautiful table with real linens and impeccable service from long-time professional waiters for less than you might spend at a trendy bistro. Even the wine prices won't make you gasp. Le Caveau does stock some expensive trophy wines in its great cellar (that's what *caveau* means), but the regular list is rich with Bordeaux, Loire Valley, and even a few Burgundy bottles at prices that are a steal in Montreal. The house wines from the Pays d'Oc are bargain-priced but serviceable merlot and chardonnay. Did we mention that Le Caveau is authentically romantic?

Restaurant Beaver Club, Hotel Fairmont Queen Elizabeth, 900 boulevard Réné-Levesque ouest; (514) 861-3511. Metro: Bonaventure. This gastronomic restaurant is the heir to the legendary Beaver Club, founded in 1785 by Montreal merchants involved in the fur trade. Members had to have endured a winter in the northwest wilderness, and their payback was the club where they could brag about their exploits while feasting like kings. Revived in the 1950s as the exclusive dining room of the Queen Elizabeth hotel, the restaurant remains a touchstone of old-style Montreal fine dining. The menu is modern French (which is to say the roasted wild bass comes with a shellfish nage instead of a cream sauce), but the most famous dish is a properly British roast prime rib. The *menu découverte* is built around local Quebec products augmented by some provender from elsewhere in Canada. Chef Martin Paquet makes it an eight-course affair that might begin with a lobster *charlotte* and move on to *foie gras,* oysters, roasted meats, and Quebec cheeses. The restaurant proposes a suite of Canadian wines as accompaniments. Diners with lighter appetites can choose the *menu petit appétit* with six courses in tapas-sized portions.

Specialty Stores, Markets & Producers

Dragon Beard Candy, 52 rue de la Gauchetière ouest; (514) 916-6252. Metro: Place d'Armes. This modest Chinatown storefront seems an unlikely place to preserve an ancient Chinese tradition. But Johnny Chin claims to be one of only 10 masters who are trained in the art of creating this delicate, nest-like confection first enjoyed by Chinese emperors during the Tang dynasty. Even the most enduring traditions benefit from an update now and then— and today Chin and his assistants start with a small frozen cube of corn syrup that is quickly warmed in the microwave, then rolled in flour to prevent stickiness. They stretch and twist this unlikely lump until it seems magically transformed into thin, spaghettilike strands that are coiled and filled with coconut, peanuts, and sesame seeds. To best appreciate the subtle flavor and texture, pop a whole candy in your mouth and let it slowly melt.

G & D Supermarché, 1006 boulevard Saint-Laurent; (514) 397-8828. Metro: Place d'Armes. The largest supermarket in Chinatown attracts a discerning local clientele who use tongs to select fresh fish sitting on beds of ice or direct the butcher in cutting meats to order. The shelves are filled with the ingredients to stock a pan-Asian kitchen: curry pastes from India and Thailand, Japanese noodle soups, tempura batter mixes, big bags of white, red, and black rice. The selection of teas—including white, lotus, green, ginger, and ginseng—is particularly strong. Big bags of spices—including crushed chile, dried orange peel, cloves, and Szechuan peppercorns—are perhaps the best bargains. Knorr packaged mixes, such as hot-and-sour soup or bok choy and tofu, make perhaps the best quick and easy meal.

La Soupière, 1611 rue Sainte-Catherine ouest; (514) 933-7885; www.lasoupiere.com. Metro: Guy-Concordia. From tart pans and silicone chocolate molds to mandolines and tagines, this packed shop has a cooking utensil for every need. But it also excels in the white serving dishes that have become almost *de rigueur* in stylish restaurants. In addition to plates, platters, and bowls in every size and shape, La Soupière carries escargot platters with little indents for each snail shell and porcelain scallop shells that are traditional for serving *coquilles St-Jacques*. To present an elegant cheese course, look for tiny white porcelain "flags" to identify each cheese.

Nocochi Cafe Pâtisserie, 2156 rue Mackay; (514) 989-7514. Metro: Guy-Concordia. "I learned to bake from my grandmother in Iran," says Shahnaz Bagherzadeh, the proprietor of this sweet little shop not far from the Musée des Beaux Arts. "Then I traveled and learned from older women around the world." Bagherzadeh named her shop for her signature chickpea powder cookie with cardamom.

A plate with a selection of 15 pastries is perfect for two people to share with a pot of tea. Fifteen may sound like a lot, but the treats are tiny and really delicious. They include the versatile nocochi enhanced with cocoa or with cinnamon, walnuts, and white chocolate. The shop also has stupendous dried fruits (dates stuffed with orange peel, apricots with ground almonds, figs with pistachio) as well as more traditional European pastries such as florentines, sablés, *macarons,* and biscotti.

Pâtisserie La Légende, 68 rue de la Gauchetière ouest; (514) 866-1628. Metro: Place d'Armes. A large seating area makes this Chinatown pastry shop a good bet for a quiet break. Try a curry beef or bacon and onion bun with honey lemonade for a light lunch or almond cookies and mooncakes with Hong Kong–style tea (with evaporated milk) for an afternoon pick-up.

Première Moisson, 1490 rue Sherbrooke ouest; (514) 931-6540; www.premieremoisson.com. Metro: Guy-Concordia. The breads from this bakery chain are things of beauty—world-class loaves that are among the real culinary treasures of Montreal. Given that Première Moisson has seventeen bakeries and supplies grocery chains in Quebec and eastern Ontario with its organic-flour breads, it's amazing how consistent the breads are. But if you can't live by bread alone, you'll also find wonderfully flaky croissants and *chocolatines,* rich Danish, and buttery *palmiers,* as well as

TCHIN! TCHIN!

It is perhaps ironic that the one region of North America that voted out prohibition almost as soon as it was established ceded control of alcoholic beverages to a provincial authority. For years that meant that Quebecers were at the mercy of the Société des alcools du Quebec, or SAQ (www.saq.com), for their wine choices. Not until 1967 did the SAQ begin importing a wide selection of wines from around the globe, and they were only available in SAQ stores until 1978, when grocery stores were allowed to sell wine. Now that restaurants can also do their own importing, the SAQ has stepped up its selection and offers more competitive prices.

SAQ has outlets all over the city in a range of categories, but here are a couple of the most unusual:

SAQ Express 22, 1176 rue Sainte-Catherine ouest; (514) 861-7908. Metro: Peel. The Express category has the most limited choice of wines, but this particular outlet has the advantage of being open 22 hours a day, seven days a week, and carries 500 wines.

SAQ Sélection, 155 avenue Atwater; (514) 932-2574. Metro: Lionel-Groulx. This outlet facing Marché Atwater has a broader selection of better wines.

SAQ Dépôt Montreal, 1001 rue Marché Central; (514) 383-9954. Metro: Chabanel. One of just a few such stores in the province, the Dépôt sells discounted bin ends and offers bulk wine (bring your own container).

SAQ Signature, Complexe Les Ailes, 677 rue Sainte-Catherine ouest; (514) 282-9445. Metro: McGill. One of only two such stores (the other is in Quebec City), SAQ Signature is the showcase boutique of fine wines. The 950 prestigious wines at this location include a huge selection of Champagnes, and *grand cru* wines in magnums and jeroboams.

gorgeous French tarts, like *tarte citronille* and others with fruit and almond combinations. A few locations, like this one near the Musée des Beaux Arts, have attached cafes where you can sit down to eat excellent sandwiches, quiche, salads, and plates of charcuterie. (The rabbit-hazelnut *pâté* is transporting.)

Suite 88 Chocolatier, 1225 boulevard Maisonneuve ouest; (514) 284-3488; www .suite88.com. Metro: Peel. The original location of this chocolate lounge is on the Plateau (see p. 139), while this shop is more boutique than lounge. The small-batch chocolates are both beautiful and delicious.

Vinum Design, 1480 rue City-Councillors; (514) 985-3200; www.vinumdesign.com. Metro: McGill/Place des Arts. You'll have to go to the SAQ for the wine, but everything you need to store it, display it, open it, drink it, and document it is right here. Flasks, drip collars, decorative stoppers, decanters, wine thermometers, corkscrews, and some of the world's finest wine glasses are all on display. The selection of wine books in both English and French (including some European references) is unparalleled in Montreal. For after drinking, Vinum also sells Jura and Nespresso espresso machines.

Food Events

A Taste of the Caribbean, Place Bonaventure; (514) 620-6612; www.atasteofthecaribbean.ca. Metro: Bonaventure. This annual May celebration of Caribbean culture is a joyful whirlwind of music, dance, traditional arts and crafts—and food. Local and visiting chefs prepare more than 100 specialty dishes representing the flavors of more than twenty different Caribbean islands, including Cuba, Jamaica, Barbados, and Martinique. You'll most likely find curried goat, oxtail stew, and jerk chicken, and maybe even the more unusual "Oil Down," a Grenadian dish that combines meat, vegetables, breadfruit, and coconut. A lot of the food is quite spicy, but sampling Caribbean rums will help to cut the heat.

Mondial de le Bière, Place Bonaventure; (514) 722-9640; http://festivalmondialbiere.qc.ca. Metro: Bonaventure. Quebec beers are certainly well represented at this five-day extravaganza in June, but organizers take the name of the event seriously and seek out beers from around the world. Of the 500 or so brands represented, expect both major manufacturers and boutique microbreweries. Organizers also take pains to spotlight new brews each year to keep visitors coming back for more. In addition to tastings, there are seminars and workshops and even a beer and cheese pairing.

Montreal Highlights, various locations; (514) 844-3500; www.montrealenlumiere.com. Usually taking place in mid-February, just as temperatures reach their nadir, the Highlights Festival (Montreal en Lumière in French) laughs in the face of winter with concerts, parties, dances, and a whole slew of food events. Most of the dining celebrations take place at restaurants across the city, but the big SAQ showcase of Quebec cheeses with a cookoff among top chefs (and public tasting of their work) happens at L'Astral (305 rue Sainte-Catherine ouest).

Salon des Vins et Fromages du Quebec à Montreal, Complexe Desjardins, 150 rue Sainte-Catherine ouest; (888) 847-2050; www.salonvins fromages.ca. Metro: Place des Arts. Taking place at the end of October, this three-day event is all about provincial *terroir*. SAQ has wine specialists on hand to guide tastings of Quebec wines, while more than two dozen cheese producers bring their specialty *fromages*. If you're in town, it's a great way to discover new cheeses and find out how the winemakers have met some of the challenges of the climate.

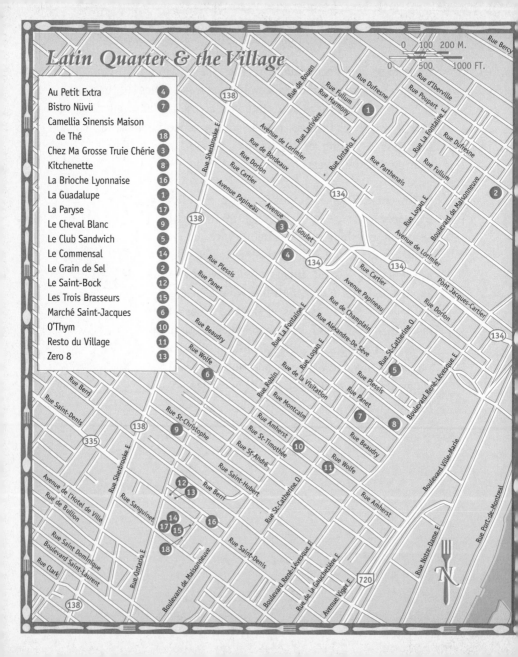

Latin Quarter & the Village

Au Petit Extra — 4
Bistro Nüvü — 7
Camellia Sinensis Maison de Thé — 18
Chez Ma Grosse Truie Chérie — 3
Kitchenette — 8
La Brioche Lyonnaise — 16
La Guadalupe — 1
La Paryse — 17
Le Cheval Blanc — 9
Le Club Sandwich — 5
Le Commensal — 14
Le Grain de Sel — 2
Le Saint-Bock — 12
Les Trois Brasseurs — 15
Marché Saint-Jacques — 6
O'Thym — 10
Resto du Village — 11
Zero 8 — 13

Latin Quarter & the Village

Perched east of downtown and below the ridgeline marked by rue Sherbrooke, the Latin Quarter and the Village (aka the Gay Village) are the most bohemian and arguably most youthful neighborhoods of Montreal. The Latin Quarter is named for the university-centric Quartier Latin in Paris. What Montreal's quarter may lack by way of history, it compensates for with sheer size. The Université de Québec à Montréal (UQÀM) was established here in 1969 and swiftly grew to a major campus of more than 45,000 students (and another 20,000 enrolled in online courses). It is the largest French-language university in the world.

French academics essentially created the business of film criticism in the halcyon early days of *Les Cahiers du Cinéma*, and UQÀM has become North America's leading Francophone center of film studies. The Latin Quarter draws film buffs who arrange private screenings at both the Cinémathèque québécoise (an archive of Québecois film) and the National Film Board of Canada's CinéRobotheque facility (a high-tech system for retrieving and screening films on individual consoles). A handful of restored old theaters in the neighborhood also function as rep houses, screening historic and art films. They are prime venues during the city's various film festivals as well as during the annual citywide Just for Laughs festival. Appropriately enough, the Latin Quarter abounds with cafes, pubs, and casual ethnic eateries where cinema students can theorize at great length and everyone else can get a caffeine buzz and a quick bite.

The Village, just south and a little east of the Latin Quarter, is the self-proclaimed largest gay neighborhood in Canada. What seemed like creeping gentrification at the end of the 20th century became galloping gentrification after the turn of the millennium as decrepit brick tenements were reborn as posh townhouses and vacant storefronts became emporia of antiques, collectibles, and modern design. The genteel residential part of the neighborhood stands in contrast to the late-night entertainment district along rue Sainte-Catherine, where most gay dance clubs and show bars operate.

The Village continues to expand its effective limits, reaching eastward into the edges of the once-hardscrabble Hochelaga neighborhood, and absorbing parts of the Latin Quarter. Boundaries, in fact, are more a figment of real-estate brokers' imaginations than anything else. But the redevelopment of once dilapidated housing has made a huge difference in the Village restaurant scene, as more and more serious chefs set up here to take advantage of less expensive rents than they would find downtown or on the Plateau.

Au Petit Extra, 1690 rue Ontario est; (514) 527-5552; www
.aupetitextra.com. Metro: Papineau. More brasserie than bistro,
this longtime favorite (it opened in 1985) has the Parisian look
down pat, with simple lacquered wooden chairs, midnight-blue
tablecloths on the pedestal tables, mirrors everywhere, and a few
fabulously padded and claw-footed bourgeois banquettes. The menu
smacks of Paris, too. The permanent stenciling on the entrance
doorways touts "oysters in season" as well as "Quebec game" and
"seasonal salads." Each day's slight permutations from the classics
are noted on a chalkboard, which might advise of specials
like roasted black cod with aioli and balsamic vinegar or a
beefsteak with fried onions instead of the usual *steak-
frites.*

Bistro Nüvü, 1336 rue Sainte-Catherine est; (514)
940-6888; www.bistronuvu.com. Metro: Beaudry. Nüvü
was a sensation from the moment it opened in August
2010 as the first upscale fine-dining destination in
the Village. So avant-garde that the ambience changes
nightly (courtesy of multiple screens and high-definition
projectors), the restaurant even publishes its own glossy lifestyle
magazine. Executive chef Bernard L'Hôte takes an equally cutting-
edge approach to contemporary French cuisine. He concocts the
likes of a fricassee of snails with parsley served with gingered sweet
potato for a starter. A typical main dish could be the duo of sea

scallops: tempura-fried and served with fish-roe aioli, and roasted and served with crushed green peas and bacon foam. Even the staff uniforms are high-fashion creations by Quebec designer Philippe de Buck. A lighter, less expensive menu is available after 10 p.m., and the glamorous martini bar stays open until 2 a.m.

Chez Ma Grosse Truie Chérie, 1801 rue Ontario est; (514) 522-8784; www.chezmagrossetruiecherie.com. Metro: Papineau. If the owners of this sweetly tongue-in-cheek bistro were Anglophones, they might have called the place "Porky's." But they're French speakers so they call it "Home of My Beloved Big Fat Pig," and the restaurant really is a paean to the French love affair with pork. Chef Loic Chazay hails from the Savoie, one of many regions where the French eat everything but the squeal. Choices range from the fairly restrained smashed roast piglet with cheddar polenta to a trio of the piglet's grilled loin, smoked and braised belly, and a confit of the shoulder roast. (The trio requires a minimum of four orders for a table.) To be fair, Chazay also offers similarly comprehensive treatments of lamb, but they didn't call this fun-filled joint My Big Fat Ewe. He also presents a terrific pheasant dish of roasted breast and braised legs in a rich sauce. The wine list is not the bistro's strong point, but they do offer a good selection of mostly local beers by the bottle and three on tap.

Kitchenette, 1353 boulevard René-Lévesque est; (514) 527-1016; www.kitchenetterestaurant.ca. Metro: Beaudry. Sitting at the very edge of the Village, far from the dance and strip clubs, Kitchenette serves the kind of food your grandmother made—if Granny was a

Cordon Bleu chef in New Orleans. "By popular demand," as chef/owner Nick Hodge puts it, Friday is always fish-and-chips day. But don't expect to see Chilean sea bass, grouper, shark, swordfish, sailfish, farmed salmon, or bluefin tuna on the menu, as Hodge eschews overfished species. Pacific halibut, Arctic char, wild salmon, redfish, oysters, crabs, mussels, clams, and shrimp, however, are all fair game, and several of them play into his "lazy cioppino" seafood stew. Oysters, in fact, are almost a fetish with this Houston-born chef who brings the taste of the Gulf of Mexico to Montreal with oyster po'boys and a luscious gumbo with oysters, shrimp, andouille sausage, and chicken. (Hodge moved to Montreal for love, he says, but it doesn't hurt that Quebec oysters are also fabulous.) Vegetarians don't have to settle for the usual grilled portobello, either, not with the likes of sweet-potato gnocchi with chipotle brown butter and spicy pecan gremolata on the menu. Hodge has assembled our favorite wine list in Montreal—not the longest or most prestigious, but the one with dozens of distinctive bottles at attractive prices. His whisky (Scotch) and whiskey (Irish and American) lists are also beauties.

La Brioche Lyonnaise, 1593 rue Saint-Denis; (514) 842-7017; www.labriochelyonnaise.com. Metro: Berri-UQÀM. During warm weather, the hidden rear terrace of this longtime pastry and coffee shop is one of the treasures of the Latin Quarter—a veritable garden of tranquillity in a very busy part of town. (Smokers tend to hang out on the much smaller front terrace.) The shop is a fine place to grab a slice of quiche, a sandwich, or an éclair or a *tarte tatin* for lunch or an afternoon break.

La Guadalupe, 2345 rue Ontario est; (514) 523-3262. Metro: Frontenac. Authentic Mexican food in Montreal is hard to come by, but if you keep walking out rue Ontario from the Latin Quarter, you soon pass Notre Dame de Guadalupe church (one mass in French, two in Spanish). As you approach the Frontenac Metro station, the neighborhood turns predominantly Hispanic. The decor at La Guadalupe makes sure that you know you're not in Quebec any-more—sunny murals show scenes of Mexican life, the furniture is all hand-carved, and Mexican folk art hangs on the walls and stands on most every flat surface. But La Guadalupe is the real enchilada— a family-style Mexican restaurant serving that country's greatest hits from *seviche* to *mole poblano* to tequila-packed margaritas. For something a little more adventurous, order the chicken in almond sauce or the *carne Tampiqueña* (roasted flank steak with guaca-mole and enchiladas in *mole* sauce). Prices are fair for Mexican fine dining, but higher than many diners anticipate. The staff speak native Québecois French and Spanish, but English is limited. Weekday luncheon specials are especially good deals.

La Paryse, 302 rue Ontario est; (514) 842-2040. Metro: Berri-UQÀM. The best way to start a friendly food fight anywhere in North America is to claim that such-and-such a place makes the best ham-burger in town. So we won't insist that La Paryse makes Montreal's best burger, but we sure like it. The menu here is very brief, really boiling down to burgers, fries, beer on tap, and wine by the glass. The standard house burger is a rationally sized patty of meat in an excellent bun topped with lettuce, tomato, raw mushrooms, cheese, and mayo. With only around 30 seats, the place fills quickly at lunch (go around 11:50 a.m. if you don't want to stand). La Paryse has been a fixture in the Latin Quarter since 1980, almost as long as UQÀM has been a major university.

Le Cheval Blanc, 809 rue Ontario est; (514) 522-0211; www.le chevalblanc.ca. Metro: Berri-UQÀM. When this little beer bar opened in 1986, it became the first licensed brewpub in Quebec. Its beers were so successful that the bar spawned a microbrewery a year later that has since merged with two others to form Les Brasseurs RJ. But the original bar persists as a favorite Latin Quarter hangout. (How could a brewpub next to a university fail?) The bar's Blanche is widely distributed around the city, but you really need to come here for the Red Rice Japanese-style ale, the At'Chouff Belgian-style pale ale, or the meal-in-itself Imperial Stout. If you're still hungry, the menu offers nachos, grilled-cheese sandwiches, grilled sausages, and bowls of popcorn. There's live music—usually jazz—on Monday night.

Le Club Sandwich, 1570 rue Sainte-Catherine est; (514) 521-1419. Metro: Papineau. Smack in the midst of the Village's "entertainment district" of nudie bars, gay clubs, and dance clubs, this tavern tucked into the ground floor of the Bourbon Hotel never closes. That's right: It's open 24/7/365. It has the air of a '50s diner crossed with a seedy bar, and true to the neon out front, serves a huge array of club sandwiches. (The official name is Cafe European Resto Bar.) During Happy Hour—11 in the morning until 10 at night—you can get two 12-ounce draft beers for less than you'd pay for one in most bars. The place also has an extensive selection of *poutine* variations, always appealing after an exhausting night at the Village clubs.

Le Commensal, 1720 rue Saint-Denis; (514) 845-2627. Metro: Berri-UQÀM. This smaller branch of the vegetarian cafeteria has most of the same choices as its big brother on rue McGill College (see p. 60). Judging by the number of backpack-slinging youth glued to their computers, it's popular with the UQÀM crowd.

Le Grain de Sel, 2375 rue Sainte-Catherine est; (514) 522-5105; www.restolegraindesel.ca. Metro: Papineau. It's hard to stop with the superlatives about this warm and welcoming bistro just a few blocks east of the Village proper. We have friends who come here just for the *foie gras,* which chef-owner Jean-François Bonin gives different treatments as appetizer or main dish. He aims to provide his clients with a *bistro-plus* experience and succeeds by putting new twists on bistro comfort-food classics. His fish-and-chips, for example, come with lime sour cream instead of tartar sauce, with pickled fennel instead of dill chips. His Arctic char with a puree of celery root and an asparagus and watercress "salsa" has both the grace and taste to be served in a fancy gastronomic palace. He makes his own black pudding (blood sausage), hand cuts the fries for his *frites,* and even makes some surprisingly complex desserts.

Cauliflower, Bacon & Clementine Salad

Like many members of the crucifer family, cauliflower thrives in the Quebec climate, so it is a popular vegetable in Montreal bistro cuisine. For this salad served at Le Grain de Sel, chef Jean-François Bonin sautés the cauliflower with bacon to bring out its sweetness before tossing with arugula and clementines. The tart citrus and tangy greens marry surprisingly well with the vegetable and bacon in a bright autumnal salad.

Serves 4

1 pound cauliflower crowns blanched 1 minute in boiling water and well-drained

½ pound slab bacon cut in medium dice

4 clementines, peeled, seeded, and cut in medium dice

2 cups arugula

¼ cup olive oil

Freshly squeezed juice of 1 lemon

Salt and pepper

Sauté the cauliflower with the bacon until bacon browns and cauliflower begins to caramelize.

In a bowl, mix clementines and arugula. Add the bacon and cauliflower.

Dress with olive oil, lemon juice, and salt and pepper to taste.

Recipe courtesy of Le Grain de Sel (p. 84).

The wine list is very good—about half it by private import—with especially strong selections from the south of France. It's hard to beat a good Côtes-du-Rhone with his Quebec lamb spare ribs seasoned with cumin and mint and served with a tangy cole slaw. Service is another big plus—and since the chef is never more than a few steps away from the tables, any question about the food that a server can't answer, Jean-François can. (See recipe on p. 85.)

Le Saint-Bock, 1749 rue Saint-Denis; (514) 680-8052; www .lesaintbock.ca. Metro: Berri-UQÀM. We are leery of novelty beer, and beer with gummies seems so misguided as to almost be inspired. But we forgive the brewer because Le Saint-Bock also offers both British and America-style IPAs, a credible porter, and a pretty nice Flemish-style red. There are always 20 beers on tap (about half brewed on premises) and many more craft brews in bottles. The food choices are a cut above most bar food, too, and include a beer-based onion soup with melted cheese, oven-roasted beer-basted "fries," and several permutations of roasted sausages. You'll spot the bar by the wall mural out front of a stein of beer with a halo over the head, and you'll sniff the heady aroma of malt and the sharp snap of hops the moment that you step in the door.

Les Trois Brasseurs, 1658 rue Saint-Denis; (514) 845-1660. Metro: Berri-UQÀM. Smaller and more pubby than most iterations of LTB (see pp. 14 and 62), this chain brewpub has to go the extra mile in friendliness to compete with Le Saint-Bock across the street. Drinkers who prefer their beer to be more predictable from week to week choose this spot.

O'Thym, 1112 boulevard de Maisonneuve est; (514) 525-3443; www.othym.com. Metro: Beaudry. Unapologetically French in both style and cuisine, this very sharp little dining room looks like a Parisian bistro, but it is strictly BYOB. (Instead of a wine list, they offer a bottled water menu.) The food menu is constantly in flux, so it's posted on a chalkboard in nice big letters, perhaps so the middle-aged business clientele at the weekday lunch can read it from across the room. O'Thym always feels like a party. That's partly because the blond-wood tables are beautifully set and because the brick walls and tin ceiling guarantee a certain level of din once more than a few tables are seated. French classics such as veal sweetbreads in mustard sauce or salmon with raspberry vinegar are augmented by Québecois interpretations like venison ravioli with cream and thyme or roasted bison steak.

Resto du Village, 1310 rue Wolfe; (514) 524-5404. Metro: Beaudry. Definitely cuter and homier than Le Club Sandwich, this 24/7 breakfast joint overflows when the Village clubs close at 3 a.m. But the place is never empty. Even during the slack afternoon hours, a few sensitive young men and their laptops hold down the tables while they surf the web and nurse their coffees. Resto du Village prides itself on serving "cuisine canadienne familiale," which translates roughly as Canadian home cooking. Mostly that means an unending number of variations on eggs (the house eggs Benedict is topped with escargot under the hollandaise), a thick ragout of shank beef and onions, and a dozen variations of poutine. The cuisine is not exactly wine friendly, but the place does have a BYOB policy.

Zero 8, 1735 rue Saint-Denis; (514) 658-5552; www.zero8.com. Metro: Berri-UQÀM. Calling itself a *resto-bar hypoallergenique,* Zero 8 is defined by the eight things that are *not* on the menu: fish and other seafood, peanuts, tree nuts, sesame seeds, milk and milk products, soy, eggs, and wheat or any other grain containing gluten. The menu apologizes for the presence of sulfites in some dishes, but notes that they occur naturally in wine, vinegar, and other foods. But all those restrictions still don't rule out tasty meals like *steak-frites,* duck breast with mushroom risotto and squash puree, rack of lamb with ratatouille, or even a vegan, gluten-free lasagna. Zero 8 is a super-stylish, contemporary bistro—the kind of place the nonallergic can love, even without a bread basket.

Landmarks

Marché Saint-Jacques, 1125 rue Ontario est/2035 rue Amherst; (514) 598-9449; http://marchest-jacques.com. Metro: Sherbrooke/ Berri-UQÀM. This corner of Ontario and Amherst has been the site of a fresh-food market since 1875—the main shopping center for what was then called le Faubourg à M'lasse, or the molasses suburb, for the strong odors emanating from the waterfront sugar factories. The working-class neighborhood went downhill through the Depression, when the current Art Deco market building was constructed. But it has become almost entirely gentrified in the 21st century as the boundaries of the Village expanded. In 2010 the completely renovated building reopened as a smaller version of **Marché Atwater** (see p. 40). A crêpe stand has a window on the plaza, which fills with farm-fresh produce during the summer. Most of the vendors inside can also be found at either Atwater or Jean-Talon markets—Première Moisson, Fromagerie de Atwater, Poissonnerie La Mar, Olive + Olives—but a few are unique to Saint-Jacques, like Milly (www.millyboutique.ca), a one-woman purveyor of fabulous teas, reserve coffees, and chocolates that will destroy your diet but let you die happy. She also has a super selection of coffeemakers, teapots, and cups and saucers.

Specialty Stores, Markets & Producers

Camellia Sinensis Maison de Thé, 351 rue Emery; (514) 286-4002; www.camellia-sinensis.com. Metro: Berri-UQÀM. The four owners of this tea company are also expert tea-tasters and make visits every year to taste and make selections for their offerings of teas from India, China, Japan, Sri Lanka, and Taiwan. So extensive is their knowledge that they even co-authored a book on the subject and seem determined to share their passion with others. The new tea shipments arrive in the spring and the owners usually do a presentation about them in June. Classes and workshops are offered throughout the year—or just grab a table in the tea salon and conduct your own tasting.

Plateau Mont-Royal

The broad tableland east of Mont Royal and northeast of downtown was farm country when it was settled in the 19th century by rural Quebecers seeking a better life (and better jobs) in the industrial and economic capital of Canada. As the Plateau became more urban, its tenements attracted successive waves of immigrants from Europe, the Middle East, North and West Africa, the Caribbean and, most recently, Latin America. The Plateau was the place where immigrants got their foothold before moving on to other neighborhoods. While only a small portion of the Montreal population now lives on the Plateau, almost everyone seems to have roots there. It is the Old Neighborhood for the children and grandchildren of immigrants as well for the *Québecois pur laine* ("pure wool"), as descendants of the settlers of New France style themselves.

No longer exclusively the home of immigrants or even the traditional working class, the Plateau has become increasingly gentrified, as young professionals and artists have colonized its triplex homes and settled into its coffee shops for long sessions with a latte and the Internet. Boulevard Saint-Laurent—still the dividing

Almost every restaurant or bar with a square meter of sidewalk sets up a terrace so patrons can eat, drink, and expound *en plein air*. Grocery stores devote ever more shelf space to heat-and-eat meals, and most casual restaurants pack large numbers of meals to take away. An incredible profusion of bakeries, pastry shops, and ice cream shops has sprung up to meet neighborhood tastes.

Like many Montrealers, the new gentry of the Plateau prize authenticity. How else to explain the nostalgic appeal of some of the survivors of an earlier era—Francophone points of reference like La Binerie, Jewish touchstones like Schwartz's? They are treasures for the whole city, but they cannot be separated from the Plateau. Neighborhood bistros have embraced locavore dining with a vengeance, as savvy contemporary chefs use traditional Québecois cuisine as a gastronomic springboard. While the *bistro-grunge* movement is a city-wide phenomenon, it is strongest on the Plateau where an ultra-casual atmosphere need not imply a lack of sophistication in the kitchen or on the plate.

Locavore dining is not cheap, even in the most casual boîte or bistro. The restaurant-dense part of the Plateau closest to rue Sherbrooke, however, remains Montreal's bargain dining district, in part because many of the small restaurants do not sell alcoholic beverages. They actively encourage patrons to bring their own bottles of wine, and never, in our experience, charge a corkage fee.

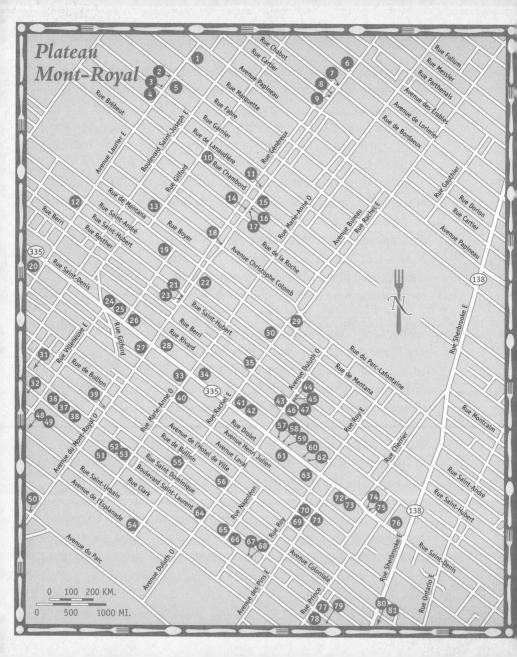

Plateau Mont-Royal

Rue Chabot
Rue Fullum
Rue Messier
Rue Cartier
Rue Parthenais
Avenue Papineau
Avenue des Érables
Avenue de Lorimier
Rue Marquette
Rue de Bordeaux
Rue Brébeuf
Rue Fabre
Avenue Laurier E
Rue Garnier
Rue Gauthier
Boulevard Saint-Joseph E
Rue de Lanaudière
Rue Dorion
Rue Chambord
Rue Cartier
Rue de Mentana
Rue Generéux
Avenue Papineau
Rue Gilford
Rue Berri
Rue de Mentana
Avenue Bureau
Rue Rachel E
Rue Saint-André
Rue Boyer
Rue Saint-Hubert
Rue de la Roche
Rue Resther
Avenue Marie-Anne O
Rue Saint-Denis
Avenue Christophe Colomb
Rue Saint-Hubert
Rue Berri
Rue Gilford
Rue Rivard
Rue du Parc-Lafontaine
Rue de Mentana
Rue Villeneuve E
Rue de Bullion
Avenue Duluth O
Rue Roy E
Rue Montcalm
Rue Marie-Anne O
Rue Rachel E
Rue Drolet
Avenue de l'Hôtel de Ville
Avenue Henri-Julien
Avenue Laval
Rue Saint-André
Avenue du Mont-Royal O
Rue Chérier
Rue Saint-Hubert
Rue Saint-Urbain
Rue Saint-Dominique
Boulevard Saint-Laurent
Rue Clark
Rue Napoléon
Rue Roy
Rue Saint-Denis
Avenue de l'Esplanade
Avenue du Parc
Avenue de l'Esplanade
Avenue Duluth O
Avenue Coloniale
Rue Ottario E
Avenue des Pins E
Rue Prince

0   100   200 KM.

0   500   1000 MI.

Name	#	Name	#	Name	#
Arthur Quentin	61	La Fabrique	75	Marché 27 Bar à Tartare	78
Au Pied de Cochon	45	La Fromagerie Hamel	6	Marius et Fanny	28
Aux Vivres	37	Laloux	71	Méliès Restaurant Bar	79
Beauty's	39	La Maison Cakao	5	Mochica	62
Bières et Compagnie	33	La Maison du Rôti	9	Moishes Steakhouse	65
Bistro Bienville	19	La Maison Thai	11	Monas & Co. Restaurant	
Bistro Cocagne	63	La Raclette	13	Equipment and Supply	50
Boutique Kusmi	60	La Sala Rosa	32	Nil Bleu	72
Brûlerie St. Denis	57	La Soupière	16	Petits Gâteaux	21
Buona Notte	80	La Vieille Europe Charcuterie		Pied de Poule	74
Buvette Chez Simone	48	et Fromagerie	67	Pintxo	70
Byblos	2	Le Canard libéré,		Point G	17
Cafe République	77	espace gourmand	51	Première Moisson	22
Charcuterie Hongroise	68	Le Chien Fumant	10	Restaurant de l'Institut	76
Charcuterie Le Traiteur du Terroir	53	Le Fouvrac	3	Restaurant Globe	81
Chez Chose	26	Le Fromentier	4	Restaurant Les Cavistes	42
Chez Claudette	20	Le Jardin de Panos	43	Restaurant Pizzaiolle	24
Chez José	56	Le Péché Glacé	7	Restaurant Vertige	47
Cocoa Locale	49	Le P'tit Plateau	40	Robin des Bois	36
Crudessence	54	Le Reservoir	64	Rôtisserie Romados	55
Cuisine et Dépendance	31	Les Aliments Picado Enr.	38	Sabor Latino	52
Diabolissimo	14	Les Chocolats de Chloé	44	St-Viateur Bagel & Cafe	18
Fonduementale	34	Les Infidèles	35	Schwartz's Smoked Meat	66
Fous Desserts	12	Le Steak Frites St-Denis	41	Suite 88 Chocolatier	58
Frango	15	Les Trois Petits Bouchons	25	Tri Express	1
La Banquise	29	Les Volailles et Gibiers Fernando	69	Ty-Breiz	30
La Binerie Mont-Royal	27	L'Express	59	Un Amour des Thés	23
La Colombe	46	Mamie Clafoutis	73	William J. Walter	8

line between east and west in the street directions—has ceased to be the frontier between English- and French-speaking Montreal.

Ethnic eateries and grocers are the chief legacy of immigration to the Plateau. But the eating and drinking culture has swiftly evolved to suit the lifestyle of the neighborhood's new inhabitants.

Au Pied de Cochon, 536 rue Duluth est; (514) 281-1114; www.restaurantaupieddecochon.ca. Metro: Sherbrooke/Mont-Royal. Chef-owner Martin Picard's Food Network Canada show is called *The Wild Chef,* and the title should warn you that eating at the Pig's Foot is likely to be a somewhat surreal experience. Picard was Normand Laprise's sous chef for the opening of **Toqué!** (see p. 18) before he set off on his own path with Au Pied de Cochon in 2001 and jump-started a trend toward upscale casual dining in Montreal. Along with his love of wild game and other backwoodsy fare, Picard is a champion of Quebec food products and a glutton for *foie gras.* The restaurant's signature dish is a pig's foot stuffed with *foie gras,* and he usually offers at least another half-dozen variants of *foie gras* on the menu, ranging from a hamburger to a salted tartare to seared *foie gras* with fresh fruit. Even after years on the menu, his *foie gras poutine* remains the talk of the town. Picard buys whole pigs and cooks them from snout to curlicue. He reserves the head (roasted for two people), chops, roasts, and feet and then makes a whole series of bold dishes (usually called the PDC cut) that employ the leftovers. Desserts lean toward maple concoctions, but that's partly because Picard not only has his own sugar bush, he also has a sugar shack in the countryside that opens during the sap run. (See p. 95.)

Sweet Retreat

The cabane à sucre, or sugar shack, is an institution in Quebec country life. Most began as simple makeshift lean-to buildings at the edge of the maple forest where sugar-makers boiled down maple sap to make syrup and sugar. Over the years, many entrepreneurial sugarmakers began to host pancake breakfasts and even maple-themed dinners during sugaring season. Chef Martin Picard of Au Pied de Cochon went them one better in the spring of 2010, when he launched his **Cabane PDC** (11382 rang de La Fresnière, Saint-Benoît de Mirabel, Quebec; 450-258-1732; cabaneasucreaupieddecochon.com) in rural Saint-Benoît de Mirabel, about 45 minutes northwest of Montreal. The cooking varies day to day, but you can usually count on backwoods standards like buckwheat crepes, pea soup, braised brisket, massive tourtières for sharing, and jugs of maple syrup. It's a veritable groaning board in the wilderness, as clouds of steam puff from the evaporator pans sending the aromas of maple and smoke wafting into the woods. Cabane PDC is only open from mid-March into May, but begins taking reservations in December.

1 boulevard Saint-Laurent; (514) 842-3479; www

tro: Mont-Royal. For diners who believe that

restrictions is no more fun than playing tennis

, Aux Vivres puts up a high barrier and still manages to

ie ball into the other court. Although you can order locally

e tofu and tempeh burgers, this vegan restaurant

is not one of those spots that concentrates on
serving meat analogs for people who still lust for
flesh. The chefs would rather come up with
vegetable dishes that simply taste good on
their own. In practice, this means a lot of
salads, soups, sandwiches, and rib-sticking
dishes like vegetarian chili. Sometimes
nothing but meat or a meat substitute will
do, so for the "BLT" the Aux Vivres chefs
stuff lettuce and tomato into chapatti (an Indian
flatbread) with a smoked pressed coconut product to give the
chewy, salty, smoky qualities of bacon. A vegan version of *poutine*
(vegetable gravy, soy cheese, real *frites*) sometimes pops up on the
specials board.

Beauty's, 93 avenue Mont-Royal est; (514) 849-8883. Metro:
Mont-Royal. Be grateful that Beauty's opens at 7 a.m. because by
the time the hipsters arrive around 10 for weekend brunch, this old
fashioned luncheonette has a line out the door. Originally established as the Bancroft Snack Bar in 1942, the joint was a fixture
of Jewish-Canadian Anglophone life along the Main. It became

known officially as Beauty's sometime in the '70s, about the time it featured as a set in *The Apprenticeship of Duddy Kravitz*, a coming-of-age movie starring Richard Dreyfuss and based on a Mordecai Richler book. The place has owned a niche in pop culture ever since, perhaps justified by the simple breakfast "special" of a bagel with gravlax and cream cheese. The house burger special includes bacon (nobody ever said Beauty's was kosher), lettuce, tomato, cheese, and pickle. Always with the pickle. Beer and wine are available, but the main liquor ordered here is a Bloody Mary at brunch.

Bières et Compagnie, 4350 rue Saint-Denis; (514) 844-0394; www.bieresetcompagnie.ca. Metro: Mont-Royal. You'd think that offering roughly a hundred beers from around the world would be enough, but this resto-pub also cooks with beer—mostly Quebec brews. The roasted chicken breast sits beneath a sauce of local raclette cheese and Griffon beer, while the lacquered bison is made with Blanche de Chambly. Several sausage dishes are also available and the kitchen prepares mussels 30 different ways. There's even a house mayonnaise made with beer to slather on the *frites*.

Bistro Bienville, 4650 rue de Mentana; (514) 509-1269; www .bistrobienville.ca. Metro: Mont-Royal. Tucked into a tiny corner building on a residential street just off the hubbub of avenue Mont-Royal, this bistro advertises "cuisine conviviale." With just 25 seats (counting seven stools at the bar), you can expect to dine in close proximity to others, and the food portioning is further designed to make sharing easy. The first five dishes on the menu are big for starters but small for mains, while the second five are big mains meant to be consumed by two people. It's an unusual format, but the house tends to be packed every night with neighborhood couples for *bistro-plus* dining. The small plates—such as a grilled piece of veal chop with some pan-fried veggies and a few slices of chorizo—tend to be simple. The large plates look like meals for a hungry family, like the meat-filled *pot au feu* or the roasted Cornish hen surrounded by grilled mushrooms and vegetables. The wine list is small but select. The entire limited menu changes daily, so call ahead if you have your heart set on a particular plate.

Bistro Cocagne, 3842 rue Saint-Denis; (514) 286-0700; www .bistro-cocagne.com. Metro: Sherbrooke. The name may hint of London, but this super-sleek and polished bistro serves locavore market cuisine. Chef and co-owner Alexandre Loiseau is one of those rare geniuses who can concoct a sophisticated dish from just a few elements—he even claims most of his plates have only four ingredients. He makes an unctuous soup that's a creamy blend of butternut squash and root vegetables, accented with a sprinkling of roasted pecans. He poaches wild sea bass with fennel and leeks, or grills a venison steak and serves it with a mound of sauteed wild mushrooms. Maybe the most complicated dishes are desserts like the lemon tart in a glass with a little crumble on the bottom and meringue on top. Before Cocagne, the space was the last home of

Toqué! (see p. 18) before it moved downtown, and it took Loiseau a couple of years to come out from under the shadow of Normand Laprise, who is the master of the complex. Loiseau has finally come into his own as a minimalist chef with impeccable taste and an ability to keep his prices unusually low. In fact, he offers a cut-rate two-plate special after 9:30 on most nights.

Buona Notte, 3518 boulevard Saint-Laurent; (514) 848-0644; www.buonanotte.com. Metro: Sherbrooke. Adjacent to the eXcentris complex that combines an art-house film screening room with cabaret rooms programming hiphop, pop, folk, and chamber music, Buona Notte caters to Montreal's "Hollywood North" movie folk with a bar/restaurant with Manhattan attitude. In true Hollywood fashion, there's a "wall of fame" of plates signed by American, Canadian, and French movie stars. It's hard to dine here after, say, 10 p.m., when the music gets cranked up and the clientele starts serious drinking. But go a little earlier and you can enjoy an icy martini with a daily risotto special or perfectly seared tuna in a black-olive crust.

Buvette Chez Simone, 4869 avenue du Parc; (514) 750-6577. Metro: Laurier. The *buvette* is a Continental French institution—a cross between a bar and a snack bar—that has never really caught on in North America. Until now. You can pop into Simone from late afternoon until early morning for a glass of wine, a portion of sausages, maybe a few oysters, and a taste of cheese. Or you and a friend can order onion soup and a half roast chicken and a couple of glasses of Pinot noir. There are two chalkboard menus: one for the wines of the evening, the other for food specials—say, a roasted sea bass to augment the charcuterie and antipasti. The wine menu is longer, and it should be. The selections are almost entirely private imports that span the globe but still make a nod to the Okanagan Valley in British Columbia and the Niagara Peninsula in Ontario.

Byblos, 1499 avenue Laurier est; (514) 523-9396. Metro: Laurier. Though not strictly vegetarian, this casual restaurant specializing in traditional family cuisine from the Middle East has plenty of tasty options that don't include meat. Some of the more unusual menu choices are the *boranis,* cold, yogurt-based dishes combined with eggplant, nuts, and mint, or with spinach. *Rouleaux* are just that—rolls filled with spinach, fresh cheese, and shallots, or with a blend of chopped meat, herbs, and onions. Delicate omelets are flavored with dill, feta cheese, or 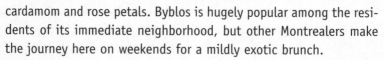 cardamom and rose petals. Byblos is hugely popular among the residents of its immediate neighborhood, but other Montrealers make the journey here on weekends for a mildly exotic brunch.

Cafe République, 3563 boulevard Saint-Laurent; (514) 840-9044; www.caferepublique.com. Metro: Sherbrooke. Coffee shops are often open early, and bistros often stay open late. This combo cafe and bistro does both, so the menu is a little schizophrenic, careening from Belgian waffles to club sandwiches to a grilled ribeye steak with *bordelaise*. Four other locations around the city complete this chain, but the low prices and good bar make this one a contender in the cutthroat competition of the Plateau. The utterly Parisian look of the room, with its high ceilings and abundant mirrors, doesn't hurt either.

Chez Chose, 4621 rue Saint-Denis; (514) 843-2152; www.chez chose.net. Metro: Mont-Royal. The decor of exposed brick wall, hardwood floors, and black-painted bistro chairs and tables may be bare bones, but Marie-France Desrosier's cooking is anything but. Chez Chose has an almost doctrinaire loyalty to Quebec ingredients, but we suspect that's because they are guaranteed to be the freshest. Stanstead rabbit gets a workout on the menu. For an appetizer, Desrosier shreds rabbit meat and layers it between triangles of puff pastry and serves the dish with a light cream sauce and sautéed mushrooms. For a main, she might stuff and roast a rabbit leg. The restaurant is a family affair, with Desrosier's mother and stepfather running the front of the house as she works her gastronomic charms in the kitchen. The menu is always on a chalkboard, since it changes with availability and chef's whim. But since everything is made from scratch (no sauce bases or other shortcuts), the staff can explain every dish and recite every ingredient—especially useful for diners with food allergies. Chances are they can also tell you the name of each farmer who raised the meat, each fishing boat that brought in the catch, and each cheesemaker behind the delectable *fromages*.

Chez Claudette, 351 avenue Laurier est; (514) 279-5173. Metro: Laurier. If a sign in the window did not proclaim "Since 1983," you would probably guess that Chez Claudette was a neighborhood fixture since at least the '50s. With a long counter and a few small tables, it has the look of a traditional Québecoise breakfast joint/ luncheonette. The menu follows suit with a selection of sandwiches and salads, a dozen variations of *poutine,* and a few specialty plates such as fish-and-chips, *pâté chinois,* and chicken in puff pastry. There's a small dining room in back for the overflow crowd. During much of the year, Claudette remains open around the clock.

Chez José, 173 avenue Duluth est; (514) 845-0693. Metro: Sherbrooke/Mont-Royal. There's something downright endearing about what passes as hiphop/slacker culture in Montreal, as French insouciance bubbles up to displace mere attitude. The exterior of this breakfast and lunch cafe is painted in a graffiti/cartoon style, as if someone started to cover up old tags and got carried away drawing brightly colored, downright weird characters. Many of the regulars have enough jewelry hanging off their faces to set off a metal detector, but the menu is ulti- mately as wholesome as the graffiti, if more limited. Fruit smoothies are popular, but the staff also makes a mean espresso. Sandwiches include **BioBon**'s *végé-pâté* (see p. 200), avocado and cucumber, or tuna and celery. Soup specials change frequently, but neighborhood foodies flock here on

Friday and Saturday for the Portuguese seafood soup, on Thursday for tomato and blue-cheese soup.

Crudessence, 105 rue Rachel ouest; (514) 510-9299; www.crudes sence.com. Metro: Mont-Royal. This tiny storefront sister of the larger raw-food restaurant downtown (see p. 55) also offers a menu that is vegan and gluten-free. Although there are a few seats here, most customers come to buy food to take away.

Cuisine et Dépendance, 4902 boulevard Saint-Laurent; (514) 842-1500; www.cuisineetdependance.ca. Metro: Laurier. Like many chefs in this corner of the Plateau bordering on Mile End, Jean-Paul Giroux is a fanatic about product and doesn't fully draw up his menu until he's been shopping. But rather than join the blackboard brigade, he has his staff write out each day's dishes on a huge roll of butcher paper that pulls down like a school room map. Maybe it's a gimmick, but we're suckers for last-minute menus. Sleek and polished, C&D is a Modernist box restaurant decorated in grays and browns and soothing earth tones—with a pop of guacamole green in the chair upholstery. Giroux's cooking follows a similar battle plan with lots of homey bistro dishes like his signature blood-sausage tart, mushroom-stuffed saddle of rabbit, or braised veal cheeks—and then a pop of brightness with, say, roasted halibut accompanied by chorizo and mussels in a saffron sauce. The wine list is a very nice mix of private imports with some SAQ classics, and features some bargains from lesser-known districts like Corsica and Spain's Empordà. C&D is so effortlessly stylish that many of the diners dress accordingly.

Fonduementale, 4325 rue Saint-Denis; (514) 499-1446; www .fonduementale.com. Metro: Mont-Royal. The tree-shaded, hidden outdoor garden is a summertime favorite, but the cozy dining room almost seems the best spot to share a homey, warming pot of fondue. The traditional Swiss fondue of Emmenthal and Gruyère cheeses with white wine and garlic is a menu standard, but the creamy cheese can be livened up with pink peppercorns, pesto or wild mushrooms. Diners can also opt to dip meat, fish, tofu or vegetables Chinese style into a pot of hot broth or *Bourguignonne*-style into a pot of hot oil. The global menu also nods to Quebec roots by adding Oka, one of the province's first artisanal cheeses, to traditional Swiss fondue and by offering marinated wild game (such as deer with juniper berries or caribou in cedar extract) to dip into a red-wine broth. The wine list features privately imported wines from small producers.

Frango, 1318 avenue Mont-Royal est; (514) 903-1228; www.frango .ca. Metro: Mont-Royal. Cooks working the grill in the front window of this tiny eatery are usually tending chicken, and occasionally throw on a piece of beef for a classic French plate of *steak-frites*. But the offerings lean more toward Portugal, with hot or mild grilled chouriço sandwiches or (by advance order) grilled sardines or calamari. There are only five tables for dining, but many people take their food to go.

La Banquise, 994 rue Rachel est; (514) 525-2415; www.restolabanquise.com. Metro: Mont-Royal. The history of La Banquise is almost a précis of everything good about the evolution of working-class Québecois food in the last four decades. Originally opened in 1968 as a hot dog and *frites* snack bar that served food 'round the clock, La Banquise began offering *poutine* in the '80s and now lists more than two dozen versions on the menu of the dining room, which enlarged into the adjoining building in 2006. Among the favorites are the classic, the Ty-Rex (ground beef, pepperoni, bacon, smoked sausage), the Matty (bacon, green pepper, mushrooms, onions), and the Taquise (guacamole, sour cream, tomatoes). The original hot dogs are still on the menu, along with a few burgers and omelets. La Banquise might not be the healthiest place to eat in Montreal, but it's hands-down one of the most fun. And they're still open 24 hours a day. No credit cards.

La Colombe, 554 rue Duluth est; (514) 849-8844. Metro: Sherbrooke. Chef/owner Moustapha Rougabi has stayed at the top of his game at this cheery and intimate Québecois bistro since he opened in 1990. He only offers two seatings each evening, which means that diners have time to linger over his *table d'hôte*

POUTINE—WHEN FAST FOOD GOES SLOW

We were surprised—even shocked—to learn that a 2007 survey by *Le Devoir* picked *pâté chinois* as the "national plate" of Quebec (see p. 26). We assumed that if Quebec were a country rather than a province, *poutine* (pronounced poo-TEEN) would have to be its national food. The dish of deep-fried potatoes sprinkled with fresh cheese curds and doused in brown gravy is the ultimate comfort food for Quebecers, who eat it at all times of the day but especially swear by its curative properties after a long night of drinking, dancing, and club-hopping. Maybe it lost out to *pâté chinois* because few people make it at home.

In fact, it is hard to make at home unless your kitchen is equipped with a professional deep-fat fryer to make golden *frites*. Moreover, it's not a dish that is easily replicated in regions that don't have a plethora of dairies making cheddar cheese and selling off the extra fresh curds in every convenience store and gas station.

The invention of *poutine* is probably as irrelevant as the invention of pizza, bruschetta, or the burrito. In essence, the dish is just one more carrier for a zillion different toppings. The most widely accepted story suggests that *poutine* was first served in a restaurant in Warwick in 1957, and was popularized by the Ashton *frites* truck in Quebec City, which began serving *poutine* in 1972. The truck has since evolved to a province-wide chain of fast-food shops.

Although *poutine* may have first found its mass audience in Quebec City, it has achieved its gastronomic apotheosis in Montreal. Since the turn of the millennium, fast-food *poutine* has inspired many a haute-cuisine chef, and it's not uncommon to see the plebeian potatoes and curds on the same plate with braised lamb shanks, sliced duck breast, *foie gras,* or salmon roe.

meals and finish the bottles of wine they brought with them. Often cited as the best BYOB in Montreal, La Colombe excels in big, bold treatments of red meat and strong-flavored fish. In the summer, Rougabi brings in wild bluefish from Boston—one of the strongest flavored fish in the Atlantic this side of anchovies—to serve with a mustard sauce and acidic fruits. His duck breast, on the other hand, usually gets a light treatment with a mild cherry sauce and a puree of the root veggie of the moment—celeriac when he can get it. His autumn treatment of *cerf de Boileau*—the trade name for pasture-raised red deer from Harpur Farms—is a medium rare chop served with red-wine risotto. In other words, when you're casting about for a bottle at the SAQ, pay most attention to the reds. BYOB.

La Fabrique, 3609 rue Saint-Denis; (514) 544-5038; www.bistrot lafabrique.com. Situated in the cluster of restos on St. Louis Square, La Fabrique—literally "the factory"—is a casual bistro with matching prices that still has edge and panache. Chef Jean-Baptiste Marchand puts the process of dinner front and center by placing the kitchen literally in the middle of the restaurant. More than just open-kitchen concept, it is theater in the round. The rest of the decor suits the theme as well with exposed heating ducts and a generally raw, unfinished look about the space. The food is what we would call well-mannered home cooking—there's a kind of studied quality about corn-flavored risotto with pan-seared scallops and little pulled-pork dumplings. The flavors might say home cooking, but the execution goes way beyond Mama's way with a skillet. The house "lamb burger" is really a croquette of braised lamb shoulder, served with dates, merguez sausage, pine nuts, and goat cheese. On the other hand, Marchand also offers a classic cassoulet, a terrine of salt cod and potato with mayonnaise, and sometimes makes a by-the-book classic Québecois pea soup. There is also a good selection of wines by the glass.

Laloux, 250 avenue des Pins est; (514) 287-9127; www.laloux .com. Metro: Sherbrooke. Easy to dismiss as just another French bistro, Laloux has a secret weapon in chef Seth Gabrielese, who brings both imagination and whimsy to traditional dishes. For example, he deconstructs ratatouille into a piquant eggplant puree with roasted cherry tomatoes and serves it with fried buffalo mozzarella, or adds the tang of pineapple and the smooth sweetness of coconut milk to the ubiquitous seared sea-scallop appetizer. The spacious, airy dining room could make you think you're in Paris rather than a block off rue Saint-Denis, and the reasonably priced wine list makes for better pairings than you could manage in the neighborhood's BYOB joints.

La Maison Thai, 1351 avenue Mont-Royal est; (514) 529-9000; www.lamaisonthai.ca. Metro: Mont-Royal. Even if you are unfamiliar with Thai cuisine, you'll know exactly what to expect when you order at La Maison Thai. All the choices—to eat in or take out—are displayed in glass cases right inside the front door of this little storefront restaurant. There is a variety a spring rolls, dumplings, and soups as well as savory plates such as Shanghai noodles with chicken, beef with ginger or with basil, and chicken with pineapple or with red curry. Many dishes have a lot of heat from peppers, so order carefully.

La Raclette, 1059 rue Gilford; (514) 524-8118. Metro: Laurier. We will attest that this charming little restaurant in a purely residential part of the Plateau is authentically Swiss, right down to the wrap-around porch where some tables are set during warm weather. This is convivial cuisine, best enjoyed by two people who are already close or aiming to get closer. In other words, it's a great date restaurant, not least because dipping fondue or scraping raclette cheese keeps you busy and covers any awkward pauses in the conversation. If you opt for the namesake raclette, it's worth the small extra charge to get a little oven on the table to melt your own cheese, which you scrape off the block and eat with cold ham and beef, pickles, pickled onions, and potatoes. Otherwise it comes pre-melted, but where's the fun in that? La Raclette also offers a number of fine traditional Continental dishes—braised rabbit with green-pepper sauce, veal sweetbreads and mushrooms, braised beef—but the cheese really stands alone. Prices are already modest, and the restaurant is BYOB.

La Sala Rosa, 4848 boulevard Saint-Laurent; (514) 844-4227. Metro: Laurier. A Spanish restaurant in every regard except the hours (they usually close around 11 p.m., when Spaniards are just starting to think about dinner), the Pink Room is essentially a Spanish social club with excellent tapas and an artsy music scene that includes live flamenco on Thursday. It's one of the few places in Montreal where you can get a slice of *tortilla española* (potato omelet) and a glass of fino sherry. As to be expected in an overseas Spanish tavern, the room also serves certain clichéd Spanish dishes like pitchers of sangria and several variants of paella, but the grilled shrimp and fried chorizo offer some authentic, less conventional tastes of Spain.

Le Chien Fumant, 4710 rue de Lanaudière; (514) 524-2444; www.lechienfumant.com. Metro: Laurier/Mont-Royal. With its motto that translates as "better the head of a dog than the tail of a lion," its cadre of staff in black T-shirts, and its uncomposed market cuisine, the Smoking Dog is the epitome of a Montreal style we like to call *bistro-grunge*. There's no dress code that says all male diners *must* wear three-day stubble, but it helps if you want to blend in. Essentially the contemporary reinvention of the neighborhood bistro, this place offers food and drink for a hipster neighborhood. From the chalkboard menu to the wide-open kitchen with all its attendant bustle, it's the dining equivalent of free jazz—it's hard to predict the next chord change, but you know it's going to be lively. The base, of course, is comfort food—fried chicken, lasagna, grilled steak with mushroom sauce, sweetbreads, roast lamb on a bed of de Puy lentils, or a boldly crisp-edged roast halibut steak. That might be one night. Show up another day and you'll choose from smoked salmon, crab claws, grilled mackerel, or a roast quail with market vegetables. Ultra-casual does not necessarily mean inexpensive, but the portions are large. The wine list is a little pricy for the selection, but the restaurant compensates with a good selection of beers. (See recipe next page.)

Le Jardin de Panos, 521 rue Duluth est; (514) 521-4206; www .lejardindepanos.com. Metro: Sherbrook/Mont-Royal. This Greek family restaurant stands out on rue Duluth for its marvelously old-fashioned architecture of white-painted brick with natural wood-framed windows. You climb the stairs to enter because the doorways of old Montreal houses were always raised to keep snow from seeping in. But in nice weather, everyone opts for the garden terrace that gives the place its name. The menu is simple, straightforward, and completely Greek— from the fried calamari, grilled squid, and lamb chops to excellent brochettes of chicken and lamb. The chicken comes from **Les Volailles et Gibiers Fernando** (see p. 136), always a guarantee of the best poultry in the city. Most dishes are accompanied by generous salads and roasted potatoes drizzled with lemon juice. BYOB.

Le P'tit Plateau, 330 rue Marie-Anne est; (514) 282-6342. Metro: Mont-Royal. Lively and loud (the tin ceiling makes the room an echo chamber), Le P'tit Plateau is a

Egg-Stuffed Pheasant

This dish from the guys at Le Chien Fumant is a great example of some of the fun cooking at a Montreal bistro-grunge. First, it uses game rather than the usual farmed poultry. Second, it is witty (egg inside a hen). And third, it's delicious. If you do not know how to spatchcock a fowl (removing the spine and trimming out the breastbone from the inside so the bird can be opened like a book), ask your butcher to do it.

Serves 4

7 ounces shredded cooked chicken (about 1½ cups)
7 ounces shredded cooked shrimp (about 1½ cups)
1 bunch parsley, chopped
up to 1 cup breadcrumbs

4 hard-boiled eggs, peeled
4 pheasants, spatchcocked
oil
salt
pepper

Preheat oven to 350°F.

high-energy neighborhood bistro additionally fueled by the fact that patrons bring their own wine. The homey French food—braised lamb shank, grilled venison with bordelaise, *cassoulet*—is augmented by a few upscale touches like the house version of poached *foie gras* served chilled with toast, raisins, and caramelized onions. The duck confit is among the best around. Note that LPP has just two seatings per night. BYOB.

Mix chicken, shrimp, and parsley thoroughly and knead in breadcrumbs until mixture forms a paste the texture of raw pasta dough.

Using your hand on a firm surface, work the paste into a thin sheet. Divide into four equal parts.

Place an egg in the middle of each sheet and fold sheet around the egg until it is completely wrapped. Repeat for all the eggs.

Place a wrapped egg in the middle of each bird and flip the sides of the pheasant to close it, making sure the legs are pointing up. Secure legs with sturdy cotton kitchen twine.

Add oil to frying pan. Sprinkle each pheasant with salt and pepper and fry it on all sides until nicely browned—about 20 minutes.

Arrange pheasants on a baking pan and place in preheated oven. Roast for 8 minutes.

Recipe courtesy of Le Chien Fumant (p. 110).

Le Reservoir, 9 avenue Duluth est; (514) 849-7779; www.brasserie reservoir.ca. Metro: Mont-Royal. A sharp little brewpub with a short list of five beers (blonde, brown and red ales and two seasonal ales, such as a porter, a white beer with cherries, or a thick Scotch ale), Le Reservoir also offers a similarly well-edited selection of food. Fried calamari, charcuterie plates, cod fritters and the like are available at all hours, while lunchtime might feature a confit breast of chicken with red cabbage, a leek risotto, or a cod fish-and-chips.

Les Infidèles, 771 rue Rachel est; (514) 528-8555; www.les infideles.ca. Metro: Mont-Royal. One of the pioneers among BYOB restaurants with serious gastronomic ambitions, Les Infidèles is ideal for diners who like classic French cuisine in a classy environment of white tablecloths and gleaming silverware, and a choice of affordable tasting menus of three, five, or seven courses. We love wonderfully old-fashioned dishes like shrimp in an anisette-scented sauce, duck confit salad, seared salmon with garlic flowers, and *crème brûlée.* BYOB.

Le Steak Frites St-Denis, 4167 rue Saint-Denis; (514) 788-4462; www.steakfrites.ca. Metro: Mont-Royal. Part of a local chain (see p. 17), this cheery spot offers a menu built around *steak-frites,* fair prices, and the opportunity to bring your own liba-tions. The meat is good, the fries crisp, and the company genial. BYOB.

Les Trois Petits Bouchons, 4669 Rue Saint-Denis; (514) 285-4444; www.lestroispetitsbouchons.com. Metro: Mont-Royal. As much wine bar as bistro, TPB has a well-studied casual look that starts with the small tables of plywood squares. The food goes beyond bar snacks, though, with starters like figs with Elizabeth blue cheese or a small cassoulet of clams. Main dishes include many of the classics, including *coquilles St-Jacques,* grilled sausages, and a selection of grilled fish and meats that changes with the season. Several Quebec cheeses are available in fifty- and hundred-gram portions. The kitchen also makes most of its own charcuterie, including but not limited to terrines and mousses. The desserts are "inspired by grandmother's cooking" and include old chestnuts such as pears poached in red wine.

L'Express, 3927 rue Saint-Denis; (514) 845-5333. Metro: Sherbrooke. Epitomizing the modern bistro with its black-and-white tiles, mirrored walls, and zinc-topped bar for solo diners, L'Express is the place Montrealers go when they hanker for a *croque monsieur,* pasta with lobster and morel mushrooms, or spring fiddleheads sauteed in bacon and topped with Mornay sauce. Once the darling of the Montreal food media, L'Express has grown up two decades later into a neighbor-hood favorite for dependable if not cutting-edge bistro fare at honest prices. The kitchen makes one of the more flavorful *steak-frites* around and some form of *foie gras* is always on the menu.

Marché 27 Bar à Tartare, 27 rue Prince-Arthur ouest; (514) 287-2725; www.marche27.com. Metro: Sherbrooke. Seating about two dozen, this delightful little bistro does a fine *steak-frites,* club sandwiches on brioche, grilled steak with blue cheese, and even a rich bowl of onion soup with grilled cheese on the side. But its real claims to fame are the tartares of tuna, salmon, smoked salmon, beef, duck, venison, and, in season, lobster. Each is available in twelve different styles that range from classic (grainy mustard, horseradish, pickles, olive oil, and shallots) to Russian (vodka, beets, chives, lime, black pepper, and caviar). You can add extras, like cornichons, quail eggs, egg yolks, or truffle shavings, but the basic flesh is so good and the cutting technique so expert that you're best off saving the cost to pay for wine by the glass.

Méliès Restaurant Bar, 3540 boulevard Saint-Laurent; (514) 847-9218; www.cafemelies.com. Metro: Sherbrooke. Maybe because it's located in the eXcentris complex, we always get the feeling that the menu here was inspired by Cannes with a strong infusion of Quebec product. Thus, the Kobe burger comes with an optional slice of foie gras and the *salade niçoise* uses salmon instead of tuna. The bar is big on martinis, and the perfect complement is the tartare du jour, served with home fries and a salad. The ambience is all-important—from the chrome stools at the glass bar to the trance music throbbing along to muffle nearby conversations.

Mochica, 3863 rue Saint-Denis; (514) 284-4448; www.restaurant mochica.com. Metro: Sherbrooke. You almost have to wonder if restaurants with uncommon cuisines are paid by their homelands to act as cultural emissaries, complete with lots of folk art in the decor and cultural lessons on the menu. Mochica is dressed to the nines in a decor promoting the ancient (pre-Inca) culture of northern

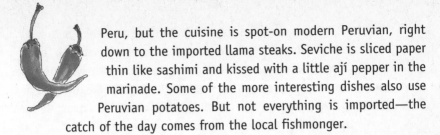

Peru, but the cuisine is spot-on modern Peruvian, right down to the imported llama steaks. Seviche is sliced paper thin like sashimi and kissed with a little ají pepper in the marinade. Some of the more interesting dishes also use Peruvian potatoes. But not everything is imported—the catch of the day comes from the local fishmonger.

Nil Bleu, 3706 rue Saint-Denis; (514) 285-4628. Metro: Sherbrooke. French-centric Europe usually fails to acknowledge it, but Ethiopia is the ultimate source for much of the world's cuisine, so calling an Ethiopian restaurant after the great river of northern Africa is going back to the source in more ways than one. For the uninitiated, the spicing resembles both Indian and Caribbean cooking, and most of the food is eaten by scooping it up with *injera,* a traditional flatbread. It's a delectable cuisine featuring dishes like split peas stewed with turmeric and fresh ginger, chicken stew with berbere spices (sort of a cross between *ras al hanout* and *harissa*), and small morsels of sauteed meats tossed with salad veggies. The jungle motif is a bit over the top, and the service is very casual. But the flavors will keep you coming back.

Pied de Poule, 3625 rue Saint-Denis; (514) 544-5404; www.pied depoule.ca. Metro: Sherbrooke. So what happens when some of Montreal's top restaurateurs tackle rotisserie chicken and take over one of the prime locations on St. Louis Square? You get finger-lickin' and people-watching at the same time. The name—French for a "houndstooth" pattern—refers to the checked pattern of the tiles, but the bird takes center stage. The menu also offers meat loaf, artisanal sausages, pork shoulder, and rosemary-rubbed lamb. Pied de Poule serves one of the stranger dressed-up versions of *poutine,* ladling the gravy over scalloped potatoes. Desserts are as homey as the main dishes—butterscotch pudding, for example, or the all-time Québecois staple, *tarte au sucre.* While the food can be replicated elsewhere, it's hard to beat the location.

Pintxo, 256 rue Roy est; (514) 844-0222; www.pintxo.ca. Metro: Sherbrooke. Chef and co-owner Alonso Ortiz brands his cuisine as Basque—as much by using the Basque term for what southern and central Spain call tapas as by the specific preparations. But he does offer a huge array of good northern Spanish dishes that use a lot of Quebec foods, like his smoked-duck tartare, or his tartare of yellow beets with smoked salmon and salty feta cheese. He goes a little farther afield in Spain for dishes like the Castillian quail (half a roast quail on pasta with smoked ham and pine nuts), or the *foie gras a la plancha* (seared *foie gras* on lentils with a sherry vinegar reduction). These small-plate pintxos give diners a chance to tour the cuisines of Spain without filling up. The large plates have an unctuous richness about them that is typical of northern Spanish cooking. The *fabada asturiana,* for example, is Asturias's answer to cassoulet: a rich bean casserole with chorizo, blood pudding, and duck breast. The lamb shank (inspired by Ségovia) is a dark, long-braised dish served with couscous. Diners unfamiliar with Spanish cooking can learn a lot by opting for the bargain-priced tasting menu where the diner chooses the main dish and the chef picks four pintxos. The wine list includes some unusual pours from Basque country.

Restaurant de l'Institut, 3535 rue Saint-Denis; (514) 282-5161; www.ithq.qc.ca/hotel. Metro: Sherbrooke. You might meet a superstar chef in the making at this hotel/restaurant/classroom facility of the Institut de tourisme et d'hôtellerie, a government-run school for training in the hotel, restaurant, and tourism industries. Under the direction of a chef from France, students prepare and serve meals in a light and airy dining room. Expect careful and cheerful service and well-made updates on classic dishes, such as breast of duck in a sauce of red wine and beet juice or grilled veal fillet and pancetta with mustard and roasted cocoa-bean sauce. Weekday lunch of appetizer, main course, and coffee is a good deal, while the evening *Menu de Terroir* showcases local products.

Restaurant Globe, 3455 boulevard Saint-Laurent; (514) 284-3823; www.restaurantglobe.com. Metro: Sherbrooke. Globe launched as a hangout for movie stars shooting films along the "Hollywood North" strip of boulevard Saint-Laurent, but lost its glam factor somewhere along the way. Chef François Nadon has refocused the cuisine on beautifully composed plates of Québecois bistro food with French flair, giving foodies good reason to reclaim the handsome, brassy room for serious dining. Salmon poached in olive oil comes out meltingly delicious, and dark and meaty braised pork shoulder mates nicely with black trumpet mushrooms and truffle oil atop a pool of toothsome cavatelli pasta. If you're in the mood for even more oomph, the pork chop with mustard spaetzle, a bit of quince, and a sprinkling of toasted hazelnuts is just the ticket. The wine list has some wonderful choices, but be aware that the per-glass pours are small and prices higher than at many comparable restaurants.

Restaurant Les Cavistes, 4115 rue Saint-Denis; (514) 903-5089; www.restaurantlescavistes.com. Metro: Mont-Royal. The point about Les Cavistes is that they import *all* their wine. Not only do they serve it by the glass and by the bottle in the dining room and the wine bar, they also sell it in the boutique. The dining room food is classic French bistro fare, with a *bouillabaisse* to represent the south and cold-water oysters with shallot vinaigrette to represent the north. The bison flank steak (*bavette*) is long-braised and served with mushroom polenta (in case you're drinking red). While sharing a bottle, you might consider ordering plates that are also designed for sharing—like platters of sea-food, charcuterie, or cheeses, or a hearty beef Wellington. The wine list—no surprise here—is fabulous.

Restaurant Pizzaiolle, 4801 rue Saint-Denis; (514) 499-9711; www.pizzaiolle.com. Metro: Laurier. This gleaming stainless steel diner has been given a new lease on life. Retrofitted with a brick, wood-fired oven and warm wood tones to offset the glint of metal, it's now an upscale pizzeria. The menu mixes classic combos, such as tomato sauce, goat cheese and basil, with more inventive pairings: tomato sauce, escargot, and cheese, for example, or duck sausage, sundried tomatoes, and mozzarella.

Restaurant Vertige, 540 rue Duluth; (514) 842-4443; www .restaurantvertige.com. Metro: Sherbrooke/Mont-Royal. **Located** adjacent to **Au Pied de Cochon** (see p. 94), Vertige serves superb French bistro food minus the Québecois swagger of its rowdier neighbor. That's not to say that most of the ingredients don't come from the nearby Quebec countryside—on the contrary. But the style is French rather than French-Canadian, the clientele skews a little older, and the prices tend to be a little lower. Wonderfully récherché classics include veal sweetbreads with Madeira sauce and celeriac, or rabbit leg braised in mustard sauce. There's also a simple grill menu with filet mignon with caramelized onions as well as half-smoked lamb chops with béarnaise for the meat-and-potatoes eater in a party. Allot plenty of time for the extensive tasting menus—it could take three hours or more to work your way through the seven-course option. If you order à la carte, you can add soup or salad, dessert, and coffee for a modest extra charge.

Robin des Bois, 4653 boulevard Saint-Laurent, (514) 288-1010, www.robindesbois.ca. Metro: Laurier/Mont-Royal. Following the example of its namesake, Robin Hood, this casual chic restaurant allows patrons to eat well while doing good. "We're a nonprofit organization," says founder Judy Servay, "and we give support to six organizations that work in the neighborhood to address poverty and help immigrants." About half the staff is volunteer, but the chef is paid. Despite their admirable mission, Servay realizes that "the food has to be good and the price has to be competitive." The fairly simple dishes—such as escargot in lemon butter, lentil soup with cilantro and lime, or a tagine of bass marinated in North African *chermoula* enriched with preserved lemon—draw inspiration and spicing from around the world. The restaurant imports its own wine and there's always a feel-good atmosphere in the large dining room. Anyone who is feeling down can purchase a cup or plate for $5, don a helmet, and enter a small room where they can smash their crockery against the wall. (See recipe on p. 123.)

Rôtisserie Romados, 115 rue Rachel est; (514) 849-1803. Metro: Mont-Royal. The Portuguese chicken rotisserie joint is a Montreal institution, and Romados happens to be our favorite, even if the place looks like a cross between a bakery and a dry cleaner from the outside. But peek in the window and you'll see cooks manning massive rotisserie grills where split chickens spin around over the heat. The lines tend to be long, but aficionados of grilled chicken call ahead, as there's a line for picking up advance orders. Most plates (OK, Styrofoam boxes) come with fries, and they are astonishingly

Robin's Olives

The scene at Robin des Bois is so comfortable that many people like to hang around at the bar drinking wine and munching on some of the lighter goodies. One of the most popular nibbles is a plate of Robin's Olives, a spiced and marinated mix of green and black olives designed to perk up your appetite.

Makes 6 cups

½ teaspoon chile flakes
1 orange, zest and juice
1 lemon, grated zest and juice
3 sprigs rosemary
3 sprigs thyme
3 sprigs oregano
1 bay leaf
3 peeled cloves garlic

1 whole star anise
2 cinnamon sticks
1 teaspoon orange blossom water
1 cup sunflower or canola oil
3 cups green olives (with pits, in brine)
3 cups black olives (with pits, in brine)

In a large pot, mix all ingredients except olives. Steep ingredients over low heat for twenty minutes. Stir occasonally but do not cover.

Drain olives and discard brine. Rinse. Put olives in a large, sealable container. Use a glass or plastic container as metal will react to the marinade.

Pour the warm, flavored oil over the olives and mix well. It is possible that the oil will not cover all of the olives—this is not a problem. Close container.

Write the date on the container and refrigerate. After 3 weeks, your olives are ready to enjoy!

Recipe courtesy of Robin des Bois (p. 122).

cheap. A few tables with stools are available for eating on site, but the primary business is take-out.

Tri Express, 1650 rue Laurier est; (514) 528-5641; www.triexpress restaurant.com. Metro: Laurier. With worn wooden chairs pulled up to white marble tables, Tri Express merges Parisian bistro style with a contemporary sushi sensibility. Master sushi chef Tri Du worked in several high-end Montreal sushi restaurants before opening his own little place on the Plateau. His light and innovative touch has made it a destination for Montrealers from all neighborhoods. Tri Du is known for his perfect rendition of "sushi pizza," a rice cake wrapped in nori (seaweed) and then fried and topped with salmon, shrimp, lobster, or tuna. Tri Express offers more than 20 choices of sushi or sashimi, but it's almost easier to simply order one of the *omakase* (chef's choice menus).

Ty-Breiz, 933 rue Rachel est; (514) 521-1444. Metro: Mont-Royal. Founded in 1959 and last redecorated not long after, Ty-Breiz claims to have been Montreal's first Breton-style *crêperie*. We have no reason to dispute the claim. Significant experience with Parisian street food has given us a soft spot for crepes, which taste even better when consumed in a cozy dining room out of the elements. There's a lot more to the menu (most notably the onion soup gratinée) but crepes—either wheat flour or buckwheat—are the main draw. We recommend the Parisienne of asparagus, ham, and cheese. BYOB.

La Binerie Mont-Royal, 367 avenue Mont-Royal est; (514) 285-9078; www.labineriemontroyal.com. Metro: Mont-Royal. This iconic eatery with eleven stools at a long maple counter and a few small booths may have changed hands a few times since it opened in 1938, but the recipes are still the same. And it's still a go-to place for Québecois dishes just like grandma used to make. In fact, the "Québecois Plate" is almost a primer of the hearty, homey cuisine. The generous plate of meat pie, pork meatball ragout, mashed potatoes, and carrots comes with a side of baked beans and is rounded out with thick pea soup to start and a dish of *pouding chômeur* (a white cake baked with a syrup of maple and cream) as an intensely sweet finish. La Binerie is also an excellent place to sample *pâté Chinois,* a layered mixture of corn, ground beef, and mashed potatoes (see p. 26).

Moishes Steakhouse, 3961 boulevard Saint-Laurent; (514) 845-3509; www.moishessteakhouse.com. Metro: Sherbrooke/Mont-Royal. Back in 1938, when boulevard Saint-Laurent was better known as The Main and the neighborhood was full of Central European immigrants, many of them Jewish, Romanian immigrant Moishe Lighter took over the restaurant where he had worked as a busboy and renamed it The Romanian Paradise. When World War II came, he redubbed it Moishes Steakhouse, and so it's been ever since. Everyone famous who ever lived in or visited Montreal seems to have eaten here, judging by the publicity photos, and there is something undeniably grand about an unrepentant, old-fashioned steak house where most diners start with the decidedly nonkosher shrimp cocktail before moving on to a char-broiled slab of beef. The wine list also seems to hail from a vanished world—a thick collection of first growths and *grand crus* that are priced accordingly.

Schwartz's Smoked Meat, 3895 boulevard Saint-Laurent; (514) 842-4813; www.schwartzsdeli.com. Metro: Sherbrooke/Mont-Royal. There's nearly always a line out front of this narrow deli that has held down the same piece of real estate on The Main since 1928.

But it rarely takes more than 15 minutes before you're seated family-style at a long table, and then things move pretty quickly. Everyone orders the justly famous smoked-meat sandwich, made from brisket that has been marinated with herbs and spices for 10 days before  smoking and then steaming. So the only choices are whether you want it lean (a little dry), medium (recommended), or fat, and whether you want a half-sour or dill pickle on the side. Drink? Black-cherry soda, which waiters refer to as the "house wine." Just don't ask for your sandwich with cheese. "In a Jewish deli?" your waiter will proclaim. "You'll get kicked out for that." Schwartz's stays open until 12:30 a.m. most days and even later on Friday and

Saturday for those who prefer smoked meat to *poutine* as a restorative after a night of bar-hopping.

Specialty Stores, Markets & Producers

Arthur Quentin, 3960 rue Saint-Denis; (514) 843-7513; www .arthurquentin.com. Metro: Sherbrooke. It's worth visiting this dignified and oh-so-proper housewares store for the wall of specialized gadgets alone. And it's almost impossible not to leave without buying something that you never realized that you needed but now can't do without—perhaps a truffle shaver, fish scaler, asparagus peeler, or the wonderfully named *guillotine à oeuf* for cutting the top off a soft-boiled egg. There are spoons for coffee, grapefruit, sodas or ice cream; forks for oysters, escargots or cakes. Of course you can also pick up a *tarte tatin* pan or *crème brûlée* set or splurge on beautiful enameled pans, dishware from France (including the rich colors of Tourron or the classic patterns of Gien), or a wooden-handled Opinel knife with corkscrew and blade for the ultimate picnic accessory.

Boutique Kusmi, 3875 rue Saint-Denis; (514) 840-5445; www .kusmi.ca. Metro: Sherbrooke. This tea specialist was founded in 1867 in St. Petersburg, Russia, where it flourished until the family escaped on the eve of the Russian Revolution to settle in Paris. Among a dizzying array of green, white, and black teas, herbal teas, specialty and flavored teas, and blends, the company still offers the tsar's favorite "Bouquet of Flowers" blend of bergamot, citrus, and flowers created in 1880 and the Prince Vladimir blend of citrus, vanilla, and spices created in 1888 to celebrate the Russian New Year. Gorgeous labels make the tea canisters great gifts.

Brûlerie St. Denis, 3967 rue Saint-Denis; (514) 286-9158; www .brulerie.com. Metro: Sherbrooke. This coffee importer and roaster has been in business on the Plateau since 1985, and while it has more than a dozen outlets around the city and nearby suburbs, this spot is coffee central for us. The roaster encourages customers to become coffee-literate by designating one of their more than two dozen single-source coffees as the "coffee of the day" for special discounts. But Brûlerie St. Denis is at its best, we think, in their artful regional blends and specific styles. Beans are available whole or ground to order, and you can also sit down with a demitasse of espresso, a cup of French press, or an honest-to-god *bol* of Montréalais *café au lait*.

Charcuterie Hongroise, 3843 boulevard Saint-Laurent; (514) 844-6734. Metro: Mont-Royal. Pretty much everything you need to know about Charcuterie Hongroise is in the windows, where you can

spy a lady assembling sausage sandwiches behind a scrim
pickled peppers and tins of paprika. Walk inside and you'
whelmed with aroma of paprika. Fresh and smoked saus
by long strings on the back wall behind glass, and the shelves are
groaning with pickled mushrooms, sauerkraut, almond paste, and all
the other essentials of Mitteleuropan cookery. At midday the shop
sells inexpensive sandwiches to go—smoked meat, smoked pork,
and sausage.

Charcuterie Le Traiteur du Terroir, 4365 boulevard Saint-
Laurent; (514) 842-5778. Metro: Mont-Royal. The proprietors of
this utterly French-Canadian charcuterie have been smoking their
pork for generation upon generation. This father and son operation
makes some of the finest, smokiest slab bacon you may ever taste.
They also craft sausages, terrines, mousses, *rillettes,* and the like,
and even sell a few plates to go (including, oddly, lasagna), but
bacon is the standout.

Cocoa Locale, 4807 avenue Parc; (514) 271-7162. Metro: Laurier/
Mont-Royal. Sweet and petite, Reema Singh is a one-woman baking
phenomenon. She makes a few cookies (including a killer ginger
cookie), and a lusciously dense and spicy brownie spiked
with cayenne pepper and ginger. But she lavishes most
of her attention and considerable skills on cakes,
which she changes frequently to suit the season
or her whim. They could range from a fairly simple
blueberry-lemon cake or a red-velvet cake colored

with beet juice to her near-legendary Valrhona chocolate cake with cardamom and chai. Singh works alone so she doesn't generally do special-occasion cakes. "I just make my cakes and by 6 p.m. they're all gone," she says. Not bad, given that she doesn't open until noon.

Diabolissimo, 1256 avenue Mont-Royal est; (514) 528-6133; www .diabolissimo.com. Metro: Mont-Royal. Fresh pasta and sauces are the main attractions of this all-Italian shop that specializes in cuisine to take home and heat. In addition to six flavors of linguine, four raviolis, two tortellinis, and cannellonis with either meat or a cheese-spinach stuffing, the shop also has freshly made gnocchi and a dozen sauces. Prepared plates vary day to day, and usually include some salads that complement the pasta dishes. It doesn't hurt that you can also purchase a dozen different olives in bulk and all the other makings for antipasti.

Fous Desserts, 809 rue Laurier est; (514) 273-9335; www.fous desserts.com. Metro: Laurier. French pastry chef Frank Dury Pavet is from Lyon and has a loyal following for his praline brioche, a typical Lyonnaise specialty with pieces of sugar-coated roasted almonds enrobed in rich pastry dough. But his plain, chocolate, and almond croissants are equally masterful. To achieve the perfect flaky texture, Pavet makes his dough fresh every day, rejecting the practice of freezing croissants the night before to bake in the morning. Pavet aims for a mix of textures in his cakes, such as the creamy and crunchy combination of chocolate cake with chocolate mousse, *crème caramel,* and a *nougatine* of three different nuts. He's also a chocolatier and the same attention to texture and interesting flavor combinations is evident in the little nuggets he fashions on the marble slab in the back of his shop. During the harvest season Pavet makes confitures—such as raspberry with cardamom or strawberry with pepper—using local fruits, a limited amount of sugar, and spices.

La Fromagerie Hamel, 2117 rue du Mont-Royal est; (514) 521-3333; www.fromageriehamel.com. Metro: Mont-Royal. While we prefer the **Marché Jean-Talon** (see p. 181) and **Marché Atwater** (see p. 40) outlets of this famous cheesemonger, it's also nice to have a somewhat abbreviated collection of Hamel's wonderful cheeses available on the Plateau.

La Maison Cakao, 5090 rue Fabre; (514) 598-2462. Metro: Laurier. Chocolatier Edith Gagnon uses mostly dark chocolate, because, she says, "It's more fun and you can taste the true flavor of the bean." She works at a marble table at the back of her tiny shop and changes her chocolate selections with the season. But you'll always find customer favorites of caramel or lemon and rosemary ganache enrobed in chocolate. "Our chocolates are very fresh and less sweet," says Gagnon. "They don't last long, but they taste better." With fillings such as strawberry and balsamic vinegar or Earl Grey tea and bergamot, it's a sure bet that the delicacies are devoured long before they might spoil. In summer, Gagnon supplements her offerings with homemade ice creams and sorbets; in winter she serves rich hot chocolate.

La Maison du Rôti, 1969 avenue Mont-Royal est; (514) 521-2448; www.lmdr.net. Metro: Mont-Royal. One storefront wasn't enough to contain this amazing butcher shop and gourmet store, so La Maison du Rôti marries two shops—enter by the west door and leave by the east. Just be sure to bring a rolling cart to get everything home. It's hard to leave without being laden with ramekins of terrines (duck and red pepper, guinea fowl and pistachio), a jar of head cheese, a container of smoked lardons, real French cornichons in bulk, a small vat of asparagus soup, a ready-to-heat container of *coq au vin* or veal kidneys, or any number of *tourtières*: wild game, duck, lamb, chicken . . . That's not even mentioning the fresh meat, cut and trimmed to order, or the best array of cheeses this side of a cheesemonger. They even make sandwiches and crepes to eat in the shop so you can gather your strength to tote your purchases home.

La Soupière, 1272 avenue Mont-Royal est; (514) 527-4626; www.lasoupiere.com. Metro: Mont-Royal. With two levels and much more space than the shop on rue Sainte-Catherine (see p. 70) this housewares emporium has enough space to display an array of sushi sets, fondue pots, tagines, bean pots, and other specialized cookware.

La Vielle Europe Charcuterie et Fromagerie, 3855 boulevard Saint-Laurent; (514) 842-5773. Metro: Sherbrooke. Need a break from Quebec product? This marvelous shop specializes in the flavors of Europe, from a zillion kinds of pasta and a nicely pungent selection of French and Italian cheeses to several types of caviar, smoked and pickled herring, and even pickled pork tongues. They sell 11 different sea salts in bulk (and dozens more prepackaged) and offer a lip-smacking array of more than 20 sausages that include a classic lamb merguez, *weisswurst,* Toulouse, a meaty blood sausage, and fragrant duck and tarragon links.

Le Canard libéré, espace gourmand, 4396 boulevard Saint-Laurent; (514) 286-1286; www.bromelakeducks.com. Metro: Mont-Royal. The country comes to the city at this outlet of the Eastern Townships operation **Canards du Lac Brome** (see p. 204). All the products available at the Lac Brome shop are offered here as well, but there's still room for a tiny kitchen where chef Patrice Gosselin turns out an array of casual but richly flavored dishes. The most popular item on the menu is the *poutine* topped with duck confit. To further gild the lily, the absolutely addictive fries are cooked in duck fat. They also make a good accompaniment to a duck sausage sandwich, a duck burger, or a duck burger with a slice of *foie gras.*

Le Fouvrac, 1451 rue Laurier est; (514) 522-9993. Metro: Laurier. Proprietor Marc Doré recently renovated his tidy gourmet shop to accommodate his inventory of 200 varieties each of olive oil and vinegar, chocolates from 40 different manufacturers, and about 15 types of tea, including Betjeman & Barton from Paris for which he is the only Montreal importer. Doré also sells Agga coffee—beans from around the world roasted in state-of-the-art Italian equipment in Quebec. His extensive line of jams and jellies includes traditional flavors such as strawberry, black currant, or rose petal from Les Comtes de Provence and more innovative flavors such as strawberry with green tea and mint or blueberry and maple from Simon Turcotte in Quebec.

Le Fromentier, 1375 rue Laurier est; (514) 527-3327. Metro: Laurier. Always a top contender for best bread in Montreal, this artisanal bakery uses flour grown and milled in the Eastern Townships and offers a dizzying range of crusty loaves such as the "trio du terroir" (made of Quebec wheat, barley, oats, and flax seed) or the sourdough whole wheat and walnut bread. With a select assortment of cheeses, sausages, and *pâtés,* this is a great place to pick up the fixings for an elegant picnic. Watch carefully for the sign since the lower-level shop is entered from a side door off the sidewalk. A pastry chef at another establishment claims that the Béarnais, a croissant filled with almond cream and chocolate, is so perfect that biting into one almost makes her weep. We're not sure if they are tears of joy or envy.

Le Péché Glacé, 2001 avenue Mont-Royal est; (514) 525-5768. Metro: Mont-Royal. This Internet cafe kicks the menu up a notch with sweet and savory crepes, delicious fruit smoothies, and homemade ice cream, sorbet, and yogurt. They are especially known for their pistachio, green tea, and ginger ice creams and for their macarons filled with coffee, caramel, chocolate or lemon ice cream. These little treats are refreshingly cool on a hot day, but the usually crisp cookies do become a little chewy.

Les Aliments Picado Enr., 4553 boulevard Saint-Laurent; (514) 289-8786. Metro: Mont-Royal. Montreal has long had a substantial Portuguese population, and this grocery store is where they come for the best selection of salt cod, dried beans from the homeland, and all the wonderful Portuguese canned goods, like sardines and tuna in olive oil, big jars of tomato pulp, and of course the olive oils from home. The freezers are full of the Portuguese catch, ranging from five sizes of sardines to blue mackerel, squid, and octopus. The store also carries Portuguese terra-cotta and glazed pottery casseroles and serving dishes.

Les Chocolats de Chloé, 546 rue Duluth est; (514) 849-5550; www.leschocolatsdechloe.com. Metro: Sherbrooke/Mont-Royal. Truffles and filled chocolates are Chloé's forte, and the secret behind the intense and complex flavors is simple. Rather than using extracts or flavoring in her fillings, she generally infuses the cream with an herb or spice before making the ganache that will become the center. Her chocolate filled with *caramel fleur de sel* might be the single best sweet bite in Montreal.

Les Volailles et Gibiers Fernando, 116 rue Roy est; (514) 843-6652. Metro: Sherbrooke. Chefs of many of Montreal's best restaurants rely on this specialty butcher for their chicken and game. You can do the same. Fernando only buys from one producer per type of animal—one chicken farm, one bison farm, one elk farm, and so on—to guarantee accountability. The shop has its own smokehouse and cure room where the staff makes all the sausages, bacon, and other cured products. A small selection of frozen heat-and-eat meals is also available.

Mamie Clafoutis, 3660 rue Saint-Denis; (514) 380-5624. Metro: Sherbrooke. Like its larger sister shop in Outremont (see p. 167), this small storefront excels at its signature *clafoutis* and fabulously recherché *tarte tatin*. It also does a bustling lunchtime business in sandwiches and salads.

Marius et Fanny, 4439 rue Saint-Denis; (514) 844-0841; www .mariusetfanny.com. Metro: Mont-Royal. This Plateau outlet of the Laval-based baker-chocolatier is especially popular at lunch time when long lines form for sandwiches and pastries. But we think that the chocolate side of the business is the most intriguing, since chef Marc Chiecchio, a past president of the

Quebec Association of Chocolatiers, offers some of his fantasy chocolate flavors (sun-dried tomato, for example) in tiny tasting bars.

Monas & Co. Restaurant Equipment and Supply, 4575 avenue Parc; (514) 842-1421; www.en.monas.ca. Metro: Mont-Royal. This supply store is a home cook's dream if you ever wanted a french-fry cutter, squirt bottles for saucing plates, chef's jackets, pizza paddles, and all the gear the big boys and girls use in their restaurants. You'll find a half-dozen sizes of chinois sieves, quotidian restaurant-grade pots and pans, every imaginable size of tart pan, and some really unusual gear, like equipment for sous-vide cookery. The store has a huge selection of both new and reconditioned commercial appliances.

Petits Gâteaux, 783 avenue Mont-Royal est; (514) 510-5488; www.petitsgateaux.ca. Metro: Mont-Royal. There's a lot to be said for specialization when the product is as sweetly charming as the "little cakes" offered here. The shop is meant to evoke the heyday of the cupcake in the 1950s. The choices range from children's birthday-party favorites of vanilla and chocolate to adult dinner-party flavors of raspberry and dark chocolate, caramelized apple and maple, or goat cheese with blueberries.

Point G, 1266 avenue Mont-Royal est; (514) 750-7515; www.boutiquepointg.com. Metro: Mont-Royal. There are two schools of thought when it comes to making the quintessentially French treat of *macarons*. Some chefs follow the traditional flavorings of legendary Parisian tearooms such as Ladurée, while others consider the delicate meringue-based cookies as almost a blank canvas for inventive colors and flavors. That's certainly the case with Julien Reignier and Thierry Andrieu, French pastry chefs who met while working at the Casino du Montreal and who are the brains and tastebuds behind this winning shop. Their twenty-two flavors of rainbow-colored *macarons* include lime-basil, lavender-blueberry, roasted pistachio, orange blossom, *crème brûlée*, and chocolate-hazelnut. The shop also serves homemade ice cream and little jars of *glace au foie gras*, or *foie gras* ice cream, to serve on crackers or dollop on soup or steamed asparagus.

Première Moisson, 860 avenue Mont-Royal est; (514) 523-2751; www.premieremoisson.com. Metro: Mont-Royal. Like the shops at the three markets (Atwater, Jean-Talon, and St-Jacques) and the one on Sherbrooke ouest (see pp. 40, 181, 88, and 71, respectively), this Plateau operation is what the company calls a Station Gourmand, which means it has the broadest choice of goods from the bakery and also offers some light sit-down meals.

Sabor Latino, 4387 boulevard Saint-Laurent; (514) 848-1078. Metro: Mont-Royal. Boulevard Saint-Laurent wouldn't be The Main without its immigrant populations. So in addition to the central European and Portuguese stores, you can also find the canned goods and kitchen staples of Latin American cooking here. Although many Latino groceries are created with Puerto Rican or Mexican cooking in mind, this store is more Central and South American in its selections. The tamales for eating at a few small tables reference the culinary traditions of Colombia, Peru, and Ecuador. At the same time, the store also sells fresh *masa* for making tortillas and tamales, tins of Argentine *dulce de leche,* and *churro* mix for making Spanish fried dough. You might forget that you're in Montreal as you get into the swing of the ever-present salsa soundtrack.

St-Viateur Bagel & Cafe, 1127 avenue Mont-Royal est; (514) 528-6361; www.stviateurbagel.com. Metro: Mont-Royal. The history-laden original shop in Mile End (see p. 156) is the place to go to pick up a bag of bagels hot from the oven. But if you want to sit down and eat your bagels, this Plateau outpost has a scattering of tables and a menu of bagel sandwiches including the "Traditionel" with smoked salmon, cream cheese, tomato, onion, capers, and lemon or "La Coque Deluxe," an omelet, grilled ham, lettuce, and tomato on a bagel. Soups and salads are accompanied by bagel chips, or for a lighter snack order a bagel spread with cream cheese, salmon spread or vegetarian paté.

Suite 88 Chocolatier, 3957 rue Saint-Denis; (514) 844-3488; www .suite88.com. Metro: Sherbrooke/Mont-Royal. Clearly the folks who operate this sleekly modern chocolate emporium don't believe that you can ever have too much of a good thing. And that is a decidedly good thing for chocolate lovers who can choose between five spice, *fleur de sel,* triple chocolate or mocha ice cream on a warm day and then sip plain, cinnamon, orange or ginger hot chocolate when the weather turns cold. The "Chocolat Chocolat" cake features five layers of chocolate cake separated by layers of chocolate fudge and butter cream. Seductive truffles, nut barks, tuiles, and even chocolate-covered pretzels are displayed like tiny works of art on rectangular platters in minimalist glass cases.

Un Amour des Thés, 781 avenue Mont-Royal est; (514) 369-2999; www.amourdesthes.com. Metro: Mont-Royal. This Montreal outpost of the Outremont original (see p. 170) has one of the largest selections of loose tea in Quebec.

William J. Walter, 1957 avenue Mont-Royal est; (514) 528-1901; www.williamjwalter.com. Metro: Mont-Royal. The William J. Walter name has spread far and wide around Montreal as one of Quebec's top artisanal sausage producers. The factory in Laval supplies most of the product, but this Plateau shop along with the one in Marché Jean-Talon (see p. 181) carries more than four dozen styles of sausage.

Food Events

Montreal Ukrainian Festival, Parc d'Ukraine; (514) 885-6419; www.ukefestMontreal.org. Metro: Beaubien. For a long weekend in mid-September, the 18,000 Ukrainians in Quebec celebrate their eastern European heritage with singing, dancing, folk-art exhibitions, and food. Ukrainian dishes resemble the neighboring cuisines of Poland and Russia. Vendors generally offer *varenyky* stuffed with cheese and potato, cabbage rolls, fried cabbage with kielbasa sausage, borscht, *shashlik* (pork kebabs) and *nalesnyky* (meat- or cheese-filled crepes). Sweet treats include *pampushky* (Ukrainian doughnuts) and *khrustyky* (cripsy fried yeast dough). The festival also serves plenty of Ukrainian beer and vodka.

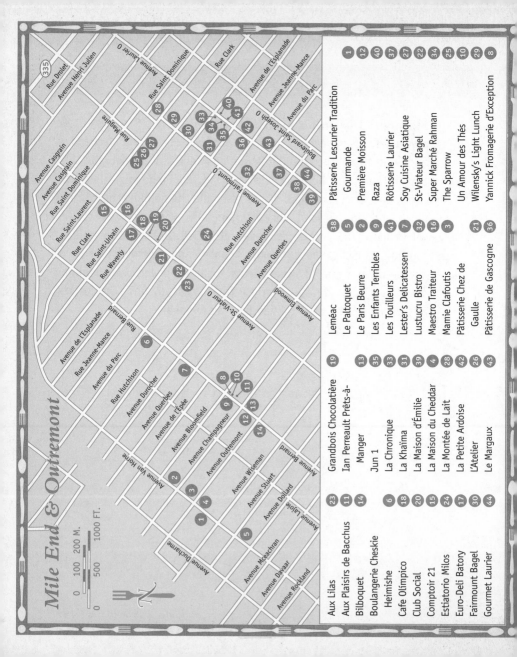

Mile End & Outremont

Montreal lore could not view the adjacent neighborhoods of Mile End and Outremont as more different. Through most of the 20th century, Mile End—an amorphous district extending east from Parc Mont-Royal to boulevard Saint-Laurent, and north from boulevard Saint-Joseph to the railroad tracks—was home to aspiring immigrants, including many Central and Eastern European Jews immortalized in the novels of native son Mordecai Richler. Outremont, which sprawls along the north slope of Mont Royal, was the home of the French-speaking upper class. Never the twain did meet.

Unless it was over lox and bagels, or as the French called it, *saumon fumé et bagels*.

Remnants of the old stereotypes persist—mostly in the peculiar jumble of cuisines. Mile End, at the very edge of Outremont, is home to the city's iconic bagel shops, while avenue Laurier boasts both contemporary French restaurants that cater to Francophone ladies who lunch, and the joint where the French-Canadian working class has tucked into roast chicken since 1936. High-end gourmet shops and kitchenware stores selling the latest in pod-system espresso makers stand only blocks from old *caffès* where real espresso *alla Romana* is considered a God-given right.

The old textile factories and warehouses of Mile End increasingly house contemporary bistros dedicated to ultra-local food and chic wine bars where the proprietors do their own importing to get around the conservative selection and high prices of the SAQ. The neighborhood is also home to some of the hippest dot-coms (mostly computer-game designers) and a bustling club and bar scene that has been the launching pad for many of North America's French-language indie bands.

Outremont remains predominantly Francophone, but about 6,000 Hasidic residents can often be overheard conversing in Yiddish and Hebrew and businesses are quick to conduct transactions in English as easily as French. Yet for all its changes, Outremont remains the home of some of the city's best classic French pastry shops, one of which may even make the finest butter croissant in Montreal. Just to confuse things, the best almond croissant hails from Mile End.

Foodie Faves

Aux Lilas, 5570 avenue Parc; (514) 271-1453; www.auxlilasresto .com. Metro: Outremont. **Montreal has a wealth of Middle Eastern**

cooking, but Aux Lilas stands out as arguably the city's best Lebanese restaurant.
Established in 1980 when the neighborhood
was still run down, the lilac-colored restaurant is now part of a bustling dining scene where
Mile End and Outremont meet. Chef-owner Christine
Faroud only opens for dinner, but her prices look more
like lunch, especially if you take one of the *tazka* tasting
plates (two-person minimum). As with most Lebanese restaurants, Aux Lilas is very vegetarian-friendly, even offering
a meatless version of the *tazka* that features a yogurt-cheese tartlet
and *qebbeh* made with fried balls of bulgur and potatoes stuffed
with olives and mushrooms. Aux Lilas has an excellent selection of
wines from Lebanon, one of the sleeper wine regions of the world
even though they've been making it for 4,000 years or so. Twenty
years as a French colony brought Rhône, Burgundy, and Bordeaux
varietals to the mountains, and the Château Ksara Reserve (a blend
of Cabernet sauvignon, Syrah, and Carignan) is always a good bet.

Comptoir 21, 21 St-Viateur ouest; (514) 507-3474. Metro:
Laurier. Curiously enough in a city that's mad for French food,
Montrealers have an authentic soft spot for the quintessential fast
food of the United Kingdom: fish-and-chips. As this book was being
written, a new fish and chips joint seemed to be popping up on
every corner. Retro lettering painted inside the window and the
long curving bar with chromed pedestal stools make this spot look
like it's been around forever, but the lunch crowd includes a lot of

dreamy-eyed youthful coders from nearby game company Ubisoft. Fries are the old-fashioned Québecois once-fried type, which means they get dry enough to take a good splash of vinegar. The lightly battered fish (haddock, not cod) is properly crisp outside and meltingly soft inside. The homemade clam chowder resembles a French *chaudière*—that is, full of clams, sea juices, and small potato chunks without being too thick and gloppy. All in all, it's a great place for cheap eats.

Estiatorio Milos, 5357 avenue Parc; (514) 272-3522; www .estiatoriomilos.com. Metro: Laurier. Owner Costas Spiliadis opened this restaurant in 1979 with the avowed goal of letting the world know that Greek cooking belonged in the pantheon of the world's great cuisines. His expansions have taken him to New York, Miami, and Las Vegas and back home to Athens, but Milos remains the cornerstone of a Greek culinary empire. Don't go looking for egg-lemon soup and its Greek diner cousins. The emphasis here is on fresh, clean flavors and pristine product. In other words, the best dishes on the menu are usually one of the fish (especially Canadian halibut) and, of course, the salads and savory pastries like *spanikopita* and *tyropita*. The reasonable prices (especially at lunch) belie the elegance of the dining rooms. Milos is blessedly a place where you can dress for dinner, if only out of respect for the impeccable cooking and service.

Jun 1, 156 avenue Laurier ouest; (514) 276-5864; www.jun1.ca. Metro: Laurier. Japanese chef Junichi Ikematsu is one of Montreal's new stars, and no wonder—he combines the skills of a top sushi chef with an authentic feel for the lighter side of Provençal cuisine. In practice, this means diners can go far east with a seaweed salad starter or a sashimi plate, then come back to familiar French flavors with mains like a duck breast sauced with spiced honey and accompanied by pan-seared *foie gras,* or a delicately roasted pork loin with pepper jelly and good old-fashioned mashed potatoes. Ikematsu often mixes crisped rice with sticky rice in his sushi, providing a nice explosion of texture, and he's not afraid to use Provençal dried tomatoes as a foil for the sashimi or dab the red tuna tartare with truffle oil. The lovely sushi bar is popular at lunch, but most diners opt for the bistro seating in this quietly swank setting.

La Chronique, 99 avenue Laurier ouest; (514) 271-3095; www .lachronique.qc.ca. Metro: Laurier. Belgian chef Marc de Canck ratchets up the bar on bistro fare, making it hard to choose. For example, his house raviolis are stuffed with roasted pork, mushrooms, and a foie gras emulsion. He does a *faux-filet* of Angus beef served with wild mushrooms and a lump of Montreal smoked meat and, of course, bordelaise sauce. De Canck has been at the top of the restaurant game for more than a quarter century, and his roots lie in French nouvelle cuisine. Although he long ago eschewed the minuscule portions of that movement, he can assemble an impeccable architectural fish dish with the best of them and knows just when to bring in vanilla or cardamom to liven up a plate. The dining room is an unassuming space—all the better to focus on the food.

La Khaïma, 142 avenue Fairmount ouest; (514) 948-9993. Metro: Outremont. Imagine if Le Mistral wind of Provence blew backwards, spreading the dust of France on North Africa instead of the other way around, and you'll have an idea of what to expect from the food at La Khaïma, which is a blend of Bedouin, Berber, and French colonial. Lentil soup is *de rigueur,* but in winter you might also find Senegalese *maffé,* an earthy stew of root vegetables and cabbage in African peanut sauce. Couscous dishes and tajines are the main part of the menu. For a good sense of the culinary fusion, try the veal tajine with prunes.

La Montée de Lait, 5171 boulevard Saint-Laurent; (514) 273-8846; www.lamonteedelait.com. Metro: Laurier. With a name that translates as "milk run" (the train that makes all the local stops) and an ever-changing menu chalked up nightly on a blackboard, you'd never guess that this modest-looking bistro has some 600 wines in its cellar or that chef Martin Juneau was Montreal's city-wide winner in the 2010 Gold Medal Plates, a Canada-wide cook-off to raise money for the country's Olympic and Paralympic athletes. His crispy pork belly with a beet glaze, Granny Smith apple jelly, and dill vinaigrette was every bit as local as the restaurant name. He suggests pairing it with a still apple cider instead of wine. Part of the fun

here is not knowing quite what to expect each night—
but knowing it will be good.

La Petite Ardoise, 222 avenue Laurier ouest; (514)
495-4961; www.lapetiteardoise.com. Metro: Laurier. A
fixture in Mile End since 1981, Petite Ardoise represents the unpretentious end of bistro fare, where French
comfort food dominates the menu, the service is utterly
casual, and you can sit for hours eating your *croque monsieur*
and chatting. Or you can tuck into a casserole of homemade
pâté chinois (see p. 26), a baked dish of corn, meat, and mashed
potatoes often translated as "Quebec shepherd's pie." At La Petite
Ardoise, they use braised beef instead of fried hamburger, which
gives it a slightly upscale twist. One of the most popular features is
the garden terrace in the back.

L'Atelier, 538 boulevard Saint-Laurent; (514) 273-7442. Metro:
Laurier. If the chums of the old TV show *Friends* were *Montréalais
amis,* you'd probably find them here eating bistro food and drinking
wine they brought from home instead of jazzing up on coffee at
Central Perk. A certain wit and whimsy informs the menu. The revis-
ited *poutine* (see p. 106), for example, tops the fries with shredded
rabbit, barbecue sauce, and five-year-old aged cheddar. All the
meat in the *cassoulet* is also Stanstead rabbit from the Eastern
Townships. In fact, the farther you dig into the menu, the more
Quebec *terroir* you find—right down to the crispy pork skins served
with *foie gras* terrine and caramelized onions. BYOB.

Le Margaux, 5058 avenue Parc; (514) 448-1598; www.lemargaux .com. Metro: Laurier. Serving food in what we like to think of as "bistro-plus" style, Le Margaux is a moderate-sized room with a short but sweet menu that wouldn't be out of place in Bordeaux. Less a date restaurant than the kind of place where two or three couples would gather, Margaux indulges the adventurous eater with starters like escargot *pissaladière* or poached frog's legs while keeping a version of *steak-frites* (ribeye with shallots, frites, and salad) on the menu most nights. Presentation is precise and often ornamental, but the modest prices do not reflect the artistic aspirations. Don't miss the lavender *crème brûlée* at dessert time.

Leméac, 1045 avenue Laurier ouest; (514) 270-0999; www.res taurantlemeac.com. Metro: Laurier. Successful bistros have a way of becoming defined by their clientele, and Leméac is clearly the table of choice for the Outremont bourgeoisie and remains, even after many years, a definitive place to see and be seen. One of the city's first bistro-plus restaurants, it is distinguished by a crisply modern decor and attentive service. Certain bistro classics never change: *steak-frites* with a good old-fashioned hanger steak and some of the city's best fries (which is saying something), the salmon *pot-au-feu,* and the salmon and beef tartares. The wine list—which includes more than two dozen by the glass—is wide-ranging and, for Montreal, reasonable. It also includes a nice selection of half bottles. Just don't try getting in on the weekend without a reservation, especially for the hugely popular Sunday brunch.

Le Paris Beurre, 1226 avenue Van Horne; (514) 271-7502; www .leparisbeurre.com. Metro: Outremont. You want to know where the merchants in Outremont go for a bite when they steal away at lunch or after they close their shops? Le Paris Beurre is where you'll find them tucking into the salad of warm baby leeks and a plate of veal sweetbreads with caramelized pears, accompanied by a Bordeaux *Supérieur*. A fixture on Van Horne since 1985, this 65-seat bistro run by Monsieur Hubert Streicher seems effortlessly lifted from Le Marais district of Paris. And in true Parisian fashion, the daily *formule* is always a bargain.

Les Enfants Terribles, 1257 avenue Bernard ouest; (514) 759-9918; www.lesenfantsterriblesbrasserie.ca. Metro: Outremont. Practically across the street from the bistro Paris Beurre, this neighborhood favorite highlights the difference between a brasserie and a bistro. For one thing, there's beer on tap, and for another, the food is even more casual. The fact that it's named for Jean Cocteau's bizarre novel should put you on notice that things are not always what they seem. Thus, the *pâté chinois* features creamed corn and truffled braised beef cheek instead of the usual canned kernel corn and fried hamburger. While the food is hardly fancy, it's always good. If you lack patience, it's probably best to skip the weekend brunch, when the staff is slammed with hungry, impatient visitors and there's often a long wait for a table.

Lester's Delicatessen, 1057 avenue Bernard ouest; (514) 276-6095; www.lestersdeli.com. Metro: Outremont. Sybil and Billy Berenholc carry on the deli business that their father started in 1951, and Montrealers still debate whether **Lester's** or **Schwartz's** (see p. 126) makes the best smoked meat sandwich. But for roast brisket (made from the same meat, but not smoked), they head to Lester's on Wednesday, Friday or Saturday. Lester's smoked meat is also distributed to other restaurants in Montreal and the Eastern Townships.

Lustucru Bistro, 5159 avenue Parc; (514) 439-6701; www.bistro lustucru.com. Metro: Outremont. Where the young owners of this very cool wine bar ever found so much matching Danish Modern furniture is beyond us, but it definitely helps contribute to the retro-louche atmosphere, where the only food offerings that don't change are the raw bar and the tartares (which usually include deer, elk, and veal). Otherwise there are five new starters, four new mains, and five new desserts per night—marked on a blackboard. In keeping with the concept of updated '50s Québecois, one of those mains is usually a roast chicken and there's an extensive choice of cocktails, classic and otherwise.

Raza, 114 avenue Laurier ouest; (514) 227-8712; www.restaurant raza.com. Metro: Laurier. The contemporary Latin cuisine from Peruvian chef Mario Navarrete Jr. crosses a lot of borders for its inspiration but stays close to home for most of its ingredients. You might find crunchy jicama in the salad, but it will be snuggling up to sweet Quebec beets and spinach. His tuna seviche (a classic Peruvian dish) seems sunny and exotic with flavors of orange, lime, ginger, and soy sauce, but it could easily be a starter before the duck breast in cranberry sauce or the shrimp with garlic and gnocchi sitting in a pool of bouillon seasoned with beer. Navarrete also teaches classes in Latin-French fusion cooking, but you'll have to go to the website and subscribe to his newsletter to know when they are being offered.

Soy Cuisine Asiatique, 5258 boulevard Saint-Laurent; (514) 499-9399; www.restaurantsoy.com. Metro: Laurier. Chef Suzanne Liu learned to cook from her Hong Kong grandmother, but at Soy Cuisine she happily jumbles the traditions of several regions of China, most of Southeast Asia, and a little bit of Japan and Korea. She also plays to some of the strengths of Quebec, sweetening the glaze for shrimp with a little maple syrup, or blending maple with coconut milk and coriander to make a sauce for fish. The occasional Chinese-Canadian stalwart like General Tao chicken becomes a deft, chef-inspired dish in Liu's hands as she sends out the chicken just lightly crisped with a perfectly balanced ginger-lemon sauce that's heavy on the ginger and light on the cornstarch. Service is "Chinese style," which means that when it's ready in the kitchen, it's served at the table for all to share. Most of the wine list is available in both full and half bottles.

The Sparrow, 5322 boulevard Saint-Laurent; (514) 690-3964. Metro: Laurier. Given the strongly Francophone character of the neighborhood, it was fairly daring for the young entrepreneurs who opened The Sparrow to go whole-hog English in concept and style. This little bird unashamedly aspires to be a gastropub, i.e., one of that breed of local bars where the food is as good as the beer. The fried battered cod hits the mark, as does an authentic rendition of the cabbage-potato side dish known as bubble-and-squeak. Even better bets are the steamed mussels, the hearty burgers, and a beef stew that prepares patrons for a night of suds in the neo-Edwardian pub decor. Cakes, by the way, come from **Cocoa Locale** (see p. 129).

Landmarks

Fairmount Bagel, 74 avenue Fairmount ouest; (514) 272-0667; www.fairmountbagel.com. Metro: Laurier. Just as Montrealers debate the best smoked meat, they also debate the best bagels. A neighborhood institution ("since 1950" says a sign in the window), Fairmount is **St-Viateur's** (see p. 156) main competition for the title. Both shops hand-roll their bagels and cook them in wood-fired

THE BAGEL TEST

In an interview in *Parade Magazine,* actor William Shatner recalls bagels as central to his Montreal childhood. "I was into onion for the longest time before I graduated to sesame, and then, as became my personality, the all-in-one, the kind that had all the seeds on it. I think that the kind of bagel you get is like a Rorschach test."

ovens. Fairmount claims lineage back to Montreal's first immigrant bagel baker and offers the classic bagel plain or with sesame or poppy seeds. Fairmount also gets a little fancy with such specials as blueberry, cinnamon and raisin, and chocolate-chip bagels. For healthier eaters, there are also spelt and buckwheat, multigrain, and whole-wheat bagels, along with the "power bagel" of honey, raisins, walnuts, sunflower seeds, and sesame seeds. Open 24/7.

Rôtisserie Laurier, 381 avenue Laurier ouest; (514) 273-3671. Metro: Laurier. You'll notice the pseudo-word "BBQ" on the sign for this institution, but it is a throwback to the day when anything grilled and slathered with sauce passed as barbecue. In this context, it means "grilled meat." This Mile End/Outremont landmark made rotisserie chicken a favorite in Montreal. Later entrants into the field may have stolen some of its thunder, but no establishment can top R-L in offering the perfect old-fashioned ambience to match its comfort food menu. You half expect to find Jell-O on the dessert menu. You can't get the gelatin, but there is still an old-time lemon cream pie, the dessert of choice after a bowl of warming French onion soup *gratinée* and a classic chicken pot pie.

St-Viateur Bagel, 263 avenue St-Viateur ouest; (514) 276-8044; www.stviateurbagel.com. Metro: Laurier. Big bags of flour and sesame seed are visible in the window of this neighborhood fixture. "We make 1,000 dozen bagels a day," says Saul Restrepo who has worked in the shop since 1981. And every one of those bagels is made by hand and slid into a wood-fired oven on a long wooden paddle. Purchasers can observe the entire process and select from a number of options including sesame-seed, poppy-seed, cinnamon, whole-wheat, nine-grain, and flaxseed. Sesame-seed bagels are the most popular by far, says Restrepo, though he prefers a poppy-seed bagel in the morning with butter. Richard Morena, son of owner Joe Morena, is also a proponent of the poppy-seed bagel, which was the biggest seller when the shop opened in 1957. Morena, however, prefers his with cream cheese. Whatever flavor or spread, nothing equals the taste and light texture of one of St-Viateur's bagels hot from the oven. Open 24/7.

Wilensky's Light Lunch, 35 avenue Fairmount ouest; (514) 271-0247. Metro: Laurier. "A lot of the element here is nostalgia," says Sharon Wilensky who works with her brother and mother behind the nine-stool counter of this lunchtime institution founded by her grandfather in 1932. Service here is quick and no-nonsense. Everyone orders the Wilensky "special" of beef salami and bologna with mustard on a grilled roll. The round sandwiches are never cut in half and are best eaten quickly while they are still warm. The Wilenskys also make the syrups for their fountain drinks. Best accompaniment to a special is a vanilla or chocolate egg cream. "We know our egg cream is good," says Sharon. "People from Brooklyn tell us that it's good."

Specialty Stores, Markets & Producers

Aux Plaisirs de Bacchus, 1225 avenue Bernard ouest; (514) 273-3104; www.auxplaisirsdebacchus.com. Metro: Outremont. SAQ may have all the wines, but this shop has all the glassware, including Riedel, Peugeot, Stölzle, Schott Zweisel, and Spiegelau. Decanters, corkscrews, wine thermometers, home cellars, wine cabinets, Champagne buckets, and tapas plates help round out the collection. In addition to selling Laguiole and Global knives, they also offer a professional knife-sharpening service.

Bilboquet, 1311 avenue Bernard ouest; (514) 276-0414. Metro: Outremont. The home base of Montreal's own inventive ice cream, this shop does offer sandwiches and a few other savories but the main attractions are the ice creams, sorbets, and gelati. Favorite flavors include chocolate-orange, vanilla-raspberry, and ever-popular salt caramel. In the summer, you can also get a scoop from the pushcart on Place Jacques-Cartier in Old Montreal.

Boulangerie Cheskie Heimishe, 359 avenue Bernard ouest; (514) 271-2253. Metro: Outremont. Get in line with the Hasidim at this popular Outremont bakery and watch what everyone in front of you is ordering, especially early on Friday afternoon ahead of the Shabbat. The overhead baskets are overflowing with challah, but hardly a customer leaves without a box of poppy seed rugelach and the thousand-layered babka filled with chocolate. The kosher bakers also make a pretty fine cherry Danish.

Cafe Olímpico, 124 rue St-Viateur ouest; (514) 495-0746; www .cafeolimpico.com. Metro: Laurier. At any time of day, chances are good that a soccer match from somewhere in the world will be blaring from the televisions, and a few of the regulars will be knocking around billiard balls on the table in the back. The limited food is forgettable, but the Italian coffees are authentically Roman—that is, not quite as burnt as Neapolitan, with a thick and perfect *crema* every time. Indoor smoking is banned in Montreal, so the cigar-chompers don't light up. Otherwise, you'd never know you're in Montreal.

Club Social, 180 rue Saint Viateur ouest; (514) 495-0114. Metro: Laurier. Half a block from Olímpico, Club Social also serves perfect

Italian coffee. If you join the club (a minimal fee), you can also order grappa for a *caffè corretto*. (The "club" designation gets around some of the baroque twists of Montreal's liquor licensing laws.) Free wifi tends to make Club Social more of a Mile End hangout for hipsters, and you'll see a lot of folks nursing an espresso while surfing the web and dreaming of a job in the neighborhood at Ubisoft.

Euro-Deli Batory, 115 St-Viateur ouest; (514) 948-2161. Metro: Laurier. Just a few doors down from the massive Byzantine-style church of St. Michael and St. Anthony—predominantly Polish and Italian these days, though built as an Irish Catholic church—Batory makes its intentions clear on the door, where it's identified in painted script as a "Polskie Delikatesy." There are a handful of tables, in case you want eat on the premises, but most of the food is sold to go. If you're a regular, you order the borscht and a plate of *pierogis*. If you're a newcomer, you should do the same. It's classically rib-sticking eastern European fare. Because it's so close to the church, Batory is open on Sunday to cater to the faithful.

Gourmet Laurier, 1042 avenue Laurier ouest; (514) 274-5601; www.gourmetlaurier.ca. Metro: Laurier. It sometimes seems that there isn't a European food delicacy that Gourmet Laurier does not carry, but we think of this gourmet shop gone wild as our mustard store. Not only do they sell Maille and Faillot from France, but they also carry Les Moutardes from Provence and A Must from Holland (including mustard with figs and with dill and honey). And despite the strong French predilections of the Outremont bourgeoisie,

Laurier displays a huge variety of British mustards next to Quebec products like the cider-vinegar mustard from Les Délices de l'Île de Orleans. Oil and vinegar choices (more than 300) put the olive-oil specialists to shame. As Americans, we find it a handy place to pick up toasty Cuban coffee. Canned goods make a gourmet's head spin (and mouth water). Not only are there the wonderful tinned fish and shellfish from Galicia and Portugal, but also blocks of *foie gras* and as many tinned terrines as we've ever seen in one place. Fresh terrines are available by the slice at the deli counter, as are about 1,000 English, French, Italian, Argentine, and Quebec cheeses.

Grandbois Chocolatière, 162 rue St-Viateur ouest; (514) 394-1000; http://chocolatsgrandbois.com. Metro: Laurier. Geneviève Grandbois is so particular about sourcing her chocolate that she even offers a small tasting box so that customers can try to discern the differences between dark chocolate from Madagascar, Venezuela, Tanzania, Cuba, Peru, and Santo Domingo. Grandbois' collection of "classic" chocolates includes such fillings as raspberry, saffron, chai tea, maple, and pepper. She also offers a "Les Chuao" collection (named for the dark Chuao Amedei chocolate from Venezuela) that features more exotic flavors such as twelve-year-aged balsamic vinegar, white-truffle oil, or the Monte Cristo which is infused with cigar leaves for a real taste of *terroir*. The confections, says a clerk, "are not for people who want very sweet chocolate."

Ian Perreault Prêts-à-Manger, 1248 avenue Bernard ouest; (514) 948-1248; www.ianperreault.com. Metro: Outremont. Once one of Montreal's high-flying superchefs, the talented M. Perreault trimmed his sails in 2007 to offer some of the best ready-to-eat and ready-to-cook meals in the city. "It's a good way to do restaurant food without the long hours and the hassles with staff," says his charming wife Mélanie Martin, who runs the shop while Perreault is working his magic in the kitchen. The store is long and shallow—essentially one long case after another offering beautiful and delicious fresh soups packed in canning jars (asparagus and ginger, cauliflower and cumin, and wild mushroom on a fall visit), salads packed in large drinking glasses, or smaller glasses with starters like a *foie gras* mousse with Quebec blueberries. Full-scale main dishes like flank steak or braised lamb leg come with directions for finishing at home. (See recipe on p. 162.)

La Maison d'Émilie, 1073 rue Laurier ouest; (514) 277-5151; www.lamaisondemilie.com. Metro: Laurier. A carefully edited cookware store for serious cooks, this shop is especially strong on French cocottes, those little flameproof dishes that go from stovetop to oven for making braised dishes. They carry a very full line of the Emile Henry glazed stoneware and several sizes of the Staub oval glazed cast-iron Dutch ovens. It's also the ideal place to pick up the full line of white bistroware for everything from *pots de crème*

Milk of Green Asparagus

Ian Perreault may have closed his restaurant in favor of cooking for his ready-to-eat emporium in Outremont, but that doesn't mean he has stopped reinventing classic French cuisine. In fact, Les Éditions GID published his fascinating Cuisine Revisitée in which he takes a classic recipe and gives it a modern twist. This "milk" is a delicious mousse that revisits cream of asparagus soup. Prep time is only about 20 minutes, and cooking time is only 10.

1 bunch of green asparagus, unpeeled, cut in large pieces
¼ onion, chopped
1 tablespoon olive oil
3 cups whole milk
half a bunch of curly parsley
3½ tablespoons butter
1 egg, boiled 5 minutes (harder than soft-boiled, softer than hard-boiled), peeled
salt and pepper

In heavily salted boiling water, blanch the asparagus for 3 minutes. Remove and plunge into ice water.

In a flameproof casserole, slowly sauté the onion in olive oil until soft but not browned.

Add the milk and bring to a boil. Add the asparagus and parsley sprigs and simmer for 4–5 minutes, taking care not to overcook the asparagus. (It should keep its bright green color.)

Remove contents of casserole to a food processor and process until smooth.

Return smooth mixture to casserole and place over low heat. Add the butter and egg in small pieces and emulsify with a small hand mixer until it becomes a hot mousse. Season to taste with salt and pepper to taste and serve.

Serves 4

Recipe courtesy of Ian Perreault Prêts-à-Manger (p. 161).

to individual soufflés. For a little more flair, consider the ovenproof painted Alsatian pottery. Ask about the schedule of cooking demos by local chefs.

La Maison du Cheddar, 1311 avenue Van Horne; (514) 904-0011; www.maisonducheddar.com. Metro: Outremont. "Everyone's getting crazy with cheese here in Quebec," says shop co-owner Jean-Pierre Gariepy. "There's almost one new cheese a month." Gariepy and partner Dominique Cormier endeavor to bring the best of Quebec cheeses to Montreal and usually stock about 300 different varieties. The selection is much broader than the cheddar that gives the store its name. But Cormier particularly loves introducing customers to what she calls the Brittany tradition of impaling a small cube of cheddar cheese on a toothpick and dipping it into hot, strong coffee just until it starts to melt. The shop grills cheddar cheese sandwiches and also offers a "sandwich of the week" to introduce customers to less familiar cheeses. The sandwiches are always served with a side of cheese curds and Gariepy seems to be on a mission to rehabilitate the much maligned but seemingly ubiquitous curds. "I've loved cheese curds since I was a kid and I was frustrated that you couldn't get good curds in Montreal," he says. To solve the problem Gariepy has curds delivered fresh from a factory every day. He has even fashioned a small paper cone to hold a serving of cheese curds—plain, or flavored with sun-dried tomato or pesto. "It brings out the kid in you," he says.

A Baker's Dozen of World-Class Cheeses

Artisanal cheese-making in Quebec has exploded since about 1995, resulting in at least 400 named cheeses. La Belle Province is beginning to rival La France when it comes to great fromage. The provincial tourism office has established La Route des fromages, or the Cheese Route (www.routedesfromages.com), for culinary explorers. The province even has its own annual cheese competition, the Sélection Caseus. The cheeses have racked up so much prestige that the top cheesemongers in Montreal offer many of the best.

Le Cendrillon, an ash-covered soft goat's-milk cheese whose name translates as "Cinderella," is made by La Maison Alexis de Portneuf. It was chosen as the best cheese in the world in an international competition held on the Canary Islands in 2009. **Le bleu d'Elizabeth,** a creamy and not overly salty blue, made by Jean Morin of Fromagerie du Presbytère in Sainte-Elizabeth de Warwick, took first prize in the 2010 Sélection Caseus. Morin's **Louis d'Or,** a hard, raw cow's-milk cheese that resembles a French Comté, makes a killer grilled-cheese sandwich.

Cheese-lovers should also try:

1608, a semisoft cheese made in Charlevoix from the milk of heritage Canadienne cattle first brought to Quebec in the 17th century, is named for the founding date of Quebec.

L'Hércule du Charlevoix, an Alpine-style cheese, is made in Charlevoix from the creamy milk of Jersey cattle.

Le Fleurmier, a creamy Brie-style cheese, is the soft sister to L'Hércule and is made from the same milk.

Grey Owl is a tart, ash-covered goat's-milk cheese from Fromagerie Le Détour in Notre-Dame-du-Lac.

14 Arpents is a farm cheese similar to the creamy, full-bodied Normandy cheese Pont l'Evesque.

Le Douanier ("the customs officer"), made by Fritz Kaiser in the village of Noyan near the Vermont and New York border, has a nutty creaminess like a young Comté or Gruyère.

Sauvagine, a washed-rind cheese with mushroom overtones from St-Raymond de Pontneuf, was crowned grand champion of Canadian cheeses in 2006.

Pied-de-Vent is a classically "stinky" raw cow's milk cheese from Les Îles-de-la-Madeleine.

Victor et Berthold, a buttery semisoft cheese, was among the first Quebec artisanal cheeses.

Riopelle de l'Île, a soft cheese somewhere between a Brie and a Camembert, is named for the painter Jean-Paul Riopelle, who often vacationed on L'Île aux Grues, where the cheese is made.

Le Paltoquet, 1464 avenue Van Horne; (514) 271-4229. Metro: Outremont. Residents of Outremont point to Paltoquet's croissants as the neighborhood contender as the best in Montreal—if not the world. The secret, they say is "butter, butter, and butter." That takes care of breakfast. For lunch in the tiny adjoining cafe, Paltoquet has an assortment of mini-quiches and sandwiches and even offers a "menu du jour" of an entree with tea or coffee and dessert.

Les Touilleurs, 152 avenue Laurier ouest; (514) 278-0008; www .lestouilleurs.com. Metro: Laurier. If you want to buy only the best sieve, frying pan, crepe pan, immersion blender, or silicone chocolate molds, this is the place to go. Instead of filling the shelves with pots and pans, the owners have selected the 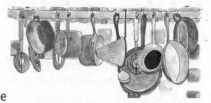 best in each category and given it the space to be admired and coveted. It will make you want to cook. And with the similarly well-edited selection of cookbooks, you can get all the ideas you need. (There's also at least one book per cooking tool, in case you wondered how to get the best from your Robot-Coupe food processor or professional-grade KitchenAid mixer.) If that doesn't inspire you, check out shop's periodic cooking classes.

Maestro Traiteur, 72 rue St-Viateur ouest; (514) 544-9333. Metro: Laurier. This French pastry shop in the middle of bagel-centric Mile End is easy to overlook, but you'll kick yourself if you do. Having tasted most of the almond croissants at Montreal's leading bakers, we nominate Maestro Traiteur for the best—a perfect blend of flaky pastry, toasted sliced almonds, and an almond cream that is both more intense than the competition's and less runny. It can even be eaten while walking without dribbling it all over you. (We can attest to that.)

Mamie Clafoutis, 1291 avenue Van Horne; (514) 750-7245. Metro: Outremont. Like its smaller sister shop on the Plateau (see p. 136), this bakery with tables upstairs excels at wonderfully old-fashioned sweets such as the eponymous *clafoutis* (fresh fruit—including cherries, apricots, blueberries, or pears—topped with batter), classic French *tarte tatins,* and artlessly scrumptious free-form fruit tarts (such as apple-rhubarb, pear-chocolate, pineapple-coconut, or chocolate-banana) called *tartes à l'ancienne.* There are croissants and *chocolatines* (of course), breads made with flour from France or Quebec, and a small choice of sandwiches and salads. In fact, the place is chaotic at lunch as people vie to place sandwich orders and wait around to pick them up.

Pâtisserie Chez de Gaulle, 231 rue St-Viateur ouest; (514) 276-5555. Metro: Laurier. A lot of folks in the Mile End neighborhood favor this otherwise French bakery's excellent pizza slices. There are even four little tables where you can sit to eat them. But don't overlook the breads and especially not the pastries. How can you fail to love a baker who makes an apricot Danish that looks like a plate of three eggs sunny side up?

Pâtisserie de Gascogne, 237 avenue Laurier ouest; (514) 490-0235; www.degascogne.com. Metro: Laurier. Gascogne is another Montreal institution that has been around so long that many foodies either take it for granted or even bad-mouth the place, but we have always had good luck—and good food—here. Their classic pastries and cakes measure up to neighborhood pastry shops in Paris, and their soups and fresh salads to take home are always competent. Best bets for cooking at home, though, are their quiches and pot pies. The shop also makes a killer *tarte au sucre.*

Pâtisserie Lescurier Tradition Gourmande, 1333 avenue Van Horne; (514) 273-8281. Metro: Outremont. It's almost impossible to choose among the beautiful sweet and savory treats in the display cases, so let the sales clerk offer some suggestions. The most popular quiche, for example, has a filling of spinach and goat cheese, but the classic ham and cheese always has its adherents. So does the traditional *tourtière* pie of beef and pork, though salmon and chicken versions are also available. For cakes, Outremont residents lean toward the "Royal" with white and dark chocolate mousses and hazelnut, but are tempted by new creations such as the "Normand" with caramel mousse, caramelized apple, and vanilla parfait. Somewhat of a stickler for details, the chef also pairs the

Quiche Lorraine

Pâtisserie Lescurier Tradition Gourmande in Outremont is a full-service pastry shop, which means that it has an extensive line of savory pastries in addition to the sweets. This traditional ham-and-cheese quiche is a favorite. Owner Eve Richard advises that it should be made in a 2-inch-deep mold that is 7 or 8 inches in diameter. She adds that any sort of precooked vegetables can be used instead of the ham or bacon to make a vegetarian quiche.

4 eggs
¾ cup whole milk
¾ cup heavy cream
salt and pepper to taste
Precooked 9-inch pie shell

½ cup ham, cut in ¼" dice, or ½ cup crumbled cooked bacon
⅓ cup grated Swiss cheese

Preheat oven to 350°F.

In a large mixing bowl, whisk together eggs, milk, cream, salt, and pepper.

Add ham or bacon to pie shell. Sprinkle with cheese. Pour egg-milk-cream mixture over meat and cheese.

Cook in preheated oven for 35-40 minutes or until the egg mixture is golden brown.

Serves 6

Recipe courtesy of Pâtisserie Lescurier Tradition Gourmande (p. 168).

filling—custard or almond cream—to best enhance the fruit flavor in his gorgeous little tarts. Seemingly ubiquitous in Montreal, caramel *fleur de sel* finds its way into cakes and the shop's specialty chocolates. (See recipe on p. 169.)

Première Moisson, 1271 avenue Bernard; (514) 270-2559; www .premieremoisson.com. Metro: Outremont. One of a handful of the company's full cafes, this branch of Montreal's dominant artisanal bakery has several tables for enjoying the quiches, tarts, pastries, and sandwiches.

Super Marché Rahman, 151 avenue Laurier ouest; (514) 279-2566. Metro: Laurier. OK, you *could* buy a loaf of bread at this *depanneur,* but the paltry selection of groceries is just a ploy to get licensing for Mile End's best selection of beers from across Canada, the US, most of Europe, some of Australia, and all of Quebec. Prices are also pretty good.

Un Amour des Thés, 1224 avenue Bernard ouest; (514) 279-2999; www.amourdesthes.com. Metro: Outremont. Stéphane Lemay opened his tea shop in 2002 and boasts one of the widest selections of loose tea in the province. One of his most popular blends is "1001 Nights," a mix of black and green teas with jasmine and berries. But Lemay really enjoys introducing customers to the unique flavor characteristics of various tea types from around the world, including the increasingly popular Rooibos red tea from South Africa. Among the 200 varieties of teas from China, India, Japan, and Sri Lanka, Lemay stocks 15 different Darjeelings from spring, summer, and fall harvests and thirty different Japanese green teas, including both shade grown and sun grown. The shop also has a lovely selection of teapots.

Yannick Fromagerie d'Exception, 1218 rue Bernard ouest; (514) 279-9376; www.yannickfromagerie.ca. Metro: Outremont. Yannick bills itself as supplying only exceptional cheeses—and the shop of roughly 200 *fromages* lives up to the billing. The emphasis is on the soft and semisoft cheeses of France, and Yannick ages each to perfection before putting it out for sale. Prices are steep, but you're paying for exceptional care in the handling—one might even say coddling—of the cheeses. In fairness, Yannick also carries some Quebec small-production artisanal cheeses.

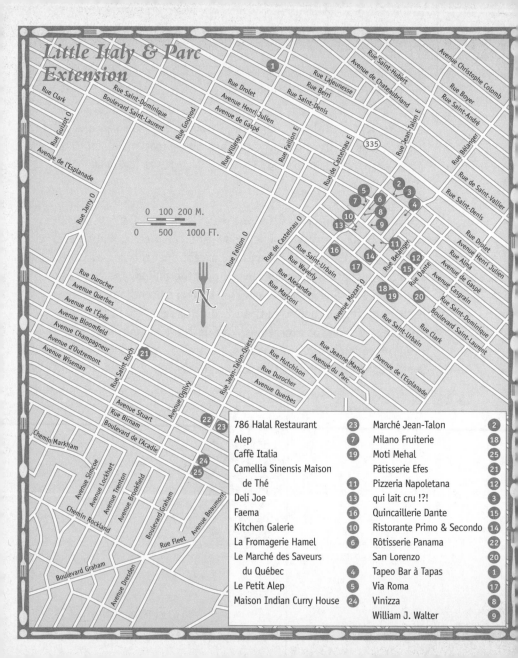

Little Italy & Parc Extension

Rue Saint-Hubert
Avenue Christophe Colomb
Rue Lajeunesse
Avenue de Chateaubriand
Rue Boyer
Rue Saint-André
Rue Drolet
Rue Berri
Rue Saint-Denis
Rue Clark
Rue Saint-Dominique
Boulevard Saint-Laurent
Avenue Henri-Julien
Rue Gounod
Avenue de Gaspé
Rue Bélanger
Rue Guizot O
Rue Faillon E
Rue Jean-Talon E
Avenue de l'Esplanade
Rue Villeray
Rue de Castelnau E
335
Rue de Saint-Vallier
Rue Jarry O
Rue Saint-Denis
Rue Drolet
Avenue Henri-Julien
Rue Alma
Avenue de Gaspé
Rue de Castelnau O
Rue Faillon O
Rue Saint-Urbain
Rue Saint-Urbain
Rue Waverly
Rue Alexandra
Rue Marconi
Avenue Mozart O
Rue Bélanger
Rue Dante
Avenue Casgrain
Rue Saint-Dominique
Boulevard Saint-Laurent
Rue Clark
Rue Saint-Urbain
Rue Durocher
Avenue Querbes
Avenue de l'Épée
Avenue Bloomfield
Avenue Champagneur
Avenue d'Outremont
Avenue Wiseman
Rue Saint-Roch
Rue Jean-Talon-Ouest
Rue Hutchison
Rue Durocher
Avenue Querbes
Avenue du Parc
Avenue de l'Esplanade
Rue Jeanne-Mance
Avenue Stuart
Rue Birnam
Boulevard de l'Acadie
Avenue Ogilvy
Chemin Markham
Avenue Simcoe
Avenue Lockhart
Avenue Trenton
Avenue Brookfield
Boulevard Graham
Avenue Beaumont
Chemin Rockland
Rue Fleet
Boulevard Graham
Avenue Dresden

0 100 200 M.
0 500 1000 FT.

N

786 Halal Restaurant ㉓	Marché Jean-Talon ②
Alep ⑦	Milano Fruiterie ⑱
Caffè Italia ⑲	Moti Mehal ㉕
Camellia Sinensis Maison	Pâtisserie Efes ㉑
de Thé ⑪	Pizzeria Napoletana ⑫
Deli Joe ⑬	qui lait cru !?! ③
Faema ⑯	Quincaillerie Dante ⑮
Kitchen Galerie ⑩	Ristorante Primo & Secondo ⑭
La Fromagerie Hamel ⑥	Rôtisserie Panama ㉒
Le Marché des Saveurs	San Lorenzo ⑳
du Québec ④	Tapeo Bar à Tapas ①
Le Petit Alep ⑤	Via Roma ⑰
Maison Indian Curry House ㉔	Vinizza ⑧
	William J. Walter ⑨

Little Italy &
Parc Extension

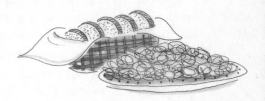

Divided from Mile End and the Plateau by the Canadian Pacific Railroad tracks, Little Italy sprang up in the early 20th century when immigrants flocked to the open land north of the Plateau where they could plant their gardens and build their bungalows. Cities to the south like Boston and New York absorbed huge influxes from southern Italy, but the immigrants to Montreal often hailed from Rome northward. In the long run, this has made for a local Italian-Canadian cuisine more dependent on rice, meat, and hard cheeses than the Italian-American fare that runs to pasta, tomato sauce, mozzarella, and ricotta. A century of assimilation has diluted the Italian heritage, but it survives in the churches, social clubs, and a few *caffès,* and the Italian flag flies high in soccer season. Of course, many neighborhood restaurants are Italian.

But a number of inventive young chefs with a bent toward contemporary Québecois cuisine have also opened in the streets surrounding the Marché Jean-Talon, which opened in 1934 and transformed the region even more profoundly than the flood of immigration. Restaurants in Little Italy became market-driven decades before local food became the fashion, and the merchants of the market cater to the needs and interests of the chefs—both the traditionalists and the *terroir* toques. No other part of the city has such an obvious give-and-take between food purveyors and cooks.

The Canadian Pacific tracks make a big curve west of Little Italy, cutting off the grid of streets known as Parc Extension from Little Italy on the east and Outremont on the south. This immigrant neighborhood is full of more recent arrivals. Many shops sell Indian and Pakistani bridal dresses or rent Bollywood videos, for example, and the restaurants are a delightful hodgepodge of ethnic cuisines from Southeast Asia, South Asia, West Africa, and the Caribbean. Because so many of the residents are Muslim, places often close on Friday—at least for a few hours while the owners attend services at their mosque.

Foodie Faves

Alep, 199 rue Jean-Talon est; (514) 270-6396. Metro: Jean-Talon/ Castelnau. Just a block or so from Marché Jean-Talon, Alep takes Middle Eastern food—specifically Syrian and Armenian—out of the snack shop and into the dining room. This formal restaurant is a good bet for a group, since the menu features a full four pages of *mezzes* that are great for sampling and sharing. The mixed plate includes hummus and grilled eggplant. But don't miss the *mouhamara* dip of pomegranate, molasses, cayenne pepper, and walnuts—so good that diners sometimes don't want to share. In any event, save room for the chicken and beef kebabs or a plate of braised lamb with port wine on rice with salted almonds and pine nuts.

Deli Joe, 7143 rue Saint-Dominique; (514) 342-4563. Metro: Castelnau. The folks at **Schwartz's** (see p. 126) like to keep things simple. Smoked meat is served on a sandwich or on a plate. But Montreal cooks are always finding other ways to incorporate the city's signature spiced-smoked brisket. At Deli Joe, it finds its way onto eggs Benedict (other choices include spinach, asparagus and mushrooms, mushrooms and brie, or smoked salmon). This breakfast- and lunch-only spot also has a large choice of omelets, crepes, and waffles, as well as sandwiches and salads.

Kitchen Galerie, 60 rue Jean-Talon est; (514) 315-8994; www.kitchengalerie.com. Metro: Castelnau. Located a chanterelle's toss from Marché Jean-Talon, Kitchen Galerie is the supercharged market cuisine restaurant of Jean-Philippe St-Denis, who learned his trade in some of Montreal's top dining rooms, and Mathieu Cloutier, whose stages in France, England, and Australia gave him an international perspective on highly local food. The menu isn't set until the chefs go shopping, but a typical fall dish might be seared scallops with a butter-caviar sauce, pureed parsnips, and a pickled beet salad. The emphasis on product tends to steer the

chefs toward the Italian side of the border with France—there's always a risotto featuring the vegetable of the moment. Bright, casual, and small, Kitchen Galerie dispenses with wait-staff—the cooks serve the tables. Always hopping, the room is an ongoing celebration of fresh food.

Le Petit Alep, 191 rue Jean-Talon est; (514) 270-9361. Metro: Jean-Talon/Castelnau. With rotating art exhibits, a more casual decor, and longer hours, Alep's junior sibling makes a good choice for lunch or a more casual dinner. In effect, Petit Alep is the cafe, while Alep is the restaurant. That means you can simply stop in for a pick-me-up of juice, coffee, or pastry or a small plate of chicken brochettes without committing to a whole meal.

Maison Indian Curry House, 996 rue Jean-Talon ouest; (514) 273-0004. Metro: Acadie. Something of a generalist in Indian cuisines, this Parc Extension stalwart effectively serves two different menus—the rice- and lentil-based cuisine of the south that includes *dosas* and a generous helping of hot spices, and the tandoori-oven cuisine of the north that emphasizes seared meats and hearth breads. Lamb dishes using Quebec lamb are especially good.

Moti Mehal, 1024 rue Jean-Talon ouest; (514) 315-8801. Metro: Acadie. As much Pakistani as Indian, this South Asian specialist occupies the building that once housed a Halal-certified Kentucky

Fried Chicken franchise. Although the Colonel has left the building, you can still get a whole chicken roasted in the tandoori oven—a healthier and, dare we say, tastier alternative. One of many things we admire about Moti Mehal is that they are straightforward (at least in the English menu) about using mutton rather than lamb. In truth, it makes a richer-flavored curry.

Pizzeria Napoletana, 189 rue Dante; (514) 276-8226; www .napoletana.com. Metro: Metro: Jean-Talon/Castelnau. Founded in 1948, this friendly pizzeria is often cited as Montreal's favorite. Certainly the chance to bring your own bottle of red wine is part of the appeal. But with 39 pizzas on the menu—from a simple Margherita with mozzarella and tomato sauce to the Vesuviano that adds olives and capers to the mix—there's something for every taste. In contrast to Montreal's typically puffy pizzas, the 10-inch pizzas at Napoletana have a thin crust, though not quite as thin as those served in the shop's namesake city. Nonetheless, as in Naples, most diners order their own pie. We prefer to split one along with an antipasto salad. Someday we'll try one of the 33 pasta dishes. Cash only. BYOB.

Ristorante Primo & Secondo, 7023 rue Saint-Dominique; (514) 908-0838; www.primoesecondo.ca. Metro: Castelnau. The first time we walked into Primo & Secondo, we had a Proustian experience.

But instead of the scent of *madeleines* conjuring our childhoods in excruciating detail, we momentarily relived the pure gustatory pleasure of a couple of great restaurants in Venice. So, yeah, this place is truly Italian, as if you couldn't tell by the chalkboard menu written entirely in that language. (The waitstaff will explain each dish in French or English if you'd like.) The kitchen hops around the peninsula a bit, seasoning the fried calamari with a Calabrese pepper, serving the prosciutto salad with San Daniele prosciutto from Friuli, and sprinkling speck from Alto Adige into the sauce for the Tuscan-style pumpkin ravioli with sage and brown butter. The proximity to Marché Jean-Talon explains the fresh-market nature of the daily menu, but being in the market district doesn't detract from the laudably formal dining experience. The tablecloths are white, the glasses gleaming, and the waiters give you time to talk and enjoy your food.

Rôtisserie Panama, 789 rue Jean-Talon ouest; (514) 276-5223; www.rotisseriepanama.com. Metro: Acadie. The name may reference the biggest canal of the Americas, but the cuisine hails from closer to Athens, with its emphasis on sliced roasted lamb and fried eggplant and summer squash. Souvlaki and brochettes are also popular, though most diners order at least one of the grill specialties (steak, lamb, or chicken) for the table. The restaurant also offers several Greek wines.

San Lorenzo, 6741 boulevard Saint-Laurent; (514) 544-1644. Metro: Jean-Talon/Castelnau. When you look at the crowds that mob

this admittedly pricey restaurant every night, you wonder why more northern Italian restaurants haven't opened in the neighborhood. The menu at San Lorenzo cuts a wide swath across Liguria, a bit of Tuscany, and Emilia-Romagna—with the exception of the signature sliders of *porchetta*, a particularly fatty and moist style of roast pork that hails from the Lazio region outside Rome. Most dishes are simple and depend on fabulous basic ingredients (grilled tuna with lentils, roasted pork with porcini mushrooms), and San Lorenzo delivers the goods. The sleek design, with modern interpretations of Art Deco, helps give the temple of eating just enough of a hard-edged vibe to make it a great drinking spot when supper is done.

786 Halal Restaurant, 768 rue Jean-Talon ouest; (514) 270-0786; www.786halalrestaurant.com. Metro: Acadie. You'll have to walk up narrow steps to find this homey spot of small-town Pakistani cooking, but you'll be glad you did. Even at dinner, few dishes go over $10—and those are intended for sharing, like the whole fish roasted on a brazier or the big bowl of mutton stewed with ginger. The family that runs 786 are observant Muslims, so the restaurant serves no alcohol and none may be brought in. A frothy mango drink better suits the food anyway. 786 is closed for Friday lunch.

Tapeo Bar à Tapas, 511 rue Villeray; (514) 495-1999; www.restotapeo.com. Metro: Jarry. We're stretching the boundaries of this chapter to Villeray East just to include Tapeo, home kitchen of one of Montreal's hottest chefs, Marie-Fleur St-Pierre. In 2010 she published a tapas cookbook and the restaurant also expanded to handle the crowds. By and large, St-Pierre replicates many of the classic tapas of Spain—anchovies on toast, Spanish omelet, scallops wrapped in bacon on quince marmalade—but she's not averse to putting her own spin on old favorites. For example, she roasts chorizo sausage with little potatoes, plates them with caramelized onions, and tops the assemblage with hot cream. Tapas restaurants are not generally known for service, but Tapeo sets a high standard. The wine list is loaded with superb Spanish vintages.

Via Roma, 7064 boulevard Saint-Laurent; (514) 277-3301. Metro: Castelnau. Despite the name, the food is more Milanese than Roman—leaning toward more roasted meat and less pasta. The tomatoes tend to be diced rather than sauced, and veal dishes predominate among the meats. Madame Caputo has been keeping Italian-Canadian diners happy here for years, so you'll find the occasional lapses from Old Country cuisine—like the pizza with onions and smoked salmon.

Vinizza, 150 rue Jean-Talon est; (514) 904-2250; www.vinizza .com. Metro: Castelnau. As much a wine bar as a restaurant, Vinizza nonetheless draws families as well as dating couples for the generous servings of heavily sauced pasta and the short list of pizzas where soft, melting swoops of mozzarella cheese are the biggest enticements. In addition to identifying as a pizzeria, Vinizza also calls itself an *enoteca*. It delivers the wines to earn the name, offering an interesting variety of lesser-known Italian wines, including La Tunella's superbly crisp Friulano on the white side and Pio Cesare's slightly ashen Dolcetto d'Alba on the red.

Landmarks

Marché Jean-Talon, 7070 rue Henri-Julien; (514) 277-1588. Metro: Jean-Talon/Castelnau. Open all year despite the paucity of fresh local produce in the winter, Marché Jean-Talon may lack the polish of **Marché Atwater** (see p. 40), but compensates by the sheer breadth of its vendors. During the height of the summer and fall, about 300 truck farmers from across Quebec bring their goods to Jean-Talon—tempting home cooks and restaurant chefs alike with salad greens, some of the world's best strawberries, all manner of row crops, mountains of freshly picked sweet corn, bins of perfect apples and pears, and—the last gasp of the harvest—pyramids of pumpkins and butternut squash. For the crops that do not grow in Quebec (and there are surprisingly few), Chez Louis Exotic Produce proffers cactus pears, kumquats, Persian limes, Spanish lemons, Medjool dates, Greek figs, Chioggia beets, exotic mushrooms, and even Provençal garlic. Stalls around the perimeter include a general fishmonger, another fishmonger who features the catch from the Gaspé Peninsula (including a dozen varieties of oysters), general butchers, Halal butchers, a butcher who only supplies Quebec game, a specialist in Eastern European charcuterie, a stand selling rotisserie chicken, several traditional bakeries and pastry shops, a Moroccan pastry specialist, a Polish pastry specialist, a vendor of olives from around the world, chocolate shops, and even a shop with artisanal fresh pasta and sauces. And that's just for starters. Several larger food specialists (see below) also have shops in the surrounding streets. If shopping in the summer, go very early in the morning as the crowds become enormous by the time most people are thinking about making dinner.

Specialty Stores, Markets & Producers

Caffè Italia, 6840 boulevard Saint-Laurent; (514) 495-0059. Metro: Castelnau. You'd think that the Italian neighborhood around Marché Jean-Talon would be awash in old-fashioned Italian coffee shops, but it's not. To get a shot of espresso that courses through your veins like a Roman office messenger on a Vespa, head to this little time capsule. The counters may be Formica and the clientele may have more furrows on their faces than a hillside in Piemonte, but the coffee is the real thing.

Camellia Sinensis Maison de Thé, 7010 rue Casgrain; (514) 271-4002; www.camellia-sinensis.com. Metro: Jean-Talon/Castelnau. Staff in this small shop almost always have a tea brewed and are happy to offer samples, but if you want to enjoy a full cup—and a sweet—visit the larger outlet in the Latin Quarter (see p. 89).

Faema, 14 rue Jean-Talon ouest; (514) 276-2671; www.faema canada.com. Metro: Castelnau. We've always thought of Montreal as a coffee-centric city, and according to Susan Angeli, interest in good coffee has even increased in the last 10 or 15 years. She should know. Her family has operated this shop that supplies espresso machines to restaurants and the public for more than 40 years. They are the Canadian outlet for the wonderful Faema machines from Udine, but also carry the exquisite, high-design Le Pavoni espresso makers and some minor brands sold in Italy in department stores. They also sell beans—their Faema blend of 12 different beans was judged to make the best *café au lait* in Montreal. You can taste it for yourself at the shop's small coffee bar.

La Fromagerie Hamel, Marché Jean-Talon, 220 rue Jean-Talon est; (514) 272-1161; www.fromageriehamel.com. Metro: Jean-Talon/Castelnau. Walking into this main outlet of Fromagerie Hamel feels like entering cheese heaven. The first case that greets you inside the door (right by the take-a-number dispenser) consists of little barrels and pyramids of soft cheeses crusted in tasty white molds or vegetable ash. Work your way around the cases and cheeses get firmer. What makes Hamel great is not just the choice of cheeses from around the world (and around Quebec), but also the fact that they coddle and care for their cheeses, holding them until they are ripe, or at least suggesting you give a particular *tomme* a few more days or that you hasten to finish the little stinky buttons before Saturday. It helps to speak a little French if you want the more glowing descriptions of certain cheeses, but they are also generous about offering samples as long as it's not a frantic Saturday morning.

Le Marché des Saveurs du Quebec, 280 Place du Marché-du-Nord; (514) 271-3811; www.lemarchedessaveurs.com. Metro: Jean-Talon/Castelnau. As the name suggests, this sometimes pricey shop specializes in the artisanal food products of Quebec, each labeled by its district of origin. You'll find *pâtés, terrines,* and *rillettes,* as well as honey, maple syrup, vinegars, chutneys, jams, jellies, conserves, pickles, mustards, dried wild mushrooms, and maple caramel sauce. You'll also find a fairly exhaustive collection of Quebec wines, hard ciders, and liqueurs in a separate section, and large case of cheeses and charcuterie. Bring an insulated bag so you can take home a container of Coaticook ice cream.

Milano Fruiterie, 6862 boulevard Saint-Laurent; (514) 273-8558; www.milanofruiterie.com. Metro: Castelnau. We have shopped in grocery stores in Italy that do not stock even half the products available in this Little Italy institution. In addition to *Arborio* rice, you'll also find *Carnaroli* and superfine *Baldo,* both of which are considered by many cooks to make a superior risotto. And then there's *Vialone Nano,* the preferred choice for a seafood risotto. The

Banana & Maple Muffins

One of the best places to find Quebec maple syrup in Montreal is *Le Marché des Saveurs du Quebec*, which carries syrup from a wide range of small producers. Montrealers do far more than pour the golden elixir over pancakes and waffles. This recipe comes from the Federation of Quebec Maple Syrup Producers (www.purecanadamaple.com), and it makes heavenly muffins where the maple syrup and the bananas meld into sheer breakfast delight. Maple butter, sold at most places that sell syrup, is made by cooking the syrup to soft-ball stage, quickly cooling, and then raising to room temperature while beating. Honestly, it's easier to buy than to make and has a super-concentrated maple flavor.

Makes 1 dozen muffins

1½ cups whole-wheat flour	2 ripe bananas, mashed
1 cup quick oats	1 egg
1 tablespoon baking powder	⅓ cup canola oil
2 pinches salt	⅓ cup maple syrup
½ teaspoon ground coriander (optional)	Maple butter, 1 teaspoon per muffin
½ cup walnuts, minced	12 walnut halves

Mix all ingredients through the minced walnuts in one bowl. In another bowl, mix bananas and other ingredients, except for the maple butter and walnut halves.

Add the wet ingredients to the dry. Stir until just moistened.

Pour batter into muffin cups. Bake for 15 to 20 minutes at 350°F. Cool slightly, remove from cups, and glaze with maple butter. Garnish with walnut halves.

pasta choices include both fresh and dried, with and without egg. Pick up some pasta, a fresh sauce, a chunk of Pecorino Romano or Parmigiano Reggiano cheese, and a few selections from the antipasto bar (marinated olives, mushrooms or artichokes) and you have the makings of a fine meal.

Pâtisserie Efes, 689 rue Saint-Roch; (514) 495-6535; canadaefes .com. Metro: Parc/Acadie. This shop is a little out of the way, even for Parc Extension, but it's worth seeking out. Talat and Zehra Tombul make all the phyllo dough by hand for their Turkish pastries, including baklava with either ground pistachios or ground walnuts. Among a variety of lovely treats, they also offer *tulumba*, Turkey's version of fried dough, soaked in sugar syrup.

qui lait cru !?!, Marché Jean-Talon, 7070 avenue Henri-Julien; (514) 272-0300. Metro: Jean-Talon/Castelnau. If Hamel feels like the public face of a cheese-aging cave, this alternative shop specializing in raw milk cheeses (though not exclusively) feels more like a small cheese factory—brightly lit and impeccably sterile. We've generally found the staff less able to expound on the cheeses and we've never been offered a sample, but the shop carries cheeses by a number of producers too tiny to supply the bigger cheesemongers. They also get loaves of Fromentier's great breads (see p. 134) delivered daily and carry the impossibly creamy butter from Beurrerie du Patrimoine, which has about 10 percent higher butterfat than most Quebec butters and has a dreamy, fresh-meadow flavor, especially in spring and early summer.

Quincaillerie Dante, 6851 rue Saint-Dominique; (514) 271-2057. Metro: Castelnau. **Don't be fooled by the displays of Le Creuset and Emile Henry cookware from France—or even by the displays of hunting knives and gun scopes for gourmets who like to bag their own wild game. For home cooks, the strength of this hardware store lies in its excellent selection of Italian food-prep tools, including tomato mills, pasta makers, espresso machines, and sausage stuffers. Sister and brother Elena Faita and Rudy Venditelli run the store and also offer classes in the basics of Italian cooking, taught in a nearby apartment on rue Dante. Inquire at the store—and be patient: Classes often have a waiting list of months.**

Eastern Townships

Many of Montreal's gastronomic pleasures originate in the Eastern Townships, one of the richest agricultural areas in Quebec. Most villages were settled just before and just after the American Revolution as colonists loyal to mother England fled north and founded communities with decidedly English names. These yeoman farmers created a district rich with dairy farms, apple orchards, maple sugar bush, and even row crops—all of which help feed the nearby hungry metropolis.

This region southeast of Montreal may be the most Anglo corner of Quebec, but even as many residents speak English, they taste in French. It seems as if most of the bakers, pastry chefs, and cheese-makers either come from France or proudly trace their heritage from little villages in Provence, Brittany, Normandy, Champagne, or Bordeaux. Even most of the grapes grown in the wine country near Lac Brome are French in origin (even if some were interbred with American grapes).

Lac Brome is also famous for raising the Peking breed of duck, introduced in the late 19th century. The area's truck gardens supply

Montreal's markets with asparagus, sweet strawberries, fancy lettuces, tomatoes, squash, corn, and fall apples and pumpkins. Rather than wait for the bounty to come to them, many Montrealers head to the Townships for gastronomic getaways along the *Route des Vins* in the western hamlets or in the "dairy bowl" of the Coaticook valley among the eastern villages. Often, such a getaway consists of holing up at a farm-country or lakeside inn that features a multi-course *table d'hôte* menu. In such cases, the most strenuous activity might be climbing the steps to the room after dinner.

The summer season begins with Quebec's National Day, June 24, when the first berries arrive and beekeepers pull the summer's first honeycombs. The days quickly grow long, and all those extra hours of sunlight accelerate the growth of plants as a northerly compensation for the short growing season. By July and August, the fields brim with berries and vegetables, leading to a harvest crescendo by Labour Day.

The remaining five weeks before Canadian Thanksgiving (Columbus Day in the United States) are the most bittersweet of the year. The late raspberries and black currants yield to the first touch of frost, and the countryside smells of apples from the quickening harvest. Grape growers switch on turbines in the vineyards to drive away the cold and eke out the last bit of ripeness before they cut the clusters and make wine. Yet even as snow blankets the orchards and vineyards, another harvest awaits: the frozen grapes and apples

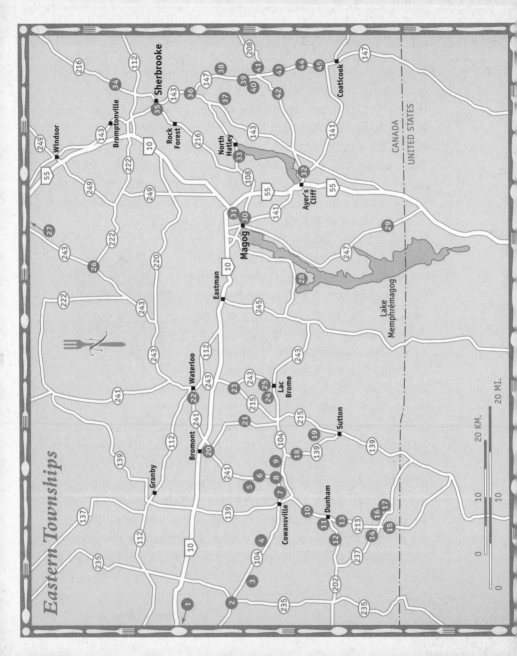

Eastern Townships

#	Name
28	Abbaye Saint-Benoît
18	Auberge & Spa West Brome
23	Auberge du Joli Vent
20	Auberge-Spa Le Madrigal
32	Ayer's Cliff Market
30	B&G Resto-Deli
43	BioBon
29	Bleu Lavande
7	Boulangerie La Mie Bretonne
24	Canards du Lac Brome
25	Chocolaterie Raphaël (Lac Brome)
30	Chocolaterie Raphaël (Magog)
11	Chocolats Colombe
40	Cidrerie Verger Ferland
43	Cinquième Elément
16	Clos Saragnat
45	Coaticook Market
7	Cowansville Friends of the Earth Market
9	Crème et Myrtilles
31	Crousset
27	Danville Public Market
37	Domaine de Courval
12	Domaine des Côtes d'Ardoise
38	Domaine Ives Hill
21	Domaine Les Brome
17	Domaine Pinnacle
5	Domaine Vitis
36	Ferme Beaulieu
20	Fleur de Cacao
2	Fromagerie des Cantons
42	Fromagerie La Station
20	Fromagerie Qualité Summum
11	Homei
30	La Chantournelle
1	Lac-Mégantic Public Market
15	La Girondine
44	Laiterie de Coaticook
11	Laperle et Son Boulanger
11	La Rumeur Affamée
41	Le Bocage
30	Le Fournil Provençal
20	Le Musée du Chocolat de la Confiserie Bromont
11	Le PUBlic House
25	Le Relais
30	Le Savarin
6	Les Jardins de la Colline
43	Les Miettes
14	Les Sucreries de l'Érable
8	Le St-Raphaël
10	Le Terroir
30	Magog Friends of the Earth Market
33	Manoir Hovey
34	Miellerie Lune de Miel
26	Racine Public Market
35	Sherbrooke Friends of the Earth Market
35	Sherbrooke Station Market
13	Val Caudalies
39	Verger Le Gros Pierre
4	Vignoble de la Bauge
12	Vignoble de l'Orpailleur
19	Vignoble Domaine Bresee
12	Vignoble Gagliano
3	Vignoble Les Pervenches
22	Waterloo Friends of the Earth Market

to be crushed to make ice wine and ice cider—the sweetest remembrances of summer.

Foodie Faves

Auberge & Spa West Brome, 128 route 139, Lac Brome; (450) 266-7552 or (888) 902-7663; www.awb.ca. The townhouse-style guest suites of this country retreat cluster in three new buildings around the indoor pool and heated outdoor hot tub. The dining room occupies the original 1880 farmhouse and its former porch, and that's where Provence-born chef Stéphane Charpentier works his magic with southern French treatments of mostly local products. His duck duo is likely to feature the breast from one producer, the confit leg from another. When the kitchen garden is in high gear (July–Sept), his authentically Provençal version of *ratatouille* is an earthly delight.

Auberge du Jolí Vent, 667 chemin Bondville, Lac Brome; (450) 243-4272 or (866) 525-4272; www.aubergedujolivent.com. During the month of March, chef Hans Christiner serves special Swiss menus—not surprising since he hails originally from Lucerne. Dishes might include jugged hare with tiny dumplings and braised red cabbage, or poached walleye with an herb sauce as it's made in Zug (about 15 miles from Lucerne). The rest of the year, he focuses on Townships provender, tempting diners with game, fish, and hearty stews. "But people scream for the duck," he declaims in mock-lament. He might complain about everyone's appetite for the region's signature poultry, but he has a long list of duck dishes to suit the season and his whim. One of his favorite presentations is to slice poached duck breast very thinly, toss it with apple slices, and serve on lettuce with an apple-cider vinaigrette. His wife, Patricia Provencher, not only manages the wine list (which features the best of the local wines), but she also runs the country-chic 10-room inn perched on the northwest tip of Lac Brome. (See recipe on p. 194.)

Auberge-Spa Le Madrigal, 46 boulevard de Bromont, Bromont; (450) 534-3588 or (877) 534-3588; www.lemadrigal.ca. Chef-proprietor Claude Massé doesn't get too fancy with his duck. He has been serving a breast of Lac Brome duck with lime sauce since 1993 and keeps his menu fairly constant because "people generally stay here three times a year, and they always want to have the same plate." Massé also works alone in his kitchen ("I am jealous of my stove," he quips), cooking every plate to order. The menu does vary some with season, as Massé features venison in the fall, lamb in the spring. A purist about flavor, Massé only serves lobster when he can get it from fishermen on Quebec's Magdalen Islands. Dinner at Le Madrigal is strictly a six-course *table d'hôte,* but it's always a very good deal. Massé features wines from three nearby wineries, but he also imports much of his well-curated list himself from France, Italy, and occasionally Australia. In addition to 11 guest rooms, the inn has a

Lac Brome Duck Breast with Maple Cider Sauce

Chef Hans Christiner of the Auberge du Jolí Vent playfully laments that his guests cannot get enough of the local Lac Brome duck. He's developed a large repertoire of recipes to indulge his creativity and keep his guests happy. This version combines three signature tastes of the Eastern Townships: duck, apples, and maple syrup.

4 duck breasts	**½ cup apple cider**
Salt, pepper and paprika	**2–3 tablespoons maple syrup, medium grade**
Oil to coat pan	
1 small onion, finely chopped	**1 cup veal jus or chicken stock**
2 Cortland apples, cored, peeled and cut in small cubes	**1 teaspoon cornstarch**
	1 tablespoon butter

Trim skin off duck breasts. Season to taste with salt, pepper, and paprika.

Heat a large (10- to 12-inch) frying pan and add oil to coat. Cook duck breasts to medium-rare. Remove from pan and reserve on a warm dish.

Add onion to pan and sauté until lightly browned. Add apple cubes and continue cooking until apples begin to soften. Add apple cider and stir to deglaze the pan, scraping the bottom to get browned bits to dissolve. Add a few tablespoons of maple syrup to taste—not too sweet—and continue heating until juices reduce and become viscous. Add jus or stock and bring back to a boil.

Blend cornstarch with a little apple cider and stir slurry into the boiling sauce to thicken slightly. Stir in butter until melted.

Pour sauce over duck breasts and serve.

Serves 4

Recipe courtesy of Auberge du Jolí Vent (p. 192).

small spa that features a number of vinotherapy beauty treatments using grape seeds from the local wineries.

B&G Resto-Deli, 290, suite B, rue Principale ouest, Magog; (819) 847-5077. If you're missing Montreal smoked meat while in the Townships, B&G is just the spot to feed that hunger. They feature Lester's smoked meat (from Montreal) in a classic sandwich with pickle, on a pizza, or as an enhancement to *poutine*. For the full "guy" experience, dine at one of the six stools at the bar and wash down your smoked meat with a beer.

Cinquième Elément, 6815 route Louis-S-St-Laurent, Compton; (819) 835-0052; www.lecinquiemeelement.ca. Before you walk in, it helps to understand that the "fifth element" was a wild sci-fi film by French auteur Luc Bresson in which the critical fifth element needed to save the world was a woman. Chef-owner Corine Descampe, who hails from Belgium, may not need to perform superhuman feats but she has come into her own in Quebec as a champion of local food, environmental awareness, and all-around good karma. These all contribute to her terrific bistro menu of such dishes as a cream of beet and apple soup, local snails in garlic sauce, or sautéed duck gizzards with frisée. She also specializes in making jarred preserves like "Plaisir Passion" of tomatoes and ginger, or preserved pears and rosemary. Descampe's motto: "Life is too short to eat sad." (It's better in French: *"La vie est trop courte pour manger triste."*)

Homei, 3809 rue Principale, Dunham; (450) 284-0522; www .homeibistro.com. Sharing the old stagecoach stopover building in button-cute Dunham with **Le PUBlic House** (see p. 197), Homei often puts an Asian twist on Quebec food. Their Chinese ribs, for example, are braised in the neighboring brewery's black stout and served with an apple slaw and french fries. Sandwiches are made with the fantastic bread from **Laperle et Son Boulanger** (see p. 214) just down the street. And, yes, Homei serves duck, most often in their spring rolls. When the weather's cool, indoor dining offers the warmth of the old stage stop. In warm weather, most diners opt for the outdoor patio shared with the pub.

La Girondine, 104 route 237 Sud, Frelighsburg; (450) 298-5206; www.lagirondine.ca. In 2006, Silvie Campbell took over this venerable duck farm about a mile outside Frelighsburg and, if anything, has expanded the variety of duck and rabbit products available in its small shop. Not only can you buy breast, confit leg, sausages, and *pâté*, you can also pick up a dozen duck eggs or *rillettes* of rabbit in Madeira sauce. The old farmhouse building serves as the farm's restaurant. Madame Campbell offers a choice of four- or seven-course dinners nightly during the warm months and on weekends during the winter. Each meal is a lesson in local product, from her charcuterie plate to the roast duck breast in black currants or the rack of lamb from a nearby farm. The longer menu also features a plate of local cheeses before dessert.

Le Bocage, 200 chemin Moe's River, Compton; (819) 835-5653; www.lebocage.qc.ca. François Dubois was a long-time customer of

Le Bocage before he finally realized his dreams in 1997 by buying the 1825 inn with four guest rooms. He expanded the summer porch into a terrace dining room to accommodate gourmets who flock to the idyllic country setting for Dubois's contemporary cooking firmly rooted in the *terroir* of the Eastern Townships. His five-course menus offer two choices each among the appetizers, main courses, and desserts. Don't dine here alone because you'd miss out on tasting your partner's plate. He never prepares chicken, beef, or pork, reasoning that diners can make those at home—opting instead for wild game, guinea fowl, or bison. Dubois is known among local chefs for his beautiful soup duos, where he plates two complementary soups of different colors in the same bowl. The garden setting in the midst of farmland is popular for celebrations. BYOB.

Le PUBlic House, 3809 rue Principale, Dunham; (450) 295-1500; www.betf.ca. Sharing a courtyard and part of the old stage stop building with **Homei** (see p. 196), this friendly bar is the tasting room and public sales side of Brasseurs & Frères. Despite the utterly French name, this small brewery takes its inspiration from English-style beer making, though the tap room fortuitously subscribes to the North American idea that beer should be chilled. While they do craft a fine Americaine Pale Ale for the faint of heart, beer lovers gravitate to Hoppy (an IPA) and the high-alcohol "Mort de Rive," which translates loosely as "Verge of Death."

Le Relais, 286 chemin Knowlton, Knowlton; (450) 242-2232; www .aubergeknowlton.ca/relais. Lac Brome duck is usually the center-piece of fine-dining menus, but this casual eatery in the heart of the Lac Brome village lets you try the local product without all the frills of a two-hour *table d'hôte* meal. In addition to duck livers in blackened butter, duck confit, and pink-centered roasted duck breast, you can also opt for cheese crepes or a hamburger before moving on to apple crumble or maple pie for dessert.

Les Sucreries de l'Érable, 16 rue Principale, Frelighsburg; (450) 298-5181; www.lessucreriesdelerable.com. Speaking of maple pie, the house specialty of Les Sucreries is *la tarte au sirop d'rable,* a swooningly sweet pie with the saccharinity and texture of pecan pie minus the nuts. As a *café-resto* (akin to a French *pâtisserie*), Les Sucreries also offers a limited menu of breakfast and lunch dishes, including waffles and crepes, sandwiches, quiches, and *croques* both *madame* and *monsieur* (that's a grilled ham and cheese, respectively with and without a fried egg on top). If you really want to gild the lily, ask for a scoop of maple ice cream on your slice of maple tart.

Manoir Hovey, 575 chemin Hovey, North Hatley; (819) 842-2421 or (800) 661-2421; www.hoveymanor.com. Neither French nor English contains enough superlatives to describe the experience of staying at Manoir Hovey and dining at the resort's fine restaurant, Le Hatley. Built in the early 20th century on the shores of Lac Massawippi and modeled on George Washington's Mount Vernon, the country estate has been a resort inn since 1950. The rooms are gracious and comfortable, and the service strikes the perfect balance between friendly and professional. Some people come here for straight R&R, others for both summer and winter sports. More, we suspect, choose to vacation at Manoir Hovey simply to enjoy chef Roland Ménard's spectacular seasonal cuisine. Ménard has led the resort's kitchen since 1981, but his ideas remain as fresh as his produce. Local growers adore Ménard because his commitment to *terroir* means that he works with them to develop consistent products and then commits to buying them. One small farm, for example, supplies him with four to five dozen ducks a week as well a great deal of *foie gras*. The heritage breed beef cattle graze on nearby hillsides. As a master of classical cuisine, Ménard could repeat himself all the time and still please his clients, but he's always doing something new. "I build the plate as I cook it," he says. "When I get sick of it, I take it off the menu." One signature dish that he will resurrect on request is his wild mushroom salad—just give him a few days to forage.

Specialty Stores, Markets & Producers

Abbaye Saint-Benoît, Saint-Benoît-du-Lac; (819) 843-2681; www .magasin-abbaye-st-benoit-du-lac.com. The monks of this abbey on a headland overlooking Lac Memphremagog live according to the Benedictine rule, and Benedict was a big believer in the sanctity of hard work. They are required to earn their living through manual labor, which has proved a huge benefit to lovers of good cheese and ciders. About 45 monks and a few outside workers manage the farm, cheese factory, and cider mill and bottling plant. The abbey was founded in 1912 and the monks began making cheese in 1943 with "Ermite," a salty cheese shot through with blue veining. But the monks gained international prominence in the cheese world in 2000 when they introduced a creamy blue cheese with a natural rind: "Bleu Bénédictin." Cave-aged at the abbey for at least 10 weeks, it blossoms with an intense "blue" nose over nutty background notes. The cheese factory also produces another seven non-blue cheeses, including a ripened goat's-milk cheese called "Le Moutier." All the cheeses are available in the abbey store, along with the abbey's dry and sweet ciders and apple-cider vinegar. The shop also features the work of monks from other cloisters, such as *Okaramel à l'érable*, a maple-syrup ganache formed into oak leaves and enrobed in chocolate. It's produced at the Abbaye Val Notre-Dame west of Montreal.

BioBon, 6820 route Louis-S-St-Laurent, Compton; (819) 835-1325; www.biobon.ca. Pasquale Beauvais makes wonderful breads and pastries at her bakery, but she is justifiably famous for her *végé-pâté*—a *pâté* of nuts, seeds, grains, and vegetables that could nearly pass as a meat product. With the texture of a moist meatloaf, the *végé-pâté* works as cubes in a salad, sliced on bread, or stuffed into tomatoes. We like to pack it in a picnic cooler along with one of Beauvais's *baguettes*. The *pâté* is so popular that it is sold in many shops besides her bakery.

Bleu Lavande, 891 chemin Narrow (route 247), Stanstead (Fitch Bay); (819) 876-5851; www.bleulavande.ca. If you want to revel in the sight and aroma of 35,000 lavender plants in bloom, plan to visit Bleu Lavande between mid-July and mid-August. Canada's self-proclaimed largest producer of fine lavender has created a whole line of body products for men, women, children, and even pets. But one variety of lavender is grown specifically for culinary purposes and the subtle flavor enhances honey, chocolate, jelly, tea, and a lavender-and-herb vinaigrette for salads. If you're inspired to create your own recipes, little tins of lavender seasoning are available. The farm's products may also be purchased in Montreal, including at La Baie department store, 585 rue Sainte-Catherine ouest, and in Les Promenades de Catédral underground shops.

Boulangerie La Mie Bretonne, 511 rue du Sud, Cowansville; (450) 955-1500; www.lamiebretonne.com. It's worth going back day after day just to see what the bakers have decided to make from their repertoire of forty different French breads. On any given day, you will probably find a multigrain bread and a couple of kinds of *baguettes*. On the weekends, the bakery even makes Parisian-style *baguettes* with imported French flour. Like many Quebec bakeries, this one is also fond of flour ground from kamut, a nutty-tasting heritage wheat well tolerated by people who have trouble digesting other grains. La Mie Bretonne also makes a sinfully rich chocolate brioche with both white and dark chocolate.

Farmers' Markets

During the growing season, farm stands open their doors and individual growers set up tables out in their front yards. But the following farmers' markets are organized affairs where you can shop the agricultural bounty of the region from a multitude of producers. In a single stop you can load up on duck eggs, farmstead cheese, and tomatoes  and zucchini. One group of mostly seasonal markets is tracked by Quebec's agricultural ministry. For more information, see this website: www.mapaq.gouv.qc.ca/Fr/Regions/estrie/Profil/prodestrie/MarchesPublics/. Another group of markets belong to the "markets of regional solidarity" of the Friends of the Earth. They tend to feature organic products, and several are open all year, though meat and preserved products displace fruits and vegetables in the winter. Check details (in French only) at this website: www.atestrie.com.

Seasonal Markets

Ayer's Cliff Market, 977 rue Main, Ayer's Cliff. Sat from 10:30 a.m. to 12:30 p.m., late June through mid-Sept.

Lac-Mégantic Public Market, City center, Lac-Mégantic. Sat from 9 a.m. to 2 p.m., mid-June through late Sept.

Racine Public Market, route 222, Racine. Sat from 8:30 a.m. to 1 p.m., mid-June to early Oct.

Year-Round Markets

Coaticook Market, 136 rue Main est, Coaticook. Wed from 8:30 a.m. to 4:30 p.m., Thurs from 8:30 a.m. to 8 p.m., Fri from 8:30 a.m. to 4 p.m.

Cowansville Friends of the Earth Market, 531 rue Sud, Cowansville. Wed from 9 a.m. to 5 p.m., Thurs from 9 a.m. to 8 p.m., Fri from 8:30 a.m. to 5 p.m., Sat from 9 a.m. to 1 p.m.

Danville Public Market, intersection of rues Daniel-Johnson and Carmel, Danville. Sat from 10 a.m. to 2 p.m.

Magog Friends of the Earth Market, 50 rue Laurier, Magog. Wed, Fri, Sat, and Sun from 8:30 a.m. to 3 p.m., Thurs from 8:30 a.m. to 7:30 p.m.

Sherbrooke Friends of the Earth Market, 843 rue King ouest. Mon and Tues from 8:30 a.m. to 4:30 p.m., Wed and Thurs from 8:30 a.m. to 8 p.m., Fri from 8:30 a.m. to noon.

Sherbrooke Station Market, 710 rue Minto, Sherbrooke. Sun through Wed from 10 a.m. to 6 p.m., Thurs through Sat from 9 a.m. to 8 p.m.

Waterloo Friends of the Earth Market, 151 rue Lewis ouest, Waterloo. Mon through Wed from 8 a.m. to 2 p.m., Thurs from 8:30 a.m. to 8 p.m., Fri from 8:30 to 11:30 a.m.

Canards du Lac Brome, 40 chemin du Centre, Lac Brome; (450) 242-3825; www.canardsdulacbrome.com. Launched in 1912 as Quebec's first duck farm, Canards du Lac Brome put the lake, the Townships, and the poultry on the map. For many years it sold almost all of its production to Chinatowns across Canada and the northeastern United States, but since the 1980s, the firm has turned its marketing closer to home. Although the ducks and duck parts are available in Montreal markets and gourmet shops (including the company's own outlet, see p. 133), this factory store has the full selection from the uncooked breast and leg portions (and whole ducks), to a couple of types of duck sausage and rendered duck fat (in case you're planning on making your own confit). Cooking demonstrations and free samples will give you an idea why the duck has become so popular with local chefs.

Chocolaterie Raphaël, 320 rue Knowlton, Lac Brome; (450) 242-2994. This modest little *café-resto* was the original home of Chocolaterie Raphaël, but when the confectioner moved to the big city of Magog (see next page) so his children could attend school there, he could barely keep this shop open. Enter Georges-Patrice Clément, a master pastry maker. M. Clément manages the cafe, makes all the fabulous tarts and cakes, and sells Raphaël's chocolates. Everybody wins. When pears are in season, he makes a killer pear-chocolate-almond cake.

Chocolaterie Raphaël, 759 rue Principale ouest, Magog; (819) 868-6698. After Raphaël Guillemette left Lac Brome (see previous page) he opened this shop in 2008 to present the full array of his exquisitely crafted chocolates. He now also sells a smaller selection of M. Clément's pastries. A big part of the fun here is to sip espresso at the bar and watch Raphaël at work across the room at his massive marble tables. Using the finest European chocolate, he crafts little jewels filled with vanilla and coffee creams, with salt caramel, or with almonds or hazelnuts.

Chocolats Colombe, 3809 rue Principale, Dunham; (450) 295-1119; www.chocolatscolombe.com. Karen Domingue, who presides behind the counter of this tempting little shop, explains that chocolates should be eaten in two bites. "The first bite prepares your mouth," she says. "On the second bite you can appreciate the full flavor." We find it hard not to scarf them down in a single bite, but the shop's delicacies—a strawberry truffle with sweet pepper, or white-chocolate ganache with Champagne—merit the more deliberative approach. Like many Quebec chocolatiers, Colombe makes delicious caramel graced with sea salt from France to cut the sweetness. The salt caramel is used to fill both milk and dark chocolate bon-bons and as a base for creating "turtles" by embedding roasted pecans. You can also buy it in small jars as a guilty pleasure to indulge with a spoon.

Cidrerie Verger Ferland, 380 chemin de la Station, Compton; (819) 835-5762; www.vergerferland.com. Martin Ferland's orchard includes thousands of apple trees and a lot of pears and plums as well. It's a popular place in pick-your-own season, but Ferland has found a way to make good use of the fruits for the rest of the year. He makes a fortified apple cider "aromatized" with pear or plum that he calls "Mistelle." And in 2010, he also began making a *cidre fort,* or hard cider, that is naturally fermented entirely from apples and reaches an alcohol level of 12 percent (which is pretty hard indeed). The blend of apples, he says, "is a secret." Open late June through Dec.

Clos Saragnat, 100 chemin Richford, Frelighsburg; (450) 298-1444; www.saragnat.com. Christian Barthomeuf is the *éminence grise* of Quebec wines and ciders—a true pioneer who keeps breaking new ground. In 1980, the immigrant from Auvergne, France, planted French-American hybrids at **Domaine des Côtes d'Ardoise** (see p. 209), the oldest Quebec winery still operating. When he planted true vinifera vines, he pioneered the radical growing method of burying the tender vines each fall to protect them from the winter cold. But Barthomeuf is most celebrated as the father of ice cider, a product he first made in 1990 by applying ice-wine techniques to apples. He continues to rave about apples as the native noble fruit of Quebec, "and I got tired of burying vines," he says with an air of ironic self-deprecation. Since 2002 Barthomeuf and partner Louise Dupuis have made Clos Saragnat into a showcase of biodynamic fruit growing, making wines and ice ciders with no chemical interventions and no additives. The "Original" ice cider is the main draw, though production is less than 3,000 bottles a year because it is all made from apples still hanging on the trees above the snowbanks. For greater yield, Bathomeuf also makes "Avalanche," an ice cider that combines fruit still hanging on the trees with fruit picked in late November. Of the unusual grape wines from Clos Saragnat, the best is the *vin de paille,* or "straw wine," so named because the Vidal and Muscat grapes are picked and allowed to partially dry on straw pallets. The labor-intensive process yields only 700 pricey bottles a year of a unique elixir that tastes a little like an amontillado sherry and a little like a German ice wine. A visit here to talk with Barthomeuf and Dupuis is a must for any fan of organic farming or cold-climate winemaking. Open June through mid-Oct.

Crème et Myrtilles, 1112 chemin de Knowlton Lac Brome, West Brome; (450) 955-1222. This tiny bakery attached to a house does not look promising from the road, but pastry-lovers in the know turn into the driveway because they would not want to miss the artistry of Jean-Philippe Moquet, a pastry chef from Dijón. Moquet, who provides the French pastry to **Boulangerie La Mie Bretonne** (see p. 201), is an artist with chocolate, cream, and butter. He makes meltingly tender *madeleines, macarons* as light as an angel's breath, and coffee *religieuse,* a cream-puff-like pastry that resembles a nun's habit.

Crousset, 190 rue Centre, Magog; (819) 868-4411; www.crousset .com. Jacques Crousset likes to remind people that the search for the spice route to India led to the discovery of the New World. Like a modern-day Marco Polo, Crousset has brought the flavors of the world to his Eastern Townships shop where he stocks more than 100 different spice blends. Among his specialties are a salmon rub with hickory and maple sugar and a lamb rub with sumac, paprika, and rosemary.

Domaine de Courval, 825 chemin de Courval, Waterville; (819) 837-0062. Not the easiest place to find—it's up a long gravel road—this tiny *fromagerie* operated by Laurie Goodhart and Raynald Hébert has a devoted following for "Kunik," a rich mold-ripened cheese made of blended cow's and goat's milks. Goodhart invented "Kunik" in New York, but kept the right to make the cheese in Canada when she sold her Nettle Meadow cheese business and moved to Quebec in 2005. Courval also produces a line of cheeses made entirely from goat's milk, including a brightly tangy fresh chevre and a mold-ripened cheese called "Perle." Goodhart altered the process of making "Perle" to suit Quebec taste. Rather than develop a creamy center as it ages, the cheese remains firm. The goats eat only organic grain and organically grown hay, giving the cheeses a distinct *terroir*.

Domaine des Côtes d'Ardoise, 879 rue Bruce (route 202), Dunham; (450) 295-2020; www.cotesdardoise.com. More than 30 years old, this lovely vineyard with a nature trail on the grounds is one of the recognized pioneers of winemaking in Quebec. That gives the operation the decided advantages of old vines and lots of experience. While their Seyval-based whites tend to find the greatest critical favor, Côtes d'Ardoise has remained committed to creating a top-quality Quebec red based on the Gamay grape augmented with Maréchal Foch. The old-vine Riesling is a nicely tart expression of the spicy grape. The winery also produces an unusual rosé ice wine, "Givrée d'Ardoise," that has overtones of blackberries and candied fruit.

Domaine Ives Hill, 12 chemin Boyce, Compton; (819) 837-0301; www.produitsdelaferme.com/aperifruits. The Quebec climate may be tough on wine grapes, but it is inordinately kind to black currants, the dark berry long used in France to produce *cassis* liqueurs. Ives Hill focuses on berry-based apéritifs (black currant, blackberry, and raspberry) that retain a striking fresh-fruit flavor. The little red barnlike shop overlooks 3,000 black-currant bushes of the 12,000 on the property. While made differently from *cassis,* the black-currant apéritif makes a fine *kir royale* (classically, *cassis* in Champagne). Open mid-May through mid-Oct.

Domaine Les Brome, 285 chemin Brome, Lac Brome; (450) 242-2665; www.domainelesbrome.com. Set high on a southeast-facing gravelly hillside above Lac Brome, Les Brome has the microclimate to grow some grape varieties too tender for other Quebec properties. The winery had great success with hardy hybrids such as Baco noir and Geisenheim, and has followed up with recent plantings of Pinot noir and Riesling that ripen nicely on the sunny hillside. While many Quebec wineries focus on growing the wine in the vineyard, Les Brome pulls out all the stops in the winemaker's playbook to craft their final wines, especially by aging in American oak. Even the ice wine (made from Vidal) is given 12 months in oak, which imparts distinctive vanilla overtones. The grounds are especially nice for picnicking, which the winery encourages.

Domaine Pinnacle, 150 chemin Richford, Frelighsburg; (450) 298-1226; www.domainepinnacle.com. Located at the foot of Pinnacle mountain, practically an apple-throw from Vermont, this pioneer producer of ice cider has expanded its product line in recent years. In addition to the "Original" ice cider that has wowed critics and won gold medals since its introduction in 1992, Pinnacle also makes a naturally sparkling ice cider and a "Signature" ice cider made with later-picked apples. The company also produces a smooth brandylike product, "Reserve 1859," made by blending ice cider and apple *eau de vie* imported from Normandy. Two of the biggest hits are cream liqueurs. "Pinnacle Crème" is similar to Bailey's Irish Cream, but has a distinct apple flavor. "Coureurs des Bois" combines ice cider with maple cream—two key flavors of the Eastern Townships. The adjacent interpretation center explains the process of making ice cider.

Domaine Vitis, 1095 chemin Nord, Bromont; (450) 263-4988; www.domainevitis.com. Pierre Genesse and Marie-Claude Lizotte only opened Vitis to the public in 2010, but the pair are no strangers to Quebec winemaking, having operated another winery from 1989 to 2001. They planted new vineyards and made the first Vitis wines in 2007. The operation is a vote of confidence in the future of the Frontenac family of grapes in Quebec. Originally released as a red wine grape from the University of Minnesota breeding program in 1996, Frontenac produced a sport with gray-green grapes that was released as Frontenac gris in 2003, and has since mutated in Quebec vineyards to produce Frontenac blanc. Vitis grows all three and vinifies them with exceeding care to produce a line of wines with pronounced taste of the local soil and climate. The "Vitis Blanc," interestingly enough, is a *blanc de noir*—that is, a white wine made from pressing dark grapes so lightly that none of the color is extracted from the skins. Even Genesse was surprised by how good it is: "I'm overwhelmed," he says. "I wasn't expecting such roundness." Perhaps the most striking wine from Vitis to date, however, is the "Glace Noir," an ice wine made entirely from Frontenac noir that strongly resembles a tawny port. It is a perfect fireside sipping wine for long Quebec winter evenings. Open May through Dec.

Ferme Beaulieu, 3750 route 143, Waterville; (819) 562-6477. A steady stream of vegetables fills the bins of this family-run farmstand at the crossroads just north of Compton. Because local farmers grow several season-neutral varieties, you can even purchase delicious Quebec strawberries into September. The stand has a kitchen attached, where the chef from France makes delectably flaky croissants, quiches, and a delicious *pissaladière* of bechamel sauce, tomato, cheese, and bacon on a pizzalike base. But the Beaulieus have not abandoned their Québecois roots—they also sell the traditional meat-filled pastries called *tourtières*. Open June through Dec.

Fleur de Cacao, 840 rue Shefford, Bromont; (450) 534-1311; www.fleurdecacao.ca. Chef Jean-Pierre Templier left France for Quebec more than 30 years ago, but his delicate lemon, raspberry, pistachio, and caramel *macarons* would be right at home in a Parisian *pâtisserie*. The multifaceted chef also makes ice creams and chocolates that look like miniature galaxies. He wraps caramel and orange flower in chocolate for the "Sicilienne" or creates a maple syrup caramel for the "Érable." Quebec's signature syrup also finds its way into a rich tart of caramel, maple syrup, and pecans.

Fromagerie des Cantons, 441 boulevard Normandie nord, Farnham; (450) 293-2498. The witty cheesemakers here must have a fascination with meteorology. They call their nutty Camembert-type cheese "La Brise de Vigneron" (the winemaker's breeze), their firm style cheese "Zéphyr" (the god of the west wind) and their two newest cheeses, "El Niño" and "Scirocco" (semi-firm cheeses, the latter with a layer of ash). All crafted from raw high-butterfat Jersey milk, the cheeses are rich and creamy and worth seeking out. The soft cheese is often available from top cheesemongers in Montreal.

Fromagerie La Station, 440 chemin de Hatley, Compton; (819) 835-5301; www.fromagerielastation.com. La Station is one of Quebec's oldest cheesemakers producing raw-milk cheeses. The signature "Comtonne" is a true *tomme* cheese, which means that it is cooked at a lower temperature than, say, cheddar, and is pressed into molds to create the signature flat wheels. The washed-rind cheese has a texture and flavor akin to a Comté, but is made in smaller wheels that age more quickly. The softer, less-aged "Alfred le fermier" is produced only in the summer. La Station also makes a very credible "Raclette de Compton" perfect for melting to eat with tiny boiled potatoes and crispy cornichons during ski season.

Fromagerie Qualité Summum, 52 boulevard Bromont, Bromont; (450) 534-0672. No one ever accused Summum of making artisanal cheese, but the company does manufacture some of the best-loved cheese products in Quebec: cheese curds. Most cheesemakers in the province, in fact, remove some of their fresh curds from production right after rennet is added to the milk and curds form. Washed in salt water and packed in plastic bags, the curds are available at the register at every gas station and convenience store in Quebec and are an essential ingredient in *poutine*. Here at the Summum factory the company has a fast-food outlet where you can get lasagna smothered in melted cheese, cheeseburgers, pizzas, and (most important of all) three different kinds of *poutine*.

La Chantournelle, 297 rue Principale ouest, Magog; (819) 847-3056. The highlight of this sweet gift shop on Magog's main drag is the "Coin de Provence" display of sunny-colored table linens made in the Provençal style. Some of the tablecloths are treated to be stain-resistant—which makes them perfect to spread out a picnic.

Laiterie de Coaticook, 1000 rue Child, Coaticook; (819) 849-2272; www.laiteriedecoaticook.com. The concentration of dairy farmers in the Coaticook valley south of Sherbrooke once earned the area the nickname of "the dairy basin" of Quebec. Founded in 1940, Laiterie de Coaticook keeps the tradition alive. The company produces cheddar, mozzarella, and even aged goat cheese, but it has earned a near-cultlike following for its ice cream. Coaticook makes ice cream with pure milk and cream and absolutely no fillers or stabilizers—8 million liters (2.1 million gallons) a year of ice milk and ice cream. It is available in a few grocery stores (and at the **Marché Jean-Talon** in Montreal, see p. 181), but aficionados favor the small dairy bar at the factory for the broadest selection of flavors. They range from the bright, pure notes of strawberry or blueberry to an almost perfect combination of chocolate and caramel.

Laperle et Son Boulanger, 3746 rue Principale, Dunham; (450) 295-2068. To clarify, "Laperle" is Julie Laperle, who makes pastry, and "son boulanger" is Bernard Bélanger, who makes the breads. This loving partnership finds expression in some of the tastiest breads in Quebec. All the sourdough breads are produced with stone-ground flour from nearby Moulin St-Pierre. Bélangᴛ also fashions a "hybrid" baguette made with a blend of western Canadian and Quebec flours, a sourdough starter, and some additional live yeast. These are breads that actually express the *terroir* of the Townships. Julie's caramel *fleur de sel* is our favorite topping for ice cream.

La Rumeur Affamée, 3809 rue Principale, Dunham; (450) 295-2399. It's hard to tell whether this shop is a deli, a *café-resto,* or just a gourmet shop from cheese-lover's heaven. The chilled cases may hold up to 150 different cheeses at any given time, about half of which originate in Quebec. It's the kind of place that when they run out of "Bleu Bénédictin" from the **Abbaye Saint-Benoît** (see p. 199), they'll apologize for offering a "Papillon Roquefort" from France in its stead. In addition to the shop's own pies, *pâtés,* and pastries, they also sell local duck and maple products.

Le Fournil Provençal, 334 rue Principale ouest, Magog; (819) 843-9009. Elizabeth Merle traces her roots back six generations to Provence, and like her Provençal ancestors, she captures the luscious flavors of seasonal fruits in such homemade jams as strawberry, rhubarb, *cassis,* and apricot. But the celebrated pastry chef is known for her chocolate cakes fashioned from Valrhona chocolate as well as chocolates from Cuba and the Dominican Republic. "I

0 recipes of chocolate cakes," says Merle. "Every week we
You might find a chocolate *génoise* cake with chocolate
nd fresh fruit, or a nut crust topped with pears, *crème anglaise*, and chocolate ganache. For an elegant lunch, purchase a few slices of Merle's quiche to enjoy before tucking into cake. It's no surprise that she represented Canadian pastry at the Culinary Olympics in Frankfurt.

Le Musée du Chocolat de la Confiserie Bromont, 679 rue Shefford, Bromont; (450) 534-3893; www.museeduchocolatde bromont.ca. We know that the main purpose of the museum is to lure visitors into the attached chocolate shop and cafe, but we

still think that the collection of old advertising posters, candy boxes, and chocolate paraphernalia has a certain charm. We learned here that the Québecois eat more chocolate (5.4 kilograms per person per year, or just under 12 pounds) than their fellow Canadians (5.11 kilos, or a little over 11 pounds). The shop's specialty "Chocolate de Bromont," with a raspberry and black-currant center, no doubt contributes to that consumption. In addition to its own small line of chocolates, the shop stocks a number of premium bars from Europe.

The small cafe serves breakfast and lunch fare, including croissants and bagels, sandwiches, and crepes.

Le St-Raphaël, 1005 rue Principale, Cowansville; (450) 263-5865. Completely unrelated to the chocolate shops bearing a similar name, Le St-Raphaël is a deli located at a strategic crossroads in the old Sweetsburg General Store. Its claim to fame is "the best carrot cake in the world," a title bestowed by owner Alain Bretón. The cake contains a touch of pineapple and a hint of cinnamon, but is much airier than most iterations of this iconic dessert. The best in the world? Probably not, but it's easily the best for miles around.

Le Savarin, 459 rue Principale ouest, Magog; (819) 843-9373; www.boutiquelesavarin.com. This kitchenware store in downtown Magog has the range of cookware and stemware that serious home cooks have come to expect. But you can also find a large selection of stovetop and electric espresso machines and an assortment of whimsical and inexpensive espresso cups. For those who prefer their coffee cut with hot milk, Le Savarin also stocks bowls for breakfast-sized servings of *café au lait*. One of the shop's more unusual products is the Vinearius Elite wine-decanting aerator and funnel. It's a handy way to instantly age a tannin-intensive young red.

Les Jardins de la Colline, 1032 boulevard Pierre-Laporte, Brigham; (450) 263-5997. This farmstand with a high peaked roof and wraparound porch used to be a seasonal operation, but now it remains open all year so that local cooks in a hurry can pick

Date Cake with Brown Sugar Cream

This old-fashioned cake with a brown sugar cream is a country favorite in Quebec. When we asked Sylvie Tremblay for her recipe, she was able to write it down from memory. She told us that she learned the topping from her father, a maple syrup maker.

Cake

1 cup dates, cut in sixths

1 teaspoon baking soda

1 cup boiling water

1½ cups sifted flour

1 teaspoon baking powder

½ teaspoon salt

1 egg

¼ cup butter, softened

1 cup brown sugar

½ teaspoon vanilla

Grease a standard (9-inch) Bundt pan.

Place dates in heatproof bowl. In measuring cup, dissolve baking soda in boiling water and pour over dates. Let mixture stand until lukewarm (about 20 minutes).

Preheat oven to 350° F.

In separate bowl, whisk together flour, baking powder, and salt.

In a large bowl, whisk together egg, softened butter, brown sugar, and vanilla until blended. Stir in cooled date mixture, then flour mixture.

Pour into Bundt pan and cook 45–55 minutes, or until toothpick inserted in center comes out clean. Cool for 10 minutes on rack before unmolding and allowing to completely cool.

Brown Sugar Cream

1 cup sugar

1 cup brown sugar

1 cup heavy cream

¼ cup butter

2 tablespoons maple syrup

1 teaspoon vanilla

Combine sugars and cream in a medium-size heavy saucepan. Cook over medium heat until the mixture begins to simmer. Cover and continue cooking for two minutes to dissolve the sugar. Remove lid and use a wet pastry brush to wash down any crystals clinging to side of pan.

Cook uncovered until syrup reaches 238° F (soft-ball stage) on a candy thermometer.

Remove from heat and add butter without stirring. Set aside until mixture cools to about 110° F. This takes 45 minutes to an hour.

Stir in maple syrup and vanilla, and beat sugar cream until cool. Pour over cake.

Serves 12 (generously)

Recipe courtesy of Les Jardins de la Colline (p. 217).

up prepared lasagna, spaghetti sauce, soups, beautiful pickled vegetables in glass jars, a quiche or a *tourtière* meat pie. The shop also stocks chicken, beef, pork, lamb, and sausages from local farms. Sylvie Tremblay's cakes—maple and coffee or date topped with brown sugar cream—are great in any season. (See recipe on p. 218.)

Le Terroir, 3115 rue Principale, Dunham; (450) 295-3266. From asparagus to zucchini, this rural farmstand has a steady supply of vegetables and berries from mid-May through October. The Rainville family also makes its own salad dressings, apple and cherry syrups, pies, and cookies. They run a pick-your-own operation during strawberry season. Open mid-May through Dec.

Les Miettes, 6770 route Louis-S-St-Laurent, Compton; (819) 835-0290. Bread baker Daniel Poirier and pastry chef Isabelle Marissal have run this splendid little bakery since 2007. She makes croissants and *chocolatines* (blocks of croissant dough with a bar of chocolate in the middle) daily and fancy pastry on request, while he creates a series of intensely flavorful sourdough breads and "poolish" breads, which are made with a conventionally raised sponge to which sourdough starter has been added. The bakery also sells a number of Fair Trade and organic products, including chocolate and coffee. Check out the striking mosaics on the front steps. They are the work of Marissal, who also teaches classes in mosaic art.

Miellerie Lune de Miel, 252 Rang 3 est, Stoke; (819) 346-2558; www.miellerielunedemiel.com. Carole Huppe and Richard Coté's apiary has breakfast covered. Their fruit-flavored honeys (including strawberry, blueberry, raspberry, and apricot) are delicious on toast, while their mint honey is perfect for sweetening a cup of tea. The husband-and-wife team started with a few hives in 1978, and now they move hives all over Quebec to pollinate specific crops. The distinctive flavors of the honeys result from those single-crop nectars. Their home base includes a playground and petting zoo for kids. Tours of the honeymaking operation (including a giant simulated hive) are available from late June through mid-October. The shop is open all year.

Val Caudalies, 4921 rue Principale, Dunham; (450) 295-2333; www.valcaudalies.com. Three friends launched this winery and ciderworks in 2005, and have made a name for their wines and ciders alike. "It is important to have both productions," says Guillaume Leroux, co-owner with Alexis Perron and Julien Vaillancourt. "The apple is natural for Quebec, and there is a real demand for our sparkling cider." They are working to create the same recognition for their wines. They vinify the grapes from 15,000 vines of Vidal blanc into a late-harvest wine (which has a honeyed steeliness) and a semi-dry style that is a gentle accompaniment to cheeses and *pâtés*. The trio reserve their ice-wine skills for the production of an unusually intense ice cider that retains an essential acidity to support the sweetness. Two principal apples go into the ice cider. Empire and Liberty, Leroux explains, will hold on the tree over the winter, and Val Caudalies usually picks the fruit in March. McIntosh apples drop when ripe, so the trio presses the juice, leaves it outside to freeze, and then ferments to a 9-percent alcohol hard cider they call "Liquoreaux Cidre." It is not as sweet as ice cider—"more like biting into a fresh apple," says Leroux. Perron and Leroux are also the authors of the authoritative book *Cidres du Quebec*. Open mid-May through Dec.

Verger Le Gros Pierre, 6335 route Louis-S-St-Laurent, Compton; (819) 835-5549; www.grospierre.com. "We're a Slow Food kind of place," says Diane Goyette of the orchard she operates with Gaétan Gilbert. "It's the concept of land to table. We graft and grow the trees and make pie, jelly, and juice." Each pie, in fact, is filled with two pounds of apples. "When people come to the farm, they want something gorgeous," Goyette says. The kitchen's specialty, however, is an apple stuffed with dark chocolate and cooked in pastry. Goyette shrugs off the richness of the treat. "You don't eat it every day—only when you are tired and have worked very hard." Of course, you can also visit the orchard just to buy or pick apples. They grow nine varieties, including Melba and Cortland, which are top pie apples. A small *crêperie* on the premises serves breakfast and lunch, which taste best when eaten on the covered deck overlooking the orchards. Open Aug through mid-Oct.

Vignoble de la Bauge, 155 rue des Érables, Brigham; (450) 266-2149; www.labauge.com. Another pioneer of Quebec winemaking, La Bauge had its first commercial vintage in 1990. The oldest vines are Seyval blanc, and they produce the exceptional flagship white "La Bauge Classique." It is an ideal complement to roast pork. Seyval also forms the base for the vermouth-style apéritif wine called "Les Folies de Vigneron" (winemaker's follies). La Bauge also makes a fortified, very caramelized red called "La Flambée" and white, rosé, and red ice wines. La Bauge has operated its formal "winemaker for a day" program since 2007. In September and October, participants take part in cutting, pressing, and vinifying grapes, and tasting wine. The following year, each gets one bottle of the wine made that day. In February and March (when the winery normally does not accept visitors), La Bauge also runs a "create your personal *cuvée*" program, where participants learn to taste, smell, and blend wine. They get to take their wine home to age. Open May through Dec.

Vignoble de l'Orpailleur, 1086 route 202, Dunham; (450) 295-2763; www.orpailleur.ca. This venerable winery is possibly the best place to start a tour of the *Route des Vins* in the Eastern Townships. Its small museum chronicles (in both French and English) the history of winemaking in the area, beginning with the clergy who made altar wine in the 17th century. Due deference is given to professor J.O. Vandal of the University of Laval who began a breeding program in 1945 to create cold-hardy wine grapes. The timeline progresses inexorably to 1981, when L'Orpailleur was founded. The displays then switch to explanations of the growing cycle and the

A Quebec Wine Primer

After Samuel de Champlain established the trading post that would become Quebec in 1608, he left for France, leaving behind thirty-two potential colonists and a large number of French wine grapevines. When he returned to Quebec in the spring of 1609, only nine of the colonists and none of the vines had survived. But a French colony without wine was unthinkable, so Quebecers kept making wine from local grapes for the next two centuries until British occupation shifted local alcohol tastes to beer and spirits. When the Quebec parliament regained some sovereignty in the late 19th century, it encouraged farmers to try some of the hardy native wine grapes, but the resulting wines couldn't compete with imports.

Shortly after World War II, J.O. Vandal of the University of Laval gathered grape varieties from all over Europe and North America and began crossbreeding to create vines that could stand the Quebec winters and still produce grapes suited for wine. Similar research by growers and university researchers ultimately bore fruit with a number of French-American hybrid grapes that now make up the bulk of the wine grapes planted in Quebec.

As long as the grapes are not entirely buried in snow, winemakers are pretty much guaranteed the conditions to make ice wines. These intense, sweet wines are fermented from juice squeezed from ripe grapes that remain on the vines until a deep winter freeze.

Quebec growers have also had success with some European wine grapes, most notably the red Gamay grape of Beaujolais, and the white Riesling and Muscat grapes of Alsace. A few growers succeed with Pinot Noir and Chardonnay, both from Burgundy. Hybrid grapes still dominate the vineyards of Quebec. Here are some of the most important:

Maréchal-Foch: This vigorous-growing dark-blue grape originally bred in Alsace has, at its best, some of the berry roundness of Pinot Noir.

Frontenac Noir: Created at the University of Minnesota, this grape is becoming the standard for Quebec red wines despite a slightly ashen aftertaste. It produces a wine akin to Beaujolais, and some producers make good Port-style sweet wines with it.

De Chaunac: This extremely vigorous grape is usually used either for sweet Rosé wines or as a tannic backbone to blend into red wines.

St. Croix: Originally bred in Wisconsin, this red grape seems to reach its maximum potential in Quebec, where the long days of summer allow it to attain higher sugar concentrations.

Sabrevois: This red grape, a cousin of St. Croix, makes wines with a distinctively Bordeaux-like character, but requires blending with sweeter grapes (usually Frontenac). Wines with a high concentration of Sabrevois have an unusual overtone of bacon.

Seyval Blanc: Developed in northern France, Seyval is the tenderest of the French-American hybrids. It can resemble Sauvignon Blanc and is noted for making excellent sparkling wines.

Vandal-Cliche: Winter-hardy and very productive, this Quebec-originated hybrid is rarely used alone in wine, as it can have a "foxy" character when fully ripe.

Vidal Blanc: Originally bred for Cognac production in France, this cross of Ugni Blanc (a Rhône Valley grape) with a hybrid grown in the Loire Valley is a winter-hardy vine that holds its grape clusters well after frost hits. With flavors akin to Muscat and Riesling, it is most often used for sweet late-harvest wines and for ice wines.

Quebec techniques for protecting tender vines. While the winery used to emphasize its red wines based on Maréchal Foch and De Chaunac, it has switched in recent years to more supple whites based on Seyval and Vidal blanc. The Vidal ice wine is a powerful, apricot-scented wine well paired with *foie gras*. The winery also has a lovely picnic area and an attached seasonal (late June through mid-October) restaurant where Lac Brome duck is the specialty.

Vignoble Domaine Bresee, 303 Draper Hill, Sutton; (450) 538-3303; www.vignobledomainebresee.com. Set on the scenic top of a gentle hill not far from the ski mountains, Richard Bresee's winery and cattle farm is an unusual combination in the Eastern Townships. Even more unusual is Bresee's commitment to the Saint-Croix red grape that forms the backbone of his red, rosé, and white wines. The "Bressoc Blanc" is a brisk wine made from Vidal Blanc and first pressings of Saint-Croix, with the green-apple perkiness of the hybrid Vandal-Cliche grape added after a separate fermentation on the skins. The "Bressoc Rouge" is a fruity red, while the "Cuvée Mackenzie-Parker" red spends more time on the skins and six months in oak barrels, producing a bigger, more tannic wine. "We like the reds with our meat," Bresee says. Indeed, many customers come in to buy their wine and their steaks at the same time. The beef comes from pastured Charolais cattle, a French heritage breed. Open July through Nov.

Vignoble Gagliano, 1046 rue Bruce, Dunham; (450) 295-3503; www.vignoblegagliano.com. Alfonso and Ersilia Gagliano took over this winery property in 2008 and proceeded to replant the vineyards. Unique in the Eastern Townships for looking to Italian rather than French wines as a model, the Gaglianos are emphasizing the Frontenac family of grapes. Their top wines include a lightly oaked white "Levante" of Frontenac gris and Seyval Blanc, a Piemontese-style big red, "Frontenac Noir," and a sweet fortified red called "Portofino." Open May through Dec.

Vignoble Les Pervenches, 150 chemin Boulais, Farnham; (450) 293-8311; www.lespervenches.com. Véronique Hupin and Michael Marler's vineyard in the northwest corner of the Eastern Townships is certified as organic and biodynamic, and its extraordinary wines are served in virtually all of the best restaurants in Montreal and the Townships. Its flagship wine is a Chardonnay-Seyval in which the chardonnay fruit finds a surprisingly full expression. The style is reminiscent of some of the more northerly growers in Burgundy. Open late June through mid-Oct.

 Food Events

Brome Fair, www.bromefair.com. Celebrated over Labour Day weekend at the fairgrounds east of Brome Village, this old-fashioned country fair is a chance for Eastern Townships farm families to show off their best products and kick up their heels a little at the end of the growing season. Ribbons are awarded for several classes of livestock as well as for best honeys, maple products, and eggs. Craft exhibitions focus on country life traditions, including lace-making and quilting.

Dunham Folk and Wine Festival, www.festivalfolkvinsdunham .com. It can be difficult to distinguish whether this two-day event in the middle of July is a folk festival of mostly French-singing artists with wine, or an extensive wine-tasting with music. Either way, it's good fun.

Fête des Vendanges Magog-Orford, www.fetedesvendanges .com. Taking place at Pointe Merry on Lac Memphremagog in Magog over the first two weekends of September, the harvest festival features 140-plus food product exhibitors. They offer tastings and sell products, which can range from artisanal goat cheeses to single-blossom honey and fine chocolates. If you're in town, it's a way to sample many of the Quebec wines without having to drive the *Route des Vins.* Don't miss the Coaticook ice cream.

Lac Brome Duck Festival, www.canardenfete.com. Given the fame of duck in these parts, one can forgive the Lac Brome folk for quacking it up on the last two weekends of September. Like many community celebrations, there are lots of entertainers and activities for children, but the big draw is the exhibition tent where you can buy all sorts of duck products, including artisanal *foie gras,* and watch as chefs demonstrate duck recipes. Many restaurants in the immediate area also offer special duck menus during the festival.

La Clé des Champs de Dunham, www.cledeschampsdunham .ca. The weather is just getting reliably warm in the Townships by the second weekend of June, when Dunham hosts this two-day epicurean event to taste wines, beers, ciders, pastry, chocolate, and charcuterie made in Quebec—mostly in the Eastern Townships.

Les Comptonales de Automne, www.comptonales.com. Not to be outdone by the villages of the *Route des Vins,* Compton and the producers of the Coaticook valley hold this *tour-des-farms* and tasting event on the last weekend of September to showcase their products with a touch of whimsy and a flair for art. Most sites along the route have exhibitions of local artists as well as tastings of such treats as tomatoes stuffed with goat cheese, lamb braised with apple and honey, duck smoked with applewood, and chocolate-dipped apples.

Appendix A: Glossary of French Terms

amuse-bouche: tiny appetizer, usually a gift from the chef; literally "amuse the mouth"

bavette: flank steak

Béarnaise: creamy tarragon sauce of egg yolks, butter, white wine, vinegar, and spices

beurre blanc: reduced sauce of butter, white wine, shallots and vinegar

betterave: beet root

boulangerie: bread bakery

Bordelaise: brown sauce of shallots, red wine, and bone marrow

café allongé: diluted espresso brewed with extra hot water

café au lait: coffee with hot milk; in Montreal often with steamed milk and served in a *bol* (bowl) instead of a cup or mug

café-resto: a coffee shop that serves light meals

cassoulet: white-bean casserole, usually made with sausage and a combination of meats that could include duck, goose, pork, lamb or even mutton

chaudière or chaudrée: A *chaudière* is technically a large iron stew pot but is often used in Canadian French to refer to a chowder. A *chaudrée* is almost always some kind of fish or shellfish chowder with potatoes.

chevre: goat cheese. Canadian French generally drops the accent used in France, i.e., *chèvre.*

chocolatine: a square of croissant dough folded over bars of chocolate, also known as *pain au chocolat*

choucroute: sauerkraut; also *choucroute garnie,* an Alsatian dish of sauerkraut with sausages, other salted meats, and sometimes potatoes

cidre fort: hard cider

clafoutis: traditional tart made with a crepe batter and fruit (often dark cherries)

confit: duck, goose, or pork cooked and preserved in its own fat. The term also refers to fruit or vegetables preserved in sugar or sometimes in alcohol or vinegar.

coquilles St-Jacques: sea scallops; often used to refer to dish of scallops mixed with a cream sauce, mushrooms, and breadcrumbs and baked in scallop shells

croque madame/monsieur: broiled ham and cheese sandwich topped with mornay sauce (Béchamel with cheese melted in) with/without a fried egg on top

dépanneur: convenience store

entrée: an appetizer, not to be confused with the identical American English word that means "main dish"

flammekueche: a hearth-baked flat bread that originated in Alsace, usually topped with bits of bacon and caramelized onions

fleur de sel: literally "flower of salt," usually refers to flakes of sea salt

foie gras: the enlarged liver of a force-fed duck or goose. In Montreal, it is usually duck.

fromagerie: cheesemonger

gâteau: cake

génoise: sponge cake

gratiné(e): having a crusty brown top, usually from melted cheese

laiterie: a dairy, but also a place selling soft-serve ice cream

magret du canard: in Montreal, *magret* is usually used to refer exclusively to the large, fatty breast of a duck raised for foie gras

mignardises: little sweets, often served post-dessert

nage: an aromatic poaching liquid that often accompanies a delicate fish

palmier: palm-shaped cookie of sugared puff pastry

pâté: literally a "paste," but can refer to a pastry dough or to meat that has been minced, spiced, and molded

pâté chinois: a Québecois shepherd's pie, usually incorporating layers of ground beef, corn, and mashed potatoes

pâtisserie: pastry shop; a *viennoiserie* is a pastry shop that specializes in croissants and other "dry" pastries made of brioche dough or puff pastry

pot-au-feu: literally "fire pot," a hot pot of beef and vegetables boiled in broth, often served as three separate courses

poutine: fried potatoes topped with brown gravy and fresh curds of cheddar cheese

religieuse: two stacked buns of cream-puff pastry filled with either coffee or chocolate pastry cream and glazed; name refers to similarity to a nun's habit

rillettes: similar to a *pâté,* rillettes are small chopped pieces of meat cooked down into a minced spread and usually packed in ramekins. Common meats for *rillettes* are duck, goose, pork, or rabbit.

sous-vide: cooking by sealing ingredients in a vacuum bag and cooking for long periods at very low temperatures to maintain integrity of raw ingredients

table d'hôte: technically, a meal at a set hour for a set price; in practice, a limited menu offering a bargain price on a multicourse meal

tarte (au sucre/tatin/au citron): sugar pie/apple pie/lemon tart

terrine: a meat, game, fish, or vegetable mixture that has been cooked (often under pressure) in an earthenware loaf pan; usually firmer than a *pâté*

terroir: traditionally, a term used in describing wines that reflect the taste of a specific place; also used to refer to local food that reflects the land, climate, and culture

tourtière: a traditional French-Canadian meat turnover or meat-filled pie

Appendix B:
Eateries by Cuisine

African
La Khaïma, 148
Nil Bleu, 117

Asian
Basilic Cuisine Viet-Thai, 52
La Maison Thai, 108

Barbecue
Bar-B-Barn, 51
Le Boucan Smokehouse, 34
Restaurant BBQ, 14

Brazilian
Le Milsa Churrascaria Rôtisserie
   Brésilienne, 60

British
Brit & Chips, 7
Comptoir 21, 145
Sparrow, The, 154

Casual
Benedicts, 32
Chez José, 102
Cluny ArtBar, 10
Cosmos, 33
La Brioche Lyonnaise, 81
La Paryse, 82
Le Club Sandwich, 83
Les Sucreries d'Érable, 198
Quoi de N'Oeuf, 39
Restaurant Orange Julep Gibeau, 41
St-Viateur Bagel, 40 and 156

Central European
Boulangerie Cheskie Heimishe, 158
Euro-Deli Batory, 159

Chinese
La Maison Kam Fung, 58
Le Piment Rouge, 62

234

Pâtisserie La Légende, 71
Restaurant Noodle Factory, 66

Delicatessen
B&G Resto-Deli, 195
Beauty's, 96
Deli Joe, 175
Espace Boutique Europea, 11
Euro-Deli Batory, 159
La Rumeur Affamée, 215
Lester's Delicatessen, 152
Marché de La Villette, 24
Pâtisserie de Gascogne, 47 and 168
Schwartz's Smoked Meat, 126
Snowdon Deli, 42

French
Accords Bar à Vin, 4
Au Petit Extra, 79
Auberge-Spa Le Madrigal, 193
Auberge & Spa West Brome, 192
Birks Cafe, 53
Bistro le Beaver Hall, 53
Bistro Nüvu, 79
Bonaparte Restaurant, 6
Buvette Chez Simone, 99
Cafe République, 100
Chez Queux, 20
Cinquième Element, 195

Claude Postel, Pâtissier, Chocolatier, Traiteur, 8
Kitchenette, 80
La Chronique, 147
La Colombe, 105
La Gargote, 12
La Girondine, 196
Laloux, 108
Le Bocage, 196
Le Caveau, 67
Le Jardin Nelson, 14
Le Maistre Restaurant-Bistro, 35
Le Margaux, 150
Leméac, 150
L'Entrecôte St-Jean, 61
Le Paris, 61
Le Paris Beurre, 151
Le P'tit Plateau, 111
Le Relais, 198
Les Infidèles, 114
Le Steak Frites, St-Denis, 114
Les Trois Petits Bouchons, 114
L'Express, 115
Manoir Hovey, 198
Marché 27 Bar à Tartare, 115
Méliès Restaurant Bar, 116
O'Thym, 86
Raza, 153
Restaurant Les Cavistes, 120

Restaurant Les Filles du Roy, 21
Restaurant Vertige, 121
Robin des Bois, 122
Steak-Frites Vieux Montreal, 17
Ty-Breiz, 124
XO Le Restaurant, 19

Fusion
Jun 1, 146
Raza, 153

Greek
Estiatorio Milos, 146
Le Jardin de Panos, 111
Rôtisserie Panama, 178

Indian/Pakistani
La Maison de Cari, 58
Maison Indian Curry House, 176
Moti Mehal, 176
786 Halal Restaurant, 179

Italian
Buona Notte, 99
Cavalli Ristorante & Bar, 55
Milano Fruiterie, 184
Monkland Taverne, 38
Pizzeria Napoletana, 177

Restaurant Pizzaiolle, 121
Ristorante Primo & Secondo, 177
Ristorante Quattro, 16
San Lorenzo, 178
Via Roma, 180
Vinizza, 180

Japanese/Sushi
Isakaya, 57
Jun 1, 146
Miyamoto Foods, 46
Tri Express, 124

Latin
Raza, 153
Mochica, 116

Mediterranean
Andiamo, 51

Mexican
La Guadalupe, 82

Middle Eastern
Alep, 174
Aux Lilas, 144
Byblos, 100
Le Petit Alep, 176
Pâtisserie Efes, 186

Pan-Asian
Soy Cuisine Asiatique, 153

Polish
Stash Cafe, 17

Portuguese
F Bar, 56
Ferreira Cafe, 57
Frango, 104
Rôtisserie Romados, 122

Pubs
Benelux, 52
Bières et Compagnie, 97
Brasseurs de Montreal, 32
Brutopia, 54
La Rôtisserie St-Hubert, 58
Le Cheval Blanc, 83
Le PUBlic House, 197
Le Réservoir, 113
Le Saint-Bock, 86
Les Trois Brasseurs, 14, 62, and 86
Pub Burgundy Lion, 38
Sparrow, The, 154

Quebec Comfort Food
Chez Claudette, 102
La Banquise, 105

La Binerie Mont-Royal, 125
La Fabrique, 107
La Petite Ardoise, 149
Les Enfants Terribles, 151
Pied de Poule, 117
Resto du Village, 87
Rôtisserie Laurier, 155
Wilensky's Light Lunch, 156

Quebec *Terroir*
Aix Cuisine de Terroir, 4
Auberge Saint-Gabriel, 5
Au Pied de Cochon, 94
Bar & Boeuf, 6
Bistro Bienville, 97
Bistro Cocagne, 98
Brasserie T!, 54
Chez Chose, 101
Chez L'Épicier, 7
Chez Ma Grosse Truie Chèrie, 80
Cuisine et Dépendance, 103
DECCA 77, 56
DNA, 10
Homei, 196
Ian Perreault Prêts-á-Manger, 161
Joe Beef, 33
Kitchen Galerie, 175
La Chronique, 147
La Montée de Lait, 148

L'Atelier, 149
Laurie Raphaël, 59
L'Autre Version, 12
Le Chien Fumant, 110
Le Club Chasse et Pêche, 13
Le Grain de Sel, 84
Liverpool House, 35
Lustucru Bistro, 152
McKiernan, 38
Newtown, 63
Restaurant Ambiance, 39
Restaurant Beaver Club, 68
Restaurant de l'Institut, 119
Restaurant Europea, 63
Restaurant Fourquet Fourchette, 15
Restaurant Globe, 119
Restaurant Le Local, 16
Toqué!, 18

Seafood
Brit & Chips, 7
Comptoir 21, 145

Spanish
La Sala Rosa, 110
Pintxo, 118
Tapeo Bar à Tapas, 179

Steak House
Gibby's, 20
Le Milsa Churrascaria Rôtisserie
    Brésilienne, 60
Moishes Steakhouse, 125

Swiss
Auberge du Joli Vent, 192
Fonduementale, 104
La Raclette, 109

Tea Rooms
Camellia Sinensis Maison de Thé, 89
    and 182
Cha Guan, 44
Le Gryphon D'Or, 34

Vegetarian & Special Diets
Aux Vivres, 96
Crudessence, 55 and 103
Le Commensal, 60 and 84
Zero 8, 88

Appendix C: Dishes, Specialties & Specialty Food

Bagels
Beauty's, 96
Fairmount Bagel, 154
St-Viateur Bagel, 40, 139, 156

Barbecue
Bar-B-Barn, 51
Le Boucan Smokehouse, 34
Restaurant BBQ, 14

Boulangeries
BioBon, 200
Boulangerie Cheskie Heimishe, 158
Boulangerie La Mie Bretonne, 201
Boulangerie Le Fournil, 43
Boulangerie Olive + Gourmando, 21
Ferme Beaulieu, 211
Fous Desserts, 130
La Brioche Lyonnaise, 81

Laperle et Son Boulanger, 214
Le Fromentier, 134
Le Paltoquet, 166
Maestro Traiteur, 166
Mamie Clafoutis, 136 and 167
Marius et Fanny, 136
Pâtisserie Chez de Gaulle, 167
Pâtisserie de Gascogne, 47 and 168
Pâtisserie Lescurier Tradition
    Gourmande, 168
Première Moisson, 47, 71, 138, 170

Breakfast/Brunch
Beauty's, 96
Benedicts Restaurant, 32
Birks Cafe, 53
Byblos, 100
Cafe République, 100
Chez José, 102

Cosmos Snack Bar, 33
Deli Joe, 175
La Maison Kam Fung, 58
McKiernan, 38
Quoi de N'Oeuf, 39
Resto du Village, 87
Sparrow, The, 154

BYOB
La Colombe, 105
Laloux, 108
La Raclette, 109
Le Bocage, 196
Le Jardin de Panos, 111
Le P'tit Plateau, 111
Les Infidèles, 114
Le Steak Frites St-Denis, 114
O'Thym, 86
Resto du Village, 87
Steak-Frites Vieux Montreal, 17
Ty-Breiz, 124

Cheese
Abbaye Saint-Benoît, 199
Domaine de Courval, 208
Fromagerie des Cantons, 212
Fromagerie La Station, 213
Fromagerie Qualité Summum, 213
La Foumagerie, 45
La Fromagerie Atwater, 45

La Fromagerie Hamel, 131 and 183
La Maison du Cheddar, 163
La Rumeur Affamée, 215
qui lait cru !?!, 186
Yannick Fromagerie d'Exception, 171

Chocolatiers
Chocolaterie Raphaël, 205
Chocolats Colombe, 205
Claude Postel, Pâtissier, Chocolatier,
    Traiteur, 8
Cocoa Locale, 129
Fleur de Cacao, 212
Fous Desserts, 130
Grandbois Chocolatière, 160
La Maison Cakao, 131
Le Musée du Chocolate de la
    Confiserie Bromont, 216
Les Chocolats de Chloé, 135
Marius et Fanny, 136
Suite 88, 73 and 139

Cider
Cidrerie Verger Ferland, 205
Clos Saragnat, 206
Domaine Pinnacle, 210
Val Caudalies, 221

Coffee
Brûlerie St. Denis, 128

Cafe Olímpico, 158
Club Social, 158
Caffè Italia, 182
Faema, 183
Le Cafe-Crème, 46

Cooking Classes & Demonstrations
Académie Culinaire, 24
Appetite for Books, 43
Ateliers & Saveurs, 25
La Maison d'Émilie, 161
Les Touilleurs, 166
Quincaillerie Dante, 187
Restaurant Europea, 63

Duck
Auberge & Spa West Brome, 192
Auberge du Jolí Vent, 192
Auberge-Spa Le Madrigal, 193
Canards du Lac Brome, 204
La Girondine, 196
Le Canard libéré, espace
    gourmand, 133
Le Relais, 198
Manoir Hovey, 198

**Farm Stands & Markets/Pick-
    Your-Own**
Cidrerie Verger Ferland, 205

Ferme Beaulieu, 211
Le Terroir, 220
Les Jardins de la Colline, 217
Verger Le Gros Pierre, 222

Foie Gras
Au Pied de Cochon, 94
Le Grain de Sel, 84
Manoir Hovey, 198
Toqué!, 18

Game
Aix Cuisine de Terroir, 4
Bar & Boeuf, 6
Le Bocage, 196
Le Club Chasse et Pêche, 13
Lustucru Bistro, 152
Restaurant Fourquet Fourchette, 15

Honey
Miellerie Lune de Miel, 221

Ice Cream
Bilboquet, 157
Fleur de Cacao, 212
Laiterie de Coaticook, 214
Le Péché Glacé, 135
Point G, 137
Suite 88, 73 and 139

Lavender
Bleu Lavande, 201

Liqueur
Domaine Ives Hill, 209

Maple
Les Délices de l'Érable, 22
Les Sucreries de l'Érable, 198

Markets
Le Marché des Saveurs du Quebec, 184
Marché Atwater, 40
Marché Jean-Talon, 181
Marché Saint-Jacques, 88
Milano Fruiterie, 184

Pâte Chinois
La Petite Ardoise, 149
Les Enfants Terribles, 151

Patisseries
Boulangerie Olive + Gourmando, 21
Chocolaterie Raphäel, 204
Claude Postel, Pâtissier, Chocolatier,
    Traiteur, 8
Crème et Myrtilles, 207
Espace Boutique Europea, 11
Fleur de Cacao, 212
Fous Desserts, 130

La Brioche Lyonnaise, 81
Le Fournil Provençal, 215
Le Paltoquet, 166
Les Jardins de la Colline, 217
Les Miettes, 220
Les Sucreries de l'Érable, 198
Maestro Traiteur, 166
Mamie Clafoutis, 136 and 167
Marius et Fanny, 136
Nocochi Cafe Pâtisserie, 70
Pâtisserie Chez de Gaulle, 167
Pâtisserie de Gascogne, 47 and 168
Pâtisserie Efes, 186
Pâtisserie La Légende, 71
Pâtisserie Lescurier Tradition
    Gourmande, 168
Petits Gâteaux, 137
Point G, 137
Première Moisson, 46, 71, 138, 170
Verger Le Gros Pierre, 222

Pizza
Pâtisserie Chez de Gaulle, 167
Pizzeria Napoletana, 177
Restaurant Pizzaiolle, 121
Via Roma, 180
Vinizza, 180

Poutine
Au Pied de Cochon, 94

Chez Claudette, 102
La Banquise, 105
L'Atelier, 149
Le Boucan Smokehouse, 34
Le Canard libéré, espace
    gourmand, 133
Le Club Sandwich, 83
Resto du Village, 87

Rôtisserie Chicken
Frango, 104
La Rôtisserie St-Hubert, 58
Rôtisserie Laurier, 155
Rôtisserie Romados, 122

Smoked Meat
B&G Resto-Deli, 195
Deli Joe, 175
Lester's Delicatessen, 152
Schwartz's Smoked Meat, 126

Spices
Crousset, 208

Steak-Frites
Le Maistre Restaurant-Bistro, 35
Le Margaux, 150
Leméac, 150
L'Entrecôte St-Jean, 61

Le Steak Frites St-Denis, 114
L'Express, 115
Marché 27 Bar à Tartare, 115
Steak-Frites Vieux Montreal, 17

Tea
Boutique Kusmi, 127
Camellia Sinensis Maison de Thé,
    89 and 182
Cha Guan, 44
Un Amour des Thés, 140 and 170

Wine
Clos Saragnat, 206
Domaine des Côtes d'Ardoise, 209
Domaine Les Brome, 209
Domaine Vitis, 211
SAQ Dépôt Montreal, 72
SAQ Express 22, 72
SAQ Sélection, 72
SAQ Signature, 72
Val Caudalies, 221
Vignoble de la Bauge, 223
Vignoble de l'Orpailleur, 223
Vignoble Domaine Bresee, 226
Vignoble Gagliano, 227
Vignoble Les Pervenches, 227

Recipe Index

Banana & Maple Muffins, 185

Cauliflower, Bacon & Clementine Salad, 85

Date Cake with Brown Sugar Cream, 218

Egg-Stuffed Pheasant, 112

Lac Brome Duck Breast with Maple Cider Sauce, 194

Macarons à l'Atelier Europea, 64

Maple Syrup Pie, 23

Milk of Green Asparagus, 162

Pâté chinois (Québecois Shepherd's Pie), 26

Quiche Lorraine, 169

Robin's Olives, 123

Scottish Shortbread, 36

Index

A

Abbaye Saint-Benoît, 199
Académie Culinaire, 24
Accords Bar à Vin, 4
Aix Cuisine de Terroir, 4
Alep, 174
Andiamo, 51
Appetite for Books, 43
Arthur Quentin, 127
Ateliers & Saveurs, 25
Auberge du Joli Vent, 192
Auberge Saint-Gabriel, 5
Auberge-Spa Le Madrigal, 193
Auberge & Spa West Brome, 192
Au Petit Extra, 79
Au Pied de Cochon, 94
Aux Lilas, 144
Aux Plaisirs de Bacchus, 157
Aux Vivres, 96
Ayer's Cliff Market, 202

B

Bar-B-Barn, 51
Bar & Boeuf, 6
Basilic Cuisine Viet-Thai, 52
Beauty's, 96
Benedicts Restaurant, 32
Benelux, 52
B&G Resto-Deli, 195
Bières et Compagnie, 97
Bilboquet, 157
BioBon, 200
Birks Cafe, 53
Bistro Bienville, 97
Bistro Cocagne, 98
Bistro le Beaver Hall, 53
Bistro Nüvü, 79
Bleu Lavande, 201
Bonaparte Restaurant, 6
Boulangerie Cheskie Heimishe, 158
Boulangerie La Mie Bretonne, 201
Boulangerie Le Fournil, 43

Boulangerie Olive + Gourmando, 21
Boutique des métiers d'art, 22
Boutique Kusmi, 127
Brasserie T!, 54
Brasseurs de Montreal, 32
Brit & Chips, 7
Brome Fair, xviii, 227
Brûlerie St. Denis, 128
Brutopia, 54
Buona Notte, 99
Buvette Chez Simone, 99
Byblos, 100

C

cabane à sucre, 95
Café Olímpico, 158
Café République, 100
Caffè Italia, 182
Camellia Sinensis Maison de Thé,
    89, 182
Canards du Lac Brome, 204
Cavalli Ristorante & Bar, 55
Cha Guan, La Maison du Thé, 44
Charcuterie Hongroise, 128
Charcuterie Le Traiteur du
    Terroir, 129
cheese, 164

Chez Chose, 101
Chez Claudette, 102
Chez José, 102
Chez L'Épicier, 7
Chez Ma Grosse Truie Chérie, 80
Chez Queux, 20
Chocolaterie Raphaël, 204, 205
Chocolats Colombe, 205
Cidrerie Verger Ferland, 205
Cinquième Elément, 195
Claude Postel, Pâtissier,
    Chocolatier, Traiteur, 8
Clos Saragnat, 206
Club Social, 158
Cluny ArtBar, 10
Coaticook Market, 203
Cocoa Locale, 129
Comptoir 21, 145
Cosmos Snack Bar, 33
Cowansville Friends of the Earth
    Market, 203
Crème et Myrtilles, 207
Crousset, 208
Crudessence, 55, 103
Cuisine et Dépendance, 103
Cuisine Gourmet Monkland, 44
Cultural Feast, 9

D

Danville Public Market, 203
DECCA 77, 56
Deli Joe, 175
Diabolissimo, 130
DNA, 10
Domaine de Courval, 208
Domaine des Côtes d'Ardoise, 209
Domaine Ives Hill, 209
Domaine Les Brome, 209
Domaine Pinnacle, 210
Domaine Vitis, 211
Dragon Beard Candy, 69
Dunham Folk and Wine
    Festival, xviii, 228

E

18th Century Public Market, 9
Espace Boutique Europea, 11
Estiatorio Milos, 146
Euro-Deli Batory, 159

F

Faema, 183
Fairmount Bagel, 154
F Bar, 56
Ferme Beaulieu, 211
Ferreira Café, 57

Fête des Vendanges Magog-Orford,
    xviii, 228
Fleur de Cacao, 212
Fonduementale, 104
Fous Desserts, 130
Frango, 104
Fromagerie des Cantons, 212
Fromagerie La Station, 213
Fromagerie Qualité Summum, 213

G

G & D Supermarché, 69
Gibby's, 20
Gourmet Laurier, 159
Grandbois Chocolatiére, 160

H

Happening Gourmand, xvii, 28
Homei, 196

I

Ian Perreault Prêts-à-Manger, 161
Isakaya, 57

J

Joe Beef, 33
Jun 1, 146

K

Kitchenette, 80
Kitchen Galerie, 175

L

La Banquise, 105
La Binerie Mont-Royal, 125
La Brioche Lyonnaise, 81
Lac Brome Duck Festival, xix, 228
La Chantournelle, 214
La Chronique, 147
La Clé des Champs de Dunham, xviii, 229
Lac-Mégantic Public Market, 202
La Colombe, 105
La Fabrique, 107
La Foumagerie, 45
La Fromagerie Atwater, 45
La Fromagerie Hamel, 131, 183
La Gargote, 12
La Girondine, 196
La Guadalupe, 82
Laiterie de Coaticook, 214
La Khaïma, 148
Laloux, 108
La Maison Cakao, 131
La Maison de Cari, 58

La Maison d'Émilie, 161
La Maison du Cheddar, 163
La Maison du Rôti, 132
La Maison Kam Fung, 58
La Maison Thai, 108
La Montée de Lait, 148
La Paryse, 82
Laperle et Son Boulanger, 214
La Petite Ardoise, 149
La Raclette, 109
La Rôtisserie St-Hubert, 58
La Rumeur Affamée, 215
La Sala Rosa, 110
La Soupière, 70, 132
L'Atelier, 149
Laurie Raphaël, 59
L'Autre Version, 12
La Vieille Europe Charcuterie et Fromagerie, 133
Le Bilboquet Westmount, 45
Le Bocage, 196
Le Boucan Smokehouse, 34
Le Café-Crème, 46
Le Canard libéré, espace gourmand, 133
Le Caveau, 67
Le Cheval Blanc, 83

Le Chien Fumant, 110
Le Club Chasse et Pêche, 13
Le Club Sandwich, 83
Le Commensal, 60, 84
Le Fournil Provençal, 215
Le Fouvrac, 134
Le Fromentier, 134
Le Grain de Sel, 84
Le Gryphon D'Or, 34
Le Jardin de Panos, 111
Le Jardin Nelson, 14
Le Maistre Restaurant-Bistro, 35
Le Marché des Saveurs du
    Quebec, 184
Le Margaux, 150
Leméac, 150
Le Milsa Churrascaria Rôtisserie
    Brésilienne, 60
Le Musée du Chocolat de la
    Confiserie Bromont, 216
L'Entrecôte St-Jean, 61
Le Paltoquet, 166
Le Paris, 61
Le Paris Beurre, 151
Le Péché Glacé, 135
Le Petit Alep, 176
Le Piment Rouge, 62

Le P'tit Plateau, 111
Le PUBlic House, 197
Le Relais, 198
Le Reservoir, 113
Le Saint-Bock, 86
Les Aliments Picado Enr., 135
Le Savarin, 217
Les Chocolats de Chloé, 135
Les Comptonales de Automne,
    xix, 229
Les Délices de l'Érable, 22
Les Enfants Terribles, 151
Les Infidèles, 114
Les Jardins de la Colline, 217
Les Miettes, 220
Les Sucreries de l'Érable, 198
Le Steak Frites St-Denis, 114
Lester's Delicatessen, 152
Les Touilleurs, 166
Le St-Raphaël, 217
Les Trois Brasseurs, 14, 62, 86
Les Trois Petits Bouchons, 114
Les Volailles et Gibiers
    Fernando, 136
Le Terroir, 220
L'Express, 115
Liverpool House, 35

Lustucru Bistro, 152

M

Maestro Traiteur, 166
Magog Friends of the Earth
    Market, 203
Maison Indian Curry House, 176
Mamie Clafoutis, 136, 167
Manoir Hovey, 198
Marché 27 Bar à Tartare, 115
Marché Atwater, 40
Marché de La Villette, 24
Marché du Vieux, 24
Marché Jean-Talon, 181
Marché Saint-Jacques, 88
Marius et Fanny, 136
Markets, seasonal, 202
Markets, year-round, 203
McKiernan, 38
Méliès Restaurant Bar, 116
Miellerie Lune de Miel, 221
Milano Fruiterie, 184
Miyamoto Foods, 46
Mochica, 116
Moishes Steakhouse, 125
Monas & Co. Restaurant Equipment
    and Supply, 137

Mondial de la Bière, xviii, 74
Monkland Taverne, 38
Montreal Highlights, xvii, 74
Montreal Ukrainian Festival,
    xix, 141
Moti Mehal, 176

N

Newtown, 63
Nicholas Hoare Books, 46
Nil Bleu, 117
Nocochi Café Pâtisserie, 70

O

O'Thym, 87

P

Paâtisserie Efes, 186
Pâtisserie Chez de Gaulle, 167
Pâtisserie de Gascogne, 47, 168
Pâtisserie La Légende, 71
Pâtisserie Lescurier Tradition
    Gourmande, 168
Petits Gâteaux, 137
Pied de Poule, 117
Pintxo, 118
Pizzeria Napoletana, 177
Pointe-à-Callière, 9

Point G, 137
Poutine, 106
Première Moisson, 47, 71, 138, 170
Pub Burgundy Lion, 38

Q
qui lait cru !?!, 186
Quincaillerie Dante, 187
Quoi de N'Oeuf, 39

R
Racine Public Market, 202
Raza, 153
Restaurant Ambiance, 39
Restaurant BBQ, 14
Restaurant Beaver Club, 68
Restaurant de l'Institut, 119
Restaurant Europea, 63
Restaurant Fourquet Fourchette, 15
Restaurant Globe, 119
Restaurant Le Local, 16
Restaurant Les Cavistes, 120
Restaurant Les Filles Ddu Roy, 21
Restaurant Noodle Factory, 66
Restaurant Orange Julep
    Gibeau, 41
Restaurant Pizzaiolle, 121

Restaurant Vertige, 121
Resto du Village, 87
Ristorante Primo & Secondo, 177
Ristorante Quattro, 16
Robin des Bois, 122
Rôtisserie Laurier, 155
Rôtisserie Panama, 178
Rôtisserie Romados, 122

S
Sabor Latino, 138
Saint-Viateur Bagel & Café, 139
Salon des Vins et Fromages du
    Quebec à Montreal, xix, 75
Salon des Vins et Spiritueux de
    Montreal, xvii, 28
San Lorenzo, 178
Schwartz's Smoked Meat, 126
786 Halal Restaurant, 179
Sherbrooke Friends of the
    Earth Market, 203
Sherbrooke Station Market, 203
Snowdon Deli, 42
Société des alcools du Quebec
    (SAQ), 72
Soy Cuisine Asiatique, 153
Sparrow, The, 154

Stash Cafée, 17
Steak-Frites Vieux Montreal, 17
St-Viateur Bagel, 40, 156
Suite 88 Chocolatier, 73, 139
Super Marché Rahman, 170

T
Tapeo Bar à Tapas, 179
Taste of the Caribbean, A, xviii, 74
Toqué!, 18
Tri Express, 124
Ty-Breiz, 124

U
Un Amour des Thés, 140, 170

V
Val Caudalies, 221
Verger Le Gros Pierre, 222
Via Roma, 180
Vignoble de la Bauge, 223
Vignoble de l'Orpailleur, 223
Vignoble Domaine Bresee, 226

Vignoble Gagliano, 227
Vignoble Les Pervenches, 227
Vinizza, 180
Vinum Design, 73

W
Waterloo Friends of the Earth
    Market, 203
Wilensky's Light Lunch, 156
Wilfrid & Adrienne, 47
William J. Walter, 140
Wine, 224

X
XO Le Restaurant, 19

Y
Yannick Fromagerie
    d' Exception, 171

Z
Zero 8, 88